PSYCHOLOGY

The Science of Behavior
The Science of Interpersonal Behavior

THE SCIENCE OF
BEHAVIOR

ROBERT L. ISAACSON MAX L. HUTT MILTON L. BLUM

PSYCHOLOGY

THE SCIENCE OF
INTERPERSONAL
BEHAVIOR

MAX L. HUTT ROBERT L. ISAACSON MILTON L. BLUM

HARPER & ROW, PUBLISHERS

NEW YORK, EVANSTON, AND LONDON

CONTENTS

Contents

vii

PREFACE TO THE COMBINED VOLUME

As separate books, *Psychology: The Science of Behavior* and *Psychology: The Science of Interpersonal Behavior* have won wide acceptance and received highly favorable comment. As introductory texts in psychology both books are new departures which have made possible the treatment of selected, contemporary issues in considerable depth. They confront the student with theories, methods, and unresolved problems with which psychologists are concerned. They invite him to come behind the scenes and participate in the scientific investigations and analyses. Each book examines psychological aspects of behavior from a single, but different, perspective: the first from a natural science orientation and the second from a social science orientation.

Reactions from many teachers have indicated the desirability of combining the two books, without, however, modifying the nature of the two approaches. The present volume is in response to this need. Many professors felt that each book contained some topics which they wanted to have available in one volume so that they could be included in a single course. This combined version will allow greater flexibility in teaching and will make the contents of both books conveniently available. The only change that has been made was to provide an integrated index for the two books so that access to selected topics might be easily available. There is some slight duplication of the treatment of introductory topics in the first two chapters of each book, but the difference in perspectives of the books may make this duplication useful to the student.

The combined volume can be used selectively and flexibly for a single semester's course, or it can be used for a full year's course, especially if supplementary materials are utilized.

One might wonder whether it would be helpful to combine the two books in some different fashion, perhaps attempting an integration of the two distinctly different perspectives. However, the current state of affairs in the science of behavior is such that an integration would probably prove to be more confusing than clarifying. At present, the use of different approaches to behavioral phenomena seems needed and offers the advantage of providing more analytical consideration of important, selected issues.

WAYNE H. HOLTZMAN

BOOK ONE

Psychology: The Science
of Behavior

PREFACE

We believe that the introductory course in psychology is an experience to be shared by professor and student. The student's own experience can be enriched greatly through his professor's encouragement to pursue and to gain mastery of those areas of psychology which are of mutual interest to them. We recognize that students do not enter an introductory psychology course as "blank slates," but that, today, most students have good high school backgrounds in biology, chemistry, mathematics, and other sciences. Some even have had partial training in psychology or sociology during their high school years, and certainly every person has developed, at either an implicit or an explicit level, ideas about behavior in general, and about his own mental processes in particular. We recognize that a student's learning is an individual accomplishment, and that the classroom and the textbook, ultimately, can serve only as adjuncts to the learning process. Thus. if the individual student is to attain the objectives of the course, he must obtain an accurate orientation of his own, a perspective with which he can identify, and plenty of encouragement to think out for himself the problems that confront psychology. Too often the beginning student comes away from his course with merely a vocabulary, a few isolated facts, and disappointment.

With these considerations in mind, we have attempted a book which has certain special characteristics. To begin with, the present book is restricted in scope to less than the whole range of psychology in favor of a more concentrated treatment of the field as a "natural science" than is given in existing texts. We have reserved for another volume (in preparation) the social-science aspects of psychology. Perception, learning, motivation, and other topics are viewed herein from an essentially experimental and behavioristic perspective. Not only has this restriction in scope enabled us to probe in greater depth than is usually the case, but we believe such an orientation lays a concrete, scientific foundation in psychology for today's student, who has already been nurtured in an essentially scientific culture. Our own experience has shown that students not only can master this more extensive information, but, in fact, become motivated by it to a more critical understanding of, and interest in, psychology as a subject, himself, his social environment, and the world in which he lives.

Further, this book emphasizes the importance of theory in psychology and in science generally. We have tried to refer to experiments in their theoretical context. Without adequate awareness of the theoretical contexts in which they are rooted, the results of individual experiments can be misunderstood and often seem trivial or insignificant. Theories themselves evolve from the collection and integration of experimental studies. In turn, they provide the basis for suggesting further, more accurate studies. In addition to its fundamentally practical value, the development of the theoretical structure of psychology is most intriguing. Thus, we have, so to speak, invited students to come behind the scenes of experimental work to listen critically as the theoretical issues are debated.

In sampling the current psychological scene, we have, of course, stressed those areas of theory and research which seem to us—in light of present trends in the field (and, more broadly, in science as a whole)—to have the greatest value for understanding and predicting behavior. Naturally, the individual professor will have his own scientific preferences, which may not be in complete accord with those selected for this book. Yet one of the most important roles of the professor in the student-teacher relationship is to share with his student his own particular interests and enthusiasm. By sharing this enthusiasm and interest, the professor can evoke and encourage the student's curiosity and initiative.

The professor who directs his students to further reading along the various lines of particular concern to himself will surely find his teaching experience enriched and facilitated. Further, the extension of regular classwork through independent reading can greatly enhance the learning experience for the student, activating in him latent areas of interest. To assist both professor and student toward this end we have provided extensive bibliographies for each chapter.

There are many individuals who have been of great assistance to us in preparing this volume. First we should like to express our appreciation to the several colleagues who have been kind enough to offer helpful criticism of different parts of the text; while we have tried to incorporate all of their suggestions, we may not always have done so, and any inadequacies in the text we must claim for ourselves. So many secretaries and typists in New York and Ann Arbor have helped prepare the manuscript that to list all of them would be impossible; however, we gratefully acknowledge the significant contribution made by Miss Judith Plekker in her handling of many of the final, prepublication details.

Finally, we would like to express our deeply felt thanks to our wives, Susan, Anne, and Naomi for their forbearance and encouragement during the time this book was being written.

ROBERT L. ISAACSON
MAX L. HUTT
MILTON L. BLUM

December, 1964

ONE INTRODUCTION: THE FRAMEWORK

In constructing a framework for the scientific study of behavior, we shall indicate how such a study differs from the layman's knowledge of behavior. In addition, psychology will be defined and differentiated from other scientific bodies of knowledge and from the layman's assumptions about it. We shall deal with hypotheses, theories, and facts, and with their use in the description and prediction of behavior. Two important tools of psychology will be introduced: descriptive and inferential statistics.

1

Observing Behavior

Most people are interested in observing and analyzing their own behavior as well as the behavior of others. The boy who wants to impress a certain girl attempts to decide whether a box of candy will be the right kind of gift for her when he visits her home for their first date. He wonders whether he should ask her out for New Year's Eve at that time or later, and if they are in the same class, whether to ask her out for a cup of coffee. In a similar fashion, a girl might wonder how she can get *the* boy in her French class to notice her. A salesman also uses his knowledge of people's reactions when he makes a sale. Even professors must have a great deal of "know how" when interacting with their students, and this knowledge is based upon their previous observation of student behavior. All these people are using information they have acquired about the behavior of others. Although the success they sometimes have indicates that their information can be useful, in every case their activities are quite different from the professional activities of psychologists, who study behavior from a *scientific* viewpoint.

In order to understand how psychologists study behavior, let us look first at the layman's use of psychology. The salesman or the lover who successfully uses his own "psychological" knowledge often cannot express exactly *how* or *why* he is able to do it. He may have learned how to deal with some people in some situations, but he has not learned how to state his findings in terms of precise principles or techniques which are easily used in other situations by different people. Whereas scientific information must be communicable, the nonscientific, private information of the layman is useful only to its holder. Its privacy may often stem from the fact that it represents and depends on a highly individualized technique. For although one salesman can do wonderously well with a "soft sell" to customers, the same approach, by all observable measures, used by another may mean dismal failure.

One might wish to specify the personality characteristics that identify people who do well using certain techniques. A salesman may have ideas about why the soft sell works for him. He may attribute its success to his friendliness and capacity to establish warm relations with others. But before we accept his hypothesis that warm people like himself should use his particular selling technique, evidence must be submitted that the hypothesis is valid. The salesman might point to one or two cases where warm persons were found to improve their sales by learning to use the "soft-sell" method. What evidence should we accept that training in "soft-sell" really makes men more effective salesmen? Perhaps we might accept the number of sales during a given month, but this figure could result from many other factors and not merely from a special kind of sales training; for example, it might be the result simply of people having more money during this period and thus buying more in general. Another kind of evidence would be the verbal reports of salesmen after they had received such training. Would the statement "I am a better salesman—I know it," be a sufficient criterion of success? The answer to this question is "No," if one is interested in the *performance* of the salesmen.

None of the questions posed in our salesman example is simple to answer. For example, can one be sure that personality characteristics, such as warmth, can be effectively measured? And even if they could, how could we be sure that our measurements were not tapping other, more important personality dimensions capable of producing the observed effects? How can we measure increased selling effectiveness? It would be a good intellectual exercise for the student to design a study to determine the effects of a training program on sales performance for the simple reason that there is no single correct answer. A good design for a study depends on creativity and thoughtfulness, among other things. Science cannot be divorced from human ingenuity. Often a problem in any science must wait for its solution until the right person comes along with just the appropriate idea for an experimental design, but basically, any good experimental design results from the methodical and careful examination of the problem by a disciplined, creative mind.

Scientists depend upon information obtained from experiments that are controlled well enough to allow precise determination of causative factors and which can be trusted to yield the same results every time the experimental conditions are repeated. Such information can be called *data*. As psychologists use this word, they mean observations which come from acceptable processes of collecting information. However, all data are not necessarily reliable. One of the values of psychology is that it hopes to teach people what data are reliable and what data are unreliable and even erroneous about behavior.

Facts of Behavior

The justification for the cliché—"psychologists seek the facts of life"—comes from the interpretation of the word *fact*. If we agree that reliable data are observations and records which come from well-controlled and repeatable experiments, then what is a *fact?* A fact is something more than data.

For example, suppose we held the hypothesis that girls with southern accents were more attractive to men than other girls. To test this hypothesis in a well-controlled and repeatable manner, we might ask every tenth girl in the student directory of a college to help us in an experiment. Let us assume that none of the girls has a southern accent. We train all the girls to speak in the manner of southern belles when instructed to do so. After completion of speech training, each girl is placed in a group situation with men. In half these situations the girls speak in their newly acquired accents and in the other half they speak in their normal manner. Ratings of the girls' attractiveness are made by the men in the groups. Suppose we find that the girls who use their southern accents are rated more favorably than the girls who speak naturally. We would have collected data that tend to confirm our hypothesis. But, would it be a *fact* that southern accents make girls seem more attractive?

To accept this statement as a fact would be to go beyond our data. All the experiment demonstrates is that in our specific circumstances girls who use southern accents are rated more favorably by men than girls who do not use them. Since the girls came from only one college and were observed by men in only one situation, our data are limited to this specially selected sample. Data are always limited to the situation from which they originate. If the southern-accent hypothesis were tested in many college, business, and professional circles, with subjects of different ages and from many kinds of social and economic classes, and if all experiments were well controlled and repeatable, then on the basis of these additional data we might be moved to accept the *generalization* that southern accents do make girls seem more attractive to men. Facts are general statements of relationships that have been supported by data from many kinds of tests. They are hypotheses about behavior that have been accepted as being generally useful and significant.

Facts and Theories

In modern science hypotheses become confirmed facts through repeated collection of data. Hypotheses are most often simple statements of relationships between variables. One way of viewing a *theory* is to think of it as a set of interrelated hypotheses. Psychological theories can also be defined as a collection of statements—verbal, mathematical, or symbolic—from which predictions of behavior can be made. When a theory has been supported by vast amounts of data it assumes the status of a fact. Newtonian theory in physics has come to be accepted as fact; synaptic transmission of impulses between the nerve cells in the brain—which only sixty years ago was a hotly debated hypothesis with which many well-known physiologists disagreed—is now a fact (see pp. 88–89).

One of the most important features of a theory is that the statements it contains act jointly to predict behavior. Since psychologists are interested in the prediction of behavior, their whole enterprise centers on the development of useful behavior theories. Their ultimate aim is to produce theories about human behavior that attain the same factual status as Newtonian theory has in its application to physical objects.

A simple theory of behavior might be something like this: As a response is repeated by an organism in a specific situation, a tendency builds up in the organism to make the same response in that type of situation in the future. Let us complicate our theory somewhat by assuming that the organism must be motivated to make any response in the situation. For the sake of simplicity, motivation in this case can be defined as the specified number of hours of food deprivation. Let us further assume that the longer the time without food, the greater will be the tendency to make the response. This is an inadequate theory of behavior, to be sure, but let us examine what we have.

The tendency to make a given response in a situation is determined by two factors: motivation and the frequency with which the response had been made in the situation in the past. The prediction of the response cannot be made knowing only one of these variables. Both the motivation and the number of past responses must be known. To test this theory, we would experimentally manipulate one or the other or both of these variables and note whether or not the predictions are borne out by the resulting data. If the theoretical predictions were fulfilled in all of the test situations, we would begin to have confidence that the theory was useful enough to be acceptable. Sometimes we talk of theories which are generally useful for predicting behavior as *laws.* Of course our simple theory model would not be supported by data, but it should serve to illustrate the idea of predicting behavior from a theory.

Most theories in psychology, as well as in any other sciences, have arisen as attempts to explain a great deal of *existing* data as well as to predict the discovery of new data. In this capacity they serve as summaries of accumulated information and provide sources for developing additional facts about behavior. The theories of color vision presented in Chapter 4 describe a great deal of what we know about the rules of color mixture, the effects of color upon perceived brightness, and certain kinds of color deficits found in humans. Results can be predicted on the basis of the theories because the theories were developed by men who had knowledge of pertinent data. Given the theory, one can accurately predict many color phenomena. Unfortunately, there are some data which cannot be explained (or predicted) by any existing color theory, but we hope that some day a better theory will be developed that will be more useful than the present ones.

Thus, psychologists attempt to predict behavior through the use of hypotheses and theories which may be more or less useful, but when they become generally useful in predicting behavior, they assume the status of facts. Facts, then, are those hypotheses about behavior which have been repeatedly confirmed through the collection of data in many situations at many different times. Theories which are effective in predicting behavior are sometimes called *laws*.

A Definition of Psychology

Many branches of science other than psychology attempt to explain behavior by formulating hypotheses and testing them; and many of the interests evidenced by psychologists in their theories and research are exactly like those of scientists in other areas. Physiologists study men and animals to understand their basic physiological mechanisms. Psychiatrists study behavior of individuals with the aim of alleviating mental disorders. Anthropologists study the behavior of men in different cultures. All seek to understand and predict behavior. Psychology is only one of many areas of science which are concerned with the study of behavior, and psychologists study many aspects of behavior that are also studied by other disciplines.

There have been many attempts to define psychology in ways which will differentiate it from other areas of science. These attempts have not been entirely successful. To understand why this is the case, let us examine some aspects of the study of psychology. Most psychologists tend to be more concerned with the entire individual than do most physiologists. The latter may study the function and activity of the liver without direct concern about the behavior of the entire organism. Although they would agree that to understand the functions of the liver one must take into account all the other operations of the body, they would focus their study upon the liver. A psychologist would rarely approach the study of behavior in such a specialized manner, but would tend to study a given function in terms of its effects on the behavior of the whole person. Thus, if there is one characteristic which acts to set psychology apart from the other scientific areas, it is the relative emphasis on understanding the individual as a total functioning unit. Looking at the kinds of things psychologists actually do, and assessing many of their professional activities, will give insight into the diversity that is psychology.

Some psychologists investigate the neural mechanisms underlying sensation and perception, studying the structure and function of the eye or the ear. Their methods and their background usually are similar to those of physiologists interested in the sensory processes. Some psychologists work with emotionally disturbed people or with patients in hospitals or in clinics. Psychologists also try to discover the best techniques for designing machines, and the most efficient ways of operating them, to take advantage of the characteristics of man. Others study the man at his job as an individual, a social, or a group phenomenon. They consider the effects on morale and attitude of joining unions and of participation in various kinds of company programs. Psychologists also work on the development of testing programs ranging from intelligence measurements, with which all of us have had experience, to the measurements of specific kinds of aptitudes or abilities. Although many psychologists are concerned with applied problems such as these, there are many others who are entirely involved with the development of theories of behavior, and who are quite removed from any immediate or practical considerations.

Theoretical psychology Psychologists working in the theoretical areas attempt to understand the basic functions and organization of man. Some want to understand why individuals differ from one another, and there are many approaches to understanding individual differences. Some psychologists work to study the development of behavior from birth onward, and there are many who investigate the influence of genetic and prenatal environment factors. The assessment of individual differences, as basic research, is a field in itself, quite apart from any practical application. Other psychologists study how we perceive the world around us. Certain of these psychologists center their attention on the sensory organs (eyes, ears, etc.) while others study the perceptual characteristics of the human in more complex environments. Quite a number of basic scientists study the physiological mechanisms underlying behavior. They seek to establish the neural correlates of learning, memory, and the emotions. Other psychologists studying these basic attributes of behavior prefer to seek understanding in entirely behavioral terms, and thus we have specialists in theories of learning and memory. Even though many people are interested in the human as he exists in global perspective, as an entire individual or a unit in his culture, their field need not be *applied* psychology. Their emphasis is on the development of more adequate conceptualizations of man, not upon predicting his behavior in the *real world*.

Applied psychology Yet, there are many competent scientists who are interested and concerned with man in the real world. They study man in his natural environments—at home, at his job, and in the marketplace. These psychologists are interested in the application of psychological knowledge to behavior. Increasingly, society is demanding psychologically trained people to work in industry, education, and government. Applied psychologists work with man and machine systems (sometimes called the general area of human engineering), as school psychologists and consultants in education, in industrial settings concerned with employer-employee relations, in clinical settings where they attempt to help emotionally disturbed people, and even in the marketplace to learn why people buy what they buy. Of course, many psychologists have found it possible and profitable to combine theoretical and applied psychology.

Historical Development of Psychology

The present-day activities of psychologists are derived historically from at least four different streams of influence:[1] philosophy, clinical studies, physiology, and mental testing.

INHERITANCE FROM PHILOSOPHY Man has always been curious about himself. Where does he come from? Where is he going? What is his purpose in life? Is he born with inherent knowledge of right and wrong? Is the mind or the body more real? Does man exist, or is he merely an idea in the mind of God? Questions such as these have persisted since the beginning of recorded human life, yet their answers have not been found and are not likely to be found. At least you will not learn them from present-day psychology. Theories are intended to predict data which arise from well-controlled and repeatable experiments, nothing more. They are to reduce trial-and-error methods in dealing with behavior [1], but do not attempt to learn the eternal truths of life. Theories, the backbone of psychology, are not necessarily absolutely true or false. They tend to offer explanations, understanding, and predictions of behavioral phenomena.

Nonetheless, one the most prominent historical roots of psychology comes from the philosophers and their attempts to understand the nature of man through reason, logic, and argument. The most important philosophic roots of psychology come from the Greeks, especially Plato and Aristotle. The Eastern philosophies (Zen Buddhism, Hinduism, Confucianism, etc.) have contributed little to our modern view of behavior. More recently, the school of philosophy called British Associationism and some German philosophy, as developed by writers such as Leibnitz and Kant, have had some influence. More will be said of the contributions of the British Associationists in Chapter 6, on learning (see pp. 212–213). Those interested in the philosophic background of modern psychology have several excellent sources available to them [2, 3]. The greatest influence of these philosophic roots can be found in the areas of learning and perception. For example, when we speak of learning as an *as-*

9

sociation between a stimulus and a response we are using a concept of association not very different from that propounded by the British philosophers several hundred years ago.

CLINICAL INHERITANCE Differentiating normal behavior from mental illness and knowing the sometimes tenuous borderlines between them are some of the demands placed on psychologists. The antecedents for this are to be traced directly to Sigmund Freud (1856–1939). Freud was an Austrian physician who founded a new method of treating the mentally ill and developed a new theory of personality. Both the method of treatment and the personality theory are called *psychoanalysis*. Freud emphasized the role of unconscious impulses (wishes, desires, drives, or motives). The behavior of the individual, and especially of the emotionally disturbed individual, is thought to reflect his unconscious motives, which are always active although unknown to him. We shall take up the contributions of Freud relating to the development and organization of personality at great length in a companion volume to this book, touching on them only briefly here.

Freud's influence is far-reaching and pervasive throughout all of psychology. While crediting Sigmund Freud, we should note that the assumption of continually active unconscious impulses had been anticipated earlier many times by philosophers. In particular, the German philosopher Herbart (1776–1841) proposed a theory of unconscious impulses that was remarkably similar to Freud's. The latter's major contribution was to make explicit the sexual nature of the unconscious impulses.

We speak of Freud's contribution as *clinical* because it is based on the clinical study of persons with mental disorders, but clinical psychoanalysis should be distinguished from the more general clinical contributions of the health or medical sciences, since these have contributed in different ways to modern psychology. Scientists in basic medicine have contributed in great part to our understanding of the sensory, nervous, and other physiological systems underlying behavior.

INHERITANCE FROM PHYSIOLOGY For our present purposes, physiological investigations represent the most direct contribution to modern psychology. Our knowledge of the functions of the brain, its sensory systems, and the anatomical substrates of behavior comes almost wholly from physiology. The indirect effects of physiological investigations can be seen in theories of learning and motivation. For example, the work of the Russian physiologist Ivan P. Pavlov (1849–1936) is clearly reflected in our current theories of learning. The work of the modern physiologists is now affecting our theories of motivation and emotion. In short, there is a great deal of cross-fertilization between physiological and psychological investigations. In one sense the behavioral study of the organism defines the problems that may someday be solved through understanding the physiological functions of the body.

Probably the most important physiologist to contribute to modern psychology was Hermann von Helmholtz (1821–1894), whose work on the anatomy of the eye and the ear as well as on color vision remains classic. Experimental psychology started in the laboratory of Wilhelm Wundt (1832–1920), a German physiologist and former assistant of Helmholtz. Another German scientist, Gustav Fechner (1801–1887), was the first to study the relation between physical stimulation and perceived sensation (psychophysics).

MENTAL TESTING The fourth historical root of psychology comes from France, where Alfred Binet (1857–1911) developed the first standardized method of mental testing. He was commissioned to develop a method for identifying mentally retarded children so that they could be educated more economically and effectively in special programs. Binet developed the first mental test, and one of the contemporary tests of intelligence, the Stanford-Binet, still bears his name.

Mental tests have been successful in predicting success in school and in industrial and military programs. Some people have argued that there has been too great a reliance upon objective testing of mental capacities especially in the United States. If this is so, it comes from the undeniable efficacy of such tests in predicting many aspects of human behavior. The success of mental-testing methods has stimulated the development of many other kinds of specific techniques and methods which have been applied in all areas of psychology.

Today we find psychologists working directly along the lines of these four historical approaches to understanding man. Psychologists work toward understanding the physiological mechanisms supporting behavior, they work in mental testing, they work as learning theorists using many of the rules developed by the British Associationists, and they work toward helping those who are mentally disturbed. But each of these historical roots has extended beyond its own domains: The psychologists working to understand the basic laws of learning know and use concepts derived from mental testing; those working with mentally disturbed patients know the many facets of intelligence which have been reported from mental-measurement efforts, and this information helps them understand the potential abilities of their patients. There is a constant process of cross-fertilization among all of the areas of psychology.

Psychology, Other Sciences, and the Student

Psychology is a kind of bridge between certain of the pure and applied sciences. On the one hand, psychology stands in a close relationship to the pure sciences of neurophysiology, biochemistry, genetics, and others; on the other, the applied areas of clinical psychology, industrial psychology, human engineering, and educational psychology are closely connected with education, medicine, industry, and engineering. Somewhere between these basic and applied sciences can be located the subareas of psychology which aim at understanding how people learn, why people show greater or poorer retention of material already learned, what motivates people's behavior, how they perceive the world around them, their personality organization, and its interaction with their social environments.

How should psychology be categorized? Should it be classified as a biological science or a social science? Parts of the study of behavior could be included in either of these academic classifications. Not only does this present a problem to the administrator, who has to make decisions for the purposes of granting student credit, but it is also a problem for the student, who must learn about the recent developments in many areas of psychology to understand what it really is.

In the past twenty-five years we have witnessed an unprecedented growth in the sciences. All areas of psychology have produced knowledge and theory at rates almost impossible to exaggerate, and as a direct result it is hard for the professional psychologist to keep abreast even of the most recent developments in his own area of specialization. Now, if it is difficult for the psychologist to keep himself current because of this fantastic growth of knowledge, imagine the student's difficulties, in his introduction to the subject.

Each subdiscipline has been so active that the cross-fertilization of one area of psychology with another has probably seemed to diminish. Ideas developed in one area do cross over to another, but so many new facts and concepts arise in each subdiscipline that they seem almost to give rise to separate sciences. Contemporary psychology, as a result, is composed of many different and partially isolated approaches to understanding behavior.

The Need for Statistical Data in Psychology

Earlier in this chapter we suggested a difference between data and facts (hypotheses about behavior that have been repeatedly confirmed by experimentation). Investigators in the subareas of psychology classified as natural and social sciences are active in collecting more and more reliable information. All areas of psychology are experimental. The personality theoretician, the clinical investigator, the educational psychologist—all collect data from well-controlled experiments just as do psychologists in the physiological or learning areas. As the student will learn, the methods of experimenting and the control over experimental conditions differ among these areas. The amount of information that can be obtained from even one experiment is nearly overwhelming. There is a universal need to be able to summarize research results so that they can be more readily grasped and be more meaningful. To do this, we use descriptive statistics. Usually we wish to describe at least two characteristics of the data coming from an experiment: (1) the central tendency of the data and (2) the variability of the data.

MEASURES OF CENTRAL TENDENCY A measure of central tendency is a combined score, a numerically expressed figure, that tells us something about the characteristics or the level of performance of a group under observation. It is the best single measurement of the set of data collected from observing the group. The most commonly used measure of central tendency is called the *mean*, which is simply the numerical average of the scores obtained from each individual in the group. To obtain the mean, the *sum* of all the scores is divided by the *number* of scores involved.

Returning to our salesman who believes in soft-sell methods, let us assume we allow him to test his theory and we advance him to an executive position and place him in charge of the company's hiring and training program. He hires twenty new salesmen and assigns ten of them to the new soft-sell program he has developed and ten of them to the regular training program. He assigns the salesmen by flipping a coin to eliminate possible biases in his assignment. After completion of the two training programs, the ten soft-sell salesmen join the other

TABLE 1.1   UNIT SALES: SPECIALLY TRAINED GROUP (A)
VS. REGULARLY TRAINED GROUP (B)

Group A		Group B	
Salesman	Units Sold	Salesman	Units Sold
1	23	A	22
2	25	B	20
3	17	C	14
4	13	D	18
5	19	E	22
6	27	F	24
7	16	G	22
8	21	H	23
9	21	I	16
10	15	J	16
Total	197		197
Mean	19.7		19.7

ten salesmen in the field. These latter, remember, have only had the benefit of the company's regular program. After three months of actual selling experience, the sales manager collects the sales records of the ten men in each group. His results are presented in Table 1.1. The total sales in terms of units of the company's product are identical for both groups of salesmen. Since the groups were composed of equal numbers of salesmen, the mean number of sales in each group is also identical. Remember, the mean is simply the total divided by the number of cases which make up the total.

Our new sales manager is downhearted at this result, since his specially trained group did no better than the salesmen completing only the regular training program. However, he argues, "Well, that's not unexpected, because you remember I predicted that my soft-sell methods would only work for those who were warm and friendly to begin with." Thereupon he determines which salesmen were rated as warm and friendly by their trainers in the training program. He finds that five of

TABLE 1.2.   UNIT SALES OF SPECIALLY TRAINED GROUP,
"WARM"-RATED VS. "COLD"-RATED SALESMEN

Salesmen Rated "Warm"	Units Sold	Salesmen Rated "Cold"	Units Sold
6	27	1	23
2	25	3	17
8	21	7	16
9	21	10	15
5	19	4	13
Total	113		84
Mean	22.6		16.8

the special group were rated warm by their trainers and he compares their sales with those of their colder associates. Table 1.2 presents the sales manager's new results. Now he finds that the mean sales of the warm salesmen who completed his soft-sell program were far above the colder personality types

TABLE 1.3.   UNIT SALES OF REGULARLY TRAINED GROUP,
"WARM"-RATED VS. "COLD"-RATED SALESMEN

Salesmen Rated "Warm"	Units Sold	Salesmen Rated "Cold"	Units Sold
F	24	G	22
H	23	D	18
A	22	I	16
E	22	J	16
B	20	C	14
Total	111		86
Mean	22.2		17.2

who were similarily trained. Here at last is evidence for his view! However, our sales manager also prepared Table 1.3, which compares warm and cold salesmen who did not have the special soft-sell training. Once again, we find those rated as warm do best, and we also note that those men with the special training were only slightly different from those rated warm but without the training. This might indicate that warm personalities tend to be better salesmen of the company's products than chillier personalities, but this could only be established as a "fact" when it could be shown that warmth and friendliness were the *only* characteristics distinguishing the better salesman. As for our sales manager's hypothesis, we can find no support for it from the data he collected.

The evidence can be summarized by the mean sales records of the groups. The means represent an estimate of the middle or central scores (sales) achieved by each group. We evaluate the effectiveness of the hypothesis by the differences among the mean scores of the various groups.

In our present example we have dealt with the *mean* (average), but there are other measures of central tendency. One can also use the most frequently obtained score in the group (the mode), or one can use that score which separates the upper from the lower half of the distribution (the *median*). The mode for salesmen in group A of Table 1.1 is 21. What is the number of sales which is the mode of the distribution of sales made by the men in group B?[1] The mean and the mode, both estimates of central tendency, differ in this example, i.e., the mean is not the same number as the mode. Furthermore, in each of the distributions the median does not equal either the mean or the mode.[2]

Which of these three common estimates of central tendency is the best to use depends upon the characteristics of the entire group of data, although where the number of cases is large, the mean score is often the most appropriate. When the number of cases in a group is small, the median is sometimes preferable. An important advantage of the mean, in general, is that it is an algebraic value, and hence it can be utilized in any further algebraic operations the investigator may wish to employ. The mode and the median do not have this advantage.

Knowledge of a measure of central tendency gives us some information about a group of numbers, whether they are sales

---

[1] Answer: 22 units.

[2] Since there is an even number of cases (ten) in each of the distributions of Table 1.1, there is no single number which has half of the numbers smaller than it and half the numbers larger than it. Therefore, the medians must be found by finding the number halfway between the fifth and sixth largest numbers. In the case of the salesman in group A it would be the number halfway between 19 and 21, i.e., 20. In the case of the salesman with the regular training it would be the number halfway between 20 and 22, i.e., 21.

figures, scores from mental tests, or whatever. When, however, we add information about the *dispersion* of the numbers about their central tendency, we gain a great deal more information about the data.

MEASURES OF DISPERSION At this point we can profit by introducing the concept of *distribution*. A distribution is nothing more than the arrangement of numbers under consideration. All the numbers representing the sales made by the two groups of salesmen arranged in sequential order from highest to lowest, as in Table 1.1, represent a distribution. Any time we have a set

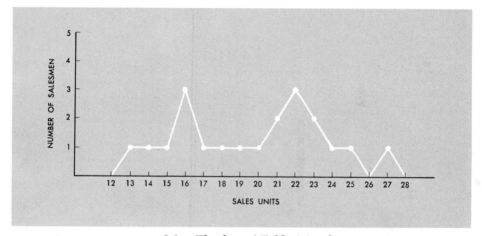

FIG. 1.1. *The data of Table 1.1 redrawn as a frequency distribution. The two groups of salesmen have been combined.*

of scores and arrange them in such a manner we can call them a *distribution*. It is often helpful to rearrange our data in a *frequency distribution;* that is, according to the number of times, or frequency, each of the scores occurs. To do this we merely make an orderly progression of scores along the *x* (horizontal or *abscissa*) axis of a graph and plot the number of individuals who obtained each score on the *y* (vertical or *ordinate*) axis, connecting each point with a line. The sales of the two groups of salesmen given in Table 1.1 are combined and drawn as a single frequency distribution in Fig. 1.1. In frequency distributions the mode will always be the score on the *x* axis that is associated with the greatest (highest) point on the *y* axis. When two scores tie for the modal average, as occurs with the salesmen's scores, the distribution is called *bimodal*.

17

Statisticians have various rules which can be applied to describe the shape of distributions, but we shall not discuss them in this book.

Even with the unusual distribution in our example we can make some attempt to describe the dispersion (or variability) of the scores which constitute the distributions. We can give the _range_ of the scores, e.g., from 13 to 27 for the salesmen of group A. The range is obtained simply by subtracting the lowest score from the highest score, i.e., 13 from 27. In this case the range is 14 sales units. We can also calculate statistical estimates of the amount of dispersion of the scores around the mean of each distribution. Some of these statistical measures are called the _average deviation_, the _standard deviation_, or the _sum of squared deviations_. Once again an extended discussion of these measures is beyond the range of our present intention. However, the student should be aware that these latter measures of dispersion are algebraic like the mean.

From the bimodal character of our frequency distribution we would be led to expect that two distinct types of individuals were represented. This is just what we found in our hypothetical example, namely, that the warm and friendly salesmen did better than the colder personalities, whether or not they received the special training.

NORMAL DISTRIBUTION Normal frequency distributions are those which are symmetrical around the mean and which fall

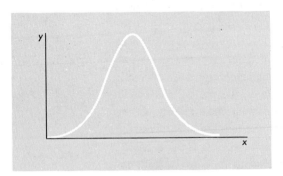

FIG. 1.2. *A normal distribution. Mathematically, this distribution describes a relationship between two variables. Often frequency distributions approximate this relationship. For frequency distributions, scores are plotted along the x axis and the number of individuals achieving each score are plotted on the y axis.*

off at a systematic rate from the mean. This phenomenon has highly desirable mathematical characteristics and, when plotted on a graph, takes on a bell-shaped curve, often called a _normal curve_, as illustrated in Figure 1.2.

When the frequency distributions of a large number of observations from many kinds of psychological experiments are studied they often tend to approximate a normal distribution. This allows the accurate description of the dispersion of the scores about the mean of the distribution through the use of the statistic called the *standard deviation*. When data approach a normal distribution and when the mean and standard deviations are known, the distribution is completely described. This is a great saving in description. By two numbers, the mean and the standard deviation, we provide as much information as by presenting all the individual scores which go into the distribution. In this sense statistics are highly valuable in their ability to summarize data.

INFERENTIAL STATISTICS Statistical description allows us to do more than summarize the data: it allows us to evaluate hypotheses about behavior. When we wish to know whether soft-sell methods are more effective than traditional methods of training, we naturally turn to statistics for summarization. We may use measures of central tendency and dispersion. However, we must be able to estimate the magnitude of the differences between groups of scores that is required for a hypothesis to be considered tenable. How large must these differences be?

For any particular experiment, we can postulate at least two possible outcomes; usually one outcome is based on a particular hypothesis or theory we hold, while the other is based on what is called the null hypothesis. From the former we might predict that, of two matched groups of subjects chosen from a larger population, the subjects in one will behave differently (or have different characteristics) from those in the other. The null hypothesis postulates that any difference between the two groups will be no greater than the chance variation normally expected to arise from the selection of our samples.

We know that in selecting any samples—particularly if they are small in proportion to the total population they represent—we are bound to obtain some differences owing to purely chance factors which may have nothing to do with the assumptions of our hypothesis. However, we can calculate the probable range of such misrepresentation that might have risen through selection of the samples; if the difference between the mean scores obtained for the two groups in our experiment (or the dispersion of individual scores) is large in relation to the *standard deviations* of the samples, the null hypothesis can be rejected. Thus, if the null hypothesis is to be disproven in favor of a test hypothesis, the differences between the two groups must be greater than those predicted by the null hypothesis. It is worth noting that all research aims at disproving the null hypothesis, rather than at proving the test hypothesis.

The following experiment demonstrates the effects of taking samples from a population. Take twenty small pieces of paper and write numbers on them according to the distribution of scores given in Fig. 1.3. On one piece of paper write the number 1; on another write the number 7. Continuing to work alternately with the scores at either end of the distribution, there will be two pieces of paper with the number 2 on them, and two pieces with the number 6 on them. Place numbers on the remaining pieces of paper according to the frequencies shown in

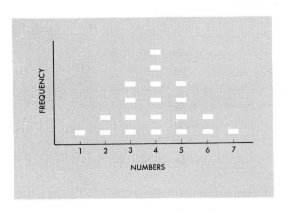

FIG. 1.3. *Example of distribution of a "population." Deviation of sample mean from population mean will decrease as the size of the sample increases.*

the figure. Place the twenty pieces of paper in a box or hat so that you cannot see the numbers and mix them thoroughly. Now draw out a sample consisting of three pieces of paper and note the average of the numbers on the three papers. Place the papers back in the box and mix them again. Now continue to take additional samples of these papers, and jot down the average in each case. Note the fact that the means of the samples of three papers differs from the mean of the entire population of the twenty slips of paper, often by a considerable margin. Now increase the size of your sample by drawing four slips of paper each time, and note the averages obtained in this part of the experiment. If you then continue to increase the size of the sample you take when reaching into the box, you will find that the means of the selected sample get closer to the true mean of the population as samples of drawings get larger.

The null hypothesis merely asserts that any difference between groups of scores comes from this kind of chance fluctuation, that is, the difference is due to the "luck of the draw" in obtaining the sample. In our original example we stated the null hypothesis; the difference between the two groups of salesmen was not significant.

When we wish to test whether two groups of scores differ, we usually test the obtained scores against those expected on the basis of the null hypothesis: We test whether the differences between groups might occur simply by chance. We usually do this kind of a test because it is simpler to test for the absence of a difference (a difference attributable to chance alone) than to test for the affirmative hypothesis. The student might do well to ponder this last statement. His understanding of why this is true will be valuable in gaining insight into the reasons why so much psychological experimentation requires this process.

We can make two kinds of mistakes in interpreting the results of experiments: we can accept the null hypothesis when we should reject it, and we can reject the null hypothesis when we should accept it. Each type of error is unfortunate, and we must avoid them both. Given the means and standard deviations of our two groups of subjects, it is possible to estimate the likelihood of obtaining a difference between means of the groups at least as large as was obtained as a result of chance factors alone. These estimates come only from information from the mathematics of probabilities and depend in part upon the extent to which the data obtained in the experiment approach well-known distributions such as the normal distribution.[3]

The results of a psychological experiment are often reported by use of a statistic that estimates the likelihood that the difference between experimental groups can be explained by sampling fluctuations from one underlying population. Some names of statistics for the evaluation of the differences between groups are the t test, the F ratio (or F) and Chi square (χ^2). For each of these, it is possible to find a related probability that

---

[3] Mention should be made of a recent development in statistical analysis. The procedures involved in evaluating the outcome of experiments for or against the hypothesis under test may change radically in the next few years with the application of Bayesian statistics to psychological research [4]. One of the major differences between Bayesian statistics and traditional statistics is that in the former the probability of acceptance of the hypothesis under test depends in part upon the experimenter's expectancies of finding support for the hypothesis before undertaking the experiment.

the null hypothesis should be rejected. In the future you will probably read a report of an experiment in a psychological journal which says that a difference between the scores of subjects in two groups in the experiment was significant beyond the .05 or .01 levels (meaning 5 and 1 percent, respectively) of confidence. Simply, this means that the difference in the scores of the two groups was large enough to justify the rejection of the null hypothesis because only 5 times in 100 attempts or 1 time in 100 attempts would drawing two samples from a single population give a difference as large as or larger than that found in the experiment. (Remember that this statement is justifiable only after making assumptions about the distribution of the underlying population from characteristics found in the data of our two groups.) Since the chances that our two groups represent one population are remote, that is, 5 in 100 or 1 in 100, we say the difference is *significant,* meaning the null hypothesis would be unlikely.[4]

CORRELATIONAL METHODS   It is often desirable to express the results of an experiment in terms of the relationship between two measurements made upon a group of subjects. One way to do this is to express the relationship as a correlation coefficient, a statistic that expresses the degree of relationship between two sets of measurements.

The relations between two groups of measurements can be presented graphically as a *scatter plot.* Numbers representing measures of one characteristic of the subjects are given on the ordinate or *x* axis and numbers representing measures of the other characteristic of the subjects are plotted on the abscissa or *y* axis. A point on the plot is determined by the two respective scores representing each subject.

Once again an example is in order. Let us devise a hypothetical experiment in which we wish to relate the amount of "exploratory behavior" shown by animals with an amount of a hormone, let's call it hormone X, in their blood. First, we allow each animal to explore a box with a checkerboard floor for $\frac{1}{2}$ hour and count the number of squares it enters. Then, we take a blood sample from the animals and make a bio-

---

[4] The .05 and .01 levels of confidence are frequently, but not always, employed to satisfy the test of a significant difference. The specific level of confidence chosen or the criterion for significance depends on the degree of risk of being wrong in rejecting the null hypothesis which the experimenter wishes to employ in drawing a conclusion.

chemical analysis to find the level of hormone X in each subject. For each animal, we have two measures:

1. The amount of exploratory activity represented by squares entered in half an hour.
2. The amount of the hormone X present in 1 cubic centimeter of blood.

Table 1.4 presents the results of our hypothetical experiment. The first measure for each animal is given in one column and the second measure for each animal in the other column. The same results are plotted in a scatter plot in Fig. 1.4. By looking at

TABLE 1.4 HYPOTHETICAL DATA OBTAINED IN THE EXPERIMENT RELATING AMOUNT OF HORMONE X PRESENT IN THE BLOOD AND THE AMOUNT OF EXPLORATORY BEHAVIOR SHOWN BY THE ANIMALS

Animal	Amount of Hormone (in Arbitrary Units)	Number of Squares Entered in Exploratory Period
Q	7	6
R	6	4
S	10	7
T	4	3
U	7	4
V	4	5
W	9	7
X	12	8
Y	8	3
Z	8	6

this figure we can see that there appears to be some relationship between the two sets of measures. The relationship is not perfect, for if it were the data would fall in a straight line.

A statistical description of the data relationship is possible by calculating the statistic called a correlation coefficient for these data. The results of this computation is +.74, which indicates the degree of relationship present in our data.[5]

Because of their specific mathematical nature, correlations (short for correlation coefficients) range from −1.00 through zero to +1.00. A correlation cannot be lower than −1.00 nor

[5] In this case a rank-order correlation was used because it best fitted the characteristics of our hypothetical data. There are many types of correlation coefficients which may be used depending upon the nature of the variables being evaluated.

greater than +1.00. The minus and plus signs are arbitrary and only indicate the direction of the relationship. In our example large scores on one rating go with large scores on the other rating and *by definition* this is a positive correlation which is indicated by the +.74 value obtained. If we had measured the tendency for the animals to remain in one place, that is, the tendency not to explore, and compared this measure with the blood levels of the hormone, then we would have had a negative correlation. The significance of the results would be the same, however: animals high in the measured hormone move around more in our maze and this result could be described by a positive correlation with activity or a negative correlation with the animals' sedentary tendencies. It must be emphasized that the sign (positive or negative) of a correlation has nothing at all to do with the strength or degree of the relationship between the two measures.

The degree of relationship is conveyed by the extent to which the absolute value (disregarding the + or —) of the correla-

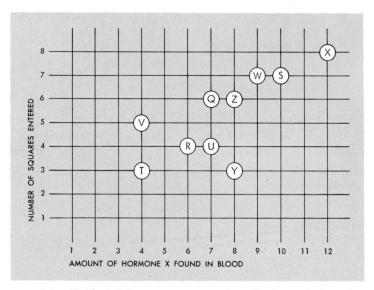

FIG. 1.4. *Table 1.4 drawn as a scatterplot. The letter designating each animal is encircled at the intersection of its hormone level and the number of squares it entered in the exploratory period.*

tion approaches 1.00. The closer the correlation is to 1.00, the greater the degree of association between the two sets of scores. A correlation of +1.00 or —1.00 represents a perfect correla-

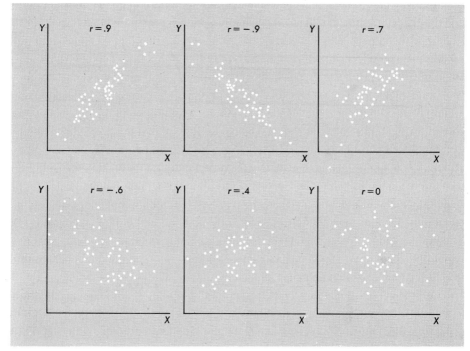

FIG. 1.5. *Scatterplots of different degrees of relationship expressed by the associated correlation coefficients.*

tion between two variables. A correlation of $+.74$ indicates the same degree of association as a correlation of $-.74$. Figure 1.5 shows scatter plots of various degrees of correlations. The reader should note that the closer the scores cluster along a straight line the greater is the size of the correlation coefficient.

Just as with differences between mean scores for groups of subjects, it is possible to determine correlation coefficients that represent a degree of relationship not likely to occur through fluctuations in the samples—that is, not due to chance factors. The technique for establishing significant correlations attempts to evaluate the probability that the two measures are completely unrelated and that they come from two populations of scores having no relationship with each other. The null hypothesis in the case of correlations would state that the obtained correlation was merely due to a peculiar stroke of chance in sampling from the two populations. From characteristics of the samples which are plotted on the x and y axes, it is possible to estimate probabilities that the null hypothesis is incorrect and that there *is* a relationship between the two sets of measures.

CORRELATION AND PREDICTION A perfect correlation allows perfect prediction of one measure or score from the other measure or score. If the correlation between exploratory activity hormone level had been $+1.00$ or -1.00 we could have predicted either of the ratings from the other. A high degree of correlation allows us to make predictions that are far better than chance.

Correlational predictions are usually made about groups of people and are often used in applied situations such as personnel selection or in the prediction of academic success. With relatively high correlation coefficients people high on one measure will tend to fall into predictable ranges on the other variable. Without a perfect correlation, however, some exceptions will occur. Thus, success in college achievement correlates approximately $+.30$ with scores obtained from the American College Entrance Examination [5]. This means that those who have low scores on the examination will tend not to do well in college and many of them will be asked to leave college. This is a statistical prediction that has been replicated many times. This information can be used in counseling prospective students and in selection by educational institutions of students who will best benefit from their programs.

This use of correlational data obtained from the performance of groups of individuals presents conceptual and ethical problems for science and society. If an organization can improve its efficiency, even by a moderate amount, by the selection of individuals who have personality characteristics correlated with success in their business, is it justified in giving personality tests to job applicants to screen out individuals who do not have the characteristics? Some of these individuals, perhaps quite a few, if the correlations are low, will not even be given the opportunity to try. Is the use of knowledge of statistical characteristics of a population justified when applied to individual cases? From the point of view of statistical conclusions the answer is "yes," since more correct judgments are made than wrong ones even though some errors also occur.

In one sense, less than perfect correlations reveal our lack of knowledge about a phenomenon. If we know that one personality characteristic correlates moderately, but far less than perfectly, with success in a business or profession, then knowing more about the characteristics of success would allow us to make the predictions approach 1.00. Then we would be able to apply the discovered method of prediction in both the group and the individual cases. But perfect knowledge may not lead to perfect predictions.

We know that many single nerve cells of the optic nerve are activated when the eye is flooded with light. Not all of them are activated, so our correlation is less than perfect. When we learn more about the codes used in the nervous system in the transmission of information from the eye to the brain, we may be able to improve our predictions about the activation of the nerve cells at the presentation of the light. However, and this point is essential, even if we know all about the functions of the nervous system, any single prediction may be only moderately accurate because of the imperfections of the measuring instruments. We may be able to know all possible responses of single cells in the visual system to light, but never be able to say with perfect certainty that our recording probe has reached any particular type of cell because of the minute size, physical similarities, and proximity of cells in the optic nerve. By the same token, we may never be able to measure, in a perfectly reliable way, those personality characteristics that we know to be related to success in business. This is most likely to be the case. Knowledge, even though it may reach perfection, may not allow the perfect prediction of the behavior of the single cell in the nervous system or of the individual in society.

STATISTICS AND DATA   Almost always, the data used by psychologists are refined by the use of descriptive statistics. Measures of central tendency and dispersion must be used to reduce the quantity of the information resulting from even the most direct experiments. Inferential statistics are useful in estimating the likelihood that the differences resulting from the experimental manipulations are substantial enough to be accepted as greater than could be expected through chance fluctuations in the samples of subjects used.

There are many ways to describe and analyze experimental data, just as there are many ways to design an experiment that is well controlled. Not all are equally useful or appropriate to test the particular hypothesis under consideration. There is no one book to read, and there is no one academic course that will prepare a person to do good research or to be a scientist. As in most areas, experience and scholarship in the area of specialization will ultimately lead to a competent level of ability in experimentation. But the factors of ingenuity and creativity, and perhaps even genius if it is different from these two qualities, are necessary for significant research contributions.

Explanation

Psychologists want to explain human behavior. Earlier we talked about the role of theories and hypotheses in the prediction of behavior, and before moving on to Chapter 2 we shall consider more generally the relation between prediction and explanation.

Explanation and prediction have a great deal in common. In predicting behavior we take information already at hand and look toward the future. Given certain behavioral data we then expect (predict) certain other behaviors to follow. We expect these other behaviors because of theories that tell us what to expect. It is theory that makes observations of the present necessary precursors of the future.

The essential role of theory in predicting behavior can be illustrated as in Fig. 1.6. Here, a horizontal line represents the separation of a theory world of variables, concepts, and theoretical constructs, from the real world of observations and data. In the theory world there are rules whereby combinations of certain concepts lead to, or permit, certain other concepts to be inferred.

In a simple experiment using biological motives, we could have a theory that relates food-seeking to a state of hunger. If we want to predict how fast an animal will run down a long passageway for food, we might predict that the hungrier an animal is, the faster will be his running speed.

Hunger, the motive factor, is a theoretical concept. We can never see hunger directly. It is something inferred from observations made in the real world. We could infer the presence of this *motive construct* from the observation of the number of hours the subjects have been without food. (Note that our theory must include a statement that relates the intensity of the motive to the number of hours without food.)

To make a prediction of behavior, we must deduce from the theory. The theory might state that when biological motives are aroused, the organism will attempt to approach stimuli that satisfy this motive. It might go on to state that the greater the biological motive, the greater attraction food will have. We test

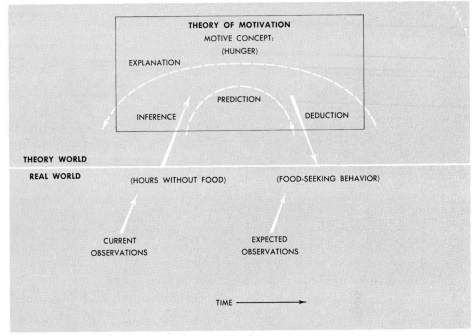

FIG. 1.6 *Schematic representation of the role of theory in the explanation and prediction of behavior.*

the deduction made from the theory by looking for data in the real world. We could measure how hard an animal works to obtain food, how much punishment it takes to deter his food-seeking behavior, whether or not it chooses food in preference to water or a sexual partner. These represent predictions generated by the general theory of motivation and by our current knowledge that the animal has, in fact, been deprived of food for a certain time.

On the other hand, explanation follows a similar pathway through the theoretical or the real world, but in an opposite direction. Suppose we notice an animal exhibiting persistent food-oriented acts. Why does it do this? We would accept the explanation that this behavior is attributable to hunger, provided that (1) we have a theory that relates hunger to food seeking and (2) we learn that the animal had been previously deprived of food.

The example is oversimplified, to be sure, but the general pattern holds even with more complicated examples. Given a theory relating academic performance to an individual's intellectual and emotional development, we can predict college success or failure from knowledge of measures of these factors made through objective tests. These allow inference to the theoretical variables and deductions from the theory are the predictions of how well individuals will do.

Given a student who is failing in college work, we feel his behavior can be explained when we have a theory that would predict such failure given certain earlier measures of personality and when the objective real-world measures of personality fit what the theory would anticipate. One can view the processes of prediction and explanation as being very similar in form, differing only in whether one is looking ahead to future events or looking back for causes.

In this first chapter, we have completed a full circle. We began by discussing the views of the layman about psychology and how the psychologist looks for firmer grounds and better observations before developing theories to explain them. The scientist wants well-controlled and highly reliable data and is not satisfied with a few observations made under uncertain circumstances. Once the real-world observations have been established, the psychologist looks for relationships between observations that are consistent and repeatable, and we have used the word *fact* to describe such firm relationships. But goaded on by a need to understand behavior, scientists develop theories or interlocking sets of hypotheses about behavior that, if useful will allow the prediction and explanation of behavior. Not all theories work well; only those theories that work best are retained in science.

Theories which are useful in predicting behavior are the goal of psychology. Theories are not necessarily true or false; they are more or less useful to explain and understand behavior. All scientific theories are evaluated against this pragmatic criterion.

Psychology comprises many kinds of theories. Some relate personality characteristics to complicated social behavior. Some relate early experiences to personality development, whereas others deal with foundations of behavior.

In this latter category we have theories concerned with the relationship between genetic influences and the development of the individual, theories relating neural structures and functions to behavior, theories describing the relation of our sensory mechanisms to perception, and theories of perception itself. We have theories of the basic mechanisms of all learning and remembering, and specialized theories of our verbal accomplishments. We have theories of motivation and emotion. But before we can have theories like these, we must have good, reliable data. This book is an attempt to provide a review of the data, facts, and theories that provide the foundations for the study of behavior.

References

1. Conant, J. B. *Science and Common Sense.* New Haven: Yale Univer. Press, 1951.
2. Boring, E. G. *A History of Experimental Psychology.* New York: Appleton-Century-Crofts, Inc., 1929.
3. Murphy, G. *An Historical Introduction to Modern Psychology.* New York: Harcourt, Brace & World, Inc., 1949.
4. Edwards, W., Lindman, H., & Savage, L. J. Bayesian statistical inference for psychological research. *Psychol. Rev.,* 1963, **70,** 193–242.
5. Fricke, B. G. *Opinion, Attitude and Interest Survey Handbook.* Ann Arbor: Evaluation and Examinations Division, Univer. of Michigan, 1963.

TWO GENETICS AND PSYCHOLOGY: A RAPPROCHEMENT

A knowledge of the causes of the resemblances and differences among individuals is one key to understanding human behavior. Psychologists have sometimes overemphasized environmental influences to the exclusion of heredity. Other psychologists have naïvely assumed hereditary factors as causes even though they have not been established as facts. The result has been an artificial separation of genetics and psychology. There is no doubt that heredity and environment both contribute to the development of an individual and to the way he is like or different from other individuals.

A basic and fundamental understanding and knowledge of psychology demands a knowledge of genetics. Genetics and psychology must be considered as interrelated if we are to truly understand behavior. The influences of genetics on the individual's behavior in many respects can be considered as a preliminary to understanding the individual's behavior from a psychological point of view.

At chronological maturity an individual has had a considerable degree of cultural training. Twenty and more years of almost constant interaction between the individual and his surroundings have produced a person whose behavior is, in some major aspects, largely predictable from the social demands found in his culture. There is no doubt that the best predictors of some kinds of behavior are merely the social expectations of society. Think of your own behavior; what you wear, what and when you eat, what you say in practically every situation from the classroom to the intimate conversation of lovers are all predictable by our current social customs. Anyone who reaches maturity has had his behavior shaped and molded by the various environmental factors that go with being reared, educated, and group living.

Environmental factors act to determine behavior at all levels of development. The ways parents enforce desired behavior patterns in children, for example, in use of the toilet and by their punishment or praise, are techniques used for transmitting the prominent social values of the culture. But, there are other kinds of environmental influences that may affect the child even before his birth. For example, the amount of oxygen or other vital substances that are in the environment of the developing fetus will have a great deal to do with his ultimate adult characteristics.

At the meeting of the sperm and the egg, the genetic information from the father and mother are joined and the rest of the determination of the individual is up to the environment. At that point our ancestors have genetically done all they ever shall for us in terms of biological inheritance. How much of adult behavior is determined at the fertilization of the egg? How great is the effect of heredity on behavior? How do genetic influences manifest their controls of behavior? These are the questions that will concern us in this chapter.

Early Behaviorism and Genetics

The leading proponent of the behavioristic school of psychology, John B. Watson, threw out a challenge to those who believed that behavior was determined in any significant degree by heredity in this famous passage:

I should like to go one step further now and say, give me a dozen healthy infants, well-formed, and my own specified world to bring them up in and I'll guarantee to take any one at random and train him to be any type of specialist I might select—doctor, lawyer, artist, merchant-chief and, yes, even beggar-man and thief, regardless of his talents, penchants, tendencies, abilities, vocations, and the race of his ancestors. I am going beyond my facts and I admit it, but so have the advocates of the contrary and they have been doing it for many thousands of years [1, p. 104].

The reader must agree that this is a rather direct and unequivocal denial of the importance of genetic factors at the meeting of the sperm and the egg. If Watson was right, then any confluence of hereditary strains doesn't matter because through subsequent socialization and training any type of person could be produced. This statement, unusual in its strength as well as its argument, needs to be set against the background of psychology as it existed prior to 1930 and against the social and political atmosphere of the culture.

Watson was attacking both introspective psychology and instinct psychology. The first attempts to build theories of sensation and perception based upon an individual's analysis of his own mental experiences. The term *introspection* refers to an individual's attempt to see within himself, to become aware of his own conscious experiences. At the time of Watson's statement, psychology was just beginning to free itself from its bondage to "a study of mental experience" which had created endless series of controversy and debate without hope of adequate empirical resolution. In other words, Watson wanted less subjectivity and more objectivity.

Instinct psychology placed great emphasis on behavior which was instinctive. For example, McDougall considered much of human behavior to be influenced by innate psychological dispositions. Instincts according to McDougall were considered to be the fundamental source of all human activity and determined the ends of all behavior. Although conceded to be modifiable, the original behavior form was considered innate.

Watson with his desire to study human behavior more objectively became interested in the study of animal behavior. He was aware of the work of Pavlov, a Russian physiologist. This blossomed into Watson's firm committment to the Pavlovian view that the relation between stimulation and response, both objectively measured, was the proper study of those interested in behavior. Soon Watson was arguing that all learning was merely conditioning and was no different from a dog learning to salivate to the sound of a bell after the bell and the food had been paired many times.

Reviewing the history of modern psychology we find a steady progression away from introspective psychology as well as instinct psychology and toward the new view of behaviorism [2, pp. 292–299]. Consciousness was first attacked as inconsequential to psychology and later rejected as illusion. The influence of heredity upon behavior declined in Watson's writings until he reached the categorical denial expressed in the quotation given above.

On the positive side it must be said that behaviorism stressed the point of view that all we can know about another person is what we can observe of his behavior; we can never directly know another's perceptions or thoughts. If we accept this position, and if we recognize that psychology attempts to provide theories to explain observable behavior then we have come to the behavioristic position widely accepted by present day psychologists.

The denial of importance of the influence of heredity in controlling behavior was not without support from the social and political spirit of the times. Think of our heritage from American history for a moment. "All men are created equal," reads the Constitution. Does not Watson's view seem to fit in better with this philosophy than a view that holds that intellectual abilities are determined by heredity and therefore that men are not created equal? If some men are smarter than others, why shouldn't they rule the others? Is a view of behavior which stresses the importance of genetic inheritance undemocratic? Of course it is not, but it should be remembered that social and political factors have always influenced prevailing opinions on the extent of genetic influences. The challenge hurled by Watson was biased in part by his society.

To a considerable degree, the antigenetic attitude made explicit by Watson has prevailed in psychology. Only in recent years have psychologists begun to pay attention to the relation between behavior and heredity, and it is likely that there will be increasing intercommunication between the sciences of genetics and psychology. This reconciliation is one which promises to help in understanding behavior and to serve as a counterbalance to the excesses of early behaviorism.

The resistance among psychologists to crediting genetic influences with much effect in governing behavior also comes from another quarter. Clinical psychologists, psychiatrists, and psychoanalysts, the group attempting to evaluate and treat personality disorders, have tended to minimize the importance of hereditary influences in such disorders. An extreme reliance upon heredity as the cause of all such disturbances would negate the effectiveness of psychological methods of treatment. Clinical psychologists have found that most mental disturbances can be helped by treatment. But hereditary factors may still contribute to tendencies toward more-or-less disintegrated behavior. Other reasons for the resistance of clinical psychologists to the significance of genetic influences in behavior have been discussed in a provocative article by Meehl [3] which essentially states that schizophrenia, while its content is learned, is fundamentally a neurological disease of genetic origin.

Genetic Material

When the human sperm and egg unite, each provides twenty-three chromosomes—the hereditary background of the potential individual. Chromosomes are bodies of material in the nucleus of cells which are darker than the other cellular material. Because of their dark appearance after staining they are called chromosomes, or colored-bodies. Every cell in the body contains the same number of chromosomes. All human cells have forty-six chromosomes. Half have come from the mother and half from the father. Each species has its own special number of chromosomes.

Through its genetic inheritance each cell becomes a specialized unit of the body. Some cells become nerve cells, some blood cells, some muscle cells, and so on. Through determination of single-cell development, the information in the chromosomes

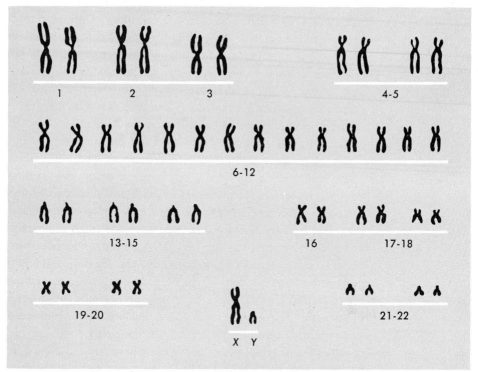

FIG. 2.1. *Normal male chromosomes. Courtesy of M. Neil Macintyre, Western Reserve University, School of Medicine.*

determines gross bodily characteristics (e.g., hair color, eye color, and the number of muscle and nerve cells). In the horse and the dog, selective breeding has isolated pure strains with special characteristics especially suitable for hunting, running, and jumping.

Just how is information stored in the chromosome and how does this information exert such a powerful influence upon the development of the individual?

THE GENETIC CODE In 1962 the Nobel Prize for Medicine and Physiology was awarded to Francis Harry Compton Crick, James Dewey Watson, and Maurice Hugh Frederick Wilkins for their discoveries concerning the structure of the material of heredity. Their investigations have provided important insights into the composition of the chromosomes and, more important, how the genetic information is encoded in them.

37

Chromosomes are made up of long organic molecules whose substance, deoxyribonucleic acid (DNA), is found in the chromosomes as two long strands periodically connected by chemical bonds. These connecting bonds are four organic *bases* (in the chemical sense of the word). The two strands of DNA are curled in the form of a helix, a configuration similar to a spiral, but which does not come to a point (see Fig. 2.2).

In normal cell division the chromosomes form images of themselves just before the cell divides. Each chromosome forms a copy of itself so that the two cells resulting from the division have exactly the same genetic composition. Before cell division, the chromosomes form copies of themselves when the two strands of DNA separate at one end and peel away from each other, progressively from one end to the other. The four basic compounds connecting the two DNA strands determine what kind of molecules will be constructed to replace the DNA strand that pulled away. Given a type of connecting basic compound, only certain molecules can be attached to replace those which tore away. The missing strand of DNA is filled in from molecules in the immediate vicinity of the breaking DNA, and since each of the original strands fills in the missing structure, an exact replicate of the original DNA double strand is produced from each of the single, separated strands. This process is illustrated in Fig. 2.3.

The most constant feature of genetic material, after many cell divisions, is the order of the four basic compounds connecting the two strands of DNA. Genetic information *must* be constant in normal cell division, and therefore, all the genetic information an individual receives is encoded into the order of the four connecting compounds. Our hereditary information is not in the long strands of DNA, itself, nor in the four connecting compounds, per se. It is in their order of appearance between the two strands of the DNA helix.

We can think of this in another way. The four basic compounds can be thought of as representing symbols in a four-letter code. Their order of appearance will be used to indicate the messages. This would be like writing in a language that has only four letters in the alphabet instead of our twenty-six. We could send any message in this four-letter code. The organic molecules in the chromosomes are so long and the interconnections so numerous that there seems to be little doubt that all of the genetic information required to designate the special func-

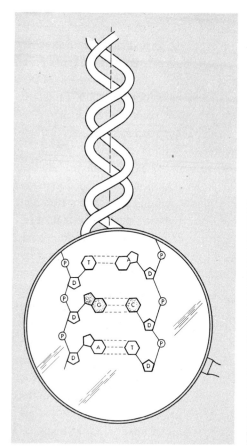

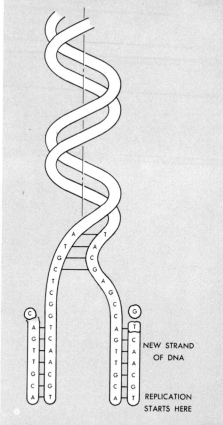

FIG. 2.2. *Highly schematic reconstruction of double helix formed by DNA molecule. Lower part of helix is enlarged to show bases adenine (A), thymine (T), guanine (G), and cytosine (C), and how these are linked with deoxyribose (D) and phosphoric acid (P).*

FIG. 2.3. *Replication of DNA during which the two strands of DNA are thought to separate, each serving as template on which new strand forms. Replication is beginning at lower ends of separated strands. Note that end result is two identical double strands.*

tions of cells in our bodies could be easily transmitted by this process—with plenty of room to spare.

Although all of the cells in the human body have forty-six chromosomes, this number is reduced by half when eggs and sperm are produced. At one stage of cell division, in the ovaries of the female and in the testes of the male, a special type of division takes place which reduces the normal chromosome number. This reduction in chromosomes prepares the way for the meeting of the egg and the sperm, each of which will have twenty-three. In this special type of cell division the regular

39

process of chromosome duplication and regrouping is altered. In this case cell division occurs without duplication of chromosomes and one member of each pair goes into each of the new sex cells. Furthermore, the individual chromosomes may not maintain their integrity. There may be a mixing up of the DNA between members of the chromosome pairs. It is this mixing at the stage of special cell division which prepares for the sperm and the egg which is responsible for the endless diversity found among people.

In normal cell division each new cell has an order of connecting bases identical to that of its former mate. If this condition prevailed in the formation of sperms and eggs, then every egg or sperm of a person would be endowed with the same order of bases. Therefore, all offspring of one set of parents would receive the same genetic information. We find a considerable degree of differences among the offspring of a given set of parents, and this diversity comes from a scrambling of the chromosomes inherited from maternal and paternal ancestors when the sex cells are made."

DETERMINATION OF SEX The sex of the offspring initiated by the union of the sperm and the egg is determined by the presence or absence of a certain chromosome. One pair of chromosomes is concerned with the sex of the child. Girls have two similar chromosomes called X chromosomes. Men have an X and a smaller Y chromosome (see Fig. 2-1). The special type of cell division which reduces the number of chromosomes preparatory to forming eggs and sperms can only result in eggs with X sexual chromosomes, because that's all there is to apportion to the new cells. The male, on the other hand, has both an X and a Y chromosome and when the sperm are produced, they may have either an X or a Y chromosome. If one of the X sperm unites with an egg, also carrying an X chromosome, then the child will be a girl. If a Y sperm meets an egg the offspring will become a boy.

Under rare circumstances chromosomal abnormalities occur. It may happen that more than two sex chromosomes result from the meeting of the sperm and egg. This condition produces a hermaphrodite, a person who has sexual organs and characteristics of both sexes. Such individuals have an extra chromosome in their genetic constitution, forty-seven chromosomes, three of which are concerned with sexual determination.

THE CONCEPT OF THE GENE   There is a considerable degree of confusion about the nature of a *gene*. The early anatomists thought the lumps which appear on the chromosomes in histological preparations were genes, but they are not. No one has ever seen a gene. Genes were inferred from an analysis of the lines of inheritance found in people and in animals. From the analysis of parents and offspring, rules of inheritance were discovered for certain bodily characteristics (e.g., eye color). When these traits are passed on from parent to progeny in what has come to be understood as a regular fashion, they are said to result from a certain gene in the chromosomes. A gene is *a hypothetical packet of genetic information determining a specific trait in the species.* Since all genetic information is in the chromosome material of the nucleus, the concept of genes in the chromosomes was invented, and it must represent a sequence of basic compounds existing between DNA strands. Recently we have learned that gene effects can be more or less localized in certain regions of chromosomes. The gene must represent the coding of information using the four organic basic compounds occurring over a limited extent of the long double-stranded DNA molecule.

Further, we know that genes controlling the same characteristics occur in matched positions on two paired chromosomes, i.e., in the same position along the extent of each pair of chromosomes. All chromosomes occur in matched pairs and the genes along one of them are related to the same bodily characteristics as the genes in similar positions on the other chromosome of the pair. We know very little as to the actual chemical composition of a gene, but we do know something of the mechanisms through which the information in the order of bases along the DNA effect the development of the body's cells.

HOW GENES WORK   The genetic information determines the development of each specific cell through the production of proteins. Protein synthesis is controlled by information encoded in the bases connecting the DNA strands. A messenger substance carries the protein-forming information in the DNA of the cell nucleus to the protein-manufacturing sites in the cytoplasm. This chemical messenger between the DNA of the cell nucleus and the extranuclear protein production sites, *ribosomes,* is a compound very similar to DNA. This substance is ribonucleic acid (RNA) and is different from DNA only in the

41

presence of an oxygen grouping in the molecule. The RNA picks up information contained in the configuration of nuclear DNA and transports this information to the ribosomes which are also made up of RNA (see Figure 2.4). The story is more complicated than this. Smaller molecules of RNA are soluble in the cytoplasm of the cell. This soluble RNA combines with specific amino acids (the stuff of which proteins are made) and with energy-packed phosphorous compounds. This package consisting of soluble RNA, a specific amino acid, and the phosphorous compounds which provide cellular energy, migrates to certain designated positions on the ribosome surface. There, the amino acid breaks free from the RNA bonds and joins with

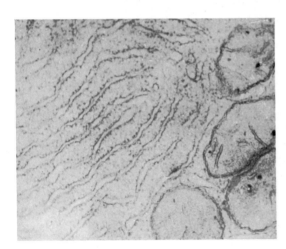

FIG. 2.4. *Ribosomes, the dark granules on the tube-like structures, are the sites of protein synthesis. The large, irregular spheres are mitochondria. The photograph was taken using an electron microscope at 50,000 diameters. From J. A. Moore.* Heredity and Development. *Cambridge: Oxford, 1963. By permission of L. D. Peachy, J. A. Moore, and The Oxford University Press.*

adjacent amino acids to form one kind of protein. The pattern of amino acid sequences, and consequently the type of protein formed, is thus determined at the surface of the ribosome and this in turn is controlled by the information brought by the messenger RNA from the nuclear DNA.

Genes are thought to be the fundamental units of biological inheritance and thus are the links of life between one generation and the next. By definition, all inherited traits are the results of genes. As we shall see, all of the genes which are inherited by the organism act together in determining characteristics. In some instances and in some species a few characteristics appear to be determined by only one or two genes. And it has been from the study of characteristics determined by a single gene that many of the rules of genetic inheritance have been discovered.

Dominant and recessive characteristics   Genes occurring in paired positions along the chromosomes carry contributions toward the same characteristics but can give information which would cause different kinds of development. One gene may act to cause the development of blue eyes, while the matched gene in the other chromosome may act to produce brown eyes. When both genes of the chromosomes act to foster the identical characteristic in the offspring, this is said to represent the *homozygous* condition. If the information concerning a given characteristic differs in the paired gene positions, the condition is called *heterozygous.* In many cases one of the tendencies of the pairs of genes found in the heterozygous condition will dominate. Thus, when a child inherits a gene for blue eyes from one parent and a gene for brown eyes from the other, the child will evidence brown eyes. Therefore, we call the gene for brown eyes *dominant.* However, the dominance of one gene over another is not absolute, and often the effects of the recessive gene can be seen in the offspring.

Mutations   Changes in genetic structure occur from time to time. There are several known ways in which these alterations can be produced. Some alterations are occurring all the time, but it has been shown that mutations occur faster than their "spontaneous" rate when the gonads of an organism are exposed to radiation. Often the effects of mutations are hidden because usually they are recessive and are obscured by the contribution of the dominant gene. However, some mutations are lethal and cause the death of the offspring. The mutant stock cannot, then, perpetuate itself. The effects of mutations are often masked by changes in the appearance of the offspring which stem from changes in the environment. Most geneticists and scientists in related fields are convinced that a low rate of mutation is preferable to a high one since few, if any, of the alterations caused by mutations help the organism to survive.

Genetic Influences

MENDELIAN INHERITANCE   In 1866 Gregor Mendel published the conclusions of his years of painstaking observations of cross-breeding strains of plants. Mendel discovered the rules of inheritance through the study of hybrid peas growing in the garden of an Austrian monastery. His principles of inheritance have been found to be applicable to both plants and animals when the particular characteristic under study is determined by a single gene. In several varieties of peas he found a number of differentiating characteristics. Once having found these characteristics that differentiated the plants, he studied the progeny that resulted from cross-breeding the different plants. Thus, he was able to study the inheritance of one characteristic at a time.

The Mendelian scheme can be summarized as follows: If a man who is homozygous for blue eyes marries a woman homozygous for brown eyes, the children of this couple will have only brown eyes. The genes determining this characteristic eye color can be called BB (brown) and bb (blue). The capital letters designate the dominant characteristic. The children of the homozygous couple will have one gene for brown eyes (B) and another for blue eyes (b). Now what happens if a heterozygous man marries a heterozygous woman? Figure 2.5 presents the outcome of this procedure. The distribution of children from this marriage will be such that one-fourth of them will be homozygous for brown eyes (BB), one-half of them will be heterozygous (Bb), and one-fourth of them will be homozygous for blue eyes (bb). Note that blue-eyed children will be born even though both parents were brown eyed. Judging only on external appearances, three-fourths of the offspring will exhibit the dominant gene trait of brown eyes.

Mendel's contribution reaches great significance because it points out that all genetic information comes to the individual in units rather than in a graduated series or continua. In other words, we receive from our ancestors genes controlling the development of specific unitary characteristics, not a mixture of various tendencies which has been blended together.

The view of Mendel that genetic inheritance came in gene packages was at odds with a long prevalent notion of biometricians (those who study the characteristics of various kinds of biological populations). Characteristics of men and animals tend to vary continuously along a dimension as is the case with intelligence. We do not find a cluster of bright people and a cluster of stupid people, but rather we find intelligence to be distributed in what appears to be a normal distribution (see Chapter 1). If our genetic inheritance comes in units, as Mendel suggests, then why do we have a continuously varying measurement of population characteristics like intelligence?

One answer to this issue was suggested by Mendel himself.

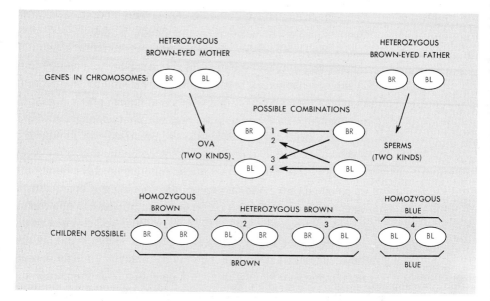

FIG. **2.5** *Probable eye colors from brown-eyed heterozygous parents. Gene for brown-eye color (BR) is dominant. Gene for blue-eye color (BL) recessive.*

He suggested that some characteristics might be determined by two or three elements (genes) acting together. In the early 1900s it was shown that if a characteristic was determined by several genes which had small but cumulative effects on the characteristic, the result would be a population which was continuous in that characteristic. Gradually the idea of continuous genetic inheritance in which hereditary influences from parents are blended was gradually discarded, and the rules offered by Mendel to explain genetic inheritance became the generally accepted rules for all inheritances.

POLYGENIC INHERITANCE The term *polygenic inheritance* refers only to the fact that some characteristics are determined by genes at more than one location in the chromosomes. Without doubt, most of the characteristics of the human that have been behaviorally studied are products of the action of many genes determining the functions of many kinds of organic systems.

SEX-LINKED INHERITANCE In some instances structural or functional characteristics of the body seem to be especially prominent in one sex rather than the other. This is due, it is

45

believed, to the fact that the genes concerned with the development of the characteristic are part of the X or the Y chromosome. Color blindness of the red-green variety is a case in point. Men tend to be color-blind much more often than women. Perhaps as much as 5 percent of the male population suffers from a red-green defect in color perception, but only a fraction of 1 percent of the female population has a similar condition. The reason for this could be that the gene for color blindness is a recessive which is only found in X chromosomes. Since women have two X chromosomes, and the gene for normal color vision is dominant, a woman could only be color-blind if she is homozygous with the recessive gene. A man on the other hand would be much more likely to be color-blind in this way because lacking a color vision gene in his Y chromosome, one recessive color defect gene in his X chromosome would produce the imperfection in vision.

Other than red-green color blindness, few other sex-linked characteristics have been identified. Certain deficiencies in blood-cell conditions and a few other organic characteristics may be sex-linked, but as we come to identify more behavioral units effected by inheritance we must be alert to the possibility of sex-linked inheritance.

LIMITING CONSIDERATIONS   The effects of genes upon behavior, as well as their effects upon the structure and function of the body, are difficult to understand fully for several reasons. One of these is the fact that the environment often acts to blur the differences among individuals which result from their various genetic backgrounds. Often environmental factors can mimic the effects of genes in the characteristics under study. Radical changes in the physiological environment can alter development of organic structures of the body. For example, a lack of oxygen in the environment of the very young fetus produces marked changes in the final structure of the organ systems undergoing the greatest degree of development at the time of oxygen privation. Less drastic alterations in the environment produce smaller changes in the developing organism, but these smaller changes tend to make the genetic inheritance less apparent.

Other confusions result from the possibility that one gene can mimic the effects of another. In lower animals it has been shown that genes located in quite different locations can produce the same behavioral effects.

Finally, it should be noted that there must be a complex interaction between genes at practically all of the gene locations. In principle this means that every gene influences the effects of all other genes in governing the developing cell. This is a most general principle and makes the study of the genetic influences upon behavior even more difficult to ascertain. At the same time this principle recognizes the fact that one gene affects bodily development or function only in concert with the many other genes inherited by the organism.

The Genetic Study of Animals

Experiments with selective breeding The most commonly used technique for studying the effects of genetic inheritance on behavior has been the selective breeding of animals. This technique takes advantage of behavioral differences which occur in a population. Animals which exhibit a similar behavioral characteristic are mated together for many generations. Fast horses are inbred with other fast horses. If there is a genetic foundation to speed in running, after several generations of such inbreeding in which only the fastest are bred with the fastest, a strain of horses should emerge which is made up of very speedy animals. If, on the other hand, there is no genetic inheritance underlying the ability to run fast, this inbreeding technique should not work. Horses inbred for speed for many generations should be no better than randomly bred horses. The obvious fact is that horses and other animals can be successfully inbred for speed in running, as well as for other characteristics, and this provides a foundation for a belief in the genetic inheritance of these characteristics.

Bright and dull rats By means of selective inbreeding, strains of rats have been isolated which have considerably greater maze-learning abilities than animals randomly mated [4]. By the seventh generation of the inbreeding procedure used by Tryon, there was little overlap between the bright and the dull maze learners. Inbreeding rats for maze-learning abilities has produced several strains of bright and dull rodent "students" [5, 6, 7].

Once two strains of animals which differed in their maze abilities had been isolated, the question remained of whether the genetic effects were due to a single gene or whether they were polygenic. If the behavior was due to a single gene, then cross-breeding the brights with the dulls should produce a type of animal represented by the dominant gene of the pair. If the strains were distinguished because of polygenic influences, the animals resulting from inbreeding the brights and the dulls should be intermediate between the two strains.

Tryon performed just this experiment. He found that the progeny of the bright animals and the dull animals fell into an intermediate position in ability and concluded that the maze skill was polygenic [4].

Research on bright and dull animals has indicated that the maze-learning abilities were but one manifestation of many differences between the strains. The bright animals were not merely smarter than the dull animals. The dull animals tended to respond to *visual* cues of the inside of the maze, whereas the bright animals responded more to *spatial* cues of the situation [8]. The dull animals were superior to the bright animals in a situation that required them to escape from water. The brights were more active in mazes but less active in the activity wheel, an apparatus which measures spontaneous running, than dull animals [9]. Some of the differences found between the bright and the dull animals may be incidental to the superior performance in the maze-learning situation. The question remains, however, which differences are incidental and which really account for the variations in maze learning of the animals.

More recently, extension of research on the characteristics of the maze-bright and maze-dull animals has developed along biochemical lines. While research has not reached a point of finality, it would appear that differences between the strains of animals may be accounted for by differences in the amounts of two chemicals in specific brain areas. As you will learn in the next chapter, one nerve cell (neuron) affects others by the release of transmitter substances. Chemical transmitters are being constantly produced and destroyed by chemical compounds at junctions between nerve cells in the brain. Efficient transmission of a nervous impulse from one neuron to the next depends upon the presence of just the right amount of transmitter substances. Rosenzweig, Krech, and Bennett [10] have argued that the balance between transmitter substances and the chemicals which act to break them down are determined through specific and separate genetic inheritance factors. It is possible that the balance between the transmitter substances and the breakdown chemicals determines the efficiency of the brain area. A favorable ratio in a visual area coupled with a less favorable ratio in nonvisual areas could act to produce animals which depend on visual cues of mazes.

Selection for other characteristics Inbreeding experiments have been used to separate strains of animals on many characteristics other than maze-learning ability. Strain differences in learning ability [11], vigor [12], wildness [13], agressive initiative [14], and the ability to win fights [15], have been reported in mice. Strain differences can be shown which are related to food hoarding and emotionality in the rat [16]. This relationship is of interest because of the work by Tedeschi [17], who found that rats hoarded food in adulthood to a greater extent if the animals had been handled early in development. It may be presumed that this early handling results in a decreased emotional reaction to fear-provoking stimuli which are present in the hoarding situations in which they are tested later in life. From the work of Tedeschi and in the light of other research it seems safe to regard food hoarding as an *innately* determined, response pattern which *can* be inhibited by excessive amounts of emotionality in later life.

Many other efforts have been directed toward the genetic separation of behavioral characteristics. But now let us turn our attention to a broad issue which has existed in the study of genetics and behavior since before the publication of Darwin's famous book which served as a foundation and stimulant to much of the later work in the area.

NATURAL SELECTION The theory of biological evolution had been advanced by the early 1800s. It had been accepted by some but rejected by others. The idea of a progressive change in the nature of animal life from lower to higher forms had a number of champions, even though the weight of many established religious and ethical organizations was thrown against the doctrine. Many famous scientists did not accept the evolutionary view of man's development on the grounds that there was just too little evidence for or against the theory. Erasmus Darwin, Charles Darwin's grandfathers had been one of the early proponents of evolutionary theory, and the famous zoologist, Lamarck, of whom we shall learn more shortly, had argued for a doctrine of transmutation of species in the course of evolutionary development. Today, however, it is the name of Charles

Darwin which is most closely associated with the establishment of evolution as a principle of biological life.

Charles Darwin's contribution stems from the fact that he recognized the need for more evidence on which to decide the acceptability of the evolutionary view. Accordingly, he sailed on the *Beagle* through the South Seas from 1831 to 1835. His detailed study of the forms of life existing in the regions visited led him to give considerable attention to the means by which nature "chose" which animals are to survive in their environments and which are not.

In the years following his trip through the South Seas, Darwin reviewed and studied his observations. He also read Malthus's *Essay on Population* during this period and this may have had an effect on his view of the determination of population sizes among the groups of animals studied. In 1859 his famous book, *The Origin of Species through Natural Selection,* was finally published. Keeping in mind that the evolutionary theory was not new, we must recognize that the importance of the work was due to its massive documentation of the theory with the result that the evolutionary view became a more reliable generalization among scientists.

The principle proposed to account for the survival of certain forms of animals and the death of others is the theory of natural selection. In this theory Darwin argues that the variations of animals which occur from time to time may be either a help or a hindrance to the preservation of that animal in its never-ending battle against the forces of nature. Today, we think of the variations found in animals of a species as reflecting mutations of the genetic material. If the mutation is of positive survival value then that animal will tend to survive and perpetuate the mutated characteristic. When the animal tends to survive, his progeny tend to survive. In natural settings the survival rate among offspring of a species is rather low. Mutations which hinder animals in their struggle for survival will result in decreased survival chances for the animal receiving the mutation; thus less progeny will occur, and the progeny will be less likely to survive. We can think of natural selection as a law of the animal world which describes the "survival of the fittest." Variations which make an animal better fit tend to be promulgated through later generations by the ever-increasing numbers of progeny arising from the mutations. Variations making an animal less fit tend to be extinguished.

Darwin also proposed a second principle of selection for survival which can be found in nature, the law of sexual selection. Darwin recognized that certain mutations occurred which were of no direct consequence for the immediate survival chances of the animal. Variation in the plumage of birds is a case in point. These nonfunctional variations of feathers could have indirect influences upon the question of survival, however. The mutation resulting in alteration of the bird's plumage could affect the sexual attractiveness of the birds. If more sexual attractiveness means more progeny then there is more likelihood that the variation would be perpetuated.

Nature selects animals which are best suited for survival through the principle of natural selection and selects others for increased chances of reproduction through secondary and indirect characteristics explained by the principle of sexual selection. But, what are the effects of the development of human societies and their cultural institutions regarding selection of the fittest humans?

When populations of animals leave natural settings of constant struggle against nature, selection for survival is based on different standards. In the laboratory situation animals are often maintained for countless generations. The principles which are important for their survival are quite different from those of the natural animals. Laboratory rats are favored for maintenance if they have a calm disposition, i.e., they do not bite their handler's fingers. The mildness of the laboratory animals would not serve the wild animals very well.

Strains of laboratory rats and wild rats have been compared. Several apparent differences were found between them which would be predictable on the basis of our current knowledge of physiology. Laboratory animals have smaller adrenal glands, for example. These glands serve the body's mechanisms for emergency reactions including aggression. Laboratory animals have sexual organs which mature more rapidly than the wild animals. In the laboratory a high fertility rate is desirable. This is an artificial selection criterion imposed by the laboratory caretakers which would favor the selection and breeding of animals with such characteristics [18]. Man's artificial environment imposes artificial rules of selection which effect the survival and perpetuation of people and their characteristics which are quite different from those favoring survival in the wilds.

In man's earliest stages of development the laws of natural

and sexual selection played a more important role than they do today. One of the effects of acculturization is to reduce the effectiveness of mutations on a person's chances to survive and contribute to new individuals. In its mercy, society acts to protect the weaker members from elimination through the harsh principle of natural selection. People with genetic backgrounds which produce rather drastic and unfavorable bodily problems can be cared for by social institutions, and the basic deficiency can often be compensated for by the use of medical know-how. Even Darwin's law of sexual selection is circumvented by the use of plastic surgery, cosmetics, and the effective use of clothes. From time to time certain objections have been raised against this role of society. People have pleaded that a continuation of genetic material which contains unfavorable mutations will ultimately result in a population of people too weak to survive despite all the remedial activities that can be undertaken. In general, people who argue for controlled breeding of humans, eugenicists, have not found a favorable reception among either laymen or scientists. There are too many unknown factors determining the structure of man to make the eugenic movement a forceful one. Even more important it is man's consideration and kindness for his fellow men that makes his perpetuation worthwhile.

LAMARCKIAN INHERITANCE   The zoologist Lamarck (1744–1829) argued a theory of *transmutation* of genetic material. He believed that changes in behavior which came about through use or disuse and those demanded by changes in the environment could be passed on to subsequent generations through hereditary mechanisms. Even Darwin suggested this might be the case. *Lamarckian inheritance,* the doctrine of the inheritance of acquired (learned) characteristics, is still prominent in some circles, despite the fact that scientific data to support such a theory are lacking.

It is not quite clear why the theory of *Lamarckian inheritance* survives at all. With but a few doubtful exceptions, all of the evidence bearing on the Lamarckian hypothesis has been negative. For many generations animals have learned various kinds of discrimination and have been subsequently mated with other animals with similar learning without any evidence that the training of earlier generations had any effect upon later ones [e.g., 19]. The doctrine of the inheritance of acquired characteristics is not accepted by the vast majority of geneticists today with the exception of some Russian workers.

Genetic Effects in the Human

It has been noted that most of the significant characteristics which come to us through genetic inheritance are polygenic. Only a few characteristics can be shown to be determined by a single gene. Again as psychologists, we shall concentrate on investigations aimed at elaborating the contributions of inheritance along lines most related to our own domain of study, that is, to studies of the inheritance of behavioral characteristics.

Before going on, however, it should be pointed out that the direct study of the genetic make-up of human cells became possible only recently through advances in techniques and methods. It is likely that the study of human genetics will advance in the immediate future far more rapidly than before. Much of what will be said in the following paragraphs will undoubtedly be elaborated, and possibly changed in conception, in the next few years.

Only in the past few years, for example, has it been possible to show that mongolism, a condition of mental retardation with a specific kind of bodily development including slanted eyes and other unusual physical characteristics, results from the presence of an extra chromosome which is located somewhere among the smaller chromosomes. Today we also know that sex hermaphrodites have an extra sexual chromosome. Both the hermaphrodite and the mongoloid have forty-seven instead of the usual forty-six chromosomes.

EARLY STUDIES OF HUMAN INHERITANCES The modern study of the inheritance of human characteristics can be said to have originated with another grandson of Erasmus Darwin, Francis Galton (1822–1911). Galton was a man of many interests and has been described as an explorer, anthropologist, and statistician, as well as a psychologist. In his imaginative study of various topics in the area of psychology, Galton attempted many approaches to the study of man which are still being utilized today. At the moment, we are concerned with his study of the nature and extent of genetic inheritance in man.

From the observation that genius tends to run in families,

Galton argued for a strong genetic influence in behavior. He was not satisfied with merely pointing out the many instances in which this apparently seemed to be true (see Fig. 2.3) but went on to collect data to support his position. In this way he was much like his cousin, Charles Darwin, who became famous for his detailed support of the evolutionary point of view.

Galton suggested ways to discover men who could truly be called eminent, i.e., men whose talents were found only about once in every four thousand men. Galton discovered that many more than one in four thousand eminent men were found in families which had already at least one eminent member [20]. Furthermore, he found decreased instances of eminence as the degree of relationship to the eminent man decreased. These data, however, were not conclusive for his hypothesis and this fact was recognized by Galton, himself. The similarity among members of a family could result from common environmental conditions rather than from a common genetic inheritance.

Galton considered other kinds of evidence to substantiate his claim of the importance of genetics for creating the correlation of abilities in families. He pointed out that the proportion of eminent men was no greater in the United States than in England despite the greater range of educational opportunities in the United States. More directly, he compared the incidence of eminence in the adopted relatives of Roman Catholic Popes, who were granted many of the finest social and environmental advantages. But Galton found this background gave rise to fewer cases of eminence than were found among the sons of eminent men.

Another innovation of Galton was the study of genetic inheritance through the use of twins. Although he recognized the existence of similar and dissimilar twins, he did not distinguish between them in his analyses. Today we know that most of the similar twins are identical twins while the majority of the dissimilar twins would be fraternal. He reported that twins who were dissimilar at birth did not tend to become more similar even though their environments were almost identical. As we shall see later in the chapter, the use of twins for the study of human genetics is now an established procedure despite serious difficulties which underly this method.

THE INHERITANCE OF INTELLIGENCE Galton began the study of the genetic influence on the development of intelligence with his analyses of the families of eminent men. Many other studies have followed this general line of investigation. Some studies have reported correlations of intelligence between pairs of members of families as approximately +.50. Based upon these reported relationships, some people have argued that we cannot safely assume that this degree of similarity in intelligence is due to genetic factors. While the arguments take several forms, the most convincing is that bright people tend to provide better environmental conditions for their children. However, data like those provided by Galton which compared the adopted children of the Roman Catholic Popes with the sons of eminent men remain to be explained if the posture of the argument is to be sustained.

Studies of twins   There are two kinds of twins: identical and fraternal. Identical twins come from the same fertilized egg. Through a mischance in cell division two individuals arise from what was originally only one ovum. Identical twins have identical genetic inheritance. Fraternal twins come from nearly simultaneous fertilization of two eggs in the mother. They have no more necessary genetic correspondence than brothers and sister (siblings), since both the sperm and the egg in each fertilization have different assortments of genes just as do other siblings. In the past few years it has been possible to determine whether twins are identical or fraternal with greater precision. Identical twins must be of the same sex and must have the same characteristics of coloration and blood composition. Identical twins have been found to be very much alike in many characteristics, including the patterns of electrical activity of the brain which can be recorded from the scalp by means of the electro-encephalogram (EEG). These findings are present even if the identical twins are brought up in differing environments from shortly after birth [21]. Identical twins have been reported to have very similar intelligence test scores even if they have been raised in separate environments, but dissimilarities in intelligence has also been reported [22]. The majority of investigations have indicated a close similarity in measured intelligence for identical twins, less similar intelligence between fraternal twins and least between brothers and sisters.

As has been pointed out, identical twins do not necessarily have identical environmental conditions. The findings of studies which compare fraternal and identical twins generally favor the genetic inheritance of some traits but are difficult to interpret, because the home environments of the identical twins *could* be more alike than that of fraternal twins. Furthermore, the development of identical twins before birth could be more uniformly effected by intra-uterine factors than the development of fraternal twins. But, positions in the uterus and other physiological occurrences could also act to make identical twins less alike and fraternal twins more alike than might be expected. Another difficulty is that studies of twins who have been reared apart often do not take sufficient account of the fact that the separated twins (separated by adoption, usually) are not randomly placed into new circumstances.

Studies of foster children   In general, the correlation in intelligence of foster children with their adoptive parents is much lower than the correlation between children and their natural parents. The intelligence of foster children tends to be fairly closely correlated with the measured intelligence of the foster parents, especially the mother [23], but the size of the correlation is much less than that of the correlation between the intelligence of mothers and their own children. Thus, the most striking resemblance is found between a child's intelligence and his true mother's intelligence even when the child has been raised with foster parents [24].

Generalizations about inherited intelligence   From the time of Galton to the present the available evidence appears to support the generalization that heredity does have an important influence on the development of the intelligence of the individual. One way to conceive of this hereditary effect is to imagine the genetic factors as setting limits, or ranges, for intelligence which can be attained by people under appropriate circumstances. Intelligence scores can be significantly influenced by differences in the environment, but the upper limit in intelligence which the person can reach through more favorable experience is set by genetic mechanisms.

What circumstances are more effective in stimulating the development of intelligence? It seems clear that the hereditary mechanism underlying intelligence is polygenic, that is, a great many combinations of genes act to produce a high score on intelligence tests. From data of other kinds of genetic experiments we know that environments which are beneficial to individuals with one set of genes may not be conducive to the proper development of individuals with other sets of genes, even though the polygenically determined characteristics produced by the two gene-types are very similar. Thus, there does not need to be any one kind of environment which guarantees to produce maximally beneficial development of intelligence. On the other hand it is clear that opportunity for development must be present in order for the "intelligence potential" to be fulfilled.

INHERITANCE OF OTHER PSYCHOLOGICAL CHARACTERISTICS

Attempts to assay the extent of genetic influence upon intelligence far surpass all other kinds of research on the genetic foundations of psychological traits. There are several reasons for this. First, and probably most important, is the fact that intelligence scores are relatively stable psychological measures. Intelligence test scores tend to remain rather constant over periods of time; and have shown themselves to be reliable and valid predictors of success in college and in certain occupations. Furthermore, they have standardized methods of administration and scoring. It is safe to say that no other kind of personality measurement technique provides as unequivocal data as come from intelligence testing. Stable test scores are absolutely necessary in order to determine the lines of inheritance which are used in tracing to establish genetic effects.

Scores on psychological tests of personality are far more variable and their interpretation is far less valid than are test scores of intelligence. In general, scores from different kinds of personality tests have low correlations with each other and there are many problems in obtaining valid predictions of behavior from such tests. Therefore, it is relatively difficult to assess traits of personality and this makes it far more difficult to assess the effects of genetic inheritance.

Personality patterns, like intelligence and other measures of performance, are most certainly the result of polygenic inheritance. A number of genes contribute to the characteristics exhibited in behavior. But, more important is the fact that several different kinds of genetic inheritance can contribute to the same behavioral effects. There is no reason to believe that one, and only one, assortment of genes underlies a given personality or behavioral characteristic. It is likely that, given the appropriate developmental environments, many different kinds of polygenic arrangements lead to the same psychological manifestation.

Studies which have used reliably measurable psychological

variables have tended to show the same pattern of findings as studies of intelligence. Correlations of motor skills, such as card sorting and manually following a moving target, tend to show higher correlations between identical twins than between fraternal twins [25]. Attempts at measuring inheritance patterns of temperament, mood, or other "personality variables" have, however, been indecisive. Some studies have reported positive results and others negative results. Here, the matter must rest for the present with an unsatisfying conclusion.

Mental disorders   The study of people with acute mental problems presents an indication of mental function that can be more or less readily agreed upon, at least when extreme. The fact that many kinds of personality disorders can be clinically recognized by many therapists makes them relatively easy to use in determination of genetic effects. The mental disorder that has been most carefully studied from the point of view of genetic inheritance is schizophrenia, a severe personality disorder characterized by a high degree of disorientation.

As a basic consideration, there can be no doubt that rates of incidence of schizophrenia are higher in families in which at least one member of the family has been previously diagnosed as suffering from the disease. For example, siblings of a schizophrenic parent have incidence rates of schizophrenia from 5 to 10 percent, whereas the incidence of schizophrenia in the general population is less than one in a thousand. The probability of schizophrenia rises rapidly when more than one sibling or one parent has been so diagnosed, and reaches probabilities of about nine in ten for identical twins of schizophrenic parents.

Those who do not favor a genetic inheritance hypothesis point out that as the genetic relationship between two individuals becomes closer, the similarity of their environments is also likely to increase.

Generally, the evidence seems to point toward a conclusion that some forms of schizophrenia are influenced by genetic factors, but such factors do not entirely account for their occurrence. In fact, Rosenthal [26] has analyzed data presented earlier (by Slater) which was obtained from the study of schizophrenia among twins, and found evidence supporting different hereditary patterns among the families of two types of twins. When both twins had been diagnosed as schizophrenic, histories of schizophrenia-like diseases were found in 60 percent of their families. When only one of the twins had been diagnosed as schizophrenic, schizophrenic case histories appeared in only 8 percent of their families.

Mental disorders indicated by psychopathic or neurotic behavior tend to have the same rates of incidence among identical twins as they do fraternal twins or siblings, [27]. While this result could imply that these two kinds of personality disorganizations have less of a genetic contribution, it could also mean that less reliable measurements or diagnoses of such disorders were made. This suggestion is given credence by the observation that scores of identical twins correlated .85 while scores of fraternal twins correlated only .22 on a "neuroticism factor" obtained from a special objective test of neuroticism [28].

Tendencies toward schizophrenia   It has been suggested that the genetic inheritance predisposing toward schizophrenia can be thought of as an inheritance of a defect in the "integrative ability" of the brain and the nervous system [3]. A precise definition of this "integrative deficit" is admitted to be beyond the present abilities of science, but Meehl argues that this concept can direct us to look for the nature of the genetic defect, namely a malfunction in the operation of single cells in the nervous system, while at the same time presenting us with the basic symptom of schizophrenia. This basic and biological deficit he labels "schizotaxia." On top of this genetic foundation the social environment adds learned reactions which tend to be common to all schizotaxic individuals. The schizotaxic individual uses characteristic type of reactions to the environment, but still may not become a schizophrenic as clinically diagnosed:

If the interpersonal regime is favorable, and the schizotaxic individual person also has the good fortune to inherit a low anxiety readiness, physical vigor, general resistance to stress and the like, he will remain a well-compensated "normal" schizotype, never manifesting symptoms of mental disease [3].

Schizotypes are people with schizotaxic tendencies but who do not come to the full degree of mental disorder resulting when individuals are not as "lucky" as those finding the favorable conditions mentioned in the above quotation. Thus Meehl suggests that the development of clinically diagnosed schizophrenia depends upon the inheritance of the schizotaxic tendency plus bad luck in having environmental conditions not hospitable to this tendency, and the inheritance of other indirectly related characteristics, such as the inability to resist stress.

One implication of such a view would be that the parents of the schizophrenic may not necessarily have the disease to the extent that it has become apparent through diagnosis, but could have less predominant symptoms which indicate the schizotype. Meehl draws our attention to the report of McConaghy [29], who found that, among parents of ten schizophrenics not diagnosed as schizophrenics, at least one parent of each had symptoms of "thought disorders" which were not disabling but still apparent. This, Meehl suggests, is support for his position and would argue that the parents were schizotaxic but more fortunate in circumstances or in inheriting other personality characteristics which act to mitigate the schizotaxic tendencies.

The significance of Meehl's ideas for us is in his suggestion of the inheritance of personality dispositions which can be controlled or modified by other genetic or environmental circumstances.

Factors Influencing Development

In a now classical article about unlearned or instinctive behavior, Beach points to the importance of understanding the relationship between environmental and genetic factors [30]. In one experiment, two strains of mice were used; one strain was susceptible to audiogenic seizures (convulsive fits induced by loud, shrill sounds) while the other did not have the susceptibility. Crossing the two strains produced an animal intermediate between the two inbred strains which of course indicated a polygenic determination of the effects. One would expect that the susceptibility of audiogenic seizures came from genetic information which was the cause of the proneness to audiogenic seizures. But, further experiments showed *this need not be the case*. Fertilized eggs were obtained from the uterus or the fallopian tubes of one strain and implanted in the uterus of the other strain. Sometimes such implants will develop in this new environment and for those that "took" it was possible to determine the seizure-proneness of the "transplanted animals." In this study mice were always transplanted from the seizure prone animals to animals of the strain which was not seizure prone [31].

The transplanted, seizure-prone mice were intermediate, that is, less seizure prone than their parental strain and more susceptible than the strain into which they were introduced. One certain conclusion from this study is that prenatal environment can play an important role in the determination of behavior, and this, as Beach points out, should make us suspicious of attempts to attribute all of the characteristics found in an inbred strain of animals to specific genes for that characteristic. The genes may actually control other characteristics, such as uterine conditions, which may in turn affect the behavioral characteristics.

Hebb [32] suggests that six factors can be distinguished which effect the developing organism:

1. Genetic. This would be merely the gene structure of the egg after fertilization. It should be emphasized that this is the entire extent of the genetic information given to new organisms.

2. Chemical, prenatal. All of the nutritive and chemical factors in the uterus as the animal develops would be included in this class. In the study of transplanted eggs of mice discussed above, one is led to believe that the uterine environment of the new mother was different from that of the natural mother. Oxygen or other deficiencies in the prenatal environment as a rule tend to effect the organ system developing most rapidly during the shortage.

3. Chemical, postnatal. In this category would be the effects on development in the chemical or nutritive atmosphere of the neonate. Continued dietary deficiencies are the most likely cause of abnormalities although other factors could be included in this class.

4. Sensory, constant. Within any species of animal, certain kinds of sensory information will almost always be presented to the developing young. To some extent, the sensory environment of one species will be different from that of any other. When we evaluate the differences in behavior between species we must keep in mind that the sensory world of each of the species has been different and this could result in different learning and perceptions of the world. Thus, the reactions of one species to changes in the environment may be quite different from those of a second species and it is possible that the differences could result solely from differences in experiences during development.

5. Sensory, variable. While many kinds of sensory experiences must be the same for members of a given species, there

always will be differences between each and every member of the species. No two animals, even identical twins, develop in the identical environments. To understand behavior, we take into account the individual experiences during development which play a part in adult behavior.

6. Traumatic. A traumatic event is harmful to the individual, often culminating in the destruction of body cells. Traumatic events are brief and are often outside the normal sensory environment of the members of the species. These intense periods of unusual stimulation can result in changes in the organism which can be influential throughout its entire life. Such occurrences may range from the "trauma" of a harsh delivery, involving the use of forceps which clamp the head of the baby too securely, or they can be accidental events which befall a developing individual. In any case traumatic events are thought to provide a basis for many unusual modifications of behavior seen in adult behavior.

From this list of classes of factors which influence the development of behavior it is apparent that it would be all too easy to mistake the effects of factors 2 through 6 for genetic effects of factor 1.

The aim of research in the area of the genetic influences can not stop when behavior can be shown to be a result of a certain pattern of genes. Even though genes can determine behavior, we must know how they do so. Do the genes affect the secretion of biochemicals? Do they change the patterns of activity in the nervous system, the muscular system, or the hormones? Do the genes affect the development of certain clusters of nerve cells in the brain? Do they affect the structure or function of receptor systems?

To describe a pattern of behavior by calling it genetic is a beginning for research rather than an end. Once the genetic influence has been determined, then we are faced with the problem of finding the underlying mechanism of the characteristic.

In summary: In this chapter we have tried to present some of the information which is available today about the effects of genetic inheritance upon behavior. Presenting information about heredity was one goal, but in addition we tried to stress the possible contribution of genetics to psychology. Modern psychology has been too greatly divorced from the study of genetics because of its own course of development, and especially because of the downfall of instinct psychology and the rise of Behaviorism. The time for a convergence of the two sciences appears to be at hand and will in all likelihood result in stimulation of new developments in research and theory for both fields.

References

1. Watson, J. B. *Behaviorism.* New York: W. W. Norton & Company, Inc., 1924.
2. Pillsbury, W. B. *The History of Psychology.* New York: W. W. Norton & Company, Inc., 1929.
3. Meehl, P. E. Schizotaxia, schizotypy, schizophrenia. *Amer. Psychologist,* 1962, **17,** 827–838.
4. Tryon, R. C. Genetic differences in maze-learning ability in rats. *Thirtieth Yearb., Nat. Soc. Stud. Educ.,* 1940, Pt. 1, pp. 111–119.
5. Heron, W. T. The inheritance of maze learning ability in rats. *J. comp. Psychol.,* 1935, **19,** 77–89.
6. Heron, W. T. The inheritance of brightness and dullness in maze learning in the rat. *J. genet. Psychol.,* 1941, **59,** 41–49.
7. Thompson, W. T. The inheritance and development of intelligence. *J. nerv. ment. Dis.,* 1954, **33,** 209–231.
8. Krechevsky, I. Hereditary nature of "hypotheses." *J. comp. Psychol.,* 1933, **16,** 99–116.
9. Searle, L. V. The organization of hereditary maze-brightness and maze-dullness. *Genet. Psychol. Monogr.,* 1949, **39,** 179–325.
10. Rosenzweig, M. R., Krech, D., & Bennett, E. L. Brain enzymes and adaptive behaviors. In Ciba Foundation symposium, *The Neurological Bases of Behavior.* Boston: Little, Brown and Company, 1958.
11. Bagg, H. J. Individual differences and family resemblences in animal behavior. *Amer. Nat.,* 1916, **50,** 222–236.
12. Vicari, E. M. Mode of inheritance of reaction time and degrees of learning. *J. exp. Zool.,* 1929, **54,** 31–88.
13. Dawson, W. M. Inheritance of wildness and tameness in mice. *Genetics,* 1932, **17,** 296–326.
14. Scott, J. P. Genetic differences in the social behavior of inbred strains of mice. *J. Hered.,* 1942, **33,** 11–15.
15. Ginsburg, B., & Alee, W. C. Some effects of conditioning on social dominance and subordination in inbred strains of mice. *Physiol. Zool.,* 1942, **15,** 485–506.
16. Broadhurst, P. L. Determinants of emotionality in the rat.

III. Strain differences. *J. comp. physiol. Psychol.,* 1958, **51,** 55–59.

17. Tedeschi, J. Infantile stimulation in rats and the genesis of the disposition to emotionality. Unpublished doctoral dissertation, Univer. of Michigan, 1959.

18. Richter, C. P. Domestication of the Norway rat and its implication for the study of genetics in man. *Amer. J. Hum. Genet.,* 1952, **4,** 273–285.

19. Agar, W. E., Drummond, R. H., & Tiegs, O. W. Third report on a test of McDougall's Lamarckian experiment on the training of rats. *J. exp. Biol.,* 1948, **25,** 103–122.

20. Galton, F. *Hereditary Genius.* London: Macmillan & Co., Ltd., 1869.

21. Juel-Nielsen, N., & Harvald, B. The electroencephalogram in uniovular twins brought up apart. *Acta genet.,* 1958, **8,** 57–64.

22. Newman, H. H. Identical twins. *Eugen. Rev.,* 1930, **22,** 29–34.

23. Burks, B. S. The relative importance of nature and nurture upon mental development; a comparative study of foster parent–foster child resemblance and true parent–true child resemblance. *Yearb. Nat. Soc. Stud. Educ.,* 1928, **27(I),** 219–316.

24. Honzik, M. P. Developmental studies of parent-child resemblance in intelligence. *Child. Develop.,* 1957, **28,** 215–228.

25. McNemar, Q. Twin resemblances in motor skills, and the effect of practice thereon. *J. genet. Psychol.,* 1933, **42,** 70–97.

26. Rosenthal, D. Some factors associated with concordance and discordance with respect to schizophrenia in monozygotic twins. *J. nerv. ment. Dis.,* 1959, **129,** 1–10.

27. Slater, E. *Psychotic and neurotic illnesses in twins.* London: H. M. Stationery Office, 1953.

28. Eysenck, H. J., & Prell, D. B. The inheritance of neuroticism: an experimental study. *J. ment. Sci.,* 1951, **97,** 441–465.

29. McConaghy, N. The use of an object sorting test in elucidating the hereditary factor in schizophrenia. *J. Neurol. Neurosurg. Psychiat.,* 1959, **22,** 243–246.

30. Beach, F. A. The descent of instinct. *Psychol. Rev.,* 1955, **62,** 401–410.

31. Ginsberg, B. E., & Hovda, R. B. On the physiology of gene controlled audiogenic seizures in mice. *Anat. Rec.,* 1947, **99,** 65–66.

32. Hebb, D. O. *A Textbook of Psychology.* Philadelphia: W. B. Saunders Company, 1958.

THREE BIOLOGICAL FOUNDATIONS OF BEHAVIOR

Thousands of millions of years ago life began. In all likelihood our development stems from the first single-celled organism, although we must acknowledge the great mystery of creation. Evolutionary theory suggests that we are in continuity with this first creation of life and that we have evolved from whatever form the spark of life had at the beginning. Human life exists in a chain of development from this primeval life.

We presume to be the highest development from this beginning, and to understand our behavior it will be helpful to recognize our connection with all other forms of life. Doing so will offer a perspective essential to understanding ourselves. We believe that we are something special in the animal kingdom—"just a little bit lower than the angels." To understand just how we are different from the other animals, while learning ways in which we are similar, it is important to trace the development of man's structure and function through his lower relations in the phylogenetic scale. Success in understanding this development will provide us with greater ability to understand the mechanisms of our own bodies. Our ultimate goal in the present chapter is to understand the mature individual in biological perspective. If we want to understand man we must understand him biologically as well as behaviorally.

The single cell of original life had to perform all of the metabolic and behavioral acts requisite to keeping alive. As we shall see, these cells grouped together and later began to specialize according to structure and function. Groups of cells began to lose their general, nondifferentiated functions and to develop highly specialized ones. Of course, in man the life of the individual cell depends upon the functions performed by an incomprehensibly large number of cells elsewhere in the body. The life of every cell in the body is extinguished when the cells comprising the kidney, heart, lungs, or parts of the nervous system fail to do their jobs.

By bonding together into complex animals, the single cells lost the thread of eternal life in the sense that some fragment of one cell would exist in the progeny resulting from the almost infinite number of cell divisions that could occur without apparent end. On the other hand, the resulting complex organism developed a new step into eternal life through sexual reproduction and the passing on of genetic materials in the sperm and the egg.

But for whatever reason, cells did come together and specialization became the rule. As psychology students we are especially interested in the cells which developed to handle the problems of communication between the cells comprising the organism. The cells which became occupied with the transmission of information from the outside world, the environment, to the other cells of the organism were the early precursors of the nervous system. In the mature animal the nervous system is responsible for the detection of changes in the environment, the transmission of information from the receptor cells to a central station (the brain) for analysis, and the conduction of command messages originating in the brain to the muscles and glands.

The complexity of the nervous system in man is frankly overwhelming. We know only too little of its principles of operation. It has been likened to a cellular city of over twelve billion inhabitants. But even more, the number of interconnections between the cells probably exceeds 300,000,000,000,000. In addition, there is recent evidence to indicate that the connections between cells may not be fixed. Time-lapse photography of cells from the human brain grown in tissue cultures reveals the cells to be in continuous motion, constantly changing their connections with one another. While our comprehension of the nervous system is meager, it is vital to even a first understanding of behavior.

Our task will begin with an examination of the development of this marvelous machine, the human brain. We shall follow the course of development of the specialized neural cells phylogenetically. After discussing the differences existing between the invertebrate and vertebrate divisions of the nervous system we shall pause to look at the building block of the nervous system—the single nerve cell—the neuron. After attaining a degree of understanding of this specialized cell we shall then attempt to understand the organization of the mature nervous system of man.

These steps shall serve us as a basis for our comprehension of psychological knowledge to be presented in later chapters, but they are important in their own right. It may be that the breakthrough needed to understand man may come from the biological world before it comes from the behavioral world. Certainly, it is man's highly developed nervous system that accounts for his place of eminence in the animal realm. It is responsible for man's humanity and great accomplishments of all kinds, but it must also be the agent responsible for his miseries and problems.

Evolution of the Nervous System

Even before we consider the animal kingdom we can observe modifications of behavior in response to external stimulation in plant life. To be sure, trees do not respond to the chop of an axe as an animal would, but plants do have growth responses and rooted plants typically bend toward light falling on them. The relatively rapid reactions to tactile stimulation of plants such as Venus's-flytrap are known to many. In general seed plants exhibit many of the characteristics of all behaving organisms: sensitivity to certain stimuli, conduction of excitation from one part of the organism to another, and some variety in response patterns. However, the plants have followed different evolutionary paths than the animals, and our primary interest is in the evolution of animal behavior.

THE AMOEBA   The amoeba has been extensively studied and is of interest to us since many basic principles of behavior can be observed in this most simple animal. If we did not know

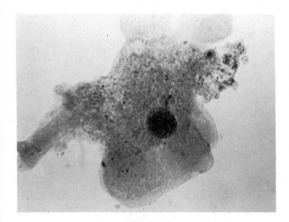

FIG. 3.1.   *Photomicrograph of an amoeba (enlarged about 130 times.) One of the simplest known forms of animal life, the amoeba nourishes itself by enveloping minute organisms and fragments of food. Courtesy of Chas. Pfizer & Co., Inc.*

that the animal was only one cell it would be easy to believe that its many responses had to depend upon the presence of many kinds of specialized cells. Consider the following facts about the amoeba:

1. *Its response is dependent upon the nature of stimulation.* When the side of an amoeba is stimulated there is an extension of protoplasm, the stuff of which it is made, toward the stimulation. If the stimulation becomes more intense the protoplasm flows away from the stimulated area and extends on the opposite side. Furthermore, the surface seems to have areas of greater or less sensitivity to stimulation.

2. *Continued stimulation alters the response to further stimulation of the same kind.* When the amoeba is brought in from the dark and placed under a microscope we observe several changes. Most pronounced among them is a general contraction. After a few minutes the animal adapts to its condition and

resumes its movements. Continued light stimulation does not produce any additional reactions.

3. *Internal states determine responsiveness to stimulation.* The amoeba will normally send a protoplasm probe toward particles near it. However, when it is well fed more stimulation than usual is needed before such a reaction will take place.

4. *The effects of several stimuli may summate to cause jointly a response neither one could elicit alone.* One level of stimulation of the surface of the amoeba may be insufficient to produce a response unless other stimulation is added. This additional stimulation may be in an adjacent area or could closely follow the other stimulation in time. The additional stimulation may be less than that normally required to elicit a response by itself. If the two stimuli, neither of which is capable of eliciting a response alone, determine a response when they are coupled in space or in time then we have a summation of their effects.

Parallels in behavior   These four principles of behavior are readily apparent in the nervous system of man. First of all, man is quite apparently differentially responsive to external stimulation. Some men are even differentially responsive to blondes and brunettes. Also, man adapts to the constant stimuli of his environment. When a new worker begins his job in a boiler factory, the noise is very obvious to him. After a few weeks he may wonder what the fuss is all about when a more recent newcomer complains. A good number of our neural cells adapt more or less quickly to a steady state of stimulation. This illustrates adaptation at the cell level in a complex animal.

Internal need states of man influence his reactions. Your usual reaction to a hamburger will be considerably modified if you have just finished a T-bone steak. More generally, we shall find that our internal states, e.g., hunger and thirst, make us differentially receptive to stimuli related to these states. Advertisers bombard us with their ads partly in the hope that the effects of stimulation will last over some period of time and affect our future behavior. They hope that a number of ads may summate their effects and alter our behavior to their advantage and profit.

At a physiological level we find that single cells in the body respond like the amoeba. The effects of two weak stimuli occurring together on a cell may affect the cell whereas neither could alone. From these considerations we can see that many of the principles of behavior of total man and his constituent cells can be illustrated in an animal as low on the phylogenetic scale as the amoeba.

On a broader scale the behavior of the amoeba has another parallel with that of higher animals. We can interpret the responses of the amoeba as attempts to maintain some specific optimal conditions in its internal chemical make-up. Maier and Schneirla [1] define these optimal conditions as those which best promote the representative metabolic conditions for the organism, in short those internal conditions which favor the survival of the animal. This tendency toward the maintenance of suitable internal conditions foreshadows the theory of homeostasis made popular by Walter B. Cannon (discussed in Chapter 8 on motivation). In brief, the theory of homeostasis argues that all behavior is motivated toward the establishment of optimal conditions in the internal environment. It would be a mistake to infer that every animal, the amoeba included, has any "idea" of what these optimal internal conditions might be. However, animals which do not act to maintain optimal internal conditions will perish. The tendency toward optimal internal conditions should be interpreted as an evolutionary development through many successive mutations of genetic structure.

STEPS TOWARD A NERVOUS SYSTEM: THE INVERTEBRATES The amoeba has only one cell and therefore it can have no nervous system, muscle system, or receptor system. Ascending the phylogenetic scale we find animals which are aggregates of single cells and above them animals that are more than collections of cells—animals which have groups of cells with specialized functions.

The phylum Porifera represents a step toward the complex individual. This group of animals, commonly known as sponges, is characterized by a group of cells organized into two layers (See Fig. 3.2). Resembling a vase, the adult sponge is fixed to one location and water is drawn in and out of the animal by the beating of some specialized cells with flagella which take in fine organic materials from water which is forced in and out through the opening at the top of the sponge. This is a primitive way of obtaining food. Each of the cells in the area surrounding the opening at the top is individually irritable. These cells jointly control the size of the opening. Each of the cells surrounding the opening acts as a *receptor* in that it is responsive to the temperature and composition of the water; but in addition, each cell can be affected by the activities of its neighbors. Stimulation of one part of the border around the opening causes the cells in that area to contract. This contraction spreads slowly throughout the remainder of cells. Thus the whole opening closes. This contraction does not depend upon cells specialized for the transmission of excitation. The initial excitation spreads in wavelike fashion from one cell to another. While one may observe the beginnings of cells which are differentiated for special purposes, as a rule each cell functions autonomously.

In the phylum Coelenterata we come upon the first true nervous system, although it is quite unlike anything found in

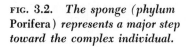
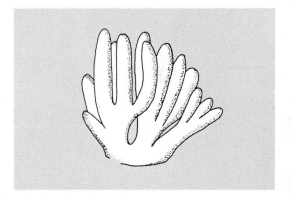

FIG. 3.2. *The sponge (phylum* Porifera) *represents a major step toward the complex individual.*

mammals. One of the representatives of this phylum is the hydra, which is probably familiar to all students of elementary biology (see Fig. 3.3). The tentacles wave about and the whole animal moves by elongation. When one of the tentacles is stimulated, the rest soon become active. The responsiveness of the tentacles to stimulation is determined by the state of the organism. The tentacles of well-fed hydra are less excitable than those of hydra deprived of food. The excitation at the point of contact in the tentacle is transmitted throughout the tentacle by specialized tissue. There are sensory cells in the outer layer (ectoderm) of the tentacle which have threadlike extensions that go to muscle cells beneath the surface. According to Parker [2], this is the second stage of development of cells in the nervous system. The first level is represented by cells which are both sensory and contractile such as those around the opening of the sponge. In the second

71

stage there is a specialized sensory cell which has an extension to a muscle system. The third stage is also found in the phylum Coelenterata and is called the *nerve net*. The nerve net is a complex mesh of cells between the receptor cells and muscles. This nerve net is diffusely organized and acts to stimulate cells of the tentacles in a widespread fashion. When one tentacle is excited, the other tentacles become excited because

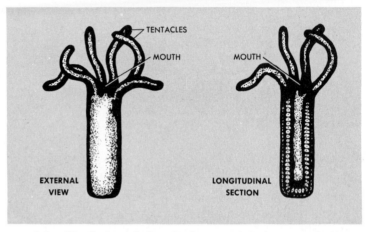

FIG. 3.3. *The hydra (phylum* Coelenterata). *Left: external views; right: internal view of longitudinal section.*

of activity of the neural net, although this excitation lacks direction.

Although some improvement in the coordination of behavior of a "nerve ring" is found in the echinoderms (starfish), we come upon our next most interesting improvements in the nervous system of the worms. One of the simple flatworms, the planarian, has been extensively studied. It is a bilaterally symmetrical animal, and has both a physiological and sensitivity *gradient* from head to tail. The head region is more active, metabolically, and is more sensitive to stimulation than the posterior regions. A drawing of a planarian is presented in Fig. 3.4. The animal has receptor cells and neural nets in the periphery. These connect with neural strands running into the head ganglia. These ganglia are merely enlargements of the nerve strands, and are thought to be responsible for the coordination of movement. However, when these ganglia are removed, the animal still moves appropriately, although more slowly and less smoothly. Excitation of the ganglia can

72

produce swimming movement. Superficially, the head ganglia would seem to be nature's first tentative step toward a brain.

Phenomena which resemble conditioning in some ways have been found in planarians. A group of investigators, led by McConnell [3, 4], has demonstrated that planarians can "learn" and, even more exciting, can pass along something of this learning to its offspring. Through a procedure called *classical conditioning* they have shown that these flatworms will contract to a light which was previously ineffective in producing the contractile response. The first step in such a classical conditioning experiment is to ascertain that the stimulus used as the conditioned stimulus does not produce the response. Therefore, in the studies under consideration the worms were exposed to light until the experimenters were convinced no contractile responses were being made. Then the conditioned stimulus (*CS*), light, was associated with a stimulus which is effective in producing the desired response. In the present case electrical shock to the worm was the unconditioned stimulus (*US*) which was used to produce the contraction response. The response produced by the *US* is called the unconditioned response or reflex (*UR*). After a number of pairings of the *US* and the *CS,* the light and the shock, the animals will come to make a response similar to the *UR* (con-

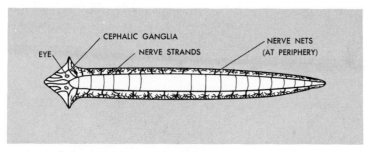

FIG. 3.4. *Drawing of a planarian.*

traction to shock) to the *CS* (light). This contraction made to the previously ineffective *CS* is called the conditioned response or reflex (*CR*). Generally speaking the *CR* is very much like the *UR,* but it is more than a matter of simple substitution of stimuli. The *CS* does not elicit a response exactly like the one elicited by the *US.* This classical conditioning model will be of importance to us throughout this book, and it may be helpful to master the simple steps in this conditioning *paradigm* early (see Fig. 6.2, p. 216).

It has been found that the planarians are capable of acquiring what very much appears to be a conditioned response, but the fascinating part of the story is yet to come. This kind of worm can reproduce by a regeneration of its separated parts. If one of these worms is cut across the middle creating a head-half and a tail-half animal, both ends will regenerate into complete animals. Interestingly, both parts show retention of the learned response acquired by the previous whole animal. The head ganglia are included in only one of the two parts of the animal. Yet the results clearly show that both the new animals learn the avoidance problem faster than animals regenerating from cut but untrained animals. If anything, the animal from the tail portion seems to relearn the contraction response faster. This means that the effects of the training, learning the avoidance response in our example, are not dependent upon changes in the head ganglia in the planarians. These studies suggest that alterations in the animal's chemical make-up could be responsible for this transmission of information from separated parents to regenerated offspring. Today we believe a great amount of learning of higher animals to be the result of changes in the pattern of interrelated activity of groups of neurons acting on one another. The fact that the tail-region animal inherits some knowledge of the avoidance problem suggests that there may be more than one bodily mechanism underlying the learning and memory processes.

In the cephalopod popularly known as the octopus we note several improvements in the nervous system and in its range of behavior. The nervous system of the animals contains several head ganglia not dissimilar to those found in the worms, but in addition a specialized receptor for visual stimuli has developed. The octopus has an eye with a movable lens which can focus light on sensory cells behind it. The effects of changes in illumination are transmitted by nerve fibers to the ganglionic lobes at some distance from the eye. This primitive visual system is efficient enough so that the octopus can use visual cues to direct attacks on its main foodstuff, crabs. The nervous system of the octopus is still rudimentary, and the behavior of the animal is limited in range. For example, it does not seem to be able to respond to barriers placed between it and the food. If it is "aware" of the barrier, it does not seem to be able to coordinate its movements to circumvent the barrier. However, the octopus can learn to inhibit its usual response of catching and eating a crab when one is placed in front of him. By appropriate administration of an electric shock as a punishment when the crab is placed on a given colored card, the octopus learns not to move about and enclose the food [5]. The octopus will continue to attack the crab when it is on a card of a different color. Surgical interference with one portion of the octopus' brain (the vertical lobe) can produce an astounding change in the animal's reactions. When the animals are tested after surgery, they can still remember not to attack a crab on the "wrong" card if the experimental trials are within five minutes of each other. When the intertrial interval is lengthened to two hours, the animal does not restrain his attack and is punished. In the cephalopod's neural lobes there must be different systems for long-term memories which are distinct from those involved with short-term memories. This represents our first contact with two kinds of memory, but it will not be our last. We will come to find that higher forms of life, including man, seem to have several kinds of memory processes.

The octopus seems to be the result of an evolutionary growth that is an offshoot from the main course of development leading to the vertebrates. The direct path of phylogenetic development is believed to run via the nonsegmented animals, the segmented worms, and insects. Herrick describes the neural organization of the segmented worms and the insects in a way difficult to improve:

The body of a worm may be compared with a loose federation of separate states, each with autonomous self government and responsible to a central power only in its foreign relations. In the insect, to carry out the analogy, the central governing power (head dominance) is stronger, the states (segments) are united in three subsidiary federations (head, thorax, and abdomen), and yet each state retains a measure of autonomy. The machinery of government is almost entirely inflexible, as if it were merely the execution of immutable laws [6, p. 143].

Both the worm and the insect can exist admirably well without their heads and even show definite signs of learning. However, some activities which occur in normal animals will not occur if they are decapitated, but changes in the external environment can compensate for this loss. For instance, decapitated moths will not lay eggs spontaneously, but will with certain special kinds of sensory stimulation. This illustrates the fact that the loose neural confederacy of the segments is not entirely dependent on the central power, the head ganglion. The organization of the nervous system of the vertebrates is entirely dependent on the centralization of the brain.

With the insect (phylum Arthropoda) we reach a peak of complex behavior for the invertebrates. The bees even have what can be described as a language of their own. The ants have a complex social order. But as Herrick has pointed out their behavior seems to be governed by certain inflexible laws. While their behavior is complex it is inflexible. It is important not to confuse these two concepts. We can obtain some insight into some characteristics of the laws which seem to govern the behavior of such animals by inspecting the spider spinning his web. Different species of spiders tend to spin their own distinctive webs. The number of webs they spin is proportional to their food intake. Again, as we have seen as far down the phylogenic scale as the amoeba, the internal environment of the animal, especially as determined by recent food intake, is important for controlling even unlearned reactions.

As with much of the behavior of insects, the spider's behavior appears to be and is indeed complex. Yet it consists largely of many fixed responses to various stimulus patterns.

To some extent the spider's motion seems dictated by the growing web, which may be considered as a gradually developing field of force. The varying tensions of long and short segments, the distances between intersections, the lengths of filaments and the angles between them—each furnish stimuli to which the instinctively driven spider is compulsorily obedient [7, p. 118].

This quotation by Savory illustrates the complex control which the environment, as interpreted by the animal's sensory system, exerts upon behavior of the lower animals.

Of a seemingly more complex nature is the communication of bees. Karl Von Frisch, an Austrian zoologist, has spent years studying how bees learn the location of food from other bees. Watching a bee's return to the hive, Von Frisch found that it communicated its find to the other bees in the hive by a dance [8]. The vigor of the dance indicates the amount of nectar left at the source. When the nectar supply is running out the bees returning to the hive dance slowly or not at all. When the supply is plentiful, the dance is more vigorous. The direction to the food source is given by the angle of inclination from horizontal. This angle is related to the position of the sun in the heavens. The intricacies of the sensory determinants of this complicated bee behavior are enormous and not fully investigated. For instance, Von Frisch has found that the bees are capable of relating direction of the food source to the sun's position even though the sun is itself obscured. (Whether this involves a capacity to respond to infrared light or to polarization of the light is unknown.)

Here at this level of insect life we find an elaborate communication system. It is a type of symbolic communication. In many ways it can be considered as similar to our use of language for symbolic communication. Equally fascinating is the capacity of these animals to use the position of the sun in the sky as a reference point in their communication of the position of the food source. Since they can use the sun's position as such a reference point, they must make use of stimuli that we do not normally use (i.e., the polarization of light or the infrared rays). Thus the sensory world of the bee must be one which is quite different from ours.

We have seen that the insects communicate symbolically. They also show what might be called social behavior.

When groups of army ants are placed on a flat surface, free of obstacles, they begin a death march. They march in eccentric circles, controlled by stimuli arising from their own group and a counteracting centrifugal force. In the jungle the army ants run into many obstacles which more or less randomly alter the group's path. Where there are no obstructions the geometry of the forces is unaltered and results in an almost certain formation of suicide mills [9]. The behavior of an individual army ant is completely determined by the group. The behavior of groups of humans is much more flexible, less determined by specific sensory patterns, than the behavior of ants.

In both the bee and the ant we can find prototypes of caste systems. For example, some bees are workers, some drones, and generally there is a queen. Each bee or ant has a certain role to fulfill in its community and generally follows a certain behavioral pattern commensurate with this role. Animals adopt such roles, however, because of their biological make-up, whereas the caste systems of human society are determined by a social not a biological heritage. Our position in any caste system is one which is subject to modification by the individual and by changes in the social structure.

Throughout the study of the invertebrates we have learned of many instances of complex behavior and even of group or social organization typified by the army ant. Yet invertebrate behavior is rigid to a great extent. It lacks the flexibility of human behavior, or even the behavior typical of vertebrates generally. Furthermore, the behavior of the insects consists largely of innate responses to stimulation. The spider builds a type of web whose structure is predictable if we know the species of spider. A particular spider's response to a strand or filament of the web is determined by genetic information acquired from his ancestors. The spider is equipped for survival by nature with innate responses. We are equipped for survival by the great flexibility of our nervous systems and our capacity to change our activities to meet the present conditions of the world. Both types of systems work effectively.

Because we are a part of the animal world, we might assume that we are born with certain kinds of responses to stimulation which are determined to some extent by our genetic inheritance. To understand the nature of any of our genetic dispositions, we should study the nature of genetically determined behaviors in other members of the animal kingdom. The general adjective used to describe responses which are exhibited by animals without any chance of their having been learned is *instinctive*.

Instinctive Behavior

Instinctive behavior occurs without being learned. We think of such behavior as species-predictable and passed on from generation to generation through hereditary mechanisms. For example, spiders build webs that are predictable if we know their particular species. The belief that this information is passed on through the DNA of the genes (see Chapter 2) is a presumption. But to classify a response as instinctive, we must be able to show that it exists even when we have deprived the animal of all chances of learning it. Since it does occur in the absence of learning and is exhibited by all members of a species, we assume that the genetic material common to the species contains the information requisite to building the physiological mechanism underlying the response.

Psychologists tend to think of instinctive responses as *elicited responses.* By this we mean that the responses are triggered by a stimulus in the environment. The notion of a stimulus-response model has been inherent in much of our discussion, but when we use the word *elicited,* we make the proposed relationship more concrete. Thus we come to a conceptualization of instinctive responses as unlearned reactions of the organism which are triggered or released by particular kinds of environmental stimulation. That the stimuli eliciting the innate behavior pattern may be complex has already been suggested by our study of the spider.

However, studies of the instinctive behavior of fish and birds suggest that the stimuli which act to release instinctive behavior can be quite restricted. The zoologist N. Tinbergen has studied the behavior of the three-spined boney stickleback. This fish displays a number of instinctive responses, some connected with the mating cycle. The male stickleback assumes control over a portion of the sandy bottom of his tank or pond. Once in possession of such a territory he will defend it from male intruders. The male stickleback will also show courtship behavior when a female comes into his area. The courting behavior leads to actions which help to squeeze the eggs from the female and which result in the fertilization of the eggs. The courting behavior, known as the zig-zag dance, is determined by heredity. Tinbergen has investigated the stimulus characteristics which are sufficient to release this courting behavior [10].

One technique Tinbergen has used is to introduce various shapes into the water near the male stickleback. By altering the character of the stimulus it is possible to determine specific attributes of the entire pattern which act to release the innate behavior of the zig-zag dance. He finds only a few characteristics of the female form are responsible for the elicitation of the response. The specific attribute which calls out a particular kind of instinctive behavior is called the *sign stimulus.* The sign stimulus for the zig-zag dance is a protruding underportion of a figure that needs be only vaguely fishlike. The characteristic of a bulging underside of a figure is the important feature of the environmental situation. The

79

bulge is the sign stimulus. In Fig. 3.5 the various stimuli used to test for the sign stimulus of the courting behavior are presented. The sign stimulus responsible for eliciting the aggressive behavior appropriate to a male intruder seems to be the size and color of the underbelly of a fishlike form.

Tinbergen can manufacture better sign stimuli than those provided in nature. He can emphasize and enlarge the sign

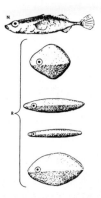

FIG. 3.5. *Models of stimuli used by N. Tinbergen in his studies of instinctive behavior in the stickleback. From N. Tinbergen.* A Study of Instinct. *Oxford: Clarendon Press, 1951. By permisson of the author and the Clarendon Press.*

stimulus characteristics in his models. When these special stimuli are presented, they exert more effect upon the animal than any stimulus naturally found in the environment. These artificial and exaggerated sign stimuli are called *supranormal sign stimuli*.

If the male fish has been stimulated time and time again to make a courting response, the presentation of yet another protruding female form will not usually elicit another zig-zag dance. In short we find adaptation of the response through repeated occurrences. However, if we present one of the supranormal sign stimuli this may be potent enough to release the behavior. On the other hand Tinbergen has observed that if the response has not occurred for some time in the past, instinctive responses often occur even when no sign stimulus is present. It is almost as if energy for a particular response builds up to a certain point and then the response will occur with a minimal amount of stimulation. The *energy* of a particular innate response is specific for a specific stimulus. The effect is not one of general fatigue. The number of recent occurrences of the aggressive responses to other males does not affect the amount of sign stimulation required to release a courting response to a female.

From this work it would seem that animals are instinctively

responsive to certain attributes of environmental stimulation. Only a part of the whole stimulus pattern is important.

From the preceding chapter we have become aware of the maturation and development of man. In the world of lower animals we find a type of instinctive activity for which genetically determined preparations have been made but whose fulfillment depends on (1) a critical period of postnatal development and (2) the occurrence of special stimulating conditions.

The sight of a group of goslings following a mother goose is a common enough sight in rural areas. But in Fig. 3.6 we find a group of goslings following Dr. Konrad Lorenz just as naturally as they would their mother. Through the work of Lorenz [11] and others we know that most fowl will follow *any stimulus* presented to them at a critical time

FIG. 3.6. *Goslings following Dr. Konrad Lorenz, having been imprinted on Lorenz at an early stage in their development. Courtesy LIFE Magazine* © *1955 Time Inc.*

after hatching. They do not *learn* to follow the object in the usual sense, rather they *immediately* follow the object presented to them. The object, whatever it may be, is *imprinted* into a following-response behavior system. When the imprinted object is presented, the birds follow it. In fact it appears now that ducks will imprint sounds and tactile sensations as well as visual objects.

Studies of the imprinting process by Hess [12] suggest that the manner of presentation of the stimulus to be imprinted is of crucial importance. Hess keeps his newly hatched ducks in the dark for about 15 or 16 hours after hatching, then they are placed in a circular runway while an object moves around it. The duck follows the object for four turns around the runway. These conditions prove to be very effective in eliciting durable imprinting. Generally, Hess finds that conditions in which the animal is aroused and required to do some work are desirable for imprinting responses. If the young animals are tranquilized with drugs, the following response is poorly imprinted.

Of greatest interest to us now is the extraordinary nature of this instinctive reaction. No innate reaction to a specific stimulus is prepared; rather the nervous system is prepared to incorporate any stimulus-object into ready-built motor sequences providing that the conditions of stimulation and of the organism are right. The work of Tinbergen, Hess, and Lorenz just discussed illustrates some of the exciting frontiers of research on the instincts found in animals. We have avoided the word *instinct* because it readily lends itself to the suggestion that a behavior is easily explained. When we use the word *instinct* we should mean no more than an unlearned response of the organism. We should not then abandon further attempts to understand the mechanisms of behavior responsible for it. The mechanisms of the instinctive responses could be the fundamental units of all behavior; in the higher, more tractable animals learned characteristics may overlie and modify the structure and functions already provided by heredity.

Development of the Human Nervous System

As Herrick pointed out, the nervous systems of the vertebrates are as different as they can be from those of invertebrates. The segmental, body-state federation character of the invertebrate plan is lost, and a central control agency of the whole organism is established in the vertebrates. The parts lose their autonomy and accept commands issued by the central nervous system and its chief unit, the brain. Messages from the senses pour into the central command station of the brain and there they are sorted, catalogued, and evaluated before being transformed into new messages for the individual muscles. All that man is, or can be, depends on the functions carried out by the central nervous system. It will be our next task to try to gain some understanding of its development, structure, and function.

Embryologically, the nervous system of all vertebrates develops from a central tube of nerve fibers. The longitudinally organized tracts of the neural tube (in man the forerunner of the spinal cord) allow the greater central control of all activities. Possessing the centralized nervous system typical of

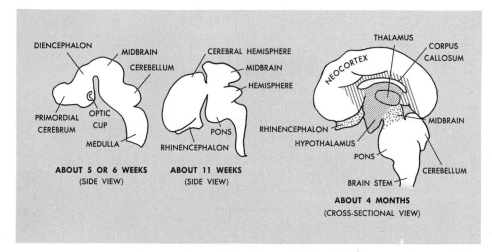

FIG. 3.7. *Stages of brain development of human embryo. Stripes show phylogenetically "old" cortex; shaded area represents the diencephalon (thalamus and hypothalamus), and the dots indicate the midbrain.*

the vertebrates, man has a vast number of elaborate reflexes and, more important, the possibility of considerable modification of behavior through experience.

Neither the brain nor spinal cord ever loses this tubelike organization. As maturation progresses, the cells of the tube in the region which will become the brain show the greatest number of divisions and alterations, and as a result certain early prominences appear which are the precursors of later adult brain structures.

Figure 3.7 shows the structure of the anterior portion of the nervous system of the human embryo at five or six weeks, eleven weeks, and four months after conception. In the four-week embryo the region that will become the medulla and the region which will become the midbrain area of the adult have begun to separate. The beginnings of the visual system are seen in the rapidly developing optic vesicles. The endbrain and the betweenbrain can be distinguished to some extent.

In the three-month embryo a great amount of further differentiation is observed. Now the endbrain has become clearly separated from the betweenbrain, and similarly the betweenbrain is distinct from the midbrain. The primitive cells from which the cerebellum will develop have begun to appear. Also the region of the medulla is more distinct from the rest of the brain or spinal cord.

The region of the medulla will contain cells which are concerned with the regulation of many internal organs and the facial muscles. The cerebellum will become a neural center controlling posture and act as one of the coordinating centers of sensory information from many of the senses. The midbrain is a region containing relay nuclei for some of the senses and contains regions concerned with modulating the information coming in from all of the senses and the outgoing information on the way to muscle cells. The betweenbrain will include in addition to certain other structural parts two regions of particular interest, the thalamus and hypothalamus. The thalamus is primarily a relay station for information from all of the sensory systems but in addition has groups of cells which act in more general fashion to regulate activity of other areas of the brain. The endbrain will differentiate into many different clusters of cells in many different kinds of arrangements. Certain of these will be cells spread over the upper regions of the brain in layers. These cells arranged in layers and overlying the upper end of the brain we call the *cortex*. We shall soon see that there are several kinds of cortices. Each kind develops at different phylogenetic stages of development and presumably each is related to different kinds of behavior in the human. We shall soon learn that the cortex is not homogeneous in structure or in function. Specialization of function is a very prominent feature of the central nervous system.

Although our discussion and illustrations may have given the impression that the brain is a discrete series of segmental structures, this is not the case. All brain regions are intimately related. The brain is continuous and interconnected, one part with the other. Some of the developing brain regions will be concerned with rather specialized functions, but each part operates in cooperation with many other parts and each cell is influenced, directly or indirectly, by almost every other cell in the brain.

THE SINGLE CELL OF THE NERVOUS SYSTEM   The units from which the nervous system is built are single cells called *neurons*. The nervous system is a massive collection of thousands of millions of neurons. To understand how the nervous system operates we must understand the construction and workings of the units of which it is composed.

There is of course a functional resemblance between the single neural cell found in the adult human and the single cell with which we started the chapter, the amoeba. Each

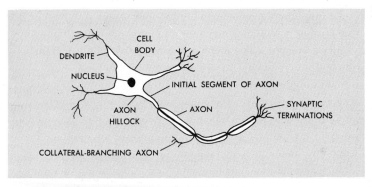

FIG. 3.8.   *Schematic drawing of a neuron.*

must have nourishment and ways to handle the elimination of waste products. Both the amoeba and the neuron have cell membranes, nuclei, other protoplasmic structures, and patterns of reactions to appropriate stimulation. Neurons differ from other cells in the body in that they are specially constructed to transmit excitation swiftly from one end to another, even though the distances between the point of excitation to the end of the neuron may be considerable.

Our brains are essential to our existence, and the brain is nothing more than interconnected masses of cells. Our perceptions, experiences, behavior all depend on the brain. Our hopes, dreams, and aspirations must be explicable in terms of the activities of the single cells of the brain. Investigations

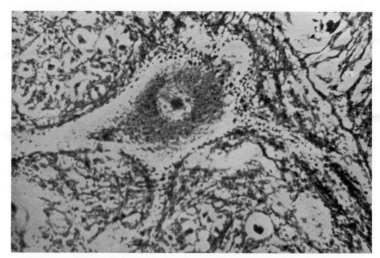

FIG. 3.9.   *Cell body of a neuron. Small dots are synaptic termi-*
nations of axons from other cells. Photomicrograph from a slide
prepared by Grant L. Rasmussen, in A. Brodal. The Reticular
Formation of the Brain Stem: Anatomical Aspects and Functional
Correlations. *Springfield, Ill.: Charles C Thomas, 1956. Used by*
permission of the author and the Trustees of the William Hender-
son Trust.

into the brain which have attempted to reveal more than mere
brain cells in action have failed. In the single cell and their
organization we must find our understanding of ourselves.

In Fig. 3.8 we have diagramed the structure of a single
nerve cell in a schematic representation, and in Fig. 3.9 we have
presented a photomicrograph of a single nerve cell. In Fig.
3.10 a photomicrograph is presented to illustrate the complexity of connections of any given cell with others. Because of
the myriad of interconnections between neurons it is misleading to think of a neuron in any other context than as
closely and intimately connected with thousands of others.

Formally, the nerve cell is thought to be divisible into
three functionally discrete parts. One part, the *dendrite,* receives excitation from preceding cells. If this excitation is
sufficient to cause a reaction in the dendrite, this reaction
spreads to the *cell body,* the second part, and then along to
the end of the *axon* portion, the third part. When this spread-
ing reaction reaches the end of the axon, its effects may cause
the next neurons to react in a similar way. Each cell is a unit,
structurally distinct from other cells. The connection between

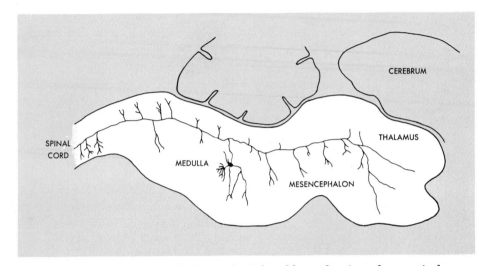

FIG. 3.10. *Sagittal section of the brain of a 2-day-old rat, showing a large reticular cell projecting forward and backward for considerable distances. Adapted from Madge E. Scheibel & A. B. Scheibel.* Reticular Formation of the Brain. *Boston: Little, Brown and Company, 1958. By permission of the authors, the Henry Ford Hospital, and Little, Brown and Company.*

the axons of one cell and the dendrite of the next is the *synapse.*

Today, we are aware of other types of junctions between cells which may be different from the axon-dendrite arrangement just described. According to Eccles [13] some axons connect directly with cell bodies of subsequent cells. This kind of synaptic arrangement can be called an axon-cell body junction. Eccles found that in some spinal-cord cells which are linked by axon-cell body connections, stimulation of the dendrites could not be great enough to cause the reaction to spread to the cell body or axon. Only the activities of cells with processes ending directly on the cell body could cause the resultant reaction, or excitation, to spread to the cell body and axon.

What is meant by excitation of a neuron? Upon examining the membrane of a neuron at rest, we find a preponderance of sodium (Na^+) and chlorine (Cl^-) ions on the outside of the membrane. (Ions are electrically charged particles of various chemical elements.) On the inside of the cell we find a preponderance of potassium ions (K^+). We are not at all sure of the chemical mechanisms that maintain the separation of the ions across the membrane; but this separation does exist and is called the *polarization* of the membrane, as it exists when the cell is in a resting state. Neural excitation refers to a change in this resting condition. During this change, the positive ions of sodium (Na^+) flow inward, and the polarization of the membrane breaks down. This process is called the depolarization of the cell membrane. Almost as soon as this depolarization has occurred, certain chemical processes begin which act to reestablish the former polarized state. The Na^+ ions are forced outward again to the exterior of the membrane. The original polarized state is reestablished. The time required for all these activities is extremely brief. The depolarization and restoration processes sufficient to allow another depolarization are accomplished in about one-thousandth of one second. Some nerve cells can fire about one thousand times a second for indefinite periods of time.

One fascinating problem of neurophysiology is how the excitation crosses the synapse. The answer now seems to be that the conduction of excitation across the synapse is accomplished by chemicals, released by one neuron, which cause the second neuron to be depolarized. When the excitation reaches the end of the axon, little pockets release certain chemicals (transmitter substances) which flow to the cell body or dendrite of the next cell. These pockets of chemicals in the terminations of the axons are illustrated in photograph made by the electron microscope in Fig. 3.11. When these chemicals reach the membrane of the next cell, a depolarization of the membrane is begun. Most likely there are several kinds of transmitter substances, or chemicals, which are released at synapses. There is evidence that some transmitter substances do not cause a depolarization of the next cell's membrane, but rather act to increase its polarization (even more Na^+ and Cl^- ions on the outside of the membrane; more K^+ on the inside). The increase in polarization results in inhibition of the activity of the neuron. There may be several kinds of chemicals acting to either increase or decrease the polarization of cell membranes.

When a depolarizing substance reaches a cell membrane, it always has some depolarizing effect. However, this effect may not spread to the rest of the cell body and in turn down the axon. There is a segment of the cell body which chemically "decides" whether the net depolarization effects of all of the transmitter substances acting on it are large enough to precipitate a complete reaction of the cell body and axon. This portion of the cell body acts to integrate all of the chemical influences acting on the cell at every moment. If the net depolarizing effect is sufficient, the cell reacts. If the totality of the influences is insufficient, no total reaction of the neuron will occur. When sufficient depolarizing influences impinge on a cell to trigger a reaction, the depolarization of cell body and axon is complete. It does not matter whether the depolarizing influences were just barely enough or much more than required.

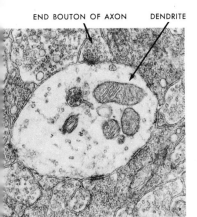

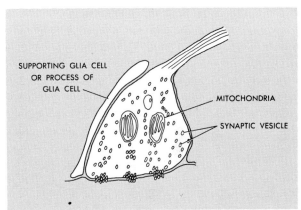

FIG. 3.11. *Photograph (left) and schematic drawing (right) of a synaptic ending based on electron microscopy. Photograph courtesy of Dean E. Hillman, Kenneth A. Siegesmund, and Clement A. Fox; drawing adapted by permission of The Rockefeller Institute Press from E. De Robertis, Submicroscopic changes of synapse after nerve section in the acoustic ganglion of the guinea pig.* The Journal of Biophysical and Biochemical Cytology, *1956, 25 (September 25), 503–512.*

If the cell responds, it responds completely. This phenomenon is the classic all-or-none law. If a cell fires, it fires all the way.

The depolarization of the cell body and axon is referred to as the *spike* potential because of the sharp spikelike waveform observed in oscilloscopic recordings of the neuron reaction. In Fig. 3.12 the reaction of an entire nerve, a collection of axons, is presented and in Fig. 3.13 a record from the axon of a single cell is shown. After the quick, sudden change the cell returns to its resting state. This recording of a spike discharge illustrates in dramatic fashion the basic electrochemical activity of the brain—the excitation of the individual nerve cells. We can record other electrochemical activities of the brain and nervous system. Records are often made of the activity of a nerve, which is composed of a group of axons.

Another technique records the gross electrical activities occurring in an area of brain tissue. Somewhat similar techniques are used in each case. Small wires or other electrically conducting substances are placed near or in the material from which recordings will be made. The electrical changes in the area under study are picked up by these conductors (electrodes) and then are sent through several stages of amplification before they become large enough to be seen on an oscilloscope or to deflect a pen in an ink-writing device. The recent advances in our knowledge of the electrical activities of the brain have depended upon the development of recording techniques and equipment. Thus our knowledge of the neurophysiological bases of behavior could only be gained when the technology of other fields, notably electronics, developed appropriate techniques and equipment.

This pattern of interdependence between technology and basic research has been prominent throughout the history of science. Investigations of the activity of the single cell and the

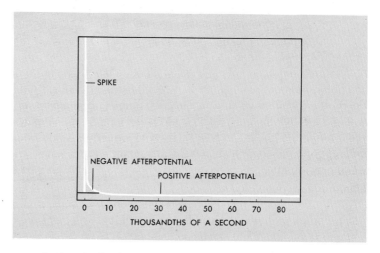

FIG. 3.12. *Scale diagram of complete action potential of a large, myelinated nerve in the cat. Adapted from H. S. Gasser. Electrical signs of biological activity.* J. appl. Phys., *1938*, 9, *88–96.*

related electrical phenomena of the brain are searches for basic knowledge. They are attempts to learn just how the nervous system works. Applications are sure to follow the accumulation of basic knowledge, but at this point the student should seek to gain understanding of the principles of neural function.

We have spoken of neurons, synapses, and the principles of their excitation and conduction in a way that the student could easily conclude that each cell is a passive unit only activated when stimulating situations are appropriate. However, the nervous system is continuously active. Cells are firing spontaneously all

FIG. 3.13.   *Action potential of a nerve fiber. Adapted from H. S. Gasser. The classification of nerve fibers.* Ohio J. Sci., *1941, 41, 145–159.*

the time. Stimulation of a cell results in an increase or decrease of the rate of activity, depending on whether the transmitter substances act to depolarize or hyperpolarize the membrane.

Even though the neurons of the brain and central nervous system are electrically active, and possibly physically active, at all times, studies of the nervous system have revealed *units of organization.* By this we mean that a given animal, e.g., man, has groups of cells whose functions are somewhat well defined and known. Understanding of the brain depends on knowledge of these organizational principles.

Anatomy of the Nervous System

To be effective a football team must work together to gain common objectives. The results of the team depend on every player doing his assigned task. In the nervous system various units act to perform different specialized functions, and again the result of their work is dependent upon the appropriate functioning by all of the parts. Just as we might analyze the functions of one player on a football team, we can try to isolate the functions of one or another anatomical parts of the nervous system. In both cases we should keep before us the fact that

91

we have isolated but one part from an ongoing process. The activity of the part under study is normally determined by activity in all of the other units and the constant flux of external events.

This section will take the nervous system apart in order to present some of the known anatomical units for study. First, we shall look at the peripheral aspects of the nervous system concerned with (1) providing us with the information about the outside world and (2) controlling muscular activities. Then we shall move inward to the central nervous system and upward toward the brain. We shall move from specific systems to more general ones which exist in the nervous system and, at the end of this section, present some of the brain structures which modulate all incoming and outgoing messages.

THE SENSES AND THE AFFERENT SYSTEMS   One of the essential functions of the nervous system is to detect changes in the physical stimuli surrounding us. We can think back to the amoeba and recall that stimuli tended to arouse the whole animal, but it is generally true that as we go higher and higher in the scale we find that more and more cells are specialized for the detection of a limited range of stimulus changes.

Cells which are sensitive to changes in specific kinds of stimulation are called receptor cells. Some are found in collections of cells with a similar function called *receptor organs* or *receptors,* others are scattered about in the skin and muscles. Receptor cells come in a wide variety of sizes, shapes, and functions. We shall discuss the general features of receptors and discuss more elaborately the nature of those in the visual and auditory systems in the next chapter.

The over-all picture of our peripheral sensory systems is presented in schematic display in Fig. 3.14. From the receptor organs, groups of axons of cells (located in or near the receptor organs) run into the central portion of the nervous system: the spinal cord and the brain. These constitute the nerves connecting the receptors to the central nervous system. In the spinal cord, the impulses originating in the receptors course toward the higher centers. Usually, the ascending fibers end on cells in restricted portions of the thalamus, and these thalamic cells in turn send axons to restricted areas of the neocortex.

The nerves which carry information from the receptors to

the thalamic areas and brain are called *afferent nerves* (afferent fibers if we are talking of single axons). The neocortical areas which receive the information from a specific thalamic area, and consequently from a specific kind of receptor, are called *projection areas*.

Receptor cells are different from other neural cells in that they can become excited by physical energy changes which do not affect other cells. In the chain of cells which carry impulses toward the brain in the afferent systems only the first cells, the receptor cells, have this function. The other cells in the chain are excited by normal processes, namely the transmitter substances of the synaptic junction.

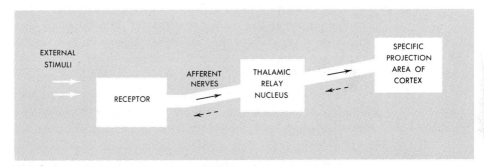

FIG. 3.14.   *Schematic representation of all sensory-projection systems. Sensory fibers run from receptors toward cortex by way of the thalamic relay nuclei. The broken arrows indicate anatomical pathways running from the cortex to the thalamic nuclei, and from the thalamus to area of the receptor, presumably allowing central control of the peripheral receptor mechanisms.*

In the receptor cell, physical energy is transformed into changes in the spontaneous activity of the receptor cells. This has great implications for us. It means that the brain does not receive *redness, loudness, burning sensations,* or *smells,* per se. But it does receive changes in the activity of millions of single neurons, and the brain in turn transforms these changes of activity in such a way that redness, loudness, burning, and smells are created. These qualities are products of the brain.

One of the most fascinating areas of research is that concerned with understanding the relationship between the physical energy changes and the changes in the activities of single neural cells. This task could be described as an attempt to crack the neural code used to transmit information about the states of the receptors to the brain.

MUSCLES AND THE EFFERENT SYSTEMS Some nerve cells have axons that end not in a synapse with another nerve cell but rather in muscle. Chemicals released at the termination of the axons produce a contraction of the muscle. The contractions of all kinds of muscles are governed by nerve fibers: both the somatic muscle system that moves the body and the muscles of the internal organs are controlled neurally by the central nervous system. The nerves that run to somatic muscles are called, collectively, the *somatic motor system.* The nerves which end in the muscles of the internal organs and glands are called the *autonomic nervous system.*

The autonomic system can be further subdivided into two categories: the *sympathetic division* and the *parasympathetic division.* Anatomically, the sympathetic division is localized by two long nerve trunks *outside of the spinal cord,* extending from the base of the skull to the "tail bone." One is on each side of the spinal column. The nerve fibers of these trunks, their fibers extending to visceral organs and their connections to the rest of the nervous system, are known collectively as the sympathetic division of the autonomic system. Generally, the sympathetic division readies us internally for stress and emergency reactions.

The parasympathetic division includes the cranial nerves supplying visceral and facial muscles and a component which leaves the spinal cord near its base and supplies internal organs in the pelvic area. Generally, the parasympathetic division acts to maintain processes such as digestion, food metabolism, and excretion, and its effect on other internal organs is to maintain the normal vegetative functions of the body.

The organization of the peripheral somatic motor system is less complex than the peripheral organization of the autonomic nervous system. Cells in the motor areas of the neocortex initiate impulses which arrive at cells in the spinal cord. These cells in turn send impulses to the appropriate muscles. If anything happens to damage the nerves from the spinal cord to the muscles, the muscles become limp and cannot be contracted by normal means. In other words, a complete flaccid paralysis is produced when the motor nerve supply to the muscles is interrupted. Interestingly enough, muscle activity also depends upon the nerves which run *from* the muscle to the cord and higher centers (the *afferent* nerves). If these afferent nerves are severed the muscles are paralyzed just as though the motor nerve was interrupted. Our muscle movements depend upon a complex interplay in the cord of afferent (sensory) and efferent (motor) impulses.

Certain simple behavioral acts are organized within the cord. For instance, when the patellar tendon is struck, the muscles of the leg contract, sending your foot forward in the knee-jerk reflex often demonstrated in the physician's office. This reflex *can* occur without assistance of the higher areas of the nervous system but normally is modulated by higher nervous centers. We should recognize the extent of this modulating effect even in simple reflexes. Even though the physician taps your crossed knee with his rubber hammer, you *can* consciously inhibit the reflex. Excitement or arousal increases the size of the reflex. The basic mechanism is built into the spinal cord, but it is under the direct influence of the brain.

THE AUTONOMIC SYSTEM   It is much more difficult to provide an overview of the autonomic system. Fibers associated with the sympathetic system seem to act in some cases as if they should be classified with the parasympathetic system. Some experts believe it would be better to divide the autonomic system into two branches on the basis of the transmitter substances involved in a chain of neurons or the effects of certain drugs on the synapses in the systems. It is sometimes difficult to separate the two systems anatomically. For example, the heart receives fibers from both divisions of the autonomic system. It is extremely difficult to separate the fibers from the cranial nerve of the parasympathetic division and those coming from the sympathetic trunks. However, for the present we shall continue with the traditional separation of the two components based on anatomic structure. Figure 3.15 shows some of the internal organs and their relation to the autonomic systems.

There are many mysteries still to be solved regarding the autonomic nervous system. One of the most pressing problems is the relation of the autonomic system to the brain areas. While we know the specific neocortical areas of origin of the somatic motor system, we know very little about the origin of the fibers going into the divisions of the autonomic system. At the moment, however, we know that portions of the limbic system and the hypothalamus exercise various amounts of control over the autonomic system.

The internal conditions of the body are partly regulated by the nervous system, as we have learned. There is another

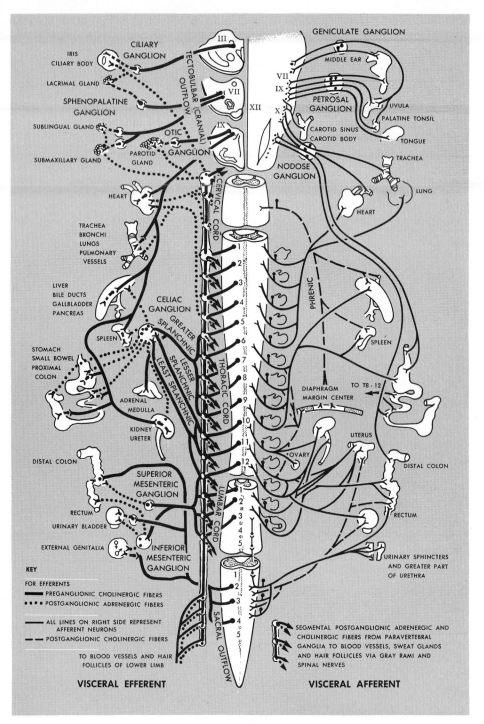

FIG. 3.15. *Diagrammatic representation of the visceral efferents and afferents.*
From T. C. Ruch & J. Fulton. Medical Physiology and Biophysics *(18th ed.).*
Philadelphia: W. B. Saunders Company, 1960.

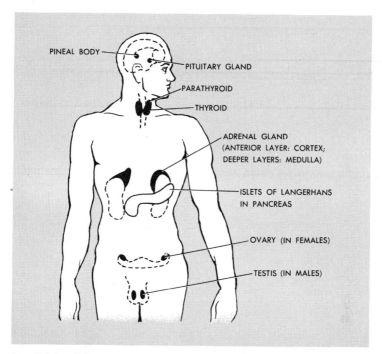

PINEAL BODY

PITUITARY GLAND

PARATHYROID

THYROID

ADRENAL GLAND
(ANTERIOR LAYER: CORTEX;
DEEPER LAYERS: MEDULLA)

ISLETS OF LANGERHANS
IN PANCREAS

OVARY (IN FEMALES)

TESTIS (IN MALES)

FIG. 3.16.   *Diagrammatic representation of the endocrine glands.*

controlling and regulating system that merits our attention: the endocrine system.

THE ENDOCRINE GLANDS   The body's glands can be categorized on the basis of whether they secrete their contents through a duct or not. If they do not secrete through ducts they are called *endocrine* glands. Substances secreted by the endocrine glands, called *hormones,* are sent into the blood stream and, therefore, may cause effects of a more widespread nature. Many hormones are of extreme importance in the individual's behavior and development. Although the endocrine glands are so important to behavior that they cannot be omitted from our discussion, their relation to behavior is so complex that much of what will be said represents a vast oversimplification. Figure 3.16 illustrates the position of the major endocrine glands.

There are many hormones secreted by the *pituitary* gland, which lies below the anterior margin of the hypothalamus. This gland is often called the master gland of the body, for its hormones influence the secretions of many other endocrine and

97

duct glands. One of the pituitary hormones is the adreno-corticotropic hormone (commonly abbreviated ACTH), which influences the activity of the adrenal gland. Other hormones from the pituitary assist in the regulation of the output of the thyroid (thyroxine) and the pancreas (insulin). Still other hormones from this body are concerned with the development of sexual organs, the secretion of milk from the mammary glands, and the conversion of fats and proteins to carbohydrates. Hormones secreted by another portion of the pituitary control the body's loss of water through the kidney. The pituitary also helps to regulate blood pressure.

The thyroid gland secretes a number of hormones which help control the basal metabolic rate of the body and its growth. The parathyroid glands work to maintain the calcium and the phosphorous balance of the blood.

Insulin is a hormone secreted by the pancreas which acts upon individual cells to allow blood sugars to enter them as nourishment. People unfortunate enough to produce too little of this hormone are commonly called *diabetics*. When there is an insufficient amount of insulin, the individual cells cannot absorb and use the available blood sugars and the blood sugar level climbs. With the injection of insulin the cells can absorb the sugar, and the blood sugar level drops toward normal. The actual mechanism whereby insulin controls the cell's membrane to allow sugar to enter is still unknown.

The adrenal glands secrete hormones from their surface layer (cortex) and their centers (medulla). The hormones produced in the adrenal cortices control the carbohydrate and sodium balances of the body, while the adrenal medulla produces adrenalin (epinephrine) and noradrenalin (norepinephrine). Adrenalin stimulates secretion of sugar by the liver, increases the heart rate, and raises the blood pressure by increasing the heart rate. Noradrenalin raises the blood pressure through constriction of the peripheral blood vessels.

Our secondary sexual characteristics, such as beard and body hair, are controlled by hormones secreted by the sexual glands. In the male these are secreted from the testes, but the female hormone system is much more complicated. There are hormones secreted from different kinds of cells in the ovary as well as from the placenta during pregnancy.

These and many other hormones act in a coordinated fashion with the sympathetic and parasympathetic systems in maintaining the body during periods of normal activities and in times of emergencies. Adrenalin produces many of the same effects as does increased activity in the sympathetic system. Thus, the adrenal medulla and the sympathetic system often are jointly referred to as the sympathetic-adrenal system. Since insulin is so necessary for body maintenance the term parasympathetic-insulin is sometimes used to describe the functional convergence of the two systems, one neural, the other hormonal.

THE BRAIN At the top of the spinal cord, we reach the pinnacle of man's neural development, the brain. We may think

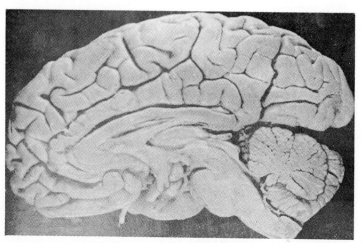

FIG. 3.17.   *Brain sectioned in the median plane.* From E. Gardner. Fundamentals of Neurology *(4th ed.). Philadelphia: W. B. Saunders Company, 1963.*

of it as beginning at the medulla oblongata and continuing upwards through pons and cerebellum, midbrain, hypothalamus and thalamus, before reaching the cortex (see Figs. 3.17 and 3.18). In man the neocortex covers the surface of the brain and is extremely convoluted, as can be seen in Fig. 3.19. The major neocortical areas are labeled in the sketch provided in Fig. 3.20. The significance of these convolutions can be appreciated when one recognizes that about one-half of all of man's neocortex lies hidden from sight in the valleys (sulci) between the convolutions (gyri). Neocortex ranges in depth from about 1.5 to 4.0 millimeters in different cortical areas.

At the top of the spinal cord is an enlarged region, called the medulla, or medulla oblongata, and pons. All of the fiber

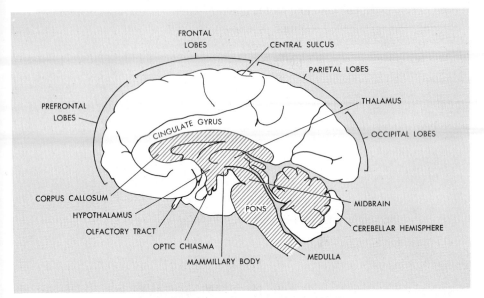

FIG. 3.18.   *Diagram of medial surface of the brain shown in Fig. 3.17.   Adapted from E. Gardner.* Fundamentals of Neurology *(4th ed.). Philadelphia: W. B. Saunders Company, 1963.*

tracts carrying information from the body ascend through this region, as do the nerve fibers descending from higher regions of the brain which control bodily movements. In the pons and medulla, however, there are groups of nerve cells which send axons downstream into some of the most important internal organs. These clusters of cells (nuclei) act as centers for the activities of the heart and lungs and their integrity is essential to life. Throughout the center of the midbrain and pons there is a network of cells which are believed to exert general and diffuse influences upon the activity of the higher regions of the brain and motor movements of the body. The central core of this region is called the brain-stem reticular system (see pp. 104–107). Finally, in this same region of the brain there are important interconnections with the cerebellum, usually thought to be important for maintaining balance and posture, and clusters of cells (nuclei) which help in the refinement and coordination of bodily movements.

Above the pons is the midbrain. The ascending and descending fiber tracts also pass through this region, and in it the reticular formation occupies a central position. At the top of the midbrain there are reflex centers for movements related to vision and audition. At the bottom there are nuclear groups which participate in coordinating motor movements.

Immediately above the midbrain is the small but important area called the hypothalamus. The border between the midbrain and hypothalamus is marked by the mammillary bodies which are part of the hypothalamus. This region contains many groups of nerve cells which function as centers for many kinds of behavior related to maintaining the individual and perpetuating the species (see pp. 328–329).

The hypothalamus is above and extends both ahead and behind the optic chiasm. This is the point at which the optic nerves, one from each eye, come together; and it is at this point that some fibers are exchanged between the two optic nerves before the fibers continue back to reach a relay station in

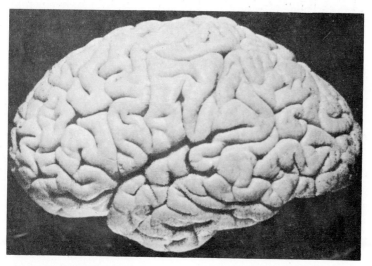

FIG. 3.19.   *Lateral surface of the human brain. From E. Gardner.* Fundamentals of Neurology *(4th ed.). Philadelphia: W. B. Saunders Company, 1963.*

the thalamus. From the thalamus (see Fig. 3.18) visual information will be transmitted by neural impulses to area 17 of the occipital lobe and then to surrounding areas 18 and 19.

The corpus callosum, a most prominent feature of Fig. 3.17, is a collection of a large number of fibers which connect areas of one hemisphere with corresponding areas of the other hemisphere.

The thalamus, located above the hypothalamus, has several

kinds of cell groups (or nuclei). One type contains cells which receive axons from one of the sensory systems and relay this information to the brain's neocortex. Another type contains cells which project to wide regions of neocortex and other higher brain regions. Since cells in these nuclei diffusely bombard brain regions, their role in behavior will be discussed in the following section on diffuse systems. We already have learned that certain thalamic areas contain cells which project to restricted neo-cortical areas.

The fibers leaving the thalamus from the relay nuclei for vision all go into the visual projection areas in the occipital lobes. The fibers from cells in the thalamic relay-nuclei for hearing reach cells in special areas of the temporal lobes, and neocortical cells just behind the central sulcus receive impulses originally arising from receptors in the muscles, joints, and skin (the somatosensory system). Note areas 1, 2, and 3 of Fig.

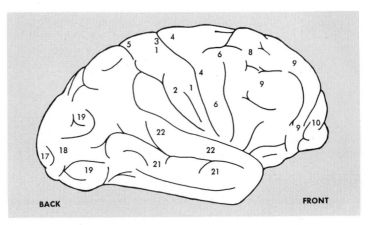

BACK   FRONT

FIG. 3.20. *Lateral surface of the human brain showing the numerical designations of cortical areas developed by Brodmann.*

3.20. These projection areas are again presented pictorially in Fig. 3.21, but in this figure we may compare the relative amounts of brain surface occupied with the reception of sensory information. As one goes higher and higher in the phylogenetic scale the amount of brain committed to a given sensory (or motor) responsibility becomes less and less. Areas of neocortex that have not been identified with specific sensory or motor tasks are called *association areas*. In passing we should note that it is often assumed, implicitly at least, that the

greater the amount of uncommitted association area the greater
will be the behavioral flexibility of the animal.

The thalamic relay cells of the somatosensory system project
to cells behind the central fissure in a rough approximation to
the location of the receptors in the body. Today, we know there
are many cells, other than those located in the primary somatosensory areas, which receive the fibers coming in from specific
body receptors. For example, the primary motor areas in front
of the fissure receive a number of afferent fibers [Woolsey, 14].
Thus, while there is anatomical and functional evidence for
describing certain areas as motor and others as sensory, we must
recognize a considerable overlap in function throughout the
cortex.

The primary motor areas just mentioned lie just anterior to
the central sulcus (areas 4, 6, and 8 of Fig. 3.20). The term
motor cortex or *motor strips* refers to areas of cortex in which

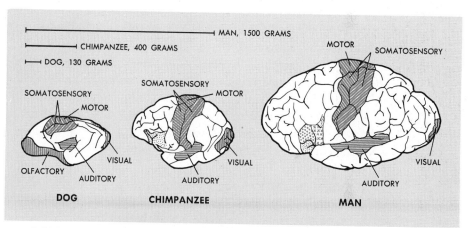

FIG. 3.21. *Lateral views of three mammalian brains drawn to scale to show the
relative sizes of primary sensory and motor areas of (a) the dog, (b) the
chimpanzee, and (c) man. Adapted from G. W. Bartelmez,* Man from the point
of view of his development and structure, *in* The Nature of the World and of Man
by H. H. Newman by permission of the University of Chicago Press. © 1926 by the
University of Chicago. All rights reserved.

the majority of cells have axons which extend down to the cell
bodies of motor neurons in the cord. These motor neurons send
projections out to the somatic musculature. The motor cortex
is not arranged haphazardly. There is a systematic organization
in which adjacent cortical cells influence neighboring muscle
cells. One interesting facet of the organization of the motor

cortex is the ratio of the number of neural cells to the number of muscle cells in a given body area. In general we observe that those areas of the body which are concerned with fine discriminations and delicate movements have the greatest number of controlling cells in the cortex.

However, the axons which run to the motor neurons in the cord originate in many other places in the cortex than the "classical areas" just in front of the central fissure. There are secondary and tertiary motor areas for most muscle groups. Lilly [15] has demonstrated that stimulation of any area of the neocortex can produce bodily movements when the animal is unanesthetized and free from physical restraints. There may be a great number of highly organized motor areas of the brain of which we know little, and *all areas* of the cortex may be involved in the production of our normal behavioral acts. There is probably no area of the brain that is entirely motor or entirely sensory in function.

The mechanisms responsible for coordinating the contractions of many muscles into a complex movement of the hands or face are poorly understood, but we know that some areas in the medulla are essential to this coordination. In addition, some neocortical areas just outside of the classical motor areas of the cortex seem to have similar functions. These cortical areas lying immediately anterior to the classical motor area are essential to the complex tactual movements, but their removal does not seem to cause any disturbance of gross movements.

THE DIFFUSE SYSTEMS   A more complex type of regulation of the motor systems is effected by the *diffuse system* of the reticular formation of the brain stem and spinal cord.

Up to this point we have assumed a simple model of neural activity: sensory pathways going toward the neocortex and motor tracts running down from the neocortex to muscles. While our presentation has been oversimplified, the underlying model represents the classic view of the afferent and efferent systems. Usually it is assumed that the *integration* of signals arising from the different senses takes place in the neocortical association areas.

Within the past ten to fifteen years a body of research findings has developed which makes it necessary for us to add some new features to our views of neural organization. These findings relate to the discovery of new functions for parts of the brain and spinal cord and may be briefly summarized as follows: Most generally, certain areas of the upper brain stem and thalamus can act so as to regulate the activity in the following:

1. The sensory afferent fibers and possibly the activity of receptor cells themselves
2. The neurons controlling muscle movements
3. The neocortex and other higher centers

Because the effects of these thalamic and brain-stem areas are generally widespread and because cells in these areas project to wide areas of cortex, these thalamic and brain-stem regions are considered to be parts of a diffuse system of brain

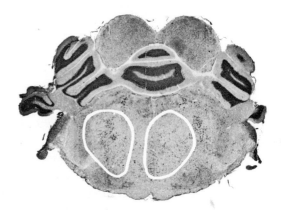

FIG. 3.22. *Photomicrograph of the brainstem of a rat. Enclosed areas represent portions of the brain stem reticular formation. Photograph by R. L. Isaacson.*

function. Most of the research on the diffuse systems has been in the brain-stem areas. Therefore, we shall discuss this portion of the diffuse systems in greatest detail.

Throughout the spinal cord and running to the forward margin of the midbrain, there is a region of nerve cells that appear netlike when stained and viewed under the microscope. In the upper regions it is referred to as the brain-stem reticular formation. Figure 3.22 shows a cross section of the upper spinal cord with this area outlined. At first it seemed to be capable of almost magical things. It was described as the neurological basis for learning, motives, and general alertness of the body and brain. As research progressed claims about its functions have become more cautious. However, there is little doubt that this region is very important in regulating many of our sensory and motor activities. We shall have occasion to speak of brain-stem reticular formation several times later in the book, and at this time we shall discuss only some of its most widely known properties.

Cells in the brain-stem reticular formation act upon cells located in upper regions of the brain with a diffuse rain of nervous impulses. Whether or not the bombardment is completely diffuse is unsettled. It may be that not all areas of the reticular formation bombard all areas of the upper levels of the brain. Brodal [16] has pointed out the likelihood of a considerable specificity in the activities of this system. In other words, certain portions of the brain-stem reticular formation may send impulses to restricted cortical areas. However, some theories in psychology have assumed a complete generality of diffuseness of reticular formation activity. Assuming a general diffuse bombardment, these theories then relate this bombardment to an activation or arousal of the brain. Evidence supporting this view can be obtained from studies of the electrical activity that can be recorded from the neocortical surface of the brain.

By electronic amplification, one can record the changing patterns of electrical potentials from the brain surface or even from the overlying scalp. These patterns originate in the neocortex and are thought to be related to the arousal or alertness of the person or animal from whom the records were obtained. French *et al.* [17] stimulated the brain-stem reticular formation electrically and found that this stimulation could alter both the waking and drowsy EEG patterns to ones that are indicative of greater arousal. Some of their EEG recordings obtained before, during, and after brain-stem reticular formation stimulation are presented in Fig. 3.23.

The brain-stem reticular formation also can produce facilitation or inhibition of reflex movements of the extremities. The response of a leg to a tap of the patellar tendon reflex (the knee jerk) is easier to obtain and of greater amplitude when certain areas of the brain-stem reticular formation are stimulated. Today we conceive of the brain-stem reticular formation as a system (or systems) of neurons which modifies the activity of the higher regions of the brain as well as the motoneurons in the spinal cord. Presumably, it does this by controlling the excitability of the individual neurons. Today we also recognize that the brain-stem reticular formation is regulated in turn by sensory stimulation from all receptors and by output from the cortex and higher subcortical areas.

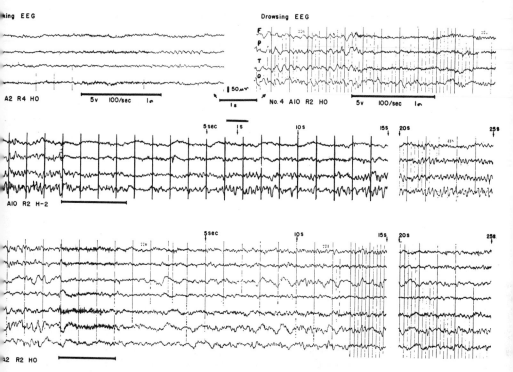

FIG 3.23. *Effects of stimulation of the reticular formation upon the waking (upper left) and drowsing (upper right) electroencephalograms. Two lower tracings illustrate long lasting effects of such stimulation on the activity of the brain in a drowsy state. From J. D. French, F. K. von Amerongen, & H. W. Magoun. An activating system in the brain stem of monkey.* AMA Arch. Neurol. Psychiat., 1952, *68*, 577–590.

Later in the book we shall discuss the theoretical significance of the brain-stem reticular formation under several topic headings. For instance, in discussing sensation we will find that the brain-stem reticular formation can influence the activity of receptor organs themselves.

THE LIMBIC SYSTEM   Between the great grey mantle of neo-cortical cells and those of the thalamus there are several varieties of cell masses which are distinct from neocortex. Some of these cell groups are related to the modification and coordination of movements (the basal ganglia). Other cell groups are collectively called the *limbic system,* and this group of structures seems to be especially important for many psychological phenomena.

The term was first used by Broca in 1878 to designate the phylogenetically old cortex which surrounds the upper portions of the brain stem. It presents a common denominator [18] of brain tissue for all of the mammals. Figure 3.24 shows the area of the brain which is called the limbic system in the rabbit, cat, and monkey. As one ascends the phylogenetic scale, the *relative* amount of brain tissue in the limbic system decreases as the amount of neocortex increases. (The neocortex is anatomically differentiated from older cortex in that it either has, or went through, a developmental stage that has six layers of cell bodies. Phylogenetically older cortex does not have, and never had, this many layers of cells.)

In general the limbic system develops from portions of the brain devoted to olfaction (smell). The limbic system is

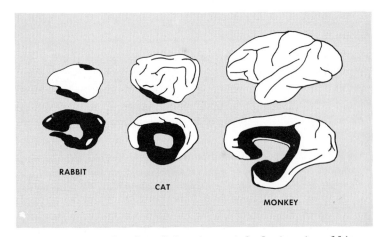

RABBIT

CAT

MONKEY

FIG. 3.24.   *Lateral and medial surfaces of the brains of a rabbit, a cat, and a monkey. The limbic lobe (shaded area) forms a common denominator in brains of all mammals and seems physiologically to be a common base for a variety of behaviors involved in self-preservation and preservation of the species. Note how limbic lobe surrounds the thalamus. (Limbic means "forming a border around.") Redrawn from P. D. MacLean, Studies on the limbic system ("visceral brain") and their bearing on psychosomatic problems, in E. Wittkower & R. A. Cleghorn (Eds.).* Recent Developments in Psychosomatic Medicine. *London: Pitman Medical Publishing Co. Ltd., 1954.*

especially large in animals that depend for their adjustment to the environment upon smell. However, in the higher animals the limbic structures do not have any important connection with the sense of smell and seem to have taken over new functions far removed from olfaction. For our purposes, the major divisions of the limbic systems are as follows:

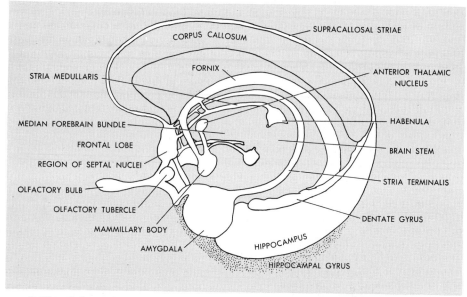

FIG. **3.25.** *Schematic representation of the relationships among various subcortical structures of rhinencephalon, as if seen through lateral surface of the brain. Adapted from P. D. MacLean. Psychosomatic disease and the "visceral brain:" recent developments bearing on the Papez theory of emotion.* Psychosom. Med., 1949, *11,* 338–353.

1. The hypothalamus
2. Nuclear masses of the amygdala, septal area, anterior nucleus of the thalamus
3. Older cortical areas: hippocampus, cingulate cortex, orbito-frontal cortex, temporal pole, etc.
4. Fiber tracts connecting various regions of the limbic system, e.g., the fornix, medial forebrain bundle

(These areas and nerve tracts are illustrated in Fig. 3.24.)

The hypothalamus is an area at the base of the brain just anterior to the upper end of the brain stem proper. About the size of a large marble in adult man, it is an extremely complex structure. In Fig. 3.25 one can see the medial forebrain bundle running through the hypothalamic areas and along the base of the brain. The fornix can be seen descending from the septal area and terminating in the posterior hypothalamus near the two prominences at the rear, the mammillary bodies. The hypothalamus itself is made up of several subgroups or nuclei.

Most of the limbic system is involved in the regulation of the internal organs, the viscera. Some refer to the limbic system as the visceral brain because of this control. Kaada [19] has shown that electrical stimulation of practically all of the various parts of the limbic system alters the activities of the internal organs. Since we believe the functioning of our internal organs to be intimately related to our mental states, emotion, motivation, and behavior generally, we can infer the importance of the limbic system, itself.

Since the limbic system is concerned with the internal organs, it must be closely involved with the autonomic branches of the nervous system. Such an intimate relationship has been found in the hypothalamus where an anterior-posterior division of function has been found.

Electrical stimulation of the anterior hypothalamus, through implanted electrodes, produces effects which are typical of those mediated by the parasympathetic division of the autonomic nervous system. Stimulation of the posterior portions of the hypothalamus results in activities of the emergency type served by the sympathetic division, such as increased heart rate, blood pressure, and respiration. These anterior and posterior divisions of the hypothalamus easily lead to a view that control centers for the respective portions of the peripheral nervous system exist in the hypothalamus.

The concept of centers in the hypothalamus which tend to control or regulate behavior has been very fruitful in our understanding of the central organization of the brain. Today, we know that there are regions in the hypothalamic area which seem to regulate the sleep-wakefulness patterns of the animal [20]. In addition, centers regulating the initiation and cessation of eating behavior, water intake, and aggressive behaviors have been reported as localized in the hypothalamus. (For an introductory review of these functions see [21].)

These represent only some of the important controlling and regulating functions believed to be localized in the hypothalamus. Considering even the ones we have listed, one cannot but be impressed by the significance of this relatively small amount of neural tissue.

Recent work suggests that electrical stimulation of parts of the limbic system may produce effects on behavior that may be most easily explained on the assumption that it elicits pleasurable sensations in the animal.

In his original experiments Olds was attempting to stimulate a specific subcortical area of the brain. He wanted to obtain an increase in the general arousal of the animal. In planning this experiment he thought that it would be desirable to have some means of controlling for possible painful or unpleasant sensations that might be produced by the stimulation. Therefore, he placed the experimental animals with electrodes embedded in parts of their brains into a large box and stimulated the brain regions with minute amounts of electrical currents when the animals wandered into one part of the box. He reasoned that if the stimulation of the brain was unpleasant the animals would not return to the region where they had had their brains stimulated. To his surprise the animals kept coming back for the electrical stimulation. Olds then set up a situation where the animals could press a bar which would close an electrical circuit and send the small electrical current into their own brains. This particular response, the bar press, is a very common type of testing situation for animals. Most often, however, the animal is rewarded by food for each depression of the bar. In Olds' experiment the reward was an electrical stimulation of a particular region of the brain. Olds found that electrical stimulation appeared to be as good a reward as food was for the hungry animal, as measured by the rate at which the animals pushed the bar [22].

Since the original bar-press experiments, Olds has found that animals will cross an electrically charged grid which gives them a painful shock to obtain this stimulation of the brain. In fact they seem to be willing to withstand a more painful shock to reach a place of electrical stimulation of the brain than they will to reach food when hungry. Generally speaking, stimulation of certain brain regions produces effects which are stronger than the effects of most, if not all, natural reinforcements [23].

In Fig. 3.26 we can see an X-ray of one of Olds' experimental animals. Under careful anesthetic and surgical techniques, a pedestal is screwed into the skull which has insulated silver wires extending beneath it. The silver wires are very small and extend into the brain region that Olds wishes to stimulate later. Only the very tips of the wires are uninsulated. When current is passed through the wires, it passes only between the tips of the electrodes in the brain and only stimulates neurons in this area. With the small amounts of current used by Olds, only cells in the immediate vicinity of the electrode tips are excited by the electricity.

With self-stimulation techniques the rat brain has now been

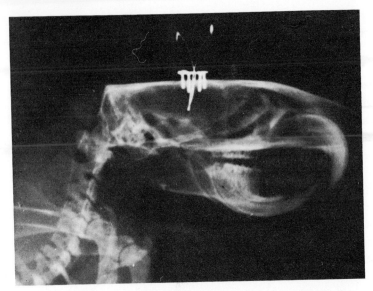

FIG. 3.26. *X-ray of implanted electrode in intact rat. Electrode pedestal is held to skull by four screws while two insulated wires, which reach deep into brain, have insulation broken only at tips, stimulating the brain only at this point.* From J. Olds, & P. M. Milner, Positive reinforcement produced by electrical stimulation of septal area and other regions of rat brain. J. comp. physiol. Psychol., 1954, 47, 420.

explored for regions that seem to act like rewards for the animals [24]. At this time it appears that positive reward behavior can be produced by stimulation of any portion of the medial forebrain bundle which courses along the base of the brain. Other areas tend to give less rewarding effects or what seem to be mixtures of rewarding and punishing effects.

From these kinds of results one can conclude that the electrical stimulation of the medial forebrain bundle produces pleasurable sensations in the animal. Indeed this might be the simplest explanation. However, psychologists are trying to explain the results obtained by Olds without recourse to inferences regarding the mental states of the animals. To date none have been entirely successful.

The hypothalamus has a plethora of neuronal connections to the rest of the central nervous system, but is more directly connected with other limbic system structures. Because of its considerable connections with the other limbic structures, the limbic system is thought to be the most direct source of regulation for the hypothalamic centers. Unfortunately, very little is known about the functions of the structures comprising the limbic system. However, some findings are so important and substantial that they should be discussed.

Evidence indicates that surgical damage in certain areas of the limbic system can alter the emotional responses of animals. If the septal area is damaged (see Fig. 3.25) the animal becomes more ferocious than he was prior to the surgical intervention [25]. On the other hand, if the damage is restricted to an area called the amygdala, a nuclear mass in the temporal lobes, the animal tends to show evidence of being more placid than before [26]. Evidence from observations and tests of human patients who have had to have surgery involving the limbic structures of the temporal lobe suggests that these people suffer deficits in recent memory [27]. These patients have difficulty recalling events happening as recently as ten minutes before testing although their memory for older, more established facts seems relatively unimpaired. However, similar results are not found when temporal lobe limbic structures are damaged in animals.

It would be exciting to be able to tie together the many present and future research findings on the limbic system at this point, but this is not possible. We have only tried to suggest some of the kinds of research that lead to the belief that the limbic system is important for many psychological functions, including the emotions, learning, and memory.

OTHER SUBCORTICAL STRUCTURES As mentioned there is more than the limbic system underlying the great neocortical layers of the brain. In the thalamus we already know of two kinds of groups of cells. There are the direct relay nuclei for vision, audition, kinesthesia, etc. Impulses arriving at these nuclei are sent by cells located there to specific segments of the neocortex. Thalamic nuclei of the other variety have more diffuse effects on the neocortex, similar to the effects of the brain-stem reticular formation. Cells in these nuclei send impulses to *segments* of the brain and regulate the excitability of cells in these segments.

There are many other masses of subcortical cells and tracts of nerve fibers. The functions of many of these are just now becoming apparent. Some have to do with the coordination of the messages arising in the motor system of the brain, others have to do with the sensory systems, and there are others whose functions are practically unknown. A thorough understanding of the actions of this enormously complicated structure, the brain, will not be attained until these other areas are better understood.

The most striking and obvious neurological feature of animals highest in the phylogenetic scale is the great grey mantle which covers the brain in man, the neocortex.

One widely held general view is that the cortex assumes the functions of many of the lower centers as the amount of cortex increases. Marquis [28] has provided evidence for this principle in the visual system. The first visual representations in the brain are subcortical nuclei found in the upper brain stem. These are used by the lower animals for every visual function, but in the higher animals these visual functions depend on the neocortex. While the subcortical centers still may subserve some rudimentary visual reflexes in higher animals, vision, as we know it, is not dependent on them. Our perception is a fortunate result of the development of neocortical development in our species.

Finally, we must remember once again that the fractionation of the living brain into centers, nuclei, areas, and tracts tends to make us forget the continuous activity and interaction between the many parts. Further, we should remember that man's great development of neocortex has provided him with the most adaptable and tractable brain yet developed. The most important and valuable characteristics of mankind are those which he *acquires* from his environment rather than those he inherits genetically.

The maturation of the human brain underlying the acquisition of speech and language and all related symbolic and intellectual performance does not proceed *in utero*. Instead, these capacities only begin to be acquired about a year after birth and go on to develop through much of our lives. While the capacity for these characteristically human developments is transmitted genetically, each individual must cultivate them for himself after birth, by education [18, p. 108].

References

1. Maier, N. R. F., & Schneirla, T. C. *Principles of Animal Psychology*. New York: McGraw-Hill Book Company, Inc., 1935.
2. Parker, G. H. *The Elementary Nervous System*. Philadelphia: J. B. Lippincott Company, 1919.

3. McConnell, J. V., Jacobson, A. L., & Kimble, D. P. The effects of regeneration upon retention of a conditioned response in the planarian. *J. comp. physiol. Psychol.*, 1959, **52**, 1–5.

4. Jacobson, A. L. Learning in flatworms and annelids. *Psychol. Bull.*, 1963, **60**, 74–94.

5. Boycott, B. B., & Young, J. Z. A memory system in octopus vulgaris Lamarck. *Proc. Roy. Soc.* (*London*), 1955(B), **143**, 449–480.

6. Herrick, C. J. *Neurological Foundations of Animal Behavior.* New York: Holt, Rinehart and Winston, Inc., 1924.

7. Savory, T. H. Spider webs. *Sci. Amer.*, April, 1960, 115–124.

8. Frisch, V. K. *Bees: Their Vision, Chemical Senses and Language.* Ithaca: Cornell Univer. Press, 1950.

9. Schneirla, T. C., & Piel, G. The army ant. In *The First Book of Animals, Sci. Amer.* (Eds.), New York: Simon Schuster, Inc., 1955.

10. Tinbergen, N. *The Study of Instinct.* Fairlawn, N.J.: Oxford Univer. Press, 1951.

11. Lorenz, K. Z. The evolution of behavior. *Sci. Amer.*, 1958, **199**, 67–78.

12. Hess, E. H. Imprinting. *Science,* 1959, **130**, 133–141.

13. Eccles, J. C. *The Physiology of Nerve Cells.* Baltimore: Johns Hopkins Univer. Press, 1957.

14. Woolsey, C. N. Organization of somatic sensory and motor areas of the cerebral cortex. In H. F. Harlow and C. N. Woolsey (Eds.), *Biological and Biochemical Bases of Behavior.* Madison: Univer. of Wisconsin Press, 1958.

15. Lilly, J. C. Correlations between neurophysiological activity in the cortex and short-term behavior in the monkey. In *ibid.*

16. Brodal, A. *The reticular formation of the brain stem. Anatomical Aspects and Functional Correlations.* Springfield, Ill.: Charles C Thomas, Publishers, 1956.

17. French J. D., Amerongen, F. K. von, & Magoun, H. W. An activating system in brain stem of monkey. *Arch. Neurol. Psychiat.* (*Chicago*), 1952, **68**, 577–590.

18. MacLean, P. D. The limbic system with respect to two basic life principles. In Mary A. B. Brazier (Ed.), *The Central Nervous System and Behavior,* Trans. Second Conf., Josiah Macy, Jr., Foundation, New York, 1959.

19. Kaada, B. R. Somato-motor, autonomic and electrocorticographic responses to electrical stimulation of "rhinencephalic" and other structures in primates, cat, and dog. *Acta*

physiol. Scand., 1951, **24,** Suppl. 83.

20. Gellhorn, E. *Autonomic Imbalance and the Hypothalamus.* Minneapolis: Univer. Minnesota Press, 1957.

21. Stellar, E. The physiology of motivation. *Psychol. Rev.,* 1954, **61,** 5–22.

22. Olds, J., & Milner, P. Positive reinforcement produced by electrical stimulation of septal area and other regions of rat brain. *J. comp. physiol. Psychol.,* 1954, **47,** 419–427.

23. Olds, J. Positive emotional systems studied by techniques of self-stimulation. *Psychiat. Res. Repts.,* 1960, **12,** 238–258.

24. Olds, M. E., & Olds, J. Approach-avoidance analysis of rat diencephalon. *J. comp. Neurol.,* 1963, **120,** 259–295.

25. Brady, J. V., & Nauta, W. J. H. Subcortical mechanisms in emotional behavior: affective changes following septal forebrain lesions in the albino rat. *J. comp. physiol. Psychol.,* 1953, **46,** 339–346.

26. Schreiner, L., & Kling, A. Behavioral changes following rhinencephalic injury in cat. *J. Neurophysiol.,* 1953, **16,** 643–659.

27. Penfield, W., & Milner, B. Memory of deficit produced by bilateral lesions in the hippocampal zone. *Arch. Neurol. Psychiat. (Chicago),* 1958, **79,** 475–497.

28. Marquis, D. G. Phylogenetic interpretation of the functions of the visual cortex. *Arch. Neurol. Psychiat. (Chicago),* 1935, **33,** 807–815.

FOUR MECHANISMS OF PERCEPTION

We live in a world of people and things—books, trees, sunshine, snow, friends, loved ones, strangers. We take our perceptions of them for granted, just as we take for granted that they really are the way they seem to us. But is this book, for example, *actually*, really, and permanently the thing that we believe it to be? We sometimes have a suspicion that some things seem different to us than they do to others. Do you see your girl friend as the rest of your friends do? Is there some doubt about whether she is quite as pretty to them as she is to you? Even the relatively stable world of objects causes us some doubts at

117

times. If this book is placed in a position at which the light strikes it from an acute angle oftentimes the color seems different. Has the color of the book changed? No, you will say, it is an *illusion* caused by the angle of incidence of the light. Yes, but how can we decide which appearance is the illusion? Plato proposed that all of our *real* objects are but illusions.

The philosophical question of the ultimate truth or falsity (the veridicality) of perceptions lies outside the domain of scientific psychology. Such questions may lead to interesting hours of discussion, but as behavioral scientists we want to understand the mechanisms whereby we perceive the world. Assuming that we live surrounded by a world of objects that we can come to know through our senses, what are the mechanisms whereby we feel, hear, see, and smell? Perceptions of the world of objects begin with the reception of changes in the physical energies impinging upon specialized organs. In the case of visual perception these energies take the form of light waves or quanta of light. In hearing, the energy is in the form of waves of increasing and decreasing compressions of the atmosphere. For touch, the skin must be compressed. Before any kind of perception can occur, there must be some interchange of energy between the environment and the individual.

In the body there are many kinds of specialized organs, collections of cells which act to achieve a common result and which are only sensitive to certain kinds of changes in physical energies. We might think of these organs, or receptors, as similar to television cameras on the outer edges of the body which tune in on events taking place in the environment. This is an especially appealing analogy in the case of the visual mechanism. However, with a little imagination one could extend the analogy to all the senses. In fact there seems to be some kind of a myth perpetuated by magazine articles and some "scientific" books intended for the layman that the actual mechanisms do work in such a fashion. Let us for the moment examine the analogy. The eye is the television camera. The receiver is back, somewhere in the brain. Electrical energies (pictures) are relayed to the receiver in the brain. But what do we have to assume then? What good would such a picture be if there was no one back in the brain looking at the picture screen? Our problem is not solved by the television analogy, for we must investigate the "someone" back in the brain who is watching the pictures transmitted to this region from the eyes.

We would have to start all over again investigating this new being watching the TV set. Our problem is much more difficult than understanding a biological TV transmission scheme. We must try to understand how the changes in energy at the receptors are utilized into a form such that the nervous system, as a whole, can alter the body's activities to reach new adjustments to the external situation.

This problem raises some important yet difficult conceptual issues. Information concerning the state of the external world is encoded into a neural code at the receptors. Changes in the physical world outside effect changes at the receptor level. Then these receptor changes are transmitted to the brain in the form of a code which uses the changes in the rate of activity of single neurons. These changes in neural firings represent the basis of the neural code. But it is not a code which is broken down into the original message once again in the brain as a TV set would do. Rather, this encoded sensory message from the receptors is integrated into the ongoing activities of the 12,000 million cells of the brain and can somehow result in changes in the neural code going out to somatic and autonomic muscles.

The assumption of a little man in the head is the easy way out. It is too bad we cannot take this way. Rather, we must learn the brain's various codes and rules of integration. We are not yet very close to this goal. However, in the first sections of this chapter we shall present some of the available information about sensory systems generally and the visual system in particular. We shall soon find that the immediate sensory environment cannot explain all perceptual phenomena. In the next chapter, therefore, we shall look at the studies which explore the effects of internal and individual factors such as sets, motives, and attitudes on perceptual phenomena.

Toward a Definition of Perception

Let us examine the problems that bear on a definition of perception. First, let us bear in mind that all we can *know* about anyone else is that which comes to us via our own receptor systems. Let us set aside, for a few moments, the problem of our own perceptual processes and concentrate on the fact that other people *behave,* and usually seem to be using information about their environment in appropriate ways. We can know only about behavior. This means that while you may assume that your neighbor *sees* a red light at an intersection, it is still only an *assumption*. You might base your assumption on the fact that he stops his car at the traffic signal you call "red." Here you are basing your assumption on his behavior, which results in his stopping his car. Still, this tells us only that he can discriminate between certain stimulus conditions. It does not tell us that his perception of the traffic light is just like yours. But, you may say, "He says it is a red light." Here you are basing your assumption on his use of a verbal labeling response. You only know that he can discriminate different colored

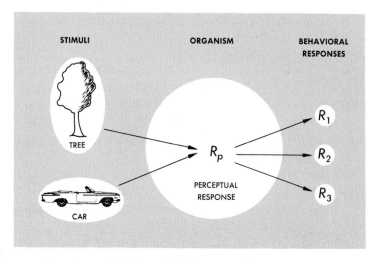

FIG. 4.1.   *A possible theoretical interpretation of perception.*

stimuli and can label them with appropriate terms. Still, you do not *know* whether the perception he labels *red* is similar to your perception of a stimulus labeled *red*. In fact you know nothing more than that given specifiable stimulus conditions he can make specific kinds of responses. We can never know about the mental processes of others except by inferences from their behavior.

Let us consider the diagram of a general perceptual situation given in Fig. 4.1. We present a stimulus to a person. Let the large circle represent the person. Then the individual emits certain verbal or other behavioral responses. Psychology's job is to build theories which accurately predict responses. As we shall see in our subsequent chapters on learning, there are psychologists who do not believe we need to say anything about perception to account for behavior, and who assume other factors to be at work (see pp. 213–232). Other theorists say we must have theories which assume that certain perceptual responses occur within the organism. (These perceptual responses are labeled *Rp* in Fig. 4.1.)

What should determine whether or not a psychologist assumes perception to occur in others? What should be the basis of a decision on whether or not to include *Rp*'s in the theoretical schema used to understand behavior? As of the moment there are many competing theoretical approaches to explaining behavior. They have not as yet merged into one stable framework. Throughout the book, the reader should be alert to the values and liabilities of each of the several types of theoretical approaches which will be presented.

In this chapter we shall be making the assumption that perceptual responses do occur in the individual and that they are susceptible to study by the use of specified *indicator responses*. Furthermore, we shall assume that it is necessary to know about the sensory apparatus of the human in order to understand perceptual phenomena properly. We would justify this assumption by our belief that the simplest explanation of a phenomenon is the best. In the present instance this means we would prefer to explain perception—insofar as it is possible—on the basis of structure and function of the sensory systems. Those phenomena not susceptible to sensory system explanations must then be handled by higher-order theories. In order to be able to know which phenomena are explicable at the sensory level we must study them in some detail.

General Properties of Sensory Systems

Conceptually, we may think of ourselves as involved in two worlds: the external physical world around us and the inner world beneath the skin. The physical world is composed of things and people and (the theorists of physics and chemistry tell us) atoms, molecules, and energy. The inner world beneath the skin is a world of atoms and molecules too, but patterned so as to constitute the person. People are made of many systems usually working harmoniously to maintain the larger system of the individual. At this point the systems of primary importance to us are the sensory systems. These systems generally are localized close to the skin, which is the membrane separating the inner and outer worlds. The skin is not simply a separating wall but also permits interchange of information between the two worlds. This interchange takes place at the receptor organs. We perceive changes in the outer world because of corresponding changes in our receptors and their associated sensory systems.

In man, we become aware of changes in electromagnetic waves through the visual sensory system, of changes in air pressure through our auditory system, of changes in the chemical composition of our environment through the olfactory and taste sensory systems. In addition we are aware of alterations of the skin itself and of the underlying musculature through other sensory systems.

SPECIALIZATION OF RECEPTOR FUNCTIONS It is a readily apparent fact that our receptor organs have become highly specialized. For example, our eyes do not respond to smells or sounds. Rather, each of our receptor organs has developed so it only responds to certain kinds of stimulation. In addition it is only sensitive to a narrow portion of the total energies which could effect it. We do not hear all possible sounds or see all possible lights. The ear is responsive to sound waves of frequencies between 20 and 20,000 cycles per second. Changes in air pressure of greater or smaller frequencies are not detected by normal auditory apparatus. We should bear in mind that other species need not have these same limitations. Dogs can detect frequencies much greater than 20,000 cycles per second, and as a result dog whistles which we do not hear can be used to call them. Some insects seem to be able to detect the plane of polarization of light waves which we cannot. Many animals can detect changes in electromagnetic waves at wavelengths beyond the spectral wavelengths visible to ourselves. The anatomical structure of the various central nervous systems of the animals leads to certain hypotheses about their perceptual world. The dog, for example, may live in a wonderful world of smells whereas we live in a wonderful world of visual impressions. This idea stems from the greater development of neural structures related to smell in the dog.

All sensory systems share various aspects in common. First

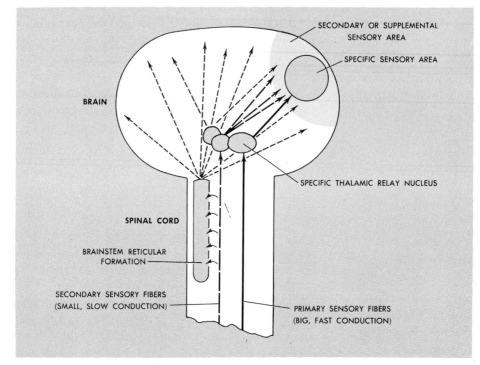

FIG. 4.2. *Primary (unbroken lines) and secondary (broken lines) afferent fibers in somatosensory system.*

of all there are specialized receptor cells grouped into a receptor. These cells act to translate activity in the physical outer world into changes in the inner world beneath the skin. Essentially, these changes are alterations in the firing of afferent neurons going to the central nervous system and the brain. *The receptor cell must therefore be sensitive to specific physical and chemical changes in its immediate environment and in turn effect changes in neurons to which it is connected.*

PROJECTIONS TO NEOCORTEX The phylogenetically most recent acquisition in the brain is the neocortex, the great grey mantle. Although the assumption is open to some discussion, we generally assume that most of the higher perceptual and intellectual functions involve neocortex. Therefore, special efforts have been made to trace the neural pathways between the receptor organs and the neocortex. In many instances it has been possible to localize these pathways and also to specify the regions of neocortex which receive information from a particular sensory modality.

The neurons connected with the receptor cells proceed to higher levels of the central nervous system. Usually, cells in the sensory systems projecting toward the neocortex go first to the thalamus, where they end on cell bodies in specialized nuclei. The thalamic cells then send axons to cells in the sensory areas of neocortex as well as to other higher brain regions. The general organization of these specific sensory systems is schematized in Fig. 4.2.

Diffuse Systems

In addition to the direct projection systems there are other routes of transmission of information arising in the receptor cells to the brain. These consist of smaller nerve fibers which reach other thalamic nuclei and project to wider regions of neocortex. These supplementary sensory systems include the diffusely projecting systems of the brain, notably the brain-stem reticular formation and certain thalamic nuclei which have cells which relay this activity to wide areas of neocortex. These other sensory systems are diagramed in Fig. 4.2. In the primary or specialized sensory systems information proceeds rapidly to highly specialized neocortical areas. Receptor activity initiating changes in the diffuse systems help to regulate the overall activity of the neocortex.

Central control of receptor activity Sensory systems are not one-way systems proceeding always upward to neocortex. It is now clear that most, if not all, sensory systems also involve efferent pathways, probably beginning in the primary sensory receiving areas in neocortex and going down to act on receptor cells or on cells near them in the chain of transmission to the brain [e.g., 1, 2]. These efferent tracts can suppress or alter the information sent toward the brain. Thus, the central nervous system itself can turn on or off the information coming to it from the peripheral receptors.

From the Physical World to Neural Changes

In order for the individual to be aware of receptor activity caused by the correlated changes in the physical world, changes in the physical world must be rewritten into a neural code. The receptor cells must alter in some way the activity of neurons. This means that the single neuron's state of membrane polarization must be broken down, and the resulting depolarization of the neuron must be sufficient to trigger the total cell body and axon depolarization so that it spreads as the *spike potential* or firing of the nerve cell.

RECEPTOR POTENTIALS The means by which changes in the external environment are translated into changes in neural activity are highly individualized for each receptor system. While all of the cells in each sensory organ operate according to the same principles, each of the sensory organs has a different mechanism to affect the neurons which will carry their information to the brain. In the visual system cells at the back of the eye initiate impulses in neurons by means of a breakdown in light-sensitive chemicals (photopigments) within them. In the auditory system cells located deep in the inner ear are physically compressed by waves of fluids induced by "sound waves" through a complex chain of bones and membranes. Other types of sense organs use still different mechanisms. In every case environmental changes become reflected in changes of activity of single neurons that reach toward higher regions of the nervous system and the brain. Electrical recordings from every kind of sensory organ reveal that there are special kinds of activities aroused in them when activated by a stimulus. These responses, found when recording from sensory organs, are called the receptor potentials.

Each specific receptor organ initiates its own particular pattern of electrical activity when it is stimulated. The receptor potential is a product of single cells. When a receptor organ is activated many single cells work together and it is possible to record the sum of the resulting electrical changes. The combined receptor potentials are referred to as the *generator potential* of the sensory receptor organ. When one floods the eye with light a characteristic change in potential is recorded in the eye which does not result from the activity of afferent axons going brainward. This is the generator potential of vision called the electroretinogram [3]. In Fig. 4.3 one can observe an electroretinogram (ERG) recorded from man. It is a complex electrical pattern. Various components of the ERG can be sorted out experimentally, and there are several of these components which seem associated with different kinds

125

of receptor cells in the eye. Generally speaking, we must recognize the fact that receptor organs are *not* simply collections of cells all of which are exactly alike. To be sure, all the cells of a receptor are sensitive to the same kind of physical energy (e.g., sound), but some may be sensitive to only a smaller portion of the energy received by the whole receptor.

In the eye, for example, there are two major divisions of receptor cells, the rods and the cones. While both are sensitive to light they are differentially sensitive to conditions of illumination and lights in various regions of the spectrum. The rods are best activated after the eye has been without light for some time and operate best at night. The cones, on the other hand, are

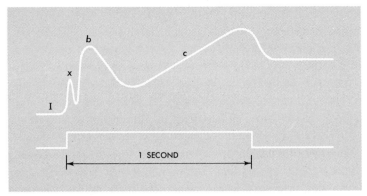

FIG. 4.3.   *Approximate representation of human electroretinogram.*

most responsive in normal daylight conditions. There are probably several varieties of rods and cones. Later in this chapter, we shall discuss the mechanisms of action in these receptor cells in greater detail.

RECEPTOR FIELDS   Up to this point we have discussed some of the general notions concerning sensory-receptor systems. Another general problem which needs to be elaborated is the concept of receptive fields. Essentially, *receptive field* refers to a characteristic of all receptor organs, namely that the functional unit of analysis of the receptor is larger than that of the individual receptor cell. For example, each axon running in the optic nerves from the eye to the thalamic relay nucleus for vision responds to stimulation of a considerable number of actual receptor cells. One inference drawn about the nature of sensory systems is simple: many receptors feed into other cells before the sensory information goes toward the brain. This intermediate cell collects information coming from many different individual receptor cells. The information reaching the brain has already been "packaged" to reflect changes of stimulation over given areas of the receptor organ. It does not receive, directly, information as to the state of any one particular receptor cell.

Research in the visual system has yielded some of the best analyses of receptor fields. It is possible to record from single axons in the optic nerve. By moving a light across the retinal portion of the eye in which the receptor cells are located, the areas which affect changes in the electrical activity of particular optic nerve axons can be determined [4]. It is the changes in rate of firing of these axons which carry visual information to the brain. There are several kinds of fields of receptor cells. Some of these clusters act to increase the activity in an optic nerve axon when the latter is stimulated by light. Others, when stimulated lightly, act to inhibit activity in the same axon.

Convergence and divergence of sensory information in the visual system   As yet, we have neglected a detailed consideration of the microstructure of the receptors. But, following our discussion of receptor fields, it is appropriate to discuss the minute structure of receptors. As with sensory systems generally, we find that several different receptor cells feed into collector cells. These collector cells sometimes feed into larger collecting cells in, or close to, the receptor organ itself. In the retinal portion of the eye the rods and cones are the primary sensory cells. These feed into bipolar cells and the bipolar cells in turn feed into what are called *ganglion cells*. The long axons of these ganglion cells leave the eye and proceed to the thalamic relay nucleus. *The axons of the ganglion cells constitute the optic nerves.* (The optic nerve also contains efferent fibers going to the retina. The locus of termination of these efferent sensory fibers in the retina is as yet unknown.) Thus, the recordings made from optic nerve fibers which indicate that these fibers are responsive to stimulation over a large area is explained by the fact that many receptors converge on bipolar cells and probably many of these in turn converge on the ganglion cells. It is likely that similar convergence takes place in all sensory systems.

127

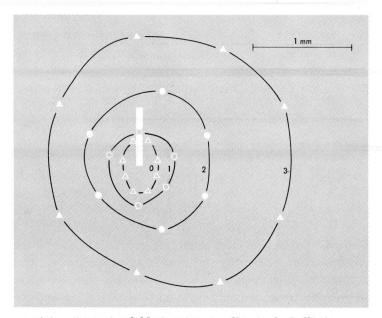

FIG. 4.4.   *Receptive field of optic nerve fiber in the bullfrog.*
Four intensities of illumination of the eye were used, represented
by the numbers (logarithms). Note that as these are increased,
area on retina, which produces responses in the fiber, increases.
From H. C. Wagner & M. L. Wolbarsht. Receptive field of
bullfrog. Amer. J. Ophthal., 1958, 46, 46–59.

Receptor fields can also be measured by recording the
responses of single cells in the visual neocortex. This type of
research uses the same method of moving a light across the
retina and recording from single cells in areas of the neocortex which receive, predominantly, input from the visual
system. Single cells in visual neocortex tend to have smaller
receptor fields than the visual fields defined on the basis of
recording effects on ganglion cell axons in the optic nerves [5].

There is a great amount of divergence in the sensory systems. Many more cells in the neocortex receive input from the
visual system than there are ganglion cells in the retina or
cells in the visual relay nucleus (lateral geniculate). Information from many receptor cells converge upon single
cells in the neocortex and, at the same time, every receptor
unit projects to a large number of cells in the neocortex.

Inhibition and excitation   The story is more complex than
that which we have presented thus far. A receptor field, defined as the retinal area which affects a cell in the visual

system, is composed of two portions. One portion is excitatory, and the other inhibitory. If the central portion of the receptive field is excitatory, that is, if visual stimulation of the retina *increases* activity in the ganglion cell axon, then there usually will be an annulus, or ring, surrounding this center which is inhibitory in nature. If the center is inhibitory, that is if visual stimulation decreases activity in the ganglion cell axon, then there often will be an excitatory annulus around it. Not all fields have a center and surrounding annulus, but receptive fields can be found which are of many different shapes with surrounding areas of antagonistic functions. A representative receptive field is shown in Fig. 4.4.

The knowledge of inhibitory and excitatory processes at the receptor level has explained some puzzling findings from studies recording from single cells in the neocortex. Many investigators have noted the remarkable observation that there are many cells in the visual neocortex which do not seem responsive to illumination of the retinal elements. But recently some of these cells have been found to be responsive to a light

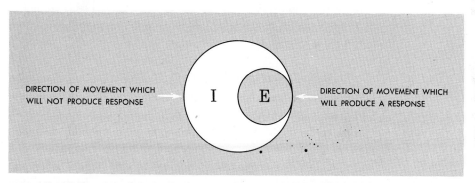

DIRECTION OF MOVEMENT WHICH WILL NOT PRODUCE RESPONSE

I   E

DIRECTION OF MOVEMENT WHICH WILL PRODUCE A RESPONSE

FIG. 4.5. *Schematic distribution of excitatory and inhibitory fields of the retina which allow cells of sensory system to respond only when light is moved across it from right to left. Movement of light in opposite direction would stimulate inhibitory field first, inhibiting reaction when light reached excitatory field. Simultaneous stimulation of both fields would elicit no response.*

source that *moves* across the retina. Some cells become excited when the light source moves in one direction but not the other [5]. We can explain this on the basis of the distribution of peripheral fields of excitation and inhibition. For example, consider a hypothetic neocortical cell which has the field illustrated in Fig. 4.5.

Under the assumptions made about the distribution of excitatory and inhibitory areas of the visual field, the illumination of both *E* and *I* would not affect the cortical cell because the *I* area would act to inhibit *E*. A stimulus moving from right to left, stimulating *I* then *E,* would not be effective either, for the inhibitory effects would prevent *E*'s affecting the cortical cell. On the other hand a stimulus moving left to right would excite the cortical cell because it would strike the excitatory position of the retinal field before striking the inhibitory portions. This would be one explanation of the fact that many cells observed in the visual neocortex do not respond when the entire retina is flooded with light [6].

We are a long way from knowing all of the different arrangements of receptive fields in sensory systems. Evidently, combinations of the inhibitory and excitatory receptive fields are many and varied. Recently, it has been demonstrated that the frog has cortical visual cells that are responsive to different shapes and curvatures entering into the animal's visual fields [7]. Probably all species of animals have somewhat different patterns of excitatory and inhibitory regions in their receptive fields. Yet, as investigators use more and more complicated stimuli, more and more cells in the visual cortex become understood.

OVERVIEW OF RECEPTOR ACTIVITY   While the idea of receptor fields is not a new one, we have only begun to scratch the surface of knowledge about them. Our knowledge, or lack of it, must make us aware of the enormous organizational complexity of the sensory apparatus. We find that every receptor generates a steady potential when activated; this in turn produces the depolarization typical of excitation in any neuron. Thus, subsequent cells in transmission chains carry information to the specialized neocortical areas by way of the thalamic relay nuclei. Throughout this chain we find increasing degrees of convergence and divergence.

Not all cells in the specialized areas of the cortex are responsive to changes in the related sensory system. Some "silent cells" have been found that will be effected by highly specialized activity in the sensory system, e.g., movement in one direction. While many of our examples were obtained from research upon the visual system, we believe the general principles of organization to be similar in all sensory systems.

The Visual System

Earlier we noted that the different specialized receptor cells acted in different ways to translate physical energies into neural activities. The actual techniques of these changes are fascinating but we shall have space only to discuss in detail the change of electromagnetic energy into neural signals responsible for vision.

Man can discriminate only a small portion of the spectrum of electromagnetic radiation. While the nature of electromagnetic waves is incompletely understood, it can be easily measured (in terms of wavelengths). The common techniques for measuring electromagnetic radiation provide us with a spectrum running from the small peak-to-peak wavelengths of gamma rays to the long peak-to-peak wavelengths of waves used to transmit radio signals. The electromagnetic spectrum is illustrated in Fig. 4.6. The small portion of this spectrum to which man can respond lies between the wavelengths of 450 to 750 millimicrons (also called *nanometers*). As mentioned before, other animals have somewhat different capacities of wavelength discrimination.

We have been careful to talk of *electromagnetic waves,* not *light waves,* a term which refers only to the wavelengths to which man is sensitive. The same problem of terminology exists with color. Within the visual spectrum we can discriminate different wavelengths. We show our wavelength discriminations in words (*red, green*) or by behavioral responses which indicate the discrimination has been modern, e.g., stopping at a red traffic light. Our discrimination between wavelengths is the basic operation, and the appearance of color is due to the organization and structure of our visual sensory system.

STRUCTURE OF THE EYE   A study of the eye reveals a finely constructed device which acts to focus the images of objects from the outer world upon the rods and cones in the retina. The electromagnetic waves come in through the cornea, the aqueous humor, the lens, and vitreous humor. The lens and cornea focus them to provide a clear image. In this process the image is inverted so that an upward pointing arrow actually is pointing downward on the retina. A simplified

131

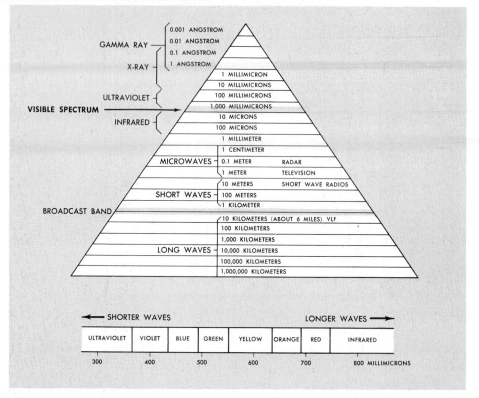

FIG. 4.6. *Diagram suggestive of the electromagnetic spectrum, with closeup of segment of visible light (below). The entire spectrum encompasses so wide a span of wavelengths that they cannot be expressed in a single unit of measurement. Adapted from John L. Chapman, The expanding spectrum, Harper's Magazine, July, 1964, pp. 70–78. © 1964, by Harper & Row, Publishers, Incorporated. Reprinted from Harper's Magazine by the artist's permission.*

picture of the eye is presented in Fig. 4.7. The image upon the retina excites, in various ways, the receptor fields. The complex changes in neural activities of the ganglion cells in the eye are transmitted to the specific relay nucleus for vision, the lateral geniculate body; then fibers from geniculate nucleus cells go to the visual cortex. Cells also project fibers to the older neural centers for vision in the midbrain (the superior colliculi) and to the diffuse systems of the brain (brain-stem reticular formation and diffuse thalamic nuclei).

The two basic receptor cells in the human eye are rods and cones. These are different in anatomical structure, although the difference is not very pronounced. A photograph of rods and cones is shown in Fig. 4.8, and the layers of the retina can be seen in Fig. 4.9. In our previous discussion of the general receptor systems we noted the fact that the rods and cones converged into bipolar and thence into ganglion cells. The actual diversity of cells in the retina is apparent in Fig. 4.10. We are not completely sure of the functions of all of the retinal elements pictured here.

Distribution of rods and cones   As we know, the rods and cones make up the sensory elements of the retina. They are distributed over the back of the eyeball and, with the ganglion and bipolar cells and the clusters of supporting cells, make up the retina. In the central portion of the retina there is a great preponderance of cones compared with the number of rods. At the approximate center of the retina there is a depression called the *fovea* or *fovea centralis* which is believed to contain only cones. In and around the fovea there is the greatest density of cones, but the ratio of cones to rods becomes less and less toward the periphery of the retina until the only receptor cells are rods.

The depression of the fovea results from the fact that in this one area of the retina the ganglion and bipolar cells are

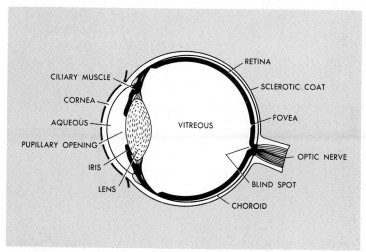

FIG. **4.7.**   *Simplified representation of the human eye.*

not piled on top of the receptors. Elsewhere in the retina the incoming light must go through the other cells stacked between the receptors and the light sources. This would seem to be an inefficient design, but the cell bodies and their processes lying between the retina receptors and the lens are almost

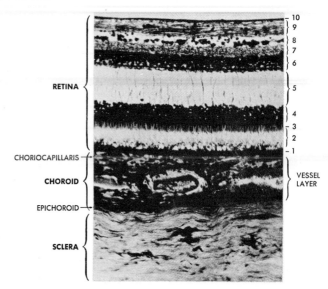

FIG. 4.8. *Low-power photomicrograph of portion of retina, choroid, and some of the sclera of the human eye. Numbers correspond to layers of the retina shown in Fig. 4.9. Adapted from* A. W. Ham & T. S. Leeson. Histology (4th ed.). Philadelphia: J. B. Lippincott Company, 1961.

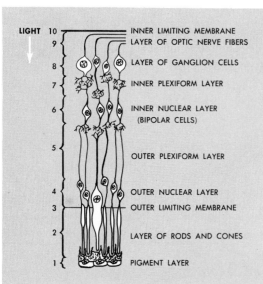

FIG. 4.9. *Diagram of layers of the retina. Adapted from* A. W. Ham & T. S. Leeson. Histology (4th ed.). Philadelphia: J. B. Lippincott Company, 1961.

transparent. We cannot complain of the results of this system for calculations made on the basis of optical properties of the eye indicate that as little as one quantum of light per receptor element may be sufficient to cause perceptible activity [8].

One other structural feature of the eye is of some importance in understanding perception. At the place where the axons of the ganglion cells leave the eye as the optic nerve there are no receptor cells at all. This region is called the optic disc.

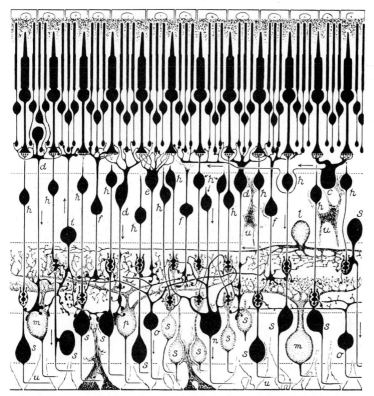

FIG. **4.10.** *Reconstruction of primate retina showing primary neuron types and their synaptic relations. c: horizontal cells; d, e, f: diffuse or polysynaptic bipolar cells; h: individual cone (midget) bipolar cell; i, l: amacrine cells; m, n, o, p, r, s: ganglion cells. Reprinted from* The Retina *by S. L. Polyak by permission of The University of Chicago Press. © 1941 by the University of Chicago. All rights reserved.*

Ordinarily, however, we do not notice any gap in our visual experience unless conditions are specially arranged for us to do so. Somehow we fill in this deficit in sensory information. In our discussion of Hebb's theory of perception (see Chapter 5) this optic disc will become of theoretical importance.

Other visual structures   The optic nerve leaves the eye at the optic disc and travels back toward the brain. A short distance from the eye the optic nerves from the two eyes cross. This junction is called the optic chiasm, and there is actually an interchange of some fibers from each optic nerve. Beyond the chiasm, fibers from the left side of the retina of the left eye and fibers from the left side of the right eye travel along together to the left lateral geniculate nucleus of the thalamus.

From the optic chiasm the fibers from the right sides of both retinas travel together to the right lateral geniculate nucleus in the thalamus. This exchange of fibers is represented in Fig. 4.11. Traditionally, the nerves which carry the visual information from the optic chiasm to the lateral geniculate bodies are called the optic tracts, and the fibers from lateral geniculate nucleus to the visual neocortex are called the optic radiations.

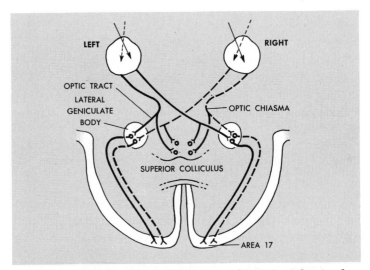

FIG. 4.11.   *Visual pathways. Light from objects in right visual field reaches left half of retina; Light from left visual field reaches right half. Note that information from right or left half of retina is transmitted to same right or left hemisphere. Collaterals from optic tracts reach visual reflex centers in the midbrain. Determine visual effects of damage to visual pathways made before and after optic chiasm.*

In higher animals, notably man and the monkeys, the lateral geniculate body is composed of six layers of cell bodies. Each layer contains cells receiving special kinds of information. Some layers receive visual information originating in one eye while others receive information originating in the other eye. Cells in certain layers of the lateral geniculate nucleus have been identified as being selectively responsible to certain wavelengths of light. This could be very important information for understanding color perception (see pp. 148–151).

In man, the visual neocortex is localized in the occipital lobes. In lower animals the cells of the lateral geniculate body project to wider areas of neocortex. Using a numbering system developed by Brodmann, we designate the area receiving neural projections directly from the lateral geniculate nuclei area 17. From this area cell axons go to other cells located in neighboring neocortex (Brodmann areas 18 and 19) and to cells in visual neocortex on the other side of the brain. Although areas 17, 18, and 19 are all referred to as visual cortical areas, area 17 is the only neocortical area to receive direct projections from the lateral geniculate nucleus. While the visual system projects directly only to area 17, messages originating in the retina reach the entire brain from axons projected from cells located in area 17.

Visual displays at the neocortex As mentioned in the first pages of this chapter, we should not think of a televisionlike arrangement whereby there is a faithful display of the retinal image on a neocortical screen formed by area 17. It would not help us to explain perceptual phenomena.

We already know that some of the cortical cells in the visual areas respond to excitation in receptor fields; we know that the different effects of excitation and inhibition at the retina "select" special groups of cortical cells to be aroused. What we need to know is more about the code used to transmit information about the changes in the outer world and how these neurally coded messages act on the ongoing activities of the brain. The sensory information must be integrated into ongoing activities and be able to change the direction of an individual's motor activities. The adjustment of the individual to his environment is the end product of all sensory discriminations and detection.

To better understand the nature of the neural codes used by organisms, we must once again return to the retina and begin with the translation of physical energies into neural information.

PHOTOPIGMENTS In every rod and cone there are outer segments filled with chemicals called, collectively, the *photopigments*. Coresponding to the rod-cone division there are two classes of photopigments: rhodopsin and iodopsin. Rhodopsin is only found in the rods, and iodopsin only in the cones.

When light strikes these photochemicals, a bleaching process begins which alters the energy state of the photopigment. This alteration is the process which acts to change the polarization of the cell membrane. This change in cell membrane polariza-

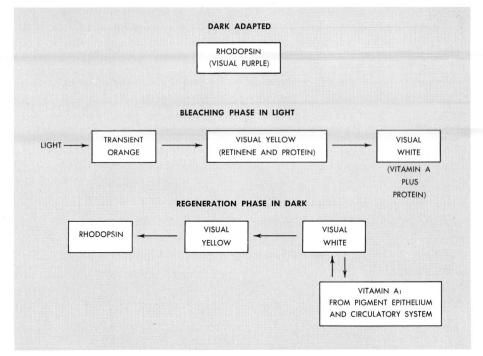

FIG. 4.12. *Diagrammatic representation of light effects on photopigment rhodopsin, and its subsequent regeneration in the dark.*

tion initiates the neural impulse used to signal a change in the electromagnetic input to the receptor cell.

The study of visual pigments has a long history and a promising future [9]. Today we know a great deal about the synthesis of rhodopsin and are rapidly learning about iodopsin. A summary of the rhodopsin cycle is presented in Fig. 4.12.

RHODOPSIN AND NIGHT VISION. Rods contain the photopigment, rhodopsin. This chemical is bleached by the incoming light and this releases energy which triggers the cell's response. After a rod's rhodopsin has been bleached, a considerable amount of time is required (in the dark) for the resynthesis of rhodopsin. This must take place before the cell can be excited again. During normal daytime vision the rods remain bleached and therefore relatively unresponsive. But after we have been in the dark for some while, rhodopsin regenerates and the rods recover their sensitivity. This process is called *dark adaptation*.

There is a period of time after entering a dark motion picture theater during which we can see only very poorly. *The recovery of our visual perception in the dark follows just about the same time course as the regeneration of rhodopsin.* The cones which contain iodopsin are less sensitive to the bleaching effects of light than are the rods of the retina, which are the cells most sensitive to even small amounts of light when they have been able to regenerate their supply of rhodopsin in the dark. Our best night vision then is accomplished by actions of our rod system. Figure 4.13 shows that the longer an animal stays in the dark, the more sensitive his eye becomes to test flashes of light. Curve (a) shows the quick drop in threshold that can be attributed to the dark adaptation of the daytime (or photopic) receptor system. Curve (b) reflects the slower but more extensive adaptation due to regeneration of rhodopsin in the night or scoptic system. Since the rods are found in greatest concentration at the periphery of the eye, night vision is best at the edges of the retina. Our chances of detecting small sources of light at night are much better if we do not look directly at the spot where we expect the light to be. By looking to the side of the light source, the light will fall on the periphery of the retina,

FIG. 4.13. *Dark-adaptation curve of frog, based on response indicated on electroretinogram. Adapted from fig. 6, L. Riggs. Dark adaptation in the frog eye determined by the electrical response of the retina.* J. cell. comp. Physiol., *1937, 9, 501.*

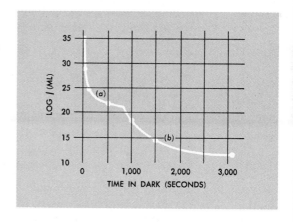

the area of greatest rod population. Lookouts scanning the horizon for lights of ships are therefore directed not to look directly at the suspected target.

CONES AND IODOPSIN. Much less is known about the cone system of the retina. Only recently have we been able to chemically identify iodopsin, although its presence had been predicted long before its discovery. The regenerative cycle of iodopsin is similar to that of rhodopsin, and the principle by which the iodopsin acts to initiate the activity of a single neural element is essentially the same; but there are some important differences.

The iodopsin reaction is faster than that of rhodopsin. Time spent in the dark will increase the sensitivity of cones to light, Fig. 4.13(a), but the cones do not achieve the same degree of sensitivity to light as do the rods following dark adaptation. While the cone system is less sensitive to light than the rod system, it provides us with the highest visual acuity in the fovea and with color vision.

THE PERCEPTION OF COLOR Color perception refers to discriminations the human and some animals can make within the realm of the visible spectrum. In order to be described as color discriminations, these discriminations must not be based on brightness or other features of the stimulation but must be based on a special sensitivity to specific wavelengths of the electromagnetic spectrum.

It is not likely that the rods are capable of providing a neural basis for discriminations of wavelengths. There may be more than one kind of rod in the eyes of higher animals, but the general belief is that they could only provide a limited discrimination between portions of the short wavelengths (blues) and the remainder of the spectrum. There is little doubt that the cone system is responsible for most color discrimination.

Let us accept the proposition that the cone system does mediate color discriminations. Does this mean that there must be more than one kind of iodopsin? In order for us to live in the world of multiple colors, which we do, we must have receptors built to discriminate among many different wavelengths. This in turn means that we must have cones containing pigments which will be bleached more effectively by one wavelength than another. This differential bleaching due to wavelength of illumination must be the peripheral basis of color discrimination.

Like all sensory experiences color exists as a response within the individual. Color is not to be found in the nervous system. All neurons are the same color, and their electrical responses are not colored either. Differential sensitivity to certain wavelengths provides us with the neural basis of discriminations in the visual spectrum.

Traditional color theories Probably the importance of vision and the beauty of the perceived world of color account for the early and continued attempts to explain color generally. Theories of color vision were among the very first theories proposed to explain behavior. Modifications of old theories and the creation of new theories proceeds to the present. No one theory is perfectly satisfactory and each contains something of special merit.

THE YOUNG-HELMHOLTZ THEORY. In 1801, Thomas Young suggested that there were three types of nerve fibers running from eye to brain. He thought these corresponded to the three primary colors. Some fifty years later, Helmholtz extended Young's theory which had not received a great deal of attention. Through Helmholtz's successful efforts to relate this theory to the facts of color mixture, the modified theory became widely accepted. It is probably the most well known of all theories of color perception.

The Young-Helmholtz theory assumes three varieties of cones which have different photopigments. Each photopigment is presumably most sensitive to one portion of the visual spectrum. One type is specially sensitive to short wavelengths (blue cones), another specially sensitive in the middle range (green cones), and the last type specially sensitive in the long wavelength area (red cones). While each type of cone has a region of greatest sensitivity, all have *some* sensitivity to other wave lengths. Color is determined by the brain on the basis of the relative amounts of excitation coming from the three different cone systems.

When we perceive a colored object we can make a discrimination of the wavelength. This reaction is referred to as hue discrimination. We say "that is aqua," "that is chartreuse," "that is magenta," and so on. We have learned to make color discriminations, and, also, we have learned to label and discriminate in accordance with the rules accepted by the majority of people in our culture.

Two stimuli can be of the same hue but differ in other visual qualities. A color can be more or less saturated. The saturation of a particular hue refers to the amount of white mixed with it. The less white mixed with a stimulus of a given hue the more saturated it is. Brightness is yet another quality which is different from both hue and saturation, and it correlates with the intensity of the light reaching the eye.

The Young-Helmholtz theory suggests that it is possible to explain saturation and brightness in terms of the responses observed in the three cone systems. The perceived hue is determined by the *relative* amounts of activity in the three cone systems. Brightness is determined by the absolute level of activity in all three systems. How can the Young-Helmholtz theory explain the quality of saturation, or the degree to which the hue is diluted with white? White light, e.g., sunlight, had been known for a long time to be a mixture of many hues. When a prism is held appropriately a ray of white light can be changed into a full spectrum of all the visible wavelengths. The Young-Helmholtz theory proposed that we see all of the spectral hues through three basic color receptors, red, green, and blue cones. White was believed to be a combination of activity in all three cone types. Thus, saturation as a quality of color perception, was explained by the balance existing between the red-green-blue cone activities aroused by the light.

HERING'S THEORY. A second major color-vision theory was developed by Hering and stemmed from the introspective analyses of color sensations. Many people who have tried to analyze impressions into primary sensory components have felt that the experience of yellow is somehow a "primary experience," not susceptible to further analysis. Today, this sort of introspective evidence is less impressive than it was historically. But introspective analysis did lead to a theory of color vision designed to accomodate *four* basic colors instead of the three of the Young-Helmholtz theory. It is based on the assumption of specialized photopigments in the cones, but it postulates rather different characteristics of photopigment reactions. Hering assumed cones contained three kinds of photopigments: (1) a white-black pigment, (2) a yellow-blue pigment, and (3) a red-green pigment.

This theory assumes a breakdown of the photopigments to produce white, yellow, and red, whereas the reconstitution of the pigments was assumed to elicit the black, blue, and green in the appropriate cones. The basic objection to the Hering theory came from the necessary assumption that a given neural fiber had to carry two kinds of sensory information, e.g., black *and* white, blue *and* yellow. This went against one of the basic notions of nerve physiology, the *doctrine of specific nerve energies*. According to this doctrine a nerve fiber could carry only one quality of sensation, and certainly the doctrine of specific nerve energies seems widely applicable in the nervous system. However, recent evidence to be presented later makes us seriously question this doctrine for all levels of the visual system. We shall also find evidence that some neural cells in the visual thalamus respond in accordance with the Young-Helmholtz theory while others act like those presumed by Hering's theory.

Today, the most widely held theory of color vision is a modification of the Young-Helmholtz theory. Its greatest strength comes from data from experiments of color mixture, and yet these very experiments present problems which suggest the incompleteness of the theory.

Color mixing Artists mix paints, psychologists mix lights. Different laws describe the results of mixtures of paints and lights, for when an artist uses a pigment that appears yellow, he is using material that reflects only electromagnetic energy of wavelengths in the region of the spectrum called "yellow." If he mixes this yellow pigment with a blue pigment he will obtain a greenish mixture. This occurs because his pigments reflect only the wavelengths common to both pigments and each pigment reflects some "green" wavelengths.

On the other hand mixing yellow and blue lights produces a whitish achromatic result. In mixing lights the wavelengths combine to form a new appearance. With colored lights the effects of one wavelength add to the effects of other wavelengths. For this reason the laws describing the addition of colored lights are called *additive laws*. Since the mixing of pigments reduces the number of wavelengths *that reach the eye,* the laws of the mixing of pigments are called *subtractive laws*.

COMPLEMENTARY COLORS. When mixing colored lights, we find that certain hues combine with other hues at appropriate intensities in such a way that their joint effect on us can best be described as neutral in hue—achromatic, or colorless. The pairs of colors that will add together to form a neutral experience are complementary colors. Mixtures of hues that are not complementaries produce a hue somewhere in between them. In theory every color has a complementary, although in fact some complementaries are practically unobtainable. The mixing and matching of colors have been studied in great detail, and we shall find it necessary to limit our discussion to some aspects most important for the development of theories of perception.

PRIMARY COLORS. If we presented a test patch of color from

any portion of the spectrum to a normal observer, we would find that he could produce a hue which matches the test-patch hue by adjusting the proportions of two of the three color primaries, taken one each from the red, green, and blue regions of the spectrum. The exact wavelengths used for the primaries have tended to vary somewhat from one experimenter to another; but the important fact is that observers are able to match the hue of test patches with combinations of two of the three primary colors.

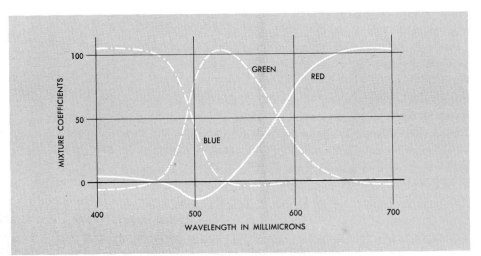

FIG. 4.14. *Color-mixing data. Curves represent proportions of each of the three primaries required to match each region of the spectrum. Adapted from S. Hecht. The development of Thomas Young's theory of color vision.* J. Opt. Soc. Amer., 1930, 20, 23.

However, even though the match made by the two primaries will be perfect for hue, the combination of our two primary colors would not always be sufficiently saturated. In order to have a perfect match for hue *and* saturation sometimes we must add some of our third primary color to the test patch. This reduces the saturation of the test patch. There is no other way to obtain a perfect match for saturation and hue for all test colors. Figure 4.14 shows the proportions of three primaries used to obtain perfect matches of test patches from each spectral region. Where a color primary curve dips below the horizontal line marked "0," that color must be added to the *test patch* to allow a perfect match.

The strength of the Young-Helmholtz theory was that it

assumed three primary color processes: red, green, and blue. The fact that all hues of the spectrum could be matched by manipulating primary colors is indirect but supportive evidence for the theory. It appeared to be more powerful than in fact it was because not everyone recognized that the third primary had to be added to the test patch to obtain a perfect test-patch-primary color-mixture match. This was partially obscured by transformations of the curves such that the curves all appear above the 0 line.

Data from color-mixture experiments provide only indirect evidence for a theory of the physiological basis of color vision. Recently, with the development of equipment and techniques that allow recording from single neural cells in the visual system it is possible to take a more direct approach to the study of the neural basis of color vision.

Neurophysiological bases of color For a number of years, it has been possible to record the electrical activities of a sensory nerve (a collection of axons); but the recording of the activity in a single cell or its axon is a much more difficult undertaking. One of the first techniques for recording from a single sensory fiber was that of dissecting out a single nerve fiber from the collection of fibers that make up a nerve. This dissection technique was extended to the visual system of the frog, and recordings were made by Hartline [4] of the excitation of single fibers in the frog optic nerve. Hartline's study of the responses of neural elements in the frog optic nerve revealed that about 20 percent of the fibers began firing and maintained an increased discharge rate while the receptors were stimulated with light; 50 percent of the fibers responded at both the onset and the termination of the visual stimulus; and 30 percent fired *only* at the termination of stimulation. These three kinds of fiber activities were labeled the "on," "on-off," and "off" responses, respectively. Not all neurons in the visual system act strictly in accordance with these three types of response patterns. In addition we should be alert to possible variations in the response characteristics of cells in the visual systems of animals in different species.

Granit [10] has studied the activities of neural elements in the retinas of many kinds of animal eyes. Unfortunately, it is not possible to say definitely which link in the neural chain from receptor cell to ganglion cell was studied, although the ganglion cell itself is the most likely candidate. Granit has

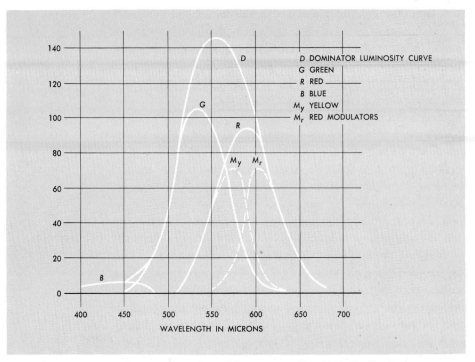

FIG. 4.15. *Basic sensation curves proposed by Granit. The photopic dominator curve (D) is a synthesis of modulator functions. Adapted from R. Granit.* Sensory Mechanisms of the Retina. *New York: Oxford University Press, 1947, p. 332. By permission of the author and Oxford University Press.*

found two general types of responding units: *dominators* and *modulators*. Dominators and modulators must be defined in terms of Granit's techniques. Essentially, after a stable location for recording from a cell in the retina is obtained through a microelectrode, the intensity of light sufficient to cause a noticeable difference in the recorded neural activity is determined for hues in all regions of the spectrum. Then for every neural unit in the retina a "sensitivity curve" can be obtained. In such a curve, wavelength is plotted horizontally and a measure of the intensity of light (of a given wavelength) required to alter the neural response of the cell is plotted vertically. Figure 4.15 shows the dominator and modulator curves found by Granit.

Modulators are defined by narrow, peaked response patterns. Retinal elements which give modulator effects are found less frequently than cells which give dominator effects. The modulator curves shown in Fig. 4.15 are found only under light-adapted conditions and are presumably initiated by activities in the cone system. Narrow response curves (modulator cells) are found with peaks at many wavelengths but they tend to cluster in certain regions. Granit believes his work supports the general position advocated by the early theory of Thomas Young, but others have interpreted Granit's findings as support for theories postulating more than three types of receptor cells. It should be pointed out that the average values of modulator curves do not resemble the three curves postulated by the Young-Helmholtz theory since rare yellow modulators have been found. If Granit's recording techniques reflect activity in single receptor elements, the yellow modulator presents another difficulty to the traditional theory of three cone types, which assumes yellow to result from the synthesis of red, green, and blue primaries.

RETINAL CONVERGENCE. There must be a considerable convergence taking place in the retina and optic nerve. In man there are 4 million to 7 million cones and about 125 million rods in the retina. In the optic nerve there are between 800 thousand to 1 million fibers. Therefore, many individual receptor cells must converge upon and feed into the ganglion cells and few (if any) receptors have "private lines" to the brain. What is the scheme of this retinal convergence?

Figure 4.16 diagrams the convergence pattern proposed by Rushton [11]. It contains some novel and important ideas about the structure and function of the visual system. Note that rods and cones feed into "excitation pools," and in turn these feed into ganglion cells. The anatomical correlate of the excitation pool is uncertain but the evidence of Rushton and others makes the assumption of some such structure necessary.

Now, let us look closely at the diagram. The existence of several types of rods seems likely, and two varieties are indicated by the filled and open rectangles. Note that *both rods and cones feed into the same excitation pools.* Also, one receptor cell sends impulses to more than one excitation pool. Several excitation pools send impulses to the same ganglion cell. All of these arrangements are necessary to account for the data assembled through the use of a technique of *silent substitution,* developed by Rushton. In one experiment, microelectrodes were inserted into the retina of the frog and the activities of neural units, presumed to be ganglion cells, were monitored. The retina was illuminated with a given intensity and wavelength of light. Then a sudden transition was made to a new wavelength

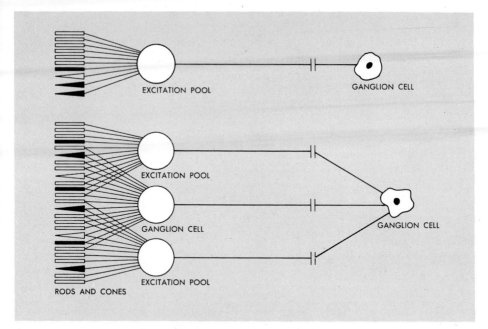

FIG. **4.16.** *Rods and cones and excitation pools. Steady excitation from various receptors is transmitted to the pool, and any changes in the pool's level are transmitted to the ganglion. The simplest model is shown above, but more recent data requires the more complicated model shown below. Adapted from W. A. H. Rushton, Excitation pools in the frog's retina. J. Physiol. (London), 1959, 149, 327–345.*

and intensity of light. If an intensity could be found for the new wavelength which makes the transition silent, i.e., no change in the ganglion cell's activity is recorded, then this would imply that the level of activity reaching the ganglion cell under the two conditions was the same. This theory assumes the ganglion cells to be responsive to the *total amount of activity* reaching it. Silent substitution can be achieved from many modifications of the basic design too detailed for presentation here. Since silent substitution can not always be made, it is necessary to assume that the retina must be organized as in the lower portion of Fig. 4.16 rather than as in the simplified version shown first.

THALAMIC ACTIVITY. Another approach to gaining understanding of the sensory systems is to "listen in" at the relay nuclei in the thalamus.

The thalamic relay nucleus for vision is called the lateral geniculate body. The lateral geniculate nucleus (LGN) is organized into six layers of cell bodies representing three *pairs* of layers. One member of each pair receives input from the right eye while the other member receives input from the left eye. In other words there seem to be three functional subdivisions in the LGN each consisting of two layers and each receiving impulses from separate eyes. Figure 4.17 presents a cross-section of the LGN stained to show the six layers of cell bodies. To record from cells in this structure, exceedingly small microelectrodes must be lowered deep into the brain.

Once the microelectrode reaches the LGN and a cell body is isolated, its responses to various illuminating conditions of the retina may be studied.

The two dorsal layers contain cells which increase their rates of activity when the retina is illuminated. Most of these cells continue this increased discharge rate for a period of time

FIG. 4.17. *The lateral geniculate nucleus of a monkey. The dark regions are densely packed cells which are organized into six layers.*

before returning to their normal rates even though the light remains on. When the light is turned off, these same cells show a decrease in discharge rate which is below the level of their "spontaneous" activity [12].

Cells in the bottom two layers respond to changes in illumination by decreasing their activity rates until the light is extinguished. Then they exhibit a burst of activity. We can think of these cells being inhibited by light and then becoming active when the light is turned off.

However, it is the activity of the cells in the middle two layers that demands our attention for their exciting implications for theories of color reception. Cells in these layers react strongly when the retina is illuminated by one wavelength but not by another, and in general their reactions are similar in form to the "modulators" discussed by Granit. However, these "color cells" show a most peculiar phenomenon: *a lateral geniculate cell may be excited (increase its rate of firing) to one color and be inhibited (decrease its rate of firing) by the complementary color.* As an example, suppose the cell increases its rate of firing when the eye is illuminated by green light, then this cell will be inhibited by red light. If it is excited by yellow light it can be inhibited by blue light.

We might recall that Hering's original proposal was discounted because of the basic physiological dictum called the *doctrine of specific nerve energies* according to which a given nerve cell could only mediate one quality of experience. In the studies of the lateral geniculate nucleus, a cell has been shown to signal the experience of one color by an increase in rate of activity and signal another color by a decrease in rate. Thus, the doctrine of specific nerve energies must be modified, and the Hering theory of color vision must be reconsidered. All theories proposed to explain color in neurophysiological terms must be able to incorporate the results obtained from the middle layers of the LGN.

The results from the LGN do not represent a clear victory of the original Hering theory. In the first place, the cells in the LGN are considerably removed from the receptor units. The excitation or inhibition of the LGN cells may come from complicated neural interaction in excitation pools or ganglion cells in the microstructure of the retina, or be the result of the summation of effects from retinal ganglion cells feeding into a lateral geniculate cell. We cannot decide upon the types of receptor cells from research on the thalamic nucleus. In addition, cells in the upper two layers of the LGN respond as modulators but without being inhibited by a complementary color. Thus, the findings obtained from microelectrode studies of the LGN suggest that our color vision must be a result of processes like those postulated by Young and Helmholtz as well as like those postulated by Hering.

But we are a long way from being able to understand color phenomenon. The theories of color vision we have studied refer to theories of the construction of the receptor organ, and neurophysiological studies are just beginning to offer hope of learning the ways in which peripheral visual information is translated into the code used by the brain. We know, on the other hand, that the quality of perceived color, the color we observe in natural objects, depends on the context in which the object occurs and the object itself. We are unable to integrate relatively simple perceptual phenomena like these into our theories as yet. Further, we still are puzzled by many of the types of color vision defects which can be found in the clinical literature.

VISUAL ACUITY The studies of the peripheral mechanisms are essential to understanding sensory phenomena, for if we know how the peripheral system is organized and responds, we will know the nature of the changes imposed upon the information coming in from the periphery to create *perception,* as we commonly use the term. We are just learning about some of the complexities that can be found in the peripheral sensory organs. A case in point can be illustrated by recent studies of visual acuity.

When we think of visual activity most of us think of the Snellen eye chart. This is the chart we read in the physician's office. Usually it hangs about 20 feet from the line on which we stand. The chart has rows of letters which diminish in size from top to bottom. This is a crude measure of visual acuity, and there are many other types of tests for acuity which reduce the unwanted effects of language attainment and letter-design cues on a person's performance. Some of these improved tests use circles with gaps in them (Landolt rings). A series of these circles with the direction of the gap varied is presented, and the subject must report this direction. In another test the subject is required to decide whether two parallel lines are actually separate or not. Most of us have had some experience with tests of visual acuity.

Visual acuity depends upon several factors. A sharp image must be focused on the retina. If the image is blurred through defects of the lens or cornea, our acuity will be decreased. On the other hand the eyeball may be too long or too short for the lens to focus a distinct image when the stimulus is far away or close up and the result is clinically either far- or nearsightedness. The ultimate limits of our visual acuity depend upon the retinal mosaic of receptor fields and their modes of action. It turns out that our visual acuity is exceptionally fine. We are able to detect lines whose thickness is *less than the diameter of one cone.* Calculations of the energy required for the perception of a visual stimulus reveal that the reception of one quantum of light by one receptor cell is sufficient to be detectable. Our vision is excellent, then, almost too good, for it poses

151

the question of how we can detect lines which are smaller than the width of a receptor unit.

EYE MOVEMENTS. The perception of stimuli smaller than a receptor cell can be accounted for on the basis of eye movements. The eye continuously exhibits several kinds of movements. Small and very rapid oscillations of the eye are sufficient to throw the image on the retina over several receptor cells and thus create patterns, or distributions, of excitation over a larger area. Resolution of this larger pattern caused by the eye movements must be accomplished by neural interaction at the level of the bipolar or ganglion cells or higher up the neural chain to the brain.

When discussing visual fields we noted that there is good evidence that one retinal area can influence an adjoining area. This interaction, in which one retinal area inhibits or excites neighboring areas, may also serve to *sharpen* the neural activity caused by the retinal figure. Thus, the images we perceive represent great accomplishments in both the anatomical system of the eyes and the neural mechanisms of the entire system beginning at the retina itself.

Other Sensory Systems

How many other senses do we have? Certainly we hear, we smell, we taste, we feel tactile sensations of the skin, we are aware of the orientation of our body in space and relative to gravitational forces, we know when our stomach "growls." On top of this, we are sensitive to changes in temperature and we can feel several varieties of pain.

As we have already mentioned, our preference is to concentrate our attention upon some of the functional characteristics of the visual system. Many of the functional characteristics found in the visual system are common to all sensory systems. For example, each kind of sensory system has some kind of a receptor field. Receptors in the skin respond to deformations over a rather well-defined spatial area. Receptor fields for these skin receptors can be mapped by recording from single neurons in sensory nerves, or by recording from the neocortical areas receiving this kind of information. Principles of transmission of sensory information from receptor to thalamus to cortex have many points of similarity in all sensory systems. The greatest *difference* among the several sensory systems is to be found in mechanisms used to change physical energies into neural activity at the receptor organs (generator potentials).

THE AUDITORY SYSTEM   The external, shell-like structure of the ear (the pinna) probably is useful in funneling changes in sound pressure into the auditory receptors of the lower animals, but in man these external features serve little function. Just inside the pinna, through a short passage (the external meatus), is the ear drum which moves in and out in response to changes in air pressure. This vibration of the ear drum is

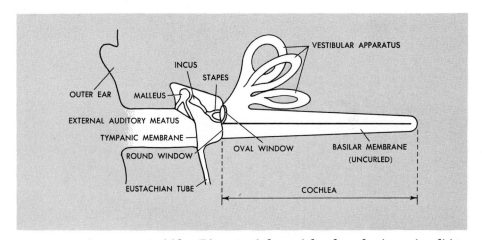

FIG. 4.18.   *Diagram of the peripheral mechanisms of audition. The cochlea, straightened here, is naturally twisted about three and a half times—rather like a sea shell.*

transmitted by a mechanical linkage of the three bones (malleus, incus, and stapes) of the middle ear to the inner ear. Inside the inner ear are the receptor cells which change physical vibrations into neural events for final translation into changes in neural activity. Figure 4.18 presents a schematic diagram of the human ear. The inner ear is filled with fluids. The mechanical vibrations of the bones of the middle ear are translated into moving waves in these fluids through the in and out movements of the oval window. The motion of the inner-ear fluids is translated into neural changes by receptor cells located on the basilar membrane.

In Fig. 4.18 the basilar membrane has been drawn as a straight, flat surface. Actually, it is curled up inside a boney structure resembling a snail's shell. The name of this boney housing of the basilar membrane comes from its appearance: it is called the *cochlea*. The basilar membrane extends throughout the length of the cochlea. Waves in the fluid medium produce oscillations of the membrane. The place of greatest oscillation of the basilar membrane is determined by the frequency of the vibration of the oval window. The actual receptor cells, *hair cells,* are located on the basilar membrane. As the basilar membrane oscillates, the hair cells are distorted and this causes them to produce neural changes just as light causes neural reactions in the rods and cones of the retina. These changes in neural activity originating in the hair cells is transmitted through a series of neurons to the auditory areas of the neocortex found in the temporal lobes, via the thalamic relay nucleus for audition (the medial geniculate nucleus). The frequency of the fluid vibrations of the inner ear is signaled to the brain by the pattern of distortion of the basilar membrane. Different patterns of distortion result in different groups of hair cells being activated.

The ears function to apprise us of changes in the air pressure around us. However, our auditory mechanism is only sensitive to changes in air pressure occurring within a certain range of frequencies. Generally speaking, the human can hear frequencies between 20 and 20,000 cycles per second. Changes in air pressure of slower or faster frequencies do not effect us. Remember that in the case of vision we found that we were sensitive to only part of the electromagnetic spectrum. In hearing we are sensitive only to a portion of the frequency spectrum. Other species are sensitive to different ranges of frequencies.

Air pressure changes of appropriate frequencies are translated into mechanical changes by the middle-ear mechanisms. These mechanical vibrations are changed into hydraulic vibrations in the inner ear. The receptor cells are affected by these changes in the movement of fluids in the cochlea. In the ear we find an interesting series of translations of air pressure changes to mechanical changes to hydraulic changes to neural changes. The signals arriving at higher centers of the brain from the auditory system are encoded as alterations in the activities of single neurons just as are signals arriving from all sensory systems.

SMELL AND TASTE Smell and taste are two of the chemical senses we have. In the nose the particles in the air combine with the fluids over the receptors to form a chemical solution to which sensory cells in the olfactory epithelium respond. The patterns of excitation set up in the receptors by these solutions are carried to the brain over the olfactory nerves, and then are projected to certain portions of phyletically old brain. The taste receptors are located on the tongue. Because of their shape they are called *taste buds*. While most of these are located on the top, tip, and side of the tongue, there are some on the top of the mouth, in the glottis, and in the pharynx and larynx.

Impulses initiated by the chemical solutions on the tongue are relayed to the brain over several nerves. Once they reach the central nervous system they become connected with impulses arising from the somatic musculature of the body, and their projection to neocortex probably is through relay nuclei which carry the somatic information. This mixing, however, does not mean that taste-initiated neural activity becomes integrated with the neural activity initiated by the muscles. The taste activity and the somatic activity are projected by thalamic relay nuclei to quite different areas of the neocortex.

Psychologically there seems to be four distinct kinds of tastes: sweet, sour, bitter, and salt. Other tastes are believed to be compounded of these four basic tastes. However, records of the activity of single taste buds reveal that none of them seems to represent a single kind of basic taste receptor. Single taste buds may respond to combinations of several of the basic tastes. A given taste bud may respond to both salt and sweet solutions, for example. Because it is possible through the use of certain drugs to eliminate the response of this kind of taste bud to sweetness but maintain its response to salty solutions, it is now believed that taste buds may have specific locations, or sites, which are sensitive to certain kinds of solutions but not others.

The fact that single receptor units do not respond in the four ways suggested by the four psychologically basic tastes implies that the latter are compounded or created by the central nervous system. (For reviews of modern information about smell see [13] and for taste see [14].)

SOMATIC SENSATION   The information about the position and the actions of our body comes from fibers embedded in muscles, from receptors in tendons, and from receptors located in the skin. For many years efforts were directed toward locating specific receptor units which corresponded to each of the types of somatic sensation. For example, investigators tried to associate a specific type of receptor cell for the sensations of heat loss (cold) and another specific kind of receptor cell for the sensation of touch. However, the work of Weddell suggests that this search for basic receptor types may be fruitless. Information concerning warmth, cold, touch, tickle, and pain can all be transmitted by free nerve endings which do not appear to have any specialized receptor units at their extremities [15]. As with the sense of taste, the organization of peripheral information into psychologically elementary sensations seems to be accomplished in the central nervous system. Different kinds of stimulation arising from the periphery of the body produce different patterns of excitation in free nerve endings, muscles, joints, etc. From the patterns of stimulation arising in the periphery of the body the central neural apparatus imposes organization.

Somatic sensations travel to the brain in the spinal cord. In general we can recognize two kinds of pathways from the spinal cord to the relay nuclei of the thalamus (spinothalamic tracts). The first system is a group of large, heavily myelinated fibers which are located toward the back (dorsum) of the body and are called the dorsal columns. These reach a thalamic nucleus and then are projected in to neocortical areas just in back of the central fissure (see p. 102). An outline of the muscles of the body can be found in the neocortical projection area and in the thalamic relay nucleus. No pain sensations are carried over this big-fiber system, and there is reason to believe this system is recent in the phylogenetic development of animals [16]. This system would represent the primary sensory stem illustrated in Fig. 4.2 (p. 123).

Somatic sensations also reach the brain from the spinal cord over other ascending columns or tracts. These are located more toward the side of the cord (lateral spinothalamic tracts) and toward the stomach (ventral and anterior spinothalamic tracts). The fibers in these somatic systems are much smaller than in the dorsal columns and reach the thalamus after many synapses with other cells. These smaller fiber systems give off collaterals to the diffuse systems of the brain including the reticular formation of the brain stem. Upon reaching the thalamus they go into different thalamic areas from those entered by the bigger fibers of the dorsal columns. Then they project to areas of the neocortex adjacent to the somatosensory areas innervated by the dorsal-column fibers.

The smaller fiber columns of the spinal cord carry different kinds of somatic messages from those in the dorsal columns. Activity in their fibers can be initiated by wider regions of the body and their thalamic nuclei receive input from more than one type of receptor. For example, a thalamic neuron in the area receiving somatic input from the lateral spinothalamic system may respond to muscle changes, tendon changes, and possibly auditory stimulation [17].

The behavioral significance of the two types of somatic sensation has not been completely specified. Yet we do know some of the functional characteristics of each kind of system. We know, for example, that neural impulses giving rise to pain are carried over the lateral spinothalamic system. This knowledge allows neurosurgeons to help people who have continuing unbearable pain in some portions of their bodies by selectively severing these tracts. This operation reduces or eliminates the sensation of pain without loss of sensation or muscular coordination of the affected region.

In summary: Although there are specialized aspects of each sensory system, in broad detail certain similarities can be found among them. Each sensory system seems to be organized at the periphery in terms of receptive fields, that is, in terms of relatively broad areas of a receptor surface. Stimulation in these areas will produce a change in the response of one of the neurons in the chain from receptor to brain. Receptive fields may be arranged in different shapes of excitatory and inhibitory areas and can be measured by recording from cells close to the receptors or at the neocortical areas receiving the specific sensory information. As a general rule receptive fields are smaller when measured at the neocortical level than nearer the receptor. This suggests, along with related evidence from many sensory systems, that the qualities of sensation result from the central organization of the brain and nervous system.

Information from the sensory systems reaches the neocortex through afferent nerve tracts and through a synaptic relay nucleus of the thalamus. There are two categories of afferent nerve fibers: the fast, myelinated nerve tracts which go to the main sensory receiving areas of neocortex and the slower, smaller fiber nerve tracts which reach the supplemental sensory areas and which give off collaterals to the diffuse systems.

Finally, we must recognize that the central nervous system is actively concerned with modifying the peripheral input close to, if not at, the level of the receptor units. This is accomplished through systems of sensory efferent fibers. The entire sensory process must be conceived of as a constantly active relationship between input from the receptors and modifying outflow to the receptors.

References

1. Kuffler, S. W., Hunt, C. C., & Quilliam, J. P. Function of medullated small-nerve fibers in mammalian ventral roots: efferent muscle spindle innervation. *J. Neurophysiol.,* 1951, **14,** 29–54.

2. Hagbarth, K. E., & Kerr, D. I. B. Central influences on spinal afferent conduction. *J. Neurophysiol.,* 1954, **17,** 195–307.

3. Granit, R. *Receptors and Sensory Perception.* New Haven: Yale Univer. Press, 1955.

4. Hartline, H. K. Impulses in single optic nerve fibers of the vertebrate eye to illumination of the retina. *Amer. J. Physiol.,* 1938, **121,** 400–415.

5. Hubel, D. H., and Wiesel, T. N. Receptive fields of single neurons in the cats striate cortex. *J. physiol.,* 1959, **148,** 574–591.

6. Jung, R., & Baumgartner, G. Hemmungsmechanismen und bremsende Stabilisierung an einzelnen Neuronen des optishen Cortex. *Pflüg. Arch. ges. Physiol.,* 1955, **261,** 434–456.

7. Lettvin, J. Y., Matwiana, H. R., McCulloch, W. S., & Pitts, W. H. What the frog's eye tells the frog's brain. *IRE Proc.,* 1959, **47,** 1940–1951.

8. Hecht, S., Shlaer, S., & Pirenne, M. H. Energy, quanta, and vision. *J. gen. Physiol.,* 1942, **25,** 819–840.

9. Wald, G. The photoreceptor process in vision. In J. Field (Ed.), *Handbook of Physiology. Section 1: Neurophysiology.* Washington, D.C.: Amer. Physiol. Soc., 1959.

10. Granit, R. *Sensory Mechanisms of the Retina.* London: Oxford Univer. Press, 1947.

11. Rushton, W. A. H. Excitation pools in the frog's retina. *J. Physiol.,* 1959, **149,** 327–345.

12. DeValois, R. L., Smith, C. J., Kitai, S. T., & Karoly, A. J. Response of single cells in monkey lateral geniculate nucleus to monochromatic light. *Science,* 1957, **127,** 238–239.

13. Adey, W. R. The sense of smell. In J. Field (Ed.), *op. cit.*

14. Pfaffman, C. The sense of taste. In J. Field (Ed.), *op. cit.*
15. Weddell, G. Receptors for somatic sensation. In Mary A. B. Brazier (Ed.), *Brain and Behavior*. Washington, D.C.: Amer. Inst. Biol. Sci., 1961.
16. Bishop, G. H. The relation between nerve fiber size and sensory modality: phylogenetic implications of the afferent innervation of cortex. *J. nerv. ment. Dis.,* 1959, **128,** 89–114.
17. Mountcastle, V. B. Duality of function in the somatic afferent system. In Mary A. B. Brazier (Ed.), *op. cit.*

FIVE PERCEPTUAL BEHAVIOR: EXPERIMENTS AND THEORIES

How many ways can we perceive the moon? Does the moon appear the same on an autumn hayride with your favorite partner as it does in an evening astronomy class? Do we *see* the moon differently after learning about its craters and landmarks in the astronomy class? Why does the large moon seen at the horizon change in size if we bend over and look at it through our legs? In asking these questions we are asking if our actual perception of the moon is different under the several conditions we have mentioned, not whether our emotion or behavior is different. If our perceptions are different then these differences must be caused by influences quite apart from the sensory determinants of perception discussed in Chapter 4. In this chapter we shall discuss experiments and theories which concern perceptual behavior of the entire individual. We have already suggested that perception is more than reactions of the sensory systems. "Man, not his eyes, sees."

In the first section of this chapter we shall discuss some modern aspects of an area of psychology called *psychophysics*. This branch of research has roots extending back to the beginnings of scientific psychology. Early research in psychophysics attempted to determine the relation between physical stimulation impinging on an individual and his mental experiences. Today, we would say that psychophysics attempts to describe the relationship between changes in physical stimulation and changes in those responses which indicate recognition or detection of the physical changes. Like all branches of psychology the aim is to understand man; in this case man as an observer. We shall discuss both early and modern techniques in this attempt to coordinate the physical world about us with our internal reactions.

Next we shall examine the reasons why some psychologists began to assert that we must study the total "form" rather than "elements" of perception. At the same time we shall consider some explanations which have been offered for the perception of forms and the relevance of psychological research using perceptual illusions. This will lead us to a theory of perception developed by D. O. Hebb which has important implications for behavior theory generally.

In the later sections of the chapter we shall discuss the influence of bodily activity, values, motives, and personality variables on perception. The fact that psychologists discuss the possibility that variables like these can affect perception reflects a relatively recent change in emphasis in psychological research. In fact research with these variables has been called the *New Look* in perceptual studies.

Psychophysics

As the name implies, psychophysics suggests a marriage of psychology and physics. If we think of the setting in which the marriage took place in the middle of the nineteenth century in

Germany, this is a reasonable union. In those days physics and psychology were very different from what they are today. Physics was fairly well established in its Newtonian tradition with a strong emphasis on measurement. In fact many philosophers of science held that it was because of this emphasis on measurement that physics advanced so rapidly. Psychology was primarily the study of mental experience. Furthermore, many scientists were active in several areas of research. What would be more natural for a scientist with biological, physical, and psychological interests to want to study and measure *sensation?* Psychophysics refers to research which aims to do just this: to study the changes in perception which occur when changes in the physical stimuli are made. While many psychologists still believe the methods of psychophysics do measure mental experiences, the behavioristic influence suggests that we confine ourselves to speaking of the relation between physical stimuli and response. It will be most useful to consider perception as a "theoretical variable" which is inferred from certain kinds of responses. We cannot know by inference the mental states of any other person but we can know and study his behavior.

One of the founders of psychophysics, Gustav Fechner, began his studies because of an interest in attacking the current materialistic philosophies existing in Germany in the middle 1800s. Fechner believed he could prove his own philosophic view through psychophysics. This view illustrates the early attempts to use psychophysical methods as a means to measure mental experiences by finding laws relating the two worlds.

WEBER'S RATIO AND FECHNER'S LAW One of the earliest psychophysical observations made was the general rule that the amount of change in sensory stimulation required to allow the observer to report that he perceives a perceptual change is proportional to the amount of the sensory stimulation. This is Weber's law. Another way of stating this, using symbols, is

$$\frac{\Delta I}{I} = K$$

where ΔI = increase or decrease in stimulation
     I = amount of original stimulation
    K = a constant which depends on the particular sensory modality and other variables

A simple example of Weber's ratio which is often found on examinations is the following:

Q. If a theater sign had a dense grouping of 1000 bulbs, and if the Weber ratio for the particular situation was 0.10, how many bulbs would have to burn out before they were noticed?

A. $\dfrac{\Delta I}{I} = K$ If $K = .1$ $\dfrac{X}{1000} = .1$, $X = 100$ bulbs

    $\qquad\qquad\qquad I = 1000$

    $\qquad\qquad\qquad \Delta I = X$

Therefore, we can predict that if less than 100 bulbs were burned out (randomly), observers would not report any change in stimulation. However, this problem is greatly oversimplified. In a real situation the Weber ratio could not be applied to the case of a theater sign where the grouping of the stimulus elements is important. In our illustration a cluster of burned-out bulbs would be noticed more rapidly than if the burned-out bulbs were evenly dispersed.

Fechner simply integrated the basic Weber equation to obtain a general statement about the relation between physical stimulation and mental sensations.

$$\frac{\Delta I}{I} = K \quad \text{(Weber's Law)}$$

$$\int \frac{\Delta I}{I} = k \log I \quad \text{Fechner's Law}$$

This result is often interpreted to read

$$\boxed{\text{Sensation} = k \log \text{stimulation}}$$

This equation asserts that sensation varies in a logarithmic relation to stimulation. In effect this means that small changes in the lower ranges of the physical-stimulus scale will produce greater changes in sensation than the same amounts of physical-stimulus changes superimposed upon stimuli of greater magnitude. We have displayed the "sensation = k log stimulation" relationship graphically in Fig. 5.1. From it we observe that a small change in skin pressure (a to a') will produce a greater change in sensation when it is imposed on a slight previous pressure than on a great previous pressure (b to b'). If the initial pressure is high enough, an increment of 2 ounces per square inch may not be reported as any change at all. This would be the case if the ratio of a 2-ounce increment to the original pressure is less than the particular Weber's constant for this type of stimulation.

JUST NOTICEABLE DIFFERENCES AND THRESHOLDS   Weber's fraction ($\Delta I/I$) is based on the concept of a *just noticeable difference* (JND). It assumes that changes in existing stimulus conditions are either large enough to cause a perceptual difference or they are not. If they are not large enough then the observer will perceive no change whatever in the stimulus. A JND refers to the smallest change in a stimulus which can be

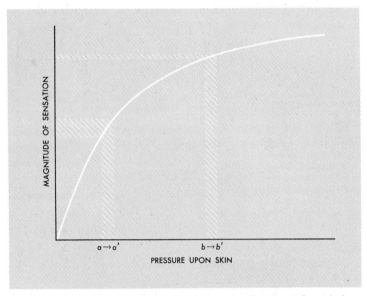

FIG. 5.1.   *Logarithmic relation between stimulation and sensation. Vertical axis presumably reflects the magnitude of observer's perception of skin pressure. The same increase in physical pressure on the skin (the distance between a-a' and to b-b') creates a greater difference in perception at lower end of stumulus scale than at higher end.*

detected by the observer. This concept rests in turn upon the concept of a threshold. The threshold is a theoretical concept which indicates a boundary condition. If one applies increasing amounts of pressure on a balloon, say by squeezing it, at some point the balloon will burst. The amount of pressure needed to break the balloon can be thought of as a threshold condition. Any pressure less than the boundary pressure will not break the balloon; any pressure greater than the boundary pressure will. Changes in any sensory stimulation which fall below a threshold will not cause any perceptual change in the observer.

Changes in sensory stimulation above this threshold amount of stimulation will produce changes in the observer's perceptions.

We can talk about two kinds of thresholds: a *difference threshold* and an *absolute threshold*. In fact they are very similar concepts, both based on change from prior conditions. An absolute threshold refers to the smallest amount of stimulation which can be *detected* by an observer. In measuring an absolute threshold we begin with no stimulation at all and add energy until the observer reports a perceptual experience. If we want to measure the absolute threshold for a spot of white light, we could present this spot to subjects looking at a dark target area in a blackened room (after sufficient time for dark adaptation to occur). We would present the spot at different intensities and instruct the subjects to respond in a certain way when they saw the white spot. If we wanted to measure difference thresholds, we must present an increment or decrement of illumination in the spot and ask when this difference is noticed. When measuring absolute thresholds the experimenter wants the subjects to report the presence of a stimulus; in measuring difference thresholds the experimenter wants the subjects to report a change in stimulating conditions.

Measurement of thresholds Psychophysical methods are techniques used to measure absolute and difference thresholds.

Measurements of thresholds can be done in several ways. The primary methods were reported by Fechner in 1860. Three methods are still widely used today.

1. The first method is often called the *method of constant stimuli,* despite the fact the stimuli presented to the observer are not constant. When using this technique, stimuli are presented to the observer one at a time in a varying order. If the method is being used to determine an absolute visual threshold the observer is asked to report when he sees the stimulus. After each stimulus has been presented many times and the observer has reported his perceptual changes, it is possible to relate the intensity of the stimulus to the number of times that the observer reported seeing it. A hypothetical curve, representing the frequency of detection for five stimuli, is presented in Fig. 5.2. As the stimuli increase in intensity, the greater is the frequency defined as that stimulus intensity which is reported as perceived Furthermore, as is typical in psychophysical experiments, the frequency of reports of perceptual changes increases most rapidly in the middle range of the stimulus intensity scale. This

is reflected in the shape of the curve which resembles a slanted *S*. Using the method of constant stimuli, a threshold is usually defined as that stimulus intensity which is reported as perceived half the number of times it was presented. This definition is

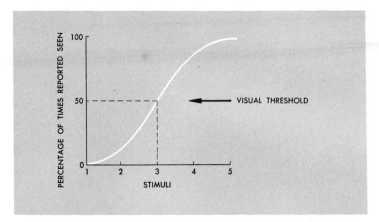

FIG. 5.2. *Hypothetical relationship between the proportion of times a stimulus is presented and reported seen and the intensity of the stimulus. Stimulus 1 is the least intense, 5 the most intense.*

arbitrary and other definitions could serve as well. For example, would not a stimulus whose intensity was such that it was perceived 75 percent of the time be an equally good threshold?

2. When an experimenter uses the *method of limits*, he presents the subject with a graduated series of stimulus intensities either from the smallest intensities to the greatest intensities or from the greatest to the smallest. The experimenter begins by presenting the subject with one of the stimuli from either end of the continuum. Then, he asks the subject if he sees the stimulus. Usually, the extreme intensities are selected so that there is no doubt that the subject will report that he sees it if the greatest intensity stimulus is presented and will not report seeing it if the minimal stimulus is presented. Each stimulus in the series is presented and the subject again reports whether or not it is perceived. The series of stimuli is presented in order through the entire range of stimuli or until the subject changes his report from "seeing" to "not seeing" or the other way around, depending on whether an ascending or descending series is being presented.

3. In the third method, *the method of average error,* the subject adjusts a stimulus until it matches some given standard.

The subject has control of a knob or dial by which he can increase or decrease the stimulus intensity. The basic operation of matching is repeated many times. The difference between this method and others is that the subject is required to make a judgment of equality between the stimulus under his control and the standard. Thresholds are determined by the mean (average) stimulus intensity set by the subject. This presumably is the point at which the sensation reaches a region of intensity indistinguishable from the standard. The conditions of the experiment influence the calculated thresholds, and the thresholds obtained by this method often fail to correspond to those obtained by the method of constant stimuli or the method of limits.

Should we assume a threshold? Each of the three methods described above produces a number, expressed in physical units of measurement, which is called a threshold. These numbers are often considered as more or less reliable estimates of some "real threshold" in the person which cannot be measured directly. This real threshold would be a boundary between sensation and no sensation or between a change in sensation and no change in sensation, depending on whether we were speaking of absolute or difference thresholds. The threshold

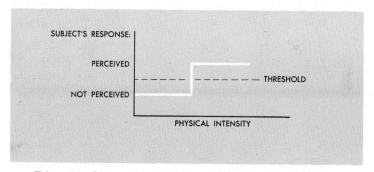

FIG. 5.3.   *Graphic presentation of the threshold assumption. As the physical stimulus increases, some point is reached when the excitation is sufficient to cause a perceptual response to it. Crossing the threshold is an all-or-none event on any presentation of stimulus.*

concept can be illustrated by the steplike graph of Fig. 5.3. Along the abscissa, we have represented a physical-energy scale. It could be a scale of light intensity, for example. On the ordinate we have represented essentially two conditions: stimulus perceived and not perceived. As the intensity of the stimulus is increased, some point is reached at which perception takes place. As we already know, this point is often called the threshold. Yet, curves like this are never found when data from psychophysical experiments are analyzed.

Usually, a slowly rising curve is obtained as represented earlier in Fig. 5.2. This, plus the fact that different psychophysical methods often yield different estimates of the threshold point, raises doubts as to the usefulness of the concept of sensory thresholds. But there are still other problems for the concept of thresholds.

REWARDS AND EXPECTANCIES   If one considers the task of the subject in a psychophysical experiment, it becomes apparent that both his expectancies about the experimental situation and the reward system set up by the experimenter must have a profound influence on behavior. Even though the subject tries to report his experiences honestly, the *sequence* of stimuli presented by the experimenter and the pay-offs to the subject affect the observer's reports.

For an illustration, let us think of a radar operator watching the face of his scope. The radar operator may be part of an early warning system and he knows that any blip appearing on his scope face could be an enemy missile on the way toward the United States. Detection of the missile is important for the initiation of countermeasures.

Radar screens tend to have some degree of background activity, or noise. The blip is really an intense point of light superimposed on a background of less intense and constantly varying light. If the radar operator has been observing the screen for months without a signal or blip occurring, and nothing has been said to make him think there is any change in the world situation, he probably believes that it is unlikely that a blip will occur. However, the payoffs for his possible responses are interesting too.

The radar operator, at any moment, can report the activity on his scope as "missile" or "no missile." At any moment a missile could be present or not. Two kinds of mistakes can be made. If a missile is on its way toward the United States, a mistake in not reporting it might have terrible consequences. The other type of mistake, reporting a missile when there is none, would waste some interceptor missiles which may be expensive; but not nearly as much damage would be inflicted by an enemy missile. Therefore, it is likely that the radar operator would tend to make the second kind of error in preference to the first. Thus both the observer's past history as it influences his expectations of the occurrence of a blip and the pay-offs for the various kinds of correct and incorrect responses influence perceptual *reports*. These factors have been incorporated into a theoretical model of how the human observer detects stimulus change.

THE DECISION ANALYSIS MODEL   Tanner and Swets [1] have proposed that our detection of sensory signals can be compared to the performance of an electronic device designed to detect signals against a background of noise which is an unpredictable pattern of activity. This comparison allows us a fresh look at the basic perceptual mechanisms. In the example of the hypothetical radar observer, the detection task faced by the human can be one where signals must be detected against more or less intense backgrounds of noise. One suggestion made by Tanner and Swets is that all sensory detection can be thought of in the same way. We all must sort out signals of interest from noisy backgrounds. Noise can be external, as in a radar screen or a poor radio, or internal, caused perhaps by the spontaneous activity of the nervous system. In any case the problem posed for signal detection is how do we reach a decision regarding whether we are observing signal and noise or noise alone. Because the theory proposed by Tanner and Swets explicitly provides a model for how this decision is reached, it is called the *decision analysis model*.

Noise and signals   In the decision analysis model every problem of sensory detection is viewed as one in which a signal is added to a noise background. Noise is postulated as a basic feature of the model and the organism. There may be more or less noise at any moment. Noise can occur in every sensory modality. While it is possible to think of various sources of noise both in the external world and in the person, *for our purposes let us merely assume that there always is some noise as part of the background for all sensory observations.*

By definition, noise refers to a pattern of activity which is unpredictable. Auditory noise usually refers to an unsystematic sampling of auditory frequencies which change rapidly. Noise in the visual system could refer to an unsystematic pattern of visual wavelengths which also change moment to moment. The intensity of the noisy background can also change moment to moment. While the precise characteristics of the noise at any instant would be impossible to predict, it is possible to make assumptions about the average values of the noise when observed over a period of time. For example, if your radio is tuned so that you get only static, you can not know how loud that static will be at any one instant. But by turning the gain (volume or loudness) of the radio you can arrange to have the average value of the static greater or less. When the radio is loud, the average value of the static has been increased. Turning the radio down would decrease the average value of the static. So it is possible to talk about average values of noise and, even more, to talk about the distribution of noise patterns. By distribution we mean the way in which the unsystematic noise occurrences of noise range about an average value. In the Tanner-Swets theory distributions are similar at all intensities.

The important parts of the decision analysis model are (1) a background noise is postulated to always exist and (2) the average value and distribution of the noise can be specified to some degree. If this is accepted, then the next assumption is that *the effect of a signal is to displace the average value of the noise distribution.*

Let us assume in a case of auditory detection that there is a background noise level with an average intensity of X. Subjects attempt to detect a signal presented against this noise background. The signal is assumed to have a *constant intensity* (not varying moment to moment like the noise) of Y. The decision analysis model asserts that the mean value of the signal *and* noise is $X + Y$. Mathematically, it can be shown that the distribution of the signal-plus-noise distribution will be the same as the distribution of the noise alone, although it is displaced along the intensity scale. Figure 5.4 shows a hypothetical noise distribution and the effect of adding a signal to this background distribution.

Moment to moment the noise distribution fluctuates about the average value of X, and the signal-plus-noise distribution fluctuates about the average value of $X + Y$.

In the normal course of events an observer in real life or in the reduced laboratory situation never can observe the entire range of either distribution. We must make decisions with less than complete information. If we must decide whether a signal is being presented we decide on the basis of a sample which can come from either of the two distributions.

Sampling from the distributions   In the decision analysis model the observer is thought to be given a sample from one or the other of the distributions. This observer's job is to decide whether the sample comes from the noise or the signal-plus-noise distributions.

In effect we can interpret this to mean that the observer is given one value from the intensity scale of Fig. 5.4. This is a

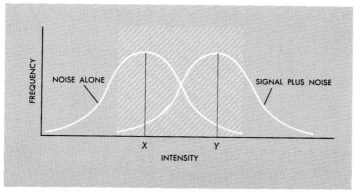

FIG. 5.4.   *Effect of adding a sensory signal to a noise distribution as proposed in the Tanner-Swets theory. Ordinate represents frequency with which a given intensity is obtained; abscissa represents a hypothetical intensity scale. Mean of noise distribution is located at X; mean of signal + noise is located at X + Y. Generally, effect of adding stimulus is to intensify noise distribution. Distributions of noise and signal + noise are assumed to be identical.*

restricted sample, of course, but can serve as the prototype for samples of larger size. Suppose we were to give our observer this sample: an intensity value below the shaded area in Fig. 5.4. Clearly, this sample must be from the noise alone. The signal-plus-noise distribution can never produce such a small intensity. By the same reasoning, intensity samples greater than the shaded area can occur only when the signal is added to the noise. But, values in the shaded area can be from either the noise or the signal-plus-noise distribution. To make decisions in this area of uncertainty, the observer must set up a *criterion,* a value on the intensity scale somewhere in the shaded area, and report any value greater than this criterion as most likely to have come from the signal-plus-noise distribution and any value below the criterion point as most likely to have arisen from noise distribution alone. What determines the point where this criterion is placed by the observer?

The setting of the criterion Tanner and Swets propose that the location of the criterion point is determined by (1) the pay-off to the subject of the possible outcomes of his responses and (2) the observer's estimates that the signal-plus-noise or the noise alone was presented.

TABLE 5.1. PAY-OFFS FOR OUTCOMES IN MISSILE EXAMPLE

	Outcome of Observer's Responses	
Actual Event	"Signal" (Missile)	"No Signal" (No Missile)
Missile coming	Save area from destruction	Destruction of area
No missile	Waste of expensive interceptor	Continued tranquility

The pay-offs to an observer can vary for each possible outcome of his response. If the subject can say only, "Yes the signal was presented," or, "No the signal was not presented, noise alone was there," then a pay-off table can be constructed. Table 5.1 presents a possible pay-off table for our radar operator in the earlier example, and Table 5.2 presents a possible pay-off table for an observer in an experiment. Tables like these represent both the rewards and penalties for correct

TABLE 5.2. PAY-OFFS FOR OUTCOMES IN EXPERIMENT

	Outcome of Observer's Responses	
Actual Event	Signal	No Signal
Signal + noise	$+10\rlap{/}c$	$-10\rlap{/}c$
Noise alone	$-10\rlap{/}c$	$+10\rlap{/}c$

and incorrect responses. Too often, in many real-life situations it is impossible to calculate the pay-off for certain entries in the table. In the laboratory, however, a pay-off system can be exactly specified and explained to the observers. Table 5.2 represents a balanced pay-off in which both kinds of correct and both kinds of incorrect responses are rewarded and penalized equally. It is easy to create pay-off tables which are not balanced. The pay-off for correct identification of the signal as a signal can be heavily rewarded and the penalty for saying "signal" when noise alone is presented can be made minimal. Such a pay-off table would bias the observer toward reporting signals at the expense of his "noise" responses. In the formulation the effect of this biased table would be to set the criterion lower, more toward the bottom of the shaded area than the top of Fig. 5.4.

The observer's estimates of the likelihood of the two events, a signal plus noise or the noise alone, will also alter the

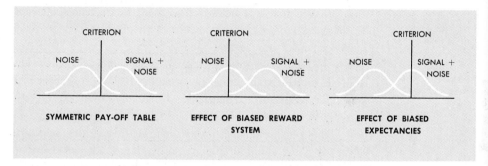

FIG. 5.5. *Effects of pay-off and observer's expectancies of outcomes on criterion placement according to the decision-analysis model. Left, placement of observer's criterion for discrimination when reward for correct identification (S + N) is balanced by some degree of penalty for incorrect identification, and observer's expectancies have not been biased; middle, observer shifts criterion when reward for correct identification is greater than penalty for error; right, criterion is shifted to accommodate observer's expectancies when he has been led to expect noise more than the signal, although reward and penalty are balanced.*

position of the criterion. The effect of increasing the probability of one or the other of these is to move the criterion away from the favored distribution. If the observer expects that noise alone is more likely to be presented to him, the criterion will be placed near the top of the shaded area. If he believes the signal plus noise is more likely to occur, then the criterion is moved lower. Figure 5.5 shows the effect of rewards and penalties and the effects of the observer's expectancies on the location of the criterion. If the pay-offs are biased and the noise-alone and signal-plus-noise presentations are not subjectively equal, then the effects of each manipulation combine to produce a joint effect. The location of the criterion can be calculated by use of a maximum likelihood ratio which takes into consideration both rewards and penalties and the probabilities of occurrence of the two possible stimulus conditions.

Significance of the decision analysis model   First, we might ask what has happened to the familiar concept of the threshold in the decision analysis model? We began by assuming a noise distribution which provides a background for all signals. Then, we assume certain effects of signals on this background noise. Next, we learned that a criterion was established to decide whether the sample should be assigned to the signal-plus-noise or the noise-alone categories. The word *threshold* did not once occur. One of the most interesting features of considering sensory detection in light of the decision analysis model is that the threshold concept need not be used. Perhaps this concept is not needed to understand perceptual phenomena.

We know of course that intense signals are easier to detect against a noise background than are weak signals. The decision analysis model explains this by assuming that weak signals add a smaller constant to the noise distribution than do intense signals. Very strong signals could displace the average value of the signal-plus-noise distribution so far along the intensity scale that there could be little or no overlap of the two distributions and thus little or no range where decisions would be uncertain. Weak signals might only displace the signal-plus-noise distribution a short distance on the intensity scale and result in making practically the entire distribution a zone of uncertainty.

One advantage of viewing sensory detection as Tanner and Swets do is that rewards and expectancies can be incorporated into the perceptual decision. Thresholds, on the other hand, are usually felt to be some inherent property of the individual and insensitive to changes in expectancies or rewards. When we think of a threshold for the detection of light, for example, we think that there is some intensity of light which is just sufficient to produce a perceptual response. But, how do we then incorporate the fact that rewards and expectancies can alter this inherent property, the visual threshold?

Perception of Complex Patterns

Hermann von Helmholtz, the great physicist and physiologist concerned with understanding the sensory systems, held that a belief in a mechanism of "unconscious inference" was needed to explain normal perception of figures. He held that we perceive those figures or objects which are most likely to have produced the sensory information reported to the nervous system from the receptors. This inference of the most likely object is based on our past experiences with objects and the stimuli arising from them. The inference was supposedly made on the basis of things we had learned about the world about us.

The concept of unconscious inference in perception has been attacked, especially by Gestalt psychologists. *Gestalt* is a German word meaning *configuration* or *form*. The basic arguments against unconscious inference have been that inference is a conscious phenomena and that it does not occur instantly, though perception itself does seem to occur at once. Yet people do not report "feeling" that they make inferences, nor do they seem to require time to make them when perceiving objects.

However, despite the fact that the battle between unconscious inference and Gestalt psychologists began before the turn of the century, no clear-cut victory has ever been won by either side. There is no doubt, however, that the work of Gestalt psychologists has resulted in the gathering of many important and interesting observations of perceptual phenomena.

THE GESTALT MOVEMENT In the later part of the nineteenth century a controversy existed between two groups of people concerned with perceptual phenomena and their origins. This controversy divided interested parties into two groups:

1. Those who believed perceptual phenomena were innately given as parts of our physiological apparatus
2. Those who believed that past experiences were crucial in determining how we see the world around us

Helmholtz belonged to this latter group, for his unconscious inferences depended upon the person's past experiences with objects. Gestalt psychologists tend to identify with the former group. The philosopher Immanuel Kant sided with those who believed in the innately given characteristics of perception, whereas the British Associationists stressed the acquired characteristics of perception (see pp. 212–213). It was in this medium of controversy that Gestalt psychology arose as a movement in psychological theory. In essence, Gestalt psychologists believe that perception is determined jointly by the nature of the stimuli falling upon the receptors and the innate organization of the nervous system. They hold that the proper study of perception involves strong dependence upon phenomenology, by which they mean the study of a person's own sensations. Because of their interests, they were drawn to consideration of erroneous perceptions, or illusions.

What is an illusion? Probably no experience exactly copies reality. All our perceptions are illusory to some extent. Because

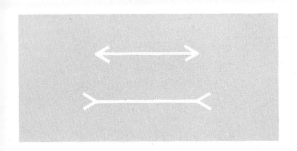

FIG. 5.6. *The Müller-Lyer illusion.*

of this we cannot usefully employ the term, *veridical perception: No perception is an entirely faithful representation of objects or qualities found in our environment.* Philosophers have struggled with many different approaches to the nature of truth and what a true perception might be. Despite the lack of a philosophic solution to the general problems of truth and falsity, we must recognize the fact that there exist a number of prominent examples of stimulus patterns which initiate perceptual activities which deviate from what we accept as appropriate perceptions.

Visual illusions The well-known Müller-Lyer illusion is reproduced in Fig. 5.6. The two horizontal lines are the same length, although the one on the bottom in the figure clearly seems to be longer. What is it about the two forms which causes the difference in the perception of length? Gestalt psychologists have pointed out, most forcefully, that our perceptions are a great deal more than any retinal figure could be. For example, we can perceive three dimensional figures even though the retinal image cannot be more than two dimensional.

One of the illusions presented in Fig. 5.7 is more aptly described as an ambiguous figure. This is the famous vase-profile form, and it is possible to see either two faces opposing one another or a vase. What determines which figure will be seen? The perception divides itself into two categories: figure and ground. The drawing will appear as a vase when the white portion acts as figure and as two faces when the black is figural. Generally speaking, ground serves as the backdrop for figures.

The figure in a figure-ground relationship always seems to have the quality of a unitary perception. This ability to separate the sensory world into figure and ground does not seem to depend upon past experience. Such figure and ground perception is found both in rats reared in darkness and in human patients following the removal of cataracts. In other words it seems to be primitive and independent of early experiences both in man [2] and the rat [3]. *In general, Gestalt psychologists believe that the illusory experiences occurring when the geometrical designs of Figs. 5.7 and 5.8 are observed are the result of the innate structure of the nervous system.* It is on this point that controversy exists. Other psychologists believe that most perceptions depend upon early sensory experiences and learning.

It is perhaps too easy to identify the Gestalt movement with the study of optical illusions. Gestalt psychologists are active experimentalists and, as is often profitable in research, have moved the study of illusions into the laboratory. Through

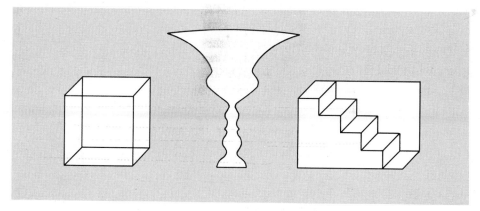

FIG. 5.7.   *Examples of reversible illusion.*

laboratory experiments the scientist is often able to isolate relationships between the variables under study. Some Gestalt psychologists use geometric patterns to isolate more easily the characteristics of stimulus patterns which affect our perceptions. It must be remembered that Gestalt psychologists are interested in explaining normal adult perception and use the study of illusory or abnormal perceptions as one approach to that end.

Two products emerged from the Gestalt studies of perception: a set of laws which described the perceptual experiences occurring as a result of specified stimulus conditions and an explanation of the ways in which perception occurred.

Laws of perception As many as 114 laws have been reported to have been formulated by Gestalt psychologists from their studies of perception [4], although this list has been abbreviated by some authors, and there are many interpretations of them. Probably the most comprehensive is the law of Prägnanz. This principle is simply that perceptual figures tend toward the "best figure" possible. This is a law of "good form."

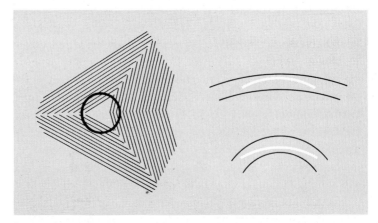

FIG. 5.8. *Examples of apparent distortion of figures by their surroundings.*

According to one of the leading exponents of Gestalt psychology, Kurt Koffka, the law of Prägnanz "can briefly be formulated like this: psychological organization will always be as 'good' as the prevailing conditions allow. In this definition the term 'good' is undefined. It embraces such properties as regularity, symmetry, simplicity and others" [5, p. 110].

Of course this law hinges upon the definition of good form. Koffka leads us to believe that the more regular, symmetrical, and simple the form is, the better it is. If this is understandable, we can now subsume a number of other Gestalt laws under it. For example, the principle of closure, one of the more widely accepted Gestalt laws, says that if a figure is presented which has an open area or gap in its boundary the observer will tend to perceive the figure with a closed boundary, *other forces permitting.* In other words, if we present a triangle with a portion of one side missing, and if the exposure is brief enough so that the forces aroused by the missing portion are not too great, then the observer will tend to see a completed triangle. By presenting the stimulus only briefly we do not allow the observer to make the gap figural—or in Koffka's terms to arouse *other forces.* Another way to exhibit the closure of the boundary of the triangle would be to present the stimulus so that the open portion of the triangle falls on the blind spot of the eye. As we have learned in the preceding chapter, no receptor cells exist in the blind spot of the eye, and so information reaching the brain would provide information about all of the triangle *except the area of the gap.* No information at all would be sent to the brain about the area of the gap. Under these conditions—perception should be in accord with the closure principle and the perception should be of a closed triangular figure.

As with many of the Gestalt laws, the principle of closure is often used in contexts somewhat removed from direct sensory or perceptual realms. For example, some might say that the reason a mystery story holds our attention is because we have been given parts of a *verbal figure* but the parts have not been assembled into a *good figure* until the end. Thus, forces are instituted toward closure (or good form), and these remain active until the author closes the figure for us.

Gestalt theory was appealing because it could be applied to many diverse phenomena. Such terms as *closure* and *Gestalt* are useful descriptive terms, but they are also vague and general. There is no doubt that the phenomena described by the Gestalt psychologists are observable and that the perceptual behaviors they describe do happen. However, the existence of the perceptions and related behaviors does not mean that the Gestalt explanations of them must be accepted. The laws developed by Gestalt psychologists may best be considered as labels for descriptions of these perceptual and response tendencies in man. They do not explain *why* these tendencies are exhibited. In this sense these laws are similar to the word *instinct,* which is a label for certain kinds of unlearned reactions (see pp. 78–82). Having stressed the more general view of Gestalt psychology—that our perceptions are unlearned reactions which depend upon the innate organization of the sensory and nervous systems and the sensory patterns presented to the observer—we shall discuss the innate properties of the nervous system which are assumed by Gestalt psychologists to account for our perceptions.

The principle of isomorphism   Gestalt psychologists seek explanations of perceptual experience in terms of physiological activities in the central nervous system. Their basic principle is that for every perception there is a corresponding physiological activity in the brain which is *isomorphic* to the mental experience. (The mathematical relation of isomorphism is that two figures are isomorphic if the points of which they are comprised are connected in the same way. If we were to draw a figure of a triangle on a piece of elastic material, like rubber, then no matter how we distort the rubber surface, the connections between the adjacent portions of the figure are always the same. Each new figure created by distorting the rubber surface is isomorphic to the original triangle and to other figures produced by distortion of the figure.) This principle asserts that when we perceive a triangle, there exists in the brain a physiological representation of a triangle which maintains certain aspects of triangularity. What kind of triangularity could exist in the brain, where the neocortex is a highly convoluted mass of cells? Almost every single portion of its surface area is curved. A perception of a flat triangle could not depend on the existence of a flat triangular form on the surface of the brain. Nonetheless, the Gestalt principle of isomorphism asserts that in the brain there must be a form of physiological excitation which maintains "triangularity" in order for the related perception to occur.

In effect, the Gestalt view holds that when a pattern of excitation on the retina is transmitted to the brain, a form is produced in the visual projection area of the brain which is isomorphic to the retinal image. Our visual perception of any geometric form is based upon the presence of a form of physiological activities in the visual projection areas of the brain.

In the Gestalt theory the form existing in the brain is in part determined by the form of activity transmitted to the brain from the receptors, but it is also determined by the structure of the brain itself. The "form" existing in the brain is a pattern of excitation in the electrical fields provided by the brain tissue. This brain form is influenced by electrical forces existing in adjacent brain areas. For example, in the Müller-Lyer illusion (Fig. 5.6) the fact that one horizontal line appears longer than the other is explained on the basis that the forms of excitation in the visual area of the brain corresponding to the horizontal lines in the stimulus are in fact different lengths. The form corresponding to the perceived longer line is longer than the form corresponding to the perceived shorter line. The field effects produced by the different types of lines at the end of the two longer lines influence the electrical brain fields of the two forms in different ways. The arrowlike endings act to shorten the figure in the brain fields, whereas the inverted arrow endings act to stretch out the electrical fields. Thus, the ends of the stimulus patterns have actually altered the *physiological forms*. The explanation is based upon electrical phenomena which would occur in any similarly constituted electrical field. Thus, the Gestalt movement explains perception on the basis of the physical characteristics of forms found in electrical fields in the brain. Our perceptions correspond to the final electrical form in the brain, according to the Gestalt view.

CRITICISM OF ISOMORPHISM. If we were to accept the principle of isomorphism and the corresponding belief that perception is some way related to the electrical form existing in the visual areas of the brain, would this be enough to explain perception? One thing we must avoid is a theory which only provides us with a display in the visual area which then must be observed by a "little man in the head." Thus far Gestalt psychology would have us assume that figures in the world are transmitted to the visual areas, and sometimes the transmitted figure is distorted because of the nature of the material in the brain and activity in other areas. But, what then? We must have some theory to explain how these physiological forms are capable of instigating behavior, and some theory by which these brain forms are translated into awareness to account for the mental experiences of perception. One of the serious problems which exist for the Gestalt theories of psychology is that these next links in the theoretical chain leading to behavior have not been forged. Whatever else, we must have a theory which gets us further than the existence of a television-like projection of images to the brain's visual cortex.

There are other bases for doubt about the usefulness of the principle of isomorphism. These center on the results of studies of the nervous system. First, the size of the visual projection area which receives fibers from the foveal area of the retina greatly exceeds the size of the visual projection area receiving fibers from the rest of the retina. Shouldn't this produce a considerable amount of perceptual distortion? Yet, our visual experiences do not seem distorted in this way. We do not see portions of figures in the center of our visual fields larger than other portions falling more on the periphery of the retina.

A second type of observation which casts doubt upon the isomorphism principle is represented by studies which create electrical or physiological disturbances of the brain tissue in the visual projection areas. It has been pointed out that tumors and accidents of brain pathology in the visual areas do not produce the expected disturbances of perception. In one study gold foil, an excellent electrical conductor, placed across the visual projection areas of a chimpanzee trained in a visual discrimination problem did not interfere with the animal's behavior in a visual task. The gold foil was placed so as to disturb any *forms* which might exist in the electrical fields of the visual brain areas [6]. Gold pins inserted in the visual projection area of another animal did not interfere with the animal's responses in the same task. These examples make it difficult to assume that the integrity of a form of electrical activity in a sensory projection area is essential to perception.

HEBB'S THEORY OF PERCEPTION   In 1949, a book by D. O. Hebb of McGill University [7] was published which has had a great influence upon certain areas of psychology. For some time previously Hebb had studied the development of perception, and his findings led him to formulate a general theory of behavior based in large part on perceptual phenomena. In Hebb's theory sensory information becomes perception. Hebb's theory is not the kind of associationistic theory against which Gestalt psychology reacted. Gestalt psychology objected to psychologies which accounted for behavior through the then current principles of association. Gestalt psychologists argued that the form of the electrical activity in the brain was responsible for perception. In their view past associations did not affect perception directly, although they could influence our interpretation of a perception. Perception, *per se,* was not influenced by experience.

From the start it should be recognized that Hebb's proposals are tentative. However, even in this form they represent one of the most thought provoking contributions yet made to behavioral theory: explanations for phenomena in the areas of learning, perception, emotion, motivation, and even abnormal psychology. The most essential of all the assumptions made by Hebb is one concerning growth processes occurring at the synapse between two neurons. This assumption, in turn, is intimately related to certain postulates about the anatomical organization of the nervous system.

Reverberatory loops   The nervous system can be considered to be a collection of individual nerve cells whose basic physiological properties we have discussed before (Chapter 3). Their arrangement is such that one can find loops of several cells through which excitation may travel around and around. It can be likened to a parking lot with so few spaces that the cars may travel around it several times before they obtain a space. Within the neural loop the firing of cell A would excite cell B and it in turn would excite cell C. Cell C then would activate cell A once again. A highly schematic loop arrangement of neurons is presented in Fig. 5.9. These loops of cells could hold recurrent

FIG. **5.9.** *Hypothetical arrangement of neurons which would underlie prolonged reverberatory activity. Neurons would fire in numerical sequence; i.e., neuron (1,4) fires first and again in fourth position. This multiple-path arrangement would "hold" activity for longer periods than simple closed loops of neurons. Adapted from D. O. Hebb.* The Organization of Behavior. *New York: John Wiley & Sons, Inc., 1949.*

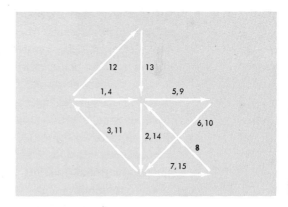

activities, although they would not continue their firing forever. These circular arrangements which would permit impulses to go around in them for some time after the stimulation originating the activity has ceased are *reverberatory circuits or holding mechanisms* [8].

The reverberatory circuits *could* provide the physiological basis of memories. If a loop arrangement like this were activated by a specific type of sensory input, then the reverberatory activity in the loop could represent a kind of memory for the input that originally started the activity. However, it is likely that activity in such closed loops would be disrupted after a short time. Therefore, it would provide a neural basis only for relatively recent memories and not what we might call permanent memories. The actual reverberations of the holding mechanisms might only last for a matter of minutes even under the most ideal conditions. *Yet, one might use these*

183

reverberating systems as the basis for developing other changes representing the physiological underpinings of more permanent memories.

The growth principle Given the assumption of the holding mechanisms, we now state the major assumption of the theory: "When an axon of cell A is near enough to excite cell B and repeatedly or persistently takes part in firing it, some growth process or metabolic change takes place in one or both cells such that A's efficiency, as one of the cells firing B, is increased" [7, p. 62].

There are many ways in which a growth process like this could take place. For instance, the axon of A might grow closer, physically, to the cell body of B. The end feet on the axon of cell A could enlarge and cover more of B's surface; and there is the possibility that the release of the chemical transmitter substances from the end feet of A might become more efficient. Despite the fact there is very little evidence for any one of these assumptions today, they are not unreasonable; and most people are willing to concede there must be some permanent changes in the nervous system which correspond to long term, or permanent, memories. Remember that Hebb does not say that these must be the mechanisms involved. He only says that as a function of reverberation cell A has greater control of the firing of cell B.

Cell assembly With these assumptions we are able to progress to the functional organization of the brain proposed by Hebb. Most of our discussion will center about the visual system, but we hope that the conclusions based on analyses of the visual system will be general and apply to other sensory systems as well.

All neocortical areas of the brain have been numbered. These numbers are labels given to the areas on the basis of their structure, function, and origins in development. There are four important numbered visual areas: 17, 18, 19, and 20 (see Chapter 3, p. 102). In man all of the visual fibers which reach the neocortex come into area 17. From area 17 impulses are relayed to areas 18, 19, and 20.

As we have learned, neurons of the brain and central nervous system have a remarkable number of interconnections with other cells. Each neuron is probably connected with hundreds, if not thousands, of cells. Any input which fires a given cell in area 17 must effect the firing of many other cells in the other visual areas and, indirectly, cells in many other brain regions. Probably, the preponderant effect is a fanning-out from the original and rather restricted region of excitation in area 17 to other regions of brain; and for any *pattern* of cells activated in area 17 specific neurons in many areas of the brain would be activated. Any group of cells indirectly excited by any particular pattern of excitation arising in area 17 could form a loop capable of maintaining reverberatory activity over a period of time. The types of cells in the loops would vary. Some would be cells which receive information from other sensory systems, some neurons which interconnect with other cortical or subcortical cells, other cells whose axons descend to motor cells in the spinal cord. The inclusion of motor cells in these reverberatory loops is important because it provides a basis for the incorporation of motor activities in perceptual learning.

As a loop of cells is activated repeatedly by identical patterns of activity in area 17, the neurons comprising the loop will become bonded together. This follows from application of our growth principle. After repeated arousal of the same pattern in area 17, the whole group of loop neurons may be so completely tied together that it functions as a unit. If any portion of the loop is activated, activity in every cell of the loop will follow. These reverberatory loops are the units of perception. They take time to form. Each loop must be activated many many times before the growth occurring between the neurons bonds them together permanently. When the connections between neurons of a reverberatory loop have become established to the extent that activity in one portion of the loop is sure to trigger reactions throughout the loop, we can consider that the loop of neurons constitutes what Hebb calls a *cell assembly,* the basic building block of all perception.

PERCEPTUAL DEVELOPMENT A collection of reports dealing with patients who were born blind [2] is quite relevant to Hebb's theory. These patients were born with congenital cataracts, a clouding of the lens of the eye. Through surgical removal of the lens the eye can function adequately when appropriate glasses are used. Thus vision is restored. When tested postoperatively these patients could distinguish between certain forms, i.e., between a square and a circle. They seemed to do this by searching for corners, which seemed to be focal points for them. They could also distinguish between figure and ground and were able to distinguish colors. However, while the patients responded quickly and directly to different forms, the patterns did not seem to have a consistent *identity*. They could name a given form (triangle, square, etc.) only after a great deal of experience with it.

It is difficult for us to imagine the difference in the perceptual abilities required to distinguish a triangle from a square and the ability to recognize a triangle *as a triangle*. Yet the patients born with congenital cataracts could not identify a triangle *as a triangle* when it was presented differently or from different angles. This ability to recognize the identity of an object took a considerable period of time to develop even though they did have the ability to distinguish between the forms.

One other observation reported by Senden needs to be emphasized, namely the role of eye movements in learning the figure identity. When presented with a visual form some patients learned to respond "triangle" only when they could count the corners and reach a total of three. After practice, eye movements followed the corners in the same way as a finger had been used earlier to pick out the corners. The counting of corners still occurred, but in a less observable way. After months of practice, some patients reached a stage where they could identify the figure at a glance.

These data suggest that adult perception, as we usually think of it, is based upon a vast amount of experience. The recognition of patterns does not seem to be the immediate and innate reaction which is postulated by the Gestalt psychologists.

Early and later perceptual learning In Hebb's theory the development of perception can be categorized into early and later stages. Normal infants and patients like those born with congenital cataracts are in the early learning stages. They have adequate visual mechanisms but the neural impulses arising from the visual receptors must be integrated into meaningful units before perception, as we know it, can occur.

In early perceptual learning individuals are developing cell assemblies for vision. What sort of stimulus patterns would be first incorporated into these cell assemblies? Hebb assumes that most of our early perceptual learning involves the development of cell assemblies which represent "lines and corners." There must be a special cell assembly developed for each of many types of corners and lines. The number of perceptual units, or cell assemblies, needed to build the adult perceptual world must be staggering. Just how many types of different cell assemblies must be formed is beyond estimate, but however many there are, they represent the building blocks for all perception. For our purpose cell assemblies can be considered as groups of cells which have been cemented into a functional unit by the growth principle. The various cells of each group may be widely scattered throughout the brain.

The phase sequence   According to Hebb's position, forms like a triangle *would be a complex perceptual entity,* which becomes recognizable only after cell assemblies for the respective

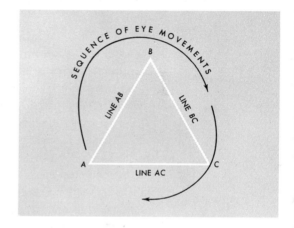

FIG. 5.10   *Triangle (ABC) and the sequence of eye movements which might be produced by observer viewing it. Eyes first fixate angle at* A; *then progress along the line* AB *to angle* C; *etc.*

angles and lines, as well as the relations between them, have been formed.

Phase sequences are defined as particular orders of cell assemblies and eye movements. Consider the triangle *ABC* in Fig. 5.10. When a person centers his visual attention at *A,* a cell assembly *a* is presumed to be activated in the brain. Then, this point of fixation of the eyes is altered and the eyes move to the line *AB,* and a corresponding cell assembly *ab* is activated. The points of fixation progress from corner to line; line to corner, etc., around the triangle. Each point of fixation elicits the cell assembly which has developed from past experiences with similar corners and lines. The eye movements which bring about a change in visual fixations are important, too, for the sensory feedback from them may act as neural units themselves, in the development of the neural counterpart of the perceived triangle.

187

The figures of our perceptual world are built from the cell assemblies, and are represented in Hebb's theory by their order and interconnecting eye movements. Thus, the triangle in Fig. 5.10 would be encoded as an order of cell assemblies and eye movements which might be: corner *a,* eye movement$_1$, line *ab,* movement$_2$, corner *b,* movement$_3$, line *bc,* movement$_4$, corner *c,* movement$_5$, line *ca.* This sequence would represent the *phase sequence* or perception of the figure triangle. Perception of a triangle would differ from perception of a square in both the types of cell assemblies and interconnecting eye movements. Triangles of all sorts would be similar in some types of corner cell assemblies and in some types of eye movements. Categories of perception, e.g., "triangle," "square," are created by the occurrence of similar perceptual elements.

Once again, it is through repeated experiences that cell assemblies and eye movements become connected into other and more elaborate perceptual units. With experience, synaptic growth occurs between the neurons of the units involved in the cell assemblies and eye movements. After repeated exposure to a triangle, a certain facilitation develops between the cell assemblies initiated by the sensory activities. It becomes easier for cell assembly *a* to instigate the subsequent eye movement, and for the eye movement, to instigate arousal of cell assembly *ab,* and so on. The occurrence of cell assembly *a* readies, prepares, or *sets* us to make the next movement and perceive the next cell assembly in the phase sequence. Ultimately, sufficient growth occurs among the clusters of neurons to allow a *short circuiting* of the cell assembly chain. When this happens a triangle can be identified before all cell assemblies and eye movements of the figure have been triggered by sensory input.

In summary: A phase sequence is the collection of cell assemblies and related eye movements which, through experience, have developed a mutual interfacilitation. Sensory information which initiates activity in any part of a phase sequence results in the facilitation of the subsequent arousal of all parts. The perception of a figure as an entity first depends upon the firing of all the elements of the phase sequence by the appropriate sensory stimulation. After further perceptual learning, however, it may be possible for a part of the phase sequence to exert strong enough facilitating effects to trigger the other units. This represents a functional short circuiting of the phase sequence. Even beyond this, however, it is possible to postulate a neural counterpart to what we think of as *perceptual classes* of stimuli.

The superordinate phase sequence   After we learn to perceive objects through phase sequences, we can develop a neural shorthand for the figure. In Hebb's theory this is a *superordinate phase sequence* and results from the development of a new cell assembly which stands for the whole complex figure. This is represented in a schematic order of cell assemblies as *t*.

Going back to our triangle example, we can diagram the perception of the triangle

$$a - ab - b - bc - c - ca -$$
$$\setminus \; / \qquad \setminus \; / \qquad \setminus \; /$$
$$m_1 \qquad\quad m_2 \qquad\quad m_3$$

When the whole triangle is identified as an entity, without demonstration of all the eye movements and all the fixations of eye movements at the corners of the figure, Hebb assumes that the phase sequence itself has built a new cell assembly, *t*.

$$a - ab - b - t - bc - t - c \qquad \text{and so on}$$
$$\setminus \; / \qquad\; \setminus \; | \; /$$
$$m_1 \qquad\quad m_2$$

According to the theory, we would recognize specific figures when a cell assembly *t* has been formed which acts as a label for the whole complex. When *t* is activated, we experience the triangle *as a figure* which can be identified, labeled, and manipulated as an entity in itself. Due to the growth assumption it becomes easier and easier for any of the cell assemblies of the complex to elicit *t,* and unless there is competing sensory input we would expect the occurrence of any constituent cell assembly to lead to *t*. Thus if an incomplete triangle was being viewed, and the incomplete portion fell on the blind spot, we would expect to see a whole triangle. No sensory input at all comes from the blind spot. If the incomplete triangle falls on the retina so that the gap is on a normal portion of the retina, then this gap would be perceived because receptors are activated which send conflicting information to the brain. In general, we would expect a facilitation for those perceptual complexes, or configurations, that have occurred most frequently in the past. This facilitation is due to the growth processes between the cell assemblies involved in each pattern in theory. This is in contrast to the Gestalt position which postulates that closure, or the tendency for figures to be seen as completed forms, results from the structure of the nervous system. Hebb's theory explains closure on the basis of interneuronal growth, taking place at the synapse and depending upon the prior sensory experiences of the organism.

Acting like one of the cell assemblies in the phase sequence, the superordinate phase sequence unit, *t,* can facilitate the occurrence of the other members. Thus, no matter how *t* is initiated, the cell assemblies and movements comprising the entire phase sequence would be easy to instigate through this facilitation. Therefore, we might expect that a subject might give evidence of the eye movements normally involved in looking at a triangle when merely told "to think of a triangle."

Motor movements and phase sequences   The cells involved in the loops of which cell assemblies are composed contain some cells which control motor movements primarily. When cell assemblies and phase sequences are acquired, these motoneurons are incorporated; perhaps even large packages of motoneurons become parts of phase sequences. From the beginning, movements are an integral part of perceptual development. In Hebb's theory movements develop along with perception and in accordance with the neuronal growth principle which underlies the entire theory. As a consequence, no little man in the head is needed to explain our responses to stimulus patterns, and no isomorphic figure of electrical activity in the visual cortex is required. The motor and cognitive aspects of perception are both natural consequences of Hebb's assumptions about neural activities and may be thought of as a possible neural basis for the phenomenon of *set.*

Perceptual Readiness, or Set

One of the most common observations made about perceptual experiences is that we tend to perceive what we expect to see. This phenomena is often ascribed to the effect of *set.* The word *set* can be used almost interchangeably with words like *expectancy* or *readiness* and refers to a disposition to perceive a certain type of stimulus in a given situation at a particular time. Outside of a perceptual framework the word *set* can be used to describe a disposition to respond in a particular way.

For example, when a sprinter on a track team is given a ready signal ahead of the starting gun, he is able to leave his position faster than if he were not given this preparatory signal. Often it is possible to observe the physical and physiological aspects of motor sets, but it is more difficult to observe preparatory sets for perceptual events. Nonetheless, there is little doubt that preparatory perceptual sets do exist and are influential in determining our perceptual experiences.

Perceptual sets may be established by the context or past experiences in a situation, by the instructions to the perceptual task, and by the general strategies we use to deal with perceptual tasks.

SITUATIONAL EFFECTS As an example of how the situation, itself, can operate to affect perception, consider the not improbable situation of being alone in a house at night. You pick a book to read, a ghost story. You get along into the book and become absorbed in the narrative. All of a sudden you see a figure on a wall or in the next room. A ghost! Whatever the stimulus might be in reality, for instance, the light from a passing car, you are *set* by the story and the circumstances to perceive a ghost. Walking at night through a cemetery while taking a shortcut home is another very good way to establish a preparatory perceptual set.

Yet the environment can prepare us for certain types of sensory experiences in a more subtle fashion. In one experiment students were engaged in what they thought was merely an attempt to determine their thresholds for a tone of 1000 cycles per second [9]. The method of constant stimuli was used in which the tone was presented at different intensities in intervals marked off by flashing lights. Some of the tone intensities were so low that none of the subjects reported hearing them, while others were so high that all subjects indicated their presence perfectly. Most of the tone intensities presented fell between these limits. The subjects were told to report *any sound at all,* and were warned that tones which are just barely audible often seem to be of different frequencies. During the course of the experiment, the experimenters occasionally substituted tones of different frequencies for the 1000 cycles per second tone. Very few subjects reported the latter tones although they were presented at usually audible intensities. Even after the experiment, the subjects had a difficult time hearing the other relatively loud tones. For example, at the conclusion of the experiment, the experimenters would turn on one of the loud tones of a different frequency which had been intruded into the 1000 cycles per second tone series and ask the subjects if they heard anything. About half the subjects heard it immediately, but the other half would not hear it until the experimenter explicitly called their attention to the tone by humming at a frequency near the 1000 cps and then "sliding" the hum to one near the different tone. When the subjects finally heard it, it appeared suddenly. Some often would claim the experimenters had just then turned it on, because it sounded so loud that they could not understand why they had not heard it before.

This experiment can be interpreted in terms of a set which was established by the sequence of 1000 cycles per second tones. When tones which were divergent from this target frequency were presented, the subjects could detect them only poorly. At times the cue tones were higher than the subsequent tones; at times they were lower. Thus the effect of the cue tone was due to the informational value of the tone.

The establishment of preparatory sets for stimuli in different frequency ranges by signals (cue tones) which indicated whether the next stimulus to be presented would be high or low has been studied [10]. The cue tones enable subjects to recognize subsequent tones better than when they are not presented.

We can look at the phenomena of perceptual set as a preparation for certain categories of stimulation: With our ghost story example we might say that the reader was prepared for the appearance of ghostlike stimuli, weird and bizarre figures. When a set was established on the basis of a sequence of 1000 cps tones or by a cue tone, we might say that the subjects were prepared for auditory stimuli in a narrow frequency range.

Many methods can be used to make one or another perceptual event most likely in any situation. Information which limits the perceptual possibilities which are likely to occur aids us in perception. The important question is, however, just how sets or information about likely perceptions act to make perception easier. In Hebb's theory we could explain this by assuming preparatory sets facilitate certain phase sequences. This partial facilitation means that less sensory input is required to initiate the activation of the entire phase sequence and, in the theory, the associated perception.

PERCEPTION AND CLASSIFICATION Some psychologists most actively concerned with understanding perceptual processes propose that we consider the process of perception as the organization of stimuli into *classes*. To these psychologists the sensory information provides us with a basis for discrimination, but this basic process of discrimination must be elaborated in the central nervous system to place these activities into classes or categories.

What do we mean when we say we perceive an apple? We usually mean that we have assigned certain sensory signals transmitting information about forms, colors, sizes, textures, and so on, to a class of objects labeled *apples*. The establishment of such classes is usually accomplished relatively early in life, but not without difficulties. Confusion among such classes as oranges, balls, and wax apples, probably takes a considerable number of years to resolve.

The basis for the establishment of perceptual classes is the effect of this classification upon the internal and external environment. We learn the perceptual classes used by our parents, friends, and playmates, because of rewards, social approval, and the ability to respond adaptively to our environment. If the effects of our perceptual classifications are not satisfactory, then reclassifications can be made, and our perceptual categories are shaped by their effects. The most fruitful ones in terms of their practical benefits and their ability to anticipate the results of dealing with objects in the class (reducing surprises) are retained.

Every perception is assigned to a large number of classes. Stimuli are assigned to *object* classes, e.g., apples, chairs, John Jones. This assignment we can call identification and labeling. However, stimuli are also categorized as good-bad, light-heavy, hard-soft and so forth. Perception depends upon a classification of the stimulus input and the related judgments of the attributes of the object class: goodness, heaviness, uses, etc.

Psychologists who hold to the view that perception can be represented by a process of categorization of stimuli, are saying that perception is the result of decisions about the categories to which a stimulus should be assigned. For them, perception is an act of judgment, and they follow in the footsteps of Helmholtz's principle of unconscious inference. The original statement of this principle was attacked on the grounds that perception was instantaneous and did not require an interval of time for inference to occur. However, with the development of Hebb's theory of perception we have a hypothetical mechanism whereby the classification (inference) could be almost instantaneous. The sensory input is classified by the nature of the phase sequences which were elicited by the particular pattern of excitation coming in from the receptors. These phase sequences in turn facilitate other, related phase sequences which could represent further classes of evaluation, i.e., goodness, heaviness, etc. The neural basis of classification could be found in something like the mechanisms proposed by Hebb. One advantage of using Hebb's concepts of cell assemblies and phase sequences as the neural basis for perceptual classification is that we tend to avoid the assumption of a little man in the head who classifies and makes inferences from these classifications.

CLASSIFICATION AND RESPONSE   Considering our earlier discussion of the effects of set upon perception, we can now rephrase the matter by use of the general concepts of perceptual classification. We could speak of set as a bias on the part of the person to expect certain classes of input. In a grocery store we are prepared to use our perceptual category for *apple*. The grocery store environment facilitates the phase sequences of all grocery store products. When we enter a toy store, we are prepared for classifications like that of *ball,* as a result of corresponding facilitation of phase sequences related to toys. After reading a ghost story, we are prepared for classification of stimuli into categories of a more terrifying nature.

This way of talking about set allows us to say that the individual and situational variables which determine perceptual sets do so by preselecting categories of classification. If the stimuli which are presented actually do fit into the preselected perceptual categories then perceptual recognition will be more rapid than if preselection were not made. On the other hand the preselection of categories will hinder proper recognition of an external stimulus if it does *not* appropriately belong to the preset categories. That is, in a grocery store a small red object will be perceived easily and quickly as an apple. However, if a boy's red ball becomes mixed up with the apples in the store we may not recognize the discrepancy between apple and ball until discrepancies in weight or texture make the distinction imperative. Generally speaking, the selection of prior categories as ones likely to be useful in a given situation will be reflected in greater facility in making responses suitable to the preselected categories.

PERCEPTION UNDER UNCERTAIN STIMULUS CONDITIONS In a normal adult with sufficient time and opportunity a ball and an apple are correctly placed into different perceptual categories. Confusion between balls and apples will only occur when we are disposed toward the perception of one or the other and when the sensory information is less than complete, for example when we only glance at the object for a moment. Greater attention to the stimulus input resolves the confusion. Yet, some of the most fruitful techniques found in the study

FIG. 5.11. *An ambiguous figure which can be seen as a pretty woman or an ugly one. The observer's "set" helps determine which profile will be seen. From E. G. Boring. A new ambiguous figure. Amer. J. Psychol., 1930, 40, 444.*

of perception use stimulating conditions in which it is *impossible* to determine the exact nature of the physical stimulus. Several techniques are used by psychologists in situations purposely designed to introduce uncertainty in perception, i.e., to prevent absolute identification (classification) of the stimulus.

Ambiguous figures In our earlier discussion of illusions we discussed the famous figure which can be interpreted as two faces or a vase (Fig. 5.7). This is typical of ambiguous figures: there is no single response which occurs when the figure is observed. In another example the figure can be seen as either a pretty or a horrible-looking woman, depending on the prior instructions given to the observer (Fig. 5.11). If a set for beautiful women is established, the more attractive profile is more often seen. Whereas if a set to perceive "your mother-in-law" is established, the alternative form is readily observed. Many kinds of ambiguous stimuli exist. They range from pictures which are interpreted by observers in many different ways to the ink blots used in personality tests.

Impoverished stimuli It is possible to reduce the clarity or details of a stimulus to the extent that responses to it become variable. Stimulus objects can be placed behind cloudy glass to give the object a hazy and indefinite appearance, they can be poorly illuminated, or they can be placed at a great distance from the subject. Probably the most common technique presents the stimulus to the observer for only a very brief time. Instruments which present stimuli for short durations at specified degrees of illumination are called *tachistoscopes*. With a tachistoscope the duration of exposure can be systematically varied so that a threshold (expressed in the length of time the stimulus is presented for viewing) can be determined by use of traditional psychophysical methods.

The effect of uncertain stimuli upon the perceiver is that the stimuli lose properties which usually allow the perceiver precise categorization of them. Therefore, these techniques can be used to force a subject to make judgments which reflect his preselected categories of perception. These preselected categories may reveal interesting qualities of the person making the observations. They could reveal information about the frequencies with which such categories are used by the person and information about his interests, attitudes, values, and motives. Looking at the problem another way, we might say that values and motives affect the perceptual categories used by the observer. Whether or not values and motives directly affect perception is still a hotly debated issue in psychology. No one questions that attitudes, values, and motives may affect the responses made to stimuli or the interpretations given perceptual phenomena. The central issue is whether we should assume that the *mental experience of the perception* can be influenced by nonperceptual variables like attitudes and motives.

THE CORE–CONTEXT ARGUMENT Many psychologists believe that the mental experiences of perception are determined solely by the sensory information. It has been argued that we should distinguish between a *visual field* and a *visual world*.

The visual field would be the composite of sensory impressions occurring at any moment, whereas the visual world would be the world of objects and things. The visual world would be created with the help of the experiences of the person, whereas the visual field would be independent of these influences. Others who support a similar distinction have argued that we should distinguish between pure stimulus processes initiated by receptor activity and the result of these pure stimulus processes interacting with memory traces of earlier perceptions, which would create something like a visual world.

Pure sensory processes, or visual fields, represent the sensory core upon which all perception is built. This core is determined only by receptor activities and the structure of the nervous system. The context, or visual world, surrounding the sensory core refers to the meaning we have attached to the components of the core. The accretions to the sensory bases of perception which we call meaning are the learned reactions deriving from our individual experiences. But in the core–context theories these only influence the outer context of perception. The central sensory core of perception remains fundamental.

In contrast, psychologists who suggest that our perceptions are really the product of almost instantaneous classifications reject the primitive and unassailable sensory core. For them our perceptions are entirely formed by the classifications which we make. This issue is lively and not likely to be resolved for some period of time. The question is which one will be the most fruitful approach? Will we be better able to understand perceptual activities if we consider them to be elaborations of a central and innate sensory core, an edifice built by experience around a base provided innately by our receptor systems? Or will it be more profitable to conceive of perception as the product of learned classification of stimulus inputs? Sooner or later, after more data and knowledge are acquired, the view which will lead us further toward understanding perception in all of its many aspects will prevail. But for now we have to be patient and explore.

General Factors Influencing Perception

Psychologists often tend to talk of visual perception, auditory perception, tactual perceptions, and so forth, as if they exist independently of one another. This fractionation of the study of perception is founded on the belief that it is possible to advance our understanding of the complex of perception fastest by the isolated study of various components of perception in the laboratory. Yet in everyday life our visual perceptions occur against an active background of auditory, tactual, and other perceptual activities. Furthermore, since perception can be influenced by the perceptual set or readiness of the individual, we must consider these effects when moving from the isolated study of one kind of perception to understanding the perception of the active individual in his busy life. If attitudes, values, motives, or even language can influence our perceptions, then these too must be studied. In this section we shall discuss information which has been gained about such general influences upon perception.

INTERMODALITY PERCEPTION   It sometimes happens that when a person receives certain auditory stimulation he has a perception which is best described as "visual." This is known as a form of synesthesia. For example, when a musical note is sounded, a person may "see" a color. It has been reported that one subject had relatively consistent color responses when tested over the period of several years [13]. This subject reported that the note C generally produced a red color, whereas F sharp tended to produce blue-green. Only a few people demonstrate a great amount of this "color hearing." However, most of us tend to think of certain kinds of visual images when auditory stimuli are presented and often associate certain colors with sounds. A soft brown color is more likely to be associated with soft auditory stimuli. Our language reflects an intermodality association of perceptual qualities by allowing us to use adjectives like *soft,* to describe visual, auditory and tactual sensations. Many words in our language produce perceptual responses which are similar in some way to the thing or object labeled. Many words in our language probably stem from phonetic similarity to the object portrayed: for example, *babbling* brook, *chirping* bird. Nonetheless, we should distinguish cases where certain verbal responses can be made to stimuli of different sensory systems through social convention from true synesthesia which is probably quite rare.

MOTOR EFFECTS   The effects of background sensory information can be rather subtle. The problem of just why the moon looks larger at the horizon than when above us in the sky has troubled many competent philosophers and scientists. According to one researcher it depends upon the eye muscles, which are used differently depending on the moon's position [14]. If a person rests on an inclined board to watch the zenith moon and does not have to rotate his eyes upward, then this moon appears as large as do moons on the horizon. This then is an example of how motor activities (and quite likely the sensory reports of tensions in the various eye muscles) alter visual perception without producing noticeable effects appropriate to their own sensory modality. The illusion of the moon being larger at the horizon than when directly above has been shown to be caused also by cues related to distance and size, e.g., trees and buildings, being present as the moon is viewed near the horizon [15, 16]. The importance of such cues can be easily observed. On a clear night make a fist so that you can see through a small hole and look at the moon when it is near the horizon. You will observe the moon's apparent size shrink. Looking through your legs at the moon will reduce its size, but not so much as will looking through the small hole of your fist which acts to eliminate other stimuli from around the moon.

In many studies the effects of other muscles and sensory systems upon visual perception have been demonstrated. For instance, a person's perception of a vertical line can be displaced by applying an electric shock to one side of the subject's neck or by inclining the subject to one side [17]. These results could be due to activities aroused in motor systems of the central nervous systems controlling the muscles or due to the sensory feedback to the central nervous system from the muscles and tendons. Evidence can be sighted for either view, although it is most frequently assumed that the sensory feedback aspect is of major importance. Since the effects of the muscle tone can play such a significant role in perception, we must keep in mind that all normal perception occurs against a background of specific muscular positions and activity. Study of the motor contributions to our perceptual activities has been somewhat neglected in the last half century. Certainly it is true that the end product of successful perception is measured in the practical usefulness of action, behavior, and effective motor responses.

EFFECTS OF VALUES AND ATTITUDES We already have discussed some effects of sets on behavior and perception. Social context, one's own past experiences, and other factors can prepare us for one type of perceptual event or another. This readiness for certain perceptions, or set, prepares us for stimuli of certain categories. Now we shall find that sets may be established by still other factors.

In one experiment, in which men who had been placed under conditions designed to provide impoverished stimuli were asked to write stories, hungry men mentioned more food-related objects than did men who were not hungry [18]. Even though the stimuli were supposed to be the basis for the stories, this experiment only provides evidence of what the subjects *wrote* in their imaginative stories. The occurrence of food-related objects could be explained by the fact that the subjects were thinking about food and incorporated these thoughts into their stories. While the hungry subjects wrote about more food-related objects than nonhungry subjects, the stories of the hungry men did not include more direct references to food than did the stories of the nonhungry men. This could have occurred because the subjects were in a situation in which going without food could have been interpreted as a patriotic duty. This might have tended to suppress any direct conscious expression of food objects.

A better example of an effect of motivation upon perception was provided by an experiment (see Chapter 8) in which subjects who were evaluated high in the motive to achieve were able to recognize achievement-related words at faster speeds of presentation in a tachistoscope than subjects low in this motive [19]. This experiment would seem to suggest that perceptual changes can be determined by the motivational states of the observers. Yet one could argue that people who were evaluated high in the achievement motive would tend to respond with more achievement-related words when they could not be sure what the word was. However, this response-likelihood explanation loses some of its strength because there was no difference between subjects high and low in the achievement motive in the number of achievement-related guess responses made before recognition of the word occurred.

Earlier, Postman, Bruner, and McGinnies [20] had studied the relation between a person's values and his tachistoscopic recognition threshold for words related to these values. Subjects were given a written test which measured the relative interest a subject had in six value areas. The experimenters predicted that people with considerable interest in one value area would have a lower threshold for words related to that area than subjects with different values. In general the predictions were upheld. A person who obtained a rather high score in the area of economic values tended to have a low threshold for words like *income*.

One basic criticism of studies dealing with the relation between motives and perception is simply that people who are high in a particular motive or value area are merely more familiar with words related to these motives or values than other people. Familiarity with words, by itself, can produce lower thresholds in tachistoscopic experiments [21]. This criticism was answered in an unusual way in one experiment. The subjects in this study were selected on the basis of the amount of motivation toward affiliation. The subjects were instructed to indicate the clearest and most apparent picture out of a group of four which were presented briefly in a tachistoscope. In every group of four pictures one contained people and three contained only inanimate objects. Subjects who were high in the motive toward affiliation selected the picture containing people as clearest more than subjects low in the affiliation motive [22]. It is difficult to explain these results on the basis of a greater familiarity with faces by the group high in the affiliation motive. The problem of how an affiliation motive could enable the subjects to see a picture of a person more clearly has yet to be solved. Perhaps subjects high in the affiliation motive have some lasting readiness to classify stimuli into categories associated with people.

EFFECTS OF REWARD AND PUNISHMENT ON PERCEPTION

Motives may operate to establish sets, that is, a perceptual readiness for certain kinds of stimuli. These then affect our perceptions of the world about us. Can we establish changes in perception through application of rewards or punishment?

In one study [23] pairs of figures were presented to subjects after a training period in which one of each pair of training figures was arbitrarly chosen to elicit a reward when named by the subject and the other to elicit a punishment by the awarding or taking away of pennies. After this training, the test figures were presented and subjects were asked which figure they saw. They could respond by naming the figure for which they were either previously rewarded or previously punished. No rewards

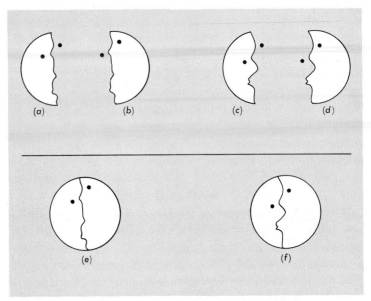

FIG. 5.12.   *The figures used in the Schafer and Murphy experiment. Perception of each pair above the line was rewarded or punished; test figures appear below the line. Adapted from R. Schafer & G. Murphy. The role of autism in a visual figure-ground relationship.* J. exp. Psychol., *1943, 32, 335–343.*

or punishments were given when the compound figure, which contained both the reward and punishment figures, was presented. The experimenters believed that the effects of the rewards and punishments would be to make the reward figure clearer and more readily perceived than the punishment figure in this compound figure. The reward figures tended to be perceptually selected by the subjects.

Before interpreting this experiment as a demonstration of the effects of rewards and punishments upon perception we must recognize that the subjects' verbal responses were rewarded, and that we have no information concerning whether their perceptions were altered. The results could be explained simply on the basis that one name could have become more frequently reported than another. Thus, the experiment could be interpreted solely in terms of reinforcement and punishment of a verbal response and not a change in perception. Supreme care must be exercised to determine the effects of other types of variables upon performance when attempting to measure perceptual changes. However, other experiments have demonstrated that stimuli associated with rewards tend to be seen more frequently and more clearly than those not associated with rewards [e.g., 24].

The effect of associating a figure with punishment is less clear-cut. Small amounts of punishment tend to have little if any effect upon figure selection. Where the punishment is stronger, say an electric shock of moderate unpleasantness, the figure associated with the shock is seen less well than figures which does not result in punishment. However, when a figure has been associated with a very unpleasant shock, there is some evidence to suggest that the figure becomes *better selected* by subjects [25], at least under conditions which allow the subjects to "get away from" the unpleasant stimulation. The names *perceptual defense* and *perceptual vigilance* are used to refer to behavior which indicates poorer recognition of some figures and better recognition of others due to degrees of pleasantness or unpleasantness. Often the pleasantness or unpleasantness is inferred from information about the subject's personality. In a moment we shall return to this topic which is a much-debated issue in perception today.

VALUE OF OBJECTS AND PERCEIVED SIZE   People who believe in a central sensory core in perception find it difficult to imagine that rewards or punishment can directly affect the perception of figures, although the evidence continues to mount in this direction. Can such an obvious and straightforward perceptual quality as size be affected by the value of the stimulus to the observer?

One of the first experiments relating the object's value to perception was that of Bruner and Postman in 1947 [26], and it has assumed the stature of a classical experiment in psychology. Two groups of children were asked to estimate the size of coins both when the coins were present and when they were not physically present. Two experimental groups were established on the basis of their social backgrounds. One group came from relatively poor and the other from relatively wealthy families. The subjects turned a knob to regulate the size of a circular patch of light projected on a screen in front of them. It was expected that the children from the poorer backgrounds would value the coins more than the wealthier children. If value affects perception, in this case perception of the size of coins, then the group of children from the poorer family conditions should overestimate the size of the coins. The experimental results confirm this prediction when size judgments were made with the coins present. In addition the amount of overestimation increased with the monetary value of the coin up to the half dollar. When the size of the coins was estimated only on the basis of memory (actual coins not present), the degree of overestimation of size by children from less wealthy families was less. The children from wealthier backgrounds only overestimated the quarter and half dollar.

Earlier, we discussed the necessity of controlling for the effects of familiarity in studies relating motivational variables to perception. The experiment in which individuals high in the achievement motive recognized achievement-related words more readily than individuals low in this motive could be criticized because the results could be due to the greater familiarity with achievement-related words in the group with high achievement motive. Can the results of the Bruner and Postman experiment be explained on the basis of familiarity with coins? To do so, we would have to assume that the wealthier children had more experience with coins and their greater familiarity led them to be more accurate than the children of poorer circumstances.

While this is a possible explanation, it does not appear to account for the results of more recent experiments. In one instance subjects under hypnosis were given false biographical information to accept as their own [27]. A subject was instructed to believe he was from a poor home at one time and from a wealthy home at another time. When provided with poor backgrounds, subjects overestimated coin sizes; with rich backgrounds they underestimated the sizes. Since every person was both rich at one time and poor at another, the experiment controls for degree of experience or general familiarity with coins. Other experiments have shown that poker chips can be overestimated after a history of association with other valued objects [28].

We must conclude that the evidence points to acceptance of a view that motives, rewards, punishments, and values can and do affect our perceptions. At the same time we must hold some reservations. Some experiments aimed at replication of earlier findings have not been successful. Furthermore, there is the possibility that motivational effects are especially effective in altering memory traces of stimuli. Probably it is safest, although least satisfying, to reserve final decision regarding whether the perceptions of figures or the memory of them can be altered. The issue can be resolved only by further experiments. Perhaps you will be one of those who help decide the issue.

PERCEPTION WITHOUT AWARENESS   The concept of threshold is a pervasive one in perception. *If* we assume a threshold to exist as a boundary between awareness and a lack of awareness, then it becomes meaningful to ask questions such as "Is it possible to have perceptual discrimination below the threshold for awareness?" Certain evidence suggests that this question should be answered in the affirmative. In one experiment nonsense words made from uncommon combinations of letters were associated with electrical shock to the skin during training sessions [29]. Other nonsense words were not paired with this electric shock. Electric shocks produce a change in the electrical resistance of the skin which reflects activation of the autonomic nervous system. This change is called the galvanic skin response, or GSR. After a number of pairings of the nonsense words and the shock, the nonsense words came to elicit a GSR which they had not done originally. Then both the nonsense words associated with shock and those not associated with shock were flashed to subjects in a tachistoscope at an intensity and for a duration such that they could not be identified. Even though they were not identified, a GSR tended to occur following the words which had been paired with the electrical shock. This result means that sufficient information must have reached the subject to alter the response of his autonomic nervous system but not enough to allow verbal identification of the words.

This finding, and others like it, present a difficult problem for psychological theories. If a GSR response occurs, and yet the subject reports he does not recognize it, how is it possible to have an autonomic alerting reaction to it? Is there a perceptual mechanism which acts to filter or censor the information arriving from the senses and which allows only certain kinds of information to reach awareness? Can stimuli influence unconscious mechanisms in the individual without influencing conscious mechanisms?

PERCEPTUAL VIGILANCE AND DEFENSE   In discussing the effects of punishment on the perception of figures, we point out that subjects defended against seeing figures associated with moderate punishment and showed vigilance for figures associated with intense punishment. It is time now to return to these concepts and dig somewhat deeper into this problem.

Both vigilance and defense can be discussed in terms of changes in thresholds. When thresholds for words are lowered we speak of perceptual vigilance and when they are raised we refer to it as perceptual defense. The mechanisms underlying both vigilance and defense *could* be operating at a "lower perceptual level," gathering and regulating the sensory data before they reach awareness. We have suggested that these perceptual mechanisms could be controlled or regulated by degrees of punishment alone, but some psychologists believe that the controlling factors are more likely to be more permanent constellations of personality characteristics in the person.

Repression is a name which describes the tendency not to remember certain information. Most personality theorists believe that the material below awareness can affect our lives in many different ways. Repression is one defense mechanism used by people to guard awareness from intrusions of painful memories. Perceptual defense could be the result of a mechanism like repression which operates to scan incoming sensory messages. The potentially threatening or painful perceptions would be prevented from reaching consciousness.

Both perceptual vigilance and defense depend upon the assumption of several levels of mental and perceptual life. This assumption is a common one for personality theorists but remains rather foreign to other psychologists. The data from future experiments will decide whether or not it is necessary to assume several levels of mental processes.

LANGUAGE AND PERCEPTION   Three separate aspects of the relation between language and perception need to be stressed. First, we can never directly be aware of the mental experiences of another person. All we can know are verbal reports, written or spoken, or indicator responses of some kind. These reports constitute the basic materials of perceptual study. We talk to each other about the view from our windows, our perceptions of others, about the colors in a painting, but the only thing available to us which can be used to understand perception in others is verbal behavior. Verbal behavior is a subject unto itself and we must be careful to recognize that it can introduce error into our experiments and into discussions of perceptual phenomena. We might fall into the conceptual mistake of assuming that every descriptive word must refer to some perceptual activity. Or we might make the opposite error of assuming the absence of a perceptual event because it is not labeled with a word. The problem exists even though we restrict the subject to "yes" or "no" responses used to signal the occurrence of perceptual events.

Second, we must recognize the dramatic yet utterly common fact that verbal messages from others are the most common means used for the establishment of sets. If a ghost story prepares us for special classes of stimuli it must do so by means of the information encoded in verbal materials. When we perceive an ambiguous figure as an old shrew rather than a beautiful woman, the set is established by words. Once again, we must admit to practically no knowledge of just how words act to perform these perceptual miracles, although Hebb's concepts of cell assemblies and phase sequences may help if we are willing to assume that the verbal labels of an object can activate at least part of the phase sequences associated with the object itself.

Third, we must recognize the possibility that language itself can act to shape our perceptions. Whorf has suggested that language influences (or alters) the nature of the perceptual processes themselves rather than merely the verbal responses and the reporting of perception [30]. One of the most common illustrations in support of Whorf's theory is that people who speak *Iakuti* do not have separate words for the green and the blue portions of the visual spectrum and that they may actually see green and blue more alike than speakers of languages which make verbal distinctions between them. The question of the effects of language is open, but it represents a fascinating although difficult area of research. It may turn out that the rules and content of a language may affect the encoding and memory aspects of perception but not the basic perceptual discriminations.

The perceptual activities of man are one exciting facet of his life, but they are far from being the only aspects of behavior which we must consider. Our next step in understanding the fundamentals of behavior takes us into studies of how we learn. Although the study of learning developed from philosophical interpretations of perception, the two area have developed rather independently.

References

1. Tanner, W. P., Jr., & Swets, J. A. A decision-making theory of visual detection. *Psychol. Rev.*, 1954, **61**, 401–409.

2. Senden, M. V. *Raum—und Gestaltauffassung bei operierten Blindgeborenen vor und mach der Operation*. Munich: Johann Ambrosius Barth, 1932.

3. Hebb, D. O. The innate organization of visual activity: I. Perception of figures by rats reared in total darkness. *J. genet. Psychol.*, 1937, **51**, 101–126.

4. Helson, H. The fundamental propositions of gestalt psychology. *Psychol. Rev.*, 1933, **40**, 13–32.

5. Koffka, K. *Principles of Gestalt Psychology*. New York: Harcourt, Brace & World, Inc., 1935.

6. Lashley, K. S., Chow, K. L., & Semmes, J. An examination of the electrical field theory of cerebral integration. *Psychol. Rev.*, 1951, **58**, 123–136.

7. Hebb, D. O. *The Organization of Behavior*. New York: John Wiley & Sons, Inc., 1949.

8. Hebb, D. O. *A Textbook of Psychology*. Philadelphia: W. B. Saunders Company, 1958.

9. Karoly, A. J., & Isaacson, R. L. Scanning mechanisms in audition. Paper read at Michigan Acad. Sci., 1956.

10. Venier, Florence A. Signal detection as a function of frequency ensemble. *J. Acoust. Soc. Am.*, 1958, **30**, I: 1020–1024, II: 1075–1078.

11. Boring, E. G. A new ambiguous figure. *Amer. J. Psychol.*, 1930, **42**, 444–445.

12. Allport, F. H. *Theories of Perception and the Concept of Structure*. New York: John Wiley & Sons, Inc., 1955.

13. Langfeld, H. S. Note on a case of synesthesia. *Psychol. Bull.*, 1914, **11**, 113–114.

14. Holway, A. H., & Boring, E. G. The moon illusion and the angle of regard. *Amer. J. Psychol.*, 1940, **53**, 109–116.

15. Kaufman, L., & Rock, I. The moon illusion, I. *Science* 1962, **136**, 953–961.

16. Rock, I., & Kaufman, L. The moon illusion, II. *Science,* 1962, **136**, 1023–1031.

17. Wapner, S., & Werner, H. Experiments on sensory-tonic field theory of perception: V. Effect of body status on kinesthetic perception of verticality. *J. exp. Psychol.*, 1952, **44**, 126–131.

18. McClelland, D. C., & Atkinson, J. W. The projective expression of needs: I. The effect of different intensities of

the hunger drive on perception. *J. Psychol.*, 1948, **25**, 205–222.

19. McClelland, D. C., & Liberman, A. M. The effect of need for achievement on recognition of need-related words. *J. Pers.*, 1949, **18**, 236–251.

20. Postman, L., Bruner, J. S., & McGinnies, E. Personal values as selective factors in perception. *J. abnorm. soc. Psychol.*, 1948, **43**, 142–154.

21. Howes, D. H. & Solomon, R. L. Visual duration threshold as a function of word-probability. *J. exp. Psychol.*, 1951, **41**, 401–410.

22. Atkinson, J. W., & Walker, E. L. The affiliation motive and perceptual sensitivity to faces. *J. abnorm. soc. Psychol.*, 1956, **53**, 38–41.

23. Schafer, R., & Murphy, G. The role of autism in a visual figure ground relationship. *J. exp. Psychol.*, 1943, **32**, 335–343.

24. Sommer, R. The effects of rewards and punishments during perceptual organization. *J. Pers.*, 1957, **25**, 550–558.

25. Reece, M. M. The effect of shock on recognition thresholds. *J. abnorm. soc. Psychol.*, 1954, **49**, 165–172.

26. Bruner, J. S., & Postman, L. Tension and tension-release as organizing factors in perception. *J. Pers.*, 1947, **15**, 300–308.

27. Ashley, W., Harper, R., & Runyon, D. The perceived size of coins in normal and hypnotically induced economic states. *Amer. J. Psychol.*, 1951, **64**, 564–572.

28. Lambert, W. W., Solomon, R. L., & Watson, P. D. Reinforcement and extinction as factors in size estimation. *J. exp. Psychol.*, 1949, **39**, 637–641.

29. Lazarus, R. S., & McCleary, R. A. Autonomic discrimination without awareness: a study of subception. *Psychol. Rev.*, 1951, **58**, 113–122.

30. Whorf, B. L. *Language, Thought, and Reality.* New York: John Wiley & Sons, Inc., 1956.

SIX BASIC THEORIES OF LEARNING

It is difficult to imagine anything we do which has not been influenced by training in social customs. Even if you select activities used to satisfy your bodily needs, such as eating and drinking, it is readily apparent that the ways in which these needs are satisfied stem largely from your early training and general culture. People living in other cultures satisfy their needs in ways which often seem strange to us. The Chinese cannot understand how we could ever eat spoiled milk (cheese) whereas we would be revulsed by the thought of eating rotten eggs. A Moslem would rather die of thirst than drink wine or beer which are prohibited by his religious creeds. We consider some foods and drinks as pleasant or unpleasant, some actions as good or bad, some goals and motives as acceptable or not, all due to *learning*. As we grow older, we keep learning more and more of the rules and standards laid down by our social environment. Psychologists want to understand the empirical relationship between our environment and what we learn, and more generally the rules which govern changes in our behavior which have resulted from changes in our experiences.

In this chapter we shall present the basic theories which try to explain changes in behavior through learning. Learning is inferred from changes in performance. However, all changes in performance are not necessarily a result of learning. Often our behavioral patterns change because we are tired or because we are under medication. These are changes in *performance* and, while they are interesting objects of study for a science of behavior, they do not represent changes in *learning* as psychologists use the term. Learning refers to changes in performance of a rather special kind.

A definition of learning is by no means easy. Underwood has mentioned several considerations which should be kept in mind when *learning* is inferred from behavior. The following considerations have been adapted [1, pp. 340, 341] with the omission of a reference to a "strict" operational definition of learning, and interested readers are recommended to Underwood's text for a more thorough consideration of a definition of learning.

1. The performance change (from which learning is inferred) must result from practice.
2. The response measured must show an increment or an improvement with practice.
3. At least two observations of performance must be made since learning is inferred from a *change* in behavior.
4. Learning is the acquisition of new responses or the enhanced execution of old ones.

The important distinction between the concepts of learning and performance will become clearer as the chapter progresses and we attempt to see how different psychologists treat them. As you will soon realize, there are many different types of theories of learning. All share a common heritage of associationism, which refers to the idea that elements of behavior become more closely tied together through learning. Most learning theories have developed rules, more or less complex, which are supposed to govern the strength of association of these elements of behavior, usually stimuli and responses.

In this chapter we shall examine (1) the background of association theory, (2) some modern examples of associational learning theories, (3) various criticisms of learning theory, and finally (4) we shall review some representative data from experiments initiated by men who try to remain independent of formal theories.

Background of Association Theory

It is impossible to understand the current status of learning theory without some idea of how it evolved to its present forms. One of the main influences upon American learning theorists stems from philosophy. The British Associationists are the men to whom psychology owes its debt for its current *rules* of learning [2, 3]. Other influences on learning theory can be found in the pragmatic and functional philosophies. The American view of learning resulted from the need for dealing only with observable behavior, from the widespread effects of the work of Ivan Pavlov, from the orientation to behavior problems provided by the evolutionary views of Darwin and from the advances made in the physiological study of the body.

THE BRITISH ASSOCIATIONISTS In the eighteenth and nineteenth centuries, philosophers were especially interested in the origin of knowledge. Where does our individual knowledge come from? Do we inherit some knowledge? Are we born with any innate knowledge? Socrates long ago had argued that knowledge of the natural laws was within each of us, and by questioning an uneducated slave about the Pythagorean theorem he showed that he had managed to elicit from the slave information that he had not directly given to him. Kant also argued for the acceptance of knowledge which seemed to come through other than direct experience. On the other hand, some philosophers maintained that people are born with no inherited information and that the mind of man at birth may be compared to a blank slate on which experiences are written. This group of philosophers denied that any knowledge was innate and believed all knowledge must come to us through sensory information provided by the receptors. The problem for this group was how we combine the mental experiences we have into a meaningful, regular, and consistent world. Their solution to the problem may be summed up as *mental chemistry;* they said we construct a perceptual world out of basic sensory elements. According to the views of the British Associationists, objects may or may not exist; we only *know* about sensory *impressions*. In fact the Bishop of Cloyne, George Berkeley, concluded that there was no objective world, but that which we call *object* is merely an idea in the mind of God.

Our debt to the British Associationists does not stem from their concern with philosophical problems but from their efforts in working out rules of association by which elementary sense data forms ideas (objects in the perceptual world). The rules developed by the philosophers of the British Associationist movement represented something like a mental chemistry. These rules varied somewhat from one philosopher to another, but they were in general agreement in regard to the effectiveness of two factors in forming associations: *contiguity* and *frequency*. In the philosophers' terms, sensations which occur close together in time or in a perceptual field tend to become associated (contiguity). The more often sense data occur together the stronger the association between them (frequency). Modern learning theories have accepted the importance of these two rules of learning, but they have rejected portions of the British Associationist theories.

INFLUENCE OF AMERICAN BEHAVIORISM   Physics and chemistry seemed to be making tremendous advances because they were able to make precise measurement of their objects of study. And so learning theories developed with the view that they could only have the same success as physics and chemistry when all things which were not objectively definable and measurable were rejected. Thus the trend in American psychology was away from the mentalistic concepts used by the British Associationists and toward the concepts of measurable *stimuli* and *responses*. These were definable in strict physical terms. The stimulus could be defined in mass and acceleration for mechanical stimuli or in other physical units for visual and auditory stimuli. Responses could be measured in terms of muscle movements or in countable acts. For example, the number of times

213

a rat presses a lever can be objectively measured. The trend was to take the subjectivity out of psychology and to make experimental manipulations open for examination and replication.

American psychologists who emphasize the importance of being able to objectively measure the *stimuli* and the *responses* of an organism in a learning situation are known as *behaviorists*. A psychologist who explains behavior by using rules associating stimuli with responses is called an *associationist*. Because behaviorists were most often associationists too, the term *behaviorist* usually implies a belief in some variety of an association learning theory.

Behaviorism has dominated the thinking of practically all of the psychology of learning. In fact the only areas of psychology not greatly affected by association theory are Gestalt psychology (treated in the previous chapter) and the personality theories based on the work of Sigmund Freud. However, it should be pointed out that there is no one universally accepted behavioristic theory today. There are many types of learning theories which are both associational and behavioristic.

CONDITIONED REFLEX   Ivan Pavlov contributed indirectly to the behavioristic movement in the United States through his studies of conditioned reflexes. The basic functional unit of the nervous system is the reflex. Pavlov summarized the reflex as follows:

An external or internal stimulus falls on some one or other nervous receptor and gives rise to a nervous impulse; this nervous impulse is transmitted along nerve fibers to the central nervous system, and here, on account of existing nervous connections, it gives rise to a fresh impulse which passes along outgoing nerve fibers of the active organ, where it excites a special activity of the cellular structures [4, p. 7].

This account of the reflex shows the mechanical, telephonelike concept that Pavlov held of the nervous system. Two kinds of reflexes could be distinguished. First, there were permanent connections built into the organism. We could think of these as unlearned and innate reflexes. Second, there were the temporary connections which came about through the association of a neutral stimulus with the first kind of unlearned reflex. This new connection was the conditioned reflex.

While there are many different kinds of reflexes available to the organism, most of Pavlov's work was with the acquisition of alimentary reflexes, which involve the autonomic nervous system, and the defensive reactions (escape or withdrawal) of the body to painful or destructive stimuli. His work with the reflex in which saliva is reflexively secreted to food is most widely known today. A picture of a dog in the experimental situation used for the conditioning of the salivation response is shown in Fig. 6.1.

In Pavlov's work we find one of the earliest examples of a laboratory learning situation. The dog stands moderately restrained in the apparatus. The equipment allows meat powder to be introduced into the animal's mouth. By earlier surgery a

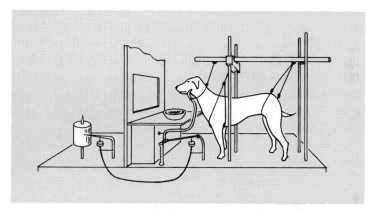

FIG. 6.1. *Dog in conditioning apparatus used by Pavlov.*

tube has been implanted in the dog that allows saliva excreted from one of the glands in the mouth to be observed and measured. Through the physiological mechanism of the innate reflex, a flow of saliva is always produced by the meat powder. Pavlov discovered that if he repeatedly presented a sound (bell, buzzer, or metronome) just before the introduction of the meat powder, the sound alone would come to elicit a flow of saliva. This kind of learning is called *classical conditioning* in which an otherwise ineffectual stimulus becomes one which can elicit a response. In the saliva experiment the learned response of salivation is very similar to (but not identical with) the natural salivation occurring to the meat powder. Because of the great similarity of the learned response to the natural response, classical conditioning is sometimes thought of as simple stimulus substitution of the new sound for the meat powder. However,

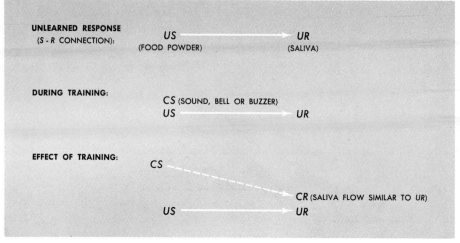

FIG. 6.2.   *Symbolic model for Pavlovian, or classical, conditioning.*

since the salivation in the two cases *is* different, it is unlikely that the learning can be understood this easily; the unconditioned reflex involves salivation with chewing, while the conditioned reflex involves salivation without chewing.

From the model of learning created by Pavlov certain terms have come to be accepted as part of the language of psychology. The meat powder used to elicit the reflexive flow of saliva is the *unconditioned stimulus* (*US*) because it always leads to the salivation response presumably without prior learning. The salivation itself is the *unconditioned reflex* (*UR*). Today it is more often called an *unconditioned response*. The stimulus which does not produce a response like the *UR* (salivation) before training but which does so after training is the *conditioned stimulus* (*CS*). The response which is acquired through training is the *conditioned response* (*CR*). Figure 6.2 presents the model for classical conditioning using these symbols. The terms can be used to describe any learning situation in which a response similar to the unconditioned response (*UR*) is conditioned to another stimulus (*CS*) previously ineffective in producing the *UR*.

We should note that the classical model of learning is a switchboard, association model. The *CS* and *CR* come to be associated so that the *CS* is more and more likely to produce the *CR*. This associative tendency is one of the vital features of all learning theories. In all of them, things become bonded together, or associated. In some theories stimuli become associated with other stimuli; in other theories stimuli and responses become associated; and in still others the association is between responses. In any case learning theories all involve some kind of association principle whereby one activity becomes connected with another activity in a more or less permanent manner.

INFLUENCES FROM BIOLOGY   At the time formal theories of learning came into prominence, scientists were very much aware of man's place in, not apart from, the animal kingdom. Darwin's work made popular the argument that man represented one point of evolutionary development. Early psychologists were aware of man's continuity with the other animals and justified the experimental study of animal behavior as one way of gaining new insights into the behavior of man. Darwin's doctrine of natural selection focused the scientific world's attention on the importance of behavioral and physiological competence in dealing with an uncertain environment. At the same time the American physiologist, Cannon, and the French physiologist, Bernard, had made popular the concept of homeostasis. Homeostasis refers to the tendency of the body to maintain a constant and generally favorable internal environment (see pp. 330–332). The effect of these ideas can be seen in the prominence of *biological usefulness* as the most important measure of the correctness or success of behavior.

In summary: Learning theories were molded into an associative pattern by the philosophic traditions of the British Associationists and the physiology of Pavlov. From Pavlov, was obtained an inheritance of a model for learning (classical conditioning) and a specific symbolism for this model.

From the evolutionary movement prominent at the turn of the century came both a stress on the biological utility of behavior and a justification for the use of animals in studying the learning of new responses. At this point we are ready to examine some of the types of theories of learning which developed largely in this century.

Modern Theories of Learning

In this section we shall first present Edwin Guthrie's views of the association process, the reinforcement theories proposed by

Thorndike and more elaborately by Hull, and then the position of Edward C. Tolman where behavior is explained on the basis of *expectancies*.

GUTHRIE'S POSITION: SIMPLE CONTIGUITY There could be no better introduction to the behavioristic learning theories than the position of Edwin Guthrie. Like many psychologists, he defines stimuli as follows: "Stimuli are changes in the world order to which sense organs or receptors respond by exciting impulses in sensory nerves" [5]. This means that physical changes must be effective in altering the state of the nervous system to serve as a stimulus for learning. Not all physical changes become registered as changes in the activity of the nervous system, and Guthrie recognizes this by his definition. His emphasis, however, is on the stimulus as a change in the physical environment which is observable and of such a nature that a number of observers would agree upon it. This is about the same thing as requiring the physical changes of stimuli to be measurable. Guthrie defines a response as specific movements whether of somatic or autonomic muscles, and he points out a distinction which we would do well to remember. This is a distinction between *movements* and *acts*. Movements are merely the contractions of somatic and autonomic muscles, whereas acts are movements which are considered in relation to the goals attained by the movements. Walking into a classroom, reaching for a pen, and opening a notebook, for example, are acts rather than movements. When we are concerned with the outcome of a series of movements, and consequently we talk of the movements in terms of their results, than we are talking about acts. Guthrie believes that it is confusing for understanding the problems of learning if we try to create laws of learning for *acts*. He prefers to think of learning as the association of stimuli with movements.

All learning theories are attempts to connect observable stimuli with measurable responses through certain rules of association. For Guthrie there is only one rule and it is taken directly from British Associationism: *contiguity*. When a stimulus occurs at the same time as a response, a maximal association is at once made between the two. On this basis, all we must do for learning to occur is to arrange for a stimulus to occur when a given response is going to take place. When the *S* is presented again, the *R* should follow. Obviously this simple rule doesn't seem to work most of the time. There are many times when movements occur in the presence of a given stimulus and yet do not occur at the next presentation of the stimulus. Most of our adult learning seems to require many training trials, i.e., a lot of practice. Certainly Guthrie is aware of this apparent contradiction between his theory and the actual conditions of learning in real life. How is this contradiction resolved? Consider yourself at any instant in time. There are millions of different stimuli impinging upon your receptors. Not only do these stimuli come from the object world around you but also from the inner world of organs and glands. Hunger, thirst, muscle tension, and internal emotional reactions all contribute to the total stimulus pattern which is constantly changing. If a stimulus is presented to us twice in succession, it will not occur in the same total stimulus context on each occasion. In fact no stimulus can appear in the same total stimulus pattern twice. Any new stimulus situation can only be *similar to,* not identical with ones of the past. Normal learning requires a large number of trials because of the complexity of the stimulus pattern. The appropriate stimulus *figure* must be isolated from the *ground* of other irrelevant stimuli through repetition.

Another reason that adult human learning requires practice and cannot be acquired at once is that most responses that we want to learn involve a sequence of movements. Remember, Guthrie believes that movements, not acts, are learned.

The learning of a sequence of muscle movements depends upon maintaining a complete sequence. There are stimulus effects for each movement we make. These effects include the new position of the body, the tension in muscles, and perhaps the effects of glandular secretions. All of these contribute to the total stimulus context to which individual movements are associated. It is important for the sequences of complex behavior to remain in a constant order.

In practical advice to parents Guthrie suggests that if you want your children to learn to hang up their coats when coming inside, you should *not* have them go back to the chair in which they flung their coats to pick them up and hang them in the closet. Rather, you should make them put on their coats, go outside, come in again, go to the closet, hang them up, and then close the closet door. By doing this, each movement produces stimuli for the next movement in the sequence to be learned.

Whether we acquire a given response pattern gradually by learning the constituent responses of the whole pattern one at a time, or whether we learn each of these small responses all at once as Guthrie suggests, is still a controversial matter. For example, some experimenters have reported evidence that word associations are not the result of a slow growth of a connection between the words [6]. However, because of the necessarily complex nature of verbal learning studies, the matter has not been finally resolved.

Thus, Guthrie's learning theory requires the immediate association of movements with the stimuli which elicited them. The stimuli must be regarded as compounds of many different types of sensory stimulation, including the sensory feedback from previous movements. Therefore, if a sequence of movements is to be learned the entire sequence should be kept intact. The basic rule of learning is *contiguity*. Nothing else is needed. We shall see that this view of learning by contiguity alone is quite distinct from the group of theories which postulate that a reward or reinforcement is essential for learning.

REINFORCEMENT THEORIES   Psychologists' use of the word *reinforcement* may at first seem somewhat different from the way it is used by the man on the street. Reinforcing a crumbling wall means to shore it up, to strengthen it. When we speak of reinforcing a response we think of strengthening the hypothetical (learned) association between a response and its stimulus. This strengthening through reinforcement is a basic feature of several theories of learning. A reinforcement is always a stimulus that is presented to the subject following his response. On certain occasions the reinforcing stimulus acts as a reward.

Thorndike and the law of effect   First, let us consider the contributions to modern learning theory of Edward L. Thorndike, a famous learning theorist and educator. Thorndike felt that *repetition* was an important factor in the acquisition of responses. Previously, Watson had held that repetition was necessary for learning, and as we have seen, it was one of the two principles which stemmed from British Associationism. However, Thorndike believed that more than repeated occurrences of stimuli and responses was necessary for an association to be built up between them, and that *motivation and reward* played important roles in learning. For efficient learning motivation must be present at least to the extent that rewards will be satisfying to the organism. Thorndike proposed three laws of learning:

1. the law of exercise
2. the law of effect
3. the law of readiness

As a function of all three laws, *connections* or *associations* are formed between observable stimuli and observable responses. The first law states that the more times the stimuli and responses are paired, the stronger is the association between the two. When psychologists use the terms *association* and *connection* they refer to the phenomenon that links a particular stimulus with a particular behavioral response which an organism makes as a result of exposure to that stimulus. The more likely a given response is to occur after presentation of the stimulus, the stronger is the association between them considered to be. An increase in the probability that a given response will follow a particular stimulus is what is meant by a strengthening in the association between the two.

The laws of effect and of readiness are closely related. The readiness law merely states that for rewards to be effective the animal must be physiologically prepared for them. Food will only be useful as a reward when the animal is hungry. A lollipop serves as a reward to a small child, but it will not be very effective if the child has just finished a box of chocolate cream candies. If the organism is ready for a certain kind of reward and that reward is given after every response that is paired with a certain stimulus, then, according to Thorndike, the connection or association between the stimulus and response will be made faster than if the reward is not given.

Reward for Thorndike means a stimulus which produces a "satisfying state of affairs" in the organism. By this he did not mean that we need to resort to an evaluation of the subjective mental experiences of the rat to determine what would constitute a reward. Thorndike said that a "satisfying state of affairs" could be inferred from the behavior exhibited by an animal. Those things which an animal approached and with which he maintained contact could be presumed to be rewards. However, with this basis of determining which objects would serve as rewards, one would have to test each and every object to determine whether or not it could serve as a rewarding stimulus. In the next section we shall see that a very much refined reinforcement theory, developed by Clark Hull, approached this problem in a different way.

The law of effect was an important milestone in the development of modern theories of learning. It represented a departure from Guthrie's theory in that the *effects* of the response determined the extent to which it was learned. If the effect of the response was to produce a "satisfying state of affairs" for the organism then the strength of association between the preceding stimuli and the response was increased. If we can

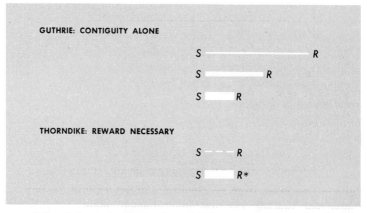

GUTHRIE: CONTIGUITY ALONE

THORNDIKE: REWARD NECESSARY

FIG. 6.3. *Schematic illustration of difference between the theories of Guthrie and Thorndike. Degree of association is represented by width of bars connecting S and R; reward is indicated by asterisk. According to Guthrie's views, only closeness determines amount of association or learning; Thorndike believes rewards are necessary to learning.*

think of those stimuli which produce a "satisfying state of affairs" as rewards, then Thorndike's law tells us that rewards act as the agents which strengthen the associations between stimuli and responses.

The theories of Guthrie and Thorndike are contrasted in Fig. 6.3. The separation of the *S*s and the *R*s indicates the amount of closeness in time or space (contiguity). In Guthrie's theory only the proximity of the *S* and *R* is important for learning. Therefore, the bottom pair of the three *S-R* pairs in the upper portion would have the strongest association. For Thorndike the closeness of association has no effect by itself. A response must be followed by a reward, indicated by the asterisk. If reward does follow, the connection between the stimulus is strengthened. If no reward follows the response, the connection is not strengthened.

We should note that the effects of a reward work *backward* in time. The reward strengthens an association between a stimulus event occurring earlier and a response which also has preceded the reward. Just what the mechanism is which allows this backward effect of rewards on prior events is not certain, although many psychologists postulate the existence of *traces* of stimuli in the nervous system as a basis of memory. The physiological effect of reward could be to act on the neural traces of preceding events. Yet, the problem is one which is very much alive in psychological research because the physiological mechanisms of learning are still obscure.

The formal theory of Hull You will be able to see many similarities between Thorndike's ideas and those proposed by Clark L. Hull. Hull was Sterling Professor of Psychology at Yale University until his death in 1951. His formulations of the laws of learning remain the closest approximation to a formal deductive theory in psychology. Yet Hull did not think his theory was in a final or complete form. He was constantly changing it through publication of articles in psychological journals and notes from his seminars. In the form of his theory which we present [7] we find typified many similarities to learning theories described earlier: (1) it is an association theory; (2) it is based on a *survival model* of life, which means it was influenced by Darwin's principle of natural selection and the popular notion of survival of the fittest; (3) it is based on biological needs and their fulfillment; and (4) many of the laws Hull derived about the nature of learning originated with Pavlov.

UNLEARNED BEHAVIOR. In Hull's system there is a recognition of the importance of unlearned stimulus-response associations. Few learning theories attempt to provide a place for such unlearned (instinctive) responses, and this is due to some extent to the rejection of any kind of inherited characteristics by the early Behaviorists. Unlearned *S-R* connections are found more frequently on the lower phylogenetic levels than on the higher, and it may be wise to view learning as a superstructure built upon these inherited connections. The nature of inherited response patterns was formulated on the basis of association doctrine. They were thought to be unlearned *S-R* connections. We shall see that Hull developed an elaborate symbolism for his theory, and in it the symbol $_sU_R$ stands for the unlearned stimulus-response connection. U was an abbreviation of *unlearned*. The $_s$ and $_R$ represent the stimulus and response components of learning respectively.

THE STIMULUS. While behaviorists measure the objective physical stimulus, their *theories* usually relate the internal neural activities (initiated at receptors) to a response. For Hull responses are conditioned to the neural aftereffects of stimuli rather than to the stimuli themselves. The effective stimulus in learning is the trace in the nervous system caused by the environmental object. The effects of a stimulus trace were postulated to be greatest about a half-second after the external stimulation begins. This figure was determined on the basis of behavioral experiments not physiological measures of neural activities. Hull did not change his behavioristic perspective, but he did remove the variables used in his theory one step beyond direct observation. Thus for Hull the stimuli in the object world give rise to stimulus traces in the organism. The first we might designate S and the second $_s$. Learning involves the $_s$ not the S.

THE RESPONSE. At the same time, we may distinguish between a tendency within the person to make a response and the actual response itself. If we designate the muscular overt response $R,$ we can refer to the preexisting neural activities which initiate the response as $_R$. These internal response tendencies are not observable, and are inferred from behavior. However, Hull postulated that learning involved an association of the stimulus trace with an "effector activity," presumably meaning the overt, observable response. At this point the authors would suggest that the more appropriate association would be with the internal motor tendency rather than the overt response. This is due in part to an experiment which indicated that a leg-lift response could be conditioned to a tone in cats who were prevented from making the response during learning [8]. These cats were trained either under a drug which blocked transmission of nerve impulses to the muscle or after the nerve which energized the muscle had been crushed, which temporarily blocked all neural impulses from reaching the leg. This experiment seems to argue convincingly for a view that the associations of learning must be between internal stimulus traces and internal response tendencies. Therefore, we have taken the liberty of modifying Hull's theory on this matter.

Symbolically the learned association of $_s$ and $_R$ is represented $_sH_R$. In unlearned reactions the connecting link U referred to an unlearned association, but in those reactions acquired through the experiences of a single organism the connecting link H should be thought of as an abbreviation for *habit* or *habit strength*. Changes in $_sH_R$ constitute learning in Hull's system. In Fig. 6.4 the distinctions between the various internal and external stimuli and responses are illustrated.

LEARNING AND BIOLOGICAL NEEDS. Hull, like Guthrie, makes a distinction between learning and performance. Many factors can affect performance, but learning itself $(_sH_R)$ is influenced only by one factor in Hull's theory: the number of times the

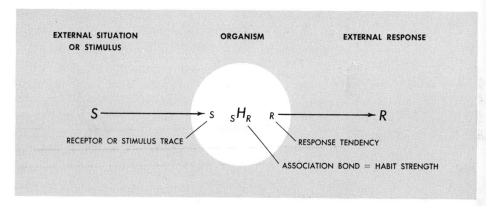

FIG. 6.4. *Modified representation of stimulus and response variables in Hull's theory.*

particular stimulus and the particular response occurring together (contiguity) *have been followed by a reinforcement.* You will find that the word *reinforcement* is often used by psychologists like the word *reward* although Hull's *reinforcement* is quite different from Thorndike's *reward*. A reinforcement is defined in a particular way by Hull and we must be careful to understand what this definition means. To do this properly we shall approach the definition through a brief historical comment.

DEFINITION OF REINFORCEMENT. Hull believed that all behavior has its origin in the biological needs, which are most demanding early in human life and in the lower animals. Yet very few of the many patterns of action we exhibit as adults seem directly related to the fulfillment of these bodily needs. To be sure, we eat and drink and sleep; but the ways, times, and places in which we fulfill our needs are not dictated by the biological conditions themselves. The means to biological fulfillment are social accruements which differ from one person to the next and from one culture to the next. Still, Hull believed all complex adult behavior to be indirectly based on our biological needs.

One insight into how adult behavior may be based on biological needs occurs when we look at Hull's principle of reinforcement. Reinforcement is like Thorndike's reward in one way; it is a *stimulus* which has the ability to alter the probabilities of certain *Rs* following certain *Ss*. When a response is reinforced this means that it has been followed by one of a certain class of stimuli. What defines this special class of reinforcing stimuli? We would like to be able to have an independent method of identifying "reinforcements" and not be confined to the observation that its presentation alters response probability because *it would then be possible to predict what stimuli would have reinforcing properties ahead of time*. Thorndike said that rewarding stimuli produced a "satisfying state of affairs in the organism." These are hard to observe. On the other hand, Hull postulated *that reinforcing stimuli were those which reduced stimuli uniquely associated with the biological drives.*

A biological deficiency in the organism produces a state of *need*. This can be defined in an experiment by depriving an animal or person of food or water over a period of time. One essential characteristic of the need is the pattern of internal stimuli which is always associated with this kind of deprivation condition. The stimuli uniquely associated with a specific need are called *drive stimuli, S_D*. It is only when these drive stimuli are diminished that the animal is reinforced. Whether or not the animal experiences a "satisfying state of affairs" is immaterial.

Drive stimuli may result from a dry throat due to thirst or stomach contractions due to hunger. In fact, they could be signals in the nervous system from hypothalamic centers or other centrally located neural systems. Reduction of S_D, reinforcement, is usually accomplished by the common method of feeding the hungry animal or watering the thirsty one. The definition of reinforcement is flexible, however, and does include the occasions when S_D are reduced by unnatural means. One could reduce the stomach contraction component of hunger S_Ds by filling the stomach of an animal with nonnutritive substances. To the extent that the stomach contractions (S_D) are reduced by the inert bulk inserted into the stomach, reinforcement would be produced.

REINFORCEMENT AND LEARNING. For Hull, learning depends on reinforcement. Neither contiguity nor frequency of S and R are sufficient in and of themselves. Hull's basic rule of learning is that a response is associated with a stimulus trace to the extent that the response has been followed by a reduction of the drive stimuli. While the definition may seem a little elaborate, it is nonetheless clear.

The learning rules for Hull can be written as follows: *A stimulus in the environment (S) is presented to the organism; this causes a neural trace of (S) in the organism ($_s$). This trace then becomes conditioned to a response tendency ($_R$) occurring simultaneously with the trace if followed by a stimulus with reinforcing properties.*

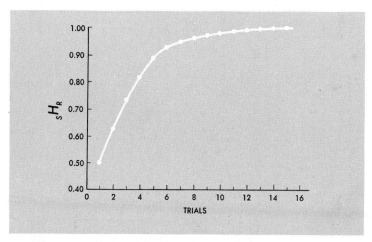

FIG. 6.5. *Representational curve of $_sH_R$ as number of trials increases.*

The growth of habit strength is a function of the number of reinforced pairings of S and R (N). *No other factors influence the growth of learning.* Hull wrote this in equation form:

$$_sH_R = 1 - 10^{-.0305N}$$

This equation implies that as N gets larger the successive increments to $_sH_R$ get smaller. It indicates that when we learn a response to some stimulus, the first few trials build up habit strength faster than do later ones.

Figure 6.5 presents the typical growth curve of $_sH_R$ as determined by the number of reinforced pairings of S and R and Hull's theoretical equation.

According to this theory, we now know all the rules necessary to describe the learning process but not all the rules which go into determination of final behavior. We must be aware of the *distinction between learning* and *performance*. Which factors operate on what an organism has learned so that this learning is evident or not evident in performance?

DRIVE AND PERFORMANCE. First of all, we must look at the role of motivation in performance. Thorndike argued that unless an animal is motivated, it will not learn. In his laws of readiness and effect we note the explicit common-sense notion that an organism must be physiologically ready for a reward for it

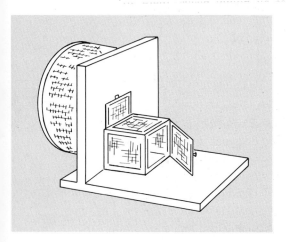

FIG. 6.6.   *Activity wheel. Animals live in small cage at right.*

to be effective in producing learning. Hull indirectly asserts the same thing when he stipulates that drive stimuli must be reduced for reinforcement to occur. But, in addition to the effects of drive stimuli on learning, Hull maintained that a general concept of drive was necessary in order that the animal alter his behavior and demonstrate what it has learned. As we have seen, Hull assumed that each different biological need produces a unique pattern of S_D. He also assumed that every need contributes *in the same way* to D (drive). Drive then is a general concept. To illustrate the general nature of D, we can consider data recorded on animals housed in activity wheels (see Fig. 6.6). The animals are kept in the housing units connected to their particular wheels. When the animals are well fed and watered, they will occasionally exhibit spontaneous running in the connecting wheels. But when deprived of food or water, all animals show an increase in the amount of time they spend running in the wheels. Generally, they will keep up this increased amount of activity until they weaken from lack of food or water. In this environment, increased running in the activity wheels is truly purposeless. No biological goals are fulfilled by running; in fact, their physiologic reserves are reduced. This increase in activity is believed to correspond to an increase in drive of the organism. Note that the increase is not dependent upon a specific deficit. Lack of food, water, or hormonal changes (in the case of the female rat) can produce an increase of drive measured in this way. (For a more detailed analysis of the role of motivational concepts in learning theories see pp. 342–348.)

While D is a common result of all bodily needs, there are differences between hunger and thirst as well as between all the other biological deficits. Hull argued that our discrimination between needs was based entirely upon the different patterns of drive stimuli associated with them.

Drive serves to energize behavior. Habit strengths formed in reaction to the many stimuli around us guide behavior. Presumably no behavior at all will occur unless there is a sufficient level of D to produce behavior. Drive does not direct behavior, it acts to arouse and intensify it, like an amplifier of our habits. It does not selectively energize the person toward one or another response. The direction of behavior depends on the relative strengths of the stimulus-response associations formed in the past and aroused by the external situation and the drive stimuli present at the moment. Drive operates in conjunction with habit strengths to produce the observable behavior.

Let us take an example of how drive, habit strength, and drive stimuli effect behavior. Class has just been dismissed. You have a free hour and *hurry* from the classroom. The fact that you are doing something and doing it with some intensity reflects a significant amount of drive. Sometimes it is possible to feel restless and move without knowing just what it is you want. This active but nondirected behavior may be a counterpart to the aimless running activity of rats in the activity wheels under food or water deprivation (high drive condition) and your behavior would only reflect the general drive level. If on the other hand you know you are hungry or thirsty, this discrimination between the biological origins of drive would occur on the basis of the S_D present. If you turn promptly and go to the coffee shop for liquid refreshment or to the cafeteria for food, these responses would be initiated because of the development of stimulus-response associations activated by the S_D present and your past experiences in the situation.

The energizing effects of drive are made explicit in the formal context of Hull's theory by the relation:

$$_sH_R \times D (\text{drive})$$

All habits active at any moment are multiplied by drive. As we shall see in the next section, other variables also stand in this multiplicative relation to learning ($_sH_R$) in the final determination of behavior.

OTHER VARIABLES INFLUENCING PERFORMANCE. Drive is not the only multiplier of $_sH_R$. The value or desirability of the goal stimulus (K), the intensity of the external stimulus paired with the response (V), and drive (D), multiply the quantity $_sH_R$ to obtain a new number called the *reaction potential* $(_sE_R)$.

$$_sE_R = H \times D \times V \times K$$

All of these other factors have an energizing effect upon reaction potential but none as strong as D. Hull has made explicit the differential qualities and specifications of each of these variables, but they are not vital to our presentation of the basic model. However, it is important to remember that the two most important contributors to $_sE_R$ are $_sH_R$ and D.

Hull was a behaviorist and as such demanded that his theoretical variables be closely tied to measurable experimental conditions. As we have seen, $_sH_R$ is defined in terms of the number of times the response has occurred followed by a reinforcement. The other variables have similar defined conditions. In the animal experiments from which the data were obtained which both lead to formulation of the theory and at least partial confirmation of it, the following were the definitions used to obtain numerical values of the theoretical concepts.

Concept	Definition Used in Experiments
D	Hours deprivation of food or water
K	Weight of food or quantity of other incentive
V	Intensity of external stimulus

The theory was recognized as only a beginning of a general theory for adult human behavior, and as such Hull did not believe it necessary to formulate definitions suitable for all learning situations. In one sense he left it up to others to extend and broaden it.

What is this $_sE_R$? First it is a numerical quantity like $_sH_R$, D, K, and V. This number represents the tendency to make the response *in the theory*. It is strictly a theoretical, or conceptual, variable, useful only in so far as the theory is concerned. It is only the product of the various numbers multiplied together. It represents an intermediate step toward the prediction of the response. It is only an intermediate step because other variables of behavior must now be considered before the response prediction can be formulated.

RESPONSE INHIBITION. We must expend energy to make any response. It costs us something in fatigue to do anything at all, and at times it seems as though the muscle fatigue is concentrated in some region of the body. One example would be the localized fatigue of the hand after continuously taking notes for an hour. After any task we have been working on for some time, there is a tendency to do something else. However, only part of the explanation of this tendency to change our behavior can be attributed to muscle fatigue per se. For example, if a person has been drawing lines on sheets of papers until he feels it is no longer possible to continue because of hand fatigue or actual cramps, it is easy for him to shift to a slightly different writing task *which uses the same muscles* without fatigue or pain [9]. Thus, there must be a considerable psychological component in the tendency to alternate performances.

Hull would explain the muscle-fatigue effects and the psychological-fatigue effect by two different inhibitory mechanisms. First, there is reactive inhibition (I_R) which is the theoretical counterpart of muscle fatigue caused by the response. The second is conditioned inhibition ($_sI_R$) which is a *learned* tendency not to respond in the same way. The two combine to form a combined inhibitory potential ($\dot{I}_R$). After a series of responses, there is this aggregate tendency not to repeat the R again. The conditioned inhibition ($_sI_R$) is akin to habit strength ($_sH_R$) in that it is learned and does not dissipate with mere passage of time. The fatigue component does become reduced with time. The aggregate of inhibition detracts from the $_sE_R$ generated by the earlier formula: $_sE_R = _sH_R \times D \times K \times V$. After the inhibition effects have been subtracted from $_sE_R$ the new quantity is the effective reaction potential, $_s\bar{E}_R$.

$$_s\bar{E}_R = {_sE_R} - \dot{I}_R$$

Both the inhibition variables are experimentally defined by the amount of work required in making the response. But we are not yet in a position to predict behavior. We must first consider the phenomenon in which a person's responses tend to show fluctuations from one situation to the next and from one time to the next.

BEHAVIOR PREDICTIONS The effective reaction potential is not considered to be constant but rather to fluctuate in an unsystematic fashion. The momentary value of $_s\bar{E}_R$ fluctuates and the effects of these fluctuations must be considered in predicting behavior. By mathematical manipulation it is possible to always subtract the oscillation effect $(_sO_R)$ from $_s\bar{E}_R$. By this subtraction a new term is defined, momentary reaction potential $(_s\dot{E}_R)$.

$$_s\dot{E}_R = {}_s\bar{E}_R - {}_sO_R$$

Behavioral oscillation does not have any important ties to experimental observation. It is a concept which lives entirely in the theory world of Hull; but it can be thought of as a device which adds in theory the spontaneous fluctuations repeatedly found in neural and muscular systems of the body.

The momentary reaction potential, $_s\dot{E}_R$, is the end product of the formulas of Hull used in the prediction of behavior. If it is greater than some necessary threshold $(_sL_R)$, then the specific behavior will occur. If the $_s\dot{E}_R$ is less than threshold, the response will not occur. If several $_sH_{RS}$ are activated in the same situation, that which is associated with the greatest $_s\dot{E}_R$ will take place. A diagrammatic summary of the Hull variables is presented in Fig. 6.7.

The quantity of the $_s\dot{E}_R$ is used to predict:

1. The probability that the response will occur (the probability that $_s\dot{E}_R$ is greater than $_sL_R$).
2. The response amplitude.
3. The response latency (the time it takes the response to occur).
4. The number of trials for which the response will continue to occur after the reinforcement is no longer given following the response.

All these are measures used by psychologists to measure performance. For Hull, these are a function of the $_s\dot{E}_R$ as derived

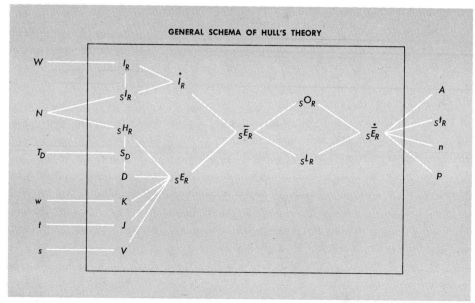

FIG. 6.7. *Schematic representation of Hull's theoretical variables. Left: antecedent measurements from which properties of first-order variables of theory are inferred (center box). Right: variables measured on response side. Second- and third-order variables resulting in momentary reaction potential are illustrated in box. Adapted from Edward L. Walker with permission.*

from his theory. Let us take a simple learning situation and try to use Hull's theory (1) to describe the problem and (2) as an aid to designing an effective situation for learning and performance.

EXAMPLE 1. Suppose we want to train an animal to solve a simple maze problem. Perhaps we would use a simple T maze of the kind illustrated in Fig. 6.8. The animal begins a training trial at the bottom of the T and proceeds to the point where the horizontal arms join the vertical section. Here the animal can choose to (*a*) turn right or (*b*) turn left. We will assume there are no significant special stimuli in the maze which would distract the animal from the task and that both horizontal arms of the maze are equally illuminated. By a flip of a coin or some other means of random selection we choose one side to terminate in a goal box containing food. Our task is to train the animal to run down the starting arm and into that arm which leads to food. To use food as an incentive we must make the animal hungry by a schedule of food deprivation.

This amount of deprivation contributes to two variables in

233

Hull's system: the S_D and the D. D arouses the animal to behavior while S_D reduction will constitute reinforcement. We place the animal repeatedly in the bottom of the T. It runs to the choice point and enters one or the other of the arms. When it reaches the end of an arm, it is lifted out of the maze and replaced in the starting box for another trial. If the animal chooses the correct arm (containing the food) it is allowed to eat for a few seconds before being removed. This reduces the S_D caused by the deprivation of food and acts as a reinforcement. As the number of times (N) that it turns to the correct side, proceeds

FIG. 6.8. T *maze often used in animal learning studies. Animals run down starting arm to choice point where they may turn left or right. Striped background is to control background around maze. Courtesy of R. J. Douglas.*

to the end of the arm, and obtains food increases , the habit strength for this behavior also increases. In this case habit strength refers to the building up of a connection between the stimuli of the maze *and* food deprivation and the response of turning toward and running to the end of the correct arm. Only the number of reinforced responses is important in the determination of the amount of learning the animal will have in the T maze.

However, all of the variables, $D, K, V,$ and $J,$ help determine the behavior of the animal once it is placed in the maze. We should obtain better performance when the animal is well motivated by hunger (D), when there is a goodly amount of food

(K), and when the stimuli of the maze are readily discernible (V).

In discussing the learning of the rat in the **T** maze, we have so far not mentioned either the inhibitory factors or the oscillation function which Hull postulated. The amount of inhibition which will become attached to the response and result in a diminution of the $_s\dot{\bar{E}}_R$ would be a function of the work involved in making the response. If we make the arms at the top of the **T** slant upwards at 30 degrees, then this would require more work of the animal to reach the ends of the arms. Inhibition would be greater in this case and thus would diminish $_s\bar{E}_R$ to a greater extent. This would result in a lower performance rate, greater latency, and fewer correct responses, especially under conditions of extinction. We could dissipate the temporary inhibition by allowing greater intervals between trials. This is important for all responses where a significant amount of work is required in making the response. Time should be allowed the subject to dissipate the temporary inhibition of fatigue. Where little work is required, the trials can occur closer together. Hull's use of the oscillation function would be apparent if we observed an animal that had a great deal of training, was well motivated, and had all of the other performance variables arranged so as to be at a maximum value. The animal would not always turn and run down the correct arm as we might expect. Occasionally the animal would still run to the wrong arm and be disappointed (along with the experimenter).

EXAMPLE 2. Let us take some liberties with Hull's strict formulations and use his terminology in the analysis of a common behavioral situation—the examination period. Let us imagine a student in college takes a multiple choice test in his introductory psychology course. A week later he receives his paper back with an F for failure written across the top. After looking at the exam once more, even the student recognizes the poor performance. What happened?

Had the student learned the material covered in the test? Hull would say that from the test itself, it would be impossible to determine the answer to this question. Why? Because any or all of the factors which contribute to $_s\dot{\bar{E}}_R$ could have been low and caused the poor performance. As we already know, the two greatest factors are learning $(_s H_R)$ and motivation (D). If the student had learned the material, then was there anything

235

wrong about his motivation which caused his poor performance? Many poor examination performances are brought about by insufficient motivation. Occasionally, we may find a detrimental effect on performance if the level of drive becomes too great. In such cases the high drive level activates responses incompatible with the ones required in the exam. As a teacher, we would want to examine the situation to see if the incentives offered for correct responses are sufficiently attractive. Are the stimuli to which the student is asked to respond clear and emphatic? Lastly, what about the student's responses? Is there any chance that inhibitions had built up through previous study or work to reduce the performance? If all else seems in order, we might then feel safe in concluding that the student had not learned the content of his course in psychology.

ANIMALS IN LEARNING EXPERIMENTS This may be as good a time as any to point out that nearly all learning theories have made great use of the laboratory rat as it solves its various tasks. Some have argued that it is useless to study the behavior of animals in any learning situation if we are really interested in principles of learning *for the human*. Naturally, psychologists *are* interested in human behavior; yet there are many impelling reasons behind the use of laboratory animals in research on learning and performance.

There is no doubt that animals are different from man. Even the inbred albino rat, who suffers from many of our own diseases, cannot be said to be similar to man in all important psychological characteristics. But probably millions of valuable hours have been spent in observing its behavior in laboratory learning tasks. Most psychologists who spend time observing this behavior believe that it is only with laboratory animals that we can control enough of the important variables (such as the amount of previous learning, capacity, motivation, rewards, etc.) to make any firm conclusions about basic learning processes. From the observations of the rat or monkey or cat or dog we hope to make better informed predictions regarding the conditions which would be relevant for the human. We do not assume that man and animals learn in identical ways, but we hope that what we find out from the lower animals will lead to *testable ideas* and *theories* which can be later tried with people. After all, from Darwin's work we can assume some form of continuity.

SECONDARY REINFORCEMENT AND MOTIVATION   In Western society little of man's behavior is directed toward direct fulfillment of biological needs. To be sure we work for money, which we exchange for the physiological necessities of life. Yet money itself does not reduce drive stimuli. It is not a reinforcement, as we have learned in Hull's theory. In addition only a small percentage of the money we earn goes toward the fulfillment of physiological needs. Millionaires who are assured of enough money to provide handsomely for themselves seem motivated to acquire more. The fruits of our labor are many beyond money itself. Words of praise or esteem and self-realization of success are but a few of the other sorts of goals toward which behavior seems to be directed. These certainly seem to be far removed from the drive stimuli of hunger or thirst.

The learning theorist recognizes that but a few of the actions of modern Western man are guided by food or drink incentives. However, a behavioristic learning theorist believes that the goals of human behavior can be understood through the same basic theory developed on the basis of direct reduction of biological needs through the concepts of *secondary motivation* and *secondary reinforcement*. These concepts allow us to extend the relatively bare theory of Hull to situations where the reduction of primary drive stimuli (biological needs) is not suitable as a condition of reinforcement and consequently to situations more relevant to human behavior.

At the outset we should like to point out that much of the literature of psychology contains references to the concepts of secondary reinforcement and motivation. Not all definitions of these terms are made using Hull's terminology. Yet, if one once understands the basic definitions used by Hull, all other modifications can be more easily understood. As with primary reinforcing stimuli, secondary reinforcements and motivations are certain *classes of stimuli*. The defining characteristics of the classes of stimuli are described below as well as their presumed theoretical effects upon the organism:

Secondary reinforcements are stimuli that have been paired with *reduction* of drive stimuli (S_D) and have the property of *reducing* drive stimuli in the organism when they are presented in the future.

Secondarily motivating stimuli are stimuli that have been paired with an *increase* in drive stimuli (and their subsequent

237

reduction). They have the property of increasing the amount of drive stimuli in the organism when presented in the future.

Both of these concepts are intimately connected with the concept of drive stimuli. Their effects on one's behavior are mediated through acquired capacity to alter the drive stimuli existing at any moment. Secondarily motivating stimuli produce drive stimuli in the person and secondary reinforcements have the acquired capacity to reduce certain drive stimuli.

An example from animal behavior In order to develop secondary reinforcements according to Hull's rules, we can train animals to value stimuli they have associated with reductions of biological needs almost as highly as the natural stimuli which reduce the needs. Chimpanzees will work to accumulate poker chips which are paired with food [10]. The animals are trained with a Chimp-o-mat, into which poker chips are inserted and food subsequently is obtained. They will seek these poker chips, work for them, hoard them—in other words act toward them as most people act toward money.

New responses can be learned to new stimuli by using secondary reinforcements with the stimulus-response pair. Even painful stimuli can lose at least some of their sting when they have been paired with drive-reducing stimuli and take on secondarily reinforcing properties [4].

The nature of secondary reinforcements and motives can be illustrated with further observations about the chimpanzees trained to value poker chips. When a chimpanzee sees a poker chip lying outside of its cage, the animal becomes agitated and tries to find sticks and tools to get the chip inside the cage. The poker chip outside the grasp of the animal does not appear reinforcing, but rather has motivational effects. The unpossessed chip acts like a secondarily motivating stimulus. The two conditions, poker chip possessed and not possessed, alter the chimp's reactions differently. The poker chip in the possession of the animal serves as a secondary reinforcement. The same poker chip not in the animal's possession acts as a secondarily motivating stimulus.

Human behavior Some learning theorists view early childhood experience in the light of reinforcement and motivation. Think how consistently a mother is associated with primary drive reductions in the infant. She is always present when the baby's needs are reduced. On this basis then, mother should be a secondarily reinforcing stimulus of the first magnitude. We have discussed poker chips not in possession of the chimpanzee. Mother not in possession should be a potent condition of secondary motivation for the child. We know that in most homes the child is firmly attached to mother and is disturbed when removed from her. The observed facts are not questionable. The issue is whether this attachment of the infant to mother is based on the close association with the reduction of drive stimuli. It is easy to be critical of such a naïve or superficial view, but it does represent a consistent theoretical position. And more, it is difficult to find more reasonable and equally consistent ones to supplant it. You might try to design an experiment to show that the child's attachment to his parents is not based upon secondary reinforcement.

Secondary reinforcements can be formed by an association with the primary reinforcements or motives, or they can be formed by association with other previously developed secondary reinforcements or motives. For example, words associated with mother's approval come to take on their own reinforcing properties. "Good-boy," "that's right," "nice going" are examples of stimuli which have reinforcing properties derived from their association with previously established secondary reinforcers. "Bad boy," "oh-oh," "that's wrong" can be considered as motivational and acquired on the basis of association with secondary or primary motivators. As an example, consider a situation when a child has done something wrong and the mother becomes angry, says, "Bad boy," and *leaves the room*. We saw earlier that mother's absence could be a secondarily motivating condition. The words, "bad boy," are now associated with conditions of secondary motivation and may come to have motivational properties themselves.

The adequacy of the theory   Are the concepts of secondary reinforcement and secondary motivation adequate to explain all of those stimuli which act to foster and consolidate new learning for us? Probably not. For one thing, we know that when a secondary reinforcer is no longer associated with the primary reinforcement it quickly loses its reinforcing quality. Yet secondary reinforcing stimuli such as our parents' approval retains its effectiveness for years after the time when they were related to the reduction of our primary drives. Experimental studies of Zimmerman [12] have demonstrated that under appropriate conditions secondary reinforcements can continue

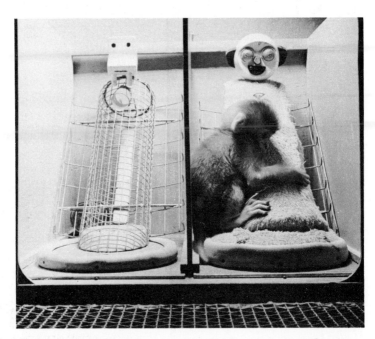

FIG. 6.9. *Mother surrogates used by Harlow. Infant monkey is clinging to surrogate which has more acceptable "skin" qualities. Courtesy of H. F. Harlow.*

to be effective for considerable periods of time. These studies are discussed in Chapter 8, (pp. 348–350).

Another line of work which indicates that traditional views of secondary reinforcement cannot entirely account for an offspring's attachment for its mother is found in the work of Harlow [11]. In his study various mother substitutes or surrogates were offered to baby monkeys. The behavior of the baby monkeys could be studied as the stimulus configuration of the mother surrogates was changed. In addition, schedules of feeding (and subsequent reinforcement qualities) could be altered. It was found that there were tactual stimulus patterns (temperature and texture of the surrogate) which influenced the infants' responses to the mother surrogates over and above its need-reducing qualities. A picture of one of the mother surrogates is presented in Fig. 6.9.

Other problems of the traditional views of secondary reinforcement and motivation arise from the definitions themselves. These problems are of a highly technical nature and concern the question of whether the onset or the termination of an unpleasant stimulus has the greatest motivational effects. (You will note that in our definition of secondary motivation the stimulus which was to come to have secondary motivating qualities had to be paired with a sudden increase and a *subsequent decrease in stimulation.*) This controversy has led to many interesting experiments and the development of an alternate theory of secondary reinforcement proposed by Mowrer. (See Chapter 8, pp. 345–348 for his views and other aspects of learning theories as they relate to motivation.)

EXPECTANCY THEORY   So far we have presented the theories of men who have viewed behavior as connections between stimuli and responses. Not all learning theorists look at learning from this same vantage point. For example, Edward Tolman argued that we learn the *relation between the stimuli* around us. Tolman's name has long been associated with "expectancy theories of behavior." For him, learning consists of mastering relations between stimuli in our environment. We learn *cognitive maps* of our surroundings. In these maps we learn various routes. These routes lead to further stimuli which have different values to the person or animal. In Tolman's theory our responses are determined by expectancies that given routes found in our cognitive maps will lead to differentially valuable stimuli.

In this view people follow the routes which will take them to goals which are important and desirable for them at any instant in time. The actual movements involved in getting to the goals are not in and of themselves essential to Tolman.

Do we learn responses?   In his emphasis upon cognitive learning we find the positive aspect of Tolman's work. Viewed from the other side of the fence, however, expectancy theories are an attack upon the foundations of *S-R* association theories. The *S-R* association is the heart of the theories propounded by Guthrie, Thorndike, and Hull, as well as by other behaviorists. Tolman suggests that theories should deal with learned associations *between stimuli,* or *S-S* associations. Which view should we hold? One in which associations are between stimuli and responses or one in which the associations are only among stimuli? Presumably the problem is amenable to experimental resolution. The following experiment has been offered as support for Tolman's *S-S* position.

Rats learned the solution to a maze problem for a food reward [13]. After the animals had learned the desired response, lesions were made in their cerebellums which produced gross impairments in motor performance. The question was, could animals with such severe motor debilities still find their way to the goal compartment? They did. The Tolmanian argument is that the rats could not have learned the maze problem in the first place as *a series of motor responses*, since the mechanisms they would have used to learn these responses were severely damaged by the lesions. Thus, superficially at least, the animals seem to have learned a cognitive map of the environment rather than to make specific responses. The *S-R* theorists, however, could maintain that since many of the muscle movements required to run the maze were common to both the pre- and post-operative phases of the experiment, the results do not provide a conclusive contradiction to their position.

Is reinforcement necessary? The expectancy theory of Tolman differs from the theories of Thorndike and Hull on the question of the need for reinforcing events in learning. Tolman argues that *S-S* associations are learned through contiguity alone and do not depend on reinforcements. For instance, we *know* the drinking fountain is out the classroom door to the left and down the hall about 15 feet. We may know this even though we have never had occasion to drink from it. However, this learning will never become evidenced through performance unless we are motivated to drink. One way to test whether a person has learned where the drinking fountain is located would be to make him thirsty. We observe the subject's reactions when motivated to obtain water. Does he go out the door, turn left, and make a beeline for the fountain? Or does he go out and begin searching in a trial-and-error fashion to find a fountain? Tolman's idea is that motivation acts to select which route is followed, and, therefore, what behavioral act occurs.

Tolman and Honzik performed an experiment with rats which attempted to illustrate that reinforcement was not necessary for learning [14]. Three groups of animals were given experience in a complex maze. The animals were deprived of food during training. One group of animals was always rewarded with food when they reached the goal box (*HR* group). Another group, equally hungry was never fed in the goal box (*HNR* group). The third and crucial group was equally hungry and was not rewarded with food in the goal box until the eleventh day of training (*HNR-R* group). The question was this: Would the performance of the critical group (*HNR-R*) suddenly improve to the level being exhibited by the *HR* group? Tolman and Honzik believed Hull would have predicted a slow learning curve to be exhibited by the *HNR-R* group with the addition to food reward, while Tolman expected the animals to show a sudden improvement because at this point the animals would start to *use* the map of the maze they had built up by their previous aimless wanderings.

On the day following the introduction of food the animals of the *HNR-R* group showed performance at least equal to that of the group that had always been reinforced by food at the goal box. In other words learning became apparent to the observers only when the animals were motivated to show what they had learned (see Fig. 6.10). Tolman believes that this is

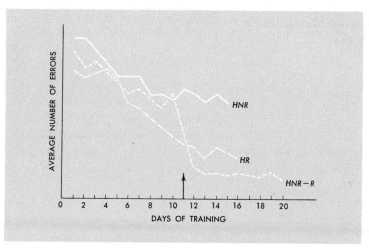

FIG. **6.10.** *Graphic representation of performances of three groups of animals in Tolman and Honzik experiment.* HNR: *animals hungry but never given food in maze;* HR: *animals hungry and always given food in goal box.* HNR-R: *equally hungry animals not given food in goal box until eleventh day and thereafter. Adapted from E. C. Tolman and C. H. Honzik.* Introduction and removal of reward and maze performance of rats. Univ. Calif. Publ. Psychol., 1930, 4, 257–275.

the *paradigm* for all learning. We learn sensory (*S-S*) associations, and when the situation makes one goal desirable we get there by the shortest route. If this short route is blocked or altered, we still can find the goal by following alternate routes developed in our cognitive maps.

The formal theory   The behavior of a rat at a choice point in a maze, Tolman believes, could be used as an example of the important determinants of all behavior in rat and man. In 1937 he confessed the following belief:

. . . everything important in psychology (except perhaps such matters as the building up of the superego, that is every- thing save such matters as involve society and words) can be investigated in essence through the continued experimental and theoretical analysis of the determiners of rat behavior at a choice point in a maze [15, p. 172].

Tolman's analysis of the behavior of the rat at a choice point enabled him to formulate a list of concepts relevant to all behavior. He postulated two general kinds of variables: (1) those concerned with the environmental aspects of choice and (2) those concerned with the differences between organisms as they make their choices. The specific variables are presented below.

1. Environmental variables

    M Maintenance schedule
    G Appropriateness of goal object
    S Types and modes of stimuli provided
    R Types of motor response required
    $\Sigma(OBO)$ Cumulative nature and number of trials
    P Pattern of preceding and succeeding maze units

2. Individual difference variables

    H Heredity
    A Age
    T Previous training
    E Special endocrine, drug, or vitamin conditions

The first category of variables are those which experimenters usually manipulate. Some researchers, for example, investigate the effect of the length of time an animal has been deprived of food or water on performance (M). Others might be curious about the effect of different incentives (G) on behavior. Tolman suggested the use of the term *independent variable* for those variables which are manipulated in experimentation [16]. Generally speaking, environmental variables are those *most often* manipulated in psychological experiments, although today we find a great number of experiments in which the H, A, T, E variables are the independent variables. In addition he suggested the use of the term, *intervening variable* to describe theoretical terms only indirectly tied to actual experimental operations. In fact, for each of the environmental variables he suggests a related intervening variable.

Tolman presents a third category: *dependent variables.* These represent the performance of the behaving organism. Let us examine a modification of a Tolman diagram which presents all three kinds of variables:

Independent variables (Environmental manipulations)	Intervening variables (Theoretical terms)	Dependent variables
M	Demand, motivation, persistence	
G	Appetite, taste, preference	
S	Sensory differentiation of situation, sensory capacities	Performance measures
R	Motor skills and capacities	
$\Sigma(OBO)$	The learning of sign Gestalts	
P	Biases toward one choice or another, perseveration, or emotional stability	

To predict behavior, we need to know two sets of relationships with this kind of formulation: (1) how each of the intervening variables is related to environmental manipulations, and (2) how the intervening variables combine to allow prediction of the dependent variables. At this time, we can say very little about this, however. Tolman's contribution remains one of an analytic scheme for future development. Tolman's organization of the behavior of the rat has influenced psychology, but no final plan has been worked out to explicate these intervening variables, nor have the rules of relationship between independent, intervening, and dependent variables been spelled out.

Additional comments The extent to which our cognitive maps range over a great number of environmental stimuli is an important attribute of our personal development. The greater the number of such associations, the wider will be our perspective. As children, our cognitive maps are limited. As we grow older, go to school, meet new people and situations, our range of hypotheses about the world become extended. In general, we tend to value the person who has a broad range of associations. Today, one prominent definition of the creative person is defined in terms of the range of associations a person makes to a set of words or concepts presented to him. As we grow old, we sometimes find the range growing narrower again. This narrowing of the cognitive map is often identified with senility. But there are other times when our maps become restricted too. Under terrific stress we can observe a constriction of our cognitive maps. When a person returns (regresses) to a mode of behavior that is more appropriate of an earlier age, we find a similar reduction in range of associations. When a person adopts a very limited set of behavior (fixation), can this be identified with a correspondingly limited map? Tolman has suggested that the cognitive map concept might be valuable in understanding these behavior patterns.

The ideas presented by Tolman foreshadowed the theories advanced by Hebb (see Chapter 5). The similarity between the two theories stems from their respective dependence upon expectancies. Hebb goes a step or two further by means of assumptions about the neural mechanisms underlying expectancies. Certain phase sequences lead to others, and synaptic facilitation bears the explanatory burden in his theory. Hebb tries to explain what *expectancy* means physiologically, whereas Tolman merely accepts it as a psychological fact.

All the learning theories discussed have been influential in shaping our concepts in other areas of psychology, and they have altered man's view of himself. These theories are not the only ways in which the professional students of behavior have attempted to understand the learning processes. Some have made models of behavior, or at least certain kinds of behavior, in the hope that these will help with the prodigious task of *understanding* man's behavior.

Machines and Models

Since the beginning of recorded time man has made images of himself. However, until this century these efforts have been aimed at producing images of the external appearances. Even the elaborate creations of the Swiss watchmakers were attempts to create *moving images* in the likeness of men or animals. Recently scientifically minded craftsmen have attempted to produce models that mimicked the psychological functions presumed to exist in man and animals. Reproduction of appearance has taken a poor second place to reproduction of function.

THE SCHEMATIC SOWBUG   Tolman designed a schematic animal called a *sowbug*, to help him understand the properties of rats as they made decisions at the choice points in mazes [17]. Presumably, when forced to design a model, even though a schematic model, one must be explicit about the intervening variables which will be built into the machine. Translating one's

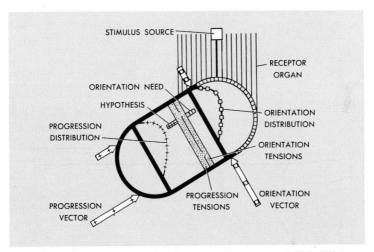

FIG. **6.11.**   *Schematic "sowbug" described by Tolman. Adapted from E. C. Tolman. The determiners of behavior at a choice point.* Psychol. Rev., *1939, 46, 318–336.*

theory into a model that works is a way of testing one's theoretical precision and may provide fresh insights into behavioral problems as well.

Tolman's sowbug incorporated many of the variables described in the preceding section. The sowbug represents a simple variety of "animal," with one receptor organ at the head and four symmetrically placed motor appendages (see Fig. 6.11). The animal would be sensitive to the direction of light falling on the receptor organ, and, in general, the left-hand appendages would be aroused by receptor cells at the right portion of the head. Correspondingly, right-hand motor appendages would be activated by light falling on the left portion of the receptor organ. This simple mechanism would produce a movement in which the sowbug would orient itself toward any illuminating light. The amount of demand for orientation, a function of maintenance schedule, is an internal variable which would create orienting movements toward the light on some occasions but not others. The effects of previous situations $(\Sigma(OBO))$ is represented in the *hypothesis area* of the bug.

The *progression distribution* represents the motor tendencies of the bug dependent on the orienting distribution and the hypothesis. Tolman suggests that with a few more assumptions and further complications of design we would have a valuable model of simple animal behavior.

MODELS FROM NEUROPHYSIOLOGY Whereas Tolman proceeded to build his model on the basis of observable data obtained from his research with rats and his theory of behavior, other men have developed models based on data and theory in neurophysiology.

Probably the neurophysiological observation most widely used in connection with model building is the *all-or-none law*. This law asserts that if a neuron fires, it does so to its maximum potentiality. This is seen as analogous to a simple electric circuit which is either open or closed. If this analogy is valid, could we not build a complete electronic model of a brain and study it as it learns, behaves, and even becomes emotional?

W. Grey Walter discussed the difficulties involved in building a model of the nervous system proceeding from the all-or-none law [18]. After presenting the problems involved in manufacturing even a single artificial nerve fiber, he goes on to say:

> Supposing a sufficient number of these simplest of imitation nerve fibers were constructed, [more] millions of cubic feet of warehousing would be required. . . .
> At this point we might have to consider cost. A cell with one fiber conceivably made for a dime—in all, say $1,000,000,-000. Wiring connection 10^{20} of them, at about two cents each, say $2,000,000,000,000,000,000. Power required would be at least a million kilowatts, even if the transistor crystal were used instead of the prodigal thermionic tube; the human brain runs on 25 watts. The cost would be incalculable. And the comparable cost of producing a first-class living brain? Twenty thousand dollars? [18, p. 117].

Walter estimates the warehouse space necessary for the 10,000,000,000 artificial brain cells at $1\frac{1}{2}$ million cubic feet!

For these and other reasons, Walter sees the road to producing a working electronic model with anything like a similar number of units as closed. On the other hand he suggests that an understanding of the functions of the brain may be based not on the number of units involved but in the richness of interconnections between units.

Machines built by Walter support his view that the richness of interconnections must be one of the more important structural characteristics of the nervous systems of man and animals. Figure 6.12 shows his *Speculatrix* on its way "home." Let us reflect upon some of the characteristics Walter built into this disturbingly alive machine [adapted from 18, pp. 126–128]:

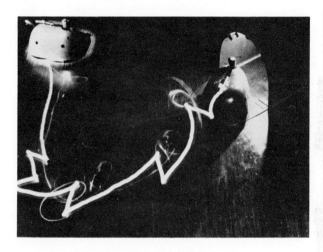

FIG. 6.12. *Speculatrix returning to its hutch.* Reprinted from The Living Brain *by W. Grey Walter. By permission of W. W. Norton & Company, Inc. Copyright © 1963, 1953 by W. W. Norton & Company, Inc., and Gerald Duckworth & Co., Ltd.*

1. *Parsimony.* The machine is very simple in construction. Two cells function as nerve cells. There are only two receptors: a photoelectric cell and an electrical contact serving as a touch receptor.

2. *Speculation.* It is always active, never at rest unless recharging batteries. Since it is always on the move it appears to be exploring. "Like the restless creatures in a drop of pond water, it bustles around in a sense of swooping curves, so that in an hour it will investigate several square feet of ground."

3. *Tropisms, Positive and Negative.* Speculatrix moves toward lights of moderate intensities. When an adequate light signal is presented it stops its exploratory operations and moves toward the light source. The photoelectric-cell eye at the front of the machine is continually scanning the horizon for light signals. Obstacles and very bright lights are repellent to this device.

4. *Discernment.* When an obstacle is met during the pursuit of an attractive light, the light temporarily loses its attractiveness. After the obstacle has been dealt with, the light becomes attractive again.

5. *Optima.* The machine seeks optimal conditions, not maximal. For example, it seeks only moderate intensity lights.

6. *Self- and Mutual Recognition.* The "animal" will be attracted to its own lead light reflected from a mirror. It will approach this light, but a circuit of the machine then extinguishes the light. The "animal" then is no longer attracted to the mirror. But since the photoelectric cell is no longer receiving the reflected input, it turns the head lamp back on. Then the machine is attracted again to the mirror. "The creature therefore, lingers before a mirror, flickering, twittering and jigging like a clumsy Narcissus" [18, p. 128]. The machines tend to group together by their tropic reactions to each other's head lamps, unless disturbed by external stimulation. In such a group the individual becomes alternately a positive or negative stimulus for others. It acts as an approachable head lamp at one time, but an obstacle at the next.

7. *Internal Stability.* In Fig. 6.12 we saw Speculatrix returning to the "hutch." The machines are built in such a way that the light of the hutch is *too* bright when its batteries are fully charged, but becomes attractive when the batteries are run down. Thus, the search for moderation in light stimulation "gives way to appetites" when the energy of the Speculatrix system is depleted.

Walter planned many but not all of the behaviors exhibited by his mechanical prodigies. The headlights were added to inform observers when the steering mechanism was on. Yet these pilot lights made possible the behaviors which could be interpreted as self-recognition and social behavior on the part of a group of the machines.

Furthermore, Walter was able to build a *black box* which has many of the same properties of real animals during learning. He called it the *conditioned reflex analogue,* or CORA for short. This machine was primarily a way of storing information so that it could be used in the future. When CORA was grafted on to Speculatrix, Walter produced a machine that could learn; he called it Docilis.

By having a whistle precede a moderate intensity light for several trials the new creature came to approach the whistle.

Used in another way the whistle could come to mean punishment-will-follow by pairing the whistle with a kick to the shell. Soon, Docilis came to avoid the area of a room associated in the past with a whistle.

In watching these "nut-and-bolt beasts" during the whistle-means-dodge training, Walter noticed an unplanned electronic phenomena. The memory circuits in the machine became reactivated with every presentation of the whistle, something that had not occurred when the machine had been trained under the whistle-means-light program. As a result, the avoidance behavior caused by the kick remained almost perfectly intact despite lack of further kicks! The whistle-means-light response disappeared in a relatively few trials after the light was no longer presented following the whistle. The persistence of the whistle-punishment behavior was unpredicted but very much like the results obtained with dogs trained to make responses to avoid high-intensity electrical shocks. These real animals continued to make responses for a considerable period of time without additional shocks [19].

The dodge response reactivated the memory trace in Docilis and this was responsible for the perpetuation of the learned response. Does an analogous mechanism exist in animals? Unfortunately we do not know enough about the physiological bases of learning or memory to decide, but certainly the findings of the reactivated memory trace in Docilis are suggestive of lines for future research.

Many other modifications of the basic machines have been and will be made with the result of greater and greater approximation to animal reactions. These may result in new ideas of how man behaves. Is Walter only investigating what happens in various kinds of models or what *may* be happening in the living brain? As Walter put it: "Of course we are considering both, hoping that the explicit clarity of the first will illuminate the implicit obscurity of the second" [8, p. 150].

MODELS AND THEORIES Models like Docilis and the schematic sowbug are, after all, merely a mechanical demonstration of an implemented theory of behavior. In current usage the term *model* is merely a synonym for *theory* [20]. For example, Hull's theory can, at least in part, be translated into a mechanical model as he showed in his presidential address to the American Psychological Association in the 1930s. Today, the types of models (theories) of behavior being constructed are more elaborate and sophisticated than ever before. They make use primarily of mathematical language, which is less ambiguous in the definition of terms and in syntactic structure than are natural languages, and more suited for use in modern calculating machines (computers). All scientists are becoming more and more aware of the power of mathematics in their fields. It is no surprise that modern theories of the learning process are formulated in mathematical languages.

Spence In a sense, Hull's model belongs at the head of any list of mathematic models of learning. Given his list of symbolic terms ($_sH_R$, D, K, etc.) and his rules for combined terms ($_sE_R = {_sH_R} \times D \times K \times V \times J$, etc.), one can know the nature of his theory. The theory or model is completely described. To use the theory one need only interpret the terms. Again, rules for this are provided. For example, the value of $_sH_R$ can be derived knowing only the number of reinforced trials in the training situations. Newer formulations of the Hull type of model have been presented by Spence [21].

Spence's recasting of learning theory has eliminated many inadequacies of Hull's theory. Through the years it was found that many facts of behavior were not predictable from the earlier formulas. The result of Spence's work is two models of learning. One is to be applied in classical conditioning situations, where the animal is trained to make a conditioned defensive response like lifting a paw when it is shocked, when a *CS* is presented. In such situations learning to respond to the *CS* is determined by the variables given in this formula:

$$R = D \times H - I_n$$

where D = function of the strength of the painful stimulus (shock)

H = joint function of strength of the shock and number of training trials where shock has been used

I_n = function of number of training trials on which *CS* was presented but animal was not shocked

On the other hand, learning to make a specific response for a positive incentive is supposed to follow quite different rules. The formula governing this kind of learning is

$$R = f(D + K) \times H - I_n$$

where H = function of number of training trials received by individual whether reinforced or not

D = function of time of deprivation

K = joint function of magnitude of reinforcement and number of reinforcements

I_n = function of number of times response has not been followed by a reinforcement, given a number of reinforcement trials

If this formula is compared with Hull's, a number of differences can be observed. Principally, these have to do with the additive rather than multiplicative relationships between drives and incentives, and the nature of the inhibitory variable I_n. Inhibition of a response is thought to occur when an animal has received reinforcements in a goal area but does not find them there on subsequent trials. This produces a frustration effect which acts to inhibit the response.

The improvements made by Spence are important since they allow much greater accuracy in the prediction of behavior. On the other hand, this line of theory building is but one of many possible methods of formulating the learning processes. Other methods have been developed and offer promise of even greater usefulness in understanding behavior.

Stimulus-sampling models An increasing number of psychologists are working to develop theorems and formulas which relate changes in responses produced by reinforcement or non-reinforcement. The complete elaboration of such theories are beyond the scope of this book. However, in the next few paragraphs we will attempt to provide a general discussion of the nature of these new directions in learning theories.

The mathematically formulated learning theories deal with three types of events: *responses, stimuli, reinforcing events*.

RESPONSES. All behavior which can be made by the subject in the experimental situation is classified into mutually exclusive and exhaustive categories. In so far as the theory is concerned this means that all the varieties of behavior which can be exhibited by the subject are brought under one of the classifications and that there is no overlap in the classifications. Since the experimental situations used by theorists must be capable of straightforward interpretation, response categories such as "a turn into right alley" or "a turn into left alley" of a **T** maze are used. In other words only simple learning situations are used where the response categories represent "either-or" types of behavior. The classes of available responses are considered to represent a mathematic collection or set.

STIMULI. An organism's stimulus condition is determined by the nature of its environment and its internal characteristics. All the stimulating conditions, or the environment, may arouse a large number of stimulus-conditions and the collection of all of these constitute a set. The elements of this mathematic set are often called stimulus elements.

REINFORCING EVENTS. It is well known that the probability of a response can be changed by presenting the individual with certain stimuli (for example, food given to a hungry animal). These stimuli are called reinforcements, as we know. For the present purposes, the nature of reinforcement is not important. Reinforcements are presumed to effect the probabilities of elements of the response set given the occurrance of elements from the stimulus set. Once again, the types of reinforcements are presumed susceptible to classification into a set of all such conditions.

Learning is defined as the changes in the probabilities of elements of the response set which come from the training trials of the individual in the situation. Every trial begins with the introduction of specific (and constant) changes in the environment, a response of the individual, and ends with one of the reinforcement outcomes. If other things are constant, the changes in response probabilities are believed to be determined by the reinforcement conditions.

In most models the changes in response probabilities are presumed to be a linear function of the probabilities existing on the preceding trial. By this we mean only that the probability of a response, X, is changed by a mathematically linear transformation by the reinforcement conditions. In other words, if the probability of response. X is P_x on trial 17, and if the response is reinforced, the probability of the response occurring on trial 18 will be increased by an amount predictable from a linear equation.

$$y = ax + b \text{ (basic model of linear equation)}$$

If y is used to represent Px on trial 18, it would be predicted as the sum of a constant factor, b, plus a multiplication operation a upon P_x of trial 17, x. The actual form of the equation depends upon specific assumptions of the mathematical model being used.

RULES OF LEARNING. One form of linear learning models involves the assumption of random sampling of stimulus elements on every trial [22, 23]. The environmental circumstances are assumed to supply a set of stimulus elements, but only a portion of this set is available for conditioning on any given trial. This portion is called the stimulus sample. They are those stimulus elements which are "available" to become completely associated with any response made with them if it is followed by a reinforcement. The learning, or association, formed on any one trial is complete and absolute. (In the theory of Bush and Mosteller [24] the conditioning of stimulus elements to the response is not assumed to be of an all-or-nothing character, but to proceed by gradual increments.)

The performance of the organism depends upon the extent to which the elements of the stimulus set become conditioned to a response. On every trial on which the reinforced response occurs in the experimental circumstances, more stimulus elements become associated with the response. In some models the number of stimulus elements sampled on each trial is assumed to be constant, while in other models different numbers of stimulus elements can be sampled.

Thus, the performance of the individual will show gradual increases in the probability of occurrence of the reinforced response, owing to the increasing number of stimulus elements associated with the response even though the mathematical theory asserts one-trial conditioning between individual stimulus elements and the response.

The stimulus elements sampled on any given trial are likely to be different from those sampled on any other trial. In Fig. 6.13 the elements sampled on trial 17 contain a combination of elements previously associated with the response A_1 (filled circles) and those associated with the response A_2 (open circles). Assuming the response A_1 was made and reinforced, all elements sampled on that trial would be associated with this response. Therefore, on trial 18 there would be more stimulus elements available for sampling which have been conditioned to response A_1 than previously. However, fluctuations in the elements selected for sampling, presumably by a random process, would make for fluctuations in the actual response produced by the animal, even though response A_1 was associated with more stimulus elements through the previous reinforcement. Thus in Fig. 6.13 two possible sampling outcomes are

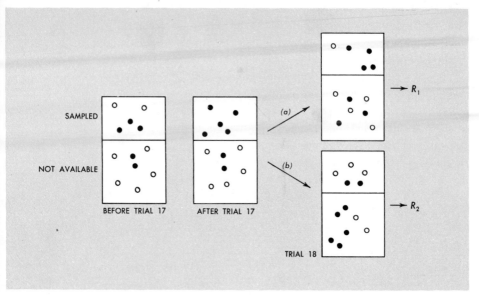

SAMPLED

NOT AVAILABLE

BEFORE TRIAL 17   AFTER TRIAL 17   TRIAL 18

FIG. 6.13.   *Schematic representation of stimulus-sampling theory.*
Total set of stimulus elements are represented by rectangles.

shown. In one case response A_1 would occur, and in the other response A_2 on trial 18. This aspect of the theory provides an explanation of the inconsistent behavior of animals during training.

The development of mathematical theories of learning is in an early stage. Interest is growing in this area of psychology, however, and ever-increasing interest can be expected. At present, several interesting contributions in this area are readily available to interested and mathematically prepared students, for example, papers by W. K. Estes, C. J. Burke, and R. C. Atkinson [25].

Reservations about the use of models   Despite the enchanting lures of model building, whether mathematical or mechanical, there are dangers inherent in embracing them unqualifiedly. Chapanis [26] has pointed out some of these dangers for us. A brief list of a few dangers would include the following:

Models lead us to over generalize about behavior. We tend to accept the theory offered as a model of the entire realm of behavior. Models are analogies restricted to a small segment of life, and their limitations should always be kept in mind.

Models lead us to make logical fallacies. If the consequence is confirmed, we tend to accept the premise. If a model predicts a given behavioral event, and it happens, this does not establish the truth value of the theory.

Model building may divert potential useful energy into non-productive directions. Chapanis suggests that the inherent "fun" in model building can take people away from the work of accumulating sound behavioral data, through experimentation. Furthermore, models may be constructed for trivial events. One might ask whether or not a toylike model, like some described earlier, actually helps us to understand behavior.

There is no doubt that model building, testing, and refinement will be major activities of many psychologists for a long time to come. Whether the current work is premature cannot be decided except by history. The enthusiasm for formal theory construction is not shared by all psychologists, even those working in the area of learning. Major contributions in the area of learning have been made by many individuals, for example, B. F. Skinner of Harvard, whose work is of a much different sort than that which has been so far discussed.

The Contributions of B. F. Skinner

Skinner is convinced that psychology should concentrate its efforts upon the accumulation of knowledge through experimentation rather than in the construction of theories. Theories are often justified by the fact that they lead protagonists and antagonists to do experiments to support their positions. But Skinner believes that experiments designed to test predictions from a specific theory are wasteful. He would prefer to explore the changes in responses which result from changes made in the situation.

TWO TYPES OF LEARNING SITUATIONS Since for Skinner the appropriate study by psychologists is the relation between situational change and response change, it is important to study the characteristics of learning situations. In general, Skinner distinguishes two types of learning. One is represented by the classical conditioning situation of Pavlov. Typically, a stimulus to which a response would be conditioned (CS) was paired with a stimulus which always *elicited* a response. We call this innately effective stimulus the US and the associated response the UR.

257

Pavlov argued that the *US-UR* association was *reflexive* in that the *US* always affected the organism in such a way as to evoke the response. These responses are termed *elicited responses*. As a general rule, he believed the study of elicited responses to be less important for understanding complex behavior than the study of responses which are not reflexively evoked.

One paramount feature of naturally occurring behavior is the large number of responses for which there seems to be no eliciting stimulus. The responses which an animal or person produces which are not unequivocally tied to certain stimuli are called *emitted responses* or *operant behavior*. They constitute a second type of learning. The essential observation about operant behavior (emitted behavior) is that it can be made more likely to occur in the situation by appropriate use of reinforcement.

It is possible for an experimenter to watch an animal and reinforce certain behavior through devices controlled by a push-button or other switch. The button could be connected to a food-releasing mechanism in the box which delivers a food pellet to the animal. With experimenter-operated devices Skinner can train a pigeon in what would appear as marvelously complex behavior in a matter of minutes. Behavior is shaped toward the desired response by a process called successive approximation. To train a pigeon to turn around, a reinforcement is given when the first small turning movement is emitted. This response usually will occur again soon. This time the reinforcement is applied after the animal has turned a little further. After a while, the reinforcing stimulus is presented only after a half or three-quarter turn is made. A few minutes later reinforcement is given only when a full turn is made. The whole training process takes but a few minutes and testifies to the efficacy of properly controlled reinforcements for learning.

REINFORCEMENT EMPIRICALLY DEFINED   Earlier we emphasized the distinction between Thorndike and Hull in their use of the word *reinforcement*. Thorndike spoke of a "satisfying state of affairs" whereas Hull referred to a reduction of S_D (drive stimuli). To this date there has been no substantial agreement in definitions of reinforcement which try to explain the nature of reinforcement. Many learning specialists have settled for a rather restricted definition of reinforcement which we may call the *empirical definition*. This restricted definition merely says that a reinforcement is a stimulus which when presented after a response will make the response more likely to occur the next time the person or animal is in the same situation. Reinforcement is defined as the increase in probability that the reinforced response will occur in the future, such as we found in the stimulus-sampling theories. This type of definition presents us with the difficult job of identifying which stimuli will act as reinforcers in a complex situation. It will surprise no one to learn that food can serve as a potent reinforcement to the hungry organism.

Reinforcements are used to guide, or shape, emitted behavior. The operation is simple. The experimenter waits until the response to be studied is emitted. Then a reinforcement is given promptly. The response tends to occur more and more frequently as reinforcements continue. Thus, the behavior of the organism is shaped by the experimenter through his distribution of reinforcements. One of the prime considerations of Skinner's view is that the experimenter must be passive until the response is produced by the subject. When the particular response does occur, the experimenter becomes active and produces the reinforcing stimulus as quickly as possible following the response.

A PROBLEM IN EXPERIMENTS Many of the tasks assigned to subjects in learning experiments produce data which must be examined in terms of what a group (of animals or people) does. The experimental results are reported as statistical descriptions of all the animals in the group. Many times the data coming from such group descriptions look regular and "smooth," whereas the behavior of the individual is neither regular nor smooth. To focus this problem consider the artificial data presented in Fig. 6.14.

In this figure the hypothetical data obtained from four animals learning a complex maze are illustrated at the left. Each animal makes a large number of errors getting to the goal in the maze early in training, but as the trials progress there occurs a point at which there is a sudden drop in the time required to navigate the maze. Furthermore, each animal shows fluctuations in speeds of maze running from trial to trial, before and after the rapid improvement in performance.

The curve on the right side is merely the average performance of the subjects. For each trial the number of errors made by all animals were added and divided by 4. The result is a curve showing gradual rather than abrupt improvement.

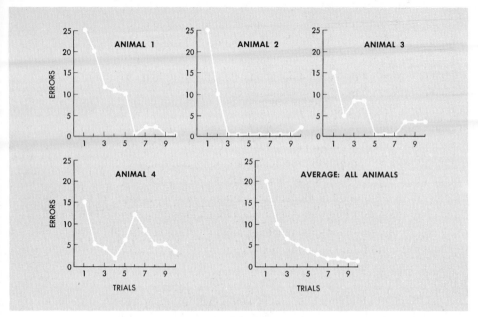

FIG. 6.14. *Graphic demonstration of the possibility that average behavior derived from a group of animals may not describe the behavior of any of the individuals in the group (based on hypothetical data). Errors in maze learning are plotted on the y axis, and the number of trials on the x axis.*

The trial-to-trial fluctuation has been eliminated. The graph of the group data does not typify the behavior of any animal in this hypothetical experiment. This example illustrates some of the possible misinterpretations of data when they are combined from all members of a group of subjects. This should not be taken to indicate that one should never use grouped data, but rather that one should be sure that the grouped data reflect what the individual subjects were doing.

THE OPERANT CONDITIONING BOX Skinner feels strongly that statistical reports of group behavior are too often misleading and that behavioral measures should be regular and reliable reports of the activities of individuals. The data obtained from *operant conditioning boxes* (sometimes called *Skinner boxes*) seem to fit his requirements best. The basic requirement of any operant box is there must be a lever that can be depressed. This depression activates mechanisms which deliver food or other reinforcements. Naturally, the bar or lever in the box does not elicit an immediate pressing response, but through accidental contact with the bar it will be depressed and a reinforcement given to the animal. Then this bar-pressing response will become shaped by subsequent reinforcements administered by the subject without interference of the experimenter. A photograph of a typical operant conditioning box is presented in Fig. 6.15. Animals are usually trained while under a food or water deprivation schedule with food pellets or small amounts of water as incentives or reinforcers. Automatic response-recording devices are connected to the box so that a continuous recording of the depressions of the lever can be made. The recording device moves a pen or writing instrument across paper at a constant rate. As the bar is depressed, the pen moves higher on the paper. If no responses are being made, the pen will make a horizontal line. The more responses made, the faster the line will ascend. A record obtained from an animal in an operant conditioning box is presented in Fig. 6.16.

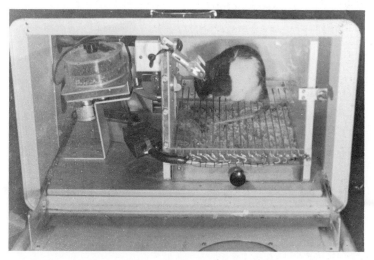

FIG. 6.15. *Rat in operant conditioning chamber depresses short bar in wall which activates feeding mechanism and causes food pellet to drop into receptacle in chamber.*

For Skinner, there are two sufficiently reliable measures of behavior and both of these can be represented in cumulative recordings. One measure is the rate of responding, which is indicated by the slope of the line as it ascends swiftly or slowly. The other is the number of responses which will be produced by the subject after no more reinforcements are applied. This is usually referred to as the number of responses from the last

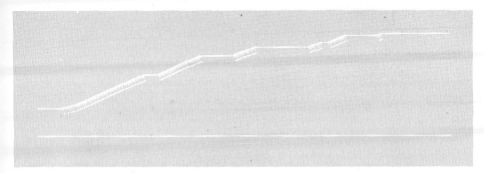

FIG. 6.16. *Sample record of animal under continuous reinforcement in conditioning chamber. Each time bar is depressed, recording mark is made slightly higher on the paper. The faster the rate of bar pressing, the steeper will be the slope of the record.*

reinforced response to that time when the animal fails to respond.

SCHEDULES OF REINFORCEMENT   In training an animal, we can reinforce it every time it makes the response we wish it to learn. On the other hand, we can ask what would be the effect of not reinforcing *every* response but reinforcing some fraction of the responses? Would the animal just make fewer responses? Would it take longer to train the animal? What would happen if we stopped reinforcing the animal entirely after training it on a schedule where we have only rewarded the response at periodic intervals?

Given Skinner's use of an empirical definition of a reinforcer, we can investigate the effects upon behavior of applying a reinforcer after each and *every* response, *continuous reinforcement,* or after only some of the responses, *intermittent reinforcement.* There are, of course, many ways we could apply reinforcements; for example, we could reinforce alternate responses or reinforce the bar-press response every four minutes. However, there are four main intermittent schedules of reinforcements that have been studied.

1. *Fixed ratio (FR).* A response is reinforced upon completion of a fixed number of responses counted from the preceding reinforcement. The word *ratio* refers to the ratio of responses to reinforcement.
2. *Variable ratio (VR).* Similar to fixed ratio except that reinforcements are scheduled according to a random series of ratios having a given mean and lying between arbitrary values.

3. *Fixed interval (FI)*. The first response occurring after a given interval of time, measured from preceding reinforcement, is reinforced.
4. *Variable interval (VI)*. Similar to a fixed interval except that reinforcements are scheduled according to a random series of intervals having a given mean and lying between arbitrary values [27, p. 5].

Combinations of these basic types could be made too. All of these intermittent or partial reinforcement techniques are in contrast to the two continuous schedules of reinforcement: reinforcing every response and reinforcing no responses (extinction training).

Fixed-ratio schedules In the fixed-ratio schedule we find an almost astounding fact. As the ratio of responses to reinforcements increases, the rate of responding also *increases*. An animal can be trained so that it makes more and more responses with fewer and fewer reinforcements.

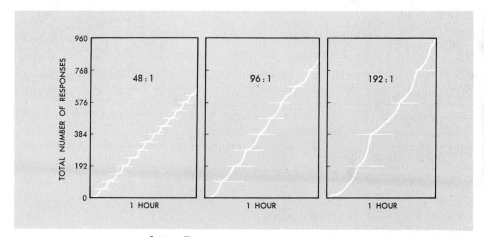

FIG. 6.17. *Rates of rat response on three fixed-ratio schedules. Adapted from B. F. Skinner,* The Behavior of Organisms, *New York: Appleton-Century-Crofts. Copyright © 1938 by Appleton-Century-Crofts, Inc. All rights reserved.*

Training an animal under an intermittent fixed-ratio schedule results in a more rapidly ascending response record than training with continuous reinforcement. Under this type of schedule the animal must produce *n* number of responses before a reinforcement will occur. As the animal moves to higher and higher rates from original training with continuous reinforcement, the *rate* of responding increases. Figure 6.17 [27, p. 152] shows

263

rates of responding for three different fixed-ratio schedules. The rate of responding is greatest in the ratio of 1 reinforcement for every 192 responses.

After each reinforcement (represented by a horizontal line on the curve) response rate slows down. This results in a scalloplike section of the curve between reinforcements. In part, this represents the time taken by the subject to ingest and chew the food but something else is going on too. For example, it should take no longer for the animal to ingest the food on one schedule rather than another. The food is the same size. At the

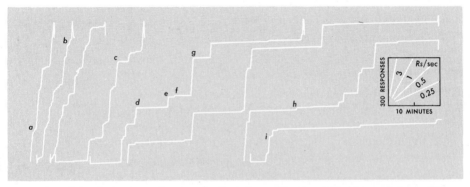

FIG. 6.18. *Cumulative records of rat undergoing extinction following training with fixed-ratio (60:1) schedule. Top of left records are continuous with bottom of right records. Note that periods when no responses are made are longer during extinction, but that otherwise rate of response remains high. From C. B. Ferster and B. F. Skinner,* Schedules of Reinforcement, *New York: Appleton-Century-Crofts. Copyright © 1957 by Appleton-Century-Crofts, Inc. All rights reserved.*

greater ratios the period between the reinforcement and the beginning of the new response period is greatest.

When the response acquired with a fixed-ratio schedule is no longer reinforced, the curves reveal that the decrease of the response rate comes about through progressive lengthening of these plateaus of no responding. When the animal responds it responds at a high rate but the periods of responding do not last long. This is illustrated in records obtained from pigeon research with the Skinner box as presented in Fig. 6.18 [28, p. 152].

One of the reasons for the high response rates obtained by the use of fixed-ratio reinforcement schedules may be that the rate of response itself is being reinforced. During the fixed-ratio schedules the animals tend to be responding at a high rate when the reinforcement occurs.

Fixed-interval schedules   Fixed-interval reinforcement refers to the administration of the reinforcing stimulus following a response occurring after some definite period following the last reinforcement. For example, a reinforcement might follow the first response to occur after a period of one minute from the preceding reinforcement. A minimum period of time must have elapsed and a response must be made by the animal. Generally, lower rates of responding are found with the fixed-interval than with the fixed-ratio schedule, and the longer the period of time between reinforcements the lower will be the rate of response. As with the fixed-ratio schedules there are also lapses in the response rate following each reinforcement, producing a scalloplike effect in the recorded records.

Variable-Interval and ratio schedules   These two more complicated schedules can change the response rates. The exact effects of the variable interval and ratio programs of reinforcement depend to a great extent on the past training histories and prior number of reinforcements given under different schedules. Generally, we may say that some of these manipulations result in response rates which do not show the pauses following reinforcement of the fixed schedules. High rates can be maintained throughout the training of the subjects.

Resistance to extinction   The number of responses which are emitted by subjects after all reinforcements have been stopped is the subject's *resistance to extinction*. The greater number of responses emitted the stronger the resistance.

An animal's resistance to extinction can be increased through intermittent, or partial, reinforcement schedules beyond that which can be obtained through training with continuous reinforcement.

Why do the partial reinforcement schedules affect the subjects so that they emit much greater numbers of responses when reinforcements are eliminated? Skinner is satisfied to report that they do. His interest is in determining the effect of various training procedures and manipulations on his two measures (response rate and number of responses to response cessation). We have only scratched the surface of the ways in which he has manipulated the many possible variables. For example, what are the effects of novel stimuli placed in the box? What is the effect of creating an emotional disturbance in the subject? What is the effect of giving the animal a "clock" to use in gearing itself to the fixed-interval procedures? All these and many more are discussed by Ferster and Skinner in their compendium of research [28].

A general summary of the findings in experiments using various schedules of reinforcement would look something like this:

Acquisition: Continuous reinforcement creates faster learning of the response than intermittent reinforcement.

Response rate: Faster rates with fixed-ratio schedules than fixed-interval schedules. Rate on fixed-interval schedules dependent on frequency of reinforcement.

Resistance to extinction: Intermittent schedules produce greater numbers of responses during extinction.

Possible explanations of extinction effects One explanation of the greater resistance to extinction of the animals trained under partial reinforcement schedules is that the subjects have a more difficult task in recognizing just when reinforcements are eliminated. If animals are trained with continuous reinforcement the transition is abrupt when depression of the lever fails to produce a reinforcement. When trained under an intermittent schedule the animals have had experience with situations when the depression of the lever would not result in the appearance of food. If the animal is on a large fixed-ratio schedule (e.g., 48 to 1), it would take longer for the animal to discover the change in conditions. This type of explanation has been generally referred to as the *discrimination-failure* explanation. The animals fail to discriminate between acquisition and extinction phases of the experiment.

While acceptable at a common-sense level, this explanation is vulnerable to the objection that it depends too much on thinking or cognition. Some psychologists believe this kind of explanation brings back mentalistic, nonbehavioristic terms to psychology. Many people who do not object to the use of mentalistic concepts in the human are not willing to be quite so mentalistic with the rat or pigeon.

Other psychologists are of the opinion that the results of intermittent reinforcement in prolonging the period of responding during extinction training can be explained if we view the "response" differently. They say we should look at the response trained under a fixed-ratio schedule as the total series of n responses animals must make between reinforcements. Then during extinction, the total responses should be counted in terms of the number of packages of n responses emitted.

Still another way of explaining the intermittent-reinforcement results is through the use of the concept of secondary reinforcement. If the bar-press response has acquired secondary reinforcing properties, then each bar depression adds to the habit strength of the bar-press response. Because of the high response rates, animals under the intermittent schedules have built up greater habit strengths than the animals which receive primary reinforcements more often. Greater habit strength should lead to greater resistance to extinction.

There are data to support and refute all of these interpretations. We cannot say which explanation will be best in the long run. At this time it is best to side with Skinner who simply reports the data and leaves the interpretation to the future.

RELATION OF PARTIAL REINFORCEMENT TO HUMAN BEHAVIOR

One of the reasons intermittent reinforcement is a lively area of psychological research is that outside the laboratory reinforcements are usually provided in an intermittent fashion. Continuous reinforcement is more the rule of the laboratory than of society. Mother's reactions to a child's behavior are seldom consistent time after time. Sometimes other things are going on in the household that make a reinforcement, positive or negative, impossible to provide. The soup may be boiling over or the phone ringing as junior emits the given response. If the behavior is undesirable, it may be that negative reinforcement is withheld because another one of "mother's angels" is doing something even worse. In any case, whether we deal with reinforcements of a positive or negative nature, whether we conceive them as physical or verbal, we can easily see that they are usually applied on less than a continuous basis. From our discussion we know that any response learned or performed on an intermittent basis is difficult to extinguish.

Punishment   Reflection on the usual patterns of social learning leads us to recognize the emphasis placed on attempts to "stamp out" undesirable acts through punishment. When a child does something undesirable, we sometimes resort to a slap, spank, or yell. We previously discussed the law of effect made famous by Thorndike. Originally he thought of positive rewards as stamping-in S-R connections and negative rewards as stamping-out S-R connections. Later, on the basis of studies

267

using negative verbal stimuli (rather weak punishments), he concluded that punishment had little effect on eliminating undesirable behavior. Hull's theory asserts that responses are learned on the basis of a reduction of drive stimuli (S_D). Drive stimuli are produced by punishment. According to Hull's view, responses most closely and consistently associated with the *reduction of aversive drive stimuli* become learned. Skinner's definition of negative reinforcers is much the same. For him, responses can be learned by their association with the termination of negative reinforcers, which are defined as stimuli that adversely affect the rate of responding.

Many things may act to reduce response rates. The presentation of novel stimuli in the responding situation, motives and emotions of certain kinds, and punishment can act to depress response rates. When a response rate is depressed by punishment, the organism can be trained to emit another type of response. This is the important effect of punishment in the Skinner analysis of behavior. If we use punishment at all, we should be careful to train the person or animal in another way of responding while the rate of emission of the objectionable response is lowered.

Through the number of reinforcement and training schedules a certain *operant strength* is built up in the organism. Skinner would define this concept behaviorally as the number of responses emitted during the extinction period. Punishment only acts upon the response rate, *not* the operant strength. Therefore, even though we punish a response, we would expect the same *total number of responses to be emitted* ultimately. This would lead to the punished animal's responding *longer* than an animal not punished following the removal of the positive reinforcement. To eliminate responses, we must have the subject emit all of the responses which constitute the operant strength without reinforcement. The faster they are emitted during extinction, the sooner the animal will stop making the response entirely. As mentioned above, if we depress the rate by punishment, it will take longer for the animal to reduce the operant strength of the response. In Fig. 6.19 we see data from an experiment by Estes in which this prolongation of response is demonstrated [29].

The group of animals punished early in the extinction period show a depression in rate which does not last long. When the punishment is no longer applied (days 2 and 3), we observe the nonpunished animals producing fewer responses than the animals in the punished groups. This in a way summarizes many of the conclusions about the effect of punishment. Punishment can depress the rate of response, but it does not effect the total number of responses that will be emitted during the extinction training. This should serve as a warning to us. *By punishment it is possible to perpetuate those very responses we wish to eliminate.*

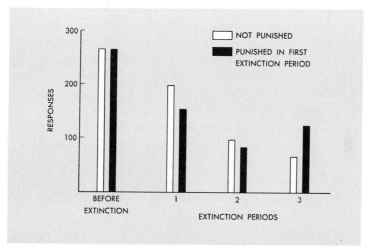

FIG. 6.19. *Effects of punishment on extinction. Note that group receiving punishment shows earlier decline in response rate, but maintains a higher rate in third extinction period. Adapted from E. R. Hilgard.* Theories of Learning. *New York, Appleton-Century-Crofts, 1953. Data from W. K. Estes. An experimental study of punishment.* Psychol. Monogr., *1944,* **57**. *By permission of E. R. Hilgard, W. K. Estes, Appleton-Century-Crofts, and The American Psychological Association.*

Through the problem of punishment and the effects of intermittent reinforcements we have been moving very close to areas far removed from necessary restrictions of laboratory work. Skinner's interests range widely, and his work upon the basic learning processes has fathered one of the more remarkable educational supports developed in recent years.

The teaching machine   One fascinating and important educational innovation which stemmed from the work of Skinner, his colleagues, and students is the teaching machine. It is based on the belief that rapid learning depends upon having the student produce a large number of correct responses. The teaching machine was designed to present many short questions, one at a time. The student writes his answers in a space provided near the question. The material used in the machines is written in a way that makes it difficult for the student to answer incorrectly. A correct response serves as a reinforcement. If there is no reinforcement, there will be no change in the student's responses. From Skinner's point of view responses are acquired through positive reinforcement, and we know that this reinforcement must occur almost immediately following the response. Since acquisition is the important dimension of learning, a continuous schedule of reinforcement is used.

It is too early to make any definite conclusion about teaching machines even though most of the preliminary studies and reports have been favorable. Generally, students using the machines learn factual material faster than students working with traditional methods. It is likely that certain kinds of materials are more amenable to presentation by teaching machines than others. Areas of learning in which a student must master a considerable amount of factual material will undoubtedly be placed into teaching-machine forms early. Areas in which conceptual frameworks must be learned and in which there are alternate interpretations may turn out to be resistant to machine instruction.

Utopia   Watson, the early exponent of behaviorism in the United States, argued that all behavior is acquired. He believed that given enough power to control a person's development he could make him into almost any kind of person: a doctor, lawyer, beggar, or thief. This may be too extreme a position, yet Skinner believes that appropriately applied reinforcements are so potent that they could shape our lives in many important ways, and he suggests a possible "utopia" that could be produced with our current knowledge of the effects of positive reinforcement [30].

In summary: In the learning theories and models we have studied in this chapter, one finds the main American tradition in psychology. They have influenced all domains of psychological activity both theoretical and applied; they have fostered controversies, and, more important, they have led to careful examination of the behavior of men and animals in many situations. Perhaps Skinner is right, perhaps the same number of exploratory experiments conducted without theoretical basis would have produced more information about behavior; but on the other hand, without the incentive of personal commitment to a certain theory, experimenters would probably not have conducted as many experiments.

Furthermore, learning theories represent the attempts of man to understand the "why" of behavior. They represent attempts to explain—even though the explanations are not complete and will likely be judged as feeble attempts by history. Yet for most psychologists, it is creative theory building and testing which represent the exciting and absorbing facets of psychology as a basic science.

References

1. Underwood, B. J. *Experimental Psychology.* New York: Appleton-Century-Crofts, Inc., 1949.

2. Boring, E. G. *The History of Experimental Psychology.* New York: The Century Co., 1929.

3. Heidbreder, Edna. *Seven Psychologies.* New York: Appleton-Century-Crofts, Inc., 1933.

4. Pavlov, I. P. *Conditioned Reflexes* (Trans. G. V. Anrep.). New York: Dover Publications, Inc., 1960.

5. Guthrie, E. R. *The Psychology of Learning.* New York: Harper & Row, Publishers, Inc., 1935.

6. Rock, I., & Heimer, W. Further evidence of one-trial associative learning. *Amer. J. Psychol.,* 1959, **72,** 1–16.

7. Hull, C. L. *A Behavior System.* New Haven: Yale Univer. Press, 1952 (published posthumously).

8. Beck, E. C., & Doty, R. W. Conditioned flexion reflexes acquired during combined catalepsy and de-efferentation. *J. comp. physiol. Psychol.,* 1957, **50,** 211–216.

9. Karsten, A. Psychische Sättigung. *Psych. Forsch.,* 1928, **10,** 142–254. (Reported in Koffka, K. *Principles of Gestalt Psychology.* New York: Harcourt, Brace & World, Inc., 1935.)

10. Wolfle, J. B. Effectiveness of token rewards for chimpanzees. *Comp. psychol. Monogr.,* 1936, **12,** 1–72.

11. Harlow, H. F. The nature of love. *Amer. Psychol.,* 1958, **13,** 673–685.

12. Zimmerman, D. W. Durable secondary reinforcement. *Psychol. Rev.,* 1957, **64,** 373–383.

13. Lashley, K. S., & McCarthy, D. A. The survival of the maze habit after cerebellar injuries. *J. comp. Psychol.,* 1926, **6,** 423–433.

14. Tolman, E. C., & Honzik, C. H. Introduction and removal of reward and maze performance of rats. *Univer. Calif. Publ. Psychol.,* 1930, **4,** 257–275.

15. Tolman, E. C. The determiners of behavior at a choice point. In *Behavior and Psychological Man.* Berkeley: Univer. of California Press, 1958. (Originally published in *Psychol. Rev.,* 1938, **45,** 1–41.)

16. Tolman, E. C. Psychology versus immediate experience. *Phil. Sci.,* 1935, **2,** 356–380. Also in *Behavior and Psychological Man, op. cit.*

17. Tolman, E. C. Prediction of vicarious trial and error by means of the schematic sowbug. *Psychol. Rev.,* 1939, **46,** 318–336. Also in *Behavior and Psychological Man, op. cit.*

18. Walter, W. G. *The Living Brain.* New York: W. W. Norton & Company, Inc., 1953.

19. Solomon, R. L., & Wynne, L. C. Traumatic avoidance learning: acquisition in normal dogs. *Psychol. Monogr.,* 1953, **67,** 1–19.

20. Simon, H. A., & Newell, A. The uses and limitations of models. In L. D. White (Ed.), *The State of the Social Sciences.* Univer. Chicago Press, 1956.

21. Spence, K. W. The roles of reinforcement and non-reinforcement in simple learning. In K. W. Spence, *Behavior Theory and Learning.* Englewood Cliffs, N.J.: Prentice-Hall, Inc., 1960.

22. Estes, W. K. Toward a statistical theory of learning. *Psychol. Rev.,* 1950, **57,** 94–107.

23. Estes, W. K., & Burke, C. J. A theory of stimulus variability in learning. *Psychol. Rev.,* 1953, **60,** 276–86.

24. Bush, R. R., & Mosteller, F. *Stochastic Models for Learning.* New York: John Wiley & Sons, Inc., 1955.

25. Marx, M. H. (Ed.). *Theories in Contemporary Psychology.* New York: The Macmillan Company, 1963.

26. Chapanis, A. Men, machines, and models. *Amer. Psychologist,* 1961, **16,** 113–131.

27. Skinner, B. F. *The Behavior of Organisms.* New York: Appleton-Century-Crofts, 1938.

28. Ferster, C. B. and Skinner, B. F. *Schedules of Reinforcement.* New York: Appleton-Century-Crofts, Inc., 1958.

29. Estes, W. K. An experimental study of punishment. *Psychol. Monogr.,* 1944, **57,** 40 pp.

30. Skinner, B. F. *Walden Two.* New York: The Macmillan Company, 1948.

SEVEN VERBAL LEARNING AND HIGHER COGNITIVE FUNCTIONS

weak rough small cold fresh
strong smooth large hot stale

A most distinctive characteristic of man is his use of language. Therefore, it is essential that the student of psychology know the relationships and factors entering into verbal learning. Such knowledge is rather basic and fundamental in understanding the nature of man, himself.

In the preceding chapter, we reviewed some of the prominent theories of learning and behavior. As noted, they are based upon the associationistic doctrine which stems, in part, from the school of philosophy called British Associationism. We shall find that the theories of verbal learning and retention, as well as the experiments generated by them, are also dominated by associationistic theories. First, we shall learn some of the basic features of verbal behavior. In the sections to follow we shall study adult verbal learning and the related explanations of forgetting, based on the assumption of an interference between verbal responses. Finally, we shall consider some of the newer approaches to the higher mental processes which have developed from work in the field of communications.

Development of Speech

We are all aware that learning to speak precedes learning to write. A baby takes a long time to master vocal communication, and we communicate with spoken sounds long before we master the art of communication through written symbols. Written communications probably came long after man had learned how to depict objects symbolically through primitive art forms.

A baby begins learning vocal communications at birth. The birth cry is a reflexive response to a sudden increase in the carbon dioxide level in the blood occurring when the umbilical cord is cut. There is a momentary lag before the lungs begin to act. Many of the early vocal acts, such as crying, are presumed to be reflexive responses to bodily changes.

In the first four to five months the infant produces just about all of the speech sounds which have been found in the known languages. The infant must learn to reduce the number of speech sounds to those used in his culture. Over a period of time, the repertory of sounds a person can make becomes narrowed to the number found in his native language.

When a baby is being fed, held, or cuddled, he tends to produce sounds which are softer (e.g., open vowels) than those he makes when he is deprived of the bottle or support (e.g., explosive sounds and grunts). Thus, from early in life we note a relationship between the type of sound produced and the state of the organism.

Before six months of age the infant has begun to learn how to control his vocalizations. This means that the muscles of the diaphragm, tongue, and jaws and the parts of the nervous system controlling them have developed to the point where fine discriminative movements are possible.

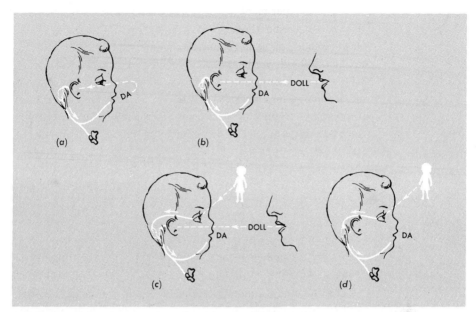

FIG. 7.1. *Stages in development of speech in infant: (1) random articulation of syllables, (2) evocation of same elements by speech sounds of others, (3) conditioning of sounds produced by others to object (doll), and (4) sight of doll produces sounds approximating "doll." From F. H. Allport.* Social Psychology. *Boston, Houghton Mifflin Company, 1924.*

Babbling and imitation After the fifth month, babies generally can be heard babbling. This refers to sounds like "uggle-uggle," "erdah-erdah," "bup-bup-bup," and other repetitive noises [1]. Babies babble when alone as well as when with others and tend to practice one sound sequence before moving on to another. Perhaps babbling affords the opportunity to master sets of muscle responses which will comprise the building blocks of later speech.

Babies learn to mimic the patterns of sounds they hear. After sufficient muscular and neural development, speech sounds created by others can be duplicated by the infant. The next step for the baby is to be able to create a pattern of sounds which he has heard in conjunction with a perceptual object. The object becomes associated with the sound created by someone else in its presence. This association provides the basis for the child's vocalization of the sound when the object alone is presented. An illustration of this phase of language learning is presented in Fig. 7.1. Here we find the behavioral origins of the verbal

275

acts called labeling. When we label an object, we attach a vocal or other specific response to a particular stimulus.

In all likelihood, labeling and many other varieties of verbal behavior are determined through timely reinforcements. Many psychologists agree that verbal behavior can be explained through the same kind of learning principles used to account for learning in animals. When an animal is placed for the first time in a experimental chamber (see pp. 260–262) in which a bar must be depressed to obtain a reinforcement, the behavior which depresses the bar can be readily inculcated through shaping. Behavior is shaped by means of judicial use of reinforcements. At first, slight movements toward the bar are reinforced. Next, only greater movements toward the bar are reinforced. Gradually, only the behaviors directly concerned with depressing the bar are reinforced. The experimenter is using a method of rewarding approximations to the final response.

Since children emit many kinds of sounds, the parents' job is to shape the child's verbal behavior so that only those responses remain which are significant in the culture. Watching parents with their children, one notices the shaping of sounds. The child's emitted response which is even a rough approximation to "Da-Da" in the presence of his father is subjected to a good bit of intensive shaping effort. Slowly, the rewarding behavior of the mother and father are withheld until "daddy" is a clear response.

Skinner believes that verbal behavior can be explained by extrapolations from his work with the empirical effects of reinforcements [2]. Whether or not all of the richness of human verbal behavior can be explained in terms of simple rules of reinforcement is a question which can not be answered at the present. Yet there is evidence that the rate of occurrence of specific verbal responses can be increased or decreased by rewarding behaviors on the part of others. In fact, the changes in verbal behavior induced by social rewards may occur without the individuals being aware of any such change [3]. The change in the rate of uttering words or word classes on the basis of reinforcing effects produced by others is called the *Greenspoon effect* after the experimenter reporting the result. The Greenspoon effect may be more complex than originally thought and the social rewards may act indirectly by inducing new sets of verbal habits [4].

Grammar   Once the ability to use labels and symbols is attained in childhood, vocabularies rapidly increase in size. We learn labels and symbols at a prodigious rate. However, even with a large vocabulary, language has not been mastered. Vocabulary is only part of language. The other part is the grammar of the language. To use or understand a language, we must know both the vocabulary and the grammatical rules. Only recently has there been much study of how the child develops knowledge of grammar, and much remains to be done [5]. It is interesting to note that most people can create perfectly good sentences in their language without being able to explicitly state the grammatical rules to which the sentences conform.

Spoken communication   The goal of speech is communication of a message from one person to another. We send vocal messages by patterns of sound waves generated by the expulsion of air across the vocal cords and through the oral cavity. No one knows just how many speech sounds the human can make. The set of sounds which are equivalent and can be used interchangeably to transmit meaning are called phonemes, and these can be thought of as the units of spoken languages. Phonemes differ from one language to another. They are the sounds which differentiate words or phrases of a language. In English we may consider them to be approximated by the sound of each consonant or vowel. Not all the different speech sounds are phonemes. There are many more distinguishable speech sounds than there are English phonemes.

We make speech sounds at a great rate. We can produce about 12.5 speech sounds every second when talking. Not all of these sounds carry information of significance for our messages, but they are units which could be used to transmit information. Information is transmitted through the use of sounds, signs and symbols, which have meaning or which elicit special kinds of responses within the perceiver.

The Sign and the Symbol

Most learning theories attempt to explain signs and symbols through the use of familiar concepts found in the study of stimulus-response learning. One could say that when Pavlov trained dogs to salivate to the sound of a metronome, the metronome acted as a signal for the introduction of food powder into the mouth. A red traffic light is a signal to stop, a green traffic light a signal to go. Animals and man both can learn to use signals.

SIGNALS FOR ANIMALS   With proper training animals can be taught to make responses which seem to involve the use of symbols. Even simple avoidance learning in a shuttle box can be interpreted as requiring symbolic activity. In the shuttle box a stimulus (*CS*) is presented some number of seconds (e.g., five seconds) before the floor of the box is electrified. If the animal runs to the other side of the box within five seconds after the stimulus is presented, it is not shocked. Why shouldn't we interpret the *CS* signal as a sign or a symbolic event? The sign in this illustration is that if a given behavior is not performed the subject will be subjected to a painful situation. If the animals can be trained to respond to signs such as this *CS* in a shuttle-box experiment then the use of signs is not a characteristic which distinguishes *man* from the rest of the animal world.

It can be argued that animals can learn to respond to signs, but only man can manipulate symbols. But what is the distinction between a sign and a symbol? As a basis for distinction we might consider that stimuli which function as signs have only one or a few associated responses. Symbols, on the other hand, are stimuli which elicit many responses in the perceiving organism. This suggests a distinction between signs and symbols which is of quantity rather than quality. This may be appropriate in as much as the chimpanzees who worked for the poker chips in Wolfe's experiment (pp. 238–239) acted as though they were manipulated objects which had symbolic value.

Psychologists have not agreed on how the words, *sign* and *symbol* are to be used. Some have used the two words as synonyms. Others have used the word *symbol* to refer to a sign which stands for other signs. The use of these words is defined by convention and theory. They are meaningful only by convention.

We may find a useful distinction between symbolic behavior and sign behavior in the observation that some stimuli can produce effects in many situations other than the original learning situation. Symbols can be used in new places and at new times. In addition they do not always act to produce one standard behavioral response. Signs merely represent learned

S-R connections manifested in behavior, symbols are something more than this.

At one time secondary reinforcements were described as symbolic incentives. Secondary reinforcers came to have the ability to change response rates in situations other than that of the original training because of their association with primary reinforcements. In fact in the experiment with the chimpanzees and poker chips we observed that the secondary reinforcing poker chips could elicit distress reactions when they were out of the animal's reach. Owing to their transituational effectiveness, the poker chips acted like symbols.

Many times it is difficult to decide whether or not stimuli are acting as signs, signals, or plain "old-fashioned" stimuli. Let us use this to underline the most important part of this problem: *A given stimulus can be a signal, sign, or symbol, depending on the theoretical position under consideration.* Again we must underscore that the evaluation of any definition of these terms must depend on the success of the whole theory and not a single definition in isolation.

STIMULUS GENERALIZATION *"Stimulus generalization"* describes the fact that stimuli other than the ones used in training can often elicit the same response. If we train a dog to salivate to a 1000 cycle tone and after conditioning is well established present a 1200 cycle tone, we are sure to obtain some saliva flow. Is this odd? In one way, we have not trained the dog on this new tone at all, and yet there has been some generalization of the salivary response to the 1200 cycle tone. The two tones are somewhat alike. Both are auditory stimuli and both are about the same loudness. Furthermore, they "sound" somewhat the same, although dogs can discriminate between the two tones.

Figure 7.2 shows curves of generalization of a learned response along a visual continuum. Visual stimuli nearest the wavelength used in establishing the response evoke the largest number of responses when tests for generalization are made. However, problems exist for any simple technique used for specifying the extent of physical similarities. For example, it has been shown that the slope of a pitch generalization curve is not uniform. Tones representing octave steps from the tone used for conditioning produce greater responsiveness than intermediate tones [7]. This implies that a tone one octave away from the original conditioning tone has "more similarity" to it than many tones which are in fact closer to it along a frequency dimension. *Primary* stimulus generalization refers to a generalization of responses to new stimuli based on *physical similarity*.

Stimulus generalization can be either a handicap or an asset. When a husband coming home late at night elicits the same responses as would a burglar breaking and entering, this may be maladaptive for the husband if the wife is armed with a shotgun.

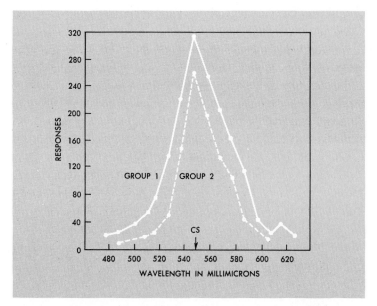

FIG. 7.2. *Stimulus generalization along visual-wavelength dimension in two groups of pigeons. Birds were trained to peck key illuminated by wavelength indicated on the x axis; and later tested by illuminating key with different wavelengths. Extent of generalization is reflected in height of response curves at different wavelengths. Adapted from N. Guttman. The pigeon and the spectrum and other perplexities.* Psychol. Repts., *1956, 2, 451–460.*

At first glance one might equate stimulus generalization with some kind of failure in discrimination. Perhaps our dog which salivated to the 1200 cycle tone for some reason failed to discriminate between it and the 1000 cycle tone. Yet, while there are instances when a failure of discrimination can explain some of the experimental results, Gibson [8] has shown that this can not be the entire explanation. She found that subjects who were best able to discriminate between stimuli in an early phase of her experiment were the very same ones who showed the greater amount of stimulus generalization later in the experiment.

It should be stressed that primary stimulus generalization is a phenomena which is found without specific training. It occurs on the basis of some prior similarity between the training stimuli and the stimuli to which the training generalizes.

Let us consider the following experiment. We train subjects to salivate when a red light is presented. We could do this by pairing the red light with the injection of a mildly acidic solution into the mouth. More humanely we might inject some food substance in the mouth. In either way we could achieve a conditioned response to the red light. Now we are in a position to perform our generalization experiment. As a test, we now say "red" or present the written words *red light,* to the subjects. Will this cause them to secrete saliva in the same way as flashing the red light did? Will this verbal symbol which stands for the light be effective through some kind of generalization? From a number of studies in the Russian and American literature the answer is that generalization will occur! [9]

Mediated generalization   What kind of explanation can we provide for generalization of a response from a physical stimulus to a verbal symbol standing for the stimulus? To understand the current directions of research on this problem we must retrace some of the historical steps which lead to the present position. John B. Watson, the great popularizer of behaviorism, argued that thinking was merely vocal movements too small to be easily observed. To test this theory people have tried to record muscle potentials in the arm when thinking of throwing a baseball. Some of these attempts to record muscle movements associated with mental acts have been rewarded with some degree of success. Yet, we know that these minute tensions sometimes found in the muscle systems can not account for the range of mental phenomena in thinking. People without arms can still think of throwing a ball. Thinking and verbal behavior generally were identified with responses occuring in the individual. Today, many learning theorists conceive of verbal behavior in terms of specific *S-R* connections although the responses are now far removed from possible detection or observation. They are postulated to exist, perhaps only *in theory,* although some psychologists propose that their neural correlates may exist in the brain.

These *S-R* connections are thought to account for the learned associations which underlie the verbal symbol's elicitation of the response conditioned to the physical stimulus. They are called *representational* or *mediational* responses. The generalization from the actual red light to the words *red light* is mediated generalization. That is to say, generalization based on learned associations between the light and the words. If primary stimulus generalization is a concept used to summarize the fact that people and animals respond in the same way to *physically* similar things, mediated generalization refers to the fact that on certain occasions people and animals respond in the same way to things that are psychologically similar. Mediated generalization must be based on acquired connections arising from the language habits and customs of the society. A Frenchman would not generalize a conditioned response to the word *red* but rather the word *rouge* after conditioning with a red light as the CS.

In language we find both similarity of sound and similarity of meaning. Will a person conditioned to respond to a word such as *style* generalize to words that sound like style more than to words that mean the same thing? Razran [10] has tested the amount of generalization of a conditioned salivation response to synonyms and homonyms. More generalization occurred to the synonyms than the homonyms. Thus, subjects responded more to the word *fashion* than to the word *stile* after original conditioning to *style*.

Experimentally created generalization The theoretical foundations for mediated generalization have been laid in our previous discussions. It may be easier to recall them if we review the work of Shipley and the subsequent experiment by Lumsdaine [11].

In these experiments subjects were first conditioned to make an eye-blink response whenever a light was presented. Shipley did this by pairing a light with a tap to the cheek. This tap elicited an eye blink. After this response was established, the subjects were trained to retract a finger from an electric shock when the cheek was tapped. The question is, after this training program, what will happen when the light is presented? Shipley found that the light would now cause the retraction of the finger. The conditioning in the Shipley experiment might have developed as follows:

Light→tap→blink
Tap→blink→finger withdrawal (shock)
Test: light→(blink)→finger withdrawal

The eye blink and the tap to the cheek were both associated with the development of the new response of finger withdrawal. Thus both should have become conditioned to the finger movement. When the light was presented after training, it elicited the eye blink which now was conditioned to the finger withdrawal. It is as though the subjects had built a link-like chain of conditioning.

The Lumsdaine experiment was important because it approached the question of whether it was actually necessary for the eye-blink response to occur. In the early stages of behavioristic theory it would have been presumed to be necessary. In present day learning theory this is not the case. The mediating eye blink may be represented by changes in the central nervous system that never become expressed in observable behavior. Lumsdaine, as reported by Hilgard and Marquis [12, pp. 230 ff.] found that while the eye blink sometimes intervened between the light and the finger withdrawal, it often did not. Many times the eye blink occurred *after* the finger movement. It is because of the evidence from experiments like Lumsdaine's that the modern learning theories have moved toward *central mediational processes.* The actual movement of the eye blink is not thought to be essential to the mediational system, but some nervous system representation of the eye blink is. This central nervous system representation of the eye blink is conceptualized as a *response disposition* or *tendency* that need not reach its fulfillment in the muscle contractions which produce actual movements.

Mediational response   Although different workers have proposed different terms and mechanisms of mediational processes, we shall follow the lead of Osgood and use the symbol r_m to refer to mediational responses [13]. Let us assume that every stimulus object produces two kinds of reactions within a person: (1) responses which are closely tied to the stimulus conditions and rarely could be elicited without the presence of the particular stimulus object and (2) responses which can be detached from the actual presence of the stimulus object. When stimuli other than the stimulus object are presented along with it, they tend to be conditioned to the detachable portion of the reaction to the stimulus object. It must be emphasized that only a portion of the total reaction to a stimulus object can be conditioned to another stimulus, namely, the detachable responses. It is some part of the detachable reaction of the total response to a red light that becomes conditioned to the words *red light*. This part would be the r_m which produces the behavioral response to the words *red light* following training to an actual red light in our earlier example. See Fig. 7.3 for an illustration of this process.

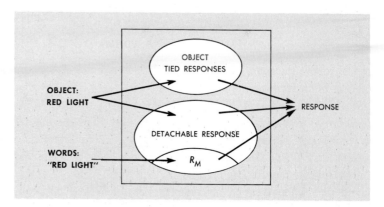

FIG. 7.3. *Physical stimuli elicit both object-tied and detachable responses. If the words "red light" have accompanied presence of a red light during the conditioning of a behavioral response, they alone can elicit the conditioned or detachable response* (r_m).

MEDIATION AND MEANING: THE SEMANTIC DIFFERENTIAL. Osgood has used the mediational response as a way to attack the difficult problem of "meaning." After our discussion of the mediating response we are now in a position to use it to gain greater definition and precision in a discussion of the relationship between words and things.

Osgood and Suci [14] have reasoned that if words have meaning because of the elicitation of mediating responses it might be possible to discover the nature of the different kinds of mediational processes elicited by a word through special statistical techniques. Their procedure calls for many people to rate words on a number of verbal scales. The data are then analyzed to determine the number of different independent dimensions needed to account for the ratings of the test words. Using this technique, Osgood and Suci have been able to find a limited number of independent scales needed to describe most of the words tested.

In Fig. 7.4 we present a sample of the semantic differential scale used to evaluate words. The dimension with the extremes labeled *good* and *bad* is what we might call the *evaluative dimension*. This dimension is the most important one for the evaluation of words. Much of the way we react to words seems to be explained on their "goodness" or "badness." In the figure we find a possible pattern of responses to the word *polite*. The differential patterns of ratings between words on these scales can be used as a very neat and precise method of investigating meaning.

OTHER VIEWS OF MEANING: CONDITIONED IMAGES. Critics of Osgood and Suci have pointed out that their technique gets at only a part of what we usually understand as meaning. Some critics have argued that this technique is only well suited to get at the evaluative aspects of meaning (goodness or badness), or perhaps even the emotional reactions to the test words, but does not attack the problem of the cognitive meaning of words. We should keep in mind that while the good-bad evaluative dimension acounts for a good deal of our reactions to words, it does not account for all. Any word which acts as a label may have an evaluative aspect (its goodness or badness), but it certainly implies other things as well.

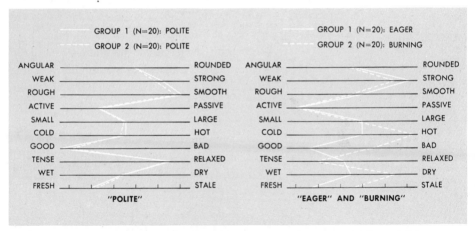

FIG. 7.4. *Preliminary forms of the semantic differential for measuring connotative meanings of adjectives. Based on median profiles of two test groups (n = 20). Adapted from C. E. Osgood. The nature and measurement of meaning. Psychol. Bull., 1952, 49, 197–237.*

Mowrer favors a theory which uses *conditioned images* to account for meaning. Images would be a kind of conditioned sensation (specific sensory attributes in Fig. 7.3) in the organism [16]. These conditioned perceptual responses represent the demonstrative or information-laden aspect of meaning. According to Mowrer's view, the semantic differential is suitable for obtaining information about the emotional but not the informational meaning of a word.

ASSOCIATION VALUE. Some of the most active research specialists in the area of verbal learning identify the degree to which a word has meaning with its *association value* [15]. Through various procedures many investigators have attempted to determine the number of associations which occur to subjects following presentation of a target word or set of letters. The more associations which are reported by subjects after the presentation of a verbal unit, the greater is its association value and, if association value is taken as a measure of meaning, the greater the meaning of the verbal unit.

It is interesting to note that association value can also be measured by other means than the number of associations elicited by a particular word. Measures of how many subjects "get" an association at all (in a limited period of time) or how fast they think they could learn lists of different verbal units all show high correlations with the number of associations produced in a specified amount of time. The association value of verbal units, even assessed by several different methods, provides a useful measure of something related to meaningfulness. As might be expected, association value is related to the familiarity of the verbal units and to the ease with which they can be pronounced. As an example, NEGLAN has less association value than does ORDEAL; ordeal is more familiar and easier to pronounce. In general the less a word is familiar and the harder it is to pronounce the less is its association value. Association value may not encompass all of the needs of people who wish to measure meaning, but, as we shall see later on it is useful as a research device.

DISPOSITIONS. Brown has argued effectively for a different sort of explanation of meaning [17]. For him words have meaning in so far as they tend to occur in connection with other words or in certain parts of sentences. This is sometimes referred to as a *dispositional* theory. Words have meaning to the extent we are disposed to use them in conjunction with other words in sentences or statements. The word *man* has meaning because we would tend to use it in front of specific kinds of verbs and behind other sorts of words. This is a somewhat mechanical approach to the subject of meaning. It leaves out a lot of the romance associated with language, to be sure. However, it may be that this kind of a definition of meaning can be scientifically useful.

As with the approach of Osgood and Suci, the dispositional theory is still in its formative stages. As previously mentioned, many think that the semantic differential can never measure more than some of the evaluative dimensions on which we categorize words. The conditioned image of Mowrer may be able to deal effectively with the informational aspect of the meaning of words. The procedure for understanding the meaning of words by understanding the verbal contexts in which they are found may provide a fresh start from which greater progress toward understanding the nature of meaning may begin.

Acquisition and Retention of Verbal Material

Even though there is a lack of agreement regarding what meaning really is, it is still possible to study and to determine degrees of meaningfulness in verbal material. For example, the word *love* has more meaning for us than the same four letters arranged as VEOL. It is obvious that words, phrases, and sentences vary in meaningfulness, and psychologists have been able to study the effect of this attribute, as well as many others, upon the time required to learn verbal material [18]. In verbal research, the effects of situational factors, the arrangement of learning sessions and materials to be learned, and factors specific to certain individuals have been studied by psychologists who expect that their findings will lead to further understanding of the organization of man.

EBBINGHAUS AND THE NONSENSE SYLLABLE Hermann Ebbinghaus was the pioneer in the study of memorizing verbal materials by rote practice. He really was a one-man research team. For the most part he was his only subject. Picture him at his desk memorizing lists of words and testing himself for retention. He found familiarity of material one very important condition which effected his ability to memorize and he sought to discover the effect of trying to memorize totally unfamiliar material. Since it was difficult to find verbal material which was unfamiliar, he created *nonsense syllables* of consonant and vowel combinations that are pronounceable but yet not words, for example, GOK, MEJ. Such nonsense syllables can be modified and, depending on the requirements of the experiment, can be long or short and can include only consonants or numbers as well. Generally speaking, a nonsense syllable such as TAL has less meaning for a typical subject in a verbal learning experiment than a three-letter word such as BOY.

Many people, however, may have unique associations formed to unusual letter combinations. A person named Terry A. Lane would have rather strong associations built around TAL, and if it was presented to him during a learning experiment, it would act more like a meaningful word than a nonsense syllable. It was found that most nonsense syllables are not free from preexperimental associations [19]. Therefore, the nonsense syllable is an artificial verbal unit which is not totally meaningless but rather has less meaning than do most naturally occurring verbal units. Nonsense syllables are useful because they can be constructed in large numbers to have greater or less meaning (higher or lower association values) for the subjects who attempt to learn and remember them.

MEANINGFULNESS AND LEARNING   It is to be expected that meaningful material can be learned more readily than nonsense material. This expectation has been confirmed many times. For instance, the times required for subjects to learn 200 items of nonsense syllables, digits, words of prose, or words of poetry, were 93, 85, 24, and 10 minutes, respectively [20]. It took over nine times as long to learn 200 nonsense syllables as 200 words of poetry! One might ask why poetry seems easier to learn than prose? The answer may be that in poetry there are additional cues of rhyme and meter which aid recall. Other studies have indicated that nonsense syllables which tend to evoke more associations in subjects are easier to master than those which evoke fewer associations [15].

One of the most satisfactory methods of explaining these results is the very reasonable assumption that subjects come into experiments knowing more about the meaningful materials. Part of their learning has already been accomplished before the experiments start.

METHODS OF STUDYING VERBAL LEARNING   Probably the most common method used to learn verbal materials is the *whole method*. You use it when you memorize an entire section of prose or poetry at once. You study the entire selection. In a verbal learning experiment using the whole method the subject is presented with an entire passage to memorize. He can be tested on how many words he has learned in a given period of time or on how many minutes it takes him to commit the passage to memory. For example, it was reported that it took subjects 93 minutes to learn 200 items of nonsense syllables and only 10 minutes to learn 200 words of poetry using the whole method.

When the whole method is used, there is very little that can be done to isolate specific variables which can help us understand the nature of the verbal learning process. For example, we cannot control the effects of the rate of presentation of the stimulus units, the effect of uncontrolled rehearsal of responses, or the effect of learning earlier or later words upon the acquisition of a particular word in the passage. Since these factors make a difference in the rate of verbal learning, it is necessary to use other techniques in which these factors can be systematically controlled and isolated for independent study.

Another technique used in studying acquisition of verbal material is called the *serial anticipation method*. It is somewhat similar to the whole method except that greater control is achieved over the presentation of the stimuli and when the responses are made. The subject must learn a list of words or nonsense syllables *in the order they are presented to him*. Usually the verbal units to be learned are presented to the subject one at a time in the small window of a *memory drum*. The memory drum is built to expose verbal items for varied durations, and it controls the length of time between presentations. Usually the list is presented at a rapid rate to reduce the possibility that the subject can rehearse one unit while waiting for the next to appear. A sketch of a memory drum is presented in Fig. 7.5.

One other common technique presents the learner with the task of learning a specific verbal response to a specific verbal stimulus. The subject learns pairs of verbal items. This method is called the *paired associates technique*. At the beginning of training, the subject is presented with a list of stimulus and response words, one pair at a time. On subsequent trials only the stimulus words are presented and the subject makes a response. For example, a subject may be asked to learn the following pairs of words:

Stimulus Words	Response Words
Apple	Canary
Blue	Table
Wide	Church
Parlor	Milk
Friend	Verb
Curse	Finger
Fly	Motion

On any given trial the subject is presented with one of the stimulus words and must try to respond with the appropriate response word. If the subject's answer is incorrect, he is informed of the appropriate response. Each time the experimenter procedes through all of the stimulus words, it is counted as a single trial. It is important to remember that the experimenter does not merely go down the stimulus list, from top to bottom, on every trial, or the subject would have only to memorize

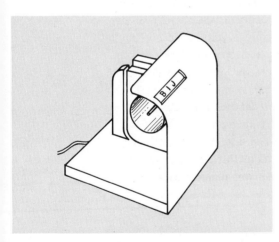

FIG. 7.5. *Memory drum used in studies of verbal learning and retention.*

their order and not pay any attention to the stimulus words at all. By skipping about in the list of stimulus words on each trial, the subject must remember which stimulus word is to be associated with which response word.

Measuring retention   Recently, another technique has been developed in which verbal units are presented only once and then subjects are asked to recall them after varying periods of time [21]. This technique has not been given any widely accepted name, so let us call it merely the *Peterson technique,* after its originators. Essentially, the subject is presented with a verbal unit followed by a number. The subject is instructed to count backwards from this number, giving one number each second, until a signal is given for him to recall the verbal unit. Then the subject must try to respond with that verbal item which was given just before the number. The delay between the presentation of the verbal unit and its recall can easily be varied by the experimenter. The subject counts backward so that he is occupied during the presentation-response interval and cannot mentally rehearse the verbal response. The Peterson method has shown itself to be a highly sensitive indicator of short-term retention. The retention of verbal materials is shown to drop drastically even a few seconds after presentation when the subject is prevented from rehearsing in this way.

Measures of learning and retention   Given these representative methods of presenting verbal materials, we are confronted with a number of possible ways to measure both acquisition and retention. We can, of course, measure the time it takes for a subject to memorize the whole passage of verbal units or measure the number of trials required for a subject to master all the paired associates given to him in an experiment. These methods require that the subject produce the correct responses on his own; yet if the subject cannot produce all the correct responses without help, does this mean he has learned nothing at all? Think of the case of a student who can not remember the answer to this examination question (see pp. 87–88): *What kind of positive ions move into the neuron when it "fires" from their position on the outside of the cell during its resting state?* Could this student pick the correct answer if he were given a group of possible responses?

(a) Na ions   (c) K ions
(b) Cl ions   (d) Mg ions

It is more than likely that he could. The fact that it is often possible to choose a correct answer from a set of possible answers when it is not possible to recall the answer in unaided fashion must indicate that learning and retention of multiple verbal units are not all-or-none phenomena, but exist in degrees.

It is often useful for the psychologist to direct his attention to two facets of learning. One is the process of acquisition of responses, whether verbal or nonverbal. The other is the process of retention. Retention refers to the subject's maintenance of his ability to perform the acquired responses. While it is easy to talk of two distinct processes, it must be emphasized that they are both inventions of the psychologist seeking the most apt ways to describe and explain behavior. They certainly are not independent processes. In an extreme instance, one can not retain that which has not been acquired. More generally, however, the lower the level of acquisition of responses, the poorer will be the retention. Acquisition and retention represent two sides of the changes in performance induced by suitable changes in environmental conditions. All we can ever observe is the performance of subjects. Despite these qualifications it may prove worthwhile to separate acquisition processes from retention processes and seek measures of each. Several measures of retention have been used:

1. *Recall.* With this technique the subject is asked to recall material previously learned. The recall score represents the percentage of the original material recalled at a later date.
2. *Recognition.* When using this method, the subject is asked to identify material previously learned. A common example would be the student picking out the correct answer in a multiple choice question on an examination.
3. *Relearning.* With this technique the subject relearns material previously studied. The savings score represents the difference in time or number of errors between the first and second learning sessions.
4. *Reconstruction.* Here the subject is presented with all of the verbal materials and asked to place the items in the order in which they were originally learned.

Retention and memory We should point out that these four techniques are used to measure what psychologists call retention. However, they may also be referred to as measures of memory. This brings up an interesting problem. If the four retention measures are used to assess how much a subject has remembered of his original learning, four scores could result. The different results obtained by different techniques are differentially sensitive indicators of retention. Material that is forgotten as measured in one way may not be forgotten if another technique is used. Think of a speech or poem you once memorized but cannot now recall. It is possible, and indeed likely, that it would take you less time to relearn it now than it took you to learn it originally. The results of a study by Luh [22] are usually considered to be representative of the differences in retention as measured by different techniques. His results, shown graphically in Fig. 7.6, present differences in the methods used to measure differential retention rates of forgetting over a period of time [23].

How often do we say we have forgotten something when we can not recall it? How often do we feel that because we can not recall it we have no *memory* of it? Must we assume a memory is gone when we can not recall it? Does the fact that our previous learning makes it easier to relearn the task mean that the memories exist at some unconscious level within us all the time? Just what do we mean by the word memory?

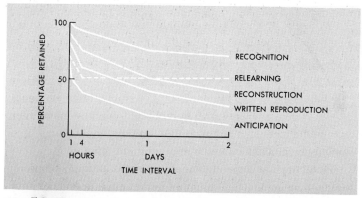

FIG. 7.6 *Percent of verbal materials retained as measured by five different techniques, over periods of one and four hours; one and two days. Adapted from C. W. Luh. The conditions of retention.* Psychol. Monogr. No. 142, 1922, *31*, 1–87.

Memory, like perception, is susceptible to many interpretations. Some psychologists think of memory as a process of retention which operates to store, or recover from storage, past experiences. Others may think of memory as composed of those things which reach conscious awareness but are not present in the person's environment at the moment. We must keep in mind, however, that memory is a theoretical concept which we infer from the observation of behavior. Our four measures of retention are measures of behavior. Our concept of memory depends on our theoretical position, and some theories seem to get along quite well without any memory concepts. The very point of studying verbal performance under various conditions is to be able to make more valuable inferences about the kind of view we should hold about the nature of memory. Through the use of the different methods for presenting verbal stimuli and measuring retention, many factors have been found which are related to the speed of acquisition and the degree of retention of verbal materials. Let us consider some examples.

AMOUNT OF MATERIAL TO BE LEARNED. When you came into the introductory course in psychology, you knew from common sense that it takes more time to learn a long list than a short list of things. When you leave the course you *may* remember that as the amount of material increases the time required to learn a *unit* of material increases as well. As the amount of material increases, the time required to learn it grows disproportionately [20]. This is true both for syllables and for prose. It took 1.5 minutes to learn 12 syllables, but it took 6.0 minutes to learn 24 syllables. Doubling the amount to be learned resulted in more than doubling the time required for learning. Thus, the time required to learn a unit (single syllable) was increased by lengthening the amount to be learned.

METHODS OF STUDY: WHOLE VERSUS PART. Given a passage of verbal materials to be learned, would it be better to break it down into small pieces to be learned separately, and then combine the pieces, or to tackle the whole passage at once? The answer is contingent upon a number of conditions (see pp. 296 ff.). Generally speaking, the greater the mental development of the learner, the better it is to study the entire passage. Also, one must consider the length of the passage and the pieces into which it can be subdivided. As we learned in the preceding paragraph the amount of time necessary to learn a passage is related to the length of the passage. Consideration of the length of the passage and possible subdivisions of it can help in deciding which technique should be followed.

MASSED VERSUS DISTRIBUTED PRACTICE. If you only have so much time which can be devoted to studying a verbal passage is it better to distribute this time into separate study sessions or to mass your study in one solid interval? While there must be some qualifications, the best procedure would seem to be mass your studying [25]. To obtain *efficiency* in studying, massed practice on verbal materials will avoid costly warm-up periods and also the time required to get your materials ready for use. In learning motor performances where muscular skills are involved, however, distributed practice results in so much greater acquisition that it overshadows the inefficient side effects. Distributed practice only seems to be advantageous when the learner must master new or unfamiliar responses [26].

In most adult verbal learning the response materials are well-practiced verbal units. The conclusions about the superior *efficiency* of massed versus distributed practice for verbal materials run counter to much professional folklore about these two approaches to studying verbal materials, but the conclusion is based upon solid experimental work.

THE EFFECT OF SERIAL POSITION. When verbal materials are to be learned in a given order, the position in which verbal units occur is an important factor. Items at the beginning or the end of the list will be recalled better than items in the middle. This serial position effect is illustrated in Fig. 7.7, where we can see that the items in the middle of the list were correctly recalled much later than items at the extremes of the list [27].

FIG. 7.7. *Effects of serial position on number of presentations necessary for learning. Learning was measured by subject's first correct response and his last error. Humps near center reflect the greater difficulty of learning verbal items in middle positions. Adapted from* C. L. Hull, et al. Mathematico-Deductive Theory of Rote Learning. *New Haven, Yale University Press, 1940.*

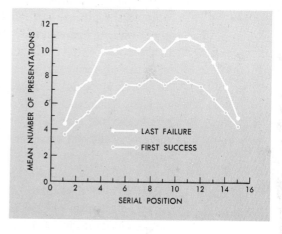

The favorable effect of coming early in the list is the *primacy effect* and the beneficial effect of being near the end of the list is the *recency effect*. These names have no deep significance in themselves and are only descriptive terms. Learning theorists want to explain both primacy and recency effects.

Many theoretical interpretations of this phenomena have been presented. Most of them have one feature in common: the concept of interference of associative connections between the different items in the list. Maximum interference would occur in the middle of the list because these units would have both forward and backward associations to items occurring earlier and later in the list. Items at the beginning or the end of a list would only have associations in one direction [24].

It is possible to overcome the detrimental effects of the middle position. If one, or even a few, of the middle items of the list are made *different* from the rest of the list the rate of learning will be comparable to that of early and late items. We could do this by printing the selected middle items in a different color or by including a set of numerals in a list of syllables. As the number of special items increases, the effect becomes less apparent. Even so, this effect of perceptually emphasizing items can still be observed when 50 percent of the list is differentiated in the ways we have suggested [28].

In summary: We have outlined a few of the variables which influence the acquisition and retention of verbal materials. Many others have been studied by psychologists interested in the processes underlying learning in men. Most studies use one of the methods of presenting verbal material and one of the measures of retention described earlier. These methods allow for a precise determination of the relationships between the variables under study. In a sense, however, they may be overprecise. We all know that it is easier to recall the substance of what we have read than to quote it verbatim. Even though it is more difficult, we must, as students of behavior, investigate learning phenomena related to substance as well as exact duplication of materials. We may find the principles of retention for ideas and concepts will be different from those of rote material.

TRANSFER OF TRAINING Many people report that they find French easier after having had Latin. If the study of Latin does assist the student in acquiring French, this represents what psychologists call a positive transfer of training. If, on the other hand, Latin hindered a person attempting to learn French this would be negative transfer effect. Of course, Latin may have no effect upon learning French, that is, there may be no transfer effect between them. Transfer of training refers to an effect upon learning a task, *B,* caused by prior learning of another task, *A.* The effect may be helpful (positive transfer) or harmful (negative transfer).

Transfer in verbal studies One common technique used to study the conditions responsible for positive and negative transfer of training involves changing the stimulus or the response words in a set of paired verbal associates. Experimenters can then study the effect of these manipulations in terms of the effects of different degrees of similarity of the substituted stimulus or response words to the original ones.

From the results of several experiments the following summary statement would seem appropriate: Learning to make old responses to new stimuli produces positive transfer, whereas learning to make new responses to old stimuli is a condition usually producing negative transfer. When one makes old responses to new stimuli, the extent to which the new stimuli are similar to the original stimuli helps produce greater amounts of positive transfer.

Let us assume a subject learns a list of paired associates similar to the one given below. The letters in the examples are used to symbolize verbal units, such as nonsense syllables:

Task 1

Stimulus Word		Response Word
A	—	W
B	—	X
C	—	Y
D	—	Z

We should expect *positive transfer* when in a second task the subject was called upon to learn pairs which kept the same response terms but had new stimulus associates:

Task 2

Stimulus Word		Response Word
E	—	W
F	—	X
C	—	Y
D	—	Z

However, if we asked the subject to learn a list like the following, he should show negative transfer because in this he must learn to make new responses to old stimuli:

Task 3

Stimulus Word		Response Word
A	—	R
B	—	S
C	—	T
D	—	U

This generalization about transfer of training was investigated by Bruce [29]. From recent work we believe that positive transfer in instances where the responses are the same is due to the subjects' learning the response items in the first learning session and having them more readily available for future use. It should be mentioned that Bruce's generalization oversimplifies the rather complex nature of transfer between learning tasks. Positive or negative transfer effects depend upon the degree of learning of task 1, the conditions of presentation of the stimulus items, and the nature of the verbal units employed.

Transfer of principles   To this point we have considered only an elementary type of transfer situation. Another type of transfer which acts to facilitate performances in situations similar to those described above is a kind of learning to learn, in which subjects learn stratagems helpful to all situations of a certain kind. Using a different variety of tasks, two groups of grade-school boys learned to throw darts at a target submerged in 12 inches of water. Subjects were then divided into two groups. One group was taught the principle of optical refraction through water, the other was not. After this instruction phase the two groups were tested once more, only this time the target was submerged in only 4 inches of water. The group of boys learning the principle of refraction of the light rays showed positive transfer of training by their quick adaptation to the new conditions. The group that had not been trained on the principle of refraction did not show as much transfer [30].

This study and others indicate more transfer when the subjects know the principle behind the task. Usually this means that one group of subjects has been told certain rules related to their performances or activities. How do the verbal principles of a task come to effect motor performances? What do we mean when we say that one group understands the principle of refraction while the other group does not? (For the present we must stay close to common sense in using words such as *knowledge* and *principle*.) We don't know, but in general it is safe to say that transfer of training is facilitated if the principles of the situation can be verbalized by the subjects. At the same time we should recognize the possibility that principles need not transfer, even though they often do. Principles must be learned in a way which makes transfer to new situations seem appropriate.

Identical elements   Early in the history of psychology, some psychologists held the view that man's mental skills were divisible into several categories, units, or processes. Each division was called a *faculty*. Each of us had a faculty for intellection (thinking), emotion, and so on. Because of this view of man, early leaders in education held that the proper aim of education was to exercise the faculties of the mind, particularly intellection, with the expected result that the mental faculty would grow stronger in the same way a muscle will grow stronger with exercise. Thinking about anything would develop the power to think. It was argued that studying Greek exercises the intellect and should therefore facilitate the learning of mathematics.

Shortly after the turn of the century, this kind of educational philosophy was changed largely because of Thorndike's work on transfer of training. Thorndike found only very limited kinds of transfer. It had been *assumed* that positive transfer would occur between subject matter areas in primary and secondary educational settings. It had been *assumed* that training in any mental or intellectual skill would result in superior performance on any other intellectual skill. The mind would be strengthened. Thorndike's findings were that transfer only occurs between two situations when they are quite similar. He postulated a theory of transfer of training based on the number of *identical elements* in the two situations. He believed that if there were a large number of similar elements (stimulus-response pairs) in two situations we would expect positive transfer. If there were few, or no, identical elements, then one could not expect transfer. His views caused a change in educational philosophy. It was found that courses like Latin and Greek will be beneficial to students only in specific situations. Even training with the use of principles must be of a kind that facilitates transfer to other situations.

Thorndike's identical elements in the transfer of training spring from basic *S-R* association philosophy. No one is sure just what an element should be considered to be. In general, one can say that whether or not performance on task B will be improved or hindered by prior experience with task A can only be predicted by a detailed analysis of the tasks, and this should include the consideration of the number of identical discrete performances found in them. In the final analysis empirical investigators of transfer among situations are essential.

Indirect transfer effects   Probably many readers of this book have noted that learning one or another type of academic material requires the development of a special orientation to it. Generally, we approach the study of a foreign language in a different manner from that of the study of mathematics. We orient ourselves differently to these two kinds of tasks. This affects both our preparation for study and what we do while studying. Whatever we do, we have learned to do it through our earlier experiences with the subject matter. We hope they represent rather optimal adjustments of our abilities to the tasks themselves. If we do better in later tasks, say advanced mathematics courses, than in earlier ones, this could be due to the learning of an effective orientation to the subject matter as much as to the gain in knowledge of mathematics.

Harlow [31] has shown that monkeys solve discrimination problems much faster when they have solved similar problems in the past. The monkeys learn to learn. Just what this ability or learning set is, is another problem. This learning to learn represents acquiring an approach to problems. On the other hand, merely assigning the effect to a descriptive category does not help us a great deal. Perhaps, the monkeys have learned to pay attention to certain aspects of the situation which are crucial for the solution of the problem and to disregard distracting influences. On the other hand, they may have learned strategies different from those followed by monkeys without a history of training. Still, they may have learned postural responses which are effective in assisting them in solving the problem. Similar findings exist in laboratory experiments at the human level. Greater speed in learning new verbal materials following previous learning of similar types of materials have been reported [32]. We call the effects of learning to learn *indirect* because they do not seem to be susceptible to explanation in terms of factors prominent in most theories of learning. This is not to belittle either the magnitude of their effects or the significance of theory for research. Rather, the word *indirect* suggests effects of a general strategic sort and not those of specific or direct effect upon the associations formed.

RETROACTIVE INHIBITION   Two of the most important concepts underlying the acquisition and retention of verbal materials are retroactive and proactive inhibition. These terms describe two sources of a decrement or attenuation of retention of verbal materials. Properly speaking, retroactive inhibition refers to a negative effect on the *retention* of a verbal task, learned earlier, by other verbal material imposed between acquisition and the test for retention. The basic outline of experiments used to study retroactive inhibition is as follows:

	Time 1	*Time 2*	*Time 3*
Group I	Learn task A	Learn task B	Test task A
Group II	Learn task A	Nothing	Test task A

In this ideal situation the extent to which the retention of task A was less for group I than for group II would reflect the debilitating effects of learning the interpolated material of task B. Several things must be noted about this model experimental situation. First, it is impossible for group II to do "nothing" in time interval 2. They could be rehearsing task A. They could be rehearsing other materials unrelated to task A. Any living animal is more or less active and the nature of the activities exhibited by group II, in time 2, is bound to be influential in determining later retention. If we do not have a time 2 for group II, but test them for retention immediately, then we have given them the advantage of a shorter period of time required for retention. Group I would then have both interpolated activity *and* a longer time before interval 3. In an ideal experiment on retroactive inhibition we would want to study only the effects of one variable: the interpolated activity.

The disruptive effects of interpolated activity on the retention of verbal materials has been intensively studied. In general the amount of retroactive inhibition (the interruptive effects on retention of task A) increases with the amount of practice on the interpolated material provided by task B. This result might be expected on a common-sense basis, of course. However, further investigations of retroactive inhibition have brought to light new facts about the interruptive effects.

Interlist intrusions and unlearning As an example of one factor influencing retroactive inhibition, it has been found that there is no consistent relationship between the number of responses from task B produced by the subject when he is being tested for retention of task A and the total degree of negative effects produced by retroactive inhibition [33]. Intrusions of words from task B account only in part for the total errors made in task A. These interlist intrusions become greatest with intermediate amounts of interpolated practice (task B).

When task B was practiced longer, the number of intrusions from task B into the retest for task A became fewer despite the fact that the over-all performance of the subjects was becoming progressively poorer. In the same study the experimenters observed that the retroactive inhibition effects persisted longest when the interpolated practice was of intermediate length. When the practice on task B was long, this effect did not last as long as when it was in an intermediate range. These results suggest that the verbal responses originally learned in task A become unavailable to the subject, extinguished or unlearned, during the learning of task B. However, with the passage of time, this lack of availability disappears and the original responses are spontaneously reactivated. We should note that this concept of spontaneous recovery of extinguished, or un-learned, responses is similar to the view proposed by Pavlov. For him, no conditioned reflex was ever permanently lost. Even after prolonged extinction training there could be a spontaneous recovery of the reflex. Furthermore, in Hull's theory the learn-ing *variable* $(_sH_R)$ can never be diminished. Other variables might act to suppress behavioral expression of the response, but learning itself was supposed to be a variable which did not diminish.

The lack of a relationship between interlist intrusions and the total amount of retroactive inhibition can be explained in other ways. Some authors have argued that the subject in a retroactive inhibition experiment becomes better able to differentiate or discriminate responses appropriate to the two lists as the amount of interpolated training increases [34]. This discrimination hypothesis receives some of its strongest support from studies of proactive inhibition.

PROACTIVE INHIBITION   The learning of one task can effect the subsequent learning of another task. Proactive inhibition refers to the negative effects on a task by prior learning of another task. Diagrammatically this can be represented as follows:

	Time 1	*Time 2*	*Time 3*
Group I (proactive)	Task C	Task D	Retest test for D
Group II (control)	Nothing	Task D	Retest for D

The superiority of Group II over Group I in acquiring task D would reflect the negative effects of proactive inhibition. As with the retroactive-inhibition model, the time interval labeled "nothing" must be considered as qualified to the extent that the living organism never does "nothing."

Underwood [35] has shown that subjects who have participated in a number of verbal learning experiments tend to forget new verbal material of a similar sort more rapidly than those

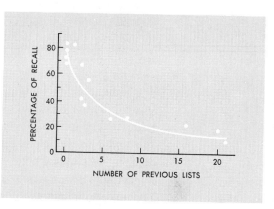

FIG. 7.8. *Effect on retention of amount of learning prior to experiment. In general, the greater the number of previous lists learned the less retention. Adapted from B. J. Underwood. Interference and forgetting. Psychol. Rev., 1957, 64, 49–60.*

who have not done so. Figure 7.8 shows this effect in graphic form. The percentage of verbal material recalled by subjects who had learned only a few prior lists of verbal units was much greater than those who had learned five or more lists of a similar kind. The effect of learning prior lists is a proactive effect since the tasks producing it come before the learning and the test for retention of the task being studied.

	Time 1	Time 2	Time 3
Proactive groups	Some number of lists similar to Task D	Task D	Retest for D
Control groups	Nothing	Task D	Retest for D

At first, these proactive effects may seem antagonistic to the principle of learning to learn. Actually, they are not. Learning to learn refers to an effect upon the acquisition of a new problem, whereas proactive inhibition effects refer to a decrease in retention. Subjects who have learned a number of verbal lists actually *learn* new lists (of similar material) faster than do less-practiced subjects. They just retain them less well.

Intrusions between tasks   In studying proactive inhibition experimenters have found that the frequency of intrusions of task C responses into responses made while learning task D is greatest with intermediate training in task C. If C is practiced longer, the number of interlist intrusions declines while the total interruptive effects of the interpolated activity increases. This suggests that two factors may be operating to produce the effects ascribed to proactive inhibition. One has to do with the subjects' ability to discriminate the two tasks and the other acts to suppress recall in a different manner.

EXPLANATIONS OF FORGETTING Experimental psychologists involved in exploring the acquisition and retention of verbal material have been torn between interference theories and unlearning theories of forgetting. According to interference theories, decline in memory comes about through factors interfering with the associations making up the to-be-remembered material. For example, associations presumed to connect stimulus and response elements in paired associate learning never decline, but they may not be demonstrated in behavior due to competition from other responses for the stimulus components. The unlearning hypothesis predicts an actual decline in associative strength between the *S-R* units. This decline is thought to occur as a function of time alone, although other factors could hasten the attenuation of the associative bonds. The battle between these two views of memory is not over. Some psychologists believe that forgetting can be adequately explained by the interference hypothesis alone and others believe that both unlearning and interference hypotheses are required.

As far as the effects of retroactive inhibition on forgetting are concerned, Barnes and Underwood [36] have provided evidence which seems to make it necessary to accept unlearning as a vital concept to explain forgetting. Decrements in performance found in the research on retroactive inhibition comes from two factors: (1) the unlearning of the original responses (task A) during practice on task B and (2) the competition between task A and task B responses. The competition of responses learned in the two tasks is increased when there is less differentiation, or discrimination, between lists. This should occur at intermediate levels of practice on the interpolated learning materials (task B). The contributions of the two components jointly produce the total amount of retroactive inhibition, and the effects of the two components vary over the time given to the subject to recall task A. Of course with the proactive inhibition situation there is no chance for unlearning of the original list since it is only presented after the other verbal materials.

General Views of Memory

Up to this point in the chapter we have emphasized interference theories of forgetting. As we have seen, interference between competing responses and unlearning represents the major analytic concepts of psychologists following in the tradition of Ebbinghaus. The success of recent refinements in interference theories in stimulating research and helping elucidate phenomena of memory can not be doubted. In the next sections we shall present brief discussions of some of the other approaches which have been made to forgetting and memory.

GESTALT PSYCHOLOGY AND MEMORY When discussing perceptual phenomena (Chapter 5), we pointed out that Gestalt psychologists attempted to explain perceptual phenomena on the basis of electrical fields located in the brain. Memories of past sensory events would be related to the reestablishment of particular brain fields by new conditions [37, 38]. There was strong appeal in their argument from basic perceptual phenomena. When a stimulus is presented only briefly and the subject looks away at a neutral field, there is a procession of after-images. These after-images resemble the prior stimulating conditions, although there usually are a series of both positive and negative after-images. (In a negative after-image the colors and light-dark relationships are reversed.) In any case the perceptual effects of the preceding stimulus conditions have effected the person so that their effects remain when the stimulus conditions have been altered. This lingering effect is often termed the *trace* of the stimulus. All memories can be thought of as traces of neural events occurring earlier. Just as perception is altered by forces operating in the electrical brain fields to cause illusions, so memory traces are subject to the same influences. Thus, our memories are represented as subject to all of the distorting influences of field phenomena, generally. The problem has always been that it is difficult to specify precisely what the distortions of the brain field will be in any but very simple perceptual or memory situations.

LEWIN'S FORCES Kurt Lewin was a social psychologist deeply influenced by Gestalt Psychology. (His contributions to motivation are discussed in the next chapter.) He postulated that our actions, both mental and behavioral, are caused by forces operating within us. These forces are produced by the joint effects of the person and the situation in which he finds himself. Memory, for Lewin, was a product of ongoing cognitive activity. To the extent that forces in the person were directed toward past events or objects' they would be remembered. When the forces directed toward maintaining the memory were reduced, the event or object would not be available for recall. One of Lewin's examples was taken from a coffee house in Germany. The waiters did not write down orders or the amounts each customer owed. These waiters were able to remember everything customers were served, even though hours went by, *up to the point the waiter was paid*. Since the waiter would be responsible for the bill if the customers did not pay, this maintained the force necessary for memory. After the customers paid the bill, this force was diminished.

On the other hand, Lewin postulated that strong forces away from events or objects would act to induce forgetting. Examples of this purposeful forgetting could be illustrated by the fact that the name of a "date" with whom you had an unpleasant time is often hard to recall. The frequency with which dental appointments are missed also testifies to the effects of anticipated discomfort upon memory.

FREUD AND REPRESSION Even though Sigmund Freud, the founder of psychoanalysis, and Kurt Lewin were contemporaries, each developed independently his own theory of purposeful forgetting. There seems to have been little communication between them. Freud developed a theory of personality based upon his study of people with behavioral problems. Through his method of psychoanalysis, he came to believe that most personality problems stemmed from anxiety. One of the theoretical mechanisms through which anxiety is minimized in the individual is called repression. Repression is a personality mechanism unknown to the person which keeps anxiety-laden memories from reaching conscious awareness. However, Freud believed that memories hidden from conscious view by repression could still influence behavior. They could be general or specific memories of previous events or situations. Specific repression would account for the loss of a given fact, for example the name of a person or an appointment. General repression could occur to such an extent that a person may have an amnesia for an entire period of his life.

FRAMES OF REFERENCE—ADAPTATION LEVELS No memory exists independently of other memories. For instance, all of our past experiences with teachers combine to some extent to influence our perception of all our current teachers. Our judgments of any stimulus depends upon our past history with similar stimuli. It has been argued that the effect of past experiences is to provide us with an *adaptation level* for particular stimuli. New stimuli will be judged using the past experiences as a *neutral point*. Judgments about immediate sensory input are based on some neutral point determined by past experiences. If the temperature of 80° F seems hot to us, it is because we have had more experiences with lower temperatures. If 80° F seems cold, it is because we have a neutral point higher than 80° F, as might occur when living in the tropics. Just how the nervous system operates to maintain some level of adaptation to all kinds of stimulating conditions is not well understood, although it is likely that the efferent sensory system is involved.

In one sense the adaptation level which we have for any stimulus condition provides a frame of reference against which future stimuli will be evaluated. Frames of reference, however, are often used in other contexts. For illustration, we might hear someone criticize a president. The critic may interpret evidence differently from the way we do, particularly if he belongs to a different political party from that of our choice. Each person, the critic and the observer, has interpreted the same evidence from different frames of reference. New stimuli of all kinds fit into frames of reference which have been learned and which exert continuing influences on behavior. These frames of reference may be so well established that they are unknown to the person. To the extent that they maintain behavioral effects on the individual they must be classified as aspects of memory, and it is often possible to "see" a person's frame of reference influencing the things which are recalled. It is possible that the memory effects produced by such global frames of reference as political identification may some day be explained through use of competing associations or perhaps selective attention to certain stimuli. In any case the frames of reference of a person act to influence his memories and selective forgetting or retention.

PHYSIOLOGICAL BASIS OF MEMORY   Gestalt psychologists proposed that memories be considered as particular kinds of electrical fields in the brain. Little has been done to further an acceptance of this view. Today, the most popular view of the neural substrate of memory is that provided by Hebb [39].

Reverberation and interneuronal growth   In Chapter 5 we learned that Hebb proposed a distinction between neural reverberating and synaptic kinds of growth (pp. 182–190). If we change terminology slightly, we could say learning must be associated with two kinds of memory systems: a memory system related to a period immediately following sensory stimulation, in which traces of the stimulation reverberate through neural circuits in the brain; and a later period in which the reverberations have resulted in changed synaptic connections between neurons. The latter would be the basis of permanent memory, whereas the reverberatory stage would represent a transient stage of short-term memory storage. Thus, interneuronal growth is the basis for the neural changes which represent memory, and these in turn are dependent upon preliminary reverberatory activity.

In Hebb's theory any neural input from sensory systems produces reverberatory activity. This activity may consist of loops of neurons which activate each other in turn. The activity of cells in these reverberatory loops does not last indefinitely; rather this activity tends to die out after some period of time, which is most likely measurable in seconds or minutes. If this reverberatory activity lasts long enough it will produce interneuronal growth. The distinction between the activities in reverberatory loops and interneuronal growth provides a neural distinction between the behavioral concepts of long-term and short-term memories.

Long- and short-term memories   If a person receives a strenuous blow on the head, amnesia may follow. Any traumatic event, expecially involving the head, can produce effects upon memories, although these are often of a special kind. Only rarely is the person's entire memory destroyed by traumatic events. Usually the amnesia extends back to only a short period, say a few minutes, before the accident. Even if the original amnesia extends back further than this before the accident, it is often possible to recover the memories up to this critical period just before the trauma.

Let us assume that reverberatory loop activity must persist

for some interval before sufficient interneuronal growth occurs to lay down a more permanent memory pattern. The evidence of short-term amnesia resulting from traumatic accidents could be explained on the basis that the accident interrupted the reverberatory activity before sufficient interneuronal growth had taken place. Furthermore, the fact that the condition of amnesia does not extend back to earlier times would suggest that interneuronal growth itself was insensitive to traumatic events. The conclusion which this evidence suggests is that short-term memories of events stretching from *now* to a few minutes ago are represented by reverberatory loops of neural activity whereas longer-term memories are represented by some kind of chemical or physical growth between neurons.

Electroconvulsive shock In certain cases of mental illness, patients are given electroconvulsive shock therapy. Usually an electrical current is passed between electrodes attached to the sides of the head. After such treatment, patients often show a marked improvement in their behavior despite an amnesia for events just prior to the treatment. This amnesia is remarkably like that occurring in cases of traumatic accidents.

Duncan sought to determine the effect of electroconvulsive shock on the performance of learned responses in animals [40]. He found that the effects of the shock depended upon the amount of time after learning that the shock was administered. Electroconvulsive shocks administered shortly after responses in a learning task tended to preclude the formation of permanent memories. If shock was administered an hour or longer after training the effect was greatly reduced. Although there have been questions raised about the adequacy of experimental controls for the unpleasant effects of electroconvulsive shocks [41], the same kind of results have been obtained in situations in which the unpleasantness of the electroconvulsion could not be prejudicial to the outcome of the experiment [42]. The basic finding that electroconvulsive shock administered within a certain period following training interferes with learning stand in support of a reverberatory basis of short-term memory.

Brain lesions At times, it becomes necessary for a neurosurgeon to remove portions of the brain. The reasons for such surgery must be compelling, of course, and the number of patients is not large. Brain removal of the temporal lobes has been done by several surgeons for epileptic conditions found localized in these areas through analysis of brain waves (using the electroencephalogram). Lesions in these temporal-lobe regions produce abnormalities in the recent memories of the patients [43]. Published reports of these patients' behavior suggest that the recall of events occurring since the operation and almost to the present is adversely effected. These difficulties of recent memory can be alleviated to some extent through the prolific use of notes and other devices to assist recall. It should be noted that the interval of impaired recall labeled *recent memory* (operation to present) is not the same as *short-term memory* (present to a few minutes ago). The involvement of the temporal lobes of the brain in memory is further supported by studies in which these areas are electrically stimulated in the awake and alert patient. When temporal lobe areas are stimulated, the patient often reports the immediate awareness of older memories [44]. While it is reasonable to implicate the temporal lobes in memory processes, we should not consider memories to be stored in neuronal packages in these areas. We do not know, as yet, the nature of the brain's techniques for storing its wealth of information and tapping it for adjustments to present situations.

MEMORY AND VERBAL BEHAVIOR   William James once likened both the future and the past to canvases upon which we create scenes amenable to present circumstances. To be sure, memories are not infallible and projections into the future cannot be. But memories are more than expressions of present needs, demands, or desires, and they are usually fairly reliable. Part of this reliability stems from the fact that we encode information with verbal symbols. Verbal labels increase memory capacities and exactness in discriminatory tasks. Therefore, to understand memory capacities, we must study, at the same time, learning and the use of words.

There are many different approaches to language and memory. We have by no means tapped all of the approaches to these two related phenomena. And, as in other sections of the book, not all of the approaches we have discussed relate intimately to one another. The work of the interference theorists does not mesh well with the work of those psychologists more interested with the physiological substrates of memory. Each group is following what it believes to be the most promising lead to understanding.

Furthermore, the principles of language may offer important

suggestions for scientists concerned with the organization of the nervous systems of man and animals. Karl Lashley, one of the pioneers in the study of behavior and the nervous system saw a close connection between the serial orders in production of verbal utterances and in all complicated behavioral patterns. He believed the hierarchical organization of verbal behavior resembled the hierarchical organization found in all behavior. In fact all behavior is patterned in serial manner, one movement closely following another, and in units of activity which help the organism attain the goals of life necessary for its existence [45]. Language acts as a bridge between memory phenomena on the one hand, and, on the other, the other attributes of the higher mental processes.

Cognitive Functions

Psychology aims at understanding all important characteristics of man's behavior. Higher processes, cognitive functions, intellection, and thinking are activities which we count as our highest capabilities, that is, those responsible for our personal accomplishments and the accomplishments of the human race. At the same time, we recognize that the ability to think and reason can be a tool for those ends we consider most reprehensible: hate, war, and destruction. Whether applied toward laudable or tragic ends, these higher mental functions can be studied for what they are.

Unquestionably there is a connection between verbal behavior and the higher mental processes. The degree of association, however, has not been clearly established and it is possible to witness behavior which seems to reflect the activity of higher mental processes without simultaneously witnessing signs of the use of verbal behavior. Since it is possible to be engaged in higher mental functions while being silent, it is possible to experimentally dissociate this activity from verbal activities which can not be silent when studied.

Is there a useful definition of what psychologists mean by higher mental processes? Many definitions have been proposed, but each derives its usefulness from the theoretical context in which it is embedded. Generally speaking, however, higher mental processes are inferred from behavior which is not readily predicted on the basis of the environmental (stimulus) conditions presented to the individual or on the basis of the individual's past reactions in similar situations. In other words if a person reacts immediately and with great regularity to a situation, it is likely that this reaction is one which can be explained on the basis of a previously acquired stimulus-response connection. If behavior is regular and swift in a given social situation, the reaction might be one which has become routine and does not require the use of the higher mental processes. On the other hand, if a response does not occur promptly, we tend to suspect that the response, when it does occur, has been produced by higher mental functions. If one is asked to solve the following mathematical problems, the time required for each will be quite different:

$$2 + 2 =$$
$$718 + 496 + 219 =$$
$$\sqrt{61} + \sqrt{23} =$$

The simple answer of $2 + 2$ requires very little time and probably does not require much in the way of higher mental functioning. The response "4" has assumed the character of a simple conditioned response to the stimulus "$2 + 2 =$."

On the other hand the longer time required to complete the other sums suggests that their solutions involve the use of cognitive functions, even though the final response may be quite uniform among subjects.

Responses may be a product of higher mental functions at one time and become, through practice, representative of the simpler *S-R* types of response. For example, when one is learning a foreign language, simple responses to questions in that language may require relatively long periods of time. After practice, the responses may become quite automatic. After more practice, quite complicated interchanges in the newly acquired language may occur without delay.

In these examples, delay in response time is used as an indicator of higher mental processes. Another indicator, of course, is variability in responses among persons, coupled with a delay in response. When we try to solve many kinds of problems, there is no one correct answer, and considerable variability can be found. The strategies devised to meet the demands of the day vary from person to person. One way of organizing our daily activities may not be superior to another, but the techniques we use undoubtedly reflect our individual approaches to problems.

Higher mental processes are inferred when there is a considerable amount of time between the presentation of the problem and the response or when there is variability between people in situations or where it is difficult to determine the single correctness of a given solution. We assume that the time lag between the presentation of a problem and the response represents the time required for the higher mental processes to occur. These processes are thought to be internal activities occurring in the person. Psychologists who believe in association learning theories think of the internal processes as series of *S-R* associations (mediational processes), whereas those disposed to accept the theories of Hebb might conceive of the internal processes as a series of phase sequences. In any case higher mental processes are based upon some kind of sequential activity in the nervous system. Furthermore, the time delay between the presentation of the stimulus conditions and the response is thought to reflect the time required for the neural events to run their course.

In the past the approaches to cognitive function have been based on personality, learning, or perceptual theories. Personality theorists, generally, see higher mental processes as one type of adjustment of the individual to his needs and desires. Learning theorists consider them to be merely another example of mediating responses. A perceptual theorist would look upon such processes in the same way as they would any perceptual situation. They would account for mental activities using the principles derived from the Gestalt psychologists (pp. 175–182). However, with the increasing interaction between mathematics, psychology, and engineering, approaches have been developed which promise new insights into cognition and a means by which most of our lives can be interpreted in a broader cognitive framework.

ORGANIZATION OF COGNITIVE FUNCTIONS The distinguishing characteristic of living systems, from the single cell to the complete individual, is its organization. Every system along this continuum can be divided into subparts on biochemical, functional, or morphological bases. Yet each system, be it a single cell or an entire person, represents a total organization of the subparts into one integrated functional unit. The organization of functions of the body into a total meaningful pattern is the most apparent characteristic of a man's life.

One approach to formalizing this organization is to think of behavior in terms of hierarchies. This is an important consideration because otherwise we have to develop separate explanations of the various levels of observable functions and behavior. We can look at behavior in terms of isolated muscle contractions, isolated movements of limbs, bodily movements of short durations, small verbal units, sentences, or other fragments of total behavior. At the same time, we can recognize that any organized sequence of behavior is organized into a hierarchical structure. Goal-directed activities are comprised of sequences of bodily reactions, which in turn are made up of limb movements, and these in turn are made up of isolated muscular contractions. In language, meaningful verbal utterances are made up of isolated phonemes, these in turn are combined by morpheme units into phrases, and phrases combined into sentences. Meaningful communication depends upon an organized set of sentences. Using either movements or verbal actions, the principle of hierarchical organization seems to be a useful conceptual device.

By *hierarchy processes,* we mean both a set of incorporative parts and a sequential pattern involved in the production of the parts. For example, the operation of hammering a nail consists of such subparts as lifting and striking. Within these categories are various groups of muscle contractions involving the arm and also other parts of the body. Miller, Galanter, and Pribram, in discussing the cognitive processes of man, have developed the role of hierarchical processes [46]. Much of the following discussion on plans and their role in behavior as well as the general perspective stems from their provocative contributions.

Feedback from the environment   The operations of hammering a nail are controlled to a considerable extent by the results of the operation upon the environment. Hammering is begun when the nail is sticking up and usually continues until the head of the nail is flush with the surface into which the nail is being pounded. The hammering operation is dependent upon the sensory information about the effects of the operation upon the environment. This information about the effects of the operations is *feedback.* For every operation undertaken and for every level of it, the activities of the operation are governed to a great degree by the feedback from the environment.

Feedback can exert various effects on the behavior of machines and men. Two broad types of effects should be distinguished: positive and negative. Feedback which results in increasing the particular ongoing operation of the man or the machine is positive feedback, whereas the results which act to decrease the particular ongoing operation are negative feedback. Positive or negative feedback refers to the effect upon the operation of a man or machine of essentially neutral information, itself neither favorable, unfavorable, good, nor bad.

In a furnace-thermostat system designed to heat a home, the thermostat provides feedback from the effects of heat produced by the furnace which is regarded as negative feedback. When the room temperature reaches a determined level, the feedback from the thermostat acts to decrease the heat production of the furnace.

It would be possible to wire a thermostat backwards so that the hotter the room became the more the furnace would produce heat. In this case the information from the thermostat would increase heat production and thus be a positive feedback system. Of course, a furnace-thermostat system operating on such a positive feedback system would be unstable in that the furnace or home would be burned. This typifies the instability of most positive feedback systems. A moth which flies toward a flame until it is consumed represents an unstable and maladaptive positive feedback system of biology. The withdrawal of a finger from a flame, on the other hand, is an example of a negative feedback system since sensory information acts to decrease the movements involved in approaching the flame.

Many of our most familiar actions depend on similar feedback. The use of our muscles at any given moment depends on the kind of sensory information the brain receives from the muscular region concerning its previous movement; in fact, complete, flaccid paralysis results in an area of the body in which the sensory fibers have been severed. In a large sense, feedback from our actions makes it possible to evaluate the degree of success or failure of these actions in executing our plans or for reaching our goals; it can tell us when to initiate an activity or when to cease it; and it can provide clues as to the qualitative or quantitative alteration of an action for the achievement of the action goal.

Feedback and plans   The importance of feedback for human behavior can hardly be overemphasized. Imagine the troubles we would encounter without it. Think of trying to strike a nail, tie our shoelaces, ski, or even walk without immediate feedback from the muscles as each action of these sequences is completed. Each of these skills represents a complicated order of movements. We have learned to expect different kinds of feedback from each behavioral component of the series. If feedback which is not anticipated results from our actions, then we try to alter our plans. We continually evaluate the effects of our behavior on the basis of whether or not our actions produce the feedback we intend or desire.

The examples of the preceding paragraph all involved motor skills, and the feedback discussed was limited to information arising from the body as a result of movements. However, it is important to understand that the concept of feedback is more broad and generalized. More completely, feedback is that which carries information about the effects of our actions upon things, upon other people, and upon society.

A girl going out on a special date may do certain things which she expects will produce a desired change in her boyfriend. Her behavior is organized about a plan. This plan may have several components: one course of action at a party before the dance, a different course of action at the dance, and yet another on the way home. Through each phase of her plan, she is very much aware of effects of these programs upon her partner. This feedback allows her to adjust her tactics according to the extent to which each part of her plan achieves its intended goal, that is, whether or not the feedback from her actions is what she expects or desires it to be. When it isn't, she can change her tactics —or in extreme cases she may drop the course of action or the total plan entirely.

Plans are organizational rules which determine the sequence of behavioral operations undertaken by an individual. The operations themselves present sequences of behaviors which have intended results. The actual feedback from the operations is matched against the expected or intended feedback as a method of evaluating its usefulness.

Psychologists interested in using plans as tools in understanding behavior must know where they come from. Since plans govern the order of behavioral operations, they must represent a higher-level process. Are we born with an innate ability to formulate plans, or must we learn how to construct plans? Given the ability to organize our activity for a functional purpose, what determines the substance and arrangement of our plans?

While each of us has his own individual plans for reaching his own individual goals, what are the determinants of the planning process which are common to all men? The answers to these questions are being sought through research. High-speed digital computers and other similar mechanisms intended to simulate human performances provide one avenue of approach.

SIMULATION OF COGNITIVE BEHAVIOR   Man has always been delighted by machines that appear to copy familiar human forms. European clockmakers designed elaborate mechanisms in the shapes of people which were the wonder of their age. These models, however, copied the external aspects far more successfully than the functional. Today, psychologists, mathematicians, and others are seeking to find ways to use the giant electronic computers as models of man.

Of course, a computer does not resemble a man. The similarity between a man and a computer is determined by how well such a machine can generate the psychologist's data obtained from people. If a computer can learn to provide data like those generated by an individual learning a maze, then in some way at least the computer has simulated the person. We don't expect the computer to walk through the maze, but the computer has produced a data sheet indistinguishable from that created by a human subject.

Data from human subjects in experiments are nothing more than systematized descriptions of the behavior. If a computer is programmed to simulate data from a human experimental session, the entire project is only worthwhile in so far as the descriptions of human behavior are useful and meaningful. Despite the romance of electronics, computers themselves are limited creations. A computer must be provided with operational instructions in order to operate at all. When referring to computer simulation of behavior, we must qualify this by emphasizing the fact that it is a computer *plus a program of instructions* which is actually responsible for the operations of the machine.

Interest in the use of computers in simulating higher functions was aroused by a theorem proposed by the mathematician Turing in 1937. This theorem stated that a machine could be built to produce any unambiguous description of the behavior of organisms. Computers have been programmed which will prove theorems in plane geometry and even draw simple drawings as a student might [47]. This is not only a demonstration of what can be done by clever design, but it also shows that many operations of a complicated nature can be accomplished by machines which do not have consciousness. More interesting to the psychologist are machines that can learn. It is possible, for example, to build a machine which can learn to play chess. More fascinating still are the self-instructional machines which are becoming increasingly possible to construct. What goes on within such a machine as it acquires knowledge that was not planned by its own builders and programmers provides an important area for psychological study. By examining the mechanical simulation of cognitive behavior it is possible to learn what changes occurred within the model as its learning progressed.

Types of problem solving   Since computers make calculations with lightning speed, they can be programmed to find solutions requiring exhaustive, humanly impossible calculations. For some kinds of problems, one can devise a program so that a solution must be obtained if one exists. Frequently, this kind of program involves making calculations of all possible outcomes and then picking the one most desired. This type of solution is called an *algorithm*. An example of a simple algorithm would be the opening of a three-number lock by simply trying all possible combinations. There are many kinds of algorithms. Some we learn informally while some we learn by formal education.

However, many problems are not amenable to solution by algorithm. Often problems are solved by use of a *heuristic,* a method which offers hope of aiding in the solution, but does not guarantee it. Polya [48] has reported many heuristics used by high school students in mathematics problems. Probably all of us have used some of these methods, such as trying to work back from the solution and trying to make a simpler problem similar to the one assigned which can be solved.

Heuristic approaches are necessary even for computers. In playing chess, for example, a computer would have arrived at an algorithmic solution if the move it decided upon at a given point in the game had been based on a consideration of all moves logically possible for each player at that point, all logically possible outcomes of those moves, all moves possible to each player as a result of those outcomes—and so forth to all check-mate situations that could possibly occur from the given point in the game. Although each move actually made diminishes the number of possible choices open to the future, it has been estimated that even if players worked at the speed of electronic computers, one game could not be completed in a lifetime. Therefore, the chess-playing computers have been programmed to play following certain kinds of heuristic rules, such as protecting the king, controlling the center of the board, developing the pawns, material balance [49]. The computer compares the situation against heuristic rules programmed into it in an order of importance. First, it evaluates its king's position. If it is not safe, it moves to protect it. If it is safe, it considers the board in terms of possible exchanges of pieces and places at which further protection is necessary. Then the machine moves on to consideration of development of control over the center of the board, and so on.

While it has proved possible to develop chess-playing machines which approach perfection, the most important direction would be the development of machines and programs which closely simulate man as *he* plays chess. If this is accomplished, we can study the characteristics of the programs in order to obtain insight into the characteristics of man.

Mathematics is contributing new ideas and approaches to psychology in this area of simulation of behavior. Earlier, we saw another contribution of mathematics in the development of mathematical models of learning and in the application of decision theory to sensory detection experiments. Developments in mathematics shape our view of behavioral problems and the techniques used to study them.

References

1. Shirley, M. *The First Two Years: III Personality Manifestations*. Minneapolis: Univer. of Minnesota Press, 1933.
2. Skinner, B. F. *Verbal Behavior*. New York: Appleton-Century-Crofts, Inc., 1957.
3. Greenspoon, J. The effect of verbal and non-verbal stimuli on the frequency of members of two verbal response classes. Unpublished doctoral dissertation, Univer. of Indiana, 1950.
4. Dulany, D. C., Jr. Hypotheses and habits in verbal "operant conditioning." *J. abnorm. soc. Psychol.*, 1961, **63,** 251–263.
5. Brown, R., & Fraser, C. The acquisition of syntax. In C. N.

Cofer (Ed.), *Verbal Behavior and Learning: Problems and Processes*. New York: McGraw-Hill Book Company, Inc., 1963.

6. Guttman, N., & Kalish, H. I. Experiments in discrimination. *Sci. Amer.*, 1958, **198,** 77–82.

7. Blackwell, H. R., & Schlosberg, H. Octave generalization, pitch discrimination, and loudness thresholds in the white rat. *J. exp. Psychol.*, 1943, **33,** 407–419.

8. Gibson, E. J. A systematic application of the concepts of generalization and differentiation to verbal learning. Unpublished doctoral dissertation, Yale Univer., 1938.

9. Razran, G. The observable unconscious and the inferable conscious in current Soviet psychophysiology: Interoceptive conditioning, semanatic conditioning, and orienting reflex. *Psychol. Rev.*, 1961, **68,** 81–147.

10. Razran, G. A quantitative study of meaning by a conditioned salivary technique. *Science,* 1939, **90,** 89–90.

11. Lumsdaine, A. A. Conditioned eyelid responses as mediating generalized finger reaction. *Psychol. Bull.*, 1939, **36,** 650.

12. Hilgard, E. R., & Marquis, D. G. *Conditioning and Learning.* New York: Appleton-Century-Crofts, Inc., 1940.

13. Osgood, C. E. *Method and Theory in Experimental Psychology.* New York: Oxford Univer. Press, 1953.

14. Osgood, C. E., & Suci, G. J. Factor analysis of meaning. *J. exp. Psychol.*, 1955, **50,** 325–338.

15. Underwood, B. J., & Schulz, R. W. *Meaningfulness and Verbal Learning.* Chicago: J. B. Lippincott Company, 1960.

16. Mowrer, O. H. *Learning Theory and the Symbolic Processes.* New York: John Wiley & Sons, Inc., 1960.

17. Brown, R. *Words and Things.* New York: the Free Press of Glencoe, 1958.

18. Noble, C. E. Meaningfulness and familiarity. In C. N. Cofer and Barbara S. Musgrave (Eds.), *op. cit.*

19. Glaze, J. A. The association value of nonsense syllables. *J. genet. Psychol.*, 1928, **35,** 255–267.

20. Lyon, D. O. The relation of length of material to time taken for learning and the optimum distribution of time. *J. educ. Psychol.*, 1914, **5,** 1–9, 85–91, 155–163.

21. Peterson, L. R., & Peterson, M. J. Short-term retention of individual verbal items. *J. exp. Psychol.*, 1959, **58,** 193–198.

22. Luh, C. W. The conditions of retention. *Psychol. Monogr.*, No. 142, 1922, **31,** 1–87.

23. Postman, L., & Rau, L. Retention as a function of the

method of measurement. *Univer. Calif. Publ. Psychol.,* 1957, **8,** 217–270.

24. McGeoch, J. A., & Irion, A. L. *The Psychology of Human Learning.* New York: David McKay Company, Inc., 1952.

25. Underwood, B. J. Ten years of massed practice on distributed practice. *Psychol. Rev.,* 1961, **68,** 229–247.

26. Underwood, B. J., & Schulz, R. W. Studies of distributed practice: XX. Sources of interference associated with differences in learning and retention. *J. exp. Psychol.,* 1961, **61,** 228–235.

27. Hull, C. L., Hovland, C. I., Ross, R. T., Hall, M., Perkins, D. T. & Fitch, F. B. *Mathematico-Deductive Theory of Rate Learning.* New Haven: Yale Univer. Press, 1940.

28. Pillsbury, W. B., & Raush, H. L. An extension of the Köhler-Restorff inhibition phenomenon. *Amer. J. Psychol.,* 1943, **56,** 293–298.

29. Bruce, R. W. Conditions of transfer of training. *J. exp. Psychol.,* 1933, **16,** 343–361.

30. Judd, C. H. The relation of special training to general intelligence. *Educ. Rev.,* 1908, **36,** 28–42.

31. Harlow, H. F. The formation of learning sets. *Psychol. Rev.,* 1949, **56,** 51–65.

32. Melton, A. W., & Von Lackum, W. J. Retroactive and proactive inhibition in retention: evidence for a two-factor theory of retroactive inhibition. *Amer. J. Psychol.,* 1941, **54,** 157–173.

33. Melton, A. W., & Irwin, J. McQ. The influence of degree of interpolated learning on retroactive inhibition and the overt transfer of specific responses. *Amer. J. Psychol.,* 1940, **53,** 173–203.

34. Thune, L. E., & Underwood, B. J. Retroactive inhibition as a function of degree of interpolated learning. *J. exp. Psychol.,* 1943, **32,** 185–200.

35. Underwood, B. J. Interference and forgetting. *Psychol. Rev.,* 1957, **64,** 49–60.

36. Barnes, J. M., & Underwood, B. J. "Fate" of first-list associations in transfer theory. *J. exp. Psychol.,* 1959, **58,** 97–105.

37. Koffka, K. *Principles of Gestalt Psychology.* New York: Harcourt, Brace & World, Inc., 1935.

38. Köhler, W. *Gestalt Psychology.* New York: Liveright Publishing Corporation, 1929.

39. Hebb, D. O. *The Organization of Behavior.* New York: John Wiley & Sons, Inc., 1949.

40. Duncan, C. P. The retroactive effect of electro-shock on learning. *J. comp. physiol. Psychol.,* 1949, **42,** 32–44.

41. Coons, E. E., & Miller, N. E. Conflict versus consolidation of memory traces to explain "retrograde amnesia" produced by ECS. *J. comp. physiol. Psychol.*, 1960, **53**, 524–531.

42. Madsen, M. C., & McGaugh, J. L. The effect of electroshock on one-trial avoidance learning. *J. comp. physiol. Psychol.*, 1961, **54**, 522–523.

43. Penfield, W., & Milner, B. Memory deficit produced by bilateral lesions in the hippocampal zone. *Arch. Neurol. Psychiat. (Chicago)*, 1958, **79**, 475–497.

44. Penfield, W., & Roberts, L. *Speech and Brain Mechanisms.* Princeton, N.J.: Princeton Univer. Press, 1959.

45. Lashley, K. S. The problem of serial order in behavior. In L. A. Jeffress (Ed.), *Cerebral Mechanisms in Behavior, the Hixon Symposium.* New York: John Wiley & Sons, Inc., 1951.

46. Miller, G. A., Galanter, E., & Pribram, K. H. *Plans and the Structure of Behavior.* New York: Holt, Rinehart and Winston, Inc., 1960.

47. Gelernter, H. L., & Rochester, N. Intelligent behavior in problem-solving machines. *IBM. J. Res. Developm.*, 1958, **2**, 336–345.

48. Polya, G. *How to Solve It.* Princeton, N.J.: Princeton Univer. Press, 1945.

49. Newell, A., Shae, J. C., & Simon, H. A. Chess-playing problems and the problem of complexity. *IBM. J. Res. Developm.*, 1958, **2**, 320–335.

EIGHT   MOTIVATION: VIEWS AND THEORIES ▶

Every human being wants food, drink, shelter, comfort, security, love, understanding, and so on. The subjective feelings which are described as wanting, desiring, or needing reflect the fact that sometimes we seem to be aware of the goals toward which our behavior is directed. There are times when we ascribe the cause of our desires to special internal conditions. For example, "I *need* a drink" or "I *need* a cigarette." At times, we are even more emphatic. "That candy bar saved my life, I was famished." Comments such as these suggest a belief that we seek objects because they fulfill a *need* within us. We must rec-

ognize that such statements as "I really needed that _____,"
and "that _____ saved my life" are overstatements and are
quite different from true cases of drastic and immediate biological deficits. Most of our desired objects are not ones that
function as life preservers.

We generally accept the idea that goals concerned with comfort and luxury must be sought secondarily to those related to
survival. A similar belief is that people can be motivated toward the loftier goals of art, religion and political freedom only
after their bodily needs have been satisfied. There are exceptions to these views and some people actually do sacrifice
their lives for idealistic objectives; in fact, many such people
have come to be highly revered by large segments of the
human society. Thus, in some individuals ideational goals can
overcome the basic biological needs as motivating factors.

This chapter presents an overview of some of the ways in
which psychologists study the motivational aspects of behavior.
It does not attempt to present the key to a complete understanding of what makes people "tick." We will be content to
select from various theories the problems that arise in the study
of motivation. After a definition of motivation, we shall outline
what is known about the body's sensitivity to changes within
itself in order to provide a basis for evaluating motivational
theories that are based on biological needs. We shall next relate motives to learning theories in an effort to point out how
theories of learning alone leave much to be desired in the explanation of behavior. In the last section of the chapter, we
shall show how the motivational theories which account for
man's social behavior provide a still further dimension in understanding human behavior.

It will be helpful for the reader to bear in mind the restricted
aims of most motivational theorists. Few would claim their
schemes account for all the motivated behavior exhibited by
man. None would assert any claim on having the one absolutely
valid approach to motivation. Rather, most would contend they
believe their approach to have some ability to increase low
knowledge of man's behavior.

Toward a Definition of Motive

Psychologists tend to use the word *motive* differently depending
upon their theoretical bias and orientation. There is no universal

psychological standard that can be used to find the meaning of the word for all psychologists. Furthermore, the forces which are presumed to be responsible for a person's choices among different objects are complex, and this complexity itself makes it difficult to formulate any single accurate statement of what motives are. One recent attempt to incorporate all that psychologists mean when they use the word *motive* ran to 244 words [1]. However, as a first approximation, we might say that *motives are theoretical concepts used to explain the direction, intensity, and persistence of behavioral patterns.*

Motives are entities inferred from observation of behavior. The statement "a hungry man will seek food and eat" implies a considerable number of assumptions; e.g., one must assume that the motive hunger *directs* the person toward certain environmental stimuli, that this action will *persist* for some finite period of time, that there will be certain *consumatory responses* when the appropriate objects are found, and usually we must stipulate something like, "all other things being equal." By "other things" we mean that this behavioral sequence (seek food, eat) would occur if there were no other more imperative motives functioning at the time. Still, we would be a long way from predicting actual behavior. The patterns of a man's food-seeking acts depend upon learned techniques for food attainment. The ways in which we make consumatory responses vary too. The time of day and many other significant variables are influential in predicting what patterns of behavior will occur.

In many cases of simple biological motives this general framework of assumptions is understood and not stated expressly, but it is nonetheless present. In predicting food-getting behavior on the basis of hunger, we have directed our attention to only one of the determining factors in an implicit, more general theory.

Biological Motives

The biological motive of hunger can be inferred from observations of behavior directed toward food, from verbal reports of hunger made by others, from what we know about a person's immediate past, and from things we can learn about certain neural or physiological conditions in the body. We may wish to accept verbal statements as a measure of hunger. They may represent a conscious awareness of a desire for food. These then are some of the ways in which presence of motives generally may be indicated.

Using one of these methods of inferring the presence of a biological motive, it is possible to study many different aspects of the motives. Some psychologists study the physiological basis of our awareness of motives, others study the brain areas concerned with the initiation and cessation of eating and drinking, and some study the mechanisms underlying other motivated behavior patterns.

THE AWARENESS OF HUNGER It is in some ways remarkable to believe that a person can be aware of changes in the condition of his stomach. We have learned about the functions of sensory nerves. There are sensory nerves from the stomach which project to several areas of the brain. But knowledge of the anatomical presence of nerves running from the stomach to the brain does not imply that activity in them signals conscious awareness of hunger.

Undoubtedly, Cannon and Washburn [2] were excited when they found that a subject's report of hunger pangs correlated with the contractions of his stomach. In their experiments subjects swallowed a balloon which could be inflated in the stomach. Pneumatic equipment was arranged to record each contraction of the stomach. Since reports of hunger followed the stomach contractions, it was inferred that contractions had *caused* the conscious experiences.

This correlation does not tell the whole story, however. In some diseases it becomes necessary for a surgeon to remove the entire stomach. Many reports have indicated the removal of the stomach does not reduce the awareness of desire for food, nor does it eliminate appropriate food-seeking responses. Experimentally, Tsang [3] reported no loss in the effectiveness of food incentives for stomachless rats. We can only say that stomach contractions may be a sufficient condition for conscious feelings of hunger or of hunger-motivated behavior in otherwise intact animals. Certainly, awareness of hunger must result from other causes too.

BLOOD SUGAR AND HUNGER There is a great deal of evidence to the effect that the blood of a hungry animal is different from that of a satiated animal. However, the absolute blood sugar level in arteries and veins has not been found to correlate with behavioral indices of hunger. Recently, it has been discovered that the *ratio* of blood sugar in the arteries to blood sugar in the veins is related to hunger. Stunkard obtained measures of the glucose levels in the arteries and veins of human subjects while the human subjects had swallowed balloons in their stomachs. When the difference in glucose levels between the arteries and veins was small, the subjects showed stomach contractions and reported sensations of hunger. When there was a good deal more sugar in the arteries, the subjects did not show these characteristics. These differences between glucose levels in arteries and veins have been interpreted [4] as reflecting degrees of utilization and availability of body sugar. When the artery-vein glucose ratio is low (*S*s hungry), there would seem to be less sugar available for the body's cells. When the ratio is high (*S*s sated) this is believed to reflect a greater amount of available body sugar.

However, even with this relationship between blood sugar and "hunger" we should be careful not to attribute all sensations of hunger to these artery-vein sugar differences. Most likely it is but one of many factors contributing to our awareness of a need for food.

We should also recognize the need for a mechanism by which we become cognizant of these differences in artery-vein sugar levels. It is not enough to know of these blood differences, we must find how the central nervous system becomes aware of them. We must find receptor mechanisms sensitive to these changes in the composition of the blood.

It is likely that such cells are located in the hypothalamus. Mayer and his co-workers have shown that cells in this brain area of the mouse are most likely to be the ones which pick up gold-thioglucose (glucose with a sulfur link to gold). This compound is taken into cells in much the same manner as plain glucose. Once in a cell, however, the cell dies and it is possible to examine the brain of the mouse *post mortem* to find maximum areas of glucose absorption and subsequent cell mortality. Destruction seems to be centered in the ventromedial nucleus of the hypothalamus. If we observe the mouse after an injection of gold-thioglucose which destroys this hypothalamic area, we find the animal becoming more and more obese. A picture of one of these extremely obese, but otherwise normal, animals

327

(called hyperphagic) is presented in Fig. 8.1. The hyperphagic effects caused by the gold-thioglucose is but one of the bits of evidence relating the hypothalamus with the biological motives.

↳ food desire motive

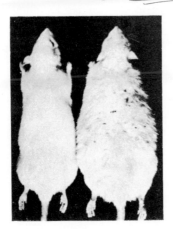

FIG. 8.1. *Comparison of normal rat (left) with one made hyperphagic by lesions in the hypothalamus (right). From Fig. 6, A. W. Hetherington & S. W. Ranson. Hypothalamic lesions and adiposity in the rat. Anat. Rec., 1940, 78: 155.*

HYPOTHALAMIC CENTERS FOR BIOLOGICAL MOTIVES   Earlier in the book (p. 110) we indicated the existence in the hypothalamus of centers controlling the initiation and cessation of eating and the initiation of drinking. Studies of the hypothalamus have usually been accomplished through evaluating the effects of lesions in, or electrical stimulation of, certain hypothalamic areas. For many years it has been possible to make reasonably small lesions in the brains of experimental animals to evaluate their effects upon behavior. But only recently have techniques been evolved to allow the implantation of tiny electrodes into various areas of the brain and pass minute amounts of electrical current through these electrodes while the animal is awake and moving about naturally postoperatively. The electrical current passed through the implanted electrodes stimulates nerve cells and fibers in the region of the electrodes.

With these two methods, lesions and stimulation, investigators have established the existence of *centers* for some of the biological motives in various hypothalamic regions. When the center in or near the ventromedial hypothalamus is destroyed, the animals will not stop eating [5]. It is as though a mechanism which normally acts to stop the ingestion of food is removed. The ventromedial region is thought to be a satiety center. Lesions placed more laterally in the hypothalamus produce animals which do not eat, and which will starve to death unless special retraining in eating is instituted [6]. This more lateral hypothalamic area can be thought of as a center acting to modulate the initiation of eating: a feeding center.

Teitelbaum has found changes in food appetites which go along with the marked increase in obesity found in animals with ventromedial hypothalamic lesions [7]. The hyperphagic animals are more sensitive to both favorable and unfavorable adulterations of their food. They will eat more or less, as the case may be, even when the amount of adulteration is so small as not to affect food consumption of normal animals.

Hypothalamic centers which seem to regulate the body's water balance have been discovered. Two types have been discovered to date. These are not exactly analogous to those for food regulation. One region in the anterior hypothalamus exerts an influence on the pituitary hormones regulating water excretion thus regulating the body's *need* for water. Another center in the lateral aspects of the hypothalamus seems to initiate the onset of drinking. By implanting electrodes into these lateral hypothalamic areas of goats, it is possible to control their drinking behavior [8]. When these centers are electrically stimulated, the animal drinks immediately and continues to drink, although the goat may have just finished drinking more than it needs.

Many other centers for behavior which are related to biologically motivated activities have been demonstrated in the hypothalamus. Once again we find that there are areas which will alter the animals' biologically directed behavior in one way or another when damaged or electrically stimulated. For example, it is possible to produce an animal that will not sleep at all, or will sleep all of the time, depending on the location of the damage or stimulation. The existence of these centers led Stellar to propose a general model for the phenomena of motivated behavior.

STELLAR'S THEORY Stellar [9] proposed that the amount of motivated behavior (used here in the sense of goal-directed behavior) is a function of the level of neural activity or excitation in appropriate "motivational" hypothalamic centers. The amount of food-directed activity exhibited by an animal reflects the state of the hypothalamic centers related to eating. Every hypothalamic center receives input from a variety of neural and chemical sources. First, as in the case of the food centers, impulses from the peripheral portions of the body (stomach) help regulate the activity in the food centers. Sensory information from all of the receptor organs is fed into these centers. The limbic system and the neocortex act to help regulate the activity in hypothalamic centers too. Finally, the center's state of excitation can be regulated by the amounts of various hormones and the artery-vein glucose ratios of the blood.

Stellar's model suggests a compensatory relationship between these various regulatory influences. Appropriate goal-oriented behavior can be elicited by combinations of the various types of controlling factors. For example, we could become hungry, from stomach contractions, from sensory input (picture or smell of steak), or from cortical influences (thinking of food). These influences could act jointly or independently or in various combinations. The hypothalamic centers are proposed as the point of summation of these several influences. Stellar's model provides us with a useful scheme for conceptualizing the roles of these different physiological factors in determining goal-directed behavior patterns. The amount of biologically motivated behavior exhibited by an animal at any moment was postulated to be a function of the excitation level of specific hypothalamic centers.

At present we had best regard Stellar's work as an admirable beginning for a neurophysiological theory of motivation. Perhaps its greatest fault lies in the fact that it does not help us understand the learned motives which are most characteristic of man. When we learn more about the subcortical and neocortical mechanisms responsible for learning it may be possible to build a suitable extension onto Stellar's basic framework. With this extension the model may have greater applicability to problems of human motivation, although it is by no means certain that the model, as it is, is sufficient to account for all of the biological motives found in animals [10, p. 1507].

Stellar's model was based specifically on experimental analysis of hypothalamic activities. However, another considerably older basis for a physiological model of motivation is based on observations of the body's activities which result in its maintaining itself in the face of changing conditions in the environment.

HOMEOSTASIS   The principle of homeostasis can be traced historically to Claude Bernard, the great French physiologist. Its greatest proponent in America was Walter B. Cannon, who receives most of the credit for its popularity. Simply stated, homeostasis refers to the body's tendency to maintain a relatively constant internal environment in the face of external changes. Fortunately, the relative invariability of the internal environment is usually a favorable one for survival of the organism. For example, when the body's supply of blood sugars becomes depleted, more blood sugars are secreted from the liver and other sources to resupply the internal environment. This tendency to maintain a relatively constant internal environment can occur through changes in the internal organs, but it can occur by means of changes in the somatic muscles too. For example, when we become cold we huddle and shiver as our internal organs make appropriate adjustments.

The concept of homeostasis provided psychologists with a philosophic perspective from which they could view behavior. Many early psychologists believed the homeostatic principle underlies all of man's behavior. Freud and Hull developed quite different theories of behavior, but both views are based on the assumption that our actions can best be considered as attempts at the restoration and maintenance of favorable internal states.

However, should we view our own eating habits as fulfilling homeostatic demands? To be sure, eating acts to provide us with the substances needed to maintain the internal conditions necessary for life. But we have already learned something of the actual physiological mechanisms responsible for hunger and eating, i.e., artery-vein glucose levels, stomach contractions, hypothalamic centers. The label of homeostatic mechanism adds little to what we already know. The word *homeostasis* is rather like the word *instinct* in that it is only descriptive and does not provide us with an explanation of the behavior under study.

THE CONCEPT OF NEED   Given the biological orientation provided by the homeostatic principle, the concept of *need* soon developed in American psychology. Needs are presumed to derive from deficits. When we are deprived of food, we *need* it. When we are deprived of water, we *need* it. Experimentally, when we deprive an organism of material necessary for survival, we have created a need for that material. This descriptive use of the term is relatively unambiguous: *deprivation produces need.*

331

Once needs were defined they could be used as explanations of behavior. Some psychologists began to use the word *need* to explain direction of behavior: a person ate because he needed food. In the same way a need for food was used to explain *persistence* or *intensity* of food-directed behavior. Thus, the simple word *need* began to be used as an explanation of behavior.

However, two types of problems arose almost immediately. First, it became clear that not all deprivations of essential substances alter behavior. If animals are deprived for example, of vitamin A or D, we can find no evidence of any special change in their behavior directed toward meeting this need. Secondly, sexual and maternal behavior patterns are not essential to the survival of the individual organism and not based on deprivation. Yet they are based in part upon internal physiological changes. Thus we are faced with these two types of problems for our definition of *needs*. Should we change our descriptive definition to say that only certain biological deprivations result in *needs* which are capable of directing behavior? Should we also say that any physiological change in the organism can become a *need* even though it may not stem from an internal deficit?

But these problems of definition have been further aggravated by the adoption of the word *need* by theorists dealing with social motives. Motives such as *need for achievement, need for affiliation, need for power* (see pp. 362–368) are defined by operations far removed from the original biological emphasis. The result is that today some psychologists argue that the concept of need is superfluous and should be dropped from current psychological usage [10].

While this suggestion may have considerable merit, it is unlikely to be adopted by any large number of psychologists. Rather, we must be alert to the several meanings and uses of the word *need*. In addition, experiments based on the concept of need have produced important knowledge about behavior. In particular, experiments investigating the relation between biological needs and behavioral preferences have proved fruitful.

NEEDS, PREFERENCES, AND SPECIFIC APPETITES Considered from a homeostatic position, we might expect organisms suffering from biological needs to become more directed toward foods which contain the materials required by the body. In many circumstances rats will tend to choose a balanced dietary fare from cafeteria-style offerings of many foods. With animals some, but not all, bodily deficiencies alter the preferences exhibited for various foods in ways which tend to restore the body's supplies of missing substances. The needs imposed on the animals resulted in specific hunger for the missing substances. Casein is a protein very low in the order of preference for rats. However, if the rats are deprived of this protein for a prolonged period of time, they will come to choose casein in preference to other foods [11].

While some changes in the kind of food sought can be produced by biological need, not all food preferences can be explained on this basis. We want to explain how it is that different people have different tastes in foods. One explanation for taste preferences might be their past association with the fulfillment of the hunger motive and the subsequent homeostatic restoration of the body's food supplies and that people and animals prefer tastes that have been associated with nourishment in their past. Thus, we like the sweet taste of saccharine (which has no nutritive value) because sweet tastes generally have been associated with actual nourishment in the past. We should notice that this explanation attempts to account for preferences on the basis of biological needs and the stimuli associated with them. The general principle is that of secondary reinforcement that was discussed in Chapter 6.

A study which poses a difficulty for this theory has been reported [12]. Shortly after birth a group of guinea pigs was fed a steady diet of food adulterated with a bitter substance. With nothing better to eat, these guinea pigs learned to associate the unpleasant taste with hunger reduction. Later in life these experimental animals were tested against a control group of normally fed guinea pigs and given a choice between food with and without this bitter substance. Despite their exclusive experience with the bitter food, the test group did *not* show any greater preference for the unpleasant taste than did the control animals. Thus, the secondary reinforcement hypothesis failed to be confirmed.

Perhaps the best way to conceptualize food or taste preferences is to assume a basic pattern of preferences to be genetically provided for each species. Sweet tastes might be one of these genetically determined preferred tastes. Transient biological needs and more stable patterns of cultural or individual learning could act to modify these basic biological preferences.

When we talk of *preferences,* we are describing behavioral choices, i.e., a person or an animal selects object A and not object B. To measure preferences we might adopt several techniques but all would use some observable and measurable behavior to indicate the preference of the individual under study. A homeostatic theory attempts to explain preferences on the basis of needs, and we have already discovered some of the difficulties of such theories. Some psychologists explain preference behavior on the basis of an inferred activity or process within the individual called *pleasure.* When we prefer object A to any other, these psychologists infer that the individual expects object A to produce more pleasure, or less unpleasantness, than the other possible choices. This kind of psychological theory has been with us for centuries and is generally called *hedonism.*

HEDONISM As mentioned above, the doctrine of hedonism refers to a proposed general tendency for organisms to attain pleasure and/or to avoid pain or unpleasantness. Let us examine this doctrine as it is related to food preferences.

For hedonists, the affective processes are the prime movers of behavior. Many psychologists believe that the affective quality of the various sensations is innately determined. Any association of these sensations with present or past reactions with need reduction is therefore inconsequential. According to this point of view we eat candy because it tastes sweet and this is a pleasant taste for us. Certain types of stimulation are pleasant, others are unpleasant or painful, and others are neutral.

Those types of stimuli which are affectively neutral can assume secondary reinforcing or motivating properties through association with other stimuli. The issue is whether or not any stimulus can have positive qualities without any association with a reduction in biological need.

In one experiment dogs were raised from birth on a diet of milk. They did not have any experience with the sight or smell of any other kind of food. When meat was first presented to the animals, the smell of it did not produce any salivation. The animals readily ate the meat, however, and after a few experiences of smell, followed by meat, the animals salivated profusely to the odor. Looking at the salivation as a conditioned response in the Pavlovian sense, the smell of meat was an unusually effective *CS*. The establishment of a salivary response to other truly neutral stimuli would have taken much longer to develop. Thus there was something special about the smell of meat which enabled it to become an effective stimulus for the salivary response with great ease [13].

We have already found that raising guinea pigs with adulterated food while they were very young did not give them an appreciable adult preference for the taste. Thus it would appear that there are preferences for certain kinds of stimulation which occur without prior learning, and also certain aversions which are hard to modify through experience.

Other studies indicate that the acts of eating and drinking have reinforcing effects over and above their physiological benefits. The reward value of eating is related to the amount of eating behavior necessary to ingest a given amount of food [14]. Several studies have compared the effectiveness of drinking milk versus having it deposited directly into the stomach through an artificially created fistula [15, 16]. The results from such experiments indicate that tasting the milk provides a more effective reinforcement condition than does the stomach injection of it. At the moment, it is impossible to decide whether the taste of the milk or the consummatory response of drinking it holds priority as the reinforcer.

An interesting experiment shows the efficacy of the sexual consummatory response as a reinforcement to animals. Sheffield, Wulff, and Backer [17] trained sexually naïve male animals to run a maze. They were rewarded by being allowed to start copulating with a female in heat. The animals were always parted before the male reached orgasm (and therefore presumably before a reduction of physiological need occurred). Nonetheless this introductory copulatory activity served as an effective incentive for maze learning. A hedonistic theory might attribute the reinforcing effects of the consummatory responses to an innate pleasurable reaction within the organism resulting from the stimuli arising from sexual act even without orgasm.

When we speak of the effects of the consummatory response on the animal, we refer to the feedback to the central nervous system from the response. In other words, it is the sensory results of the response that will have the reinforcing or affective properties. Which word is chosen to describe the behavior depends to a large extent upon one's theoretical orientation toward behavior.

To this point we have only talked of *affect* as a theoretical concept inferred from behavior. But we do know something about physiological activities more or less closely associated with the hedonistic qualities of pleasure.

PHYSIOLOGICAL CORRELATES OF AFFECT   Some of the results found by Olds have been discussed earlier (Chapter 3, pp. 110–113). The locating of various zones of positive, negative, and neutral affective, or reinforcement effects, in the brain was a major neurophysiological breakthrough, and at the same time a major problem to theories which asserted that affect must be related to reductions of biological need. In the work of Olds and others working with brain stimulation, we find that reinforcing effects are produced without any reduction of biological need. The electrical stimulation is such that it could not have been paired with need reduction in the past. How do the advocates of the homeostatically based theories interpret these results from stimulation of the brain?

First and foremost, the fact that animals prefer intracranial stimulation to other forms of reinforcement does not mean this produces pleasure in the animal. We can never fully know the subjective experiences of animals or people. One type of explanation tried to show that intracranial stimulation produced compulsive, automatic behavior patterns, only superficially appearing to have positive affect for the animal. However, the great number and variety of tasks on which animals have exhibited preferences for stimulation of certain brain areas makes this alternative explanation seem doubtful. But we can not dismiss so easily the arguments that stimulation obliterates ongoing unpleasant neural activities or that the stimulation activates the same neural systems aroused naturally when needs are reduced.

What about pain? Consider the seemingly prodigious effects of this experience upon behavior. There are few impelling motivational conditions which approximate the effects of pain. But the physiological basis of pain is still relatively uncertain despite the considerable research activities devoted to understanding it.

Olds has found areas of the brain of the rat which appear to have punishing or unpleasant effects when stimulated. Areas producing behavior indicative of positive or negative effects are shown in Fig. 8.2 [18]. If depression of a bar acts to produce electrical stimulation in a negative affect area, animals will make special efforts to remain clear of the bar. Other tests indicate that animals will do nothing to produce and actively strive to prevent stimulation of these areas.

Neuroanatomically, pain tracts can be located within the spinal cord and followed to the thalamus. However, at this point the trail ends, and no higher representation of pain has been found in the brain. Stimulation of the neocortical surface of the brain in the human produces no painful sensations [20]. It is for this reason that neurosurgery on man can be performed when necessary with only local anesthetics.

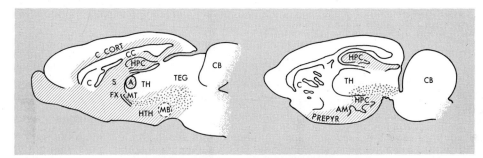

FIG. 8.2. *Locations of brain areas which produce positive (lined areas) and negative (stipple) effects when stimulated electrically. Adapted from J. Olds. Positive emotional systems studied by techniques of self-stimulation.* Psychiat. Res. Rep., *1960,* 12, *238–257.*

In some cases where patients suffer from relentless pain, neurosurgeons have severed certain neural tracts connecting the extreme forward portions of the frontal lobes (called the prefrontal lobes) with other portions of the brain. This operation seems to produce an interesting and, at present, inexplicable result. The patients on whom the operation was performed still report pain existing with the same severity as before the operation, but this pain no longer "bothers them" [19]. The operation seems to free them from domination by the sensation of pain. These results have yet to be satisfactorily incorporated into any theory of behavior.

Another fact about pain which remains unexplained is that a hypnotized subject, given appropriate instructions by the hypnotist, can inhibit pain responses and the memory of pain. Hypnotized subjects have reported no painful sensations from burning or puncture wounds which actually cause tissue damage. The mechanisms underlying these phenomena are unknown.

Finally, evidence from dogs reared under conditions where they were deprived of the normal pains and stresses of puppy life react as though their perception of pain was missing or reduced in adult testing [20]. Time and again these dogs would approach a burning match and extinguish it with their noses without a trace of any painful response and without a lessening of approach tendencies to the match. The suggestion is that certain kinds of early experiences may play a crucial role in development of our sensations of pain, but the mechanisms responsible for development of pain and pleasure are not really understood.

HEBB'S THEORY RELATED TO MOTIVATION Only a few behavioristic theories attempt *to explain* the phenomena of pleasure and unpleasantness. Many theories use pleasure and pain as conceptual tools to explain behavior, but only Hebb has undertaken to explain these tools themselves, in a way acceptable to many psychologists, using reasonable assumptions about the operation of the nervous system. In Chapter 5 we discussed the major features of Hebb's theory, including the basic unit of neural functioning, the cell assembly. Cell assemblies become related to each other through past sequential associations to form phase sequences. Phase sequences can be facilitated by environmental stimuli or by previous phase sequences. This facilitation of phase sequences was related to behavioral expectancies. One individual in a given social group builds expectancies, or phase-sequence chains, differently from an individual in another social group. An animal raised in one background will have different expectancies from one raised in a different setting. Thus far, we can account for the different cell assemblies and phase sequences; but why should we prefer one set of phase sequences over another, or one set of neural conditions to another?

This problem is resolved by postulating a principle of optimal conditions for growth in the nervous system. Let us assume that the optimal nervous system condition is one in which some small phase-sequence growth is possible. Hebb assumes this small growth to be a result of conditions where the sensory input from the receptors is *almost* what is expected, *almost* the phase sequence which has been facilitated, but not quite. A small amount of disparity between expected and obtained allows a dominant phase sequence to continue without disruption and allows some few new cell assemblies to be incorporated into the ongoing phase sequence. This condition of small disparity is assumed to be desirable for the preservation of the organism and *is the physiological correlate of pleasure.*

On the other hand when the disparity between the expected and the obtained is too large, there is insufficient sensory support for the dominant phase sequences. The ongoing sequences are disrupted. This disruption is defined as unpleasantness or

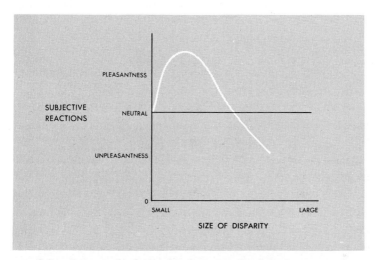

FIG. 8.3. *Presumed relationship between disparity in expected vs. obtained sensory experiences and affective reaction. Note that greatest positive affects occur with small disparities; negative affects occur with large disparity.*

subjective pain. When there is an exact matching of expected and obtained, Hebb assumes that no affect is involved. Figure 8.3 presents this theory in diagrammatic form.

We should note that this theory predicts that as the sensory stimulation deviates from our expectancies, we first experience positive affect or pleasure. This diminishes as the discrepancy between the expected and obtained becomes larger until a disruptive amount of discrepancy is reached. At this point and beyond, greater discrepancies are perceived as unpleasant.

The discrepancy between expected and obtained simuli is predicated, of course, on the basic theory of cell assemblies and phase sequences. The expectancies are the facilitations produced by the dominant phase sequences, and these account for the direction of behavior. Since dominant phase sequences determine the direction of behavior, they are motivational in nature.

In 1949 Hebb believed that the direction of behavior was the only aspect of motivated activity that needed explanation. He argued that we need not explain the initiation of behavior because all living organisms are constantly active. Later modifications of this type of theory have recognized the need to account for levels of activation or arousal, presumably mediated by diffusely projecting systems [21, 22]. At least in his original theory the most important motivational concept was the ongoing phase sequence. He believed that an organism is food-oriented when food-related phase sequences are dominant. The same organism is sex-oriented when sex-related phase sequences predominate the central nervous system activities. Because of the nature of the phase sequences activated, different expectancies for certain kinds of stimuli are activated in each case. When sex-related phase sequences are dominant, the presentation of food stimuli may produce large discrepancies.

What is widely divergent from what is expected, would therefore be unpleasant. When food-related phase sequences dominate, the presentation of sexual objects may be unexpected and irksome. Of course, these new stimuli may trigger off new phase sequences appropriate to the new type of object. If the object remains in the presence of the organism, it may soon present only a slight discrepancy from the altered phase sequences and might tend to become an object of pleasure.

What are the conditions which are responsible for ongoing phase sequences at any moment? First of all we must recognize the importance of stimuli from the receptors. Sights, sounds, tastes, and smells may trigger phase sequences which dominate the central nervous system activities. For example, how often have you suddenly become hungry while looking at a picture of a sizzling steak? Another source of phase-sequence control consists of stimuli arising within the body; for example, stomach contractions or certain patterns of activity in cells located in the hypothalamus may initiate new phase sequences. Perhaps, the hormones in the blood facilitate certain phase sequences while inhibiting others. According to Hebb's views, any or all of these factors could initiate food-related phase sequences.

The similarity of these regulating factors to those postulated by Stellar (pp. 329–330) should be apparent. The differences between Hebb's and Stellar's position is in the mechanisms controlled by these factors. In Stellar's model each factor contributes to the excitation in specific hypothalamic centers. The amount of excitation in them is correlated with the amount of appropriate motivated behavior. In Hebb's theory each factor facilitates one or more types of phase sequences which may actually exist in many areas of the central nervous system. The two theories could prove to be complementary in explaining motivated behavior.

While disruption and unpleasantness most often occur from large discrepancies, Hebb also has postulated that activity in some of the peripheral nerves which reach the brain through the cord have the inherent ability to disrupt ongoing neural activities. These nerve fibers are what we call the pain fibers. In Hebb's views these neurons are painful *because they disrupt the ongoing phase sequences,* not because of any mysterious perceptual quality received or elaborated in the brain.

It is too early to tell if the motivational aspects of Hebb's theory will stand the test of time and research. We do know that there are times when sensory experiences, widely divergent from our expectancies, do produce unpleasantness, and there are occasions when small discrepancies produce pleasantness. Yet we can find exceptions to the predictions based on the discrepancy hypothesis. If someone were to promise you 50 cents for doing a job and gave you $5000, this should be a large discrepancy; but there is some question of whether unpleasantness would be associated with it. In the more prosaic world of research, subjects report that small discrepancies between new salt solutions and salt solutions to which they have adapted (and have come to expect?) are pleasant and greater ones unpleasant, but the same relation is not found for sugar solutions (see Fig. 8.4). Why should the discrepancy hypothesis work for one type of solution and not for others?

It is difficult to accept the simple discrepancy hypothesis as the entire explanation of pleasure and pain. On the other hand we should recognize its merit as one of the few attempts to explain the subjective affective states. Further, Hebb's theory provides a rather different approach to the direction and persistence of behavior. This approach relates direction and persistence in behavior to direction and persistence of phase sequences in the brain which are initiated, supported, or disrupted by sensory experiences.

In Chapters 6 and 7 we discussed theories of learning which did not postulate anything about neural events or physiological events between stimuli and responses. These theories, generally, do not attempt to deal with subjective experiences of any kind, including affective experiences. Yet these theories do attempt to explain the direction and persistence of a person's behavior, and in this manner may be said to be motivational

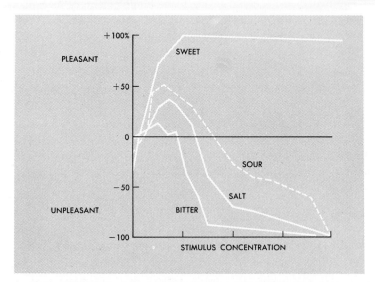

FIG. 8.4 *Pleasantness and unpleasantness of various tastes as a function of stimulus intensity. Based on data obtained by R. Engle, adapted from R. S. Woodworth.* Experimental Psychology. *New York, Holt, Rinehart and Winston, 1938.*

theories. In the next section we shall discuss some of the concepts in learning theories which are most invoked to account for motivational aspects of behavior.

Motives in Learning Theory

Earlier, we suggested that motivational concepts were those which were related to the direction, intensity, and persistence of behavior. To begin, let us examine the learning theory proposed by Hull (pp. 223–232) to determine those concepts with motivational properties.

HULL'S THEORY In Hull's theory, behavior is predicted from a formula which considers the following factors:

Hull's th

1. Past learning, or number of stimulus-response (*S-R*) pairings that have been followed by a reinforcing stimulus, which contribute to habit strength ($_sH_R$).
2. The amount of biological need experienced by the animal. This is called *drive* and is the sum of all deficits (*D*).
3. The incentives at the goal region experienced by the animal in the past (*K*).
4. The intensity of the stimulus eliciting the response (*V*).
5. The interval between the response and the presentation of the reinforcing stimulus (*J*).

In the chapter on learning (Chapter 6), we discussed the additional postulates regarding secondary reinforcement and secondary motivation, as well as the role of the drive stimuli (S_D) in performance.

It is hard to decide which of Hull's many terms should be called motivational. Each plays a part in directing and maintaining behavior. Drive, for example, is one of the most frequently occurring words in the motivational literature. Certainly, its nondirective energizing characteristics qualify it for inclusion in a list of motive terms. What about $_sH_R$? It provides the direction of behavior in any stimulus context, yet it is seldom used as a motivational term. Perhaps, it is because the value of $_sH_R$ is in part a result of other concepts more directly related to the direction of behavior

The drive stimuli (S_D) have properties which are important for the analysis of motivational phenomena. For example, we can think of S_D as those stimuli which occur whenever a drive is activated by deprivation or by pain. Thus S_D are those stimuli uniquely associated with a specific need. Of course, the S_D are a component of the *s* variable in $_sH_R$. If learning to navigate a maze depends upon the learning of a series of $_sH_R$'s (habits) which will lead to the goal, then S_D, being a component of each $_sH_R$ in the series, can act as a common link uniting the whole series. If a hungry rat is learning to reach a food goal through a complicated maze, each response it acquires will be made in the general context of "hunger stimuli." Hunger stimuli, the S_D, occur in the animal at the beginning, the middle, and the end of the behavioral sequence. Each response is learned to the specific cues of the maze *and* the hunger stimuli arising inside the animal. To understand Hull's learning theory analysis of sequential acts (like learning a

343

maze), we must consider other theoretical concepts as yet un-introduced, the r_g-s_g mechanism.

In Chapter 6 we introduced the concept of a goal response (R_G). Hull's theory asserts that a portion of the response at the goal becomes conditioned to stimuli present at the goal and is generalized to cues earlier in the sequence. After a few trials, as an animal enters the maze a portion of the actual goal response occurs. It is not the entire goal response but fractions of it which do not interfere with successful navigation of the maze. This fractional and anticipatory goal response, r_g, in turn elicits its own unique pattern of stimuli, s_g. The r_g and s_g usually occur together and may be considered inseparable; therefore they are joined with a hyphen, r_g-s_g, in theoretical symbols. The r_g component is learned as any response is learned in Hull's theory and the s_g component acts in the same way as any stimulus in the theory.

The persistence of any behavioral sequence stems in part from the drive stimuli (S_D), and the direction of behavior is a joint function of the environmental stimuli (S), the anticipatory goal reactions (r_g-s_g) and the drive stimuli (S_D). These variables are used to account for both the direction and persistence of behavioral sequences.

Now let us examine the variables which have the function of energizing behavior. We tend to think of the variables of drive (D), the amount of incentive (K), the stimulus intensity (V), and the reciprocal of the delay in reinforcement (J), in this way. Each acts as a multiplier of $_sH_R$ to obtain *excitatory potential,* $_sE_R$.

$$_sE_R = {_sH_R} \times D \times K \times J \times V$$

We should pause to note that the relation between all of the variables is the same. Each variable acts as a multiplier of behavior and each thus acts to influence the amount of excitatory potential. Because behavior at any moment is determined by the excitatory potential having the greatest numerical value at that time, each can contribute to the observed direction of behavior.

Where we have two possible responses leading to different incentives, the response which occurs will be the one whose components multiply together to obtain the greatest $_sE_R$.

$$_sE_{R_1} = {_sH_{R_1}} \times D \times K_1 \times J_1 \times V_1$$

and

$$_sE_{R_2} = {_sH_{R_2}} \times D \times K_2 \times J_2 \times V_2$$

According to Hull's theory, D is constant for all excitatory potentials. Let us arbitrarily assume the delays in reinforcement and stimulus intensities identical in the two equations. The equations then hinge upon $_sH_R$ and K. Then if the habit strengths

$$_sE_{R_1} = {_sH_{R_1}} \times K_1 \times \text{(constant terms)}$$
$$_sE_{R_2} = {_sH_{R_2}} \times K_2 \times \text{(constant terms)}$$

of the two habits ($_sH_R$'s) are nearly the same, the response which will occur is dependent upon only the incentives. In the same fashion, delays in reinforcements or stimulus intensities could exert directional influences.

Inasmuch as drive level (D) is identical for all behavioral potentials evoked at any time, we can consider it as a general concept. Some psychologists think of drive (D) as an activating or arousing concept. As such, it is a concept which is related to the intensity of behavior exhibited by an individual. Drive level is sometimes identified with the level of physiological arousal, although this is not assumed by most theories of learning. Drive is most clearly defined by strictly behavioral operations, like hours of deprivation.

Perhaps learning theory's important contribution to our understanding of motivation has come through the elaboration of the ideas of secondary motives and secondary reinforcements. We have discussed the traditional aspects of these concepts earlier (Chapter 6), but at this point we shall extend our treatment of acquired motives and reinforcements by presenting some of the contributions of Mowrer.

MOWRER'S ANALYSIS OF SECONDARY REINFORCEMENT It will facilitate our discussion if first we note a difference in the meaning of terms used by Hull and Mowrer [23]. Hull used the terms *secondary motive* and *secondary reinforcer*. He argued (see Chapter 6) that the term *secondary motive* should be applied to stimuli associated in the past with a rapid *increase in drive* (and its subsequent diminution), whereas *secondary reinforcement* should be applied to stimuli which have been associated in the past with a *reduction of drive*. When stimuli with these different associational histories are presented, secondary motives should act to raise drive level and secondary reinforcements should act to lower drive level. In Mowrer's terminology we use only secondary reinforcements. However, he postulates two kinds of secondary reinforcements. One is associated with drive increments and the other with drive decrements. Thus, the distinction between the effects of stimuli associated with drive increases and drive decreases is maintained.

Basically, Mowrer is an advocate of drive theory in psychology. All behavior stems from drives which are produced by biological needs. He believes that two kinds of drive conditions are of central importance for behavior: (1) *incremental reinforcement,* in which drive is increasing; (2) *decremental reinforcement,* in which drive is decreasing.

Four types of secondary reinforcements can be produced on the basis of the association of neutral stimuli with these changes in drive:

1. Stimuli associated with incremental reinforcements which act as danger signals. These produce an emotional response which can be called *fear.*
2. Stimuli associated with the termination of incremental reinforcement which act as safety signals. These produce an emotional response which can be called *hope.*
3. Stimuli which are associated with termination of safety signals. These produce an emotional response which can be called *disappointment.*
4. Stimuli associated with the termination of danger signals. These produce an emotional response which can be called *relief.*

The association between stimuli and the increments and decrements in drive requires only the simple association of the stimuli with alterations in drive. These primary drives and secondary reinforcements are presumed to be the basis of all behavior. They represent primary and secondary emotional reactions which are acquired by simple association. Mowrer assumes that an individual will act to seek decrements in primary drives and to avoid increments in them. Similarly, an individual should react positively to secondary reinforcements of types 2 and 4, hope and relief, and react negatively to reinforcements types 1 and 3, fear and disappointment. Responses which lead to reinforcements of types 1 and 3 will be dropped, whereas responses leading to reinforcements of types 2·and 4 will be enhanced.

For Mowrer, emotional reactions are conditioned by contiguity alone. Fear is his most popular example. A fear reaction is learned when a neutral stimulus is paired with a primary incremental drive, some noxious stimulation or drive, usually electrical shock. Reduction of drive provides a suitable condition for response learning (habits), as well as for the learning of secondary reinforcers, type 1. In a typical laboratory experiment a rat learns to avoid an electric shock by crossing to the opposite side of a shuttle box within a certain time interval after the onset of a buzzer or bell (*CS*). Both types of learning take place. The animal learns to *fear* the bell, through its contiguous appearance with shock, and responses which terminate the buzzer are learned because they reduce this learned fear response. Avoidance responses are difficult to extinguish in the sense that they persist for many trials even when the animal is no longer shocked if it fails to respond. Of course, the animal must fail to respond to find this out. But one reason the response is so persistent may be that the response is *always* useful in reducing the conditioned fear response to the *CS*.

Mowrer believes that both fear and pain are produced by noxious stimulation, and the fear component is conditionable to neutral stimuli. Animals will work to terminate or otherwise eliminate this fear-producing stimulation. When the fear-evoking stimulus is eliminated the animal experiences *relief* (type-1 secondary reinforcement). However, if one were to present a neutral stimulus with the termination of a painful stimulus, this neutral stimulus should evoke *hope* (type-2 secondary reinforcement).

Some of Mowrer's examples are informative. In one of them he imagines the relief of desert weary travelers who see a mirage in the distance. Although their thirst is not reduced, they feel better. For Mowrer, this would represent the effect of conditioned hope, or type-2 secondary reinforcement. To take another of Mowrer's examples, think of the relief we usually feel after a temporary sickness has been diagnosed by a physician. His presence and reassurance that we soon will be well again provide another example of type-2 secondary reinforcement. Yet another example comes to mind when we think of common experiences in the office of a dentist. As we arrive, we become fearful (conditioned fear). When the dentist begins to drill a cavity, the fear mounts—fear of both an unconditioned portion of the slight pain and of an indefinite continuation of the slight pain. Fear of fear, itself! When the dentist tells us, "just one more minute," or some action of his signals the imminent end of the drilling, we feel better, even though he might still be drilling (type-2 secondary reinforcement). And, when he stops at last, we experience relief (type-1 secondary reinforcement).

There is a similarity between the effects of type-2 secondary reinforcement and those of "suggestion." Mowrer states this is one of the few instances in which a learning theory has attempted to deal with phenomena like suggestion. How often do we attribute the effects of the reassurances of a physician to some mysterious concept like suggestion? It may be possible to equate positive suggestion with secondary reinforcement, type-2, and negative suggestion with conditioned fear. Mowrer's elaborate analyses of secondary reinforcement make this concept a much more influential one. However, many psychologists believe that it is impossible to explain all behavior on as simple a basis as secondary reinforcement.

A GENERAL PROBLEM OF SECONDARY REINFORCEMENT
Critics of secondary reinforcement explanations of adult human behavior have dwelt on one major problem in any such explanation: many experimental studies have shown secondary reinforcers to be ephemeral in nature. In short, the experimental evidence from animal studies indicates that secondary reinforcing stimuli have to be continually associated with primary drives to maintain their potency for any length of time. Since men tend to seek goals which are not primary reinforcements year after year, these critics claim that these goals can not be explained through secondary reinforcement theory.

Zimmerman [24, 25] has shown that one *can* establish secondary reinforcers that retain their effectiveness for considerable periods of time after they are dissociated from changes in primary drives. Zimmerman's technique involves the use of what is called *double intermittent reinforcement*. For some while we have known that reinforcing responses on every other trial or every third or tenth trial will make the response more difficult to extinguish than reinforcing it on each trial. It remained for Zimmerman to demonstrate that by (1) *intermittently* associating the neutral stimulus with primary reinforcement and (2) using this new secondary reinforcer only intermittently following a response, the response will become much more difficult to extinguish.

Let us examine one of Zimmerman's procedures in greater detail to clarify this method. Laboratory rats were placed in a small box which opened into a runway. A few seconds after the animal was placed in the box, a door opened and the rat could go into the runway. The rats were moderately hungry and food could be found in the goal box at the end of the runway. Soon the animals ran directly to the goal box when the door was opened. After some fifteen to twenty trials, the animals were running swiftly to the goal box. Additional trials did not improve their running speeds. At this point food was not placed in the goal box on every trial, but rather only on every other trial. Then, after a few more trials, food was placed in the goal box more rarely, until it was found there on only one trial in every eight, on the average. Actually, whether or not the food was placed in the goal box was decided randomly, with the probability that it would be there one time in eight. This did not mean every eighth trial is reinforced. There was no regular pattern of reinforcement. Remember that on each trial the door separating the starting area from the runway had been opened a few seconds after the animal was placed in it. It had been a neutral stimulus associated with primary drive reduction and should have come, therefore, to have secondary reinforcing properties itself.

Now the entrance situation is changed so that the animal has a bar in the starting box which will open the door leading to the runway if it is depressed. *From this point on food is never again placed in the goal box.* The animal begins to press the bar, opening the door. After five or six trials, the experimenter changes the situation so that it takes many depressions of the bar to open the door. The door will be opened once every eight bar depressions, on the average. The effectiveness of the bar-press response is placed on an intermittent schedule. Because both the reinforcement and the door operation have been learned on intermittent schedules, the procedure is called *double intermittent reinforcement.* If we were to watch an animal in the final stages of the experiment, we would see a rat pressing a bar in the starting box over and over again until the gate lifts, allowing it to run to an empty goal box. Then the animal is returned to the starting box, and the whole sequence repeated.

Using this technique an animal will press the bar about 2000 times to enter the continuously empty goal box. This is a great many more responses than has previously been obtained with only secondary reinforcements. While this double intermittent technique does not produce entirely permanent behavior, Zimmerman's results show that secondary reinforcers can be quite effective even when no longer associated with primary drives. Perhaps, they would be even stronger if further intermittencies were incorporated in the training procedure. For many years it seemed unlikely that secondary reinforcers could account for the persistence of human goals and incentives because of the transient nature of their potency once they are no longer associated with primary reinforcers. Since secondary reinforcement was the main conceptual link between laboratory research based on learning theories and human behavior, this tended to limit learning theories to explanations of animal behavior. However, the persistence of behavior based on secondary reinforcements illustrated by Zimmerman's work tends to strengthen the position of all learning theories in so far as they may be applicable to adult behavior.

Drive and Anxiety

For Hull, as well as for many other learning theorists, drive is a general concept. All biological needs contribute to drive (D). Drive increases as biological need becomes more and more acute. Tissue damage resulting from electrical shock, or other noxious stimulation, can also produce an increase in drive level; and, as we have seen, Mowrer's incremental reinforcement refers to situations where the drive level of the animal or person is increasing. Hull's concept of secondary motivation also refers to situations in which D increases. But, which way D is caused to increase is unimportant to these theories. The effects of hunger, thirst, and pain (and other sources) all add together to achieve the resultant D level.

One factor related to the D level of an individual is his own individual characteristic responsiveness to emotional situations. In general one can say that D is a joint product of the situation and the way in which the person reacts to it. How can we measure this variable in the human being?

Janet Taylor developed a self-report questionnaire which was designed to determine the number of clinical symptoms of anxiety evidenced by subjects. Questions were selected by clinical psychologists so that the answers to them reflected internal anxiety levels. It was assumed that anxiety test scores indicate the individual's emotional responsiveness, and a person with a higher anxiety score will have generally a greater D than subjects with low anxiety test scores. If this assumption is justified, it should be able to predict the differential behaviors of groups of people with high and low test anxiety on the basis of different drive levels.

Both Hull and Spence have models with a multiplicative relationship between habit strength and drive:

$$_sE_R = f(_sH_R \times D)$$

In a simple situation which involves only one response (or habit strength, $_sH_R$) the greater the level of drive (D) the

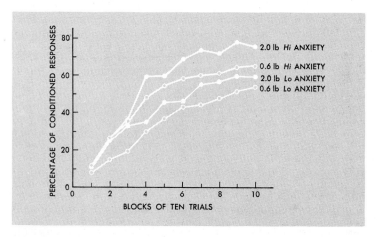

FIG. 8.5. *Performance in eyelid response conditioning as a function of* US *intensity (in pressures) and position of subjects on anxiety scale. Adapted from K. W. Spençe & Janet A. Taylor. Anxiety and strength of the UCS as determiners of the amount of eyelid conditioning.* J. exp. Psychol., *1951, 42, 183–188.*

greater the response should be. In one experiment [26] subjects were trained in an eyeblink conditioning experiment. A puff of air to the eye (*US*) was paired with a previously neutral stimulus (*CS*). As training progresses we can observe the increased tendency for the *CS* to elicit the eye-blink response. The data are presented in Fig. 8.5. We observe the subjects with high anxiety scores to show a greater percentage of conditioned responses than those with low anxiety scores *for a given pressure of air puff.* We observe also two factors influencing drive and operating to increase the conditioned response: the anxiety levels of the subjects and the strength of the puff of air used to condition the response.

In this experiment highly anxious subjects, as measured by an anxiety scale, showed faster conditioning than did the less anxious subjects. What would we expect in a more complex situation? To predict an answer from our theory of drive, we must consider the significance of the multiplicative relationship between drive and habits. Because drive multiplies habit strength to form (with other factors) the response tendency, it acts to magnify the differences between response tendencies. Suppose there are only two responses which can be made in a given situation. Let us assign a strength of .60 to one of them ($_sH_{R_1}$) and a strength of .70 to the other ($_sH_{R_2}$) for a given subject. If we can place the subject into the situation at different drive levels, it is possible to calculate the effects of these levels on performance. If we assign values of 1, 2, and 3 to three drive levels and multiply these values with the two habit strengths, we would obtain the following results:

Under drive level 1:

	Drive	$\times$	habit strength	=	response tendency
Response 1	1	$\times$	.6	=	.6
Response 2	1	$\times$	.7	=	.7

Under drive level 2:

	Drive	$\times$	habit strength	=	response tendency
Response 1	2	$\times$	.6	=	1.2
Response 2	2	$\times$	.7	=	1.4

Under drive level 3:

	Drive	$\times$	habit strength	=	response tendency
Response 1	3	$\times$	.6	=	1.8
Response 2	3	$\times$	.7	=	2.1

At increasing drive levels the differences between response tendencies become larger. This means that the probability of R_2 becomes greater as drive increases. If R_2 is the response which is the one which the experimenter desires, this condition is advantageous. In the eye-blink experiment just reported there was only one response involved and increased drive acted to accelerate the growth of the response tendency. However, if the desire was to increase the weaker habit strength, higher drive would interfere with learning.

Spence, Farber, and McFann [27] tested this type of reasoning in an experiment in which subjects had to learn two kinds of lists of paired associates. One list was prepared so that the responses were readily available and had relatively high habit strength before the experiment. For this list, high drive helped acquisition of the list. The other list was constructed so that the correct responses were of lower habit strength than incorrect responses. On this list subjects with high anxiety (drive) were poorer in acquisition. Therefore, the effect of drive upon performance depends upon place of the response to be learned, relative to other possible responses in the situation. When this response is already nearly dominant in the situation, drive will facilitate performance. When this response is less dominant than other responses, high drive will interfere with performance.

Since everyone's drive level is, to some extent at least, a unique property of the individual, it is difficult to formulate any general statement of whether a person should take steps to increase or decrease his drive level before an examination. For individuals with normally high drive or anxiety levels, it would probably be best to try to reduce anxiety by going to a motion picture the night before the examination and trying to relax and not to think of it. For individuals with normally low drive or anxiety levels, steps should be taken to raise the drive level. Black coffee and jangling nerves may actually improve the performance of a person with a normally low drive level. We should remember that this discussion of drive level and examination performance has assumed learning to be constant for all individuals; but we should recognize that examination performances are jointly determined by drive and learning.

Other Views of Anxiety

Behavioristic theories have been developed by people who view anxiety somewhat differently from the way Taylor and Spence do. Some psychologists believe that it may be best to consider anxiety as a response to specific conditions. A situation that is anxiety producing in one person may not be anxiety producing in another [28]. A questionnaire that attempts to measure anxiety symptoms specifically occurring in testing situations has been developed [29]. These authors believe that anxiety interferes with performance through elicitation of responses which are aimed at reducing anxiety rather than at the task at hand. This view of the effects of anxiety is based on the assumption that anxiety fosters task-irrelevant responses.

Anxiety is a conceptual term in these behavioristic theories, defined on the basis of a test score. A score on an anxiety scale is presumed to be an indicator of individual drive level, as defined by the theory behind the scale, and not an indicator of *real anxiety,* whatever it may be.

FRUSTRATION BEHAVIOR   It seems likely that some behavior can not be explained on the basis of goal-directedness. Maier [30] believes that some behavior is not goal-directed at all;

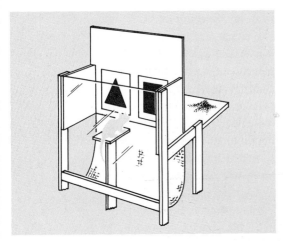

FIG. 8.6.   *One form of the Lashley jumping stand.*

rather, he believes some responses become *fixated* through frustrating circumstances. Once a response becomes fixated, it will occur again and again quite apart from any beneficial or detrimental effects produced by the responses. Only through special retraining procedures can this fixation be altered, according to Maier.

In a typical experiment rats are trained to jump to a given pattern in a window of a Lashley jumping apparatus which is illustrated in Fig. 8.6. Cards are *placed in the two windows of the jumping stand.* There are different figures on each card. The animal is forced to jump from the stand to the platform behind the windows. The windows can be fixed so that a card can be locked in place or just lightly held so that the rat's jump will knock it down and allow entry to the platform. If the animal jumps and strikes a window with a card locked in place, it falls into a net below. If the animal jumps at a window which is blocked by a card, lightly held, it lands easily on the platform behind. Usually the animals are trained while on mild food-deprivation schedules and food is available on the platform behind the windows.

Let us assume that the card with a circle painted on it is always locked in place and a card with a square painted on it is only held in place lightly. The cards are placed in the right or left windows on a random basis. The animals soon learn to jump to the card with the square on it. By doing so, they gain entry to the platform and do not bump their noses and fall into the net below as happens when jumping to the card with the circle.

The next step is to change the situation by randomly locking the cards in place so that there is *no solution* to the problem. Now a jump to either card may or may not pay off. Half the time a jump will result in bumped nose and a fall. What happens to the behavior of the animals? Quickly the animals adopt an invariant position response. For example, an animal will jump toward the right window on all trials. This is the *fixation* of a response. It occurs on every trial and in a stereotyped fashion. If an animal has fixated a jumping response toward the right window, and the left window is completely open, the rat will lean out toward the open window, sniff at it, then jump at the closed right window on trial after trial. Maier's argument is that frustration (in this case the insoluble problem) leads to response fixation, and this fixation serves no goal. When an individual's frustration toleration has been exceeded there is a complete loss of adaptivity as stereotyped behavior is initiated.

Many things may lead to the frustration-instigated fixation of responses. In the jumping-stand experiment above it was the introduction of an insoluble problem. In other instances frustration-instigated fixation could be caused by punishment, anxiety, a series of business failures, disappointments in love, in short any frustration. Maier uses the term *frustration* somewhat more broadly than many psychologists who restrict the term to instances where an individual is thwarted in attaining a specific goal.

The fixated responses discussed by Maier are similar to those exhibited by mentally disturbed individuals who exhibit compulsive behavior. Any one may show fixated behavior when frustrations have temporarily exceeded tolerances; but the compulsive person evidences fixated, stereotyped responses day in and day out, relentlessly. Both temporary and permanent fixation responses are a phenomenon which we cannot deny. They exist in animals and in man. Whether they will best be explained in terms of anxiety-reduction, frustration, or more elaborate personality dynamics is an empirical problem which future research must decide.

Behavior in Society

To this point in our discussion of motivation we have concentrated our attention on the physiological and behavioristic analysis of motivation. We have, it is true, discussed the concepts of hedonism and anxiety, but restricted our discussion to approaches to these problems which are very close to the behavioristic learning theories. Next, we shall attempt to explore other kinds of motivational theories that have been developed to account for man's behavior in the society in which he lives.

LEWIN'S AHISTORICAL APPROACH   One of Kurt Lewin's more widely quoted statements is that behavior is a joint function of the person and of his environment [31]. This means we cannot

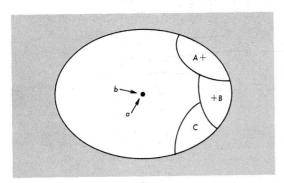

FIG. 8.7.   *Simplified drawing of life space as used by Lewin. Regions A, B, and C are differentiated by the individual; A and B have positive valence and forces "push" subject toward these regions.*

understand why a person behaves knowing only one of these factors. More important, we must know the environment as the person perceives it. As we already know, our perception of the world may correspond to a greater or lesser degree with others' perceptions of the world. Behavior is a joint function of the person and *his* perceived environment. Lewin expressed this relation as

$$B = f(P,E)$$

Behav Person , Environment

Lewin incorporated this assertion into his conceptual term, *the life space*. The life space is a psychological space representing the person in his perceived environment and describes relationships between its various subspaces, forces, and valences. A simplified example of a drawing of the life space is presented in Fig. 8.7. The life space is the entire enclosed region. The enclosed subareas *A, B,* and *C* are regions of the life space. The regions may be objects, other people, institutions, or ways of behaving. The arrows *a* and *b* represent forces in the life space

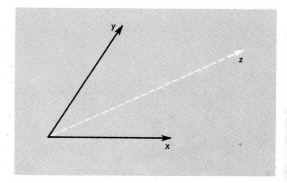

FIG. 8.8 *Vector summation.* z *represents sum of vectors* x *and* y. *Lewin believed that all behavioral choices represented the summation of all motives (forces) acting upon an individual at a given moment, which could be represented as vectors in the geometry of life space.*

directed toward regions *A* and *B*. The plus signs indicate regions that have a positive valence for the individual who is represented by the point. Region *C* is discriminated by the individual but has no valence for him. Since there is no valence, there is no force toward or away from this region. If the valences in regions *A* and *B* were negative, the forces in the life space would be acting to push the person away from these regions. In most situations we should recognize that our conceptual life spaces would be very complex with numerous subareas more or less clearly differentiated from each other. Many different forces act upon us, many valences appeal to us. Each varies in quality (positive or negative valence) and quantity. How do we reach decisions when faced with these complex situations where many competing forces place us in situations of conflict?

Lewin conceived of the forces operating in the life space as vectors. The resolution of conflicting forces is made by the mathematical rules governing addition of vectors (a vector is a quantity with a direction). Vector addition can be represented rather easily. Consulting Fig. 8.8 we see two vectors, *x* and *y*. The dashed line, vector *z*, is simply the addition of vectors *x* and *y*.

357

The same principle can be applied when adding a great number of vectors. According to Lewin's position all of our decisions are made this way. Therefore, our behavior is influenced by all the forces and objects with valence operating on the individual at any moment in time. Any force operative in one's life space will have some effect, however slight, on behavior.

This analysis serves to introduce the concept of *overdetermination of behavior*. If some of the forces acting on the person are known, Lewin's rule (vector addition) enables us to combine the forces. Suppose we use the word motive in place of force. Then we would say behavior is the result of many motives and seldom reflects the operation of any single motive. In general it is wise to recognize this as a useful principle: any given behavior is usually determined by more than one motive.

Lewin's terminology also allows us to illustrate a possible danger in interpretation of behavior. It is impossible to safely infer similar underlying motives from similar behavior patterns. If we were to observe two students working hard in a high school study hall, we might be impressed with the great similarity of their behavior and be *mislead* into concluding that their actions were produced by similar motives. This is not necessarily true. One student's behavior could be produced by the motives for academic achievement and for power over others. This student might believe success in high school will lead to these goals. The other student's behavior may be a result of motives for affiliation with the teacher and to avoid failure in an impending examination. Both students might believe that studying hard will help them fulfill these differing underlying motives. The issue at hand is whether motives represent hidden determinants of behavior which can or cannot be inferred directly from behavior. Two individuals may exhibit identical actions resulting from widely divergent motive patterns. Along the same line, we can imagine two people with similar motive patterns who exhibit different behavior because each believes divergent courses of action will be instrumental in motive fulfillment.

Lewin believed the life space to exist on both conscious and unconscious levels. There can be different subregions and valences in the various possible levels of awareness. Behavior can be a result of forces on the conscious or unconscious level, or on both. In any case behavior is only determined by forces operating at the moment of the behavior; about this, Lewin was emphatic. If the forces do not exist *now,* they do not influence present behavior. It would be important to know about an individual's past only if we knew just how the past influences the present life space. Since we know little of the relation between past and present, Lewin pressed the point that psychologists should seek to understand the present psychological environment. Surely forces and valences of the present have origins in the past, but the best we can do is to assess the present representation of the past. Similarly, we can not be influenced by events yet to happen in the future, but we can assess how an individual anticipates the future. Our anticipations or expectations of the future can and do influence our actions.

Lewin's emphasis on understanding the present life space can be thought of as a *cross-sectional* approach to understanding behavior. He would advise us to take a cross-section of a person's life space and use this segment, containing perceived objects, valences, and forces, to understand the individual. Compare this approach with that of a learning theorist who studies the development of behavior patterns over some period of time or of a personality theorist who studies the effects of different early childhood experiences on later characteristics. In these cases the psychologist takes a *longitudinal view,* studying the changes in behavior over a period of time. Lewin's belief that we must concentrate on the current make-up of the individual foreshadowed much of the recent investigations into modern theories of motivation where attempts are made to assess the current motive structure of the individual.

MURRAY'S VIEW Murray collaborated with others in an interdisciplinary study [32]. The investigators were from varied professions and included psychiatrists, psychoanalysts, psychologists, physicists, and anthropologists. They undertook to study in depth a large number of "normal" individuals, in the hope of arriving at a conceptual scheme that all of the experimenters could use and understand. This goal was not reached completely, of course, but a novel framework of analysis of personality stemmed from their efforts. Many of the important variables in this framework can be regarded as motivational because they represent attempts to explain energizing and goal-directing aspects of personality. Murray called certain of these concepts *needs,* defined much more broadly than a physiological deficit. Needs, for Murray, refer to some hypo-thetical brain activity which disposes an individual to respond in certain ways in certain specific situations. The reference to hypothetical activities in the brain indicates a hope that needs can someday be related to physiological activities and a belief that they *must* depend upon neural activity in some fashion yet to be determined.

Needs are described in terms of the effects produced by be-havior. When people do things or say things which produce similar behavioral effects, Murray believed the actions to be motivated by the same or similar needs. The normal individuals at the Harvard Clinic who served as subjects were exhaustively studied to find the common behavioral effects and, conse-quently, the pattern of common needs. The results of the study were interpreted to reveal two broad categories of common needs: the biological needs of the body (viscerogenic needs) and needs unrelated to the biological urges (psychogenic needs). Some of the viscerogenic needs are similar to those studied earlier in this chapter, for example, need for food and need for water (symbolized *n* food, *n* water). Other needs related to our physiological well-being were added, for example, need to avoid cold (*n* coldavoidance) and need to avoid harm (*n* harmavoid-ance).

The list of psychogenic needs was a product of the analysis of common behavioral episodes found in the subjects. While Murray makes passing comment that the psychogenic needs "are presumably dependent upon and derived from the vis-cerogenic needs" [32, p. 80], this is not an important feature of his system. The important aspect is that the list of psycho-genic needs was to represent the motive systems apparent in the majority of subjects.

To give the flavor of Murray's analysis, some brief descrip-tions of some of the secondary or psychogenic needs are pre-sented below:

1. *n* Acquisition (acquisitive attitude). To gain possession and property. To grasp, snatch or steal things. To bargain or gamble, to work for money or goods.
2. *n* Conservance (conserving attitude). To collect, repair, clean and preserve things. To protect against damage.
3. *n* Order (orderly attitude). To arrange, organize, put away objects. To be tidy and clean. To be scrupulously precise.

4. *n* Retention (retentive attitude). To retain possession of things. To refuse to give or lend. To hoard. To be frugal, economical, and miserly.
5. *n* Construction (constructive attitude). To organize and build.
6. *n* Superiority (ambitious attitude). This has been broken into two needs: *n* achievement (will to power over things, people, and ideas) and *n* recognition (efforts to gain approval and high social status).
7. *n* Achievement (achievement attitude). To overcome obstacles, to exercise power, to strive to do something difficult as well and as quickly as possible. (This is an elementary ego need which alone may prompt any action or be fused with any other need.)
8. *n* recognition (self-forwarding attitude). To excite praise and commendation. To demand respect. To boast and exhibit one's accomplishments. To seek distinction, social prestige, honors, or high office [32 pp. 80–81].

These are but a few of the social, or psychogenic needs listed by Murray. As the thinking of Murray and the group developed, four observable indices became most prominent for evaluation of needs:

1. Statements by individuals of their desires or wishes for certain end situations.
2. Behaviors which tended directly to bring about a specific end result.
3. The occurrence of special amounts or kinds of affect with special types of behaviors. For example, anger may be used as a sign of aggression. When a behavior sequence is blocked and anger or aggression results, we can infer there was some underlying need being blocked.
4. Some motor patterns are more or less stable indicators of underlying needs. Movements of striking out or hitting represent aggression; crying represents the need for succor; smiling, the need for affiliating with others.

In effect, Murray suggested that we can view motives or needs in terms of end states resulting from behavior and from some other reliable indicators. The origin of these motives was not a paramount interest to Murray; rather, attention was focused upon determining what motives are found in normal individuals. Most important, perhaps, is the conceptualization of human behavior as motivated by urges toward such abstract goals as achievement, affiliation, and recognition. Motives are assumed to be socially acquired, and transmitted through our culture. Furthermore, this conception of motives makes them the prime, dynamic movers of behavior rather than merely passive traits or habitual modes of behavior.

McCLELLAND AND THE ACHIEVEMENT MOTIVE   Both the types of common needs found by Murray and the methods used to establish the presence of motives served as useful background for McClelland and Atkinson in their work on the motive for achievement. McClelland *et al.* published [33] an extensive elaboration of one of the motives suggested by Murray in which a new theory of motivation was delineated, based in part on the theory of hedonism.

Certainly, on a subjective level it would seem that much of our behavior is determined by our expectations of future pleasures or pains. In fact one might inquire why hedonism has not been accepted as a general principle, or even *the* general principle underlying behavior. Probably the reason why hedonism was virtually ignored in American psychology for its first fifty years stems from the emphasis on measurement and objectivity that marked the behavioristic movement in general. For many years a behavioristic point of view was identified with a scientific one. However, the current work on hedonism (discussed earlier) along with a growing discontent with motivational explanations of *S-R* learning theories have caused workers to return to hedonism as an important principle in the explanation of behavior. However, the behavioristic influence can still be seen in the newer brands of hedonism. Today, psychologists tend to define pleasure and pain as theoretical concepts defined in terms of behavioral or environmental changes. McClelland *et al.* believe that motives are learned through the association of affective states with stimulus conditions, and they define affect in a manner somewhat similar to the discrepancy hypothesis mentioned earlier (pp. 338–342 ff.). For our current purposes, let us use *affective qualities* to define the term *motive*. McClelland and his co-workers define motive as follows: "a reintegration of a change in affect by a cue and an anticipation of future change in affect contingent upon certain actions." [This definition, condensed from several, captures three important features of the McClelland model: the motivated individual (1) is experiencing affect, (2) anticipates a further change in affect, and (3) expects these further changes to be contingent on certain of his behaviors.]

According to this view, an individual is motivated when a cue in the environment elicits an affective response in him, and the individual anticipates a further change in affect depending upon some subsequent behavior. A person is motivated by hunger when a cue produces a part of the pleasure experienced in the past through eating and expects that doing something, like heading to a restaurant or dormitory, will produce even more pleasure. A person high in n achievement is one in whom a competitive situation elicits some of the positive affect which has been experienced in the past in competitive situations and at the same time expects that some action on his part, such as studying long and hard, will lead to even more pleasure. n Achievement refers to a positive motive to attain success in competition with a standard of excellence. Other people might be motivated in a negative or aversive fashion by competitive situations. For these people, cues of competition suggest some of the unpleasantness experienced in past failures and even offer the possibility of greater pain through yet another failure.

The person who experiences positive affect from competitive situations has a need for achievement (n achievement), whereas the person who experiences negative affect is motivated by a fear of failure (f failure). A person for whom competitive situations elicit positive affect will act so as to continue and enhance the situation; whereas a person motivated to avoid failure would try to leave the competitive situation or at least to terminate it as soon as possible.

The types of motives which dominate an individual's life develop as a function of an individual's past experiences. The motivation model of McClelland postulates that affect is conditioned to stimuli by mere association. The more frequently pleasure or unpleasantness is associated with neutral stimuli, the stronger will be the association formed and the more likely it is that this formerly neutral stimulus will evoke affect in the future.

If one's parents provide pleasure for the child as a reward for engaging in competitive activities, or if the child is often successful and wins the pleasures of victory, then we would expect the child to develop strong achievement motivation. If a child has learned to expect the worst from competitive activities, one would expect him to have more fear of failure.

Individual patterns of rewards will determine the extent to which one is motivated by achievement, failure, power, affiliation, or by any of the other motives discussed by Murray. At the moment, most research in this area has centered on the achievement motive. Even a cursory view of our culture would suggest that everyone is motivated to some extent by needs for achievement, failure, and affiliation. The job of the motivation specialist then is to establish an order or *relationship* among a group of individuals for a given motive.

McClelland's *n* achievement is currently assessed through a written test given in one of several forms. Subjects are asked to write creative stories based on stimuli which are sufficiently ambiguous to allow many possible interpretations After the stories are written, they are scored on the basis of the amount of "achievement imagery" in the stories. It is assumed that the stories reflect the motives of the writers.

Projective technique is the generic term for tests which result in subjects revealing things of theoretical interest about themselves through stories created as a result of ambiguous or unstructured stimuli allowing various interpretations. The McClelland system for measuring motivation is objectified to allow a minimum of subjective evaluation. One of the techniques used by the McClelland group to measure motivation stems from the earlier work of Murray.

Murray developed a method for evaluating various aspects of personality. The subject would be shown several different kinds of pictures and would be asked to tell the experimenter what he believed the individuals in the pictures were doing. The experimenter might ask the subject about the outcome of the activities, intentions, or emotions of the person in the picture. This general procedure and the set of pictures is known as the *Thematic Apperception Test* (TAT). The name comes from Murray's interest in the over-all nature of the stories (thema). As with most projective instruments the information obtained from the TAT is evaluated in relation to all that is known about the subject (or patient, in a clinical setting).

For many reasons, for example, different theoretical approaches of the interpreters and different previous experiences with the person being examined, the interpretations of TAT stories are known to vary among interpreters. Another difficulty is that the training of those who interpret TAT stories is long and intensive. These difficulties led McClelland and his colleagues to search for new techniques to assess human motives that would be more amenable to research purposes.

The method McClelland developed as an attempt to find a more objective way to score imaginative stories for motives was as follows. The scorer for a particular motive, say need achievement, would examine the stories for their themes. A significant portion of a story had to concern attempts to reach achievement goals in order for it to be scored for *n* achievement at all. A passing mention of achievement behavior is not sufficient to represent *n* achievement in the protocol. The determination of whether or not a character of a story was trying for achievement ends was made using at least one of several objective criteria.

Once it has been determined that the story contains achievement imagery, other categories of possible behaviors which indicate strength of interest in success may be scored. For example, the scorer scans the story for statements indicating that the character(s) is anticipating possible outcomes of the activity and is experiencing emotions related to his possible success. For every type of behavior exhibited which is related to the act of achieving, the person writing the story is given another point; having started with a point for a story containing achievement imagery in the first place. In review: The scorer (1) judges whether it is an achievement theme and then (2) looks for certain specific types of activities in the stories postulated as represented indicating strength of motivation.

This scoring system attempts to approximate a counting procedure. Ideally, the scorer should only have to search the story for certain statements, emotions, activities, etc., and enumerate their frequencies. However, some interpretation is still required of the scorer, although much less than required for an interpreter of a traditional TAT or a Rorschach test. Instructions for scoring stories have been published [34]. With practice scorers can reach high levels of agreement in their scoring in a relatively short period of time—a week or so. Thus one of the aims of McClelland has been accomplished, at least in part: a system for evaluating projective tests with a vastly reduced subjective component. But even if scorers can agree, on what are they agreeing? Does the score which is the total of the achievement points have anything to do with motivation for achievement?

Atkinson and McClelland [35] showed that responses to ambiguous stimuli could reflect the arousal of a biological motive. Stories written in a projective test situation by adult human beings under food deprivation contained more references to food deprivation and food-related objects than did stories written by subjects not food deprived. The number of direct responses concerning food did not increase with increased deprivation, however. Would it be possible to arouse experimentally the motive for achievement and show corresponding increase in achievement imagery?

It is worthwhile to note a difference between the arousal of hunger and the arousal of n achievement in the McClelland system. Hunger was elicited by deprivation of food in the Atkinson and McClelland experiment; but deprivation of achievement (or failure) would not be an appropriate condition to arouse the achievement motive. The McClelland view sees n achievement as an affective response in the person aroused by hopes for success. In broad scope it is a fulfillment theory; success feeds on itself.

One type of experiment has effectively demonstrated the effect of situational stimuli in arousing achievement imagery. Imaginative stories written after prior experiences with success and failure contained more achievement imagery than stories written by comparable students at other times [36]. Presumably, the examination provided cues which raised the hope of successful competition with a standard of excellence. While both environmental circumstances and the cues of the TAT pictures can contribute to the achievement imagery produced in creative stories, the most important factor for evaluating n achievement is the contribution of the individual. The theory assumes each person to be differently disposed to produce achievement imagery. The standard practice is to use the achievement-imagery score obtained under what are defined as *neutral conditions* (using certain pictures) as the measure of an individual's n achievement.

The next logical step would be to show that people attaining high achievement scores will work intensely to obtain success in situations where doing so would likely result in reaching achievement goals. Rather than go into the many experiments which have been done to demonstrate the ability of n achievement scores to predict behavior [e.g., 37], we shall discuss an experiment in which n achievement scores predict behavior only under certain conditions.

Atkinson and Reitman [38] performed an experiment in which two tasks were given to two groups of subjects under different conditions. In all conditions the instructions asked the subjects to do their best on the tasks. In one group they were told these tests were ones which in the past had been useful in predicting those who would "do well in life." The subjects in this group worked at the tasks alone in private rooms. The subjects in the other group were told the same thing but in addition they were told cash prizes were to be given to students doing best. The subjects in the latter group worked on their tasks in a group situation in which the experimenters walked around more or less proctoring their work. It could be presumed that the group situation and the experimenters' actions increased the motivation of the subjects to affiliate with the other students and to favorably impress the experimenters.

The results of this experiment indicate that people who were measured as having high achievement scores performed better than those with low achievement scores only in the first group. When the additional sources of motivation were added (money, affiliation) the performance of the high and low achievement groups was indistinguishable. This experiment shows that differences in behavior can be predicted on the basis of the achievement motive only when the situational cues elicit achievement cues and little else. Atkinson and Reitman recognized the principle that almost all of our behavior is overdetermined, i.e., it serves many motives. Typically, we measure only one motive, the others left uncontrolled and unassessed. In their group situation they purposely introduced situational cues for money and affiliation motives. True to their prediction, the introduction of cues for these other motives obscured the predictive ability of the achievement scores. This experiment serves to bring to our attention the point made before that it is only possible to observe the effect of a motive when the person perceives that an activity can serve as a means to fulfillment of that motive.

Progress has been less rapid in the research in other motives stemming from Murray's theoretical contributions. Scoring systems have been developed for n power, n affiliation, and f failure by workers of the McClelland orientation [37]. While such primary efforts are, by and large, encouraging, there remains much to be accomplished in regard to all of these motives.

Perhaps the most urgent need is to develop measurement devices for these needs which are even more objective than the McClelland system. While trained scorers correlate highly with each other in the McClelland technique, there are other practical measurement problems in the system. This may indicate one administration of the test is all that can be used profitably. The measure can be made only once. Correlations between *n* achievement scores on different stories in a set are low, and sometimes show a cyclic effect from story to story. Does this mean achievement is not as general a motive as we have thought? Should the *n* achievement score be considered as a sum of scores representing similar yet different motives?

As with many areas in psychology, a great deal has been learned about motives, but a great deal remains to be learned. This chapter has presented a variety of theories and frameworks to stimulate thinking. It remains for the student of psychology to evaluate the work and points of view represented by Stellar, Hebb, Hull, Mowrer, Lewin, Murray, and others and to continue the exploration of behavior so that new and more effective theories may be developed. It is today's student who will be tomorrow's researcher in man's never-ending attempt to understand himself.

References

1. Littman, R. A. Motives, history, and causes. In M. R. Jones (Ed.), *Nebraska Symposium on Motivation*. Lincoln: Univer. Nebraska Press, 1958.
2. Cannon, W. B., & Washburn, L. An explanation of hunger. *Amer. J. Physiol.,* 1912, **29,** 441–454.
3. Tsang, Y. C. Hunger motivation in gastrectomized rats. *J. comp. Psychol.,* 1938, **26,** 1–17.
4. Mayer, J. Regulation of energy intake and the body weight: the glucostatic theory and the lipostatic hypothesis. *Ann. N.Y. Acad. Sci.,* 1955, **63,** 14–53.
5. Hetherington, A. W., & Ranson, S. W. Hypothalamic lesions and adiposity in the rat. *Anat. Rec.,* 1942, **78,** 149–172.
6. Anand, B. K., & Brobeck, J. R. Localization of a "feeding center" in the hypothalamus of the rat. *Proc. Soc. exp. biol. Med.,* 1951, **77,** 323–324.

7. Teitelbaum, P. Sensory control of hypothalamic hyperphagia. *J. comp. physiol Psychol.*, 1955, **48**, 156–163.

8. Andersson, B., & McCann, S. M. A further study of polydipsia evoked by hypothalamic stimulation in the goat. *Acta physiol. Scand.*, 1955, **33**, 333–346.

9. Stellar, E. The physiology of motivation. *Psychol. Rev.*, 1954, **61**, 5–22.

10. Stellar, E. Drive and motivation. In J. Field (Ed.), *Handbook of Physiology*. Washington: Amer. Physiol. Soc., 1960.

11. T. Tomita, data reported by P. T. Young. The role of hedonic processes in motivation. In M. R. Jones (Ed.), *op. cit.*, 1955.

12. Warren, R. P., & Pfaffman, C. J. Early experience and taste aversion. *J. comp. physiol. Psychol.*, 1959, **52**, 263–266.

13. Cytovich, I. S. Dissertation, Petersburg, 1911. Reported in J. Konorski, *Conditioned Reflexes and Neuron Organization* (Trans. S. Garry). England: Cambridge Univer. Press, 1948.

14. Wolfe, J. B., & Kaplon, M. D. The effect of amount of reward and consummative activity on learning in chickens. *J. comp. Psychol.*, 1941, **31**, 353–361.

15. Berkun, K. J., Kessen, M. L., & Miller, N. E. Hunger-reducing effects of food by stomach fistula vs. food by mouth measured by a consummatory response. *J. comp. physiol. Psychol.*, 1952, **45**, 550–554.

16. Miller, N. E., & Kessen, M. L. Reward effects of food via stomach fistula compared with those of food by mouth. *J. comp. physiol. Psychol.*, 1952, **45**, 555–564.

17. Sheffield, F. D., Wulff, J. J., & Backer, R. Reward value of copulation without sex drive reduction. *J. comp. physiol. Psychol.*, 1951, **44**, 3–8.

18. Olds, J. Positive emotional systems studied by techniques of self-stimulation. *Psychiat. Res. Rept.*, 1960, **12**, 238–257.

19. Freeman, W., & Watts, J. W. *Psychosurgery in the Treatment of Mental Disorders and Intractable Pain*. (2nd ed.) Springfield, Ill., Charles C Thomas, Publisher, 1950.

20. Clark, R. S., Heron, W., Fetherstonhaugh, M. L., Forgays, D. G., & Hebb, D. O. Individual differences in dogs: preliminary report on the effects of early experience. *Canad. J. Psychol.*, 1951, **5**, 150–156.

21. Hebb, D. O. *A Textbook of Psychology*. Philadelphia: W. B. Saunders Company, 1958.

22. Milner, P. M. The cell assembly: Mark II. *Psychol. Rev.*, 1957, **64**, 242–252.

23. Mowrer, O. H. *Learning Theory and Behavior*. New York: John Wiley & Sons, Inc., 1960.

24. Zimmerman, D. W. Durable secondary reinforcement: method and theory. *Psychol. Rev.*, 1957, **64**, 373–383.

25. Zimmerman, D. W. Sustained performance in rats based on secondary reinforcement. *J. comp. physiol. Psychol.*, 1959, **52**, 353–358.

26. Spence, K. W., & Taylor, Janet A. Anxiety and strength of the US as determiners of the amount of eyelid conditioning. *J. exp. Psychol.*, 1951, **42**, 183–188.

27. Spence, K. W., Farber, I. E., & McFann, H. H. The relation of anxiety (drive) level to performance in competitional and noncompetitional paired associates learning. *J. exp. Psychol.*, 1956, **52**, 296–305.

28. Sarason, I. G. Empirical findings and theoretical problems in the use of anxiety scales. *Psychol. Bull.*, 1960, **57**, 403–415.

29. Mandler, G., & Sarason, S. B. A study of anxiety and learning. *J. abnorm. soc. Psychol.*, 1952, **47**, 166–173.

30. Maier, N. R. F. *Frustration: The Study of Behavior without a Goal*. New York: McGraw-Hill Book Company, Inc., 1949.

31. Lewin, K. In D. Cartwright (Ed.), *Field Theory in Social Science*. New York: Harper & Row, Publishers, Inc., 1951.

32. Murray, H. A. *Explorations in Personality*. New York: Oxford Univer. Press, 1938.

33. McClelland, D. C., Atkinson, J. W., Clark, R. A., & Lowell, E. L. *The Achievement Motive*. New York: Appleton-Century-Crofts, Inc., 1953.

34. Smith, C. P., & Feld, Sheila. How to learn the method of content analysis for *n* Achievement, *n* Affiliation, and *n* Power. Appendix I in J. W. Atkinson (Ed.), *Motives in Fantasy, Action, and Society*. Princeton, N.J.: D. Van Nostrand Company, Inc., 1958.

35. McClelland, D. C., & Atkinson, J. W. The projective expression of needs: I. The effect of different intensities of the hunger upon perception. *J. Psychol.*, 1948, **25**, 205–222.

36. McClelland, D. C., Clark, R. A., Roby, T. B., & Atkinson, J. W. The effect of the need for achievement on thematic apperception. *J. exp. Psychol.*, 1949, **37**, 242–255.

37. Atkinson, J. W. (Ed.), *Motives in Fantasy, Action, and Society*. Princeton, N.J.: D. Von Nostrand Company, Inc., 1958.

38. Atkinson, J. W., & Reitman, W. R. Performance as a function of motive strength expectancy of goal attainment. *J. abnorm. soc. Psychol.*, 1956, **53**, 361–366.

BOOK TWO

*Psychology: The Science
of Interpersonal Behavior*

PREFACE

This introductory textbook in psychology represents a departure from the traditional approach found in other introductory texts. Its focus is on the broad area of interpersonal behavior. It attempts to utilize consistently a social-science orientation rather than to view behavior from differing, and sometimes irreconcilable, perspectives. The implicit question we have asked throughout the book is, "How well does a social-science approach to interpersonal behavior enable us to comprehend and predict behavioral responses?"

This approach has enabled us to examine theory in considerable depth. Our hope was that a careful study of theory would lead to a meaningful and critical understanding of basic issues. Moreover, we have tried to select and present parsimoniously the data—experimental, clinical, social, and cultural—which are relevant for such a study, and to give the student a forthright and relatively complete presentation of such findings. The relative values and limitations of alternative theories in explaining important aspects of interpersonal behavior should therefore become more clearly evident. Our analysis of the different theories is presented with the expectation that they will be viewed not merely as conflicting interpretations of behavior, but as supplementary and perhaps complementary. We have invited the reader behind the scenes, so to speak, to participate in the kind of thinking psychologists do, without foreclosing issues prematurely. Too often, we believe, students are given inappropriate feelings of false closure in regard to basic issues.

The sequence of chapters is designed to provide cumulative growth of understanding. The early chapters deal with basic concepts, primary methodological issues, and competing philosophical perspectives concerning the psychology of interpersonal behavior. The later chapters build on theories and data presented earlier. This arrangement makes possible the presentation of fairly complicated problems which are often omitted from an introductory textbook or are given superficial treatment. The arrangement of topics makes it necessary for students to master the concepts and theories presented in the earlier chapters before studying those in the later chapters.

The first chapter deals with the nature of theory in psychology and with some basic tools needed for analyzing the data of behavior. Following this, basic principles and facts concerning the development of behavior are presented. In subsequent chapters we discuss theories and evidence about personality development, the nature of conflict, and methods of resolving conflict. This enables us to consider the problem of defining the structure of the personality and to examine theories offered to account for the organization of the personality. The phenomena of personality disorganization and some theories to account for them are examined next. Then we consider methods that have been proposed to promote the reorganization of the personality. In the light of prior material, it is possible, finally, to evaluate methods of assessing different kinds of interpersonal variables and to introduce the student to some basic considerations about social phenomena and group behavior.

Of course, some topics which some instructors may believe to be important have been omitted. The long lists of references given at the end of each chapter suggest that a specialized treatment is required in an introductory text—as our book is designed to be. These references, and others which may be suggested, will enable the individual professor to emphasize those topics which he believes are most significant. It seems to us that such individual emphases in instruction make the teaching and learning of psychology most rewarding and stimulating.

A companion volume to this book, *Psychology: The Science of Behavior,* prepared by the present authors and published in 1965, selects those topics which permit a natural-science orientation to psychology, and treats them in depth. The use of that book may provide coverage of other basic issues required in introductory courses which are designed to provide broader coverage than the present volume can provide alone.

The preparation of this book has involved the close interaction of the three authors. Each has a different type of background. All have had extensive experience in college teaching and in research. One is a clinical psychologist with varied experience in the diagnosis and treatment of individuals with either mild or severe personality problems. Another has specialized in the area of physiological psychology. The third author has been involved in the field of industrial psychology. Yet all of us have agreed on the significance of the basic issues presented in the present volume. We hope that the final product represented in the text has benefited because of the balanced set of interests and perspectives represented by the authors.

We have been particularly fortunate in having the critical but sympathetic counsel and detailed review of our text by our two professional editors: Wayne H. Holtzman and Gardner Murphy. We have labored hard in attempting to make full use of their advice and suggestions. We are also extremely grateful to the many colleagues who read individual chapters of the book and offered many helpful criticisms. We have not always agreed with the advice we were given, but we have considered it most carefully. We owe a very special debt of gratitude to George A. Middendorf, psychology editor of the college department of Harper & Row, not only for his patient encouragement during the preparation of the manuscript, but for his invariable helpfulness in meeting complex problems during this period. We must, of course, assume final responsibility for whatever merit and limitation our book has. Once again, we wish to offer our humble thanks to our long-suffering wives, Anne, Susan, and Naomi. Without their forebearance, tact, and encouragement this work would never have reached fruition.

Max L. Hutt
Robert L. Isaacson
Milton L. Blum

January, 1966

ONE INTRODUCTION: THE MEANING OF INTERPERSONAL BEHAVIOR

The perennial questions about man are: "What is man really like?" and "How did he get that way?" From time immemorial, writers, philosophers, and others have been concerned with these questions. Above all else man is a social being. His behavior occurs in relation to some other person, real or imagined. Even when he is alone, his behavior reflects how he feels about himself. But this, in turn, is a product of how others have felt and acted toward him in the past. This book is about man's personal and *interpersonal behavior,* or about how man relates to himself and to others.

Man lives in a constant state of flux, but some aspects of his behavior remain constant. Since present behavior evolves out of previous physical and psychological contexts, we need to learn what factors are significant for this development. To be understood, development must be studied over a life-span. We also need to know whether a particular man's behavior has the same impact upon the various people with whom he is in contact. Indeed, the same man may behave quite differently with different people. Moreover, different people may perceive him as being quite different. Is he really the "same man" under all of these circumstances?

Some literary writers have stated that man is a "prisoner of his own skin." The same physical man may be in that skin, but he may behave in significantly varying ways in his relations with other people. He may, at times, be arrogant; at other times, obsequious. He may be kind to his employees or friends but horrid to his wife. He may appear to be passive and submissive to all or most people but then suddenly and apparently inexplicably erupt in a fit of rage. Even when you think you know a man very well, he may surprise you and reveal qualities you did not suspect. In short, the "same" man within the "same" skin is always something of an enigma. He can be understood if his behavior is studied *in relation to the social situation which evoked it.* At the same time, his behavior can have greater meaning to us if we understand the nature of his needs and the mechanisms through which these needs are expressed.

This book presents the findings derived from the scientific study of these aspects of man's behavior. We shall study the ways in which these findings have been accumulated: from controlled observations of behavior; from clinical studies of disturbed people; from experimental research in the laboratory and social settings; and from theoretical attempts to assimilate and integrate these findings into a coherent and meaningful set of propositions which can help us to predict behavior with greater precision. And we shall examine critically the scientific conceptions of man's personality and his social behavior in order to see their advantages over the layman's conceptions. We shall also seek to evaluate the limitations of the present stage of our knowledge.

Simple and Complex Behavior Functions

Every behavioral act is *multidetermined*. Some kinds of responses, like the reflex reaction of the pupil of the eye to a
bright light or the response of the leg to a tap on the patellar
tendon below the knee, appear as unvarying, highly specific,
simple bits of behavior. These simple acts are, however, modifiable in a number of ways. The internal state of the organism, or
the setting in which the behavior is elicited, may increase or
diminish the response. Previous learning may affect the response. The focus of the person's attention may modify it. In
other words, the intensity of a simple reflex response is determined by a complex of factors. This modifiability of response is
far greater for more complex behavioral acts. But, whether
simple or complex, each response is the end product of many
intervening factors. If, for example, we consider such behaviors
as pursuing a vocational or professional goal or selecting a mate
for marriage, we become aware that many factors influence our
responses. The choice of a vocational goal depends, in the first
instance, on previously developed interest patterns. The potential satisfactions of attainment of the goal constitute another set
of important factors. Other possible factors are intellectual and
special abilities, the availability of training and employment
opportunities, the kinds of experiences involved in the training
program, and social and cultural pressures and prohibitions.
Similarly, in choosing a husband or wife, our behavior is
determined by many interrelated factors which influence the
particular pattern we display. The contrast between the factors
involved in simple behavior responses and those involved in
complex behavior responses is shown schematically in Figure
1.1.

In both simple and complex behavior, not only are our
responses multidetermined, but we have varying degrees of
awareness of the significant causal factors. We shall have more
to say concerning these differences in degrees of awareness; at
this time, we simply wish to point out that such differences are
present. For example, when we say, as in the familiar song, "I
want a girl just like the girl that married dear old Dad," we are
acknowledging the fact that our choice of a marital partner is
somehow influenced by both *conscious factors,* of which we

379

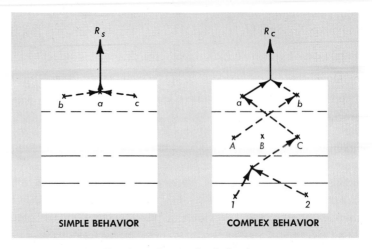

FIGURE 1.1 *Simple and complex behavior responses contrasted. In the simple response* (R_s), *the response is determined mainly by factor* a, *supplemented by factors* b *and* c, *all from the same level. In the complex response* (R_c), *the response is determined by the interaction of factors from many levels of the organism; it is truly multidetermined.*

Responses are varied and multidimensional. Zimbel from Monkmeyer

may be fully aware (such as Mom's charm, intelligence, emotional stability, and the like), and by *unconscious factors* (like the degree of emotional identification with Mom, the degree of emotional dependence upon Mom's approval, and the like). Psychologists attempt to define all of the significant *parameters* (or psychological variables) which are relevant to the behavioral response in order to find more effective methods for predicting the nature of the response.

As we shall see, in subsequent chapters, motivation, emotional state, degree of conflict, degree of perceptual awareness, and defense patterns are all highly influential in determining any particular behavior. Complex behavioral acts, especially those carried out over an extended period of time, appear to be far more significantly influenced by the interactions of these internal factors than are simple responses. Although even simple reflex responses may be influenced, to some degree, by psychological factors, the more complex a response, the more likely it is that it will be influenced by such factors. Simple acts, like turning on the light switch, may involve a number of "inner determinants" (in unusual instances, such as when some irrational fear is connected with the act, these may be crucial), but complex behaviors are much more likely to be significantly influenced by such factors.

Since we cannot "see" the operation of these internal factors, psychologists postulate the theoretical existence of certain *intervening variables* to help explain the behavioral outcome. The process of such theory construction involves a number of steps. On the basis of *observed facts* about behavior, psychologists formulate *hypotheses* (tentative explanations) about it. An interrelated set of hypotheses to predict behavior is called a *theory*. Many hypotheses concern events which are not directly observable, and such hypotheses deal with the postulated *intervening variables* that may help to predict the behavioral outcome.

Let us now turn to a consideration of such variables.

Phenomenological and Dynamic Views of Behavior

Today, few would deny the operation of "inner determinants" of behavior. Psychologists, like other people, take different philosophical approaches to behavior. Thus, they construct different theories of behavior, each with differing views concerning the nature of the intervening variables. The phenomenological approach in psychology, which represents one extreme on this problem, takes the position that what the psychologist should be concerned with is how the person perceives the events in his own life [1]. From this viewpoint, what really matters in determining behavior is the individual's *phenomenological field*. Data about unconscious factors or about the individual's developmental history are irrelevant in predicting behavior, they say. The only significant factors are how the individual feels about experiences in his life.

In contrast to this position is that of *dynamic psychologists,* in general, and of psychoanalysts, in particular. Psychoanalysts (those who stress the importance of unconscious factors) maintain that to understand behavior one must be fully appreciative of the *unconscious motivations* (those of which a person is unaware) that are largely responsible for it. What a person tells us about his feelings and actions has relevance, but the nature of the relevance cannot be understood without comprehension of unconscious factors. Dynamic psychologists cite examples of many kinds of irrational aspects of behavior to emphasize their position that unconscious factors must be postulated.

As we stated, however, no one disagrees that intervening variables must be postulated. What really differentiates psychologists on this score is how they view them. Some believe that they can define behavior more precisely, and predict it more accurately, by focusing on external conditions rather than on internal variables. Others believe it is necessary to emphasize internal factors. There are at least two basic questions which such differences in orientation pose for the student of psychology. The first is, Which approach leads to better predictions of behavior? This is an empirical question and could be a relatively easy one to answer with appropriate research data. However, the second question indicates that the problem is more complicated than this.

The second question is, What *kinds of questions* should one raise about human behavior? Those who take a dynamic position, like that taken by psychoanalysts, say that one cannot ask the most crucial questions about human behavior unless one recognizes the significance of unconscious forces. They would claim that the phenomenologists raise only trivial questions and neglect the really vital ones. Dynamic psychologists view such problems as symbolism in dreams, inconsistencies between values and behavior (as, for example, *believing* one has no racial prejudice but *acting* in such a manner as to invalidate this belief), and irrational fears (like being fearful of harmless moths) as critical to any adequate theory of behavior. Phenomenologists might reply that they can predict behavior without answering some kinds of questions and that the problems cited are beyond the province of psychology—or of any science, for that matter.

To make the problem more understandable, let us view the issue by considering some specific examples of behavior. In doing this, we shall be attempting to conceptualize two major aspects of behavior: the *overt* and the *covert.*

Overt and Covert Behavior

Overt behavior may be simply defined as that which is observable and measurable by the observer. In contrast, *covert* behavior is inferred from overt behavior by the observer. Some simple illustrations may help. When a person kicks a dog without provocation, most observers will agree that the observable behavior may be characterized as angry or aggressive. They are describing the overt aspects of the person's behavior. Consider, next, the following behavior. A person is "appropriately but coldly polite." Many observers might believe that, in this instance, the person is actually angry or annoyed. They are making the inference that the overt polite behavior conceals some covert feelings of anger.

Now, let us examine more complex behavior.

In a certain Midwestern town, according to a newspaper account, a man who was well known for his kindness and courtesy in dealing with others was found to have murdered a number of women. He had cut their bodies into small pieces and buried them in his cellar. He had never publicly shown any indications of extreme anger or of emotional instability. When confronted with the evidence of his misdeeds, he made no attempt to deny that he was responsible but maintained that he had simply been slaughtering cows! When shown the dismembered pieces of these women's bodies, he insisted that they were parts of cows, not women.

Psychological study of this man indicated that he was suffering from a severe form of mental disturbance (a psychosis). It

383

Overt behavior developing.

Motivation can be inferred although the stimulus is not apparent. United Nations

was learned that there were many indices that he had very strong, hostile feelings toward women. For instance, although he had always been known to be polite to women, he would frequently "forget" appointments with them. Although he had never made deprecatory remarks about men, he had been known to refer to some women in a highly derogatory manner. During the psychological study of this man, it was learned that he frequently had dreams in which he "saw" horrible-looking women chasing him or inflicting pain upon him. He responded on projective tests (see Chapter 8) with considerable indication of latent hostility toward female figures.

This man's overt behavior was that of an essentially stable, polite, and well-mannered individual. On the covert level, there were indications of severe emotional conflict and disturbance and very marked hostility toward female symbols and figures. There was little or no overt evidence of these intense feelings of anger and little or no evidence of the severity of his perceptual distortions. Yet it seemed clear that his overt criminal behavior was determined, in part, by these covert feelings and conflicts.

Another illustration concerns the severe inhibition of cognitive (or intellectual) functions in a college student.

This young man had a very superior high-school record and a very superior record in his first two years of college work. In his third college year, however, his schoolwork fell off very sharply. He failed four of the five courses he was taking, and three of these were continuations of courses in his own field of concentration (English literature). He stated that he was employing his usual, or even a larger than usual, amount of study time. He found that he could not concentrate, that he had difficulty retaining what he had read or studied, and that, for the first time, he was panicking on examinations and could not function effectively on them even when he was thoroughly familiar with the subject matter. Later he developed physical complaints, such as stomach pain, headaches, and low back pains. Medical examination revealed no physical basis for these complaints.

The young man sought psychotherapeutic help for his problems. (See Chapter 7 for a discussion of psychotherapy.) In the course of this work it became clear that he had had mixed feelings about going to college. He had told others, and he had tried to tell himself, that he wanted to go to college. He did not wish to disappoint his parents, who wanted him to have a college education. He believed that he loved his parents and that their counsel in such matters was kind and wise. He felt that he could not discuss with them his apparently irrational wish to leave college. Later he became aware that he had considerable resentment toward his parents, but he had never "permitted" himself to confront these "dishonorable" feelings within him. He had always found it difficult, in fact, to express any overtly hostile feelings toward his parents. This was due to his overly dependent emotional attachment to them. They had never let him feel that he could really disagree with them. When this young man resolved his conflicts about himself, he decided that *he* wanted to stay in college. He chose a different field of concentration from the one his parents had selected for him, and he was able to complete his program with good scholastic grades.

In this case we note, again, that there were unexpressed feelings of anger. There was also an excessive degree of emotional dependence upon well-meaning but authoritarian parents. There were conflicting attitudes about the desirability of a college education, with rationalization and other defense mechanisms (see Chapter 4) "piled one upon the other." He was conflicted about what he thought and what he felt. His severe internal conflicts had led him to "try to escape" from the college situation by producing a severe disturbance in the effectiveness with which he used his mental and other abilities. At the overt level he functioned as though he were limited in scholastic ability, although he really had quite superior competency. Finally, he had developed secondary, overt symptoms of his disturbance—his physical complaints—which gave him some apparent justification for doing poorly in college. In considering this case, we may note how complicated the total end product of behavior is and how many internal, covert behaviors were significant in determining its outcome.

To further illustrate, let us examine the results of some studies of perception. Bruner and Goodman asked children of

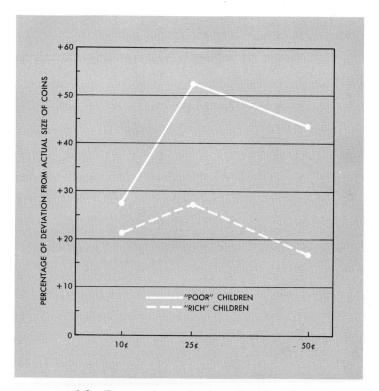

FIGURE 1.2   *Degree of error in size-estimation of coins by "rich" and "poor" 10-year-olds. Adapted from J. S. Bruner & C. C. Goodman. J.* abnorm. soc. Psychol., *1947,* **13**, *33–44.*

approximately ten years of age to adjust the size of a circular aperture to the size of common coins [2]. Under laboratory conditions in which this study was done, children tended to overestimate the actual size of the coins. Even more important, poorer children tended to overestimate the size of these coins far more than did richer children. The difference in degree of overestimation was greater for the larger (and more expensive) coins such as a quarter and half-dollar. (See Figure 1.2.) This study was interpreted to indicate that <u>internal needs</u> influence

387

visual perception since children from low economic background were presumed to have a greater need for money than those from high economic backgrounds. Although the study has been criticized on methodological grounds (because poorer children have had less actual experience with large coins than richer children, this factor may have influenced the results), the conclusion that "need" can affect behavior—in this instance perceptual behavior—has been confirmed in a number of other studies. For example, in order to control for familiarity with the size of coins, Ashley and his co-workers, in another study, compared the degree of overestimation of the size of coins in subjects who were hypnotized and given posthypnotic suggestions [3]. Those who were "instructed" that they were poor tended to overestimate size more than those who were "instructed" that they were rich.

Once again, we are confronted with the fact that there are internal factors influencing behaviors. Psychologists develop hypotheses about these factors and their interaction. When this has been done, we refer to the factors as *intervening variables*.

Clinical cases and research data such as these indicate that, to understand overt behavior completely, we must have some knowledge of what is going on "underneath." Sometimes, as in the studies of perception, we are able to evaluate these covert factors by experimentally manipulating them. At other times we may have to make reasonable inferences about such factors by careful evaluations of behavior, by an analysis of the history of the person's experience, or by other means. From various kinds of evidence we are finally able to hypothesize the nature and characteristics of such covert phenomena. Much of our study of interpersonal behavior will reflect the psychologists' attempts to construct theoretical explanations of the interaction of covert and overt parameters of behavior in order to arrive at better understanding and prediction of human behavior.

Man: A Machine or a Creative Organism?

Many scientists, both in the social science field and in the biological science field, have struggled with the age-old problem concerning the nature of man. Social scientists, attempting to emulate the physical scientists in their search for precision of definition and measurement, tried to reject the idea of man as an irrational being, with unknown impulses, unreasoned purposes, and unconscious levels of motivation. Many conceptualized man as a machine—infinitely more complex, perhaps, than man-made machines, but a machine, nevertheless. If man were constructed of many specific parts and observable mechanisms, one could treat his behavior much like that of some inanimate contrivance. One could then more easily understand him and could *control* him more effectively. And, his behavior could be viewed with objective, detached, and "scientific" precision.

THE MECHANOMORPHIZATION OF MAN   This whole mechanomorphization of man must be understood as a revolt against mysticism and conceptions of the world as composed of two separate and distinct kinds of matter: animate and inanimate. Inanimate objects were expected to obey "natural" laws about matter. However, animate things were thought to contain a "life-spirit" (*animus*) whose presence made their behavior either unpredictable or understandable only in terms of special "life-spirit laws." Since the time of the Copernican revolution some 300 years ago, when man was displaced from the center of the universe, scientists searched for an explanation of man as an objective, mechanical contrivance whose behavior was determinate and predictable with absolute accuracy. Psychology and the other "social sciences" borrowed a page from classical physics and began to conceptualize man as an organism "with regular motions according to mechanical principles" [4]. Physics departed from the classical traditions concerning mechanics with its discovery of the quantum theory. But, a great many of the disciples of psychology, lagging behind, did not greet this revolution with enthusiasm. Instead, they clung to the traditional and "classical" scientific orientation and, indeed, attempted to reinforce this position with considerable vigor.

John B. Watson, an "animal psychologist" and the founder of Behaviorism, became the protagonist of this mechanical conception of man and of his machine-like characteristics [5]. He saw psychology as "a purely objective, experimental branch of natural science which needs introspection as little as do the sciences of chemistry and physics." (Introspection refers to the reporting by an individual of his subjective or conscious feelings and thoughts.) *Meaning* and *intent* were stripped from consideration in studying man's behavior. Similarly, subjective feelings were mercilessly removed for the good of an "objective science"   389 of behavior. Behavior was to be understood solely in terms of stimulus and response! With such a view, said Watson, "The possibility of shaping [of behavior] in any direction is almost endless." Man was now a mere technological device; irrationalities of behavior were simply due to imperfections in the construction of the machine. As Kuo, a disciple of Watson's, put it, "The duty of a behaviorist is to describe behavior in exactly the same way as the physicist describes the movement of a machine. . . . This human machine behaves in a certain way because environmental stimulation has *forced* [*sic*] him to do so" [6].

Watson had a great impact upon American psychology. The major theoretical conception of behavior, in general, and of personality functioning, in particular, was in the direction of the mechanomorphization of man. There were significant exceptions, however, in this country, and much of European psychology did not follow the "new" direction of American thought. At the present time this trend toward mechanization and stimulus-response models of human behavior is being carried forward with highly sophisticated theoretical formulations by B. F. Skinner, among others. (See reference [7] for a detailed consideration of Skinner's position.) In his book, *Science and Human Behavior* [8], and in his treatment of this scientific orientation as a novel, *Walden Two,* he spells out the assumptions and principles he has derived.

Skinner sees man as an *organic machine.* It is not necessary, he believes, to assume that his behavior has any unusual properties. It is based solely on physical construction, and its actual attributes are entirely determinable on the basis of factors in the external environment. Skinner wishes to avoid the error of subjective anthropomorphism. He therefore views psychology's task as that of reducing everything to physical terms. In this process, such concepts as purpose, spontaneity, and meaning would need to be excluded from scientific study. Excluded, too, would be the need to postulate consciousness.

His conception made it possible to visualize a new kind of society—one in which people are controlled for their own good. Since behavior should be entirely predictable, people could be trained to behave in any prescribed way. This training would be under the control of a hierarchy, which would decide what is good for man and would seek to implement this goal by prescribing appropriate conditions of living and learning. The

Can one readily avoid an anthropomorphic interpretation of behavior? Both photos, Godsey from Monkmeyer

ultimate criterion in such behavior-control practices would be the survival of the culture. And it follows that the managers of society, not the individual members of society, should have the responsibility of deciding what the right kind of culture should be.

OPERATIONAL ANALYSIS This mechanistic orientation toward man was given great additional impetus by the formulations of a mathematical physicist, P. W. Bridgman, in 1927 [9]. Bridgman introduced and defined a process of scientific study known as *operational analysis*. By this was meant that any hypothesis or proposition should be formulated and tested in

391

terms of specific and objectively defined operations. Such an orientation in the behavioral sciences would mean that behavior could be studied "from the outside" by the experimental observer, who merely had to define objectively the sequence of external events that would produce a given consequence. Thus, "inner man," with its vague, ill-defined, and subjective characteristics, could be eliminated.

It is interesting to note that Bridgman himself not only disavowed this position as a result of his own further studies and the impact of the then new quantum principle in physics but wrote, repeatedly, very careful expositions of the limitations and fallacies of his own earlier position [10]. He had become convinced that operationalism was inadequate because no scientific phenomenon—and no act of human behavior—was understandable except in terms of the uniqueness of that phenomenon *in relation to the field of which it was then a part.*

For human beings this meant that behavior could only be understood if the uniqueness of the individual in his specific interaction with another individual was considered. Thus, the observer, even a "neutral" scientific observer, was an essential part of the field, for, whether he intended it or not, he participated in determining the behavior of the subject. (He was part of the significant "field.") This viewpoint has been vividly expressed by a contemporary philosopher, Karl Mannheim, who said, ". . . a human situation is characterized only when one has . . . taken into account those conceptions which the participants have of it, how they experience their tensions in this situation and how they react to the tensions so conceived"[11]. There is research evidence on this issue, some of which, relating to psychological testing, is reviewed in Chapter 8.

MAN AS A PURPOSIVE ANIMAL   In opposition to the mechanistic conception of man, other social scientists conceive of him as a dynamic, striving, purposeful, and creative organism. Beginning with McDougall, who in 1912 championed the cause of *hormic psychology* (or purposivism in psychology), some psychologists recognized that man's behavior could not be understood adequately without considering his *goals* [12]. As McDougall put it, there are some things that are inert and mechanical, and there are others, especially human beings, that "seem to have an intrinsic power of self-determination, and to pursue actively . . . their own ends and purposes." In more recent years, some learning theorists like Edward Tolman [13], some psychotherapists like Horney [14] and Fromm [15], and some Gestalt psychologists, like Wertheimer [16] and Lewin [17], have offered views which have this fundamental concept in common: that man is conscious, striving, purposeful, and capable of spontaneous and creative behavior.

Our discussions in later chapters, especially in Chapters 5–7, introduce the student to these dynamic conceptions of man in some detail. At this point, it may be sufficient to indicate that science tries both to understand more completely and to predict more accurately the nature of man's behavior. The student, as well as the scientist, has a responsibility in judging which viewpoint is most congenial and which is most useful. Like the modern physicist, we have to ask which theory explains phenomena most adequately. The theory which does this best will replace other theories. In turn, it will be supplanted by still more adequate theories which explain still more.

The Nature of Behavior Variables

In order to study behavior we have to select some aspects of it for close scrutiny or for experimental manipulation. We could study the development of walking in many ways. For example, we could select the sequence from crawling to erect walking. We could study the development of speech, similarly, by selecting the variable of sentence length in relation to age. We could study the process of thinking by selecting the variable of logical structure shown in a person's speech. In each of these examples the variable selected is itself an abstraction that is deemed important in the study of behavior.

BEHAVIOR VARIABLES—AN ABSTRACTION Any "item" of behavior can be utilized as a behavior variable. Some items will prove to be useful because their study leads to a better theory of behavior and better prediction, whereas other items will be found to be less useful. Some items will need reconceptualization, or better definition, as our knowledge of behavior improves and as our study of the interrelationship of these items of behavior with other items progresses. In any event, a behavior variable is a *response of the organism* that is conceptualized by the observer in a specified, systematic manner. It is therefore always an abstraction derived from repeated and refined observations of examples of behavior. Certain behavior variables have a concreteness to them, as in the examples we have given. Others, like "honesty," "passivity," "depression," and "dominance" represent higher degrees of abstraction in that these variables represent greater degrees of inference about the behavior than do the more concrete examples given above.

PARAMETERS OF BEHAVIOR VARIABLES The scientific study of interpersonal behavior presents special problems of conceptualization and definition. In the first place, we may conceive of both overt and covert behavior variables, as we indicated in a previous section of this chapter. Suppose, now, we wish to deal with some overt, and presumably more explicit, variable of interpersonal behavior. Such a variable might be defined in a great many ways, and the results of our study would depend upon the definition we utilized. As we shall see, this leads to the problem of the degree of *generalizability* we can make about our hypothesized behavior variable.

As a specific illustration of the kinds of problems which are inherent in the investigation of behavior variables, let us consider *aggression*. This term may be roughly defined as an attack made by one person upon another, in other words, as assaultive behavior. But what is an attack and what is an assault? Each of us can think of different kinds of aggressive behavior. We seldom pause to consider whether these different behaviors have much in common. Is aggression a single factor, or does it consist of many factors? And how can we measure it? Should we define it in physical terms, like hitting or striking, or should we also include verbal assaults, like sarcasm and irony? If we decide to use both physical and nonphysical manifestations, we then have the problem of determining whether these two types of aggression "go together." Are they really expressions of the same underlying factor? If we find that people who are physically assaultive are also as frequently and intensely verbally assaultive, we can then conclude that these are expressions of some underlying aspect of behavior. But thus far we have considered only two *types* of aggressive behavior. Of course, there may be many other types of aggression.

Another dimension of aggression may be conceptualized as *direction*. Aggression may be *outwardly directed* or it may be *inner-directed*. A child may, for example, express his aggression

Aggression is not always directed outward. United Press International

by hitting his mother, or he may express it by refusing to comply with her request that he do something. Inner-directed aggression (which is usually passive) may take other forms than negativistic rebellion. It may take the form of sulking or of becoming depressed.

There are, of course, many other possible dimensions of aggressive behavior, e.g., *frequency, intensity,* and *pattern.* Consider such questions as the following. Does a given individual display a specified type of aggression with similar frequency during different periods of his life? Does the intensity of this behavior vary over time? Does the particular pattern of aggressive behavior remain constant? The psychologist who studies aggressive behavior will need to determine how each of these dimensions is related to the others.

A different kind of dimension concerns the *object* of the aggressive behavior. The term "object" is used here to refer to a person, situation, animal, or physical object toward which the aggression is directed. Some men, for example, display aggression more readily toward women than toward other men. Some display this behavior toward people whom they perceive as weak or helpless. Some are more likely to display it in group situations.

We can begin to see how complex any study that undertakes to investigate the behavior variable of aggression may turn out to be. Psychologists, therefore, have to keep two things in mind in their study of aggression or any other behavior variable. (1) They have to specify the nature of the variable under study and relate this to some theoretical model in order to give it some "anchorage." Otherwise, both the measure of the variable and the research done with it can be entirely fortuitous. (2) They have to limit the *degree of generalizability* of their findings to those aspects of the variable under study which have been specified in (1). To illustrate this point, consider the finding that children from the lower socioeconomic classes tend to exhibit more physical aggression than verbal aggression. This finding must be restricted to the measures of aggression used in the research, to the definition of "lower socioeconomic classes" specified in the theory, and to the types of samples of subjects employed in the study.

Some psychologists recognize that any definition of a behavior variable is incomplete if it does not consider the field conditions under which it is observed or measured. As we have noted previously, the observer exercises some degree of influence upon the behavior under study, even if he tries to be as inconspicuous and as neutral as possible.

Assessment of Reliability and Validity

In order to utilize behavior variables in theory and research, they must be defined and must be measured in some manner. As we shall see, later in this book, there may be value in "fuzzy" or unprecise definitions in the early stages of theory development because overly precise definitions at this stage may unduly restrict the development of alternative modes of explanation. At the moment, however, we shall be concerned with problems in obtaining relatively precise assessment of behavior variables.

One of the most direct methods of assessing a behavior variable is through direct observation of the behavior in question. In this case, the variable has to be defined so that different observers and raters of the behavior can agree on its presence and, possibly, on its intensity. The degree of agreement among judges is known as the *reliability* (interjudge reliability) of ratings. However, although judges might agree perfectly in their ratings—and thus achieve a perfect degree of reliability in their ratings—they would not necessarily be measuring what it was intended that they measure. The latter attribute is known as *validity*. Validity refers to the degree to which a measure truly represents the variable which it is intended to measure. We shall shortly have more to say about the concepts of reliability and validity.

A behavior variable can be measured in many ways, depending in part upon the nature of the variable. Sometimes the intensity of behavior is measured in terms of the effect this behavior has upon some instrument. An example of this is the effect upon an electroencephalograph (a machine used to record electrical activity of the brain) of an increase in an individual's anxiety. There are also various kinds of psychological tests which attempt to measure psychological attributes. As examples, there are questionnaires (called *personality tests*) which measure such variables as anxiety or suspiciousness by summing the person's responses on a "paper-and-pencil" test which contains questions about such phenomena. There are *projective personality tests* which can be used to measure an individual's anxiety or hostility in terms of the degree to which the individual "projects" or interprets relatively ambiguous or neutral test stimuli in terms of these phenomena. In Chapter 8 we discuss measures of this kind, like the Thematic Apperception Test, in which the individual is asked to tell stories about a series of standardized pictures. Another widely used projective test is the Rorschach Psychodiagnostic Ink-Blot Test, in which a person is asked to interpret ambiguous inkblots.

To understand the adequacy of the measures which are employed, we must understand two basic attributes of any measure: validity and reliability. Let us consider the concept of validity first. As we have said, validity represents the degree to which a measure accurately assesses that which it is supposed to measure.

VALIDITY If we are to know how well something is measured, we must have some criterion or yardstick of this attribute. In the domain of psychological attributes, establishing the validity of a test is often a complex and long-term task. A measure of the validity of a test or of a rating requires some reference criterion, yet this criterion may be as difficult to obtain or define as the construction of the test itself. If, for instance, we wish to measure "general intelligence," we must first assign some meaning to this concept (or have some theory about it) and then find some criterion which reflects it adequately. If we agree that general intelligence is represented in behavior by how well we learn the academic subjects of reading and arithmetic, then we can establish performance in these subjects as our criterion of intelligence. The validity of our test of intelligence would then be determined by ascertaining the degree to which it accurately predicted performance in these courses. However, we might be unable to agree on a definition of intelligence. Then we would need a considerable period of further observation of various kinds of supposedly intelligent behavior, as well as research studies, to investigate the relationships among these several kinds of intelligent behavior. This would then lead to refinements of the theories of "intelligence."

The selection of a suitable criterion of some behavior variables is even more complex than in our example, the variable of intelligence. In some instances we have less adequate theories about the phenomena in question. In others we have less adequate means of finding suitable external criteria. Suppose we wished to measure a variable known as "ego strength." (The reader will find in Chapters 3, 6, and 7 considerable discussion of the concept of "ego.") We shall learn that ego functions have been defined in terms of the relative adequacy with which an individual is (1) aware of both internal drives and external reality, (2) able adequately to integrate conflicting internal drives in his behavior, and (3) effective in carrying out sequences of behavior in terms of the situation in which he is involved. Measures of the strength of the ego would, presumably, then represent the effectiveness of all these aspects of personality functioning. Even if we assume that we are agreed on our preliminary definition, what kinds of criteria might we select to represent these phenomena? How could we construct measures that would predict them? In attempting to establish suitable criteria, we might find our theory and our definitions insufficiently explicit, and we might find it very difficult to obtain satisfactory criteria of the phenomena in question.

On the basis of these illustrations, we are now in a better position to understand the meaning of the concept of validity in the study of interpersonal behavior.

The concept of validity is usually subdivided into four types. The first of these is called *construct validity*. If we have a fairly clear idea of what it is we wish to assess, either in terms of theory or arbitrary definition, we can develop some methods for ascertaining the degree to which an individual shows this characteristic. In our illustration of the construct "general intelligence," suppose our theory demanded that: "Intelligence represents the ability of an individual to reason logically." We would not necessarily be concerned with the question of how well this ability predicts school performance, or ability to hold a job, or ability to remember, or ability to get along with people. Instead, we would be interested in trying to find measures of "the ability to reason logically." It would remain a task for subsequent research to discover whether this ability was related to other characteristics, such as school performance. Given our "logical reasoning" definition, the task now would be to select items that would presumably measure reasoning ability. We might search through books on logic, or we might try to think up "new" reasoning problems.

In any case, we would select samples of logical reasoning as the first step in developing our test. We would then, perhaps, subject this list to the close scrutiny of a group of experts on logical reasoning to determine whether there was agreement that all of the items represented "logical reasoning," and we would eliminate those items on which we could not obtain substantial agreement. Next, in our refinement of the measure, we might give this preliminary test to individuals who differed widely in reasoning ability. (The reader might wish to consider how this could be done.) After gathering the responses from a large sample of individuals, we could then examine the data to see "whether the items went together," i.e., whether each item discriminated between subgroups of "bright" and "dull" reasoners. This would give us some indication that, whatever the items were measuring, they tended to measure the same kind of thing. Then we might further refine our test by eliminating ambiguities or crudities in the wording of the items. We might wish to place the items in order from easiest to hardest. In these and other ways we could finally produce a fairly good measure of the phenomenon we had chosen to call "reasoning" and would have a measure of intelligence based on our construct of it. Figure 1.3 shows how the concept of construct validity might be represented schematically.

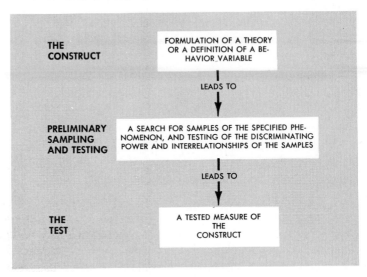

FIGURE 1.3　*Schematic representation of the process leading to a test based on* construct validity.

A second type of validity is called *predictive validity*. Again, referring to our illustration of the phenomenon of intelligence, suppose we defined it as "the ability to learn reading and arithmetic." In this case, we would try to construct a test that would predict how well individuals could learn these subjects, and our criterion would be "ready made." We would be trying to develop a measure that could predict how well people would do in these known areas. Now the psychologist's task would be to select items for the test that would predict the known scholastic behavior—the *external criterion*. Having made up a preliminary form of this test, he would then "test the test" by seeing how well it did predict the criterion. This could be done in a number of ways, e.g., by giving the test to a group of pupils *before* they began to study reading and arithmetic and then determining, at a later date, how well the scores on the test predicted the rate of learning in these subjects. Many tests of psychological variables are constructed in this fashion. Tests of selling ability, mechanical aptitude, artistic ability,and mathematical ability are examples of tests that are frequently based on how well they can predict subsequent performance. And, as with tests based on construct validity, these tests have to be refined many times before they are really effective testing instruments. Figure 1.4 illustrates the concept of predictive validity.

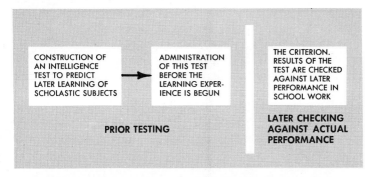

FIGURE 1.4 *Representation of the process involved in testing for predictive validity. The test is given before the experience which is to be predicted actually occurs. Results on the test are then compared with later performance.*

A third type of validity is called *concurrent validity*. As the name implies, this is validation based on comparison with some already existing measure of the phenomenon in question. Usually, the existing method is considered only reasonably satisfactory because it may take too much time, or it is too subjective, or it is too expensive. Many tests of personality attributes are constructed in order to improve on already existing methods of assessment. A good example of a test based on concurrent validity would be one for determining whether a person is suffering from "mental illness" like a psychoneurosis or a psychosis. Such a determination can be made by extensive clinical examination and evaluation, utilizing the services of a psychiatrist, a psychologist, and a psychiatric social worker. After extensive evaluation and psychiatric examination, a diagnostic decision is made concerning the nature of the person's possible mental abnormality. In recent years a great many paper-and-pencil personality tests have been constructed to provide measures of these phenomena. Most of these are based on the principle of concurrent validity. (See Chapter 8 for discussion of such tests.) The validation problem for such tests is to determine empirically how well the new test measures the attribute that is already being evaluated by the former, less satisfactory means. Usually, the aims of such tests are to provide greater objectivity and more efficient or less expensive methods of measurement. Figure 1.5 presents a schematic illustration of concurrent validity.

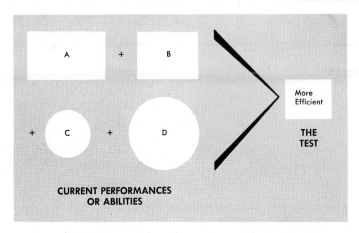

FIGURE 1.5 *Schematic representation of a test based on* concurrent validity. *The more efficient and more objective test measures the* current *performance in four areas much more simply.*

In some areas a fourth type of validity may be obtained—*content validity.* Suppose you wished to measure the extent to which a student had mastered the content of a course in introductory psychology. In this instance, the content of the course is known (on the basis of the textbook or the instructor's lectures). The task, now, is to construct a test which measures this content in a fair and representative manner. Items of psychology information based on some other psychology course would not be suitable, for example. The test must represent an adequate sampling of the content of this particular course. And the test would be so constructed, therefore, that it provided an appropriate sampling of this content. Content validity is often combined with construct validity in efforts to measure personality variables. For example, would it be possible to develop a test of aggression based on the definition of aggression (the construct) and of known examples of aggressive behavior (the content of actual behavior)? Figure 1.6 illustrates the concept of content validity.

As our last comments have implied, validation may involve one or more of the four types of validity we have been discuss-

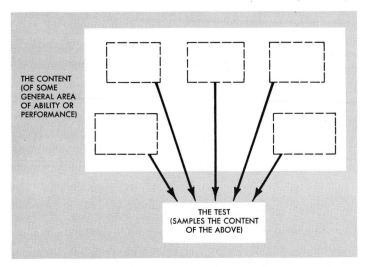

FIGURE 1.6 *Schematic representation of* content validity. *The test samples the content of some area of ability.*

ing. The particular method (or methods) of validation chosen will depend upon the purpose for which the test is developed as well as upon the nature of the phenomenon to be measured.

RELIABILITY Assessment also depends upon the *reliability* of the measure that is being employed. Reliability refers to the *consistency* of the results obtained with a test or testing method. Just as, in speaking of a person's reliability for "honesty," we are referring to the question of how consistently this behavior is manifested, so in speaking of the reliability of a measure of honesty or some other personality variable, we are referring to the consistency with which our method of evaluation can obtain similar results.

Inconsistency in measurements can come from a number of sources. There may be *inconsistency in the phenomenon.* An individual may vary at different times in the extent to which he manifests some behavioral characteristic. Not only do people change over time, but their performance is influenced by such factors as current motivation, effort required in the performance, and attention to the task at hand. Hence, even if we had a perfectly reliable measuring instrument, we would not necessarily obtain entirely consistent results on repeated tests of the same person due to *factors operating in the individual.*

But the instrument itself may be unreliable. If, for example, we constructed a test to measure knowledge of European history, with perfectly valid items, the test would tend to be relatively unreliable if it were too short. Chance factors could unduly influence the results. Thus, length of the test, or the number of items involved in the observation or measurement, affects reliability. In general, as a test is lengthened, assuming that other factors remain constant, its reliability increases. Increasing the length of a measure, or enlarging its sampling of the phenomenon under study, tends to increase its reliability. However, *rate* of improvement in reliability does not increase directly in proportion to the length of the test. Instead, the relationship is curvilinear, so that increasing a very short test produces relatively greater improvement in reliability than increasing a longer test. Figure 1.7 shows the nature of this relationship.

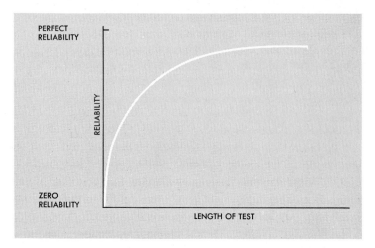

FIGURE 1.7 *The probable relationship between the length of a test and its reliability.*

Another factor that may lower a test's reliability is the operation of *chance or unpredictable effects*. These represent effects that are essentially unknown or unforeseeable. If the person being observed or measured is distracted, this may temporarily lower his score. Similarly, fatigue in the person taking the test may fortuitously influence the measurement. One way of reducing chance effects is to take repeated measures over a short time interval; this tends to average out such factors. Another is to increase the size of the sample of the behavior— as we do when we increase the length of a test—or to take many observations rather than a single one.

A measure of the reliability of the instrument we are using may be obtained in a number of ways. One such method is to give a test to the same subjects twice or to take sample observations on two separate occasions and then compare the results. We can then obtain a mathematical measure of the amount of reliability in the test instrument by determining how much difference there is between the two sets of results. This is called the *retest method.* Another method is to employ two different but equivalent measures of the phenomenon under study, give both of these to the same individuals, and then determine the degree of comparability of results. This is called the *method of equivalence.* The items of a test may be randomly divided into two tests, each half the length of the original test and each half theoretically the equivalent of the other half. The scores on the two halves could then be compared and a measure of reliability (the *split-half reliability*) obtained. A fourth method involves a variation of the retest method. This time the individual is retested, but an equivalent form of the test is used for the second administration. This has sometimes been called the *delayed parallel retest method.*

Measures of validity and reliability can be expressed in mathematical form and thereby treated with greater precision and economy. In order to understand such summary statistics, as well as to be able to interpret the results of reported research and clinical evaluation, we should know the meaning of certain basic statistical measures.

Some Basic Statistical Tools

In studying human behavior, psychologists often acquire large masses of data. These data have to be summarized in some meaningful manner so that their implications can be understood. But, more than summaries are needed. Methods must be found to determine the nature and degree of the relationships among various behavior variables. The significance of various factors must be weighed. We shall now examine some of these techniques—the statistical tools—so as to understand their values and limitations. Our short introduction to this material can do no more than provide an orientation in such matters. Underlying theoretical assumptions and statistical derivations must be mastered if statistical methods are to be used intelligently. Such mastery requires extensive study and is not possible in this introductory presentation.

DESCRIPTIONS OF GROUPS OF DATA   Psychologists gather data from observations and from controlled experiments. Once these data have been accumulated, they must be summarized and analyzed so that their meaning may be clear. One of the first problems in dealing with data is to summarize them in some convenient and appropriate form. Procedures devoted to this task are part of *descriptive statistics.* To describe a group of data statistically, we need to have at least two measures: a measure of the *central tendency* of the data and a measure of the *dispersion* (or the variability) of the data. With these two measures we can describe the data with sufficient accuracy so as to be able to talk about them intelligently and so as to compare groups of data with each other.

Measures of central tendency   The measure of central tendency tells us about the "level" of the variable which characterizes the "average value" of the group. It tells us, in other words, what the typical "score" is. If we observe a hundred individuals for the amount of aggression they display, the first thing we may wish to know is how much aggression the group showed "on the average." Suppose that, to simplify our illustration, we have not 100, but 10 scores representing the intensity of aggression shown by each of 10 members of an observed group. The scores might be: 1, 2, 2, 3, 3, 3, 3, 4, 4, 5. A score of 1 represents one act of aggression, a score of 2 represents two acts of aggression, and so on up to 5, which represents five acts of aggression on our scale. Now, our first question is, "What is the average number of aggressive acts displayed by our group?" There are three measures that might be used to answer this question.

The most commonly used measure is one that we are all familiar with: the *arithmetic mean,* or "average," as it is popularly called. To obtain the mean, we simply add up all of the scores and divide the total by the number of cases, as is indicated by the formula for the mean: $M = \Sigma X/N$. In this formula, M represents the arithmetic mean, X represents a score, and N represents the number of cases. For our illustration, $\Sigma X = 30$, $N = 10$, and $M = 3.0$. The mean of 3.0 tells us that, on the average, our group had 3.0 acts of aggression during the observation period. If now we studied another group's aggressive behavior and found that its mean of aggressive acts was 4.0, we could say that the means of the two groups differed by 1.0 aggressive acts. Thus, the mean enables us to describe a group in terms of an average characteristic, and the comparison of two means tells us something about the difference in the two samples of scores.

The mean is the most widely used measure of central tendency, and it is the most appropriate measure of this kind in most instances when large groups of scores are being considered. It has two desirable characteristics: (1) it is a highly stable score, and (2) it is computed by simple algebraic operations (i.e., $[X_1 + X_2 + X_3 + \ldots X_n]/N = M$) and can therefore be used in further computational work (such as in combining data from different groups and computing other algebraic measures based on the mean). It is stable because it is equally influenced by every score in the population. Therefore, comparison of two random samples of scores from a large population will generally yield closer agreement of the means than will other measures of central tendency.

The two other measures of central tendency are the *median* and the *mode*. Generally speaking, these measures have special and limited uses, and we shall, therefore, consider them only briefly. The median is simply the value of the "middle" (hence, median) score when the scores in a population have been arranged from lowest to highest. In our illustration, which involved an even number of scores (10), the median would be the value halfway between the fifth- and sixth-largest scores. In this instance, the median score of 3.0 would be the same as the mean because the distribution of scores is symmetrical. If it were not, the values of the median and the mean might differ considerably since the median is determined only by its *position in the distribution* of scores and it does not give equal weight to each score. To make this clear, suppose we compare two distributions of scores, the one we have already described, which we shall call distribution A, and another distribution of 10 scores, which we shall call distribution B, as in Table 1.1 (p. 408).

The student will note that the mean for distribution B is 3.0, just as it is for distribution A. But the median for distribution B is 2.5 (halfway between the scores of 1 and 4), whereas the median for distribution A is 3.0. In short, the median is always determined by the position of the midmost score. It is not affected by the relative size of the other scores in the distribution. When a distribution is asymmetrical, the median is some-

TABLE 1.1. DISTRIBUTIONS AND MEASURES OF CENTRAL TENDENCIES
FOR A SYMMETRICAL AND AN ASYMMETRICAL SET OF SCORES

Distribution A	Distribution B
5	5
4	5
4	5
3	4
3	4
3	1
3	1
2	1
2	1
1	1
$M = 3.0$	$M = 3.0$
$Md = 3.0$	$Md = 2.5$
$Mo = 3.0$	$Mo = 1.0$

times preferred to the mean, since extreme scores are likely to be atypical or unduly influenced by chance factors.

The *mode* is simply the most frequently occurring score. When there are two or more such scores, there are two or more modes. In our illustrations, the mode of distribution A is 3.0 (note that in a symmetrical distribution the median, mode, and mean coincide), whereas the mode of distribution B is 1.0.

Measures of dispersion In order to describe a group of data adequately, a measure of dispersion (or variation) of the scores around their central tendency is needed. As with measures describing the central tendency, there are also a number of measures of dispersion. Again, for reasons similar to those we discussed in connection with the arithmetic mean, we shall emphasize the algebraic methods of measuring dispersion.

Returning to our illustration in Table 1.1, distribution A contains 10 scores, each of which differs by a certain amount from the central tendency of the distribution. One measure of dispersion that might be used to describe the scatter of this group is the *average deviation,* or *AD* (also called the "mean deviation"). As this name suggests, *AD* is simply the average of the deviations of all the scores from their mean. Thus:

$$AD = \frac{\Sigma x}{N}, \qquad (x = X - M)$$

where (x) is the deviation of a score (X) from the mean, and Σx is the sum of these deviations without regard to the

TABLE 1.2. CALCULATION OF THE AVERAGE DEVIATION FOR TWO
DISTRIBUTIONS OF SCORES

Distribution A		Distribution B	
X	x	X	x
5	+ 2	5	+ 2
4	+ 1	5	+ 2
4	+ 1	5	+ 2
3	0	4	+ 1
3	0	4	+ 1
3	0	1	− 2
3	0	1	− 2
2	− 1	1	− 2
2	− 1	1	− 2
1	− 2	1	− 2
$\Sigma x =$ 8		$\Sigma x = 18$	
$AD = \dfrac{8}{10} = .8$		$AD = \dfrac{18}{10} = 1.8$	

direction of deviation ($+$ or $-$). Table 1.2 shows the calculations of AD for both distribution A and distribution B. The
value of the AD tells us that the average amount of dispersion of
these scores around their mean is 0.8 for distribution A, while it
is 1.8 for distribution B. Group B, therefore, as can be seen
from inspection, has a greater amount of variation around the
mean than group A. Another way of saying this is that the
scores in distribution A cluster more closely around their mean
than the scores in distribution B cluster around their mean.

A more refined measure of dispersion, which has important
mathematical advantages over the AD, is the *standard deviation*
(*SD* or σ). The *SD* simply represents the square root of the
sum of the squared deviations around the mean divided by the
number of observations, thus:

$$SD = \sqrt{\frac{\Sigma x^2}{N}}$$

Since the deviations are squared, the sign of the deviation is of
no significance. We shall not illustrate the calculation of *SD*,
since it is usually employed with larger samples of data, but we
can note that it has three major advantages over AD. (1) It is a
more stable measure. (2) It can be dealt with algebraically, just
like the mean, and can therefore be used in further statistical
treatment of data. (3) Related to advantage 2 is the fact that
the *SD* has certain known mathematical qualities, which makes

it especially valuable. All the student need remember at this point is that it is, mathematically, a better measure of dispersion than any other measure for most statistical purposes, especially when large masses of data are to be summarized.

As with measures of central tendency, there is a very simple measure of dispersion that may sometimes be employed, namely, the *range*. The range is a measure of the difference between the highest and the lowest scores. In both distributions A and B the range is 4.0 (or 5.0 − 1.0). Since the range is entirely determined by the two extreme scores, it is highly unreliable and may fluctuate widely, depending on what these extreme scores may happen to be. The range is therefore used only to give some indication of the total size of the dispersion and cannot be employed in further treatment of the data.

RELATIONSHIPS BETWEEN GROUPS OF DATA Whenever we wish to test some hypothesis, we ask whether the results which have been obtained might have arisen on the basis of chance factors or whether they do in fact arise from factors related to our hypothesis. To illustrate this point, let us consider the hypothesis that ministers show fewer aggressive acts of behavior than a group of laymen. Suppose, then, that we have randomly selected 25 ministers from the population of ministers of a state and have also obtained a random sampling of 25 laymen from the same state, equated for sex, age, and religious affiliation.

In order to test our hypothesis, we have trained observers observe each group for a specified period of time, counting the number of aggressive acts shown by each member of each group. We can then obtain the means and *SD*'s in number of aggressive acts for each group. If the means and the *SD*'s do differ between the two groups, we have to ask whether the obtained difference might not have arisen by chance. This involves a number of considerations which define the *significance of the difference*. In the first place, we have to determine how well our groups of 25 ministers and 25 laymen represent the respective populations from which they were drawn. In other words, was the obtained mean for ministers sufficiently close to what would have been obtained from another sample of 25 ministers (or from the total population of ministers) to be considered a sample from the same population mean value, and was the mean for the laymen similarly representative? Other factors than problems in sampling might affect the significance of the results, such as: the reliability of the scoring of aggressive acts; the possible effect that observers might have upon the manifestation of aggressive acts; and so on.

Therefore, we must ask what the probability is that the results which have been obtained might differ from other, repeated samples of the same population? In problems such as these, we are attempting to compare a given set of findings against other samples of the finding to determine the stability of the finding or the difference between groups of scores. We have to compare two groups of data (within a given population or across two or more populations) and determine the size and significance of the difference.

Another kind of comparison between two groups of data gathered on the same individuals asks the question, "What relationship exists between the two groups of data for individuals?" We might be interested in learning whether children who come from families with high socioeconomic background differ in displayed aggression from those who come from families with low socioeconomic backgrounds. But instead of merely comparing means and *SD*'s of the two sets of scores, we might determine the degree of relationship between aggression and socioeconomic background. We would then be asking, "What is the size of the correlation between socioeconomic level and frequency of aggressive acts?" (And of course, we would need to determine the statistical significance of the correlation.) As a simple illustration of the use of correlational analysis, we might consider the question of the degree of relationship between height and weight. As is well known, height and weight have a considerable degree of correlation with each other, but, to express the degree of the relationship accurately, we would have to determine the size of the correlation coefficient between these two variables.

These two kinds of questions—the significance of a difference between groups of data, and the degree of correlaton between groups of data—may thus be seen to be closely related. Both involve the problem of inferring the nature of possible relationships from some given data. Both are, therefore, problems in *inferential statistics,* as contrasted with the problems discussed in the previous section—those of descriptive statistics. We shall briefly consider the methods pertinent to problems of this kind.

First, we must consider the general question of how one goes about testing any hypothesis about behavior. Any hypothesis about behavior states that a certain prediction concerning this behavior will be borne out by experimental study of the phenomenon. We can state our prediction in one of two ways. (1) We can say that a particular difference (or a relationship) exists between two variables (or two groups). This is a positive statement of the hypothesis. (2) We can say that there is no significant difference (or no significant relationship) between the two variables. This is the *null hypothesis*. The null hypothesis simply states (1) that there is no real difference between our groups or the variables being investigated or (2) that any difference which was found might have arisen on the basis of chance alone. In scientific studies, it is simpler to test for the null hypothesis, i.e., to determine whether a difference or relationship can be explained only on the basis of chance factors. If the null hypothesis is disproved, this is evidence that a meaningful difference or relationship may exist, and the theory on which our hypothesis is based in then given some credence.

Differences between groups of data   We have stated that in testing for a difference between groups we must evaluate the probability that the difference has not arisen by chance. What we are really asking, therefore, is whether, if we had repeated samples of the data under study, we could be sure that the obtained difference truly represented other possible samples of the data that we might have obtained from the different populations.

The following experiment demonstrates the effects of taking samples from a population. Take twenty small pieces of paper and write numbers on them according to the distribution of scores given in Figure 1.8. On one piece of paper write the number 1; on another write the number 7. Continuing to work alternately with the scores at either end of the distribution, you will have two pieces of paper with the number 2 on them and two pieces with the number 6 on them. Place numbers on the remaining pieces of paper according to the frequencies shown in the figure. Place the twenty pieces of paper in a box or hat so that you cannot see the numbers, and mix them thoroughly. Now draw out a sample consisting of three pieces of paper and note the average of the numbers on the three papers. Place the papers back in the box and mix them again. Now continue to take additional samples of these papers, and jot down the average in each case. Note the fact that the means of the samples of three papers differ from the mean of the entire population of the twenty slips of paper, often by a considerable margin. Now

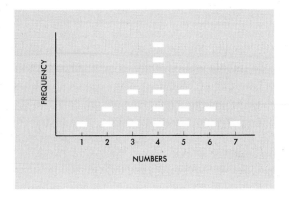

FIGURE 1.8 *Example of distribution of a "population." Deviation of sample mean from population mean will decrease as the size of the sample increases. From R. L. Isaacson, M. L. Hutt, and M. L. Blum.* Psychology: The Science of Behavior. *New York: Harper & Row, 1965, p. 20.*

increase the size of your sample by drawing four slips of paper each time, and note the averages obtained in this part of the experiment. If you then continue to increase the size of the sample you take when reaching into the box, you will find that the means of the selected sample get closer to the true mean of the population as samples drawn get larger.

The null hypothesis merely asserts that any difference between groups of scores comes from this kind of chance fluctuation, that is, the difference is due to the "luck of the draw" in obtaining the sample.

There are a number of methods, too technical to discuss in an introductory treatment, for estimating the significance of a difference between groups of data. Some of these methods are called: the standard error of the difference, the t test, the F ratio (or F), and the chi-square (or χ^2). These are simply statistical methods for estimating the probability that a difference between groups of data might not have arisen by chance. Thus, an experimenter might report that the probability of obtaining a difference of this size between two groups of data (referred to as p), was at or beyond the .01 level. This would mean that the obtained difference would not have arisen on the basis of chance fluctuations in sampling more than 1 time in 100 samples (or attempts). Hence the null hypothesis could be rejected, since the difference was sufficiently large that the probability that the difference was due to chance was small. The probability of differences is called the *confidence level* and represents the degree of confidence with which one may reject the null hypothesis. In different kinds of experiments the confidence level which the experimenter will accept before he is willing to reject the null hypothesis will differ, depending, in part, upon the rigor of his theory, the adequacy of his sampling methods, and the adequacy of his measuring devices.

Correlation between groups of data   The correlation coefficient expresses the degree of relationship between two sets of data. These coefficients may range from -1.0 through 0.0 to $+1.0$. The sign of the coefficient indicates the direction of the relationship, while the numerical value represents the degree or size of the relationship. A coefficient of 1.0 is indicative of a perfect relationship, while a correlation coefficient of 0.0 indicates that there is no relationship. To give some idea of the nature of correlation coefficients, the size of the relationship between height and weight in adults is approximately $+0.7$. This would mean that these variables are strongly and positively related but that the relationship is by no means perfect. Another example of a positive relationship is that which indicates the test-retest reliability of good intelligence tests. Many of the better tests show a reliability coefficient of about $+0.9$, indicating that the two sets of data are highly correlated. An example of a negative relationship is that between anxiety and intelligence test performance. In some studies, a relationship between level of anxiety and performance on intelligence tests of about -0.2 has been reported. This would mean that there is a slight negative relationship between these two factors, as measured. In other words, high anxiety tends to go with low intelligence test performance, and vice versa.

There are various methods for calculating the degree of correlation between two sets of measures. One of the most commonly employed methods is known as the Pearson *product moment correlation coefficient.* In calculating this coefficient, a mathematical formula is employed to determine the degree of the relationship. We can best understand the meaning of correlations by considering the graphic method of portraying relationships.

When the relations between two groups of measurements are plotted on a *scatter diagram,* we can see by inspection how they are related. In this procedure, numbers representing measures of one characteristic of the subjects are given on the ordinate, or *x* axis, and numbers representing measures of the other

TABLE 1.3. DATA FOR HEIGHT AND WEIGHT OF 10 ADULT SUBJECTS

Subject	Height (in.)	Weight (lbs.)
A	74	220
B	72	190
C	70	168
D	68	174
E	68	170
F	68	174
G	68	170
H	66	176
I	64	124
J	62	154
	$r = .70$	

characteristic are plotted on the abscissa, or *y* axis. Suppose we had the following data, as represented in Table 1.3, showing the figures in height and weight for each of ten adult subjects. These same figures are presented in a scatter diagram in Figure 1.9.

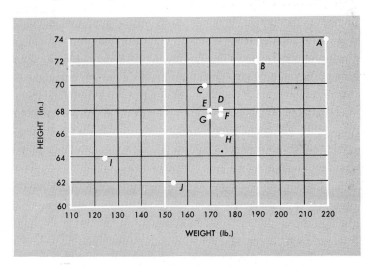

FIGURE 1.9 *Scatter diagram for data in Table 1.3, showing the relationship between height and weight.*

We can see in this figure that measures of height and weight tend to go together, so that when an individual is tall, he is also likely to be relatively heavy. If the Pearson product moment correlation coefficient were calculated for this scatter diagram, the coefficient would turn out to be + .70.

The data from studies such as these can also be represented on *scatter plots,* in which each dot represents the scores on the

415

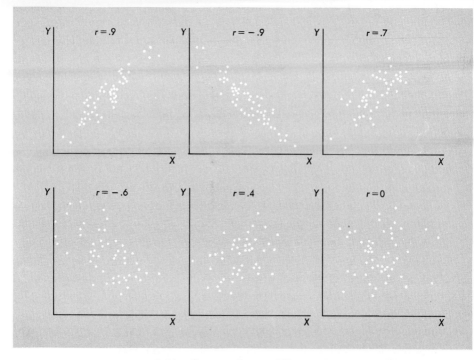

FIGURE 1.10 *Scatter plots of different degrees of relationship expressed by the associated correlation coefficients. From R. L. Isaacson, M. L. Hutt, and M. L. Blum.* Psychology: The Science of Behavior. *New York: Harper & Row, 1965, p. 25.*

ordinate and on the abscissa for each subject. Figure 1.10 shows six scatter plots for different degrees of relationship varying from − 0.9 through 0.0 to + 0.9.

ANALYSIS OF MULTIPLE VARIABLES In the study of an individual's personality, evaluations or scores on a number of different personality variables are often obtained. The question then arises as to how one can best summarize such results. Of course, the individual's score on each variable can be reported, or each score can be reported in relative terms, such as whether it falls above or below some critical point. But it often happens that the particular *pattern* of scores may be important in revealing something which the separate scores do not. For instance, suppose we know that, if a person (*a*) has strong homosexual tendencies, (*b*) is highly compulsive in his behavior, (*c*) tends to be withdrawn in his interpersonal relations, and (*d*) engages in a great deal of fantasy, he is very likely to become a *paranoid*

416

schizophrenic. (See Chapter 6 for a discussion of this condition.) We are thus stating that this particular pattern of personality variables is correlated with this psychiatric condition. To be able to use such information for accurate predictive purposes, or to use such data in the comparison of individuals or groups, we would attempt to summarize these patterns in terms of some mathematical formula.

In the illustration given, let us suppose, further, that we knew the degree of correlation that each of the four factors had with the criterion, paranoid schizophrenia, and with each other. We could then develop a formula by means of which the probability that an individual would fall within the criterion group (schizophrenia) could be objectively stated. Using such a formula, after assigning *weights* to each factor, we could summate the scores on each factor multiplied by its appropriate weight to make our prediction. To give our illustration more concreteness, suppose that we called the four predictor variables $a, b, c,$ and d and called our criterion S. Let us assume that scores on S could vary from 20 to 90 points and that any S score above 50 represented a strong likelihood that the individual had schizophrenia. We shall also assume that the four scales, $a, b, c,$ and $d,$ are equivalent in mean and $SD,$ so that the numerical values on any one of these scales are equivalent to the values on the other scales. Our predictive formula might then look like this:

$$2.0(a) \times 1.0(b) \times 0.7(c) \times 2.0(d) = S.$$

Each factor has now been assigned a weight in terms of its significance in predicting S. If an individual then had the following scores:

$$a = 12 \qquad c = 20$$
$$b = 11 \qquad d = 8$$

his total S score would be 65.0, and this score would place him well above the *critical* score of 50. Thus the probability that, as measured on this set of scores, he was schizophrenic would be relatively high. There are methods for estimating the degree of probability of such predictions.

In this illustration, we assumed a linear relationship between each predictor variable and the criterion. Although this is frequently the case, it is not necessarily so. Sometimes a high score on a given predictor variable may have quite a different meaning than usual, depending upon the configuration of the

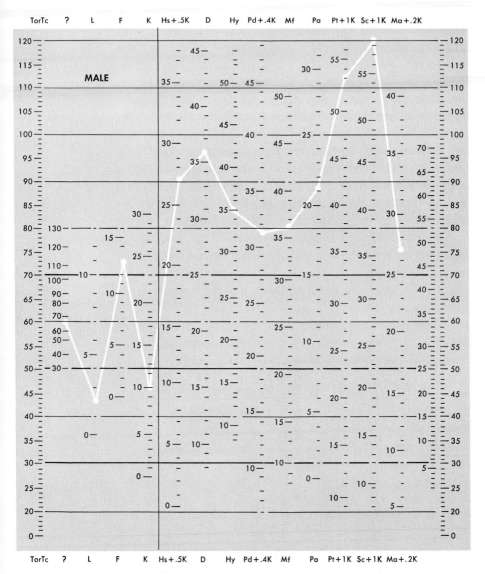

FIGURE 1.11 *The profile presentation of the data from the Minnesota Multiphasic Personality Inventory on a male psychiatric patient.* From E. S. Schneidman (Ed.). Thematic Test Analysis. New York: Grune & Stratton, 1951, p. 221. Courtesy of Dr. Harry M. Grayson and The Psychological Corporation. Profile form, copyright © 1948 by The Psychological Corporation.

remaining scores. For example, the variable *fantasy* can operate in quite different ways depending upon other factors in the individual's personality configuration of variables. An individual with high fantasy capacity but who is in good contact with reality and has good interpersonal relations may be quite different from another individual who is also high in fantasy but is poor on the other factors. The first person might be able to use his fantasy constructively and adaptively, while the second might use his fantasy to escape further into withdrawal and reduce his adaptive efforts.

Patterns of scores, all reduced to a common base, are therefore frequently presented as *profiles* (sometimes called configurations). This is especially likely to be the case when there is a large number of scores to be dealt with. One of the best examples of such profile summaries of scores is that of the Minnesota Multiphasic Personality Inventory (MMPI). This is a personality test on which a number of scores for each of several personality attributes may be obtained. (See Chapter 8.) Originally there were nine scales, consisting of such items as hysteria, paranoia, schizophrenia, and the like. The results of the test can be reported on a profile sheet especially prepared for this purpose. Figure 1.11 presents such a profile for a mental patient who was exhaustively studied as part of a research program [18]. The clinician who interprets this profile must be acquainted with the significance of this type of profile, and this in turn means that he must know the research findings that have been obtained with each variable (or subscale) and with various kinds of profiles.

Profiles, like other assessment methods, can be evaluated for reliability and validity and can be subjected to evaluation so as to compare their utility in relationship to other measures.

References

1. Snygg, D., & Combs, A. W. *Individual Behavior: A New Frame of Reference for Psychology.* New York: Harper & Row, 1949.
2. Bruner, J. S., & Goodman, C. C. Value and need as organizing factors in perception. *J. abnorm. soc. Psychol.,* 1947, **13,** 33–44.
3. Ashley, W. R., Harper, R. S., & Rynyon, D. L. The perceived size of coins in normal and hypnotically induced economic states. *Amer. J. Psychol.,* 1951, **64,** 564–572.

 4. Burtt, E. A. *The Metaphysical Foundations of Modern Physical Science.* New York: Doubleday, 1954.
 5. Watson, J. B. *Behaviorism.* Chicago: Univ. Chicago Press, 1958. (Orig. Ed., 1924.)
 6. Woodworth, R. S. *Contemporary Schools of Psychology.* New York: Ronald, 1948.
 7. Isaacson, R. L., Hutt, M. L., & Blum, M. L. *Psychology: The Science of Behavior.* New York: Harper & Row, 1965.
 8. Skinner, B. F. *Science and Human Behavior.* New York: Macmillan, 1953.
 9. Bridgman, P. W. *The Logic of Modern Physics.* New York: Macmillan, 1927.
10. Bridgman, P. W. *The Way Things Are.* New York: Viking, 1961.
11. Mannheim, K. *Ideology and Utopia.* New York: Harcourt, Brace & World, 1949.
12. McDougall, W. *Psychology, the Study of Behavior.* London: Williams & Norgate, 1912.
13. Tolman, E. C. *Purposive Behavior in Animals and Men.* New York: Appleton-Century-Crofts, 1919.
14. Horney, K. *Neurosis and Human Growth.* New York: Norton, 1950.
15. Fromm, E. *Man for Himself.* New York: Holt, Rinehart and Winston, 1947.
16. Wertheimer, M. *Productive Thinking.* New York: Harper & Row, 1945.
17. Lewin, K. *A Dynamic Theory of Personality* (trans. by D. K. Adams & K. E. Zener). New York: McGraw-Hill, 1935.
18. Shneidman, E. S. (Ed.). *Thematic Test Analysis.* New York: Grune & Stratton, 1951.

TWO   BEHAVIORAL DEVEL-
OPMENT

Our study of human behavior begins with an examination of the principles of human development, and this chapter considers both the knowns as well as the unknowns concerning development. Our major purpose is to obtain an overview of the general nature of development before discussing relatively specific aspects of behavior because, as we shall see, adult behavior cannot be fully understood without an understanding of the prior experiences which affect the development of this behavior. So much of what we take for granted as "human behavior" turns out to be attributable to either consistencies or variabilities in the developmental experiences of the individual and not, as is generally but incorrectly believed, to inherent and unmodifiable characteristics of the genus *Homo sapiens*.

How did they get that way? Olin Mathieson Chemical Corporation

In order to concretize the nature of our problem, let us ask some questions about some commonly accepted beliefs relating to nationality and sex differences. We frequently hear that, for example, adult Frenchmen are quite different from adult Americans. Is it really true, as we are so often told, that Frenchmen are better lovers than American men? Are they also more emotional, more sensitive esthetically, and more pleasure-oriented? And if we believe that these questions should be answered positively, can we be sure that these answers characterize all Frenchmen or all Americans?

To evaluate the nature of such real or suspected differences,

we have to ask some additional questions. Are Americans living in the deep South more like "typical Frenchmen" than Americans living in the northern portions of our country? And similarly, are southern Frenchmen similar to northern Frenchmen, or are they more similar to southern Americans? But even more important than the answers to such questions, at least from a developmental viewpoint, is the question, "How did they get that way?" In other words, are such similarities and differences due primarily to inherent genetic factors, or to developmental experiences, or to some combination of both?

Or consider some commonly accepted notions concerning sex

differences. Is it really true that women are more emotional than men? Do men have better aptitude for mathematics and for business? Do women gossip more? Are women able to provide better or more affectionate care in rearing youngsters than men are? Are men more intelligent? And if these differences exist, how shall we explain them?

If we really consider such questions deeply, we can begin to see that knowledge of the principles of development of the human organism is necessary. Such knowledge can contribute to a more adequate understanding of these and related problems. Of course, this poses the immediate problem of how one can determine whether obtained differences—such as those which purportedly exist in the areas of nationality and sex—are the result of genetic or experiential factors. Would it make any difference, for instance, if it was found that French children are more similar to American children than French adults are to American adults? Would it be useful to learn at what ages national or sex differences appeared and what life-experiences were correlated with such differences? Or, in more general terms, would it be useful to learn something concerning the developmental patterns of specific aspects of behavior and to determine whether various aspects of constitution or experience were related to such developments? And, how would knowledge about the stages at which differences in behavior of individuals appeared and the influence of varying conditions of learning upon these differences assist us in understanding and guiding such development?

The foregoing questions and considerations point to the importance of viewing all behavior from a *developmental* framework. In the first place, if we study developmental phenomena, we are able to ascertain whether there are characteristic patterns in development and whether these patterns are modifiable under specified conditions. Thus we can begin to tease out the principles which govern the development of certain behaviors. We can learn whether these principles are universally applicable or whether they hold true only under certain conditions. We can then study the effects of various conditions, both *internal and external to the individual,* which influence development. And all of these findings set the stage for a more accurate understanding of the behavioral phenomena which psychology, together with other sciences, attempts to explain, predict, or control.

Prenatal Development of Behavior

The beginning of the development of behavior of the individual starts with conception, and not with birth. By the time the individual is born he has already acquired a variety of specific skills and potentialities which will determine his later development. Therefore, it is important to understand how behavior develops during the prenatal period. It is also true that both biological and social heredity may contribute to development during this period, but we shall reserve these aspects of the problem for discussion in the next section.

We have to begin with the process of cell division and differentiation following conception. Conception results from the union of the male sex cell with the female sex cell. Some 280 days later, on the average (or from a minimum of 180 days to a maximum of 334 days later), birth occurs. This total period of gestation is customarily divided into three phases: the *germinal* phase, the *embryonic* phase, and the *fetal* phase.

THE GERMINAL PHASE This period lasts about two weeks from the moment of conception. Ordinarily, or in about 99 percent of conceptions, a single *zygote* results from the union of the two sex cells of the male and the female. In some instances, the two male sex cells, or spermatozoa, may fertilize two female sex cells, and *fraternal* or *dizygotic* twins result. Another possibility, and for reasons that are not understood, is that the single union of a male and a female sex cell may split into two groups of cells during the process of early cell division, and *monozygotic* or *identical* twins result. (See Figure 2.1.) In either case, when twins (or plural pregnancies) occur, the prenatal environment is different from what it is when a single zygote occurs: the same uterus now has to accommodate two organisms instead of one, and the presure on the developing tissues, as well as the location within the uterus, affects subsequent growth and development differentially.

The process of cell division begins when the original fertilized cell (or cells, as the case may be) divides into two cells, each with components identical to the original cell. In turn, each cell redivides, and gradually a mass of cells develops, with a cavity inside. Three kinds of cells develop from the original cell: cells

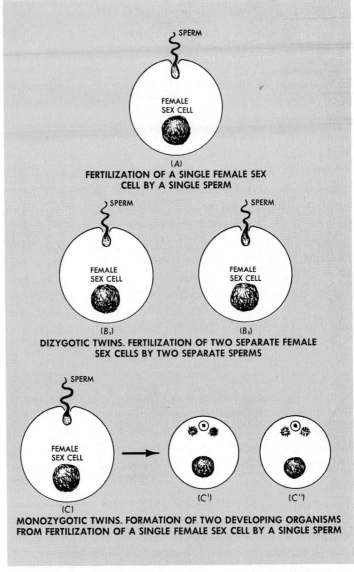

FIGURE 2.1 *Schematic representation of the development of a single individual in* (A), *dizygotic twins in* (B), *and monozygotic twins in* (C).

constituting the outer layer, or *ectoderm;* cells constituting the middle layer, or *mesoderm;* and cells constituting the inner layer, or *endoderm*. Figure 2.2 is a schematic presentation of this differentiation of cells. The question as to how this differentiation occurs is a provocative one. It is probable that different internal conditions of growth, such as amount of nutri-

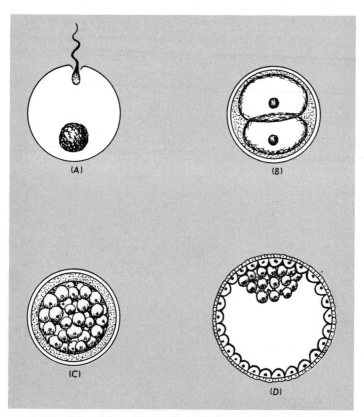

FIGURE 2.2 *Schematic representation of the beginning differentiation of organs and tissues. At* (A) *the female sex cell is fertilized. At* (B) *the process of cell division has begun. At* (C) *further differentiation has occurred. At* (D) *the differentiation of an outer layer which will become* ectoderm, *a middle layer which will become* mesoderm, *and an inner layer which will become* endoderm *is shown. Note how the mass grows in size during the process.*

tion (dependent on distance from the umbilicus or place through which nutrition arrives), pressure (related to location), and the like, account for cell differentiation. At any rate, the three major types of cells tend to develop into different tissues and organs. Note that we said *tend to develop.* For conditions within the uterus can affect the course and rate of growth. It has been learned, for example, that there are *critical stages* in the growth of tissue during which both the type of growth and the speed of growth may be profoundly affected. Studies have shown that, with animals, transplantation of cells before specialization of certain functions occurs will result in the acquisition

427

of new characteristics for these cells [1]. And studies of humans have shown, similarly, that disease occurring during certain stages of development has a profound influence on the fetus, while the same disease occurring before or after these stages has relatively little or no effect.

Not only does growth proceed by *differentiation* in structure and function of parts, but, as growth proceeds, the various parts function in *subordination* to the whole organism. This principle of subordination of parts to the whole means that the growth of each part is dependent upon the whole with respect to rate and characteristics of development.

THE EMBRYONIC PHASE During the next six weeks the "germ" develops into a clearly recognizable human being. Gesell terms this period one of "structural organization" [2]. At the end of this period the approximately one-inch-long organism has crude limbs, rudimentary fingers, a head, definite facial structures, and rudimentary internal organs, such as heart, lungs, and kidneys.

The most important evidence we have thus far about embryonic behavior in humans comes from histories of embryos removed surgically from their mothers for medical reasons [3]. Another source of information comes from studies of the intrauterine behavior of embryos as recorded on various instruments attached to the mother's abdominal wall, such as the cardiograph, the electroencephalograph (see Figure 2.3), and instruments for automatic recording of embryonic movements. Such studies, from which preliminary conclusions, only, can be offered thus far, indicate that embryos do have movement and that specific reflexes occur, the earliest of which is that of the heart reflex, which occurs at about the sixth week of embryonic age.

THE FETAL PHASE This period, which lasts from about eight weeks until birth, is marked by the very rapid differentiation of both structure and function. By 28 weeks of age the organism is *viable,* i.e., its physiological functions are so well developed that it is capable of maintenance in an extra-uterine existence. Thereafter, growth is focused mainly on increase in size and weight.

There is a very rapid development of the nervous system during this period, and particularly of the brain. At birth the

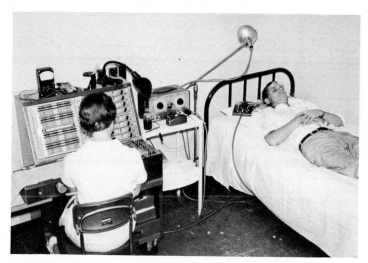

FIGURE 2.3 *Administration of an Electroencephalographic Test. Courtesy of Grass Instrument Company and the University of Iowa, Department of Psychiatry.*

brain comprises approximately 10 percent of the total body weight. The nervous system develops out of the neural plate, and the anterior portion develops most rapidly, becoming greatly enlarged and differentiating into three main portions: the forebrain (or cerebral hemispheres); the midbrain; and the hindbrain. Thus the organism has a highly developed communication system early in its life, and this fact influences the ways in which the other portions of the organism develop.

Various kinds of evidence (morphological, histological, and electrical recording of brain activity) indicate that the forebrain, and the cortex in particular, is immature in structural and functional development at birth. Since this portion of the brain is associated with such processes as reasoning, memory, and imagining, it is not surprising that the organism is not capable of such behavior at birth. The subcortical portions of the brain have a relatively more advanced maturation, and since these portions govern postural adjustment and the transmission of incoming and outgoing impulses, these aspects of behavior become manifest before birth. Fetal behavior is essentially under subcortical control. The fetus can and does respond to tactile stimulation, it is capable of responding to other sensory types of stimulation, it can engage in motor responses of head, legs, and even lips, and it can engage in respiratory activities and use its vocal chords.

Although the fetus is, thus, capable of relatively specific responses, its activities are generally characterized as *mass behavior*. The reasons for this become clear when we study in detail the development of the nervous system. Present evidence suggests that mass behavior occurs because of the slow development of myelin tissue in the fetus. This myelin, or sheathing around the nerves, develops first in the subcortical areas of the brain and in the spinal cord, and, even at birth, myelinization of brain neurons is incomplete. Thus, specific behaviors cannot emerge, it is believed, until myelin development is advanced. Before this development, the reflexes which occur are essentially subcortical responses.

Evidence concerning prenatal behavior is based on three kinds of studies: animal fetuses; human fetuses removed surgically from the uterus; and human fetuses within the uterus whose behavior was reported on by mothers under careful conditions of experimental study. One of the most elaborate studies of the latter kind was undertaken at the Fels Research Institute in Yellow Springs, Ohio, in which mothers reported fetal activities under a variety of conditions of the mother, such as after eating, after resting, after smoking, and the like [4 and 5]. All of these studies indicate that fetal behavior tends to develop in a highly orderly sequence. After the initial mass responses which the fetus is first capable of, there later develops a variety of specific and relatively discrete responses. Still later, some of the specific responses are integrated into newer patterns of total responses. Thus, prenatal behavior includes both (1) the *individuation* of more specific responses out of mass and stereotyped general patterns of behavior and (2) the *integration* of newer patterns of behavior out of relatively specific responses that have emerged.

Another general conclusion that various studies have contributed to is that, although there is an orderly development of fetal behavior related to the age of the fetus, some intra-uterine and some extra-uterine factors may significantly influence the course of behavioral development of the fetus. It is known that conditions affecting the mother cannot *directly* influence the behavior of the fetus, since the fetus has its own separate circulatory system separated from that of the mother's by a semipermeable membrane (the *placenta*), and substances are absorbed into and expelled from the baby's system by capillary action. (See Figure 2.4.) However, both physical and emotional conditions

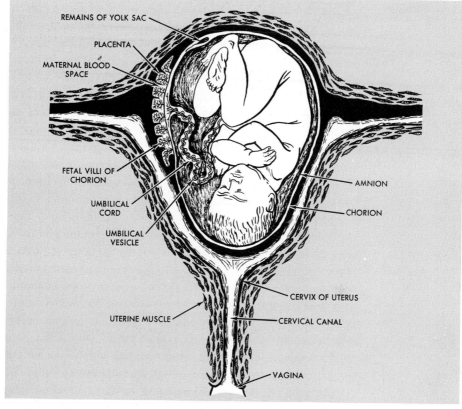

REMAINS OF YOLK SAC

PLACENTA

MATERNAL BLOOD SPACE

FETAL VILLI OF CHORION

UMBILICAL CORD

UMBILICAL VESICLE

UTERINE MUSCLE

AMNION

CHORION

CERVIX OF UTERUS

CERVICAL CANAL

VAGINA

FIGURE 2.4 *Relationships between the uterus, fetal membranes, placenta, and embryo.*

affecting the mother may and do indirectly affect the development of the fetus. In considering these effects, it should be borne in mind that those tissues which are in the process of rapid differentiation at the time are the ones most vulnerable to various influences. This finding, that there are *critical stages* in the development of tissues during which they may be more radically affected, is paralleled by the finding concerning psychological development following birth—that there are also critical stages in behavior and personality development. (See Chapter 3.)

The sample of findings which will now be presented has been based, usually, upon relatively small numbers of cases and should be taken as *strongly suggestive* rather than *conclusive*. However, only those results will be reported which are based on carefully controlled studies or on studies which have been replicated.

First, we should note that severe malnutrition of the mother may adversely affect the fetus, even producing retarded mental development in some cases [6]. A few diseases of the mother, notably smallpox, chicken pox, German measles (rubella), and syphilis may have adverse effects. Such consequences as still-birth, cataracts, and retardation may follow.

When drugs are taken to excess, the baby may be harmed. Cases of asphyxiation and brain damage have been reported. Cigarette-smoking by the mother during pregnancy produces increased heart activity in the fetus, especially toward the end of the pregnancy period [7]. Various other conditions may reduce the supply of oxygen to the fetus and cause abnormalities in development [8].

A condition that has special relevance in our consideration of prenatal influences is that of X-ray irradiation, especially since X-ray diagnosis has been so frequently employed in diagnostic studies of pregnant women. Excessive exposure of the mother to such irradiation can produce extremely harmful results in the infant. A special form of mental retardation, called micro-cephaly (small head; pin-head) may result [9]. A recent experimental study in the Soviet Union throws some light on the specific effects of irradiation (in this case ionization irradiation) [10]. A group of rats and rabbits were exposed to X-irradiation antenatally and compared with control groups. They were studied extensively by means of electroencephalographs, behavioral conditioning experiments, and morphological analyses. It was found that X-irradiation significantly reduced the total cerebral mass, caused cellular instability of the cortex, and disturbed certain reflexes. Finally, it was found that these effects varied according to the time in the organism's life when X-irradiation was applied and that different layers of the cortex were thus affected. It was concluded that the usually stable prenatal conditions which guarantee orderly prenatal development *can be influenced by certain radical means* and can have long-lasting effects.

Findings such as these indicate clearly that the usually stable conditions which surround the fetus can be altered and that such alterations can affect subsequent development. The physical condition and the activity of the mother do influence the development of the fetus, speeding it up, slowing it down, or producing abnormal development or even disease.

Emotional conditions of the mother have also been shown to

influence the course of the fetus's development. In general, maternal emotions, especially if severe, tend to increase fetal activity. This result is produced through an increased rate of metabolism in the mother, by means of increased cell activity and hormonal discharge. Postnatal aftereffects may include hyperactivity, malnutrition, increased bodily movements, and disturbances in sleep and gastrointestinal upset. In the most serious cases, stillbirth may result [11]. Even unconscious attitudes of the mother may adversely affect development of the fetus, especially if severe or prolonged [12].

As can be imagined, experimental manipulation of humans to investigate the effects of prenatal conditions is extremely difficult and limited. Suggestions coming from experimental work with animals support the belief that prenatal conditions can significantly influence later behavior. For example, it has been demonstrated that when pregnant rats are stressed with a conditioned fear stimulus, the offspring behave differently from a control group which did not have this experience [13]. It has also been shown that tranquilizing the mother can produce significant effects on the offspring [14].

Our present knowledge in this field indicates that, although we can dismiss the "old wives' tales" that a physical marking of the baby can result from the mother's fright over a wild horse, the mother's emotional state, her physical condition, and her physical activity may influence the subsequent development and behavior of the infant. In fact, we might go so far as to say that appropriate physical and mental hygiene for the mother are prerequisites for effective pre- and postnatal development of the baby. We still have a great deal to learn concerning the specifics of such influences.

Biological and Social Heredity

We have chosen to include these two topics in the same section in order to emphasize the interdependence of the one upon the other. Although it is possible to separate the two sets of factors, especially since one refers to the physical and the other to social factors, we shall see that the line of separation is not as precise as the use of the two terms would imply. As a matter of fact, the term *biosocial* inheritance was coined some years ago to acknowledge the finding that there is an interaction of some kind.

We have seen in the previous section that conditions during pregnancy can alter potential modes and rates of development during and after this period. We shall soon note that different cultures prescribe different methods of dealing with children after birth, thus further modifying tendencies in behavior that were already present. There is now available evidence that specially adapted and enriched environments can offset deleterious physical factors, even when they are surgically produced. Even the genes are modifiable, as our later discussion will demonstrate. Thus, we must be clear at the outset that the human organism is, in fact, a biosocial organism and that both biological and social factors must be considered as they interact in behavioral development.

Let us now examine briefly some of the most important findings concerning biological inheritance. This inheritance *starts* with the kinds of genes we are born with. But what are genes? At one time, anatomists thought that these were little lumps that could be detected in histological preparations. The presence of genes was *inferred* from evidence that certain bodily characteristics followed specified patterns in studies of "families" of men and animals. Today we think of genes as hypothetical packets of genetic information determining a specific trait in the species. These "genes" have recently been localized in certain regions of the chromosomes (see below). They are thought of as representing certain coded information which determines the development of trait behavior—that is, they are believed to be mechanisms through which inheritance operates.

Each germ cell in the human contains 46 chromosomes, half of which come from the mother and half of which come from the father. The chromosomes are present in pairs, but the ones that occur in a given cell, resulting from the process known as *reduction division* that is part of the development into spermatazoa and ova, for the male and female respectively, are present on a random basis. In other words, one member of each pair of chromosomes comes from the sperm or egg. Which member is so selected is presumed to be due to chance factors. When the male germ cell and the female germ cell unite during the process of conception, each with its own set of 23 pairs of chromosomes, the union produces a fertilized ovum, and once again there are 23 pairs of chromosomes. Millions of different pairings can thus occur on the basis of chance. And since the determiners of inheritance are carried in the much larger numbers of genes, the process of inheriting traits or tendencies is very complex indeed. On this basis it can readily be seen why brothers can be so different from each other.

In 1962 a team of investigators, Crick, Watson, and Wilkins, was awarded the Nobel Prize for Medicine for its work on chromosomes. These men had learned, among other things, how genetic information is encoded in chromosomes. The substance of chromosomes contains deoxyribonucleic acid (or DNA, as it is more conveniently known). There are two strands of DNA which are periodically connected by chemical bonds—adenine, thymine, guanine, and cytosine (see Figure 2.5). When the chromosomes separate during cell division, the two strands of DNA peel away from each other. The four basic chemical compounds determine what kind of molecules will be constructed to replace the DNA strand that is no longer present. An exact replicate of the original DNA strand is produced from each of the single, separated strands. (See Figure 2.6.) It has been learned that the genetic information (i.e., the specific growth patterns) is encoded in the *order* of the four connecting compounds. This order, then, and not the compounds themselves, determines the genetic code. The endless diversity found among people is accounted for by the scrambling of the chromosomes during meiosis, some coming from paternal and some from maternal ancestors.

Some determiners of hereditary transmission contribute to *unitary traits,* i.e., specific biological structures, while others simply determine general predispositions toward the development of constitutional traits or structures. Some genes are dominant whereas others are recessive, so that when the corresponding genes from the respective germ cells are present in the fertilized ovum, the characteristic depends on the balance of these factors. Two dominant genes produce the trait associated with the gene, whereas the combination of a dominant and a recessive gene produces the dominant characteristic, while the recessive characteristic is carried in the germ cell. Thus, there is an interactive effect of the pairs of genes with respect to a given trait. Moreover, since chromosomes may *cross over* from maternal to paternal segments of the respective chromosomes, the resulting chromosome may be partly determined from one ancestral strain and partly from the other. And, finally, there is the process of *spontaneous mutation* of the genes, in which, usually over long periods of time, the characteristics of the

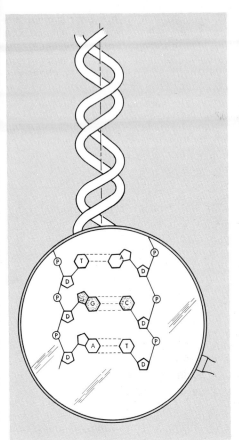

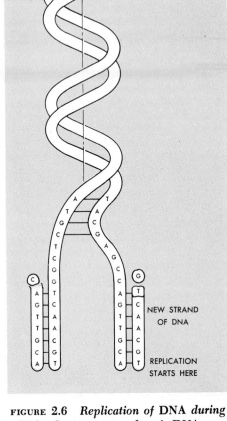

FIGURE 2.5 *Highly schematic reconstruction of double helix formed by DNA molecule. Lower part of helix is enlarged to show bases adenine* (A), *thymine* (T), *guanine* (G), *and cytosine* (C), *and how these are linked with deoxyribose* (D) *and phosphoric acid* (P). *From R. L. Isaacson, M. L. Hutt, & M. L. Blum.* Psychology: The Science of Behavior. New York: Harper & Row, 1965, p. 39.

FIGURE 2.6 *Replication of* DNA *during which the two strands of* DNA *are thought to separate, each serving as template on which new strand forms. Replication is beginning at lower ends of separated strands. Note that end result is two identical double strands. From R. L. Isaacson, M. L. Hutt, & M. L. Blum.* Psychology: The Science of Behavior. New York: Harper & Row, 1965, p. 39.

genes change. Sometimes severe stress may produce changes in such characteristics, as in the effects of prolonged exposure to X-ray or in the effects of exposure to nuclear radiation, and the genes may be adversely and rapidly affected. Taking all of these considerations together, we can infer that many factors can influence the course of the presumptive heredity. We still know extremely little concerning the effects, if any, that styles of living in the parents may induce in hereditary characteristics, but we cannot assume that there is no effect over long periods of time.

A child is equipped at birth with a certain kind of constitution, but the way in which he develops does not depend alone on the nature of his constitution or on his genetic background. Even the way in which he is born may strongly influence the kind and the development of his constitution. We have already discussed briefly the nature of the relation of prenatal conditions to the development of the neonate, and we have seen that a person's characteristics do not simply *unfold* but are molded by internal and external factors. The birth process may further affect these characteristics. For example, the baby may be injured during the process of delivery by excessive pressure, by too much oxygen administered to the mother during labor and delivery, by the excessive use of drugs, and by other factors. [See 8, 13, and 15.] Moreover, as we have noted, the mother's attitudes, both conscious and unconscious, may affect the condition of the neonate, depending on such factors as her cooperation and activity during the delivery and her emotional acceptance of the anticipated neonate.

Only in recent years have studies been initiated on the long-term effect of various conditions occurring during pregnancy and delivery. The long-term effects of brain damage incurred during delivery are part of the concern of Pasamanick and Knoblock's work [16]. A very large collaborative study involving 14 different medical institutions is gathering data on genetic, pregnancy, and delivery factors on 40,000 cases [17]. Even the possible relationship between complications attending the birth process and very severe personality disorganization is being intensively studied [18]. (See Chapter 6 for a discussion of this problem.)

And following birth, the influence of social factors as they condition the behavior of the parents toward the infant may influence the ways in which he develops. In fact, each child may be said to have a *social heredity*. A child is as impotent to modify the circumstances of the world into which he is born as he was to influence the course of his biological inheritance. Culture may dictate that the baby be treated very indulgently, as the Hopis, a southwestern tribe of Indians, have been reported to do, or he may be treated with severity and with rigor, as the

Child rearing and relationships in another culture.

Jack Ling from UNICEF

Pueblo do [19]. What the baby is fed and the great variety of ways in which this food may be offered are also greatly influenced by the culture [20]. The amount of physical handling, of cuddling, of rocking, and so on, also varies tremendously from culture to culture. Moreover, the attention given to the baby, the way his bodily functions are reacted to, and the extent to which the baby is permitted to move about also differ significantly among different peoples. These and other conditions may significantly condition both physical and psychological development—or may even produce an abrupt end to life itself [21]. We are still at the beginning of discovery of the story of the short- and long-term effects of such variations in the early life of the infant, but there is little doubt how striking some of these effects may be—in some cases producing emotional disturbance of the proportion of insanity (*autistic psychosis*) [22].

As we follow the infant into the period of childhood, we find that other factors condition both the kind and extent of his physical and psychological development. It has been shown, for example, that many personality characteristics are *class-linked,* that mental illness tends to be distributed differently in different classes (this may be due to both selective mating and sociological factors in mental health), and that physical development is affected by habits of diet and activity, which are surely linked to cultural patterns [23, 24, and 25]. How much, one wonders, may the influence be of the current fads for vitamin-enriched diets!

The point of all of these observations is to stress the interaction of so-called "nature" and so-called "nurture." We might say that we can only assess the effects of nature when we are able to vary tremendously the effects of nurture, keeping nature constant. Conversely, we can only assess the effects of nurture by varying greatly the effects of nature, keeping nurture constant—and for obvious reasons such a study has not been done. But we can point out how, when children live together with their parents from birth on, the correlation between the intelligence of parents and children tends to be of the order of 0.5 to 0.6, whereas, when children are separated from their own parents, at or near the time of birth, the correlation drops markedly [26]. This kind of finding, for one phenomenon only, is presented simply to emphasize the interactive aspects of nature and nurture. One has only to consider how much the infant's development may be influenced by other social factors, including the amount and kinds of sensory stimulation to which he is subjected, the kinds and amounts of contacts he has with people, and the interest or lack of it which is shown the infant, to realize how varied is the pattern of social experiences to which he may be subjected. Although it is not our present purpose to appraise any or all of these variations in social phenomena, it is important to stress the fact that the infant is a captive subject with respect to such events. It is in this sense that we can begin to see that he "inherits" a culture—not through the genes, to be sure, but through the act of being born into a particular culture—and that this culture forms an inescapable part of early, and therefore highly important, personal experience.

Behavioral Characteristics of the Neonate

The *neonatal period,* of approximately two weeks, is the period during which the newborn baby stabilizes its adjustment to the external world. It is highly important to recognize this fact, since the nature of this experience may exert its influence upon subsequent behavioral development. Stabilization of behavior is necessary because the neonate has to learn to adapt to its new external and stressful environment after its long period within a remarkably stable internal environment, the womb. Moreover the "rough passage" into the external world has produced its own share of stresses.

Following the baby's loss of its circulatory relationship with its mother at birth, it has to change its circulation to that of the adult type, with blood flowing into the lungs instead of into the placenta. It has to start breathing, change its methods of elimination, use new methods of ingesting food, and adapt to new methods of digesting its food. The variations in temperature to which it is now subjected require adaptation by its own regulatory system to maintain a reasonably constant body temperature. Blood pressure and blood oxygen level have to be stabilized to meet the requirements of the newer modes of living. The impact of a wide variety of sensory stimulations requires that some physiological adaptation be made to this new input, and sense organs which were not required to operate before birth are now brought into action. It is not surprising that during this period of stabilization the baby loses weight; this loss is related to the amount of physiological activity which has been provoked. Nor is it surprising that the neonate is unable to make a significant selective attention to such a bombardment of stimulation; he is literally fighting for his life, and without the assistance of modern medical methods his chances for survival would not be so great as they are. (See Figure 2.7.)

We have already noted that the nature of the birth process conditions the newborn's behavior and activity. Although we

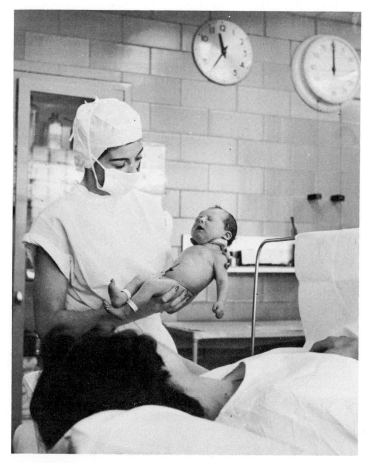

FIGURE 2.7 *The neonate. University of Michigan News Service.*

have only tentative answers concerning the effects of various kinds of birth experiences, one example of a well-controlled study will indicate the significance of this factor. Hughes made a comparison of the electrical activity of the brain of babies whose mothers had been given sodium seconal (a sedative) during the birth process with other babies whose mothers had not been given this drug [27]. It was found that for some time later, even after clinical signs in the babies no longer suggested it, those whose mothers had been given this drug showed significantly more depression, even striking depression, of brain activity (as measured by electroencephalograph) than the other group of babies.

All babies show a pronounced tendency to engage in sucking activities shortly after birth. The sucking reflex is certainly related to the neonate's "need" for survival. But both controlled observations and recent research have indicated that even survival itself is not guaranteed by the sucking reflex. For example, a number of studies have indicated that when the baby does not have adequate *mothering,* that is, cuddling, rocking, and handling in general, it may fail to gain in weight and may otherwise behave in a retarded manner despite being given adequate

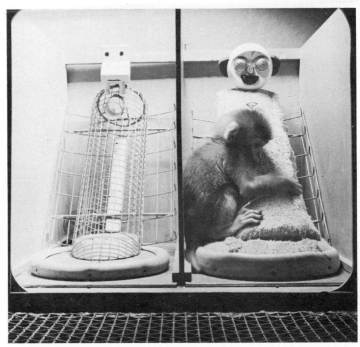

FIGURE 2.8 . *Mother surrogates used by Harlow. Infant monkey is clinging to surrogate which has more acceptable "skin" qualities. Courtesy of H. F. Harlow.*

amounts of nourishment. Moreover, recent studies by Harlow with monkeys [28] have shown that even these animals are greatly influenced by the kinds of contacts they have with their mothers. Using artificial mothers made of soft and rounded materials versus mothers made of hard and sharp materials, respectively, and keeping amount of nutrition constant, Harlow showed that monkeys that had available the "softer" mothers were far less fearful, timorous, and agitated but, on the other hand, were more adventurous with respect to their environment than the others. (See Figure 2.8.)

Nevertheless, the weight of present evidence indicates that

the ways in which the neonate (and later, the infant) is fed—not so much the mechanics of feeding but the attitudes connected with the whole feeding process and the general consistency of the patterns of child-parent interaction—influence the further course of behavioral development for shorter or longer periods of time. We shall discuss this problem in the next chapter, on personality development, but we wish to call attention at this time to the importance of these early experiences. Two relevant studies may emphasize this point.

In one study, Marquis compared the behavioral reactions of three groups of infants from the second day of life on to the next few days [29]. The babies were divided into three groups on the basis of the feeding schedules that were maintained. One group was fed every four hours, another every three hours, and the third group on a self-demand basis (i.e., whenever they seemed to indicate by their behavior that they "wanted" food). A comparison of the activity of the four-hour group with the three-hour group showed that the former group increased its activity sharply during the fourth hour, indicating that there may have been a need for earlier feeding, but that prior to this last hour the activity rates of both groups were comparable. When, however, the three-hour group was changed to a four-hour feeding schedule on the ninth day, this group now showed a much higher rate of activity during the fourth hour than did the group that was continuously maintained on a four-hour schedule. These results indicate that *change in the consistency* of the methods of feeding (in this case frequency of feeding) produced a change in behavioral reactions. We can interpret the change as a response to *experienced frustration* resulting from the change.

In another study, the amount of crying by neonates was correlated with the amount and kind of nursing and other care they were given in two ways [30 and 31]. In the first place, the amount of crying during a period of observation in 1944 was compared with the amount of crying done by a supposedly comparable group of babies in the same hospital in 1945. In 1944 the babies were given 0.7 hours of nursing care, on the average, whereas in 1945 they were given 1.7 hours of such care, on the average. The amount of crying was 117 minutes per day in 1944 and was 55 minutes per day in 1945, on the average. Moreover, in the 1945 study, controlled observations showed that there was a relationship between the amount of crying and the kind of care given the babies. Other observations supported the conclusion that babies cried less in proportion to the amount of care they were given and the degree to which they were made to feel "more comfortable."

Such studies indicate, then, that certain kinds of neonatal behavior are rather closely connected with (1) the amount of basic satisfaction of primary physiological needs and (2) changes in the patterns of meeting such needs which may ameliorate or affect unfavorably the behavioral responses as needs are experienced as being satisfied or frustrated, respectively.

In general the behavior of the neonate appears to be under the domination of stimulation from the gastrointestinal and genitourinal systems, as studies by Irwin have shown [32]. However, the neonate soon begins to learn to adapt to his environment, although this learning is, at first, unstable and relatively nonpersistent. He responds with a great deal of fairly diffuse activity and responds reflexively to both internal and external stimulation.

The neonate is capable of showing distress reactions and satisfaction responses. The amount of each of these two major kinds of "emotional" responses appears to be related both to constitution—and particularly to level of autonomic activity, in which babies differ at birth—and to external conditions of stimulation. All babies suffer some degree of stress as they learn to adapt to their new extra-uterine environment, but stress can be minimized when conditions of rearing are kept relatively constant and basic physiological needs are met with dispatch.

Postnatal Growth and Differentiation of Behavior

The baby *matures*. This statement implies that postnatal growth is determined, in part, by internal regulatory factors and that growth follows orderly and predictable patterns. In the strictest meaning of the term maturation, the reference is to growth which occurs without opportunity for specific learning experiences. Before birth it is difficult to determine the extent to which such "unfolding" occurs independently of other factors, but studies of animal fetuses removed from the uterus before birth indicate that specific structures and functions do, in fact, appear at regular and well-defined points in the developmental curve.

Even here, however, there is evidence that factors other than maturation influence both the speed at which development occurs and, to a lesser extent, the patterning of prenatal behavior.

In postnatal development of the infant, maturation occurs in a regular and orderly manner provided minimal conditions necessary to support development are present. The development of the walking response illustrates this kind of phenomenon. In Shirley's studies it was shown that progression toward the end of relatively mature walking proceeds through predictable stages, although the ages at which different infants reach each stage differ [33]. (See Figure 2.9.) This kind of finding is supported by studies which show that even when certain kinds of activity are restricted or are practiced, as the case may be, the rate and order of development of many kinds of motor responses are little affected, if at all [34, 35].

Experiential factors seem to affect the rates of maturational development when minimal conditions are not present, however. Recent evidence by Dennis indicates that extreme deprivation of opportunities for stimulation necessary to produce normal maturation can cause serious retardation in maturation [36]. The data for children in an orphanage in Teheran were examined to determine whether Shirley's norms in locomotor development were applicable for such children. For children up to three years of age, sitting was greatly retarded, and in many cases creeping did not occur at all. Some of these children learned to "scoot" instead of to creep. Commenting on his observations, Dennis writes: "These facts seem to indicate clearly that experience affects not only the ages at which motor items appear but also their very form."

Further analysis of such studies has led to more precise statements concerning the nature of maturation. Not all structures and functions are equally impervious to external—or indeed internal but nonmaturational—factors. However, within rather wide limits, basic skills develop, even with varying degrees of stimulation, at a relatively uniform rate. When such skills are practiced before the effects of maturation have become fully evident, whatever greater progress is made is not retained over a longer period of time. In fact, premature training of such maturational skills may, in certain instances, impede growth for a time [37]. It has also become clear that certain psychological skills, such as crying and smiling, appear

FIGURE 2.9 *Postural and locomotor development. From M. M. Shirley*. The First Two Years, A Study of Twenty-five Babies, Vol. II: Intellectual Development. (*Institute Child Welfare Monogr. Series, No. 8*) *Minneapolis: Univ. of Minnesota Press, frontispiece. Copyright 1933 by the University of Minnesota.*

at about the same ages for different children, even when such children lack opportunities to observe other children. But, in the case of psychological skills, the nature of the stimulation provided by the environment, and more specifically the nature of the communication between child and adult, does influence these early personality characteristics significantly under certain relatively extreme conditions [38].

There are important differences in the constitutional equipment with which different children are born and which influence both the amount and kind of activity that they manifest. For example, research by Jost and Sontag has shown that babies differ in the amount of nervous excitability (autonomic stability), which in turn conditions many aspects of motor learning [39]. It is now known that siblings are less alike than identical twins in nervous excitability. The correlation among siblings and the greater correlation among identical twins indicate the influence of heredity. But other factors affect even this rather basic constitutional factor. The size of the correlation in identical twins on the index of autonomic excitability is approximately 0.4. It is clear that nonhereditary factors play their part.

PRINCIPLES OF DEVELOPMENT It is also important to recognize that growth does not proceed at a constant, continuing pace but instead proceeds in spurts, lags, and even by regression (i.e., there may be a loss of some previously acquired function). This characteristic of the growth curve has been called the *spiral effect* [40]. A striking illustration of this phenomenon is the spurt in height that often occurs during preadolescent development. When there is a lag in growth, one may frequently infer that behavior is becoming integrated and that the plateau in the growth curve may be due to such integration. Sometimes a child who has been developing slowly in some characteristic begins to develop more rapidly and may even surpass others who have previously been further ahead in the characteristic. Thus, there are *discontinuities* as well as *continuities* in growth.

Another important developmental principle is that of the *directional sequence* of growth. Growth proceeds more rapidly in the region of the head than it does toward the opposite end of the body; this is the principle of *cephalocaudal* development. At the same time, growth proceeds more rapidly near the center of the body than near the peripheral sections; this is the principle

447

of *proximodistal* development. These two phenomena constitute the general directional sequences of growth. Not only do structures of the body follow these conditions of growth, but motor development follows the same general pattern; thus, the peripheral muscles of the body develop later than the others.

One of the principles of development which came to the foreground in recent years is that of *total-organ involvement*. In order to understand how the person develops, it is necessary to note that development of any part is conditioned by the larger whole of which it constitutes a part. Thus, in a fundamental sense the growth of any part is subservient to the development of the organism as a whole. More than this, the development of any organism is dependent to some extent on the organ system of which it forms a part. For example, although a particular part of the brain may be focal in governing motor responses (as in the case of the motor area), nevertheless the brain tends to act as a whole, and the general activity and condition of the total brain play their part in the motor response. Even specific reflexes are modifiable in terms of the conditions affecting the nervous system. Not only function but growth itself is governed by the principle of total-organ involvement.

Still another principle which must be understood in order to comprehend fully the nature of development is that of *continuous activity* of the organism. Studies of the physiology of the brain indicate that there is a constant autonomous process going on within the brain, even when the individual is asleep. Hence, an incoming stimulus impinges upon an organism in an active, not passive, state, and it is the nature of this active state which in part determines what the response will be. In fact, the state of the organism is an important determiner of the kind of response it makes. The human being is not a passive object, upon which forces impinge, but an active one, which attends to, selects, and governs the nature of its own responses to stimulation. This is one of the reasons why people respond differently even though the sources of stimulation are similar or even identical. (Chapters 3, 4, and 5 offer theory and evidence concerning this important principle.)

THE DEVELOPMENT OF ADAPTIVE BEHAVIOR This principle of continuous activity leads us into a discussion of the development of adaptive behavior. As the child develops, he learns to adapt himself to the circumstances which confront him. He becomes increasingly adaptive as he grows older, under normal circumstances.

Piaget has proposed an explanation of the principles of adaptive development which elucidates the growth of intelligence [41]. The formulations which follow are the result of repeated informal observations by Piaget and his collaborators and a number of research studies. Piaget has not tried to separate, as carefully as some workers would like, theory from validated research findings, but his provocative and creative constructions have given rise to many experiments in the current era.

The infant's earliest behavior is determined in large measure by the specific reflexes of which he is capable, largely by reason of his inherited structure. Thus, he sucks reflexively, not having to learn to utilize this behavior. But the earliest sucking activity does not merely get repeated. As the reflex occurs, it also produces an *assimilation* of the experiences which are thereby generated. Thus, for example, in connection with the original sucking reflex, the infant may put out its tongue and may happen to place its fingers in its mouth. These additional elements in the pattern of behavior not only prolong the use of the sucking reflex but produce an adaptation of the sucking response itself—primitive and not very complicated adaptation by adult standards, but highly significant in its portent for future behavior development. For here, along with the purely reflexive elements which were already present, we see that the infant begins to accommodate its behavior. And in this accommodation, the beginning of *means-ends* behavior emerges. To be sure, one does not have to assume the presence of *intent* on the part of the infant to put these newer activities together with the old one of sucking. The association may first have been accidental, and one does not have to assume knowledge of the end of this process; but the old simple circular behavior involved in sucking has now been replaced by a new pattern. Moreover, since the sight of the fingers may now stimulate the sucking response, just as, previously, contact of the lips with the nipple produced the sucking response, and since sight of the nipple may produce placement of the fingers in the mouth, we can say that the situation has become *reciprocal*. What this means is that older schemata of structural and self-stimulating reflexive behaviors have been replaced by newer and co-ordinated schemata in which the older schemata have been integrated. The newer

Intention in behavior. Children's Bureau, DHEW

organization of behavior therefore brings with it the development of newer needs—needs which were not evident before and
which are no longer based on the primitive reflexes. These kinds
of co-ordinations—of sight with prehension, of reaching with
grasping, and of each of these with other sensory modalities—
constitute the primary *circular responses.*

The next stage in the development of intelligence involves
secondary circular responses. Here, during infancy, the child
learns to repeat behaviors which involve objects external to his
own body. He learns, in other words, to utilize objects from his
environment to satisfy his emerging needs and tends to reproduce such behavior whenever the need is present. At this stage
the child is not yet aware of time, but he is beginning to become
aware of space. Thus new schemata are introduced into the
child's behavioral organization. Later, when the various elements in these newer schemata can be dissociated from one
another, when they can be recombined in newer ways, when, in
fact, activities are not engaged in simply to take advantage of the

450

greater complexity of the extended environment in space but are deliberately sought in time to produce the desired ends, *intention* in behavior may be said to have truly emerged. But during the *secondary-circular-response* phase much more highly complex organizations of behavior are possible than during the previous phase.

The subsequent development of intelligent behavior through the remaining four phases which Piaget proposes as part of his theory is similar to those we have already discussed. In the final stage the child learns to manipulate his environment actively, by experimentation and evaluation or by mental analysis of previously acquired knowledge, and thus acquires new means of mastering his environment and dealing with his needs. The process is always reciprocal, since newer behaviors with their newer schemata of organization always generate newer needs, and newer needs generate newer behavior. In essence, this constitutes the dynamics of behavior, which we shall be discussing in some detail in the chapter dealing with personality development.

The Development of Physical Behavior

We shall now take one specific aspect of total development— that of physical development—to illustrate some of the phenomena of developing behavior in the human.

The physical development of the various parts and organs of the body does not proceed at the same rate. Various studies of physical growth have shown that the rate of increase is different for different parts of the body. An examination of Figure 2.10 will show that the body as a whole does not increase in size in a regular, consistent pattern over the years from birth to adulthood but rather that the specific parts of the body have significantly different rates and patterns of development. Moreover, there is a rapid spurt in the lymphoid tissues in childhood, and there is an even more abrupt increase in rate of growth in the genital tissues around puberty.

At birth the head is more than one-fourth the length of the entire body, whereas in adulthood the proportion will be about one-tenth. During the first year the cerebellum, a portion of the brain important for postural control, increases by about 300 percent, but the rate of growth of the cortex slows down during

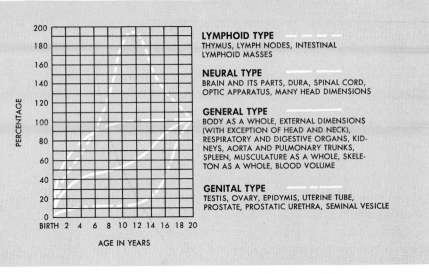

FIGURE 2.10   *Four major types of postnatal growth curves. Adapted from R. E. Scammon. The measurement of the body in childhood. In J. A. Harris et al. The Measurement of Man. Minneapolis: Univ. of Minnesota Press, 1930, p. 193.*

the same period. The nervous system as a whole reaches its adult status at about twelve years of age.

Neuromuscular development shows a number of important developmental characteristics. At first, the grosser muscles gain in strength relatively more than the smaller muscles. The striped muscles show a relatively slow developmental rate at first, and consequently many motor responses and sphincter responses cannot be learned until appropriate development has occurred in this part of the body tissue.

We have noted previously how diffuse are the earliest motor responses; they are not directed specifically to external objects as such. The limp tonus of the baby's muscles makes it impossible for him to engage in many forms of specific motor behavior. For example, he is unable to co-ordinate the movements of his eyes, and he is unable to fixate his vision upon a particular external object for some weeks. Prehension is also rather diffuse for the first few weeks, and, as we have seen, coordination of prehensile and visual behavior is at first impossible. The baby is unable to sit up, even with support, until about the third month; he cannot yet hold his head up. The baby goes through fourteen differentiable stages in learning how

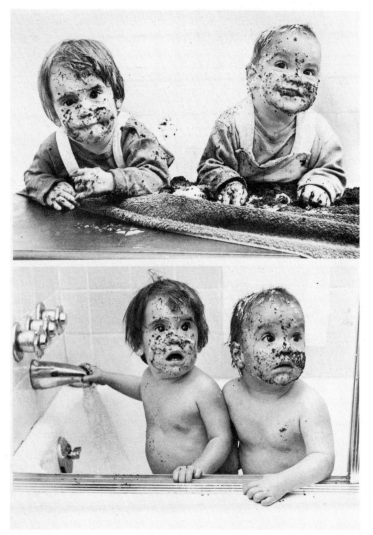

From ecstasy to disillusionment via chocolate cake.
Both photos, Wide World

to creep. Learning to walk follows an orderly but slow pattern. Until maturation of the neuromusculature is sufficiently advanced, training has little and only temporary effect; it may even hinder subsequent development if pushed too rapidly and severely. In fact, babies may become quite fearful of walking activities if great stress is associated with learning such behavior, and walking may be greatly delayed.

By two years of age the baby will ordinarily have become quite adept at basic forms of locomotion. He will be able to

453

walk by himself, he will be able to climb a few steps, and he will try climbing other objects. However, there will still be some flaccidity of the leg muscles; anyone who has tried to put shoes on a baby will know that he will be unable to keep his leg or his foot stiff. Again, it should be noted that emotional factors may exert their important influence upon the baby's motor behavior. If he is pushed too fast, or if he is frustrated in his relationships with adults in other ways, not only his motor skills may suffer but he may develop fearfulness in situations he did not originally fear, and this may contribute to his general insecurity.

During the second and especially the third year of life, growth in manipulatory skills increases significantly. From simple prehension of objects there is progression to manipulation of objects, in which co-ordination of visual and motor functions is involved. Specific manipulatory skills become differentiated out of the cruder forms of prehension, and finally finger-play, holding and throwing objects, rotating objects such as a doorknob, and even imitating a scribble and later a circle of a crude sort will be possible. Skills in dressing oneself begin during this period, too, and during the third year the child can assist in the dressing activities, particularly in taking some of his things off. It is during the third year that the child will display, characteristically, some negativistic behavior. This negativism appears to be related to his frustration with his inability to do some of the things he sees others do and with his growing sense of being controlled by others when he is making his first steps toward some degree of independence. Patience and tolerance will bring rewards both with respect to the specific negativism as well as with respect to the relevant aspects of physical development.

During the next three years gross physical development slows down perceptibly, but muscle weight and muscle development proceed more rapidly. It now becomes possible for the child to engage in prolonged physical activity with remarkable endurance, sometimes to the adult's great distress. By the age of six years he has developed many fine motor skills and generally good co-ordination. Such skills are now markedly influenced by appropriate training and appropriate motivation.

If one plots the physical growth of height and especially of weight during the first six years of life, one is impressed with the variability in these phenomena over the total period. The usual growth curves for height and weight obscure this characteristic variability in rate of growth, for they are based on averages obtained on cross-sections of the populations at different age levels. The longitudinal study of single individuals, however, reveals that a smooth curve is not characteristic. In one of the relatively recent studies of this type, a study of individual variability in weight over the first ten years of life, this feature of growth was abundantly documented [42]. Figure 2.11 shows

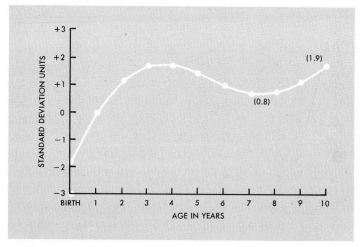

FIGURE 2.11 *Weight of an individual in terms of variability units. Adapted from data in W. Sontag.* The Fels Research Institute for the Study of Human Development. *Yellow Springs, Ohio: Antioch College, 1946.*

the relatively marked variability in weight for a single child. Note that this child's weight changed from considerably below average at birth to far above average at three years, back to slightly above average at seven years, and again up to far above average at ten years.

During the prepubertal period there is a characteristic spurt in growth, especially in height, for both boys and girls. Girls show this spurt earlier than boys, on the average, so that for a period of time girls are bigger than boys of the same age, but later boys overtake the girls and become both taller and heavier. During puberty, when the pituitary glands become more active, hormonal activity influencing the development of sexual characteristics in particular, and general body growth as well, increases rapidly. A new glandular balance has to be achieved,

455

and the tissue development of the body shows considerable variability. Skeletal development may increase rapidly while muscular development proceeds at a constant rate. All of these factors produce considerable internal tension (conflicting physiological characteristics) within the body and considerable conflict in total adaptation. The typical awkwardness accompanying the new sexual roles arising out of pubertal changes may be accompanied by and enhanced by other kinds of awkwardnesses. Adolescents may feel and appear awkward, not only because their skeletal development has outstripped their muscular development, but also because all of this is going on during a time that their physical skills and related social skills are being put to rather severe tests. Some may withdraw during this period and try to live more within "their own shells," while others may overcompensate and attempt to develop exceptional physical skill to cover their feelings of awkwardness. Others, whose previous repertoire of both physical and social skills has added to their feelings of security, may be able to withstand the rigors of this transitional period without much overt evidence of internal tensions.

Thus it may be seen that the complex interaction of maturational and developmental factors, on the one hand, and the interaction of physical and social skills, on the other, constantly operate during the total developmental period. In the beginning, the emergence of certain abilities and skills is largely dependent upon the given constitutional situation but is not entirely uninfluenced by "external" factors, whereas, later, skills may be markedly influenced by opportunities for training and practice. Yet the accompanying self-attitudes which develop as a result of the ways the environment chooses to react to the emerging skills may markedly influence the further development of these skills, and, in turn, the ways in which these skills develop may condition the self-attitudes and the total psychological adaptation of the individual. We shall do well to keep in mind that the organism, whether human or animal, is conditioned and limited by the equipment which it has at its disposal; but, unlike machines, organisms can modify within certain limits both their original equipment and the environmental factors which operate upon this equipment. Above all else, we shall see again and again how the previous experiences of the individual affect the ways in which he perceives, reacts to, and adapts to the constantly changing panorama of his life.

References

1. Pratt, K. C. The neonate. In L. Carmichael (Ed.), *Manual of Child Psychology.* (2nd ed.) New York: Wiley, 1954.
2. Gesell, A., & Amatruda, C. S. The *Embryology of Behavior: The Beginnings of the Human Mind.* New York: Harper & Row, 1945.
3. Hooker, D. Reflex activities in the human fetus. In R. G. Barker, J. S. Kounin, & H. F. Wright (Eds.), *Child Behavior and Development.* New York: McGraw-Hill, 1943.
4. Sontag, L. W., Reynolds, E. L., & Torbet, V. Status of infants at birth as related to basal metabolism of mothers in pregnancy. *Amer. J. obstet. Gynec.,* 1944, **48,** 208–214.
5. Sontag, L. W., & Wines, J. Relation of mother's diet to status of their infants at birth and in infancy. *Amer. J. obstet. Gynec.,* 1947, **54,** 994–1003.
6. Burke, B. S., Stevenson, S. S., Worcester, J., & Stuart, H. S. Nutrition studies during pregnancy. Relation of maternal nutrition to condition of infant at birth: A study of siblings. *J. Nutrition,* 1949, **38,** 453–467.
7. Sontag, L. W., & Wallace, R. F. The effect of cigarette smoking during pregnancy upon the fetal heart rate. *Amer. J. obstet. Gynec.,* 1935, **29,** 77–83.
8. Benaron, H. B. W., *et al.* Effect of anoxia during labor and immediately after birth on the subsequent development of the child. *Amer. J. obstet. Gynec.,* 1960, **80,** 1129–1142.
9. Courville, C., & Edmondson, H. Mental deficiency from intrauterine exposure to radiation. *Bull. Los Angeles Neurol. Soc.,* 1958, **23,** 11–20.
10. Piontkovsky, I. A. Features specific to the function of the higher division of the central nervous system in animals subjected to the effects of ionizing irradiation at various periods of antenatal development. *J. comp. physiol. Psychol.,* 1961, **54,** 314–317.
11. Squier, R., & Dunbar, F. Emotional factors in the course of pregnancy. *Marriage and Family Living,* 1944, **6,** 1–5.
12. Despres, M. A. Favorable and unfavorable attitudes toward pregnancy in primaparae. *J. genet. Psychol.,* 1937, **51,** 241–254.
13. Thompson, W. R., Watson, J., & Charlesworth, W. R. The effects of prenatal maternal stress on offspring behavior in rats. *Psychol. Monogr.,* 1962, **76.**
14. Werboff, J., & Haulena, J. Postnatal behavioral effects of tranquilizers administered to the gravid rat. *Exp. Neurol.,* 1962, **6,** 163–169.
15. Krech, D., Rozenzweig, D. R., & Bennett, E. L. Effects of complex environment and blindness on rat brain. *Arch. Neurol.,* 1963, **8,** 403–412.

16. Pasamanick, B., & Knobloch, H. Brain damage and reproductive casualty. *Amer. J. Orthopsychiat.*, 1960, **30**, 298–305.
17. *Collaborative Perinatal Research Project, Five Years of Progress.* Bethesda, Md.: Nat. Inst. Neurol. Dis. Blindness, National Institutes of Health, 1963.
18. Taft, L. T., & Goldfarb, W. Prenatal and perinatal factors in childhood schizophrenia. *Develpm. Med. Child Neurol.*, 1964, **6**, 32–43.
19. Goldfrank, E. D. Socialization, personality, and the structure of the Pueblo society. *Amer. Anthrop.*, 1945, **47**, 516–539.
20. Kardiner, A. *The Psychological Frontiers of Society.* New York: Columbia Univ. Press, 1945.
21. Spitz, R. A. Anaclitic depression: An inquiry into the genesis of psychiatric conditions in early childhood. In R. S. Eissler, A. Freud, H. Hartmann, & M. Kris (Eds.), *The Psychoanalytic Study of the Child,* Vol. II. New York: International Universities Press, 1946.
22. Hutt, M. L., & Gibby, R. G. *Patterns of Abnormal Behavior.* Englewood Cliffs, N.J.: Allyn and Bacon, 1957.
23. Honigman, J. J. *Culture and Personality.* New York: Harper & Row, 1954.
24. Escalona, S. K. Feeding disturbances in very young children. *Amer J. Orthopsychiat.*, 1945, **15**, 76–80.
25. Carter, H. D., & Krause, R. H. Physical proportions of the human infant. *Child Develpm.*, 1936, **7**, 60–68.
26. Neff, W. S. Socioeconomic status and intelligence: A critical survey. *Psychol. Bull.*, 1938, **35**, 337–357.
27. Hughes, J. G., Ehemann, B., & Brown, W. A. Electroencephalography of the newborn. III, Brain potentials of babies born of mothers given seconal sodium. *Amer. J. Dis. Child.*, 1948, **76**, 626–633.
28. Harlow, H. F., & Zimmerman, R. R. Affectional responses in the infant monkey. *Science,* 1959, **130**, 421–432.
29. Marquis, D. P. Learning in the neonate: The modification of behavior under three feeding schedules. *J. exp. Psychol.* 1941, **29**, 263–282.
30. Aldrich, C. A., et al. The crying of newly born babies. II, The individual phase. *J. Pediat.*, 1945, **27**, 89–96.
31. Aldrich, C. A., et al. The crying of newly born babies. IV, A follow-up study after additional care had been provided. *J. Pediat.*, 1946, **28**, 665–670.
32. Irwin, O. C. The distribution of the amount of mobility in young infants between two nursing periods. *J. comp. Psychol.*, 1932, **14**, 429–445.
33. Shirley, M. H. *The First Two Years, A Study of Twenty-five Babies, Vol. II: Intellectual Development.* (Institute Child Welfare Monogr. Series, No. 8.) Minneapolis: Univ. Minnesota Press, 1933.

34. Dennis, W. Infant development under conditions of restricted practice and minimum social stimulation. *Genet. Psychol. Monogr.,* 1941, **23,** 143–189.
35. Dennis, W., & Dennis, M. G. The effect of cradling practices on the age of walking in Hopi children. *J. genet. Psychol.,* 1940, **56,** 77–86.
36. Dennis, W. Causes of retardation among institutional children. *J. genet. Psychol.,* 1960, **96,** 47–59.
37. Hilgard, J. R. Learning and maturation in preschool children. *J. genet. Psychol.,* 1932, **41,** 36–56.
38. Goldfarb, W. Effects of psychological deprivation in infancy and subsequent stimulation. *Amer. J. Psychiat.,* 1945, **102,** 18–33.
39. Jost, H., & Sontag, L. W. The genetic factor in autonomic nervous system function. *Psychosom. Med.,* 1944, **6,** 308–310.
40. Gesell, A., & Ilg, F. L. *Child Development.* New York: Harper & Row, 1949.
41. Piaget, J. *The Origins of Intelligence in Children.* New York: International Universities Press, 1952.
42. Sontag, L. W. *The Fels Research Institute for the Study of Human Development.* Yellow Springs, Ohio: Antioch College, 1946.

THREE   THE DEVELOPMENT OF THE PERSONALITY

In this chapter we begin the discussion of human personality. If we are to understand any phenomenon, we must first of all define the phenomenon in such a manner that all of us who are concerned with it understand precisely what it is that we are studying. Hence we shall be compelled to define and conceptualize "personality" to meet this requirement. As we shall see, the definition of "personality" involves a number of complexities. To deal with these complexities, it will be necessary to study "personality" from different vantage points.

The introduction to this subject, in the present chapter, will be concerned with the *development* of the personality. Then the *dynamics* of personality functioning will be discussed in Chapter 4. Following that, the focus will be on the *organization* or structure of the personality. These three perspectives should enable us to understand more fully the major aspects of the phenomenon that is termed "personality."

Toward a Definition of Personality

Some theorists approach the study of personality from the viewpoint of *individual differences*. They are concerned with the relatively persisting modes of behavior which differentiate people. Their study includes all forms of human variability. It includes the almost infinite variety of highly specific aspects of behavior—from simple reflex reactions to individual differences in the highly complex patterns of behavior in, let us say, choosing a marital partner.

Another approach to this problem is that which is concerned with the *general* aspects of human behavior and general principles of human adjustment. It attempts to understand the problems of human uniqueness in terms of such factors as personal identity, modes of organization of behavior, and continuities and discontinuities. One of the widely accepted definitions of personality, viewed from this orientation, is that of Allport, who states: "Personality is the dynamic organization within the individual of those psychophysical systems that determine his characteristic behavior and thought" [1]. This definition accents the interaction of physical and psychological characteristics. Moreover, it emphasizes that these inner determinants of behavior lead to generalized modes (systems) of behavioral outcomes.

We can accept this formulation as a starting point in our study of personality. However, we must add, at the outset, that personality may be defined not only in terms of persistent inner systems but also in terms of the constant interactions of these systems with events that are external to the organism. It is an interesting metaphysical problem to attempt to define the boundary of the organism. Is the boundary the skin, which seems to mark the physical separation of the physical man from the rest of the physical universe? Or is it, in psychological terms, somewhere beyond the skin as various external events around the physical man—other people and other stimuli—impinge upon the individual, stimulate him, and affect his development and behavior?

This addition to the conception of personality considers the organism and the environment as the *field* which is the unit of study. The personality does not, in this view, exist within the skin. It is the emergent system of behavior which is determined by the psychophysical-social field of which the individual is a part. Behavior can change as any of these three major components, or their interactions, changes. Personality is thus not infinitely stable but is in a constant state of flux. Its tendencies are defined by the total field of which it is a part. In Figure 3.1 the total area within the outer circle constitutes the "personality," while the physical organism and its current inner organization are defined by the inner circle.

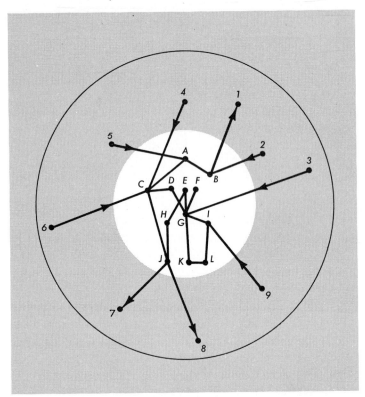

FIGURE 3.1 *Relation between the organized system within the individual (inner circle) and the surrounding field of forces (outer circle) in a field conception of the personality.*

The Early Emergence of Personality

At birth, babies differ in many aspects. In general, we may note that some babies are quite active, others are generally passive, and some are in between [2]. Some authorities speak of these

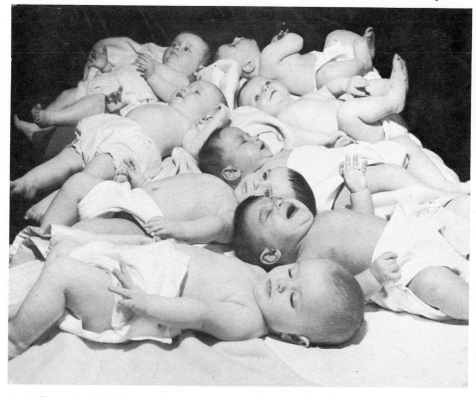

A small sample of infinite varieties in excitability. Pinney from Monkmeyer

differences as differences in *excitability*. There are other rather broad types of differences among babies, so that we are able to say that babies differ in general temperament at birth. These differences in temperament, or level and pattern of moods in behavior, may be correlated with differences in physical conditions. However, aside from such general differences, babies do not have *personalities,* if by personality we mean more or less persistent and patterned characteristics of methods of adaptation to the environment. It therefore seems reasonable to assume that personality is, to a large extent, learned. Whatever may be the limits of this learning experience, psychologists are agreed that it is learned rather than inherited. The old saying that "as the twig is bent, so is the tree inclined" still is appropriate regarding our present judgment concerning this problem. But note that even the old saying does not account for all of the tree's characteristics in terms of its early experience in being bent.

If, then, the infant does not inherit a specific and preformed personality which then merely unfolds, how does his personality develop? We need to examine the evidence concerning the effects of the child's early experience on his personality development during childhood and later years. Although psychologists are agreed on the general importance of early experiences, they are by no means agreed on which factors are most important or on how long-lasting or significant the effects of these experiences may be.

It seems clear that the ways in which primary biological needs are satisfied—the methods by which such needs are gratified and the speed and consistency with which such satisfactions occur—have important effects upon the emerging personality. The behavior of the neonate is under the domination of the gastrointestinal and genitourinary tracts. Let us examine some of the evidence and see what theories have been developed to explain the observed facts.

EFFECTS OF EARLY FEEDING EXPERIENCES   Before examining some of the relevant data on this topic, we would do well to consider the perplexities involved in gathering and interpreting such data. If it were possible to assemble a considerable number of infants who were equivalent in personality characteristics and then subject them to varying feeding experiences in order to assess the effects of such variations, we would be faced with an apparently simple problem. However, the problem of defining the variations in "feeding experience" is, in fact, extremely complex. For example, we might vary the foods which were given the infants, we might vary the ways in which the foods were prepared, we might vary the methods by which the foods were "given" to the infants, we might vary the emotional climate in which food was given, and so on ad infinitum. "Feeding" can thus be seen to be a highly complex kind of experience, and how are we to know which aspects are most salient for research and study? In a general way we could categorize the most significant dimensions of the total food-getting experience as a first step in the process of investigation. Then we could experimentally change one part of each dimension while keeping others constant (or use statistical methods to evaluate their effects). In this way we might eventually begin to evaluate the effect of various factors upon later behavior.

But the problem is much more complex than even these considerations suggest. In the first place, we must remember that although babies may not be born with specific personality characteristics, they do vary in reactivity or general temperament and possibly in other tendencies. These differences may selectively alter the ways in which they respond to feeding or other types of early experience. Hence, we should have to consider how different types of babies respond to the different types of feeding processes. This might lead us to find that certain feeding variables interact differently with different temperamental and neural-excitatory processes. Then, there may be, and probably are, a whole series of co-ordinate conditions which affect the total feeding experience. For example, Ribble has suggested that infants require an optimal amount of "mothering" in order to survive and prosper physically and emotionally [3]. Lest Ribble be accused of sentimentality in ascribing to infants a "need for mothering," let us make clear that what Ribble meant by "mothering" involved various kinds of "physical handling" of the baby, such as picking it up, rocking it, turning it over, and so on. Ribble's contention is that the infant requires physical handling in order to stimulate the circulation of blood and lymph. An infant's physical development is inadequate to take care of this vital process for some time after birth. During the fetal stage of development, the physical movements made by the mother in the normal course of her own activity served to stimulate the baby's physiological behavior. In fact, Ribble found that infants who did not obtain what she termed "minimal mothering," or physical stimulation, frequently developed disorders in breathing and digestion. We shall have more to say about Ribble and related observational and research studies later in this chapter.

Aside from all other considerations, the food-getting experience is highly significant for the infant because of its tremendous biological need for food intake. For example, on the average, weight is doubled during the first five months of life. During this period the body requires considerable food satisfaction if biological needs are not to be frustrated. Depending on the infant's original excitability or reactivity, the amount of distress he is likely to experience will have some relationship with satisfactions derived from appropriate food intake, and later, as he becomes conditioned to them, with the conditions involved in this food-getting experience. Dissatisfaction in obtaining food is likely to precipitate excessive physiological arousal and may generalize diffuse activation of the brain.

Some cultures
encourage close
mother-child
relationships
through physical
handling.

Breast feeding   Freud believed that the *oral orifice,* that is, the mouth and the regions immediately surrounding the mouth, such as the gums, teeth, the upper and lower palates, and the upper gastrointestinal tract, was of primary importance during infancy in organizing the discharge of oral satisfactions. This region of the body was very sensitive to stimulation. The ways in which these primitive oral-sexual drives were satisfied were seen by him as of critical importance in early personality development. His position, sometimes inaccurately summarized in the psychological literature, was that either *over-* or *under-indulgence* of these drives resulted in frustration of oral-sexual needs and led to personality disturbance which was *likely* (not *necessarily*) to have long-lasting effects. Moreover, he postulated another condition of this hypothesis, namely, that this frustration, to be significant, should occur during the period of *oral primacy,* usually during the first eight months. Thus he postulated a *critical period* for the importance and primacy of the oral-sexual drives.[1]

Some observational evidence seems to support the importance of these propositions. Anthropologists and ethnologists report that in those societies which provide minimal deprivation of oral needs along with positive support for the infant, the adults demonstrate secure emotional adjustments and are able to test reality very well. Studies of the Comanche [4] and of the east-European Jewish culture [5] support this thesis. Of course such evidence is neither universal nor meets the rigorous tests of scientific control of other possibly relevant factors. Nevertheless, direct observational evidence, over many years, of children under laboratory conditions at Yale University leads Gesell to state, "Breast-feeding is the most favorable condition for the initiation of a self-demand schedule" [6]. What Gesell suggested is that the absence or limitation of frustration, which letting the baby set his own pace in feeding involves, is most effectively determined during breast feeding.

The experimental evidence on this problem is not conclusive and is far from easy to interpret. There are a number of reasons for this. In the first place, how is one to conceptualize "under-indulgence of oral drives," for example? Is breast feeding a

[1] Freud conceived of the sexual drives as biologically derived drives related to the *total process* of developing and maintaining affectional relations with people. In infancy these affectional drives were satisfied through oral gratification; hence the term "oral-sexuality" was coined to describe this phase of sexual development.

more effective method of obtaining adequate indulgence than bottle feeding? Is the age of termination of such feeding crucial? Are supplemental methods of feeding significant? Or is the complex pattern of infant-parent interaction during feeding, as well as during other activities, relevant?

Then there is the criterion problem: the kinds of evidence concerning adjustment which one utilizes. Should one consider highly specific aspects of personality response, such as amount of physical activity, thumb-sucking, and the like? Or should one consider more general aspects of personality, such as amount of security, capacity for independent behavior, or absence of pathological adjustment?

There are other problems. How is one to measure the phenomena in question? What kind of sampling of subjects should be studied? For example, are results the same for boys and girls? Does the position in the family among other children make a difference? And still other problems arise to plague the investigator in this field. Must the behavior be observed at first hand, or are retrospective reports by adults about their own childhood experiences adequate? And what about the duration of the effects of the early experience upon later behavior? If one conducts long-term studies, should one look for specific relations between particular early experiences and, later, particular outcomes? These difficulties must be kept in mind in evaluating findings from research studies.

Results are quite ambiguous in studies in which the duration and age of initiating or terminating breast feeding were considered as isolated variables. Thus, Goldman-Eisler [7], trying to investigate the relationship between early weaning and later adult personality characteristics, rated 100 English adults on 19 personality traits. It was found that there was a small but significant tendency for the pattern of "oral pessimism" to be associated with early weaning. On the other hand, Maslow and Szilagyi-Kessler [8], who gave 400 college students an emotional-security inventory, found that the difference between bottle and breast feeding was not of crucial importance. They found, for example, that those who reported having been bottle-fed from birth rated themselves as secure as those breast-fed from birth to over a year of age. The limitations of this latter type of study are fairly apparent, since reports of what may have happened and self-ratings of traits leave much to be desired in the way of adequate research procedures. A more carefully controlled study at the Fels Research Institute in Yellow Springs, Ohio, in which accurate data on bottle and breast feeding were obtained, may be more to the point [9]. In this study, the complex emotional interactions of an "average" group of children with their mothers were evaluated by means of ratings based on direct observation. No correlation was found between duration of breast feeding and ratings of security in adolescence. The better-educated mothers used more subtle forms of discipline and nursed their children for shorter periods. It was concluded that the duration of breast feeding, per se, did not appear to be of crucial significance. The complex pattern of emotional interaction between child and mother seemed much more relevant.

In contrast to this study is the one by Brody at the Menninger Foundation at Topeka, Kansas [10]. In this research, 32 mothers and their infants were observed both in the clinic and at home. Observations were intensive and repeated. Very great variations in the patterns of breast and bottle feeding were observed. The amount and type of bodily contact, communication, and expressed attitude also varied greatly in the two extreme groups of mothers, as Table 3.1 shows quite clearly. The findings of this study suggested that breast feeding, by itself, did not insure "gentle procedures, intimacy, or restfulness." However, breast feeding by mothers who were not in conflict about this practice or, in other words, who probably employed breast feeding as part of a total, accepting, and warmly secure relationship with the infant, was related to highly favorable responses by the infants. This is a conclusion of the investigator which her data seemed to support but which is not rigorously tested by her own data. The study did clearly demonstrate, however, that the total feeding pattern, rated on the basis of reasonably objective and replicable observational scales, was more indicative of the nature of the relationship between mother and infant than any other pattern or single variable. *Only a study of the total feeding relationship was significant in predicting the emotional relationship between mother and infant.* It was also learned that, when this total relationship was favorable, the mother responded in a consistently sensitive way to the baby's expressed needs. This sensitivity to the baby's needs was not present when the relationship was "unfavorable." In the latter case, the mother was likely to be consistent in her methods of dealing with the infant but so rigid that she frequently frustrated not only the hunger drives of the baby but his oral needs as well. This research clearly does not tell us much about the effects of "a favorable mother-child relationship" which result from good breast-feeding practices, but, of course, this was not its purpose. Nevertheless, it does highlight many important aspects of the nature of the total feeding experience of the baby.

TABLE 3.1. COMPARISON OF THE INTERACTIONS OF MOTHERS AND INFANTS IN CONNECTION WITH INFANT FEEDING

Category of Behavior	Group A Mothers ("Good" mothers) $N = 7$	Group D Mothers ("Poor" mothers) $N = 11$
Bodily contact	Mother (M) holds child securely; M and infant (I) relaxed; feeding tempo consistently moderate; M waits for I to show cessation of interest in feeding.	M does not use position comfortable for both M and I; M's tension interferes with I's feeding; feeding interrupted abruptly.
Communication	M is able to respond to both I and others; talks gently to I; M and I smile frequently to each other; M shows tenderness, pride.	M frequently urges I to eat; frequently withdraws and restores nipple; occasionally teases or threatens not to offer food.
Expressed attitude	M prefers breast feeding; reasons for breast feeding: brought up that way, most natural, most satisfying; M uses flexible schedule because I's moods vary; usually considers latter part of 1st year best for weaning from breast; none in hurry to wean.	Most M's breast-feed for few days only and offer such reasons for cessation as: insufficient milk, nervousness, nipple irritated; most M's said they preferred self-demand schedule but showed markedly contrasting behavior.

SOURCE: S. Brody, *Patterns of Mothering*, New York: International Universities Press, 1956, pp. 287–371.

Fortunately, there is available a comprehensive study in which the separate and interactive effects of five major independent variables were considered in relation to subsequent adjustmental behavior. Heinstein published a monograph in 1963 that dealt with the relations of type of feeding, duration of nutritive sucking, marital adjustment of the parents, warmth of the mother, and nervous stability of the mother, on the one hand, and behavior of the children, on the other [11]. The subjects were 47 boys and 47 girls, part of the Berkeley Guidance Study conducted by Macfarlane. They had remained in this study from infancy through 18 years of age.

Insofar as breast feeding and duration of nutritive sucking, considered separately, were concerned, no significant advantage could be demonstrated for either variable. There were some sex differences, however. But when feeding practices and interpersonal factors were considered together, the story was different. Thus, for example, it was found that girls who were formula-fed by warm mothers had fewer adjustment problems than girls formula-fed by cold mothers or than girls who were breast-fed by either warm or cold mothers. There were no significant interaction effects, of this kind, for boys. In the case of boys, interaction effects did show up for interpersonal factors and duration of nutritive sucking. For example, when boys from good interpersonal milieus were nursed for longer periods of time, there was better personal adjustment.

This type of study is very significant in many ways. In the first place, it is a longitudinal study and is not based on retrospective reports made by adults about their early childhood. In the second place, results are analyzed separately for each sex. And, finally, both single-variable and interactive-variable analyses are available. Among other things, such research demonstrates how complex the problem of personality development really is. However, this study does not evaluate adequately some aspects of the problem we posed at the beginning of this section on breast feeding. For example, are there critical periods which affect subsequent development differentially? And are results of over- and undergratification similar or different?

There is an earlier study which gets at some of these other aspects of the problem. Yarrow presents the findings from a longitudinal study which considered breast feeding, duration of nutritive sucking, and length of feeding sessions [12]. There were 26 males and 38 females in this study. The findings do not seem explicable in terms of simple reinforcement theory, but they are compatible with a phase-specific hypothesis such as Freud and others have suggested. It was found, for instance, that late-weaned children show more indications of problem behavior (thumb-sucking) than early-weaned children. But it was also found that short individual feeding sessions during the first six months are significantly related to thumb-sucking. These kinds of findings suggested to Yarrow that oral drive varies as a function of the developmental level. During early infancy insufficient feeding experience (underindulgence) leads to fixation. But prolonged oral satisfaction (overindulgence) after oral drives begin to wane also leads to fixation.

Lois Murphy and her associates have been conducting an extensive study of factors influencing "coping behavior" during the preschool years [13]. (See Chapter 4 for further discussion of coping behavior.) Such items as sense of security, sense of self-esteem, clarity of perception, and ability to deal effectively with factors in the environment were considered as part of coping behaviors. She found significant positive correlations between appropriate oral gratification and these measures. She concluded that such experiences lead to lower tension levels, good differentiation of the self from the environment, and effective self-concepts.

Two other kinds of evidence will be cited which bear upon the present problem. One of these shows that babies are very responsive to the personality of those who nurse or take care of them. Margaret Fries compared the behavior of babies who were taken care of by compulsive nurses with a supposedly equivalent group of babies who were taken care of by noncompulsive, secure nurses [14]. Both groups of babies had the same diet and the same feeding schedules. The compulsive nurses treated all of their babies in much the same way, paying attention to the mechanical details of feeding in a careful manner but not paying particular attention to the reactions of the babies. On the other hand, the noncompulsive nurses were much more gentle with their babies and varied their behavior to attempt to adapt it to the apparent needs of the babies. The most significant differences seemed to be that the babies handled by compulsive nurses developed more anxious, startled reactions to usual stimuli, whereas the other babies not only showed fewer reactions of this kind but ingested more food and became more responsive to their nurses.

The other evidence is derived from a study that Escalona made of the relationship between the personality characteristics of infants and their mothers [15]. Attention in this research was focused on the problem of feeding disturbances, e.g., refusal to eat. It was found that feeding disturbances tended to occur much more frequently when the mothers were emotionally "high-strung." Their babies also were "high-strung" and showed difficulties in the whole food-intake process. Whether constitutional and possibly hereditary influences contributed to the relationships was not determined, but the evidence is suggestive that such factors were not the primary determinants.

We must conclude from the evidence available at the present time that many of the issues related to early feeding experiences are still largely unresolved. That early experiences have some significant effects cannot be denied. However, the duration of these effects is still speculative; the evidence that a warm, secure relationship between mother and child during the feeding experience leads to less disturbance in the child, or to more security in the total personality in the child, seems likely. It has not been demonstrated, as yet, which factors in this total relationship, singly or in combination, are most significant. Nor has it been demonstrated how long such effects persist or what other factors may counteract such effects or reinforce them. Only longitudinal studies with appropriate controls, based on replicable and objective types of observations or measurements, can supply conclusions that can be relied on with great confidence.

THE EFFECTS OF OTHER EARLY EXPERIENCES In considering the possible influence of various kinds of experience upon the individual (human or animal), we shall have to be constantly alert to two interrelated problems. One of these is the possible significance of a *given kind of experience,* by itself or in combination with other types of experience, for *short-* and *long-term* effects in subsequent behavior. The other is the relative *availability (or deprivation)* of the total pattern of experiences. Some kinds of *deprivation* tend to enhance the effects of the experiences available to the organism, since the latter now become more prominent. Increased *availability* of some kinds of experience tends to reduce the availability of other kinds of experience, since these now occupy less time in the individual's life-space. In both cases an increase or decrease in the set of experiences influences the amount of time remaining for the other experiences. For example, if an infant experiences two hours of rocking and caressing experiences each day, he has available *less time each day* for other types of experiences had

Emotional deprivation? Bayer from Monkmeyer

by another infant who is rocked and caressed for only one hour per day.

Deprivation experience in animals   Experimental psychologists have become interested in the effects of deprivation experiences in animals because of the relevance of this issue to human personality development. It is much easier to employ experimental manipulation of environmental stimuli with animals than with humans, but it is important to exercise caution in generalizing from animal studies to the possible significance of any conclusions for humans. Recent studies have centered on the relative effects of handling (i.e., stroking and petting) versus deprivation of such handling. In one such study, rats "handled" a great deal in infancy were compared with another group in which this was not done [16]. Both groups of rats were later given tests involving severe environmental stress, such as immobilization and deprivation of food and of water. The "handled" group was able to withstand the effects of the stress (deprivation) far better than the "nonhandled" group. There was less physiological damage to internal organs and the gastrointestinal tract. In fact the "handled" group was even able to survive, for many more hours than the other group, the effects of deprivation of food and water.

In another study, by Thompson and Heron [17], the effect of social isolation in the lives of puppies was studied. Two groups of puppies were compared, after an experimental period, upon a variety of tests involving the learning and retention of mazes which were thought to measure "memory," "attention," and learning ability. One group was raised in cages in which they were isolated from external stimulation (except for relatively short periods during feeding) for the first seven and a half months. The other group had "normal" stimulation in the laboratory. They were able to see and interact with other puppies and humans during this same period. A comparison of the two groups after these differential experiences showed that the deprived group was significantly inferior on all of the behavioral tests.

In another study, the effects of the deprivation upon the behavior of puppies was explored with respect to the period when the deprivation was applied. In this study, Pfaffenberger and Scott [18] found that the critical period for the most significant effect of "social experience" was at twelve weeks of age. If puppies were "ignored" after this age, that is, if they were not handled, played with, and the like, they were unable to learn to "take responsibility" or successfully to complete guide-dog training. Deprivation before this critical time (12 weeks) did not have similar effects.

Riesen investigated the effects of light-deprivation in kittens and chimpanzees [19]. Deprivation was begun shortly after birth and continued for varying periods through infancy and beyond. It was found that, when light-deprivation was continued beyond infancy, chemical and atrophic changes occurred in the retina and that these changes were then irreversible. The effect of light-deprivation was more marked in the higher than in the lower mammals.

That the effects of deprivation are not altogether on the negative side is indicated in a study by Seitz [20]. In this study the effects of social isolation on kittens were investigated. Kittens were removed from their mothers and placed in individual isolation. Some were isolated at two weeks of age, others at six weeks, and still others at twelve weeks. At nine months the three groups were compared on various indices. The twelve-week group (considered the overprotected group) showed greater fear responses in shock situations than the other groups. However, this group seemed less fearful in other situations. Kittens in the two-week group showed more alertness but at the same time were more "anxious" and aggressive. They were also slower in some learning tasks and were less able to compete for food. Some even developed an asthma-like state. The six-week group showed the least over-all disturbance in most situations.

Over the past decade, studies on the effects of deprivation in animals have become increasingly more frequent. More to the point, these studies have become more sophisticated with respect to research design and theoretical orientation. The results have not been unambiguous, and many issues remain to be explored. However, a number of important inferences may tentatively be drawn. The first of these is that, generally speaking, deprivation of sensory and other experiences during early stages of development does influence the subsequent development of behavior in various ways. The second is that for many functions there is a *critical period* in development, different for different functions and different for different species, before and after which the effects are significantly different. The third is that the effect of deprivation tends to be differential, so that, while some functions are impaired, others are enhanced. The fourth is that deprivation during a critical period serves to reduce the effectiveness of the over-all adaptiveness of the animal even though some functions may be temporarily improved. And, finally, there is clear evidence that some effects of early deprivation, especially if continued, are so severe that they lead to irreversible effects and to profound physiological and structural change as well as to behavioral change.

Effects of different kinds of experience in young animals
The work of the Wisconsin laboratories with monkeys offers a great deal of insight into the effects of differential types of early experience. In one series of studies, Harlow investigated the effects of various kinds of "mothering" [21]. One group of young

monkeys was separated from their mothers and "nursed" by surrogate, mechanical mothers. Two such surrogate mothers were available, one made of wire mesh, which offered no soft physical contact, the other made of wood that was was covered with sponge rubber and terry cloth and thus offered soft physical contact. As Harlow puts it, the soft mother was "soft, warm and tender, a mother with infinite patience, a mother available 24 hours a day, a mother that never scolded her infant and never struck or bit her baby in anger." The "hard" mother had the same characteristics except for her lack of softness. Under varying conditions of experimental manipulation to stressful situations, it was concluded that, when monkeys were free to choose the preferred surrogate mother, they showed increasing responsiveness to the cloth mother. They would often clutch her, rub against her, and rush to her. When frightened, they would turn to the cloth mother. Monkeys raised with cloth mothers were found to be less fearful, showed more exploratory behavior, and were more able to withstand stress. The converse findings were true of the monkeys whose experience had been with the wire mother. Thus, Harlow concluded that the evidence favors "the overwhelming importance of the variable of soft body contact that characterized the cloth mother, and this held true for the appearance, development, and maintenance of the infant–surrogate-mother tie." He also concluded that "nursing or feeding played either no role or a subordinate role in the development of affection . . ." [22].

Two other studies highlight additional findings which are relevant for our present discussion. One is interesting because it demonstrates the different effects that can be caused by varying the *intensity* of experiences [23]. In this study, mice were subjected to different levels of electric shock during infancy. When the magnitude of the shock was low, it facilitated avoidance-learning in later adulthood, but, when it was high, it interfered with this later learning. Thus, in addition to the type of experience and the age at which an experience affects an individual, as we have noted in our previous discussion, the intensity of the experience (in this case, shock) has a differential and possibly opposite effect. Another study, with Siamese kittens, in which the factor of "gentling" as an experiential variable was investigated, showed that this factor influenced even the speed and depth of coloring of the kitten [24]. These authors believe that the differential effect is produced indirectly as a result of hormonal and neurophysiological changes produced by "gentling." This kind of inference about the effects of favorable or unfavorable "emotional" experiences upon aspects of physical functioning and indirectly upon behavior of the organism is supported by a wide variety of studies upon both animals (principally) and human infants.

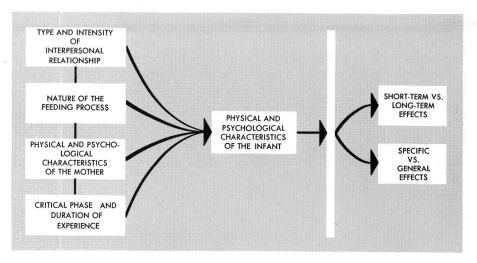

FIGURE 3.2 *Some of the interacting factors influencing early personality development.*

Studies of the kind we have described, and related studies, suggest that early experience has significant consequences for the maturation of the organism, for the time and quality of the performance which is manifested, and possibly for the enduring aspects of personality development. In the case of Harlow's monkeys, the type of body contact experienced in infancy certainly had long-lasting effects upon adult behavior—effects which profoundly altered the course of even sexual behavior in adult life. Figure 3.2 summarizes the kinds of factors which have been proposed as important in influencing the early development of the personality.

Attitudinal Orientation to the World

One of the critical questions concerning the dynamics of personality development is that which asks, "How does the individual develop an attitude toward himself and toward the world which, in general, may be characterized as trustful?" Some writers have referred to this attitudinal orientation as one of *basic trust* [25]. Others have characterized the variable which is involved as that of security-insecurity [26]. In any event, many observers have noted that people differ with respect to the degree of self-confidence they display in meeting new situations in life. On the one hand, some people show a high degree of appropriate self-regard and have the attitude that they can succeed in dealing with most life-situations. Even if they fail, they are not utterly crushed. On the other hand, there are those who seem to anticipate failure, have little regard for themselves, and show disruptive behavioral consequences when they are thwarted. The first group tends to be optimistic, friendly, realistically oriented, and strives appropriately toward accomplishment of immediate and long-term goals. The other group tends to be pessimistic, is suspicious of others, is critical of their lot in life, and becomes easily frustrated in dealing with difficult problems.

BASIC TRUST   What we are concerned with, then, is how this orientational attitudinal variable toward life is learned. One writer (Erikson) suggests that the learning of this attitude is unlike the learning of specific skills or specific behaviors but depends instead upon the opportunity afforded the individual to develop his potential for action, thought, and feeling without undue threat and interference [27]. It may depend, then, upon a pattern of early conditions which fosters positive self-regard, so that the individual learns to anticipate that his psychological needs will usually be gratified. It does not depend, primarily, on the mere satisfaction of physical needs but upon *the ways in which these needs are met*. Erikson suggests that it has its beginnings as the infant develops a sense of self-awareness, particularly during the second half of the first year of his life. During this period the nature of the total relationship between the infant and the person who takes care of him (in our culture, usually the mother) exerts a profound impact upon his developing sense of basic trust in himself and the world. When this total relationship conveys *security* in meeting his needs, *warmth* in the relationship, and *minimal frustration,* the infant learns that the world can be trusted. And, when the world can be depended upon in this way, basic trust extends to the self-system as well as to the attitudinal orientation to the world.   *479*

Erikson's formulation, which is sketched here without consideration for all of the relevant detail, is based upon clinical observations of disturbed youngsters who failed to develop a sense of basic trust and is supported by reference to anthropological research in varying cultures. This viewpoint clearly suggests that it is the whole pattern of the interrelationship between infant and mother that must be considered as crucial rather than specific needs and their gratification or frustration. It does not imply that specific methods of handling child-training (such as control of elimination or weaning from the breast or bottle) have no significant effects upon the general attitude of trustfulness but rather that these effects can be properly understood only in terms of the total pattern of the child-mother relationship.

The Basic Mother-Child Relationship

A recent comprehensive study by Sears and co-workers has shed some light upon this problem [28]. In this study 379 mothers and their kindergarten children were evaluated by means of intensive interviews with the mothers. The mothers were selected from two suburban communities and comprised samples of Protestant, Catholic, and Jewish faiths of varying socioeconomic levels. The interview data were recorded mechanically and were analyzed into 44 scales of parental child-rearing practices. On the basis of the analysis of these data, five clusters of factors were isolated. These were highly significant in predicting the personality attributes of the children. One cluster, called *permissiveness-strictness,* consisted of scales of severity in toilet training, use of physical punishment, restrictions in making noise, and permissiveness in using aggression toward siblings. Another cluster was called *warmth of mother-child relationship.* These two clusters were the most important ones in terms of their relationships to (and possible effects upon) child personality. When the relationship was one that could be characterized as *warm,* the children tended to be secure, whereas, when the relationship was characterized as *cold,* the children tended to be aggressive, had frequent feeding problems, were persistent bed-wetters, and, in general, could be characterized as insecure.

480   Many other patterns of relationships and their consequences

were explored. The data indicated, in general, that the over-all pattern of the relationships, as reported, was important in determining whether children tended to be secure or insecure. It should be noted, however, that a particular pattern was *not* invariantly accompanied by the typical personality effect. This indicates that other factors must have contributed to personality development. For example, the effects of the pattern of relationships seemed to depend on other factors in the familial environment, such as whether the parents were middle-class or lower-class individuals. Although these data do not bear precisely upon the nature of the formative period in the development of basic trust, as conceptualized by Erikson, they lend suggestive support to his thesis.

Some research support for the thesis that the pervasive nature of the relationship between mother and child is highly significant in determining the general way in which the personality develops, whether it is secure and matures progressively or whether it is insecure and fails to mature, is offered by Spitz in his study of three groups of children [29]. These infants lived under three types of conditions: one group lived with their mothers in their own homes; another group lived in a nursery in which they had contact with other infants and some regular attention by substitute mothers; the third group lived in a hospital and had no regular substitute mothers. Spitz found that when infants were deprived of regular, consistent "mothering" (which might and did vary from "mother" to "mother"), they were retarded in their over-all development, both physical and psychological. They tended to become progressively more apathetic, were unable to respond to good diet or even medical care as they became physically more debilitated, they became ill, and many died. Spitz concluded that when infants were deprived of consistent "mothering" they failed to mature in either physical or psychological characteristics. He thought that his study showed that infants needed some consistent type of relationship with a mother-figure. He found that the effect of separation from the mother was most devastating (1) when it occurred during the second half of the first year of life and (2) when a consistent relationship had already been established.

Spitz's studies have been severely criticized on the ground of inadequate methodology, mainly in terms of inadequate controls of several important variables [30]. Although the methodology can justifiably be criticized, the extremely great differences among groups, the frequent highly abnormal conditions in the hospitalized group, including many deaths despite very good physical care, and the progressive nature of the deterioration when consistent mothering was unavailable, can hardly be overlooked. It is clear that some specific conclusions of Spitz's concerning the value of handling, rocking, and other physical and psychological interchanges between "mother" and infant which he regards as important may be questioned. But the overriding conclusion that a period of consistent relationships is necessary for healthy personality development—or its corrollary, that loss of such a relationship, when it has once been available for a period of time, can have devastating effects upon the security of the infant—seems entirely justified.

Another study, by Dennis, completed a few years before Spitz's, has been interpreted by some as being in opposition to that of Spitz [31]. Dennis reported that two infants who were raised under conditions of restricted practice and minimum social stimulation from the age of one month to fourteen months showed no retardation in behavioral or emotional development. The two fraternal twins in the study were raised in two adjoining cribs with plain walls and nothing else in view. They had no toys to play with, and they were restricted during eating and bathing so that they could not practice "sitting up" or reaching during these periods. They were left alone except for feeding and bathing. When they cried, they were fed or were changed with reasonable promptness. In these and other ways the effort to provide restricted practice and minimal social stimulation seems to have been satisfied. Dennis reported that during the first nine months no retardation was noticeable. Physical and emotional development seemed to proceed in accord with normative standards. Later, however, there were definite indications of progressive retardation in various abilities. Dennis reported, however, that neuromuscular learning, which was retarded, was easily compensated for by subsequent practice. It was not reported, nor was any attempt made to determine, whether the transient retardation was accompanied by emotional disturbances in either of the twins. Nor could the effects of the study be definitive in other respects, since there was no way of knowing how comparable these twins were to other infants with whom they were compared on various types of normative data. Furthermore, it was later learned that one of the twins had a disability on one side of his body (a condition diagnosed as hemiplegia, likely due to brain injury at birth).

In evaluating this study, one can raise many questions. However, we should like to focus on the problem of *consistent relationship* with a "mother-figure." If, indeed, the restricted conditions did not produce any significant retardation in general physical and emotional development, it may have affected the development of basic trust in these children. On this point, unfortunately, there is insufficient evidence. In any case, there was a consistency in the relationship—a consistency which the infants were able to rely upon completely. Thus, if the results are to be accepted at face value, they are in agreement, or at least are not in contradiction, with Spitz's finding that consistency is essential for avoidance of traumatic effects upon physical and emotional development. Dennis' study does not support any hypothesis which argues for the necessity of other elements in the "mothering" process, such as the need for fondling, rocking, frequent social stimulation, and the like. It does, however, offer support for the effectiveness of a highly consistent pattern of infant-adult relationship—one that could lead the infant to trust his world.

From evidence of the kind we have cited, it may become clear how complicated is the problem of deducing causal connections between conditions of rearing children and personality consequences. One question concerns the meaning of the term *consistency*. What is the optimal condition of consistency and during what period or periods? And for which personality consequence are these conditions relevant? Since, even in Spitz's studies, not all children were equally affected or affected to the same degree by separation or by deprivation of consistent "mothering," what factors exaggerate the effect and what factors minimize it? Under which conditions is the basic attitudinal orientation toward the world of trust or distrust enhanced or decreased? The reader will wish to consider other questions which this general problem suggests.

Nevertheless, the evidence cited and other observational, anecdotal, cross-cultural, and experimental evidence seem to indicate that children do differ in the kind of basic attitudinal orientation they have to themselves and the world and that conditions during infancy and early childhood are highly important to such an orientation, at least as primary contributors.

483

The Family in Relation to Personality Development

For a long period of time in the life of the child, during his formative years of development, the family is the main social institution which directly affects, guides, and controls him. In most Western cultures the primary agent for these responsibilities, during infancy and at least early childhood, is the mother. It is therefore not surprising, as we shall learn, that most studies of the effects of family experiences have focused on interactions between mother and child, with relative neglect of the father's influence. During preschool years the father usually begins to assume a more important and direct role in relation to the child's upbringing. It is during this same period that the influence of siblings and other relatives also acquires greater importance. During this whole period, and even in later years, the effects of the culture in which the child lives are experienced through the focus of the family's interactions with the child. Thus the nature of this complex set of family experiences must be understood if we are to gain some comprehension of factors which affect the child's personality development. Because it is so complex, various investigators have tried to limit their studies to some major aspects of the family constellation. Similarly, we shall focus our attention on a few major considerations, such as the interactions between child and parents, the interactions among siblings, and the general emotional climate of the family.

THE FREUDIAN POSITION Sigmund Freud focused attention on the importance of intrafamilial experiences upon the personality development of the child through his highly creative theory of psychosexual development. As we shall see in Chapter 5, he tried to develop a "metapsychology" of personality development in which the bases were formulated for a systematic theory. His comprehensive formulations, based primarily upon clinical observations of neurotic adults, were constantly revised by him during his own lifetime, and revisions have continued to be made by his disciples, as well as by his dissenters, to this very day. The impact of his theorizing, whether for "good or bad," has been tremendous, not only upon psychology but upon many aspects of human endeavor, such as art, education,

Future mothers of America.

science in general, and even religion. We shall discuss, primarily, the central importance which Freud attributed to certain aspects of the family situation as a basis for reviewing some important empirical evidence which has been gathered in recent years.

The anal period   We have already commented briefly on some aspects of Freudian theory in discussing, earlier in this chapter, the oral period of psychosexual development. We shall therefore turn our attention to the next period in psychosexual development which Freud suggested—the anal period. According to Freudian theory, from about the eighth month of life through the third year, the anal zone becomes the primary zone for "erotogenic" or psychosexual stimulation [32]. The child experiences pleasurable sensations when pressure upon the anal sphincters (valvelike muscles which control defecation) mounts to the point that defecation results. Involved in this activity are not only the anal sphincters but also the lower end of the intestinal tract, the anus, the buttocks, and the surrounding region. Indeed, it might be said that the whole child participates in the act of defecation as he becomes perceptually aware of his own reactions and of the reactions of those around him who participate with him in various ways as he performs this function. Central to the Freudian position on the pleasure or pain which the child originally experiences in defecating is that it is the *relative* reduction or increase of tension (through pressure on the anal sphincter) which produces these phenomena. As the tension builds up, it is experienced as painful, and, as it is decreased in the act of defecation, it is experienced as pleasurable. Moreover, anal behavior, that is, retaining or expelling feces, may become a method through which tension arising in other parts of the body may be dealt with.

Even more important from the viewpoint of the developing personality of the child, the complex set of experiences which are involved in so-called toilet training is part and parcel of the child's first social interactions or first form of social learning. The child's need to defecate when and where he wishes is in conflict with the social needs of reality as represented by his mother, who wishes to teach him to behave in a socially more appropriate manner. The interactions of the needs and capacities of the child, on the one hand, and of the needs and methods employed by the mother, on the other, furnish significant models for conflict and resolution or frustration. Children vary in the rate of biological maturation and their physical readiness to develop voluntary control over anal activity. They also vary in their temperament and emotional reactivity at the time when toilet training is instituted. On the other hand, mothers vary in their "philosophy" of toilet training, their methods of toilet training, and their own personality attributes, among other things. All of these factors are relevant to the way the child experiences the learning of appropriate toilet habits. They also become relevant to the concomitants of this learning —his attitudes toward his own competency in gaining mastery over a basic biological need, his pleasure or pain connected with the total act of defecating, his methods of dealing with the conflict situation which the mother's demands create in relation to his own inner needs, his attitudes toward his mother as a punishing or rewarding or understanding person, and the like. The child may learn to perceive the mother as hostile or demanding, or he may learn to perceive her as supportive and accepting. The Freudian theory posits that the child's *narcissistic* position during early infancy, during which he loves himself, sees himself as omnipotent, and tends to respond only in terms of his own needs, is gradually abandoned in favor of a reality-testing position in which he learns to gain pleasure by pleasing his mother while gaining mastery over his own biological functions—if conditions are favorable. He begins at this stage to interiorize his mother's values; in other words, he *identifies* with her. He learns to obey, conform, and to inhibit behavior according to his mother's wishes. Her wishes and values gradually become his own. He also gradually learns to master his *ambivalence* toward his mother, that is, he learns that it is possible to continue to love his mother even though she is a frustrating object at times. And he learns to give up some of his feelings of omnipotence. He thus prepares the stage for achieving a less dependent attitude as he gains mastery in terms of reality rather than fantasy.

The child's learning during this stage of development may be significantly influenced by his mother's overindulgence or over-punitiveness. If he is praised excessively for exercising bowel movements upon command, he may learn to overvalue this activity, and thus he may begin to learn the general principle that it is highly important to please others. The generalization may then follow that it is important, in getting along in this world, to please others even at one's own expense. On the other hand, if the mother is overly punitive in dealing with the problem of bowel control, the act of defecating may become an arena in which wills are pitted against each other, and the child may begin to learn that it is necessary to be defiant or to be excessively compliant. These are but a few of the many complex derivatives in character development which have their beginning and may become "fixated" (i.e., overlearned) as a consequence of this highly emotion-laden early learning experience, according to Freudian theory. Fixated anal traits which *may* persist into adulthood include: *parsimony, petulance,* and *pedantry.* There is some evidence that, at least in cases of psychopathology, these traits in adulthood had their origins during the anal periods of development (see Chapter 6).

The oedipal period The next period in psychosexual development is that which involves the *oedipal conflict,* according to psychoanalytic theory. This is the phallic stage of development, during which the primary sexual organs assume erotic primacy. The third year normally marks the beginning of this period, and the sixth year normally marks its termination. It should not be assumed that, with the onset of the oedipal period, oral and anal drives have been eliminated. The theory maintains, rather, that such drives become subordinated to phallic drives, which now assume ascendancy. It is also suggested that the onset of this period is largely determined by the biological maturation of the individual, and evidence has been accumulated which indicates that the genital region does produce pleasurable reactions from stimulation at this time [33].

The psychosexual development of the two sexes differs during this stage, owing presumably to both biological and cultural factors, and we shall sketch the characteristics of the personality development of the boy at this point, referring to that of the girl a bit later. Typically, the boy, who has already developed some identification with his mother and who has interiorized some of her personality characteristics, now becomes aware of increased sexual longing for her. At this time he also becomes more critically aware of the dangers he faces because of these longings since they bring him into more or less direct conflict with his father. The father is perceived as a rival for the mother's love and affection and is feared because he is: (1) bigger and stronger; (2) loved by the mother; (3) needed as a model for identification by the boy if the latter is to assume some of the attributes of the masculine role. The oedipal conflict acquires high emotional intensity as the boy's sexual wishes for the mother and his intense fear of his father come into focus. He becomes fearful that he will be punished because of his sexual longings and that his penis will be cut off in retribution.[2] This fear is partially overcome through the work of repression (see Chapter 4), but that the conflict is very active may be inferred from the changing content of dreams and an increase or emergence of night terrors during this period [34]. The castration threat finds expression in our culture in several ways, such as: (1) the taboo against the public expression of sexual behavior; (2) the increasing awareness in the boy of the differences in the anatomy of the two sexes, which he has difficulty in understanding and is often given little opportunity to discuss; and (3) the boy's sexual drives require that he begin to assume a more "masculine" role, but the familial pattern clearly relegates him to a more subordinate (i.e., less masculine) role than he might have in other types of cultures.

According to Freudian theory, the oedipal problem is only partially solved during the phallic period. Several things normally occur. In the first place, the boy begins to ally himself with his father through identification with him, and he gains some satisfaction from this new relationship. In the second place, since, in fact, he is now more able physically, mentally, and emotionally to be more independent of his mother, he begins to rebel against his mother as he becomes less dependent upon her. This newer orientation concerning his relatively more independent role has been termed *satellization* by Ausubel, a social psychologist [35], who accepts the dynamics of the Freudian explanation but rejects the specific role of sexuality as a primary causative factor. And finally, repression of his oedipal wishes enables the child to renounce his sexual strivings, in part, and to sublimate them into other channels of activity. Freud accounts for the child's intense intellectual curiosity during this period and the extensive character of his exploratory activity as a function of his heightened sexual curiosity. Similarly, he accounts for the reduction in sexual interests at an explicit level, as well as for the increasing inhibition of exploratory behavior, during the next phase of psychosexual development—the

[2] This fear, called the *castration complex,* was first noted by Freud when his patients recounted anxieties of this kind. The phenomenon has also been reported in research studies of children's fears. See [34], for example.

latency period—when repressive forces have succeeded in their operations. But we shall delay discussing the latency period for a moment while we examine the model of interpersonal relationships which the oedipal period suggests.

Prior to the oedipal period the child had developed an intense relationship with only one person—his mother. In this relationship he was first omnipotent during infancy. His every wish seemed to be gratified upon command (typically crying). Yet, at the same time, he was highly dependent in almost all respects upon this very significant person. As he moved through the next period of psychosexual development and gained his first experiences in situations where his "will" opposed that of his mother's, he became somewhat less dependent, less omnipotent, and gradually and increasingly more ambivalent toward his mother. These experiences enabled him to learn to deal with the bilateral relationship in a primitive but realistic way. At this stage he learned the prototypes of all forms of interpersonal relationships. The third party to the familial drama, the father, had not yet fully entered the sphere of interpersonal relationships except as a distant or ghostlike character. However, during the oedipal period the problem became one involving a trilateral relationship, in that two other persons were significant in determining the kind and amounts of gratification the boy would experience as well as the kind and amount of frustration. Thus, the beginnings of a general pattern of interpersonal relationship began to take shape in the oedipal phase of development, for now the boy had to learn to deal with two different and significant people in a close, emotionally charged pattern of relationships. Not only this, but he had to learn to deal with two people of different sexes who had different stimulus values for him since each could only gratify him in somewhat different ways. Thus, during this phase of development he had to learn to deal with the complex patterning of means to satisfy his affectional requirements—how to learn to like, and be liked by, two individuals at the same time without fear of rejection by one if he favored the other. He also had to learn to maintain positive interpersonal relationships while experiencing satisfactions as well as frustrations (in other words, how to solve the problem of dealing with ambivalences).

The development of the girl's personality during the oedipal period is purportedly more complicated than that of the boy's, according to psychoanalytic theory. Like the boy, the girl learns to identify with her mother, but, since the two are of the same sex, there probably are some differences in this identification. Also like the boy, she learns to identify with her father. But, following this, she must re-identify with her mother as she progresses toward her adolescent status. She must, therefore, modify some of her newly acquired phallic attributes and develop feminine modes of behavior which, biologically and culturally, are appropriate for her. Thus she not only has one more general phase in her identification than the boy, but she also has the problem of relinquishing pleasurable modes of behavior as she attempts to assume new roles: passivity, less active physical experiences, and other feminine attributes. Biologically, she will later have to adapt to erotic stimulation from the vagina, rather than from the clitoris alone.

Many of the interpersonal problems involved in this transition from the preoedipal to the postoedipal period involve learning social skills in relating to different people at the same time. The progression in the development of these skills is schematically presented in Figure 3.3.

The Freudian position on the nature and solution of the oedipal problem is highly important because it offers general and creative hypotheses concerning relevant factors in personality development during this formative period. Whether these hypotheses are valid and consistent remains for empirical validation; but they have stimulated a large number of studies and, by proposing at least one way of explaining some aspects of development, have challenged theorists with other viewpoints to present alternate theories which were more rigorous or more compelling, on some or all aspects of the problem. As examples of formulations arrived at by Freud, other than those already mentioned, we may note the following propositions: (1) failure in resolving the oedipal conflict produces a persistent oedipal complex which is the basis of continuing neurotic behavior in later life; (2) excessive harshness in dealing with sexual strivings during the phallic period results in regression (return) to earlier modes of sexual gratification and thus to perversions; (3) inadequate identification with the same-sexed parent results in homosexual development of the individual; (4) an accepting and warm relationship among all three partners in the familial drama encourages more rapid personality maturation and secure general relationships in later life. These are only a few of the most general propositions which have stemmed from

491

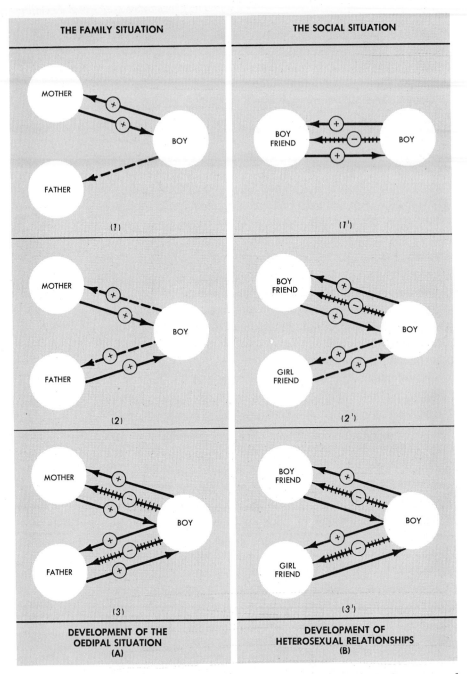

FIGURE 3.3 *Comparison of familial and heterosexual progressions in interpersonal relationships. In column (A) a boy in the first phase (1) is positively attracted to his mother, who loves him, while he is scarcely aware of his father; in phase (2) his positive attraction to his mother has weakened, while a moderately positive relationship with his father has begun; in phase (3) he has positive but slightly ambivalent relationships to both parents. In column (B), the boy has a positive but slightly ambivalent relationship with his boy friend in (1′); in (2′) he has become positively aware of a girl; in (3′) he has developed positive but moderately ambivalent relationships with both sexes.*

Freud's theory. Many others are available in some of the recent reviews of this theory [36, 37].

The latency period   Following the phallic phase of development, the latency period begins, and it continues until physiological changes at puberty usher in the genital phase of development, when sexual strivings arise with increased intensity and old oedipal problems are revived. These and the emerging problems of adolescence have to be dealt with. During the latency period, overt sexual interests and behavior decrease. Boys become more self-conscious, tend to be embarrassed in the presence of girls, and prefer group activity with other boys [38], and the nature of intellectual behavior changes as repression of sexual impulses increases. There is evidence to show, for example, that when the oedipal period is *traumatic* (that is, when there are serious frustrations), far more inhibition of intellectual development occurs than when it is not [39]. There is also evidence to show that even in normal individuals there are significant personality and intellectual differences in the behavior of pre- and postlatency individuals which are consistent with the theory of psychosexual development during latency [40].

The genital period   The last phase of psychosexual development is the genital period. The object of the sexual drives during this period is sexual union with a member of the opposite sex. Since such union is sanctioned only by marriage in our society, and since the age of marriage is generally delayed until well beyond the teens because of the increasingly longer periods of vocational or professional preparation which are required, the individual meets considerable reality frustration in gratifying his sexual needs in a mature manner. Adult genitality involves appropriate "object love," in which the aim of sexual drives is satisfaction from the total interpersonal relationship between the partners. This involves not only satisfaction from the genital sexual experience but mutual and reciprocal satisfactions in offering and receiving affection, adaptation to the needs of each of the partners on a psychological as well as a physical level, and the retention of pregenital satisfactions, such as looking, fondling, and kissing, as an appropriate, but subordinate, part of the genital experience. The genital phase continues until senility, which often brings a return to markedly regressive behavior.

Normal genital development in the psychosexual sense is

dependent, in the first place, upon adequate development through the previous stages of psychosexual development or upon correction for prior maldevelopment. It leads to a successful choice of a partner in marriage (in our culture), to effective work habits, to the capacity to be creative in interpersonal relationships as well as in work, and to adequate sexual gratification as part of the total pattern of effective living. Many individuals never attain true adult sexuality, and many others, having attained it in some precarious fashion, regress under stress or frustration to pregenital forms of adaptation.

Since the crux of the Freudian position on healthy personality development lies in the nature of familial experiences during the preschool and early school periods, we shall now examine some of the evidence concerning this problem.

PATTERNS OF FAMILY RELATIONSHIP On an a priori basis one could attempt to categorize the possible patterns of relationships within the family in an almost infinite number of ways. Nevertheless, both in terms of common observational evidence about the ways in which families function and, more specifically, on the basis of curent theories of personality development, we can make some decisions on how to go about this very complex job. To begin with, we shall examine some important attributes of the child-parent relationship, then consider some evidence on the more general aspects of the emotional climate of the home, and finally turn to problems concerning the effect of sibling relationships on personality development. Clearly, we may be excluding from consideration some important aspects of the problem, but we shall have to content ourselves with the knowledge that, at least, we have sampled the more important aspects of intrafamilial relationships. We shall conclude this section by considering the problem of the degree to which parental attitudes are consistent. The relative consistency of parental attitudes may be expected to have important effects upon the child's personality.

Child-parent relationships The first question to which we shall direct attention is the effect on personality development of acceptance or rejection of the child.

It appears that acceptance or rejection of the child is one of the basic dimensions of child-parent interactions which affect personality development. When the child is rejected, for instance, he is denied other factors which might be useful to him

Child-parent interactions.

in his development. Studies of severely neglected children have shown that they are unable to make use of even intensive help provided by an experienced psychotherapist or are able to make only minimal use of such help [41]. Baldwin and his co-workers have concluded that "acceptance-rejection" is the "fundamental dynamic" which delimits all other aspects of child-parent interactions [42]. But what, exactly, is this "fundamental dynamic"? What is meant by "acceptance" or by "rejection"? Is it the degree of emotional compatibility between child and parent? Is it the degree to which the parent meets the child's biological and psychological needs? Is it the relative *appropriateness* with which the parent *deals with* (methods of child management) the child's needs? Or does it refer only to extremes of overt and communicated acts of acceptance and rejection of the child by his parent? Any or all of these ways of looking at "the dimension" of acceptance-rejection might be useful, but we should expect that different results would be found in studies using different approaches.

Any definition of the acceptance-rejection dimension implies that certain attributes of the behavior of the parent can be assigned to positions along a continuum of this dimension. If this is the case, then we have to examine the effect of acceptance-rejection in terms of the degree to which the phenomenon is manifested rather than in terms of its presence or absence. Unfortunately, most studies have dealt only with the over-all effects of accepting or rejecting parents without defining the degree of the behavior that was present.

Other problems with which psychologists have had to contend in studying this dimension of family life have also beclouded the issue and produced results which sometimes seem contradictory. One of these is the consistency with which a parent behaves in an accepting or rejecting manner over a period of time. It is clear that parents change in this aspect of their behavior. Some parents may find it difficult to accept an infant but easy to accept an older child; some parents may be able to act acceptingly when they are not under severe stress but are unable to function this way when they feel anxious; and some parents may be unable to accept the first child in the family but may later be able to accept this child when there are other children in the family.

Another problem concerns the degree to which the child *feels* accepted or rejected whether or not it was the intent of the parent to have this effect upon him. For example, the same behavior of the parent which the younger child may have experienced as accepting when he was, say, two years old, might be experienced as rejecting when he was four years old and *his* (the child's) attempts to be more assertive or independent had come to the fore. And still another problem concerns the concurrence or disparity in acceptance-rejection by both parents, as opposed to each one singly. This problem may be illustrated by considering the possible effects on the child when he is accepted by the same-sexed parent but is rejected by the opposite-sexed parent, as compared with the reverse condition, when he is rejected by the same-sexed parent but is accepted by the opposite-sexed parent.

We are now ready to summarize three lines of evidence. The first deals with the effects of extreme rejection of the child by both of his parents, or by his mother, during the early formative years of his life. The studies by Spitz, to which we have referred earlier, have indicated that rejection of the child when he is deprived of his mother has devastating effects upon his personality. These findings have been confirmed in studies by Bowlby [43] and Aubry [44]. The effects of rejection differ, however, depending upon the point in the child's life when the rejection occurs. Other studies of "broken homes," in which either or both parents were unable to meet the needs of the child, have indicated that personality disturbances are often (and significantly often) the consequence. For example, delinquency occurs about twice as often among children from broken homes as it does from unbroken homes [45]. These results were not attributable to other variables, such as socioeconomic status, sex of child, and age level of the child when the home was "broken." Studies of institutionalized children, in whose case rejection of needs or failure to meet needs occurs with significant frequency as compared with situations in which children are in their own homes [46], clearly indicate the tendency for such children to be retarded in general behavioral as well as personality development [47].

A second line of evidence deals more specifically with the effects of the relative degree of acceptance and rejection. A series of studies at the Fels Research Institute in Ohio has shown that accepted children tend to be confident and friendly. In addition they tend to be mentally alert and responsive. In contrast, rejected children tend to be lacking in confidence, unstable emotionally, and apathetic or rebellious. They are also apt to do poorer in schoolwork and are less alert mentally [48].

Another way of looking at the problem of acceptance-rejection is to examine the effects of *permissiveness-strictness* of the parent upon the child's behavior. Several lines of evidence converge upon this problem, all of them purporting to demonstrate the effects of such behaviors, which seem to imply acceptance or rejection, respectively, of the child. Some workers from Yale University studied the relations between infant care and illnesses in 75 primitive societies. Whiting focused his analysis on the permissiveness-versus-strictness continuum [49]. It was found that societies which were not permissive and did not gratify the dependency needs of their children had a greater frequency of illness in their children and explained them in terms of possession by spirits or loss of soul, thus attempting to deny their own culpability or responsibility for them. Quite the opposite was found to be true in more permissive societies.

Of course it is a far cry from evidence of relationships of this kind to the assertion that acceptance or rejection *causes* the resulting behaviors. Demonstrations of a causal relationship may be gleaned from the studies of animals as well as from studies of child-parent patterns of interaction. Marx studied the relationship between food deprivation and behavior in a group of rats. One group was deprived of food in infancy, while a control group did not suffer such deprivation [50]. It was found that in adult life the experimental rats, in contrast with the control rats, showed significantly increased tendencies to hoard food. They also displayed a significantly faster eating pace following deprivation of food in adult life than did the control rats.

Goodwin Watson conducted a very carefully controlled study on children coming from homes which differed in permissiveness-strictness [51]. Permissiveness and strictness as concepts are comparable to acceptance and rejection, respectively. All of the children came from "good homes," so that variability in socioeconomic status did not enter into differences found between homes which were "permissive" and those which were "strict." The contrast in his study was made between 34 children in elementary school coming from *fairly permissive* parents (he could not find extremely permissive parents in his relatively middle-class group!) and 47 children coming from homes with extremely strict discipline. The behavior of these two groups of children was evaluated by means of personality tests and by direct observation. He found that those children coming from the strict homes showed no clear personality advantages, whereas, on four of the most reliably rated personality characteristics, those coming from the relatively permissive homes were significantly superior. The permissive group was more independent, more mature in social behavior, more co-operative, and had less inner hostility. Although Watson is cautious in implying a direct causal relationship between the permissiveness-strictness of the home background, on the one hand, and the personality characteristics on the other—for many reasons—his evidence is at least highly suggestive that such a relationship is possible.

A third general line of evidence comes from innumerable clinical studies of children who were found to have been rejected. In evaluating the findings of case studies, we must be careful to note that the usual rigorous controls which thorough research studies require are only rarely possible in this approach and that the bias of the clinical investigator may contaminate the results. Nevertheless, the very massive documentation, from many very different kinds of clinics from different parts of the world with clinicians of different theoretical persuasion, lends credibility to the almost universal finding that rejected children are much more likely to show significant disturbance in their general personality development than accepted children [52, 53]. Rejected children tend to become behavior problems, delinquents, lacking in self-confidence, prone to high anxiety, and unable to function up to the level of their mental capacities. There are exceptions to the general rule, sometimes even remarkable exceptions, and careful study of such cases can lead to more sophisticated hypotheses concerning the specifics of parent-child interactions and their effects. However, exceptions do not necessarily invalidate general findings.

A short presentation of one case of rejection may make some of the mechanisms which produce the aberrant behavior more understandable. The case is presented only for illustrative purposes, and the student who is interested in the problem may refer to the more general literature that has been cited.

A mother brought her nine-year-old boy to one of the writers for clinical evaluation and assistance in guiding him more effectively. She was convinced that her son was somewhat retarded in mental development because he was unable to function in his academic work in school at the level of his chronological age. This was true despite the fact that he had received fairly intensive individual tutoring by a competent remedial teacher. Prior to this tutoring offered at school, the mother had tried to help her son by coaching him at home, but to no avail. She felt that she could not account for her boy's school difficulties other than in terms of inadequate mentality for the work. Investigation revealed that there were no physical factors that might have interfered with his school learning and no special problems in his school experiences which might have handicapped him. In fact, his developmental history and his school experiences were all favorable.

The mother's explanation of her boy's difficulties seemed plausible, at first glance. Her view that his scholastic problems were caused by inadequate mental capacity for his grade seemed consistent with the facts, and her suggestion that, perhaps, he might profit by placement in a "special" class for slow learners seemed reasonable. She also felt that his moderate personality difficulties, such as negativistic behavior, withdrawal tendencies, and lack of self-confidence might be overcome if he were given schoolwork that did not place an undue burden upon him. The mother's orientation seemed to have much to commend it.

However, clinical study of the youngster by means of formal individual tests of intelligence revealed that he was not inferior in intelligence but on the contrary was remarkably superior! He obtained an intelligence quotient of 145 on one of these tests, for example, indicating that he ranked in intelligence well within the upper 1 percent of children of his age. On the other hand, clinical study also showed that he *felt* inferior, believed he was not liked by his mother or by his peers, and had considerable anxiety. He was functioning more than one year below his age level in reading and arithmetic.

Interviews with the mother and the boy brought out the following facts. At the time the mother was pregnant with her son, she was having considerable marital difficulty with her husband, and divorce seemed imminent. She resented being pregnant, for she felt that this would "trap" her; i.e., she would have the additional burden of being responsible for this child when she already had enough problems of her own. She reported that she had another boy, born three years prior to this one, whom she liked and admired because he "was so much like me in so many ways." She reported that when the younger child was born, she resented him, and she noted, soon afterward, that he seemed to resemble his father in some characteristics. She regarded the older boy as "extremely bright," and her evaluation was confirmed by his extremely superior performance in school. She noted that, by the time the younger boy was three years old, the home situation had improved a great deal, and she began to feel more fondness for her younger child. She tried to "make up" to him for the neglect she felt he had suffered during his earlier years. Moreover, since she noted that he was inferior, she tried to "encourage" him to do better, often suggesting he take his older brother as a model and try to emulate him. She found herself pointing out his inadequacies and trying to get him to correct them.

On the other hand, the boy reported that his mother had always liked his older brother better than him, that he "knew" how inferior he was to his brother, that he was always being reminded that his behavior and his school functioning were inadequate, and that he often felt alone and unwanted. He also spoke longingly of his father, who was frequently away for long periods because of his business, and of how little time his father had for the family during the periods when he was at home.

These few statements about this case may suggest some of the factors that were involved in this boy's "retarded" development and his inadequate functioning. Intensive clinical study of the family confirmed the impression that this boy had been severely rejected at both the conscious and unconscious levels. Rejection by his mother was subtle as well as direct; he had also been rejected by his father and by his supposedly "superior" brother.

Corrective measures enabled this boy to function at a superior level in his scholastic work. This process took almost two years' time. During this period the mother became able to deal with her own feelings toward her youngster and to resolve her guilt reactions; she also became able to perceive him in a very favorable light. His improvement during therapy helped her, in turn, to accept him more fully. The youngster needed a considerable amount of psychotherapy to work through his own feelings of rejection and inadequacy and to begin to accept his mother and, in turn, be accepted by her. The schoolteachers needed guidance in managing this boy's school program so as to implement his total progress. Unfortunately, it was not possible to work directly with the father, but he gained some vicarious assistance through the work done with the mother and the boy. When psychotherapy was terminated, this youngster's schoolwork was superior, his social adjustment was quite favorable, he was co-operative at school and at home. He was able to function in a relatively independent fashion, and he had acquired a number of "good friends," with whom he was very happy most of the time.

The case illustrates many things, but in one respect it is typical of what has been reported in the psychological literature about the effects of parental rejection: rejection tends to retard development of the personality, it tends to produce less effective utilization of mental abilities than might otherwise be the case, and it adds a considerable burden to the individual's attempts to

501

adjust to environmental demands. Fortunately, in this case, it was shown that these effects, at least in part, were reversible.

Emotional climate of the home   In recent years considerable research attention has been given to defining, measuring, and evaluating the influence of the emotional climate of the home upon the personality development of the child. As will be seen, some significant degree of convergence in areas to be evaluated and in the significance of the findings has occurred.

Again we must emphasize that the effect of a particular climate in the home depends on factors other than the climate alone. The nature of the child's temperament must be taken into consideration, since the same external conditions of the home would not be presumed to have the same effect upon children with different temperaments. Similarly, the previous experience of the child conditions the way in which he may respond to any given set of conditions defining the climate of his home. Then, too, the consistency in the climate of the home is likely to have important consequences. And, finally, the relation of the home climate to the nature of the culture outside the home, to which the child is exposed, may be of crucial importance, as, for example, when the child is treated indulgently at home but suddenly finds that the world expects him to respond to severe discipline. These illustrations may help to demonstrate how the total complex of factors to which the child is exposed, as well as the nature of the child who is exposed to them, affects the developing personality. The nature of this complex of factors, as well as the degree of its consistency, is significant.

We have already noted the studies by Sears and his co-workers in which types of behavior of the mother, as revealed in interviews and rated by trained workers, were divided into clusters of traits. The most significant clusters that were precipitated by statistical analysis were: permissiveness-strictness; warmth of mother-child relationship; general family adjustment; and responsible child-training. In this study it was found that there were marked differences in the general climate of the home among, for example, middle-class as compared with lower-class homes. This general finding is consistent with many other studies which report the effects of socioeconomic status on home climate and child-parent interactions. (See the book by Symonds for an excellent review of this evidence [54].) It was also learned that the two general characteristics of *permissiveness-strictness* and *warmth* were closely related to personality

The emotional climate of the home.

characteristics of the child in the home. Children coming from *cold, strict* homes tended to be more aggressive, have more feeding problems, and were more persistent bed-wetters than those coming from *warm, permissive* homes. The latter group tended to be more secure and showed far fewer behavior problems. Each of these pairs of conditions was not inevitably associated with the predominant personality characteristics that were obtained. The lack of complete relationship could be due to the unreliabilities of the measuring instruments (as applied to parents and to children), the effect of other concurrent variables, and the constitutional nature of the children—among other possible conditions.

But perhaps we should consider, now, the more general character of the home rather than specific attributes, such as warmth, strictness, and the like. We should like to consider the general attribute of *anxiety*. (See Chapter 4 for a full discussion of this attribute.)

When parents are tense, when they are worried, or when they are in constant conflict with each other, the home atmosphere is likely to be characterized by an emotional turmoil which may be more or less persistent and more or less intense. Anxiety in the parents may take a wide variety of forms and may be manifested in a great variety of ways. (See Chapter 6 for a discussion of the kinds of disorganization in behavior which attend such anxieties.) Such a home climate tends to affect the personality development of children, depending on its intensity and persistence. In a series of studies, MacFarlane was able to show that homes that were high in what we choose to call anxiety (but which she referred to in other terms) tended to have children who were insecure, unco-operative in behavior, quarrelsome, and lacking in intellectual curiosity [55]. Moreover, she and her co-workers were able to show that "high tension" in the home could be measured (as judged by its effects on the behavior of children) very simply by the *number* of unfavorable factors that were present. When only two or fewer unfavorable factors were present, the adverse effects noted were not likely to be present; but when three or more were present, problem behavior, in some form, was very likely to follow. Other studies have reported similar findings [56]. Not only the immediate effects on the personality of the child can be shown to be related to such high-anxiety homes, but the subsequent effects on the poor marital adjustment of children coming from such homes is also demonstrable [57].

High-anxiety homes also produce their inordinate share of children with poor sexual identification, that is, an ambiguous sexual self-picture [58]. This can easily be surmised from our theoretical model of sexual identification presented in the preceding section of this chapter. As far back as 1938, Terman was able to offer empirical evidence that children who came from unhappy homes tended to have unhappy marriages themselves [57]. High anxiety in the home makes it difficult to maintain a consistent relationship with either parent in a healthy, nonconflictful relationship. The constant struggle to maintain loyalties to both parents, to avoid antagonisms, to avoid stirring things up still more by showing any preference for either parent, and to find a secure model from which to learn appropriate modes of behavior—all contribute to an ineffectual identity as well as to other personality problems.

Recent evidence suggests that it will be possible to describe adequately the major aspects of the home climate in terms of perhaps four or five major dimensions [26]. Among these, the dimension of *autonomy-control* surely seems to have an important place. This dimension refers to the relative degree of independence which is fostered in the child by virtue of parental attitudes which maximize his growth toward autonomy in his behavior, i.e., independence from external controls and spontaneity derived from effective internal controls. "External control" seems to refer to the degree to which parents impose upon the child an authoritarian regime, i.e., dependence upon strict, rigid, suppressive discipline.

Some years ago, Adorno and others proposed the concept of the authoritarian personality [59]. Evidence derived from many types of observation and measurement indicated that, when parents are severely supressive in their modes of discipline, the members of the family tend to become authoritarian in their orientation toward the world. Children in such families are unable to express their hostile feelings against the parents and tend to repress them. They find it necessary in later life to find models of identification which are strong, sadistic, and prejudiced in their orientation toward others. They give vent to their aggression against minority groups and against passive and less dominant individuals. Moreover, such individuals externalize

505

blame for their faults and tend to be rigid in their thinking processes.

Recent evidence from the California Growth Studies [60, 61] indicates that a high degree of control in the home produces a number of unfavorable effects in the children. These effects differ, depending upon whether or not there is consistency in the behaviors of the pair of parents and depending on the age and sex of the child.

Generally speaking, when one parent is hostile, the other tends to be similar [62]. Hence, the effects of this factor are likely to be maximized. Moreover, it appears that aggression in parents tends to have more adverse effects upon girls than upon boys, at least during the early years of life of the child. This latter finding may be an artifact in that most of the studies investigated the behavior of the mothers and not the fathers, so that, when differences in severity of control or in hostility did occur between the parents, it was the mother who was high on these characteristics in the studies cited, and her effect upon the girl may have been more devastating than upon the boy. In such cases, when the father was less severe and hostile, the boy was able to identify with a more democratic father and experience less frustration in his need-satisfaction. Therefore, he may have shown less aggression in his behavior. The major findings, however, should not be lost sight of since, in the main, they confirm the general conclusions of the previous authoritarian studies as well as the recent studies by Sears and his group. The personality characteristics which seem to result from controlling homes include rudeness, irritability, impulsivity, and the like.

Another of the dimensions of home climate upon which recent evidence has converged is that of warmth-coldness [62]. Again, the student should refer to the study by Sears, reported earlier in this chapter. That warmth-coldness is, indeed, a most powerful factor is shown by the consistency with which numerous studies report similar findings. Again, there are differences between children of the two sexes, but these are not as striking as in the case of the dimension of autonomy-control. The studies by Symonds and the recent work of the California Growth Studies show similar trends. Warmth in the home (defined operationally as concern over the children, affection in the relationship, and sensitivity to the needs expressed by the children) tends to beget secure, affectionate, happy, and co-operative behavior in the child. Intellectual curiosity is heightened. Emotionally stable behavior tends to become characteristic.

We still do not have adequate evidence about at least two major questions related to the problem of the effect of such a climate upon the personality. One of these is the extent to which these effects persist into later childhood and adulthood, although there is some evidence to suggest that the correlations between degree of warmth shown by the parents and the personality characteristics in the child diminish as the child gets older. This decreasing correlation may be due to the diminishing effect of the parental behavior as the child becomes older. Then, too, many other factors outside the home have increasingly greater effect as he gets older. The relatively lower correlations may also be due to the inadequacy of the devices employed to measure the behaviors that are involved. However, as the study by Brody on the interactions of mothers and their infants showed, at least the beginnings of personality development in the child are strongly influenced by the degree of warmth shown by the mother [10], and since the effects during early years of life are also pronounced, as shown by other studies, the dimension of warmth-coldness is a powerful one indeed, no matter what the subsequent variations in personality development may be. It is certainly important to get a good start in life, and warmth in the home seems to be highly important in this regard.

The other question concerns the kinds of behavior which warmth-coldness encompasses. One writer calls this dimension warmth-hostility, for example [64]. Is this dimension related— and, if so, to what degree—to anxiety or to autonomy in the parents? In other words, we are asking whether these dimensions are truly independent aspects of parental behavior or home climate. It will remain the task of future research to clarify the definitions of these, and possibly other, dimensions, to provide increasingly more effective methods for assessing them, and to investigate the nature of th causal connections between them and personality development.

Becker has attempted to integrate the findings from a number of studies, including his own, concerning the primary variables necessary to categorize parent behavior [63]. His analysis leads him to postulate at least three general dimensions: *warmth-hostility, restrictiveness-permissiveness,* and *anxious-emotional involvement versus calm-detachment*. This organization of parental behavior makes use of the repeated findings from various studies of the interrelationships of various kinds of more specific parental behaviors.

In his review of the research literature, Becker finds support for the importance of warmth and permissiveness in the home in "facilitating the growth of sociable, independent children. . . ." He notes the ". . . debilitating effects of parental hostility." He also finds it possible that the use of threats to the love relationship between parent(s) and child is so powerful that the ". . . development of independence is jeopardized."

An interesting subsidiary finding is that, when the effects of both the mother's and the father's behavior are evaluated in relation to the development of the child, the influence of the father turns out to be at least as great of that of the mother. Since most studies, in the past, have neglected to consider the influence of the father (and many workers have considered it to be negligible), it is apparent that the importance of the father cannot be overlooked.

Although no final answers have been given, the current status of our evidence is that certain child-parent patterns of interaction and the general nature of the emotional climate in the home exert a powerful impact upon personality development of the child. Moreover, the evidence to date, taken as a whole, is not inconsistent with the major premises of the Freudian theoretical position, although there are many questions still to be answered, and some other theoretical view may· prevail in the end. We have attempted to represent our current knowledge concerning the factors in child-parent relationships and their consequences in Figure 3.4.

Sibling relationships   The case that was discussed in a previous section illustrates some of the possible effects of the relationships between siblings in the family. In this instance, it was suggested that the more favorable attitudes of the mother toward the older brother, as well as the superior accomplishments of this older brother, adversely affected the development of the younger brother's personality and school achievement. All of us have known of instances in which the relationships between siblings presumably influenced the development of each of them. The older good and kind brother who was a mountain of strength to his younger brother may have compensated, in a particular family, for tension between parents and even for neglect by such parents. The "baby" brother in the family who was "spoiled" by all of his older siblings may have become a

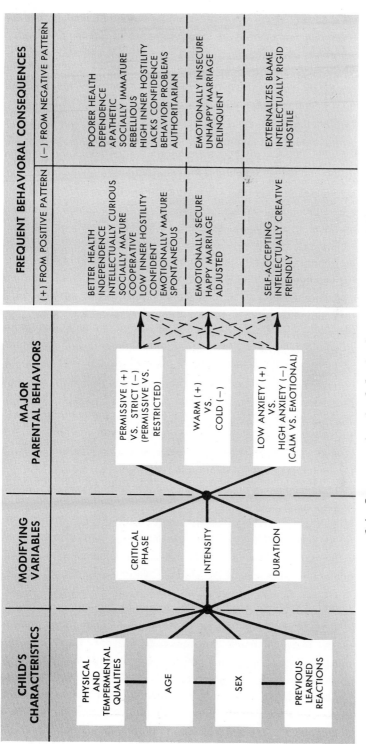

FIGURE 3.4 *Summary of major behavioral consequences in children resulting from three patterns of parental behaviors and other interacting factors.*

very passive, self-indulgent, and dependent individual. Or the older sister in a family of four younger brothers, who was given the chore of taking care of her younger siblings and who was considered less important in the family simply because she was a girl, may have learned to dislike not only her brothers but most males as well.

The effects siblings have upon each other are likely to have significant repercussions upon personality development, because, aside from the parents, siblings are long-term and relatively consistent agents in the socializing process, and they serve as close-range models of behavior for each other. These effects are difficult to determine precisely. The research problems involved in analyzing the possible effects of various types of sibling relationships take into consideration all of the variant and complex conditions of the home which we have discussed previously. In addition, the relative comparability of different sibling patterns may be a function of the characteristics of the parents. These characteristics may affect the number and age distribution of their children. Moreover, cultural factors affect the different kinds of roles assigned to siblings quite apart from other conditions which exist within the family. For example, older children in Western working-class families have real and important authority in supervising their younger siblings, whereas older children in Western middle-class families have relatively little authority in such relationships [64]. Consequently, the effect of being an older or younger child in a given family tends to vary in relation to these "external factors."

It shall be our purpose in the remaining portion of this section to discuss a few of the many problems concerning the impact of sibling relationships upon personality development. It is interesting that only one psychologist, Alfred Adler, has attempted to propose a relatively comprehensive theoretical analysis of the effects of sibling relationships on personality development, and he emphasized the effects of the *ordinal* position of the child on his personality characteristics.

Quite a good deal is now known concerning the relationships of the factor of being "an only child" to personality development. For one thing, only children are far more likely to occur in families of upper socioeconomic status than in lower-class families. For another, only children are more likely than children who have siblings to show emotional problems in adjustment [65] and are more likely to be overindulged and to suffer from "Momism" [41]. However, research evidence has not completely demonstrated this to be a specific consequence of being an only child, since emotional and situational characteristics of parents who have only one child may be different from parents with several children. Thus it may be that the combination of special parental characteristics plus the fact of being an only child may produce the personality characteristics found in the youngster.

Now what happens when there is more than one child in the family? Although there is no inevitability about it, research evidence clearly indicates that the birth of the second child tends to have an adverse effect, at least temporarily, upon the first child [66]. This finding is, in some respects, contrary to the commonly held belief (less common now than it was before some of the research findings became widely known) that the older child is bound to love his new sibling, greet him with excitement and tenderness, and constructively assimilate him into the household. The adverse effects upon the older child constitute a kind of *syndrome,* that is, a more or less characteristic cluster of reactions. He tends to regress in his behavior (see Chapter 4 for a discussion of this phenomenon), he becomes jealous and hostile, and his relationship with his parents becomes more unstable. These effects may be minimized by a number of conditions, such as the age spread between the siblings [67] (an age difference of four or more years produces quite different reactions than a smaller age spread), the total number of children in the family, and, perhaps most important of all, the emotional security of the older child [68, 69]. The adverse effect upon the older child may occur with greater likelihood when other conditions are unfavorable. When other conditions are favorable, the adverse effects are likely to be only temporary and may even assist in emotional maturation if the older child, by learning that he can express negative feelings, thus gains more security in dealing with frustration.

It is also clear that the *ordinal* position of the child in the family influences his personality development. Present evidence points to a few important generalizations about ordinal position, but the student should be reminded that these conclusions need further research appraisal. There is a tendency for the youngest child in the family to be more ambitious, more competitive, and more outgoing than his older siblings [67]. One possible effect of having older siblings, who appear to be in more favorable positions by virtue of their greater maturity, is that they act as models against which one must compete. Aspiration levels may be raised by the constant presence of these visible older competitors. On the other hand, the oldest child is more likely than his siblings to be withdrawn, perhaps shy, and to show more variability in mood [67]. The position of middle children tends to be intermediate between these two extremes.

We should emphasize that the range in ages of the siblings as well as the distribution of the sexes may significantly affect the influence of ordinal position. It is also evident that the size of the family group has important bearings upon the personality development of the several members of the family. Although it is hard to pin down specific cause-and-effect relationships between each of the several factors in sibling relationships and personality attributes, the cumulative evidence, both research and clinical, has clearly indicated that these relationships are relevant and substantial.

Consistency of parental attitudes   We have noted that the behavior of parents changes as they get older. As they gain more experience in dealing with each other and their children, as they react to favorable and traumatic events in their lives, and as they acquire new values in the very process of living and adapting, they become at least a little different. After all, *parents are people,* and people do change even though the "core" of personality may remain relatively stable. One of the puzzling questions we need to consider is how relative consistency or inconsistency over time in parental attitudes toward their children affects the personality development of their children. To provide answers to the implications of this broad question probably requires long-term longitudinal studies of both parents and their children, and as yet we have no definitive evidence on this problem. This lack of information is due to many factors, such as the great expense of conducting such studies, the operational and methodological difficulties in such studies, and the need for development of appropriate measuring instruments which are useful over a wide span of ages. Some of the longitudinal research projects we have referred to in preceding sections may soon produce evidence on some phases of this broad problem. However, in the past, investigators have assumed that parental attitudes have remained stable over time.

Pertinent to this problem is the work that has been done on

consistency of traits among adults. The general finding that may be summarized is that adult personality tends to remain reasonably consistent but that, with increasing age, predictable trends in certain directions occur. The first half of this conclusion may be better understood if it is stated in some numerical fashion, as follows: there is a tendency for most personality characteristics of adults to show self-correlations between about .40 and .60 over a relatively short period of time (say, over a five-year span). Such a finding indicates that the individual tends to rate or score about the same, within reasonably wide limits, on specific personality characteristics. Nevertheless, such correlations are far from perfect, and considerable fluctuation may occur for any given individual. The second half of the conclusion may be made more explicit by indicating that, with increasing age, there is a tendency toward more rigid moral attitudes, more conservative ethical and political thinking, and more rigid behavior [70].

There is also evidence that, as adults get older, particularly after thirty–forty years of age, they tend to show diminished interest and participation in athletic activities, they become more anxious, and they change in their self-concepts in that they become more uncertain about their values and have more self-deprecatory attitudes [70, 71]. Some of these changes may be attributable, in large part, to physiological changes associated with aging, while others may be attributable to increasing concern with physical limitation due to illness, the process of physical aging, and death.

Two recent studies concerned with a longitudinal approach to personality attributes are of special interest. The first, by Kagan, studied the stability of passive and dependent behavior [72]. From the latency period to the adult years, these personality attributes remain fairly stable in women, but they are far from stable in men. Thus, there is a difference between the sexes in the relative stability of these traits, possibly associated with cultural factors which enable women to retain more stable passive and dependent roles than men.

Kelly has reported on the follow-up results obtained from a group of 300 engaged couples over a time span of approximately 18 years [73]. Because of various factors, a certain number of these individuals were unable to participate in the follow-up testing. Nevertheless, a large number of cases remained, upon whom original and retest results were obtained

(215 males and 231 females). Kelly's findings represent unique types of data on the problem of consistency of the adult personality. But first, we must note that the subjects were a highly select group of individuals, not representative of the general population. They were superior in intelligence, superior in education (75 percent had at least one year of college), mostly between 21 and 30 years of age at the time of initial testing, and were living in New England when the study began. The retest correlations for personal values (as measured by the Allport-Vernon Scale) ranged from about .30 to about .60. The attitudes of these individuals (as measured by Remmers' Attitude Scales) were far less stable, the retest correlations ranging from about .06 to about .35. In fact, the retest on "attitudes toward marriage" indicated that there was no consistency for these individuals on this factor over the approximately 20-year span. On the other hand, vocational interest (as measured by the Strong Interest Test) remained the most stable of any of the attributes measured; the median retest correlation over the several categories of vocational interest was .62 for men and .57 for women. The retest correlations for personality attributes as measured by the Bernreuter Personality Test were almost as high as for the Interest Scales; .61 for self-confidence and about .46 for sociability.

The highest consistencies were found in values and vocational interests, and the lowest were found in attitudes. Of course, the absence of very high correlations may be due, in part, to the fact that none of the measures used has perfect reliability, but the fact that the obtained correlations were lower than the reliabilities of the instruments indicates the absence of absolute consistency in these attributes of the adults. Kelly interprets his data to show that "absolute changes in personality scores tended to be small but similar in direction and magnitude for men and women." He also adds, "But we also found evidence for considerable change in all variables measured," and "Our findings indicate that *significant changes* [our italics] in the human personality may continue to occur during the years of adulthood."

Taking all of the known evidence into consideration, we may conclude that some parents show very considerable change in personality, although most show only moderate change. Changes in attitudes toward others and toward the self are likely to be far from stable, and these attitudes tend to become more conservative, rigid, puritanical, and punitive as the adult gets older.

Not only may the same child receive different treatment from his parents as he and they get older, but children coming into the family at different times in the lives of the parents may receive quite different treatment from the "same" parents. Children born when the parents are relatively young may be treated with greater tolerance and beneficence. Those children who happen to have parents who are highly inconsistent in personality and attitudes over time may be subjected, therefore, to the traumatic impact which such inconsistency imposes.

We stated at the beginning of this section that evidence on the consistency of parental attitudes was far from adequate. Our survey of the literature reveals very little that is directly pertinent to the problem of changing attitudes of parents toward their children. We have even less evidence on the possible effects such inconsistencies may have on the specific personality characteristics of the children. We can only surmise that such inconsistencies have an important bearing on the developing personality. There is considerable suggestive evidence from clinical psychology, especially from case studies in which psychotherapy of the parents was associated with changes in parental attitudes. Such changes seem to have highly significant effects on the personality development of the children involved. This appears to be especially the case when parents move from more negative to more positive attitudes toward their children's behavior and toward more accepting relationships with them. Such clinical evidence is consistent with the empirical studies on the effects of rejection and acceptance on the development of the personality characteristics of the child.

References

1. Allport, G. W. *Pattern and Growth in Personality.* New York: Holt, Rinehart and Winston, 1961.
2. Gesell, A., & Ilg, F. L. *Child Development.* New York: Harper & Row, 1949.
3. Ribble, M. *The Rights of Infants.* New York: Columbia Univ. Press, 1943.
4. Kardiner, A. *The Frontiers of Society.* New York: Columbia Univ. Press, 1945.

5. Benedict, R. Child-rearing in certain European countries. *Amer. J. Orthopsychiat.*, 1949, **19**, 342–350.
6. Gesell, A., & Ilg, F. L. *Infant and Child in the Culture of Today*. New York: Harper & Row, 1943.
7. Goldman-Eisler, F. Breastfeeding and character formation. In C. Kluckhohn & H. A. Murray (Eds.), *Personality in Nature, Society, and Culture*. New York: Knopf, 1953.
8. Maslow, A. H., & Szilagyi-Kessler, I. Security and breast-feeding. *J. abnorm. soc. Psychol.*, 1946, **41**, 83–85.
9. Peterson, C. H., & Spano, F. L. Breast feeding, maternal rejection, and child personality. *Charact. & Pers.*, 1941, **10**, 62–66.
10. Brody, S. *Patterns of Mothering*. New York: International Universities Press, 1956.
11. Heinstein, M. I. Behavioral correlates of breast-bottle regimes under varying parent-infant relationships. *Monogr. Soc. Res. Child Develpm.*, 1963, **28**, No. 4.
12. Yarrow, L. J. The relationship between nutritive sucking experiences in infancy and non-nutritive sucking in childhood. *J. genet. Psychol.*, 1954, **84**, 149–162.
13. Murphy, L. B., et al. *The Widening World of Childhood*. New York: Basic Books, 1962.
14. Fries, M. E. The child's ego development and the training of adults in his development. In R. S. Eissler, A. Freud, H. Hartmann, & M. Kris (Eds.), *The Psychoanalytic Study of the Child*, Vol. II. New York: International Universities Press, 1946.
15. Escalona, S. K. Feeding disturbances in very young children. *Amer. J. Orthopsychiat.*, 1945, **15**, 76–80.
16. Weininger, O. The effects of early experience upon behavior and growth characteristics. *J. comp. physiol. Psychol.*, 1956, **49**, 1–9.
17. Thompson, W. R., & Heron, W. The effect of restricting early experience on the problem solving capacity of dogs. *Canad. J. Psychol.*, 1954, **8**, 17–31.
18. Pfaffenberger, C. J., & Scott, J. P. The relationship between delayed socialization and trainability of guide dogs. *J. genet. Psychol.*, 1959, **95**, 145–155.
19. Riesen, A. H. Brain and behavior. Session 1. Symposium, 1959. Effects of stimulus deprivation on the development and atrophy of the visual sensory system. *Amer. J. Orthopsychiat.*, 1960, **30**, 23–36.
20. Seitz, P. F. D. Infantile experience and adult behavior in animal subjects. II, Age of separation from the mother and adult behavior in the cat. *Psychosomat. Med.*, 1959, **21**, 353–378.
21. Harlow, H. F. The nature of love. *Amer. Psychologist*, 1958, **13**, 673–685.
22. Harlow, H. F., & Zimmerman, R. R. Affectional responses in the infant monkey. *Science*, 1959, **130**, 421–432.

23. Dennenberg, V. H., & Bell, R. W. Critical periods for the effects of infantile experience on adult learning. *Science,* 1960, **131,** 227–228.

24. Meier, G. W., & Stuart, J. L. Effects of handling on the physical and behavioral development of Siamese kittens. *Psychol. Repts.,* 1959, **5,** 497–501.

25. Erikson, E. H. *Childhood and Society.* New York: Norton, 1951.

26. Becker, W. C. Developmental psychology. In P. R. Farnsworth, O. McNemar, & Q. McNemar (Eds.), *Annual Review of Psychology,* Vol. 13. Palo Alto: Annual Reviews, 1962.

27. Erikson, E. H. The problem of ego identity. In M. R. Stein *et al.* (Eds.), *Identity and Survival.* New York: Free Press, 1960.

28. Sears, R. R., Macoby, E. E., & Levin, H. *Patterns of Child Rearing.* New York: Harper & Row, 1957.

29. Spitz, R. A. The importance of the mother-child relationship during the first years of life: A synopsis in five sketches. *Ment. Hlth. Today,* 1947, **8.**

30. Pinneau, S. R. The infantile disorders of hospitalism and anaclitic depression, *Psychol. Bull.,* 1955, **52,** 429–452.

31. Dennis, W. Infant development under conditions of restricted practice and of minimum social stimulation. *Genet. Psychol. Monogr.,* 1941, **23,** 143–189.

32. Freud, S. *General Introduction to Psychoanalysis.* New York: Garden City, 1943.

33. Katcher, A. The discrimination of sex differences by young children. *J. genet. Psychol.,* 1955, **87,** 131–143.

34. Jersild, A. T. Studies of children's fears. In R. G. Barker *et al.* (Eds.), *Child Behavior and Development: A Course of Representative Studies.* New York: McGraw-Hill, 1943.

35. Ausubel, D. P. *Ego Development and the Behavior Disorders.* New York: Grune & Stratton, 1952.

36. Gill, M. The present state of psychoanalytic theory. *J. abnorm. soc. Psychol.,* 1959, **58,** 1–8.

37. Rapaport, D. The structure of psychoanalytic theory: A systematizing attempt. In S. Koch (Ed.), *Psychology: A Study of a Science,* Vol. III: *Formulations of the Person and the Social Context.* New York: McGraw-Hill, 1959.

38. Bonney, M. E. Sex differences in social success and personality traits. *Child Develpm.,* 1944, **15,** 63–79.

39. Friedman, S. M. An empirical study of the castration and Oedipal complexes. *Genet. Psychol. Monogr.,* 1952, **46,** 61–130.

40. Gurin, M. G. Differences in psychological characteristics of latency and adolescence: A test of relevant psychoanalytic propositions, utilizing projective material. Unpublished Ph.D. dissertation, University of Michigan, 1953.

41. Levy, D. M. *Maternal Overprotection.* New York: Columbia Univ. Press, 1943.
42. Baldwin, A. L., Kallhorn, J., & Breese, S. Patterns of parent behavior. *Psychol. Monogr.,* 1945, **58,** No. 3.
43. Bowlby, J. Maternal care and mental health. *World Health Technical Monogr.* (series), Geneva: World Health Organization, 1951.
44. Aubry, J. The case of Monique. In K. Soddy (Ed.), *Mental Health and Infant Development,* Vol. I. New York: Basic Books, 1956.
45. Louttit, C. M. *Clinical Psychology.* New York: Harper & Row, 1947.
46. Rheingold, H. L. The modification of social responsiveness in institutional babies. *Soc. Res. Child Develpm.,* 1956, **21,** No. 63.
47. Goldfarb, W. Infant rearing and problem behavior. *Amer. J. Orthopsychiat.,* 1943, **13,** 149–165.
48. Baldwin, A. L. *Behavior and Development in Childhood.* New York: Holt, Rinehart and Winston, 1955.
49. Whiting, J. W. M., & Child, I. L. *Child Training and Personality.* New Haven: Yale, 1953.
50. Marx, M. H. Experimental analysis of the hoarding habit in the rat. III, Terminal reinforcement under low drive. *J. comp. physiol. Psychol.,* 1957, **50,** 168–171.
51. Watson, G. Some personality differences in children related to strict or permissive parental discipline. *J. Psychol.,* 1957, **44,** 227–249.
52. Bettleheim, B. *Love Is Not Enough.* New York: Free Press, 1950.
53. English, O. S., & Pearson, G. H. J. *Emotional Problems of Living.* New York: Norton, 1955.
54. Symonds, P. M. *The Dynamics of Parent-Child Relationships.* New York: Teachers College, 1949.
55. MacFarlane, J. W., Allen, L., & Honzik, M. P. A developmental study of the behavior problems of normal children between twenty-one months and fourteen years. *University of California Publ. Child Develpm.,* 1954, No. 2.
56. Becker, W. C. The relationship of factors in parental ratings of self and each other to the behavior of kindergarten children as rated by mothers, fathers, and teachers. *J. consult. Psychol.,* 1960, **24,** 507–527.
57. Ternan, L. M., & Oden, M. H. *The Gifted Child Grows Up: Twenty-five Years' Follow-up of a Superior Group.* Stanford, Calif.: Stanford Univ. Press, 1947.
58. Rabbah, M. Sex-role identification in young children in two diverse social groups. *Genet. Psychol. Monogr.,* 1950, **42,** 81–158.
59. Adorno, T. W., et al. *The Authoritarian Personality: Studies in Prejudice Series.* New York: Harper & Row, 1950.

60. Schaefer, E. S., & Baylor, N. Consistency of maternal behavior from infancy to preadolescence. *J. abnorm. soc. Psychol.,* 1960, **61,** 1–6.

61. Schaefer, E. S. Converging conceptual models for maternal behavior and for child behavior. Paper presented at Conference on Research on Parental Attitudes and Child Behavior, Washington Univ., St. Louis, Mo., March, 1960.

62. Becker, W. C., *et al.* Relations of factors derived from parent-interview ratings to behavior problems of five-year-olds. *Child Develpm.,* 1962, **33,** 509–535.

63. Becker, W. C. Consequences of different kinds of parental discipline. In M. L. Hoffman & L. W. Hoffman (Eds.), *Review of Child Development Research,* Vol. I. New York: Russell Sage Foundation, 1964.

64. Hutt, M. L., & Miller, D. P. Social values and personality development. *J. soc. Issues,* 1949, No. 4. (Whole issue.)

65. Sewall, M. Two studies in sibling rivalry. I, Some causes of jealousy in young children. *Smith College Stud. soc. Work,* 1930, **1,** 6–26.

66. Bossard, J. H., & Sanger, M. The large family. *Amer. sociol. Rev.,* 1952, **17,** 3–9.

67. Koch, H. L. Some personality correlates of sex, sibling position and sex of sibling among five- and six-year-old children. *Genet. Psychol. Monogr.,* 1955, **52,** 3–50.

68. Schachter, S. Birth order, eminence, and higher education. *Amer. sociol. Rev.,* 1963, **28,** 757–768.

69. Schaefer, E. S., & Bayley, N. Maternal behavior, child behavior, and their intercorrelations from infancy through adolescence. *Monogr. Soc. Res. Child Develpm.,* 1963, **28,** 1–127.

70. Cavan, R. S., Burgess, E. W., Havighurst, R. J., & Goldhammer, H. *Personal Adjustment in Old Age.* Chicago: Science Research, 1945.

71. Havighurst, R. J., & Albrecht, P. *Older People.* New York: Longmans, 1953.

72. Kagan, J., & Moss, H. A. The stability of passive and dependent behavior from childhood through adulthood. *Child Develpm.,* 1960, **31,** 577–591.

73. Kelly, E. L. The re-assessment of specific attitudes after twenty years. *J. soc. Issues,* 1961, **17,** 29–37.

FOUR CONFLICT, ANXIETY, DEFENSE, AND COPING

Introduction

We shall now turn our attention to some of the important ways in which an individual deals with external frustrations and internal sources of conflict. Even under the best of circumstances, the development of one's personality is never smooth and regular. It follows an irregular path as the individual moves from infancy to adulthood, sometimes moving rapidly ahead and at other times halting in its development or even moving backwards.

The sources of this irregularity in development lie both within the organism and in the conditions to which it is exposed. In the

520

present chapter, we shall learn how the individual, whatever his resources may be, copes with the problems of living and adapting to varied situations. Such problems often lead to conflict within the individual, and in turn anxiety may be aroused. As we shall see, the ways in which an individual learns to react to conflict and anxiety are of critical importance in his over-all development.

In the following sections we shall discuss the nature of conflict, and we shall learn how conflict leads to various kinds of anxiety reactions. Then we shall discuss the kinds of defenses which the individual learns to employ in dealing with conflicts and anxiety. In short, we shall learn how the individual contends with the stresses and strains of living.

Conceptualization of Conflict

The term *conflict* has been defined in a number of ways, but we shall consider its theoretical meaning as first developed by Kurt Lewin and which has received wide acceptance [1].

We should first distinguish between *conflict* and *frustration*. Let us assume that the individual wishes to reach some goal. If, now, some obstacle is placed in the path toward this goal, the satisfaction of the wish is frustrated or blocked. Frustration may be thought of as some thwarting circumstance which impedes progress toward a goal. Figure 4.1 illustrates schematically two kinds of thwarting circumstances: one in which the path toward a goal is blocked by a barrier and another in which the goal cannot be fulfilled because the situation lacks the means with which to achieve the goal. In the first instance, for example, a person is frustrated when motivated to eat, but something in the situation prevents him from getting to the food. In the second instance, he is motivated to eat, but there is no food available to him. Psychologists have studied reactions to frustration extensively. They have shown that at times frustrations lead to anger and aggression, produce an increment in the motive (the person "struggles harder to reach his goal"), lead to withdrawal from the situation or to other "defensive" reactions, but sometimes lead to problem-solving responses that circumvent the frustrating agent.

By contrast, conflict refers to certain *internal* conditions which block effective goal-directed behavior. At any given

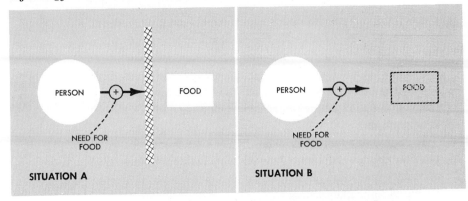

FIGURE 4.1 *Two types of frustrating situations. Situation (A): need for food is frustrated by an obstacle. Situation (B): need for food is frustrated by absence of food.*

moment, each person is being "prodded" by many motives. The term "motive," as we use it here, refers to the condition of the organism which influences the direction, intensity, and/or persistence of a behavioral sequence. The essence of a conflict condition, then, involves the *simultaneous arousal of two or more motives which are, in some degree, competing with each other*.

TYPES OF CONFLICT Lewin suggested that there are three types of basic conflict situations. In the first, the individual is simultaneously motivated to approach and to avoid the same

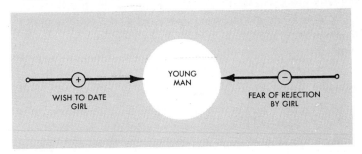

FIGURE 4.2 *Approach-avoidance conflict. Young man wishes to date girl (+), but is fearful of rejection (−).*

goal. This is called the *approach-avoidance* conflict. (See Figure 4.2.) Examples of such conflicts in human affairs are legion. A young man wishes to call a girl for a date, but he is fearful of rejection. Until he can resolve this dilemma, he is in a state of conflict. If the approach and avoidance motives are equally strong, tension may become very high. Such conflict states are called *ambivalent states,* and the individual may be unable to make any decision. Other examples of approach-avoidance conflicts will surely come to the reader's mind. College students are frequently faced with such conflicts in taking examinations. They wish to take the examination and do well on it but are fearful of failure. They may, therefore, engage in a variety of defensive behaviors. They may "forget" to study; they may leave the examination room very early because of high anxiety; they may try to study more intensively; they may "freeze" during the examination.

As our subsequent discussion in this chapter will demonstrate, approach-avoidance conflicts are both extremely important and frequent in human adjustment and personality development. There are many examples of this type of conflict situation. Such conflicts are likely to lead to disorganized and more primitive response patterns of behavior. Clinical studies and research have shown that in many approach-avoidance conflict situations the individual is "drawn" toward the goal by the approach motivation, but, as he gets nearer to it, the strength of the avoidance motivation becomes rapidly greater. The phenomenon is like that of the young man who finds that a certain girl seems attractive and exciting to him, so he hurriedly arranges a date, "forgetting" meanwhile that she has many undesirable characteristics. It is like the problem of the mountain-climber who "remembers" how much fun it is to climb a mountain, but, until he reaches the site of the mountain climb or until he is well up on its slopes, he "forgets" that there are many dangers. In such instances, the sudden emergence of anxiety as the "goal" is approached may lead to disorganized or defensive behavior.

These illustrations also involve the principle of the *approach-avoidance gradient.* In the first illustration, for example, the young man may remember the girl's negative qualities more readily as the time for his date approaches. Even closer to the date, he might "forget" his appointment entirely. This is an example of the psychological effects produced by different *slopes* of approach and avoidance gradients. They were first found in studies of animal behavior [2]. Measuring the amount of effort expended by the animals in reaching a positive goal or in trying to get away from a negative, unpleasant goal results in observations like those in Figure 4.3. This means that the positive,

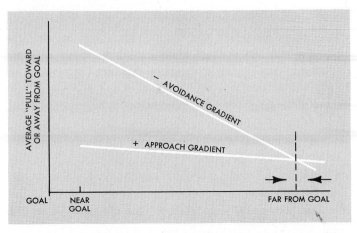

FIGURE 4.3 *Illustration of approach and avoidance gradients based on amount of effort expended by animals in attempting to approach or move away from a goal. Note greater steepness of avoidance gradient as compared to approach gradient. Arrows indicate points at which animals would run toward or away from goal. Adapted from N. E. Miller. Experimental studies in conflict. In J. McV. Hunt (Ed.),* Personality and the Behavior Disorders. *New York: The Ronald Press, 1944, p. 434. Copyright 1944 The Ronald Press Company.*

approach tendencies are exhibited over a larger area than the negative, avoidant tendencies. The avoidance tendencies have steeper slopes and are more concentrated near the goal.

The second and third types of conflict situations have much in common. In both there are *two goals,* and the response tendencies are in a *similar direction.* One of these types of conflicts is called the *approach-approach* conflict. The other is termed the *avoidance-avoidance* conflict.

In the approach-approach conflict situation, the individual is faced with two positive, approach alternatives. (See Figure 4.4.) His problem now is to decide between them. Should he date Sally or Mary, both of whom he finds very attractive? Should he go to a large or a small college, both of which have advantages for him? Should he go to a movie or attend the basketball game? In situations such as these there may be some vacillation in choosing a course of action, but a choice will probably be made after a period of time. However, if the goals are about equally attractive or if there is strong personal involvement in the choice, the decision may become much more difficult [3]. In such instances, there may be long delay or even

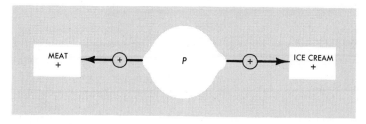

FIGURE 4.4   *The approach-approach conflict situation. The person P is faced with two approach alternatives.*

inability in making a choice, or there may be alternation in the choices, if this is possible. Some form of compromise solution may also be sought.

When we have to face two unpleasant goals that we wish to avoid, so that in either we are confronted with an avoidance-avoidance type of conflict, the appropriate behavior would involve avoidance or withdrawal. Many situations of this type arise in the course of daily living. (See Figure 4.5.) For

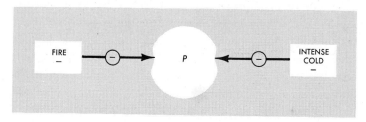

FIGURE 4.5   *The avoidance-avoidance conflict situation. The person P is faced with two avoidance alternatives.*

example, we may be offered a choice of two kinds of food, but both are disliked. Or we may have to choose between two courses to fulfill a college requirement, but both are uninteresting. In such instances, we might try to avoid the entire situation or do nothing. If forced to make a choice, we might vacillate for a long time.

LEVELS OF CONFLICT   There is another way in which conflicts may vary. This relates to the degree to which the individual is aware of the presence of various motives. It is a commonplace observation that one may "suddenly" feel very tired, or develop a headache, when faced with an unpleasant obligation. Sometimes the presence of conflict leads to these reactions. It may become known to us only after we have already developed the

525

somatic reactions. In puzzling over the tired feeling or the headache, we may become aware that we were ambivalent about the obligation that we did not wish to discharge.

It is difficult for some of us to grasp or accept the idea of our own unconscious determinants of behavior. We would like to believe that we are rational animals and have full control over our actions. However, it remained for Freud to discover the great significance of unconscious motives and unconscious conflicts in everyday life as well as in neurotic problems [4]. In the next chapter we shall discuss the theoretical significance of these discoveries. At this point we merely wish to clarify the meaning of the concept of unconsciousness.

Mental activity goes on at various levels. At one level we are fully aware of what we are thinking, striving for, and feeling. On another level there is no awareness of some of these activities. For convenience, the whole range of awareness may be subdivided into three major categories: the *unconscious level* (of which we have no awareness but of which we can become aware under certain conditions); the *preconscious level* (of which we can become readily aware if we simply focus our attention on the relevant mental phenomenon); and the *conscious level* (of which we are currently fully aware). (See Chapter 5 for a more complete exposition of these constructs.) Some psychologists dislike the use of the term "unconscious," preferring other terms which are more "operational," that is, which refer to more overt and explicit behavior. For others, the concept implies a dichotomy between consciousness and unconsciousness which they find unacceptable. However, most psychologists assume that there is a continuum on which mental events may be ranked with respect to the person's awareness of them.

As we shall see later, there are many types of data which are consistent with the hypothesis that mental activities occur at an unconscious level. Our present purpose, however, is to illustrate how unconscious conflicts may influence behavior. The following three examples of unconscious conflict indicate that we sometimes behave with only partial or with no awareness of the nature of our conflicting motives. At the same time, in each of these illustrations, the subject was aware of some of his motives, or was aware of them in some distorted manner.

One of the authors, who is a psychotherapist (a person who seeks to assist people in resolving debilitating emotional conflicts), was working with a college student. This student was very uncomfortable in some of his classes, felt anxious in them, and could not perform satisfactorily. As his psychotherapy progressed, he gradually became aware that his difficulties occurred in those classes in which he felt attracted to his male instructors. He came 20 minutes late for the next session following the one in which he had talked about his "discovery" of these feelings. He "explained" that, in driving to the psychotherapist's office, he had "accidentally" taken a wrong turn, and before he knew it he had driven to the opposite side of town. During this session he made no reference to his discussion of the previous meeting. Instead, he spent his time talking about the subject matter of the courses in which he was having difficulty. At his next appointment, the psychotherapist asked him why he had discontinued discussing his feelings about the instructors. He disclaimed having discussed this problem, but, before the session was over, he got up and prepared to leave, although there were some 15 minutes left in the session. He was embarrassed and stated that he had looked at his watch and had thought that his time had run out. It was only after a number of additional sessions that he became aware of his conflict over his undiscovered homosexual impulses. He became aware that he was attracted to these men and was, at the same time, anxious about the anticipated disapproval of the therapist, of his family, and of himself for having such motives. Much more therapy was needed before he was able to resolve his conflicts and work effectively.

Our second illustration is taken from a study using hypnosis [5]. In this study, neurotic patients were first hypnotized and were then told that chocolate candy was very "bad" for them. They were instructed not to remember that they had been told this when they were awakened from their trance states. In the posthypnotic condition none of the patients remembered what they had been told under hypnosis. Each was then offered some chocolate candy. Each reacted differently to this situation, but all showed the effect of the hypnotically induced but "forgotten" motive. One patient became blind temporarily and did not see the candy when it was offered. Another patient ate the candy but developed nausea and intestinal pain. She finally regurgitated the candy. It would be interesting, but not relevant to our main point, to discuss the various methods used by different patients to attempt to resolve their conflicts. Our point at this time, however, is to demonstrate how conflicts of which the person is entirely unaware may dramatically affect behavior.

For our third illustration we shall refer to some research work by a group of investigators studying the influence of the "achievement motive" (the motive to perform well in some task) upon behavior. In one study these psychologists were interested in studying the relative effectiveness of consciously experienced motivation to achieve as compared with the effectiveness of this motive when it was not consciously perceived [6]. They measured the former by asking the subjects to rate themselves (using a questionnaire) on the strength of their motivation to achieve. They rated the latter by inferring the strength of this (hidden) motivation from stories about people in picture situations (see Chapter 8 for a discussion of such methods) which these subjects told. This indirect measure of achievement motivation correlated significantly with various criteria of superior performance under laboratory conditions, while the conscious, direct measure of this motivation did not so correlate. In other words, performance was influenced by motivations of which the subjects had little or inaccurate awareness.

Findings such as these have some further implications. One is that conflicts occurring within the individual may produce a temporary state of disharmony. The second is that conflicts that one is unaware of contribute to the development of a chronic state of anxiety and may lead to more serious disorganization of behavior and personality [7]. If we are unaware of what it is that is bothering us, or about which we are conflicted, we are, to that extent, less able to make appropriate decisions or to function efficiently [8]. Conscious conflicts, on the other hand, may often be resolved more readily, and such resolutions may even be productive of more healthy development of the personality. Unconscious conflicts tend to have a spiral effect in that they produce behavior which makes it ever more difficult for the individual to become aware of his internal difficulties and to resolve his problem. Karen Horney offers the example of the individual who has learned to be overly submissive and obliging toward others because he is very fearful (for reasons of which he is unaware) of criticism and rejection [9]. He becomes unable to express himself spontaneously and assertively and becomes, in turn, ever more fearful and bitter. But to avoid further discomfort, he all the while persists in being sweet and overly submissive to others, becoming ever more fearful and hostile inside. In this way the conflict tends to be increased, since there is no awareness of its origins, and effective resolution or adaptation becomes increasingly more difficult. In severe cases of unconscious conflict, personality disorganization may become persistent. (See Chapter 6.)

The Nature of Anxiety

In the previous section we introduced the term "anxiety." Now we shall attempt to define this term and differentiate it from other concepts.

ANXIETY AND FEAR   The terms *fear* and *anxiety* have usually been used interchangeably in popular literature and thought. However, they are distinguishable. In a technical sense fear refers to an apprehensive reaction to some external danger that is known to the individual. For example, the young child is fearful of falling off his bicycle, the teen-ager is fearful of getting into a fight with a much stronger boy, and the adult is fearful of swimming across a wide lake when he knows his own limited swimming ability. In situations such as these the individual is able to assess rather accurately the source and degree of danger which confronts him and, barring unforseen circumstances, is able to make appropriate adaptive responses to the situation. In fear situations, the source of the danger is external to the person, is known to him, and can be assessed fairly accurately if previous experience has been adequate to teach something of its characteristics and its possible consequences. A response may be made to approach the situation, in an attempt to cope with it and overcome the feared situation, or the response may be avoidance or an attempt to find some compromise solution if the problem cannot be dealt with directly. The fear can then be reduced in a relatively efficient manner.

   In contrast, anxiety refers to an internal state, of which the individual has only partial awareness. Its source is in some conflict which is not fully known. The direct expression of needs or the solution of the conflict is blocked because the individual is unaware of the source of the danger and because the direct expression of the conflicting drives would tend to suffuse and overwhelm the normal adaptive functions of the person. (See Chapter 5 for a discussion of the concept of ego.) Because he does not "know" what is troubling him, the individual is unable to make an effective response which would resolve the conflict. As a result, he makes some ineffective response which is *not* entirely appropriate, and the original conflict is reinforced. Anxiety reactions are thus likely to be increased.

Persistent anxiety may lead to an anxiety state, in which the individual suffers from diffuse and persistent apprehension but cannot ascribe any known cause to it. Such states are known as *anxiety neuroses*. (See Chapter 6 for a discussion of neuroses.) A phobia (a persistent, specific, and irrational anxiety) is another form which anxiety may take. There are many types of phobias. The following is one example of a phobic reaction. A man becomes highly anxious when he enters an elevator. He "knows" that modern elevators are well engineered and have many safety features. He "knows" his anxiety is unreasonable, but he dreads entering an elevator and, if forced to do so, sweats profusely, shows increased heart rate, begins to tremble, and dashes out at the first opportunity. In this kind of phobia the man "knows" that he fears elevators, but he does "not know" why he is anxious about them. The source of his anxiety is just as well hidden from him as from the person with more general, less specific anxiety. In a phobic reaction the individual "attaches" his anxiety to some external object in an attempt to gain some degree of control over it. Clinical study has often revealed that phobias of this kind have developed on the basis of previous experiences in which the person was rejected or was left alone and helpless. Finally, small, closed spaces trigger off the current phobic reaction. The true source of any phobia lies in past events in which important needs were thwarted and the individual's entire security system was somehow endangered. Phobias, which on the surface may resemble fears, are actually anxiety reactions in which the individual is unaware of the nature of his conflict. Figure 4.6 illustrates the relations of fear and anxiety states to their origins.

Many theories have been offered to explain the source and the nature of the anxiety. Some theorists regard anxiety as a specific response to specific conditions [10]; anxiety is thus roughly equated with the fear response. For others, anxiety is conceived as a *drive* (in this respect like any other biological drive), and it is defined as a "non-directive energizing function assigned to D in Hullian theory" [11]. In terms of this theory, in simple situations (those uncomplicated by other drives and motives), persons with high anxiety would learn more rapidly than those with low anxiety. There is experimental evidence that this is the case [12]. The effect of the anxiety drive varies, however, depending upon other response tendencies of the organism, other competing drives, and so on.

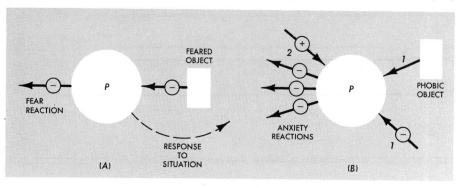

FIGURE 4.6 *Origins and responses to fear and anxiety. In (A) the feared object is "known" and the person P circumvents the difficulty. In (B) the source of anxiety (needs 1 and 2, which conflict) are "not known" and P experiences anxiety reactions and displaces his anxiety to some "known" but irrelevant object (the phobic object).*

Freud proposed an elaborate theory to explain the source and manifestations of anxiety [13], but he was never satisfied with his theory and kept reformulating it on the basis of new observations and more refined analyses. His last formulation conceived of anxiety as a "danger signal" from within to warn the individual that the expression of certain "instincts" under certain circumstances would be dangerous. In other words, anxiety arises when an individual tries to avoid dangers which would occur if he behaved in a certain way. However, he is not aware, or is not fully aware, of the source of the danger that lies within him. What he does become aware of is the danger that the external situation provides. Thus, in this theory, the individual *fears* some external event (objective anxiety) due to apprehension over some internal motives whose expression in that situation would prove dangerous.

This formulation was illustrated by Freud in connection with his analysis of the case of a five-year-old boy, Hans [14]. This boy was afraid to go into the street (the fear) because of his phobia about horses (the symptom). But the source of the anxiety was really unknown to this boy. It turned out that Hans felt strongly attracted sexually to his mother, but he was very much afraid of his father, who he feared would destroy him for having such impulses. He also liked his father when this did not bring him into conflict (competition) with him for his mother's love. Thus, he feared retaliation by his father for both his love of his mother and his hostile feelings toward his father. Hans learned

531

to displace his fear of his father upon horses. He felt anxious about horses and thus could avoid the danger of expressing his sexual attraction for his mother. He could thereby avoid awareness of the real cause of his anxiety.

To summarize, in Freud's theory anxiety is seen as the perception by the subject of some *internal danger* which is unknown at the time (is *repressed*) but which is displaced to some *external* situation (as fear or objective anxiety). Anxiety thus contains both external referents and internal referents. The major source of the anxiety is the classic oedipal situation (see Chapter 5 for a discussion of this problem), which reinforces the original anxiety level of the individual.

CHRONIC AND REACTIVE ANXIETY   Further study of anxiety enables us to distinguish between its *chronic* and *reactive* manifestations. Chronic anxiety refers to a more or less persisting state of anxiety with which the personality is suffused. We often refer to an individual as "being in a constant state of anxiety." This type of anxiety is characteristic of some types of neuroses. What we mean by this notion is that a certain high level of anxiety is constantly present, and no new traumatic event is necessary to instigate it. This kind of persistent anxiety, termed *anxiety state,* can be measured, and can be shown to have significant correlates in behavior [15]. Chronic anxiety may vary in level of intensity and when high may be indicative of a persistent psychoneurosis [16], whereas, when it is relatively low, it may simply represent a generally heightened state of drive-arousal conducive to more rapid conditioning and more effective learning of many simple types of tasks.

On the other hand, reactive anxiety (also called transitory anxiety, by some) is the anxiety level produced by transient events in the life of the individual [15]. In terms of our discussion in the preceding sections, reactive anxiety would represent some combination of a fear response and an associated anxiety response which act together to produce a temporary increase in the anxiety level. This type of anxiety is also measurable and is experimentally different from chronic anxiety [15].

We do not yet know many of the correlates of these two types of anxiety manifestations, although the preponderance of recent research seems to indicate that (1) a high level of chronic anxiety is found in many, but not all, types of psychoneuroses and (2) a strong tendency toward reactive anxiety is character-istic of emotionally immature personalities.

OVERT AND COVERT ANXIETY Hutt has attempted to distin-guish *overt* from *covert* anxiety [16]. A number of other workers, deriving their insights from somewhat different sources, have reached similar viewpoints [16, 17]. Overt anxiety is a behavioral *trait* (i.e., characteristic). The parameters of overt anxiety are more easy to distinguish than those of covert anxiety by the very nature of the phenomena. In overt anxiety, the behavioral reactions are visible to the naked eye, so to speak. The individual feels anxious, may have motor tremors, may flush easily, feel his heart pounding, and be aware of increased tension and increased sweating. The behavior in overt anxiety may be quite similar to that of fear, but the individual "doesn't know why" he behaves like that. Overt anxiety may typically occur in some specific life-situations for the individual. Some people are very anxious on tests, while others are very anxious in benign social situations. Mandler and Sarason have developed the Test Anxiety Questionnaire (TAQ), which pre-sumably measures the characteristic anxiety level an individual shows in academic test situations [18]. On the other hand, overt anxiety may be more generalized and be elicited over a wide variety of life-situations or even be "ever present." Thus, Janet Taylor has developed her Manifest Anxiety Scale (MAS), which attempts to measure this kind of phenomenon [19]. Although measures such as these have been quite useful in a wide variety of research studies, they also present a great many problems. The correlation of test scores of manifest, or overt anxiety, with each other tend to be positive but low (usually of the order of $+ .20$ to $+ .30$) and their relations with other behavioral phenomena inconstant over different types of popu-lations. In other words, the scales, as presently derived, tend to measure relatively specific rather than generalized features of the personality, except perhaps at the extremes on these phe-nomena.

Covert anxiety, which is construed as an intervening variable, refers to anxiety which is not directly observable but must be inferred from behavior. In other words, the consequences in behavior are attributed to this hypothesized factor. We should note that scientists have frequently conceptualized some factor which is not directly observable. Electricity cannot be observed, but its presence can be inferred from its effects. Similarly, atmospheric pressure can only be inferred and not observed directly. The presence of covert anxiety may similarly be inferred from its effects. An individual may be unaware that he is anxious yet may, for example, develop migraine headaches (induced, in some instances, by increased blood pressure in the frontal area of the head because of increased anxiety). Many forms of psychosomatic disturbances, in which there is no organic or structural defect but in which there is a malfunction of an organ or organ system, are believed to be the result of high levels of covert anxiety [20]. Peptic ulcers may be caused by this condition; so may essential hypertension, spastic stomach, colitis, and even cardiac disturbances. The inference that covert anxiety is a factor in the development of such conditions (in many cases) is based on the fact that psychotherapy which acts to reduce the anxiety assists in reducing or eliminating the psychosomatic disturbances [21]. Another line of suggestive evidence is furnished in the dreams and nightmares of such individuals, which reveal how anxious they may be without "knowing" it. Still another line of evidence comes from projective tests, as in the research cited above on the achievement motive.

Covert anxiety may also take a *symbolic* form. In such cases there may be little overt anxiety and there may be no gross psychosomatic disturbance, in the usual sense, but the individual may show a dysfunction which has a specific symbolic meaning for him. Such symptoms may be attributable to anxiety. Cases have been reported in which the individual shows psychogenic blindness, or peculiarities of visual function such as tunnel vision (he cannot see outside the confines of a limited "tunnel-like" area), or psychogenic deafness, or psychogenic paralysis of the fingers [22]. In such cases there is no anatomical or physiological defect, but an inhibition of function has occurred. Moreover, the dysfunction does not follow the usual physiological pattern that is present when, for example, a nerve is paralyzed but rather follows the individual's specific conception of the supposed nature of his organic disability. Many years ago, *glove anesthesia* was described, a phenomenon in which the anesthesia corresponded to the area of the hand that might be covered by a glove but which made no sense in terms of the biological nature of the nerve distribution in the hand and in which no organic defect was present [23]. Such symptoms are found most frequently in cases of *hysteria*. In all of these instances, the symptoms of the individual *symbolize some underlying conflict*.

Not only does the dysfunction correspond with the individual's unconscious conflict, but it clears up when the underlying conflict and anxiety have been reduced or resolved. Moreover, the presence of symbolic anxiety can be dramatically demonstrated when the clinician working with this kind of patient exposes the conflict by making a relevant interpretation and "triggers off" the anxiety. At this point the patient may become highly agitated and overtly anxious, as though the anxiety had been suddenly released.

The distinctions between fear and anxiety, chronic and reactive anxiety, and overt and covert anxiety may now be applied to a brief review of some behavioral phenomena, as in learning, in regression, and in psychological defenses, which are the next subjects for discussion.

ANXIETY AND LEARNING The research literature is replete with studies suggesting that subjects who are high on anxiety tend to perform well on simple learning tasks. The reverse is not so frequently found, namely, that subjects who are low on anxiety do not perform well. Moreover, the findings on the learning of complex tasks, such as abstract reasoning, problem-solving, and the like, are far from consistent with the theory that high anxiety serves to increase general drive level and so tends to facilitate all learning [24]. This theory has received a critical review by Spence, in which a more careful formulation of anxiety as constituting a high state of drive is made and the nature of the critical factors involved in such studies is analyzed [11]. As Spence says: ". . . D [or Drive, in his terms] is a function of the strength of the emotional response made by the organism to *noxious stimulation* . . ." [11, p. 133; italics ours]. The Manifest Anxiety Scale was developed by Janet Taylor in order to differentiate subjects in terms of "the degree to which they admitted to possessing overt or manifest symptoms of emotionality. . . ." Spence points out that his theory is concerned with the effects of aversive, stressful stimulation which may arouse activity "under the control of the autonomic nervous system. . . ." In relation to the learning of complex tasks, the problems involving the effects of anxiety are far more complex than the relatively simple theory introduced to account

535

for learning of simple tasks or in conditioning studies. As he says: ". . . in order to derive implications concerning the effects of drive variation in any type of complex learning task, it is necessary to have, in addition to the drive theory, a further theoretical network concerning the variables and their interactions that are involved in the particular learning activity."

We have tried to present the complexity of the problem of conceptualizing, defining, and measuring anxiety. We have noted that various measures of anxiety, especially those of the paper-and-pencil questionnaire type, have only approximate validity and do not correlate very highly with each other. It is especially true that covert and overt anxiety tend to show little or no relationship with each other. Hence, if we are to understand the nature of the relationships of anxiety to learning, we have to specify not only the types of anxiety and how they are measured but the types of learning and how they are measured.

Moreover, anxiety is only one of many possible contributors to performance, that is, it is responsible for only a small portion of the variance in behavior. This really means that other motivational variables, the capacities of the individual, previous learning experience, and the nature of the learning situation contribute their share to learning and performance.

One of the interesting findings by Sarason and his co-workers is that individuals who are high on specific test anxiety (a special form of overt anxiety) tend to do better than average on test situations for which they are able to prepare themselves. They tend to do worse, however, on examinations for which no immediate preparation is possible [25, 26, 27]. In such instances we can speculate that relatively focused overt anxiety (focused, that is, on the immediately relevant task) tends to increase general drive level, alerts the individual to events or facts which he must master (therefore produces better input of information), and so improves his performance. Why, however, does it not improve performance on tests where specific preparation does not help? We might speculate, again, that such drives are not highly pertinent in complex learning tasks.

These speculations are not inconsistent with some of Freud's earlier formulations which proposed that moderate degrees of anxiety not only did not "flood the ego" (i.e., did not overwhelm the individual) but acted as "warning signals" which alerted the individual so that he could perform the tasks more efficiently or avoid apparent dangers [13]. In short, relatively moderate amounts of overt anxiety may facilitate simple learning since this may assist in marshaling attention, increasing drive state, and promoting appropriately vigilant behavior. On the other hand, relatively extreme amounts of overt anxiety (and most laboratory studies do not even approach this condition[1]) may not only impair learning, even of simple tasks, but may disorganize behavior and produce a tendency to function less effectively in future situations of a similar nature.

When we recall that covert anxiety is the result of excessive amounts of anxiety which may have been overt originally, we can begin to understand that covert anxiety may retard or inhibit learning, especially of complex tasks, since the individual is unable to produce the correct response (he does not know what danger threatens him and therefore may make many more irrelevant than relevant responses), and he may be unable to persist in making the correct response even when it occurs "by accident" (since he may not respond to relevant rewards or information in his environment). Another way of stating this is the following. When an individual's learning efforts are interfered with by drives toward inappropriate or diffuse behavioral responses, the "cause" may lie in a relatively high level of covert anxiety. Complex learning tasks are therefore more likely to be unfavorably influenced by covert anxiety than simple tasks, since the likelihood of initiating the correct response and thereby reducing the anxiety is smaller.

Our speculations concerning the involved relationship of anxiety to learning are intended to stimulate the student to consider how much more we need to know before we can begin to offer general principles which govern their relationships. It would be well to emphasize, also, that the concomitant effect of other intervening variables must be considered. Recent studies have shown, for example, that the effects of level of anxiety, the severity of the stress which the situation imposes, as well as the difficulty of the task, produce far different results from those one could predict on the basis of level of anxiety alone [27]. Some studies have shown that one must take into account *both* the level of anxiety and type of personality organization (or its degree of integration) if predictions of responses to conflict are

[1] With the exception of some studies of sensory deprivation, like those discussed in Chapter 3, most research studies have dealt with anxieties already present in their subjects or have tried to induce only mild anxiety reactions.

to be made [28, 29]. Other studies, especially on learning to make more effective personality adaptation through the use of psychotherapy, suggest that the individual's strength of ego and his self-percept may markedly influence the curve of growth [30]. We can conclude, however, with the thought that the various types of anxiety have important bearings on the nature of the learning process.

ANXIETY, DEFENSE, AND REGRESSION As anxiety increases, no matter what type is involved, the individual begins to respond differently to the task at hand. In the course of time an individual learns to defend himself against anxiety of almost intolerable amounts. He learns relatively specific types of *defense mechanisms*, which he then utilizes in order to reduce anxiety. In the next section we shall discuss some of these mechanisms and see how they are employed. At this point we wish merely to indicate that defensive behavior is, in general, an inefficient and usually somewhat inappropriate behavioral reaction to the anxiety situation. It is less effective than "coping" or "adaptive" behavior, which does reduce the anxiety more efficiently. A defense mechanism involves behavior that is a response to only part of the stimulus situation because the individual has been previously unsuccessful in coping with similar situations which produced the higher levels of anxiety.

An example may make this general point more meaningful. If we have not learned to cope with certain social situations and we feel shy (anxious) in a social gathering, we may get "butterflies in our stomach" or may suddenly develop a headache. The physiological reaction enables us to defend ourselves by giving us an excuse to leave the situation, but the defense is inefficient, since it does not solve the underlying problem. Another type of defense, which we shall presently discuss, that of repression, vividly dramatizes the inefficient manner in which defenses serve us. We may repress a person's name or we may repress some factual information we need for a test answer (that is, we inconveniently forget what we knew quite well) because of anxiety, the source of which we are unaware.

When anxiety is severe and persistent, it may lead to *regressive* behavior. Regression is the substitution of more primitive (i.e., earlier) modes[2] of behavior for more mature modes of

---

[2] The term "mode" is used here to mean the patterns of behavioral adaptation which an individual characteristically employs.

behavior. Hysterical crying (or crying "like a baby") is an example of such behavior. Psychotic persons (called insane by the layman) may show bizarre forms of regressive behavior, like playing with feces or having very severe temper tantrums, which had not occurred for years until regression produced by very severe anxiety induced this extreme kind of behavioral reaction. In regression, the primitive behavior is not exactly like that which was previously employed, since the individual has had many years of experience since he first learned these behaviors and is physically and psychologically a different person from what he was in earlier years. Nevertheless, it is a *reversion to an earlier mode of behaving.* Regression may be thought of as an example of impaired learning in which more primitive behavior is substituted for more mature behavior which had already been mastered by the individual.

Defensive Behavior

When anxiety reaches very high levels, behavior becomes severely disorganized. Anyone who has seen an individual in a severe state of anxiety recognizes the terrifying anguish that it entails. Sometimes, as in the case of intense anxiety precipitated by severe traumata like an accident or an experience during war conditions, there is acute reactive anxiety. In other cases in which intense chronic anxiety has been developed, some trivial incident may trigger off highly disorganized behavior. The person, in either case, seems to lose control. He is unable to use his intelligence effectively; behavior is impulsive and highly erratic, and, finally, aimless, frantic behavior or withdrawal into complete passivity or into the world of fantasy may result. To ward off such intense states of panic when other more rational, problem-solving methods of adaptation are not available, the individual employs *defense mechanisms.* Defense mechanisms may be thought of as secondary methods employed, by the individual who has failed to resolve a conflict, to ward off the further buildup of anxiety. They are adaptive techniques to prevent further loss of self-esteem, and they avoid, to some degree, confrontation with what seems to be an insoluble conflict.

The concept of the defense mechanism was proposed by Freud and elaborated by his daughter, Anna Freud [31]. It has been subjected to intensive experimental study. Sometimes the defense mechanisms have been divided into two subgroups, primary defenses (or primary defensive processes) and secondary defenses (or secondary defensive processes). The former are thought of as the basic, or front-line, protective devices, while the latter are conceived of as supportive devices to assist in the process of inhibiting the development of extreme anxiety.

Defense mechanisms are not the only means of reducing anxiety. Problem-solving, for example, in which cognitive processes are utilized with the maximum degree of efficiency to find a solution to difficulties, is a more effective means of reducing anxiety. But when anxiety mounts in degree and its source is unknown to the individual, problem-solving cannot successfully occur since the factors causing the difficulty are not available for inspection and evaluation. It is when the individual is unable to cope with his conflicts on some realistic basis that defense mechanisms are likely to be employed.

This lack of ability to cope appropriately may be constitutional (e.g., due to some inadequacy of the organism, such as its deficiency in some ability or its immaturity), it may be experiential (e.g., due to lack of appropriate experience in dealing with some kinds of situations), or it may be environmental (e.g., due to factors in the external environment which make a reasonable solution impossible or very difficult). It may also be due to the intensity of the internal conflict and the intense anxiety which has accumulated within the individual, despite adequate constitution, experience, and opportunity. For example, the severe inhibition which some students suffer when confronted with writing a term report for a course may result in endless delay in getting started or the inability to finish the report, despite good intelligence, ample skill in writing, and adequate time for completion of the project. The behavior doesn't "make sense," it is beyond the capacity of the student to conquer, and it gets him into increasingly greater difficulty. It might be due to any one or more of a number of causes which have little to do directly with the present situation, such as: excessive fear of failure which is not realistic; a fear of exposing one's efforts to public scrutiny; an irrational fear of the particular professor or the subject; a low self-esteem system; an unconscious wish to leave the school situation; an unconscious wish to be punished; excessive dependency needs; a phobia about writing; and the like. In any event, it is defensive, and it leads to inefficient ways of dealing with the problem. It may even lead to complete avoidance of the problem or the problem situation.

We have stressed the negative aspects of the defense mechanism because it is an inefficient means of dealing with conflict and it tends to avoid the real problem. Nevertheless, defense mechanisms have their positive features. In the first place, they serve, even if only temporarily, to allay or reduce anxiety. More than this, they may serve to maintain some degree of self-esteem and thus stave off further disorganization of the personality. The defensive operation gives us an "excuse," as it were, and prevents further self-deprecation.

Thus we can see that defense mechanisms have their place in our lives, since none of us is forever exempt from conflict and since none of us can always find the means of dealing appropriately with conflict situations. When used in moderation, defenses give us "breathing space," and they enable us to avoid a more severe personality disturbance. *It is only when we employ very primitive defenses as a characteristic mode of operation or when we rigidly rely exclusively upon one or two defenses that our personality becomes psychopathological.* In other words, even the healthy individual uses defense mechanisms at times, but their use becomes pathological (unhealthy) when they have displaced reasoning and other more appropriate methods of adaptation.

PRIMITIVE DEFENSE PATTERNS Experimental psychologists have, as yet, given little attention to the problem of the development of defense mechanisms in early life. The reasons are manifold, but the most important ones are probably a lack of adequate methodology for measuring such behaviors and a lack of an adequate systematic theory of defensive development in the individual. Most of our present knowledge of the early development of defenses comes from the work of clinical investigators and theorists, and much of it is open to controversy and further speculation. Moreover, clinical workers have based much of their evidence on a kind of inferential reasoning. They have inferred that the types of defenses they have seen in severely disturbed and hospitalized mental patients are not only "primitive" defenses but are those which necessarily evolve earlier in the lives of all normal individuals. Although such

541

evidence is reasonable and is, in some measure, confirmed by laboratory studies, it is nevertheless based on clinical inference rather than controlled observation or experiment.

Anna Freud has suggested that, although it is difficult to classify the various defenses into a chronological order, there are some which clearly come early in the life of the individual [31]. She lists *regression* and *reversal* as among the earliest modes of defense. Other psychoanalytic writers suggest *projection* and *introjection*[3] as the earliest forms of defense [32]. But all agree that those defenses emerge first which enable the developing personality to defend itself against the most elemental threats which a highly vulnerable organism has to contend with: the threats of nongratification of basic biosocial needs, including the bodily satisfactions of hunger, thirst, temperature, and such security needs as affectional gratification, consistent attention, and protection against severe physical traumata.

It seems reasonable from what is known of the behavioral development of the infant and child that the organism tends to satisfy its needs, at first, in a highly passive manner. That is, its needs can only be satisfied (i.e. reduced) as someone else provides the means for this satisfaction. Thus, the infant *tends* to operate predominantly with an *approach orientation* to stimuli which impinge upon it, but it does so relatively passively. The major exceptions to this approach orientation occur in connection with withdrawal reflex responses to noxious stimuli. Gradually the infant learns to *avoid* some stimuli which produce or increase tension, as it simultaneously begins to learn to differentiate among stimuli and especially between internal and external phenomena. It learns an *avoidant orientation* when it is frustrated. One can assume that the first defensive operations of the emerging personality involve avoidance behaviors. As internal and external events become more clearly differentiated, the infant begins to seek actively (by looking, listening, and reaching) those objects which may offer some gratification —principally the mother and her attributes.

Since the infant's adaptive behaviors are severely limited by its physical immaturity and it cannot move bodily toward the object which might offer gratification, and since it is limited in its bodily movements away from irritating stimuli, it must rely

[3] See later discussion of these terms, pp. 546–550.

primarily upon *perceptual defenses* to reduce internal tensions. It must learn to avoid those stimuli which irritate by shutting them out of *perceptual awareness*. It can learn "not to see," and later it can learn "not to hear," as primitive means of avoidance. In most instances what may occur is some decrease in visual or auditory intake as a basic defensive operation. If the irritants which the infant experiences are very severe, these perceptually avoidant behaviors may become markedly reinforced, and perceptually approach-oriented behavior may be simultaneously reduced. On the other hand, if conflicts are not severe, approach-oriented perceptual behavior is reinforced.

This primary perceptual dichotomy of approach- versus avoidance-oriented behavior may therefore be conceptualized as the most primitive form of defense mechanism. Some studies suggest that perceptual *adience* (or perceptual behavior which is approach-oriented) is clearly related to greater personality maturity, greater capacity for dealing with traumatic events, and greater capacity for effective behavioral adaptation than is perceptual avoidance-oriented behavior [33]. Such studies suggest that perceptual *abience* (or perceptual avoidance) is related to immaturity, difficulty in dealing with traumatic events, and difficulty in effective behavioral adaptation. To illustrate what perceptual abience involves, we can list such specific phenomena as the following, which were used in one of the studies: perceiving things as smaller than they are; a tendency to perceive stimuli as rotated from the vertical to nonvertical position; a tendency to reduce the dimensions of objects. Perceptual abience may be related to some of the defenses which have been observed and studied experimentally in older subjects; these are principally repression, denial, and regression (see next section).

Recently Solley and Murphy reviewed the clinical and the limited experimental literature on what has been called "autistic perception" [34], which can be defined as the tendency to perceive largely or predominantly in terms of inner personality determinants (as contrasted with outer or environmental determinants). The perceptual response is therefore not veridical (i.e., it does not correspond to external reality). Autistic perception appears to be characteristic of children in the preschool years and is gradually replaced with more veridical perception in normal development. The accumulated evidence indicates that frustration of inner needs in infancy and childhood reinforces autistic perception. The two concepts, autistic perception and abient perception, appear to be closely linked. Both suggest that a primary mode of defense involves avoidance on the perceptual level.

It may well be that perceptual abience is a precursor of and an important determinant of other primitive defense mechanisms. Such behavior reduces appropriate input for the organism and may therefore leave it in a poorer position to cope with other conflict situations. Consequently, additional defenses have to be employed to deal with increasing anxiety or with increasingly lower self-esteem. Such defenses continue to produce distortions of reality for the individual and make it ever more difficult to become aware of inner needs and conflicts. Present evidence supports this view, in that *repression, regression, projection,* and *denial* are the predominant mechanisms of individuals who have strong perceptual abience tendencies [35].

OTHER PRIMARY DEFENSES   We shall now discuss some additional defenses which are employed early in the life of the individual. Athough such defenses are used occasionally by presumably healthy adults, they usually occur only under great stress, or they do not predominate in the pattern of behavior which such persons usually employ.

Repression   Psychologists have learned that forgetting cannot be explained solely in terms of the adequacy of the original learning or the time interval since the learned material was last practiced or rewarded. Forgetting is facilitated by emotional factors associated with the learned material. In general, we tend to forget unpleasant memories more quickly, for instance, than pleasant memories [36].

Repression represents a special case of forgetting in which there is unconscious blotting-out of awareness of impulses that are unacceptable to the self. We noted in the discussion of the experiment on hypnosis how conflict in the individuals produced "forgetting" of the negative instructions although the behavior of the subjects indicated that the instructions were still influencing behavior. This is characteristic of all repression. The individual is unaware of his blocked impulses, but these impulses find some expression in more indirect ways. Repression results in less trauma or negative impact upon the individual, and so the defense serves a "useful" purpose. The student can undoubtedly think of many examples of repression in his own life

Too much mother? Drawing by Mary Petty; Copyright ©
1952; The New Yorker Magazine, Inc.

but can probably think of more instances in the lives of others. Some cases of *amnesia* (or loss of memory) are vivid examples of repression. In such instances the person may forget who he is or what his life was like until the amnesia "lifts." If it does, he is able to remember what he had repressed, and it is discovered that his amnesia represented an attempt to avoid intolerable feelings or impulses. In much the same way, we sometimes "forget" the names of people who were unpleasant to us or the memory of an experience that would make us think less highly of ourselves.[4]

When repression is "massive," that is, when it obliterates a whole area of one's impulse life, then some form of psychopathology is likely to result. As we shall see in Chapter 6, repression is the characteristic defense in *hysteria,* in which sexual or aggressive impulses are intolerable to the individual.

Repression should be differentiated from *suppression.* The latter refers to the conscious inhibition of an act which is socially unacceptable. Such inhibition may become habitual and require little conscious attention, after a time. Cultural conditions teach us to suppress some behaviors which would be obnoxious, thereby enabling us to develop appropriate self-control. When suppression of impulses is very severe or persistent, this cultural practice may cause us to develop repression. When, for example, society, or some section of it, takes an excessively severe, negative attitude toward the expression of sexual impulses, the individuals involved may learn to repress these "threatening" sexual drives. This may explain why hysteria was more common in the Victorian period (near the end of the last century) than it is now and why more women than men tended to develop hysterical personality reactions.

Some degree of repression probably is involved in all defensive behavior [31]. Freud suggested that repression represents the most basic and general of all defense mechanisms. However, in most cases the work of repression is supported by other learned defenses, and this enables the person to retain more flexibility in his behavior than would otherwise be the case.

Regression   This type of defense has already been discussed briefly in an earlier section of this chapter. A considerable amount of experimental work has confirmed the fact that

---

[4] The content of what is forgotten depends on other factors besides its pleasantness or unpleasantness. The nature of the individual's personality (especially his general disposition), for one thing, is also influential.

regression does occur and that it is greatly facilitated by frustrating external circumstances. However, experimental work
rarely involves the degree of stress that real-life conditions may
exert. Laboratory conditions of regressive behavior are less
likely to be severe or to persist for any considerable period,
whereas regression in severely disturbed persons may be quite
pronounced and be very difficult to remove.

Common examples of regression may be observed at parties
when people "let their barriers down" and behave like children.
These are usually only mild forms of regression. Somewhat
more severe forms of regression may occur when a person is
hospitalized for a serious illness and behaves like a child, has
temper tantrums, and requires that everyone wait on him.

A classic study of the effects of frustration which produced
temporary regression is that by Barker, Dembo, and Lewin [37].
In this study, children were first permitted to play with a
fascinating array of toys; later, parts of these toys, such as the
iron that went with an ironing board, and the pond of water that
went with the toy boat, were made inaccessible by a wire screen.
Many of the children then showed regressive behavior; according to the authors they engaged in behavior that was at least a
year more immature than that which they had previously displayed.

Recent studies in sensory deprivation (in which the individual is deprived of or has restricted visual or auditory stimulation, for example) have shown that this type of experience can
produce severely regressive behavior under certain conditions
[38]. It is interesting to speculate about the types of frustration
involved in such studies. In the limitation of the usual types of
sensory input produced by such deprivation, these subjects
were prevented, in many cases, from effective modes of adaptation. They had relatively fewer ways left to them with which to
discharge their impulses or had fewer external frames of reference against which to evaluate their own responses. Hence they
had to find means to meet their needs in less mature ways than
was normally the case.

In psychopathological regression the individual avoids current conflicts by resuming modes of response that were once
more appropriate under earlier and simpler conditons. In such
instances he usually utilizes behavior patterns that were highly
overlearned in the earlier period. He not only acts as if he were
living in more primitive circumstances, but, in doing so, he

gains a certain amount of security by doing well those things that once worked well for him.

Projection   This defense has been studied experimentally more extensively than any other. The term has been defined in various ways (see [39] for examples of such varied uses of the term), but it was originally employed to connote that kind of behavior in which the person unconsciously attributes to others those motives within himself which he finds unacceptable. Freud, who coined the term, used it in this sense and saw its most intense manifestations in paranoid individuals who attributed their own undesirable characteristics to others. Paranoid individuals, for example, see others as hating them, whereas in reality it is they who hate others. In this way they are able to deny their own unacceptable impulses. They can also justify their behavior and feel that they must defend themselves against the hatred of others.

Projection, like all other mechanisms of defense, may occur in normal individuals. A series of studies by Sears and others [40 and 41] demonstrated this phenomenon in children and also in college students. In the former study, severely punished children were observed, during doll play, to attribute aggression to the dolls with which they were playing. In the latter study, it was found that college students who were least aware of their own undesirable traits tended to be the ones who were most likely to attribute these traits to other students whom they were asked to rate. Some writers distinguish between *assimilative* and *defensive* projection. In the former, the individual assumes that other people are like him and erroneously, therefore, attributes his feelings to them. In the latter, he assumes that the individuals are unlike him, and he attributes his own unacceptable feelings to them.

Of course, attributing motives or traits to others may be employed with full awareness of what one is doing. The boss who takes out on his secretary the anger he feels toward his wife may be fully aware that he is "projecting." Such behavior is usually called *displacement* rather than projection. It is far less likely to lead to maladjustment than "classic" projection, since one can readily find substitute ways of coping with the known frustrations or one can learn to adapt to the frustrating experiences.

The classical form of projection is probably closely related to another important, but little understood, mechanism, namely,

Introjection. De Wys from Monkmeyer

introjection. As we shall see in Chapter 5, introjection seems to explain a great deal of the child's learning of value systems. This mechanism refers to the process by which one unconsciously assimilates the attributes of others. The young infant introjects the values of his mother, the young child introjects the values of his hero-ideal, and even the young man may introject the values of great public figures of his generation, without being aware of the process that is taking place. Witness, for example, the current marked increase in interest of high-school students in atomic physics.

It seems to some writers that both projection and introjection are necessary to explain some important aspects of personality development in young children (see [42] and [43]). They believe that these mechanisms help us to understand how the healthy infant takes over some of his mother's personality attributes. First he introjects (interiorizes) her feelings and attitudes. Those that are frustrating or uncomfortable for him he projects upon her. Later he introjects his newly formed perceptions of his mother. The continuing process of introjection and projection gradually enables him to test out effective and reality-oriented ways of behaving that are satisfying and keep his tensions within reasonable bounds. However, under "unhealthy" conditions, as, for example, when the mother is "cold" and severely disapproving, the testing-out of the self is frustrated. In such circumstances, these primitive mechanisms may persist and become markedly reinforced. Under "healthy" circumstances, these mechanisms are replaced by more efficient defenses and other coping methods of behavior which are much more adaptive.

Denial This mechanism is one in which the very presence of unpleasant reality is blotted out, i.e., denied. One can observe this behavior in very young children who behave as if they were oblivious of intense stimuli impinging upon them. When a young child is brought into a new and frightening situation, he may behave as if he sees and hears nothing. All strong threats may produce this inhibition of responses that might prove dangerous. Denial can be observed in the adult who "shuts out" responses to stimuli which would interfere with his satisfaction, as when he concentrates upon a problem he is working on or when he shuts out distracting noises at a concert.

Another form of denial is known as *negative hallucination*. Here the person hallucinates some stimulus (i.e., has the experience of seeing or hearing something that is not present) in order to conceal the painful experience of missing something that he needs. The young child may hallucinate his mother when she is not there and he feels lonely and insecure. Rapaport believed that this type of thinking underlies fantasy and creative thinking in later life. [44] It is presumed to be a healthy mode of adjustment in the early years of life but becomes pathological when it persists as a recurring tendency in later life.

Denial may occur in fantasy (or in negative hallucinations) or in words and behavioral acts. Its use becomes untenable when the individual's reality-testing no longer permits him to tolerate simultaneously a "make-believe" and a real world. Our previous discussion of perceptual abience suggests that denial may be one consequence of a high degree of such tendencies.

SECONDARY DEFENSES We shall now consider some of the defenses which are fairly common among healthy adults and then contrast them with other modes of adaptation called "coping behavior."

Reaction formation Another common defense mechanism involves the substitution of a pattern of behavior that is opposed to some other, objectionable pattern. If, for example, an individual is anxious about his tendencies to be dependent or

passive, he may develop an exaggerated pattern of assertive or even aggressive behavior. Such phenomena are normal in the course of personality development, but they become pathological when they are extreme and compulsive. In reaction formations the behavior appears inflexible or rigid even when the situation is not appropriate. Moreover, the behavior can be recognized as pathological because it is clearly out of proportion to the situation.

Reaction formations are accompanied by repression. One might say that the individual becomes anxious about some impulse or behavior tendency and tries to eliminate it from awareness. Repression of awareness is thus the first step in reaction formation. The development of the reaction formation reinforces the repression, thus supporting the inhibition of the original tendency and assisting in reducing awareness of it.

Phobias represent good examples of reaction formation. The mother who develops a fear of knives and is anxious because she might harm her child with them has developed a phobia about knives. As the phobia increases in intensity, all that is left in awareness is the irrational fear of knives. The aggressive impulses toward the child have been repressed. In their place, there may appear only love and tenderness for the child. This defensive behavior can be recognized as such because the mother becomes overly solicitous of her child's welfare and becomes overweening and engulfing in her affectionate behavior.

There are many other examples of reaction formation. Some prohibitionists develop a reaction formation against their own wish to drink and not only refrain from drinking themselves but wage a "war" against all others who attempt to drink. Thus they "convince" themselves that they have no need for alcohol, disguise the true nature of their anxiety, and are fearful of the possible effects of alcohol on others. Some people who are fearful of their own assumed feminine characteristics try very hard always to appear masculine. They may then detest femininity in other men but be unaware of their own tendencies in this direction.

Reaction formations often assume the form of a caricature of the true trait because they are exaggerated and appear, to the observer, to be irrational. Their irrationality becomes most clearly evident when they are utilized in situations when they are inappropriate.

551

Compensation The tendency to increase the strength of one motive in order to minimize the threat of some other motive is termed compensation. In extreme cases compensation may be part of a psychopathological reaction pattern. For example, the individual who feels insecure may develop bizarre methods of calling attention to himself by virtue of some special but eccentric behavior and thus gain some compensatory measure of security. People who have a strong need to "clown" all of the time may be showing this kind of behavior. Another example of an extreme form of compensatory behavior is that of the nymphomaniac—the girl whose sexual drives are so strong that she engages in a rapid succession of affairs in an attempt to gratify frustrated needs for affection. The male counterpart, the "Don Juan," similarly engages in countless love affairs to "prove" his potency as a male.

Most instances of compensation are, however, far less extreme or bizarre than those just noted. The short person may, for instance, compensate for his feelings of inferiority in the physical sphere by learning to excel in academic or artistic pursuits. Used in this way, the defense may actually contribute to greater self-esteem, more favorable feedback from others through their praise and attention, and finally to a decrease in the need for further compensatory activity. In such cases, compensation may lead to effective techniques for self-enhancement.

A specific form of compensation known as *overcompensation* was first discussed by Alfred Adler [45]. In this form of behavior the individual compensates for his weakness, real or imagined, by striving to excel in the same area. Thus, the person who is physically weak may overcompensate by trying to excel in physical abilities. Demosthenes, who had a stutter, overcompensated by putting marbles in his mouth, learning to speak with considerable fluency, and finally becoming a great orator. Cunningham, who suffered severe leg injuries, overcompensated by becoming a champion mile runner. In general, when successful, overcompensation acts as an incentive to intensive learning efforts and to relatively high degrees of success in some activity. Too often, however, this specialized success is accompanied by deleterious effects on the individual's personality because it leads to compulsive attention to the specialized goal and to the neglect of other needs and abilities of the person.

Rationalization This is a form of defense in which the

individual justifies his behavior in terms of some relevant but not completely valid reason. The behavior is seen as inadequate or even humiliating, it is usually an impulsive act, and the individual wishes to find some excuse for it so as to make it more acceptable to himself and others. Rationalization is therefore a form of self-deceit. It is frequently employed without conscious awareness of the basis for the original behavior but with reasonable awareness of the attempt to make it "seem rational" to others. That it can result from unconsciously motivated behavior may be observed in the cases of hypnotized persons who are given some posthypnotic suggestion to do something which embarrasses them. Usually they will offer some lame excuse for doing what they did, not knowing what motivated them to do it.

Rationalization tends to be employed, then, when one's self-esteem is threatened. It may serve to reduce guilt or self-deprecation momentarily; but, since it is a form of self-deceit, it may lead to decreased reality-testing as well as inaccurate self-appraisal if engaged in frequently. Used as an occasional defense, it may serve effectively in preventing unnecessary self-hurt.

Sublimation Freud suggested that in successful psychosexual maturation the energy of the sexual drives was redirected to other than specifically sexual objects and that civilization itself was based on the capacity of individuals to sublimate their sexual drives into the forms of behavior required for cultural and social advance [46]. He believed that sublimation is the highest form of defensive behavior. It was supposed to account for the resolution of the oedipal problem, at least in part. The term has been employed by other psychologists to denote any type of activity in which an impulse is redirected from its original object to some other object or activity, and sometimes the term *substitute activity* or simply *substitution* is employed in its place. Such uses of the original concept of sublimation are defensible only if it is made clear that a really different concept is being used. There is little doubt that many drives are redirected in the course of learning. However, Freud's contention that the redirection of the sexual drives is all-important for psychosexual maturity is a separate hypothesis and needs study in its own right.

Freud believed that many of the highest forms of art and science could be explained, in part, on the basis of sublimation.

Sublimation. Gregor from Monkmeyer

He also indicated that many simpler forms of personal and social behavior, such as "doodling" and dancing, involved sublimation. Sublimation, it was believed, led to reduction of the sexual drive and thus reduced tension when the drive could not be satisfied directly. Some clinicians dispute the validity of this hypothesis, but many offer striking case illustrations of successful and unsuccessful sublimations. The experimental literature is far from conclusive but thus far suggests that sublimation does not always reduce tension level [47].

SOME PROBLEMS CONCERNING DEFENSES We have discussed the defense mechanisms as if (1) they were mutually exclusive and operated independently and (2) our list of defenses was exhaustive. Neither of these statements is true.

Defenses tend to operate plurally rather than singly, one of them often supplementing the other. Moreover, there is not sufficient evidence to suggest that our list of defenses, or the lists of others, is either complete in describing all defensive operations of the personality or that each of them constitutes a really separate entity. These are some of the problems that current and future research on personality dynamics may enable us to understand more adequately.

We have considered some of the ways in which defenses are learned. We know now that different socioeconomic classes tend to employ somewhat different patterns of defenses [48]. We have learned how certain cultural conditions influence the development of preferences for some defenses rather than others [49]. And we have also learned how some defenses may be modified through conditioning, psychotherapy, and even through traumatic experiences. But the final word in the development and meaning of defenses has not yet been written.

Coping Behavior

In learning to deal with inner needs while at the same time responding effectively to the external demands of the environment, the child develops many strategies and techniques which prove more or less useful to him. The complex set of skills which enable him to gain this kind of mastery may be subsumed under the term *coping behavior*. Although some writers prefer to include defense mechanisms within the broader concept of coping (see [50], for example), it seems more reasonable in the light of present evidence to distinguish between these two terms. This does not imply, of course, that the two do not often occur together, forming a more general pattern of adjustment and adaptation, but rather that they seem to constitute at least relatively distinct ways of dealing with frustration, conflict, and tension.

Coping behavior may be conceptualized as behavior which is primarily directed at the external world in the attempt to deal with or master it. The infant is consciously, even if dimly, aware of the obstacles to his gratification and tries to find effective ways of avoiding them, circumventing them, or mastering them. These three basic modes of adaptation to obstacles may assist the individual in gratifying his needs. When successful, coping

555

behavior represents a pattern of behavior which leads to reduced tension and increased mastery of the world. Behavioral drives can thus be executed more readily. There is less need for defensive behavior, reality is not significantly distorted or is not distorted at all, and the individual's orientation toward the world tends to be generally approach- rather than avoidance-oriented.

Lois Murphy presents a general review of a series of studies of normal children, seen in infancy and evaluated periodically to adolescence, in which very careful documentation of the development of coping behavior is discussed [50]. She thinks of coping behavior as "a matter of strategy, of flexible management of different devices for dealing with challenges from the environment." But she also states, ". . . coping methods use such resources as alert perception, a reservoir of memories, and so forth, as well as defense mechanisms such as denial and repression. . . ." Thus she seems to include defensive operations within the category of coping behaviors. Yet she also adds, "If his first [coping] efforts fail . . . they may lead to defensive rigidity . . . , which prevents further exploration of potential gratification." As we have noted, it seems appropriate to differentiate between the concepts of defense and coping. It is only when coping behavior (in our sense) is insufficiently effective in gaining gratification or overcoming obstacles, and when tension mounts, that defensive operations are brought into play.

Coping behaviors may involve quite different patterns in different individuals, and the patterns learned in infancy and early childhood may be modified by later experience. Some of the primary elements in such patterns include: the direction and control of attention; inhibition of motor activity which might increase frustration; the employment of spontaneous responses in a flexible manner; the management of anxiety so as to maintain it within tolerable levels; the appropriate expression of feelings; the use of earlier experiences (memory) in solving new problems with cognitive efforts; and the like. These more fundamental coping strategies may be employed quite differently at different times, depending on many other learned skills (verbal, motor, and fantasy) which have become part of the individual's specific learned behavior.

As the individual grows older, he utilizes his coping strategies and techniques in characteristic ways, and we may then speak of his "personality style" (see Chapter 5 for a discussion of this

concept). His style will involve a healthy adjustment if his coping patterns are effective for him, whereas it will involve an unhealthy adjustment if it involves a characteristically high frequency of primary defensive operations. It is reasonable to suggest, it seems to us, that a high reliance upon defenses, especially primary defenses, is accompanied by failure in learning effective coping methods, whereas a low reliance upon such defenses is accompanied by success in learning effective patterns of coping.

There is some evidence to indicate that certain kinds of infant and early childhood experiences lead to highly effective coping methods. In the series of studies which Murphy reports, it was found, for example, that many significant positive correlations were obtained between ratings of infancy behavior in feeding situations (infancy oral gratification) and later clarity of perception, sense of self-worth, "level of reality," and ability to control the impact of the environment. Similarly, significant negative correlations were obtained between oral gratification and criticalness of people, loss of perceptual clarity, and tendency to get fatigued. It was also found that the degree of autonomy permitted by the mother correlated positively and significantly with later (preschool) internal integration (absence of disorganizing defenses), resistance to discouragement, ability to fend off excessive stimulation, and the like. These correlation coefficients in the case of boys were generally in the range of .50 to .65, and some were even higher.

As we noted in the previous chapter, when discussing the effects of early experience on the later characteristics of personality, the problems of establishing causal connections between these two sets of events are not solved by the finding that there are significant correlations between them. Careful control is needed of many other intervening factors which may contribute to such correlations, but the findings are highly suggestive of such a connection. What is critically needed in such studies, or in other studies, is evaluation of cases in which apparently less favorable (or different) conditions in early childhood were still associated with favorable personality outcomes in later life. Frustration and conflict do not lead inevitably to defensive operations and maladjustment; they may, at least in some instances or under certain conditions, also lead to effective coping behavior and healthy personality integration.

One study, in particular, that has attempted to differentiate

557

between defense mechanisms and coping mechanisms and to relate these two general modes of behavior to relative increase or decrease in measured intelligence deserves special note. Haan studied the performance of 49 male and 50 female subjects on a test of intelligence when these subjects were adolescents and, later, when they were in their middle adulthood [51]. The subjects were carefully rated in terms of their defense mechanisms and their coping mechanisms. Haan based her measures on a conceptual model which assumes that the mechanisms have identical *processes* but exhibit different *properties*. She offers the following list of properties which distinguish the two mechanisms:

Properties of a defense mechanism:

1. Behavior is rigid, automatized, and stimulus bound.
2. Behavior is pushed from the past, and the past compels the need for the present.
3. Behavior is essentially distorting of the present situation.
4. Behavior involves a greater quantity of primary process thinking, partakes of unconscious elements, and is thus undifferentiated in response.
5. Behavior operates with the assumption that it is possible to remove disturbing affects magically.
6. Behavior allows impulse gratification by subterfuge.

Properties of a coping mechanism:

1. Behavior involves choice and thus is flexible and purposive.
2. Behavior is pulled toward the future and takes account of the needs of the present.
3. Behavior is oriented to the reality requirements of the present situation.
4. Behavior involves secondary process thinking, . . . conscious and preconscious elements, and is highly differentiated in response.
5. Behavior operates within the organism's necessity of "metering" the experiencing of disturbing affects.
6. Behavior allows forms of impulse satisfaction in an open, ordered, and tempered way.

As noted in our own discussion, the conception of coping mechanisms is based on the premise that they are responses to external threats but that, at the same time, they are responses to internal conflicts, as well. Haan believed that persons who utilized coping rather than defense mechanisms, preferentially, would show acceleration in their relative intellectual performance over a period of time. She also believed that defensive behavior would be correlated with a reduction in intellectual performance. These hypotheses were confirmed in her study. She also discovered certain sex differences, as, for example, that men were more accelerative in intelligence than women. These differences seemed to be related to cultural factors associated with sex roles.

Findings such as those cited suggest that the healthy individual "copes" rather than "defends" and that both types of patterns of adjustive behaviors are related to experiential factors.

References

1. Lewin, K. *A Dynamic Theory of Personality.* New York: McGraw-Hill, 1935.
2. Miller, N. E. Experimental studies of conflict. In J. McV. Hunt (Ed.), *Personality and the Behavior Disorders.* New York: Ronald, 1944.
3. Barker, R. G. An experimental study of the relationship between certainty of choice and the relative valences of the alternatives. *J. Pers.,* 1946, **15,** 41–52.
4. Freud, S. *The Psychopathology of Everyday Life,* in *The Basic Writings of Sigmund Freud.* New York: Random House, 1938. (First German ed., 1904.)
5. Wolberg, L. R. Hypnotic experiments in psychosomatic medicine. *Psychosom. Med.,* 1947, **9,** 337–342.
6. DeCharms, R., Morrison, H. W., Reitman, W., & McClelland, D. C. Behavioral correlates of directly and indirectly measured achievement motivation. In D. C. McClelland (Ed.), *Studies in Motivation.* New York: Appleton-Cen-century-Crofts, 1955.
7. May, R. *The Meaning of Anxiety.* New York: Ronald, 1950.
8. Solomon, R. L., & Wynne, L. C. Traumatic avoidance learning: The principles of anxiety conservation and partial reversibility. *Psychol. Rev.,* 1954, **61,** 353–385.
9. Horney, K. *The Neurotic Personality of Our Time.* New York: Norton, 1937.
10. Jersild, A. T., & Holmes, F. B. *Children's Fears.* (Child Develpm. Monogr. No. 20.) New York: Teachers College, 1935.
11. Spence, K. W. A theory of emotionally based drive (D) and its relation to performance in simple learning situations. *Amer. J. Psychol.,* 1958, **13,** 131–141.
12. Taylor, J. A., & Chapman, J. Paired-associate learning as related to anxiety. *Amer. J. Psychol.,* 1955, **68,** 671 ff.

13. Freud, S. *The Problem of Anxiety* (trans. by H. A. Bunker). New York: Norton, 1936.

14. Freud, S. Analysis of a phobia in a 5-year-old child, in *Collected Papers,* Vol. III, pp. 149–289. London: Hogarth & the Institute of Psychoanalysis, 1948.

15. Cattell, R. B. *Anxiety, Motivation and Measurement.* New York: Harcourt, Brace & World, 1957.

16. Hutt, M. L., & Gibby, R. G. *Patterns of Abnormal Behavior.* Englewood, N.J.: Allyn and Bacon, 1957.

17. Mowrer, O. H. *Learning Theory and Behavior.* New York: Wiley, 1960.

18. Mandler, G., & Sarason, S. B. A study of anxiety and learning, *J. abnorm. soc. Psychol.,* 1952, **47,** 166–173.

19. Taylor, J. A. A personality scale of manifest anxiety. *J. abnorm. soc. Psychol.,* 1953, **48,** 185–190.

20. Weiss, E., & English, O. S. *Psychosomatic Medicine.* (2nd ed.) Philadelphia: Saunders, 1949.

21. Diethelm, O. *Treatment in Psychiatry.* (2nd ed.) Springfield, Ill.: Charles C Thomas, 1950.

22. Reed, C. F., Alexander, I. E., & Tomkins, S. S. (Eds.). *Psychopathology: A Source Book.* Cambridge, Mass.: Harvard, 1958.

23. Breuer, J., & Freud, S. *Studies in Hysteria.* In *Standard Edition,* Vol. II (trans. and ed. by J. Strachey). London: Hogarth, 1955. (First German ed., 1895.)

24. Child, I. L. Personality. *Annu. Rev. Psychol.,* 1954, **5,** 149–170.

25. Sarason, S. B., Mandler, G., & Craighill, P. G. The effect of differential instructions on anxiety and learning. *J. abnorm. soc. Psychol.,* 1952, **47,** 561–565.

26. Sarason, I. Effect of anxiety, motivational instructions, and failure on serial learning. *J. exp. Psychol.,* 1956, **51,** 153–160.

27. Sperber, Z. Test anxiety and performance under stress. *J. consult. Psychol.,* 1961, **25,** 226–233.

28. Haywood, H. C. Relationships among anxiety, seeking of novel stimuli, and level of unassimilated concepts. *J. Pers.,* 1961, **29,** 105–114.

29. Sarason, I. G. Empirical findings and theoretical problems in the use of anxiety scales. *Psychol. Bull.,* 1960, **57,** 403–415.

30. Cartwright, R. D. The effects of psychotherapy on self-consistency. *J. consult. Psychol.,* 1961, **25,** 376–382.

31. Freud, A. *The Ego and the Mechanisms of Defense.* New York: International Universities Press, 1946.

32. Klein, M. *The Psycho-Analysis of Children.* London: Hogarth, 1932.

33. Hutt, M. L., & Feuerfile, D. The clinical meanings and predictions of a measure of perceptual adience-abience for a

deaf-retarded group. Paper presented at Amer. Psychol. Assoc. Convention, Philadelphia, Pa., Sept., 1963.

34. Solley, C. M., & Murphy, G. *Development of the Perceptual World.* New York: Basic Books, 1960.
35. Fenichel, O. *The Psychoanalytic Theory of Neurosis.* New York: Norton, 1945.
36. Stagner, R. The redintegration of pleasant and unpleasant experiences. *Amer. J. Psychol.,* 1931, **43,** 463–468.
37. Barker, R. G., Dembo, T., & Lewin, K. Frustration and regression: An experiment with young children. *Univ. Iowa Stud. Child Welf.,* 1941, **18,** No. 386.
38. Zubek, J. P., Sansom, W., & Prysiazniuk, A. Intellectual changes during prolonged isolation (darkness and silence). *Canad. J. Psychol.,* 1960, **14,** 233–243.
39. Cattell, R. B. *Description and Measurement of Personality.* New York: Harcourt, Brace & World, 1946.
40. Sears, R. R. Survey of objective studies of psychoanalytic concepts. *Soc. Sci. Res. Council Bull.,* 1953, No. 51.
41. Sears, R. R. Experimental studies of projection. I, Attribution of traits. *J. soc. Psychol.,* 1936, **7,** 151–163.
42. Hutt, M. L., & Miller, D. R. Social values and personality development. *J. soc. Issues,* 1949, **5,** 2–43.
43. Cameron, N. *Personality Development and Psychopathology.* Boston: Houghton Mifflin, 1963.
44. Rapaport, D. *Organization and Pathology of Thought.* New York: Columbia Univ. Press, 1951.
45. Adler, A. *Study of Organ Inferiority and Its Psychical Compensation.* New York: Nervous & Mental Disease Publishing Co., 1917.
46. Freud, S. *Civilization and Its Discontents* (trans. by J. Riviere). London: Hogarth, 1930.
47. Taylor, W. S. Alternative response as a form of "sublimation." *Psychol. Rev.,* 1932, **39,** 165–174.
48. Miller, D. R., & Swanson, G. E. *Inner Conflict and Defense.* New York: Holt, Rinehart and Winston, 1960.
49. Seward, G. *Psychotherapy and Culture Conflict.* New York: Ronald, 1956.
50. Murphy, L. B., *et al. The Widening World of Childhood.* New York: Basic Books, 1962.
51. Haan, N. Proposed model of ego functioning: Coping and defense mechanisms in relationship to IQ change. *Psychol. Monogr.,* 1963, No. 571, 1–23.

FIVE THEORETICAL AP-PROACHES TO PERSONALITY STRUCTURE

We shall focus our attention in this chapter on the major theoretical approaches which attempt to explain the organization and structure of the concept known as personality. Our previous discussions were concerned with the ways in which personality *developed,* as well as the *dynamics* and *functioning* of personality. Now we are more interested in those conceptualizations which describe the *structure* of the fully developed personality or, in other words, the ways in which the various attributes of personality relate to each other.

From the earliest times recorded in history, man has attempted to describe his own nature. Philosophers from the time of Plato and Aristotle offered their views concerning the basic attributes of man and the nature of the interrelationships among them. The early philosophers based their views primarily upon observation and introspective analysis. In more recent years, beginning with the latter portion of the nineteenth century, scientists attempted to study personality more systematically and utilized empirical methods. Clinical observations or other methods, largely of a crude experimental character, were used to derive a more substantial theory of personality organization. Perhaps the most impressive first attempts in this direction began with the medical clinicians who were interested in the pathological conditions of their patients. In such early clinical studies of emotionally disturbed people, by Charcot and Freud, speculations were introduced concerning the nature of the maladies suffered by their patients which the known facts of anatomy and physiology were unable to explain. Freud was able, by virtue of long-term observation and therapy, to ameliorate some pathological states. He developed some highly creative hypotheses concerning the origins of their conditions and arrived at some far-reaching theories concerning the nature of the organization of the personality. At the same time, in Germany, the Gestalt psychologists were studying the personality of people by experimental methods and arrived at a different theoretical explanation. In their view, attempts being made by other contemporary psychologists to understand behavior solely in terms of isolated or fragmented aspects of behavior were highly inadequate. They provided us with a theory of man's personality which differed both in emphasis and in conception from the Freudian view of personality organization.

In more recent years extensive experimental studies have led psychologists interested in learning and motivation to develop more general theories of behavior which presumably could explain attributes of personality. Still another path was followed by psychometricians interested in the more precise measurement of behavior. They too have contributed views about the ways in which personality is organized.

We should state at the outset that we are still probably quite far from developing a single theory of personality organization which is entirely satisfying to any one "personality school," let alone to all behavioral scientists. An adequate personality theory should embrace a set of explicit assumptions concerning the major dimensions of man's behavior and the interrelationships among these dimensions. Moreover, the postulated dimensions must be rigorously defined, capable of reliable observation or measurement, and significant in the prediction of important aspects of behavior and adjustment. No theory exists today which meets these criteria and which embraces sufficiently the major dimensions of man's behavior. Nevertheless, we do have a number of important theories of personality organization which provide valuable insights about significant aspects of behavior and adjustment. They enable us to make some significant predictions and, most important of all, are highly stimulating for further observation, research, and constructive theory development.

We shall therefore sample a few of the views of the way in which man's personality is organized and thereby attempt to summarize both the nature of our progress in this field and the problems which still beset us. We should keep in mind the general assumption of these theories, namely, that the various aspects of the personality remain relatively consistent over the life-span and that their interrelationships are also relatively stable.

Freud's Psychoanalytic Theory

Freud's contributions concerning the structure of the personality deal with two interrelated sets of hypotheses concerning (1) the basic components of the personality, namely, the *id,* the *ego,* and the *superego;* and (2) the levels of mental life, namely, the *unconscious,* the *preconscious,* and the *conscious.* These two sets of hypotheses were frequently revised during the course of Freud's thinking and writing, roughly from the last decade of the nineteenth century, during which he wrote his first book, *The Interpretation of Dreams* [1], and culminating after his death in 1939 with his posthumously published work, *An Outline of Psychoanalysis* [2]. Moreover, the definitions of the ego and its functions were revised considerably after Freud's death by his followers, given far greater emphasis, and now comprise an essential part of psychoanalytic theory. We shall not attempt to trace the many ramifications of these hypotheses but shall, instead, discuss their characteristics as they are now accepted by Freudian psychoanalysts. In the case of the definition of the concept of the ego, however, some necessary developments in the reformulation of the theory will be considered.

In order to understand Freud's theories, one should be aware of his viewpoint concerning the nature of scientific discovery. He believed that in developing theories to explain human nature—as in other types of theories—there was necessarily a long period of *describing, classifying,* and *relating* phenomena. During this general phase the development of "abstract ideas," i.e., creative hypotheses, was of chief importance in explaining the observed interrelationships of the phenomena. He spoke of these "abstract ideas" as "conventions," and said of them:

. . . everything depends on their being chosen [these conventions] in no arbitrary manner, but determined by the important relations they have to the empirical material—relations that we seem to *divine* [italics ours] before we can clearly recognize and demonstrate them. It is only after searching investigation of the field in question that we are able to formulate with increased clarity the scientific concepts underlying it, and progressively modify these concepts so that they become widely applicable and at the same time consistent logically. Then indeed it may be time to immure them in definitions. *The progress of science, however, demands a certain elasticity even in these definitions* [italics ours] [3].

Freud tried to develop his theory beyond the stage which is described above, but he himself did not believe that he had yet achieved this goal, although contemporary psychoanalysts now believe (about a quarter-century after Freud's death) that they are in the beginning phases of this development. Thus, Freud would probably have agreed with some critics of his theory who argue that it is "hazy," "nonrigorous," and "abstract." At the same time he would have argued that it was stifling to further discovery to demand more precise and measurable interrelationships prematurely.

THE ID, EGO, AND SUPEREGO   To Freud the *id* constitutes the central core of the personality, and its properties are based on inheritance. It is the inner source of psychological energy and thus the source from which all psychic energy is derived. According to Freud, it is the source of all of our instincts (or drives, as they are now often called), including the primary sexual drives. Through the behavioral manifestations of the functions of the id, the individual may be enabled to become somewhat aware of his inner world of experience.

Impulses from the id constantly strive for discharge or expression. As tension builds up when internal or external excitation is present, the energy of the id seeks discharge through some form of behavior and thus returns the organism to its former tension level. The discharge of id energy in this manner is always experienced as pleasurable. Functions of the id are governed by the pleasure principle. The id functions in such a manner as to gain *immediate discharge* and is not significantly influenced by external factors. Gradually, as id energy is expended in this way, the individual may learn the reality principle, that is to say, he learns ways of adapting to the demands of the external world while keeping internal tensions at a comfortable level.

The characteristics of id process were described by Freud as primary processes which are amoral and alogical—uninfluenced by time or space relationships. It is difficult for the normal adult to comprehend the nature of primary process phenomena because, in his own developmental history, he has learned to substitute logical, realistic thinking and behaving for irrational thinking and behaving. Nevertheless, he can catch a glimpse of the operation of such phenomena in his dreams and in his fantasy. In dreams these features of primary process thinking are encountered; the realities of time, place, and size are disregarded, and wish-fulfillment guides the formation of fantasies. The thinking of psychotic (mentally deranged) people is also often characterized by primary process phenomena. The very young child's thinking is also often subordinated to this primary process, when wish or hallucination is experienced as vivid and real.

Another aspect of the id is its reliance upon inborn reflexive patterns of behavior. Response to increased internal excitation, such as pressure upon the bladder, or to strong external excitation, such as increased intensity of light or sound, is effected by reflex mechanisms. Together, primary process behavior and reflex behavior serve to reduce tension and offer discharge of id impulses. The fact that they are, nevertheless, not sufficient to maintain adequately low tension levels causes the organism to develop a secondary structure of the personality—*the ego*.

The *ego* is that aspect of the personality which makes it possible to adapt to reality. It is comprised of those systems which function to fulfill demands of the id, delay or inhibit them if there is conflict with other demands, and act in executive

Symbolic-irrational language of dreams. 'Man at the Top' and 'Come In.' Both paintings by Tomi Ungerer, courtesy D'Arcy Galleries, New York

manner to attend selectively to, or to respond to, external reality. According to Freud, the ego derives all of its energy from the id and develops out of the id in the course of maturation and learning. Unlike id functions, which are not directly responsive to external demands, the ego comes into being as a requirement of the organism in dealing with reality. At the same time, it has to meet the demands of id forces and is essentially a mediating mechanism.

In this original formulation of the nature and functions of the ego, Freud believed that the ego was a derived system, having its entire source in the id. The ego was said to develop out of the id because of two sets of factors. On the one hand, reality does not permit ready gratification of id demands. On the other, the developing organism, as its sensory, motor, cognitive, and affective functions mature, becomes capable of responding in new ways. More recent developments based on both clinical and experimental investigations have suggested that ego functions also have an autonomous origin and development [4], but we shall delay further consideration of this viewpoint for a moment.

In contrast to the operation of the id, the ego operates by the *secondary process*. It enables the organism to seek gratification in newer and more complex ways in coping with the demands of reality. In sum, there are three major aspects to ego operations: (1) it modulates the discharge of id impulses through delay or inhibition, when necessary, and, as a result of this experience, perceptive awareness of inner or subjective needs is developed; (2) it perceives, evaluates, and integrates incoming stimulation; and (3) it develops skills in integrating internal drives into appropriate patterns of discharge. By this means, patterns of response that maximize the fulfillment of id impulses are developed. The development of ego skills takes a lifetime of experience and, as we have noted, is in part dependent upon the biosocial development of the individual. In recent years various methods have been developed for assessing the strength of the ego [5] and for assessing any (psychopathological) damage it may have suffered [6]. We should also note that the ego has still another mediating function, that of keeping an appropriate balance between *id* and *superego* demands, and we shall discuss that function when we consider the "structure" known as the superego.

It became clear that individuals differed considerably in the extent to which they could develop ego skills. Some of this evidence came from studies of the inheritance of various ego abilities. In addition, clinical evidence indicated that some of the variance in ego skills could not be accounted for in terms of differentiation out of id functions; some individuals seemed to show limited capacity for ego function from the earliest days of infancy; psychotherapy proved to be ineffective in overcoming psychopathology in some individuals because they seemed to be deficient in ego strength. Moreover, the accumulation of experimental evidence concerning such phenomena as exploratory behavior (or *curiosity*), perceptual development, and cognitive functions led many workers either to attempt reformulations of the old drive theories[1] or to reconsider the source and nature of ego functions.

It should be noted that Freud himself proposed a tentative reformulation concerning the source of ego functions [7], in which he indicated that there were probably some inborn ego functions not essentially dependent upon derivation from id sources; but he did not carry this idea very far forward, and he died only two years after the publication of this reformulation. In 1946 Hartmann, Kris, and Lowenstein suggested that the ego had its own independent source of energy and that the exercise of some ego functions (like motility, perceptual clarity, and the like) had both pleasurable effects of their own and increased the possibility of adaptive behavior [4]. In an important paper, Hartmann developed this theory still further some twelve years later [8] and proposed that there was an innate ego apparatus (the "autonomous ego") which had its own laws of development and which was important in explaining the development of locomotion and language development. Erikson carried this line of thinking still further and offered a schema for understanding the development of ego functions as part of an interplay between the organism and social forces impinging upon it [9]. These social encounters provide a series of crises in the life of the child, and the outcome determines the nature of the individual's identification and his sense of adequacy. Klein [10] and later Gardner [11] were able to offer evidence that the "high-level" ego functions involved in cognition apparently had their own sources of growth and contributed significantly to the differences among individuals in their capacity for effective

---

[1] See pp. 323-370.

interpersonal behavior. Although it has not often been related directly to this problem, Piaget's theory, based largely on observational studies, which proposed that there are inborn *schemata* (or mechanisms for assimilating external stimulation) which change in the course of the individual's growth, and are replaced by new schemata when they prove to be inefficient, has some obvious similarities to these newer developments in the conception of the ego [12].

The *superego* is the third basic structure of the personality, according to Freud. Once ego functions have become fairly well established, the superego begins to develop in childhood. It results from the interactions of the child and his parents (or other supervisors of his activities in early childhood). When the child is punished for certain behaviors, he gradually learns to internalize these inhibitions, which then become that part of his superego known as the *conscience*. He does this to retain the love of his parents, whose love he seeks. These internalized controls then make him do what he was originally unwilling to do. When he engages in behavior in accordance with these internalized controls, he avoids displeasure (or *guilt*). But the child not only internalizes the inhibitions known as conscience; by a similar process, he also internalizes his parents' value systems, which tell him what he should do or positively strive for. These become part of the superego known as *ego-ideals*. Thus the superego inhibits expression of id impulses or, when it fails to do so, in accordance with internalized prohibitions of the conscience, it produces guilt; and the superego facilitates those aspects of behavior that are in accord with its ego-ideals and thereby enables the individual to experience pleasure (or *pride*).

This structure of the personality, consisting of the three basic components—id, ego, and superego—functions as a whole, the three subcomponents being closely interrelated. During periods which are regarded as "healthy," there is a harmonious interplay among these three systems, and energy is expended while being experienced as pleasurable. There are crises during the course of every individual's life when these three subcomponents are not in harmony. Relatively normal crises occur during adolescence, and there are crises which occur more frequently or persistently in disturbed individuals when there is moderate or extreme disharmony. Maturation and learning increase the strength of one component relative to the other, and thus the relative balance among the systems is in a constant state of growth and change. Both the ego and superego are considerably affected by life-experiences, whereas the id presumably is never directly influenced by these factors.

CONSCIOUS, PRECONSCIOUS, AND UNCONSCIOUS LEVELS

In trying to understand the nature of human motivation, Freud gradually came to the conception of "levels of mental life." Like others before him, he recognized the operation of unconscious forces in the behavior of the person, but, unlike others, he came to believe that these unconscious forces were not trivial phenomena to be occasionally taken into account in explaining behavior. He believed these unconscious forces to be the mainspring of much significant behavior. Today, many psychologists acknowledge the importance of unconscious processes, although they may prefer to describe them in terms other than Freud utilized. For example, Murray and his co-workers deal with the significance of unconscious factors in the production of fantasies and in the relationship of such factors to achievement as well as to adjustment [13].

Freud postulated three levels or layers of the mind, the conscious, the preconscious, and the unconscious. He described the *conscious layer* as that which is immediately within our perceptual awareness. Freud believed that this area of the mind was relatively "narrow" in that it contributed only a small fraction of awareness of what was going on in the personality. Moreover, he ascribed much less importance to conscious phenomena than most other psychologists of his day. Although people ascribe conscious motivations to what they do, and these conscious motivations have some role in our behavior, man is not as rational as we would like to believe. Much of our motivation is not on the conscious level. The conscious level of mental life is most closely linked with "ego operations" of the personality and enables us to deal with objective reality or to find ways of defending against it.

The *preconscious layer* of the mind consists of those experiences which are not within immediate awareness but can be called into play with moderate or minimal effort. Thus, memories of things past which we do not recall immediately but which can be recalled when we make the effort are part of the preconscious and play an important role in our behavior. We sometimes are aware of this role of the preconscious as we note that our behavior was prompted by information resulting from past experience which was not focal in our attention as we performed the behavior. In buying clothes, making a date, or in selecting a route for a journey, we may be able to isolate previous experiences which guided our decisions. Freud postulated the presence of an unconscious level of the mind to account for the vagaries of attention (later called *selective attention* by the psychiatrist, Sullivan, and more recently called "scanning" or "field dependence" by experimental psychologists). Figure 5.1 is a diagram of the relations of these three layers, or levels, of the mind.

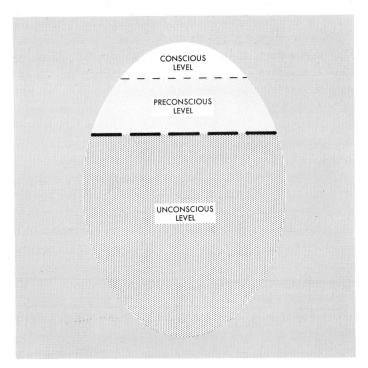

FIGURE 5.1 *Graphic representation of relations of the three levels of the personality.*

The *unconscious layer* of the mind is not available to consciousness except under unusual circumstances and only with very great effort. It consists of those aspects of one's psychological experience which have been repressed or have otherwise become unavailable to one's awareness. Nevertheless, unconscious processes are highly important in our everyday lives and guide much of our thinking, feeling, and motor behavior. Our most important choices concerning such things as friendships, marriage, vocational decisions, and prejudices are based on levels of experience of which we are largely unaware. Freud believed that unconscious processes revealed themselves through (1) *slips of the tongue,* in which we reveal unconscious factors of which we are unaware; (2) the phenomena of *hypnotism,* in which the subject can be shown to be motivated by unconscious forces; (3) *dreams,* in which important memories and affects that have been repressed appear in disguised or symbolic form; (4) *sudden insights* or creative solutions to seemingly insoluble problems that occur without conscious awareness of the factors leading to the behavior (5) *hysterical symptoms* (often physical), with no known organic basis and with no known psychological causes (to the person who is ill); (6) the emergence in psychoanalysis of *deeply buried memories* which appear to be significant in determining the person's personality reactions.

Many studies have demonstrated the utility of the concept of the unconscious. Sears summarized many of these in his monograph [14]. Recent studies on attention [15] and on perception [16] have been influenced by the assumption of the unconscious and have provided evidence for its plausibility. As we shall see in Chapter 8, many of the devices for assessing personality are based on the assumption of an unconscious and have been used not only in the study of individual personality but in many types of studies of social interactions. *Projective tests* are devices of this kind which attempt to get at deeper levels of motivation by offering the subject a relatively unstructured stimulus which is interpreted by the subject in his own unique way. The trained psychologist in turn interprets these responses by recognizing that they are derivatives of the subject's unconscious.

Factor Analysis and Personality Structure

Quite a different view and approach toward understanding personality structure is sponsored by those who may be called "factor analysts of personality." These workers base their view of personality structure on empirical findings derived from statistical studies of the intercorrelations among various measures of personality functioning. Sometimes they have been guided in the selection of the measures to be studied by the findings of clinicians; more often they have been stimulated by the evidence derived from developmental and experimental studies of human personality.

THE NATURE OF TRAITS   To understand the factor-analytic findings, we must understand, first, the meaning of the term "trait" which is at the base of all studies employing this method. A trait is usually thought of as a relatively persistent way of behaving in a number of different, but related, situations. For example, shyness may be thought of as a trait if we assume that a person who is shy in one situation also tends to be shy in other, related situations. The presumed trait of shyness is not an entity that exists in reality; it is rather an abstraction, derived from repeated observations of behavior which appear to have a common characteristic. Some workers, as for example Eysenck [17], suggest that the concept of trait is based upon a lower-order concept, that of *habitual responses*. Habitual response patterns may be defined as ". . . specific responses which tend to recur under similar circumstances," that is, similar responses to similar life-situations. And, of course, underlying habitual response patterns, one can describe more detailed specifics of behavior, i.e., those responses which occur only once in a given type of situation. An example of such a specific response would be that of an eye blink in response to stimulation of the eye by an increase in light intensity. As we proceed up the ladder of hierarchical organization of the personality, we move from specific responses to habitual response patterns to traits. The trait may be seen as a kind of group factor, and it depends upon a group of responses which have an organizational unity or coherence. A trait is based upon the observed correlation of behavior patterns across a number of different situations. Figure 5.2 may make this concept more clear.

One of the persistent problems with which psychologists have attempted to deal is that of determining the minimum number of traits necessary for describing personality or required for predicting responses of an individual in new situations. Obviously, if the number of traits required to do this job is very large, then little can be said concerning the major characteristics of personality organization, for we would need as many traits as there are possible behavior patterns.

574   Some psychologists object to the use of trait-names as an

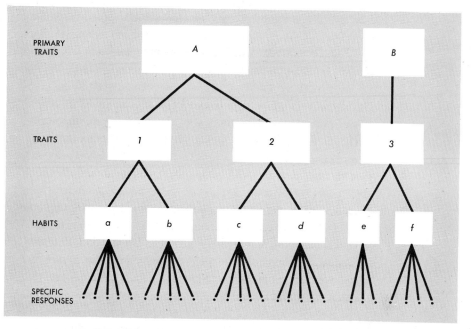

FIGURE 5.2 *Diagrammatic representation of hierarchy from specific responses to primary traits.*

approach to characterizing personality structure on the ground that their research indicates that a very large number of traits is needed to describe personality. For example, Odbert and Allport, who made a very thorough study of this problem, found that about 18,000 terms were needed to account for all of the subtleties of human behavior and that even this number of traits did not account for all of the variability [18]. However, factor analysts have tried to demonstrate that the personality structure can be defined by a relatively small number of general categories, each of which is composed of several traits which have relatively high intercorrelations among themselves. If this can be done, they argue, then it may be possible to develop not only an economical method of measuring the major general components of the personality, but these components, or *factors* as they are usually called, may become highly effective in predicting personality reactions.

Before these factors can be isolated, it is necessary, therefore, to have some idea of which traits are likely to have some high degree of significance; effective ways of measuring such traits must be developed; and the various measures of a given trait must be shown to be measuring the same behavioral attribute.

Although none of these conditions has yet been fully satisfied, factor analysts have already gone a long way in demonstrating the usefulness of the factor-analytic method.

THE EXTRACTION OF FACTORS Some factor analysts have taken a large number of measures on a given population of subjects and have obtained the intercorrelations among all of the measures. Then they determine the least number of general factors necessary to account for the intercorrelations by one of the statistical techniques involved in factor analysis. Finally, appropriate names are assigned to these factors. Such an approach has been criticized on several counts. In the first place, the selection of traits to be included in the factor analysis should include a wide variety, and not a narrow sampling, of personality attributes. In the second place, factorial investigations should be based as broadly as possible on a variety of measures of the same behavioral characteristics. If only a single type of measure of some trait is employed in the measures used in the factorial analysis—such as responses to questionnaires or rating scales—there is no assurance that a given factor obtained from the analysis has any meaningful generality. Therefore, several very different types of measures of the same characteristic should be employed. Unfortunately, this has not been true in most factorial studies. And, in the third place, the demonstration that there is a factor can be useful only if the factor can be shown to occur in several subject populations. Otherwise, it may be only an artifact of the selection of the sample in which it was discovered, or it may only have applicability in a small sector of the general population. Once again, factorial studies have seldom been applied to enough widely divergent types of populations, such as to both normal and abnormal groups, or to both adults and children, or to well-educated persons and not-so-well-educated persons.

In recent years, studies have been made which have attempted to meet the criticisms noted above. These studies have been rather large-scale projects involving large numbers of subjects and varied types of populations and have only been made possible by the recent availability of high-speed electronic computers. Even so, they often take years to complete. Summing up the results of such studies, most psychologists believe we are just scratching the surface—just beginning the development of satisfactory techniques of studying the personality by factor-analytic methods. Cronbach reviewed the major factorial studies of personality and concluded, "There is at present no consensus among factor analysts as to the number of factors that have been reliably identified, the best organization of them, or their most appropriate names" [19]. Nevertheless, the future promise of the method suggests that it will become an increasingly powerful tool in personality research.

The method of factor analysis begins by calculating the intercorrelations among several measures. Suppose, for example, that in a large population of subjects we find the following intercorrelations among four tests of personality, as in Table 5.1. We note that tests A and B have a great deal in common with each other but have little in common with the

TABLE 5.1. THE INTERCORRELATIONS AMONG FOUR TESTS

	Test B	Test C	Test D
Test A	.85	.10	.05
Test B		.08	.15
Test C			.75

other tests, C and D. We can also note that C and D have a considerable correlation but that neither of these is highly correlated with either A or B. Thus, we might assume from these data that these four personality tests show the presence of two rather distinct sets of factors: Factor A-B and Factor C-D. If we concluded that only two factors were necessary to describe personality, on the basis of these results, we would be making an unwarranted generalization, as we indicated in our previous discussion of the general criticisms of factorial studies. For, if we had chosen to work with only tests A, B, and C, we might just as unwisely have concluded that personality consisted of one group factor, A-B, and one specific factor, C. In other words, the degree of generalizability one can obtain from intercorrelations depends, at the very least, upon the number of measures one has used.

But suppose that we start with a large number of personality measures and apply these measures to a variety of subject populations. Then we obtain the intercorrelations among all of the measures. Mere inspection of the table of intercorrelations will be very confusing. Some method is needed for obtaining a statistical evaluation of the intercorrelations to find clusters of highly correlated items which represent presumptive factors. Mathematically it is possible to determine the smallest number of factors needed to account for all of the clusters of correlated items. Once the minimum number of factors has been obtained, it is possible to describe each individual test measure by its relationship to the newly discovered factors. Mathematically, it is possible to transform the original factor analysis to accomplish, more efficiently, certain predictive results. Most American psychologists attempt to locate "pure" personality dimensions. This type of decision is related to the goal of the study, whether this is to describe the data by as few broad factors as possible or to describe the data by means of clear-cut, specific factors.

Generally speaking, when personality tests are factor-analyzed, a large number of factors emerge. More factors emerge when variables related to personality are being analyzed than when items are selected which measure some more selective characteristic of behavior, for example, musical ability. The problem of describing personality is very complex, and the measures of personality traits can emphasize quite different aspects of what may be the same trait. The tests used to determine a trait can be measured in terms of a person's behavior or in terms of how well he performs that behavior. They can be measured by objective tests, or they can use evaluations of a person's behavior made by observers. Even physiological variables can be used in traits defined by factor-analytic techniques.

SOME FINDINGS Having noted the difficulties as well as the promise of factor-analytic methods of studying personality structure, let us now review the results of this approach. We shall follow the summary provided by Guilford [20], who bases his conclusions on the reported findings of a large number of investigators. Guilford describes four aspects of personality: somatic, aptitudes, temperament, and hormetic disposition (or motivational traits). Most pertinent in this context is the analysis of temperament. On the basis of factor-analytical studies he believes it possible to divide temperamental factors into three subgroups: general, emotional, and social. Each of these, in turn, is divided into five categories. (See Table 5.2.)

The *general* category of factors of temperament consists of three factors which Guilford believes have been widely accepted (at least among factor analysts) and two about which there is far

TABLE 5.2. GUILFORD'S MATRIX OF TEMPERAMENT FACTORS

Kind of Dimension	Areas of Behavior Involved		
	General	Emotional	Social
Positive vs. negative	Confidence vs. inferiority	Cheerfulness vs. depression	Ascendance vs. timidity
Responsive vs. unresponsive	Alertness vs. inattentiveness	Immaturity vs. maturity	Socialization vs. self-sufficiency
Active vs. passive	Impulsiveness vs. deliberateness	Nervousness vs. composure	Social initiative vs. passivity
Controlled vs. uncontrolled	Restraint vs. rhathymia	Stability vs. cycloid disposition	Friendliness vs. hostility
Objective vs. egocentric	Objectivity vs. hypersensitivity	Poise vs. self-consciousness	Tolerance vs. criticalness

SOURCE: J. P. Guilford, *Personality,* New York: McGraw-Hill, 1959, p. 409.

less consensus. The factor of *confidence vs. inferiority feelings* has been found in quite diverse types of populations, such as adults, children, normal people, and abnormal people. It therefore deserves recognition as an important group factor. The factor is assumed to be a continuous variable. It has a "negative end," which may be defined by such characteristics as discontent with oneself, guilt, and egocentrism. This constellation may surprise us; one might have suspected that guilt would not be a necessary part of feelings of inferiority and that egocentrism would not inevitably be associated with this factor. It may be that there are various forms of guilt, some of which are not integrally associated with inferiority, and the same thing may be true for egocentrism. At any rate, this constellation has been *measured* and does, in fact, occur. Only further experimental factor-analytic work will tell us more about the final meaning of the factor of inferiority.

The second of the three subcategories of the general aspect of temperament may be called *objectivity vs. hypersensitivity.* The hypersensitive end of this continuum may be defined by such characteristics as recoil from reality, worry over humiliating experiences, and hypersensitivity (at the extreme, *paranoidal*)

579

concerning the presumed critical attitudes of others toward oneself. Some workers have linked the hypersensitive end of this scale to Jung's concept of introversion (see p. 588 ff.). It is also worth noting that the hypersensitive characteristics have been more clearly established than the objective aspects of this group factor.

The third general category is that of *alertness vs. inattentiveness*. This factor has resulted from quite recent factorial studies and may be defined as ". . . a matter of keeping in rapport with the environment versus being inattentive or absentminded" [20]. The characteristics found in this factor seem to relate to *spontaneous* rather than *directed* attention. The potency of this variable in determining the capacity for learning and for tolerating changing conditions as well as in characterizing some aspects of the adjustment of the individual (see Chapter 6) has been attested in a great variety of research studies.

At this point the reader may have become aware of the fact that these three factors seem, in common-sense analysis, to have some things in common. Isn't egocentrism part of both inferiority feelings and hypersensitivity? Isn't being inattentive more likely to be found among inferior individuals than among others? The point is that whether these factors are or are not really independent is a matter for experimental study and not a matter of semantics alone. Our common vocabulary is suffused with terms which have arisen out of popular conceptions (perhaps misconceptions), and one of the virtues of factor analysis and of correlated experimental study is that it can help us to clarify and add precision to present-day "fuzzy" conceptions.

Often the factors emerging from factor-analytic procedure contain characteristics which do not seem to fit together in any common-sense rubric. At other times there does seem to be a label which could characterize the items making up part of a factor. Some workers (like Cattell [21]) have invented entirely new verbal names of factors to avoid the confusion that might be introduced by the use of popular terms to describe factors.

The major grouping of *emotional factors* which Guilford has proposed consists of scales related to: *cheerfulness vs. depression; emotional immaturity vs. maturity; nervousness vs. composure; stability vs. cycloid disposition; poise vs. self-consciousness*. Again, as with the category of general factors discussed previously, not all of these factors have been found in all factor-analytic studies. Depression, for example, seems to be a multifaceted phenomenon. It is quite difficult to obtain self-ratings of depression because of the withdrawal and resistance character-istics of many depressed individuals. Further, it is quite different in children and adults. The term *depression* is used to cover many different kinds of things, both in popular usage and in clinical diagnosis. It will remain for clinical and experimental studies to define the characteristics and to determine the specific parameters of the phenomena covered by this rather broad spectrum of behaviors. On the other hand, the factor of *sta-bility vs. cycloid disposition* has been pretty well established and well defined. The cycloid person shows wide swings or abrupt swings in mood, largely independent of external cir-cumstances. This characteristic has been linked to certain kinds of psychopathology, as we shall see in Chapter 6.

The social-disposition category consists of scales purportedly measuring *ascendance vs. timidity; socialization vs. self-sufficiency; social initiative vs. passivity; friendliness vs. hostil-ity;* and *tolerance vs. criticalness.* Research studies have shown that these factors are related both to specific environmental conditions and to previous learning and conditioning. Never-theless, the factors tend to emerge regularly from factor-analytic studies undertaken in Western cultures and especially in popula-tions of college students and other "captive populations." They are related to various kinds of social capabilities and have been found useful in many kinds of predictive studies. They may be thought of as social skills which the individual has developed out of his past experiences; they may also be dependent in part on inherited characteristics of the individual.

Factor-analytic studies have provided fresh insights into many aspects of personality, they have challenged some pet clinical theories, and they have stimulated much research. They do not appear to be the final word, and they depend, them-selves, upon theories and hypotheses which have been devel-oped from clinical or other types of observations and upon experimental studies which have produced significant findings about various traits and the antecedent conditions.

The contrast between the clinical and psychoanalytic ap-proach to the theory of personality organization, on the one hand, and the factor-analytic, on the other, is quite striking. The former lays stress on a few fundamental characteristics of the personality which are assumed to embrace its most significant aspects, while the latter tries to encompass the whole organization of the personality with a much larger number of group or primary factors.[2] The former has emerged out of the clinical study of disturbed persons, while the latter has placed its trust in the mathematical analysis of various measures of presumably significant traits. Perhaps the greatest contrast lies in the dynamic interrelationship posited to exist among the components of the structure, as viewed by the psychoanalysts, whereas the interrelationships, if any, proposed by the factor analysts are those found in behavior as it is observed and measured. Despite these differences, the two approaches are not necessarily in opposition to each other, although the means of reconciling and integrating them may not yet exist. They rest upon different methodological assumptions and have different subgoals. But both are attempts to provide a more parsimonious explanation of the nature of the structure of the personality than a common-sense view can offer.

Type Theories of Personality Organization

INTRODUCTION The general goal of *type theories* of personality organization is not so far removed from the factor-analytic approach as at first might seem to be the case. Both have as their object the description of personality structure in terms of an economy of factors. And both assume that an individual's structure, so far as personality is concerned, remains more or less constant over the life-span.

Most type theories have attempted to describe the major components in the personality by means of a very few all-encompassing characteristics, which were thought to be so important that they could safely be used to predict most of the significant behavior of the individual. People were thought to fall into "types" describing their central personality characteristics. The layman is prone to accept this line of reasoning about personality because it makes for easy generalization and does not require painstaking attention to the highly complex and unique qualities of each human being. Such characterizations as "the incurable optimist," "the sad sack," "the bull in the china shop," "the smooth, oily salesman," and "the human dynamo"

---

[2] "The major exception to the relatively large number of factors suggested by factor analysts may be found in the work of Eysenck, cited previously [17].

seem to tell us at one fell swoop all that we need to know about the person. Although they may, in fact, call attention to some outstanding characteristic, they hardly begin to describe the variegated nature of human behavior. They lend themselves to easy stereotyping of people by class, by race, by nationality, and even by political conviction. They leave unsaid the tremendous differences among people who are characterized as being of the same "type." Therefore, they distort the very characteristics of the people they seek to describe. They assume that a "type" characteristic is an all-or-none phenomenon and that people of a given type are alike (and alike to the same degree) in the essentials of the "type." In this respect they deny the validity of the scientific discoveries of psychology which have demonstrated that each of the characteristics with which a person may be described is a "more-or-less" phenomenon, falling on a *continuum*. They tend to assume some genetic basis for the type characteristic and utterly neglect the influence of cultural conditioning and learning. Thus, once a person has been "typed," he must unfailingly and forever display the appropriate characteristics of that type.

Nevertheless, attempts to develop type theories of personality have characterized man's search for an explanation of human nature from time immemorial; they still are much in evidence today, although most modern psychologists are highly critical of such approaches. Hippocrates, usually thought of as the father of modern medicine, proposed about 400 B.C. that all men could be grouped into four main types of temperament: the *phlegmatic;* the *choleric* (or irritable); the *sanguine* (or optimistic); and, the *melancholic* [22]. He believed that each person could be characterized as belonging primarily to one of these four groups and that the dominant temperament of the individual was based on the dominance of one of the then four basic humors (body fluids); phlegm, yellow bile, blood, and black bile. Neither the types of temperament nor the conception of body humors has withstood the accumulation of evidence from the fields of personality research or human physiology.

However, Hippocrates' contributions in this area went largely unchallenged for centuries. Much later, in the nineteenth century, with the advance in the field of physiology, revisions and refinements of his theories were proposed. Attempts were made to relate aspects of human physique to physiological characteristics, on the one hand, and to personality characteristics, on the other. These explorations culminated in the work of Ernst Kretchmer, who in 1921 published his *Physique and Character* [23]. This psychiatrist was interested in demonstrating the inherent relationship between type of physique and type of major personality adjustment. He believed that he could demonstrate that physique was a major determinant of the personality mode not only in psychosis (or insanity) but also within the range of normal adjustments. It may be worth while to examine some of his formulations and some of his evidence.

Kretchmer devised a system of classifying the major parts of the human anatomy by means of "objective" check lists. On the basis of an analysis of his data, he proposed a fourfold classification of types of bodies. The *asthenic* was described as having ". . . a deficiency in thickness combined with an average lessened length." In common parlance such people would probably be described as frail and thin in general appearance. The *athletic* was described as ". . . (having) a strong development of the skeleton, the musculature and also the skin." This was the characterization for a middle-sized to tall man, with a powerful body build. The *pyknic* was classified as ". . . characterized by pronounced peripheral development of the body cavities . . . and a tendency to a distribution of fat about the trunk. . . ." These are people with short, plump bodies. And, finally, the *dysplastic* characterizes those individuals who show marked inconsistencies in the various parts of their bodies so that they may show athletic features in some part or parts while manifesting pyknic features in another part or parts.

Having developed what he regarded as a reliable rating scheme for these body types, Kretchmer proceeded to check his hypothesis that each type was associated with a particular mode of adjustment. His major findings concerned the relationship between two body types and two psychiatric conditions. His prior observations had convinced him that there was a biological affinity between the asthenic physique and schizophrenia and that there was, similarly, an affinity between the pyknic physique and manic-depressive psychosis. (See Chapter 6 for a description of these psychiatric conditions.) In a study of 260 psychotic patients suffering from either schizophrenia or manic-depressive psychosis, he obtained the findings presented in Table 5.3. It will be noted that the evidence seems to favor his hypothesis, since 81 schizophrenics were rated as asthenics and only 4 asthenics were manic-depressives, whereas 58 pyknics

TABLE 5.3. KRETCHMER'S FINDINGS ON RELATION OF TYPE OF
PHYSIQUE TO SCHIZOPHRENIA AND MANIC-DEPRESSIVE
PSYCHOSIS

	Type of Physique		
Type of Psychosis	Asthenic (*N*)	Pyknic (*N*)	Others (*N*)
Schizophrenia	81	2	92
Manic-depressive	4	58	23

Source: E. Kretchmer, *Physique and Character,* New York: Harcourt, Brace & World, 1925.

were manic-depressives and only 2 were schizophrenics. Of course, there were 27 manic-depressives who were *not* pyknics, and there were 94 schizophrenics who were *not* asthenics. However, even if the relationships between body build and tendency toward a particular form of psychiatric disorder held up in other investigations of this type, the validity of the hypothesis would still remain in serious question. The student would do well to consider what questions remain before the hypothesis can be either rejected or accepted. For example, do the relationships hold up when sex of the subjects or their culture is controlled in such studies? Do the relationships hold up when age, which is a factor in weight gain and change in body type, is controlled? (Schizophrenia tends to occur earlier in life than manic-depressive psychosis.) How much *contamination* (or observer bias) enters into the findings?

SHELDON'S TYPOLOGY A more sophisticated approach to the study of the relationship between physique and temperament was made by William H. Sheldon, a psychologist and physician [24]. He devised a method for *scoring* individuals on three basic components of physique. His method, called *somatotyping,* rejects the idea that people can be grouped into distinct physical types and instead evaluates them on the basis of the *degree to which* they possess each of a number of components. This method was developed on the basis of painstaking empirical research. He secured three standard photographs (frontal, lateral, and dorsal views of the naked body) of about 4,000 male college students taken against a standard background. Examination of these photographs by Sheldon and his collaborators led him to conclude that *three dimensions* were sufficient to describe the structure of the body. Each of these three primary components could be rated on a scale from 1 to 7 (from low to high) based on carefully specified anthropomorphic measurements and ratings. The three components were termed *endomorphy, mesomorphy,* and *ectomorphy.* The *endomorph* is a person who is high on the scale of endomorphy and low on the two others. He has highly developed digestive organs, is soft and round, and shows an underdevelopment of bone and muscle. The *mesomorph* is a person who shows a predominance of muscle and bone. The *ectomorph* is a person with an elongated body, a large central nervous system in relation to his size, is fragile, and has relatively little connective tissue. A person rated 1–6–2 would thus be low in endomorphy and ectomorphy and high in mesomorphy. The terms used to describe the three primary components were selected to indicate the cell layers in the body from which the body tissues developed. The concept of somatotype was coined to differentiate the measure from those of the *phenotype* (the overt, and perhaps transient, aspects of the physical build which might be influenced by aging, nutrition, and disease), on the one hand, and the *morphogenotype* (the underlying characteristics giving rise to the phenotype). It is thus, in Sheldon's own words, ". . . a prediction of the future succession of phenotypes . . ." other conditions (notably nutrition and health) remaining constant (see [24]).

In developing his Temperament Scale, Sheldon first selected a list of 650 traits from the relevant literature. He reduced this list to 50 traits and then, by means of an intensive study of selected individuals, discovered the clusters of traits that were necessary to define the temperament of these subjects. By means of this procedure, three primary clusters of traits were isolated, the traits within a cluster correlating with each other to the extent of + .60 and with those in the other clusters at the level of + .30. Each cluster was defined by twenty specific traits, and each of these could be rated from 1 to 7. A person's temperament on each of the primary components was based on the total of the twenty rated traits comprising that scale. The three scales were labeled: *viscerotonia* (high in sociability and a glutton for affection and food); *somatotonia* (liking for physical activities, strong need for the use of the musculature, and aggressive and callous toward others); and *cerebrotonia* (restrained, secretive, self-conscious, and overreactive to stimulation). In using the scale, the observer makes a prolonged study of the individual and then rates him on each of the twenty traits for each of the three primary scales.

Sheldon was interested in discovering how much relationship there was between the somatotype ratings and the temperament ratings. In an initial study of 200 white male college students, he reported surprisingly high correlations according to his predictions [25]. Thus endomorphy correlated with viscerotonia to the extent of + .79, mesomorphy with somatotonia to the extent of + .82, and ectomorphy with cerebrotonia to the extent of + .83. All of the other intercorrelations among these variables were negative. These findings would appear to be a significant demonstration of the relationships between body build and temperament. They are, clearly, much higher degrees of relationship than have generally been reported in the personality research literature between physique and temperament or, for that matter, between various measures of personality in general. What do they mean, and how well do the findings stand up?

The first question that one must ask of evidence presented in support of some theoretical position is whether the reported empirical findings are replicated by other investigators. In the case of Sheldon's findings this question is particularly important since the ratings made of temperament, even though made with great care and after a considerable period of study of his subjects, were made by Sheldon himself. Sheldon argues that his temperament ratings were made *before* his subjects were somatotyped and that, in any case, the ratings were objective. Both of these arguments are cogent and true, but it is quite possible, nevertheless, that in his intensive studies of his subjects Sheldon got to know (i.e., to contaminate because of this bias) both the temperament and the physical qualities and thus "loaded the dice" in his favor. The criticism can be answered appropriately, however, only by the presentation of findings from other research, with suitable controls for testing the reliability of the findings. Unfortunately, other studies using *ratings* have found, at best, only limited support for Sheldon's findings. And when the studies have employed *tests* of personality characteristics rather than ratings, there is almost no support at all for his thesis [26]. Sheldon argues that his somatotyping procedure is quite intricate and requires careful training by the rater, but other careful workers have, nevertheless, been unable to replicate his results.

Other criticisms of the theory proposed by Sheldon to account for his findings point out that there is practically no theory at all. There are no carefully developed postulates, no set of interrelated hypotheses to explain the alleged relationships, and no significant derivations from the theory that are amenable to testing. One test of the powerfulness of a theory is how much related and expanding research it stimulates. The answer on this score must also be on the negative side. And on the empirical side, some investigators have shown that Sheldon's three primary kinds of somatotype can be accounted for on the basis of two variables, not three [27], and that, moreover, the somatotype is, in fact, variable in the face of various environmental factors [28]. Thus, despite Sheldon's arduous labors and his impressive methodology and statistical findings, his general proposition, that it is possible to predict personality structure (in this case, persistent temperamental characteristics) from an invariant kind of somatotype, has not been sustained.

JUNG'S INTROVERSION-EXTRAVERSION Still another typologist, although he himself would probably disclaim this categorization of his personality theory, is C. G. Jung, who is most popularly known for his exposition of *introversion* and *extraversion*. The fact is that Jung has contributed far more significant concepts to the field of personality theory than his exposition of the introversion-extraversion problem, but we shall confine our remarks to this aspect of personality structure as he views it. Jung also accepts the concept of the personal unconscious, as does Freud, but he conceives of another "structure," the *collective unconscious*, as having great importance for the functioning of the personality. He also discussed other aspects of the personality structure, which we shall not detail here [29]. But for all of these he considers the various structures or factors in the personality as dynamically interacting systems.

Returning, now, to the concepts of introversion and extraversion, these are posited as two opposing attitudinal orientations to the world, the first of which involves orientation of the person toward his inner, subjective world and which is attended by social shyness and preferences for being by oneself, while the second involves orientation of the person toward the outer, objective world and is manifested by a tendency toward gregariousness, with an "open and ready disposition, at ease in any given situation." These temperamental attitudes are thought to be inborn characteristics and can be observed from birth on.

People can be typed as being either introverts or extraverts. Moreover, these basic orientational qualities are highly significant in all interpersonal relationships, determining such things as the type of occupation one finds congenial, the kinds of companions one selects, and even one's basic philosophy of life. Jung presented both clinical and various kinds of empirical evidence to support his contentions.

But unlike typologists who conceive of people as belonging in one category or another and who possess all or none of a given characteristic, Jung believed introversion and extraversion were matters of degree and that *both* orientational attitudes were present in every human being. Further, he believed that both orientations were necessary for effective living, since they complement each other. A given individual, then, has a certain degree of, let us say, introversion in his makeup, which is the predominant characteristic. He also has the counterpart of extraversion, which is then subordinate. As he develops and *consciously* strengthens his predominant characteristic, the greater is the *unconscious* development of the opposing orientation. The unconscious attitude thus remains undifferentiated, that is, it grows in strength but does not mature and enter into a reciprocal and interacting pattern in the individual's total adjustment. Jung cautions against the one-sided development of the naturally predominant attitudinal orientation; for, when this happens, some form of psychopathology or maladjustment is likely to occur, and psychotherapy, in some form, becomes essential for restoring some degree of harmony to the personality.[3]

Research with introversion-extraversion in relatively recent years has shown that this characteristic of the personality is probably a multifaceted phenomenon, for factor analysis of tests purportedly measuring it indicate that, for example, social introversion and cognitive or "thinking" introversion are relatively independent features of the personality [30 and 31]. Research findings support Jung's contention that people differ in degree of introversion-extraversion; in fact, the distribution is close to that of the normal probability function [32]. Some writers on personality theory and structure have taken this kind of finding to be a disproof of Jung's position, but the error is not

---

[3] Eysenck has devoted a number of years to factorial studies of personality and has concluded that extraversion-introversion is one of the three primary dimensions of the personality [30].

Jung's. Jung simply maintained that some people (normal or pathological) were on the extremes in this characteristic (which is consistent with the evidence) and *not* that there were two modes in the distribution or that most people clustered at either extreme.

Field Theory and Personality Structure

A theory which is unique in conceptualizing the nature of psychological organization is that proposed by Kurt Lewin [33]. Unlike other theorists who tackled this task, Lewin attempted to conceptualize the structure of personality in relationship to the forces impinging upon man from the outside world and upon which he, in turn, impinged. He was interested, as were other dynamically oriented psychologists, in conceptualizing the internal structure of man's personality, but he believed that it was impossible to evaluate this structure properly without *simultaneously* considering the "facts," as he called them, of the psychological and physical worlds. Hence he termed his theory a "field theory," in which the field was defined as both the person and the environment. As we shall see, Lewin conceived of personality structure not as a fixed, static, and immutable organization of traits or habits but rather as a contemporary field of dynamically interacting forces which was constantly in a state of flux. In this respect he departed radically from those psychologists, and from that philosophical viewpoint, conceiving of man in mechanical or machine-like terms. For Lewin, man was not an *object* whose behavior was to be predicted entirely in terms of stimuli applied to it. Lewin also differed from Freud in at least two respects: (1) he viewed man as changing continuously and interacting with his environment, and (2) he attempted to understand man's behavior in terms of factors operating within and upon him *contemporaneously*. His orientation may be seen as a revolt against the mechanistic conception of man, on the one hand, and, as we shall learn, as a protest against those theories which made difficult the empirical testing of derivatives of the theories.

Lewin proposed, first of all, that the nature of psychological reality could be depicted in terms of mathematics and physics. He attempted to represent the nature of ever changing or dynamic structure. He frequently used spatial representations of the forces that were operating in the person to produce behavior, and he termed his spatial representation *hodological*, in order to indicate that it was concerned with *paths of influence* of the forces. Theoretically, the person was conceived as operating, at every moment in time, within a *life-space*. The life-space, in turn, was conceived as operating within a *physical world*, described by Lewin as "the foreign hull of the life space." The accompanying simplified diagram represents the rudiments of this conceptualization. (See Figure 5.3.) Usually, the person is

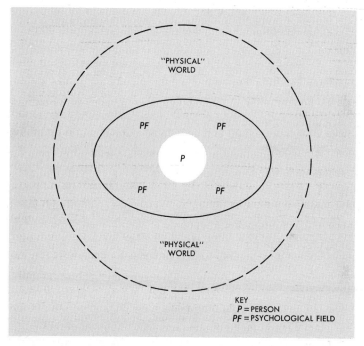

FIGURE 5.3 *Lewin's basic conceptualization of the person in his life-space.* P = *person;* PF = *psychological field.*

represented as a circle (*P*), and the life-space consists of the person and the *psychological field* (*PF*) within which this person is enclosed (*P* and *PF*). The person has his own circle, and the life-space has its own boundary, represented by the perimeter of the ellipse. Note that not only is the person enclosed by the ellipse but that no part of the boundary of the person touches the boundary of the ellipse. The boundaries of both the person and the life-space are conceived of as permeable, meaning that there can be lesser or greater degrees of influence or interaction between life-space and person and between the physical world and the life-space. This diagrammatic representation of the person-in-the-world may suggest that personality can only be understood, in terms of this system, as that behavior which emerges, at a given moment, as a result of the complex interplay of forces from the individual, his life-space, and the physical world. According to Lewin's theory, it would be inaccurate to conceive of a person as having this or that amount of aggression or any other trait. Rather, his manifest personality is *always the interplay of the fields of forces operating within and upon him.* Whether a particular person will act aggressively in a given situation depends upon the total interaction of the person in the situation. The situation acts upon the individual, just as the individual acts upon the situation. This is in sharp contrast to the classical behaviorist's view that the organism contains definite behavioral potentials from which the environment elicits certain responses (the classical stimulus-response view).

Before further defining the nature of the person and the nature of the situation, as well as the boundaries of each, as conceptualized by Lewin, it would be well to consider in more detail the concepts of *force, valence,* and *tension.* Lewin thinks of *force* as any tendency toward movement of an individual within a psychological field. This is a logical construct and does not imply any particular assumption about the nature or source of the forces that may be involved. More simply stated, it is a conceptualization concerning what motivates behavior. Force only exists as a function of the field. It is based on the relations of organism to environment. *Valence* is defined as ". . . that which attracts or repulses this individual." A region has valence when it is within the life-space of the individual and arouses some force.*Tension* is understood as a condition of the inner-personal region (i.e., the inner forces) and is related to the particular activity which generates it. As an additional assumption, Lewin believed that tension always tends to become equalized in terms of surrounding or adjacent regions of the life-space. That is, there is a tendency for tension reduction through a process of equalization. Sometimes, as tension is reduced in one region, it may rise in another region, but the whole system works toward the establishment of a state of equilibrium. When tension arises, pressure is exerted against the boundary of the region in which it occurs and, depending upon the nature of the

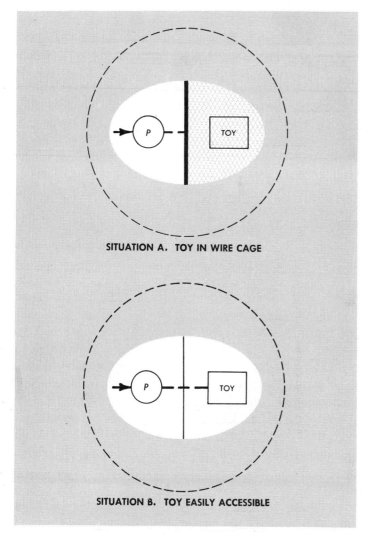

SITUATION A. TOY IN WIRE CAGE

SITUATION B. TOY EASILY ACCESSIBLE

FIGURE 5.4 *Two different interactions between a person,*
P, and his life-space.

boundary (see below), will flow into adjacent systems of regions easily, or with difficulty, or not at all.

Now, to return to the conception of the interactions of the
person with his life-space as the structural definition of personality, consider the diagrams in Figure 5.4. As the situation
varies, the person reacts differently in interaction with it; i.e.,
his personality is different. In situation *1* the personality is
defined as the area of the ellipse which is polarized by the
interaction of the person (*P*) with the situation (*1*). Thus, in

an experiment by Wright [34], situation *1* involved presenting a toy to a child, with the toy in a wire cage. In situation *2* (using the same study by Wright as illustration), the personality is defined as the area polarized by the ellipse resulting from the interaction of the person and this situation—in this case, the toy is freely available-to the child. The same toy is perceived by the child differently in the two situations (the toy seems more attractive in situation *1*), and the same child behaves differently in the two situations. In this illustration the *positive* valence toward the toy varied in the two situations.

One can think of everyday illustrations of differential reactions to unpleasantness, as when a person shows aggressive behavior in one situation, is passive in another, and feels angry but acts politely in still another. It is not the person who is characteristically aggressive or passive, but rather these are behavior reactions which differ in different situations; i.e., the person and the situation change as part of the *total interaction* or of the *field of forces*.

Lewin conceives of the person as consisting of separate but intercommunicating parts or regions. The life-space of the person becomes more differentiated as he grows more mature. The life-space consists of differentiated regions, some being more and some less accessible to the person. The degree of accessibility of regions between the person and his environment depends upon the nature of the boundaries of each, the closeness of the regions to the person and to each other, and the valences of each of the regions. Let us look briefly at each of these qualities.

A boundary may be highly permeable or highly impermeable. When the boundaries are impermeable, it is difficult for interactions between regions to occur; i.e., there is resistance. When two regions are adjacent, interactions are more likely to occur than when they are more distant from each other. Certain regions may be more *fluid* (or less *rigid*) than others, that is, they may be more susceptible to change. These are among the most important characteristics which determine the nature of the interactions which occur at any given moment. We say "at any given moment" because the characteristics of each region are themselves capable of change as the person and the situation change.

Let us consider now how the field of forces affects the personality reaction of the person. In Figure 5.5 the person's

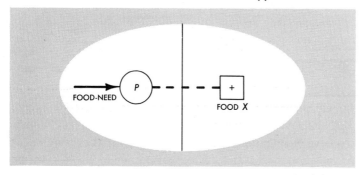

FIGURE 5.5   *Effects of field forces on a person's reactions.*

need for food has been heightened because he has had nothing to eat for several days. The food, in this case food *X*, has high positive valence for him because his need is high. In Figure 5.6

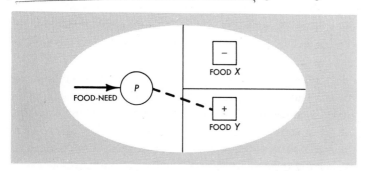

FIGURE 5.6   *Effects of field forces on a person's reactions.*

this same person is represented as having a high aversion toward food *X* on this particular day (suppose he is Catholic, this is Friday, and food *X* is meat), although he is equally hungry; yet because food *Y* is also available, this has high positive valence for him, while food *X* now has negative valence. In Figure 5.7, when the person's immediate needs for

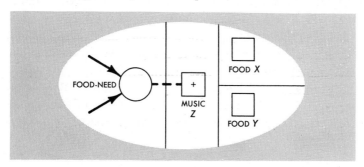

FIGURE 5.7   *Effects of field forces on a person's reactions.*

food have been sated, neither food X nor food Y has much positive valence, but stimulus Z, let us say a musical recording, now has high positive valence. Of course, we have not attempted to represent the interactions taking place within the person in these illustrations, but it might be an interesting project for the student to work out some examples which do involve the "regions" within the person as they might affect the total person-in-situation reaction.

Lewin's contributions have spurred many investigators to attempt to carry out experimental tests of his theoretical formulations, as Lewin himself did. Several illustrations of these experimental studies, briefly cited, may demonstrate the kind of impact he has had upon the development of personality theory. Two studies were aimed at demonstrating the phenomenon of tension level. In 1927 Zeigarnik asked her subjects to perform a series of tasks, some of which they were permitted to complete while others they were not permitted to complete [35]. According to Lewin's theory, the tension aroused by the task should be reduced only when the task is completed (the goal region is reached in the life-space). This would mean that behavioral tendencies toward the tasks would remain active only when the tasks were unfinished. Zeigarnik was able to show that her subjects recalled significantly more of the interrupted tasks (especially on memory tasks) than of the uninterrupted tasks (the so-called "Zeigarnik effect"). Ovsiankina interrupted her subjects in activities which they had been given; then she left the room and observed them through a one-way screen when they were left to themselves [36]. Many of the children continued with the interrupted activities once she had gone. These studies indicate that, when a tension has been created, the need persists and the increased tension has demonstrable effects until the tension is reduced.

We have cited Wright's study, which indicated that the perceptual and affective response to a stimulus varies with the nature of the barriers that are present. That the nature of the differentiation within the person has an important bearing on the field properties of a task was illustrated in the experimental work of Köpke [33]. It had already been demonstrated that, when subjects are interrupted in a task but are given a substitute task following this, the more similar the new task was to the interrupted task, the less need there would be to go back to the interrupted task. Köpke applied this finding to an experiment with mentally retarded children. They nearly always went back to the interrupted task even when they were given a nearly identical substitute task afterwards. This was interpreted as showing that mentally retarded children in contrast with normal children have less-differentiated personalities and more rigid boundaries between cells.

A series of studies was performed by Lewin, Lippitt, and White in which the same children were exposed to three different atmospheres in small social clubs: *an authoritarian atmosphere*, in which the leader was highly dominant and authoritarian; *a democratic atmosphere*, in which policies were a matter of group discussion and decision; and *a laissez-faire atmosphere*, in which the leader had no leadership functions and complete freedom was allowed both individuals and the group [37]. The autocratic group was found to show increased aggressiveness and evidenced increased disruptive behavior either within the group or outside. The laissez-faire group also produced disruptive behavior but of a different type. The democratic group learned to engage in more constructive and productive behavior. Thus the climate of the group was shown to have important valence for the personality reactions of the individuals, although there were important individual differences.

AN EVALUATION OF LEWIN'S CONTRIBUTIONS Lewin's formulations have been criticized on several counts. One made by theorists who view behavior over long periods of time is that Lewin fails to take adequately into account the past history of the individual and the tendencies toward certain kinds of behavior which this history makes probable. Although Lewin did engage in longitudinal studies, these usually covered only short periods in the life of the individual. His theory, therefore, can still be called "cross-sectional." Lewin took for his unit of analysis one moment in time and tried to study the dynamic forces operating upon the individual *at that moment*. He believed that, if the forces of the life-space could be known at any moment, behavior could be predicted and it would not matter how the forces came to exist. The opposing view—that one must know the past development and experiences of the individual in order to predict behavior—is called the "longitudinal approach," because it holds that one must view the individual in temporal perspective. One great difficulty for Lewin's theory is that he failed to formulate any principles, let alone explicit laws,

597

to explain why the life-space and its regions develop in particular ways.

Perhaps the most telling criticism of Lewin's theories is that they fail to explain how the perceived environment exerts an influence upon the person in his life-space. Lewin does offer explanations *after the fact,* but he does not indicate what independent variables must operate to produce behavior. In fact, some critics of Lewin argue that he falls into "the trap of subjectivism," since he fails to specify the variables in the life-space which are influenced by independent variables in the environment.

It has also been suggested that Lewin has really failed to specify in any precise way the origin or the nature of the concepts he employs, such as valence and tension. This criticism is related to the point previously made, since in neither case is there a clear developmental treatment of how the person-in-the-life-space came to the point at which he is being studied.

Perhaps the critics are asking more of Lewin than he himself intended to do and are ignoring the fact that he died before completing his theory. It cannot be denied that Lewin exerted a tremendous influence on the field of personality theory and upon the many psychologists who designed hosts of ingenious experiments to test out the theory and its implications. He certainly supplied a needed corrective to the viewpoint that all of personality exists "within the individual" and insisted that the importance of the perceived environment should not be ignored. One of his greatest contributions (as part of the "external world" that influenced the life-space of all psychologists) was, and still is, his catalytic effect upon social psychology, in general, and upon group dynamics, in particular [38].

"Recently Discovered" Personality Dimensions

FIELD-DEPENDENCE In a recent book, Witkin and his co-workers summarized their own work, and the work of others, on conceptualization of what Witkin originally termed "field-dependence and field-independence" [39]. He suggested that people could be distinguished by the degree to which they were perceptually field-dependent, i.e., passively dependent in their orientation, or contrariwise were field-independent, i.e., actively and analytically oriented toward the world. The latter terms have been replaced more recently with such terms as "differentiated" and "articulated," while the former have been replaced with "global." The "articulated" style of perception characterizes the more mature person, who is less dependent upon external cues in his perceptual judgments. It also seems to characterize a different kind of personality adaptation; for example, it has been found that male alcoholics tend to be more global or field-dependent than male nonalcoholics [40]. The type of perceptual style which a person employs remains relatively consistent over years, although with maturation there is a general tendency to become articulated rather than global. Because measures of the perceptual style are significantly correlated with personality characteristics and with various kinds of ability and social influence and also show a consistency over time, they are thought to tap an important dimension of the personality.

A clearer conception of the nature of the perceptual phenomena may be gained by a study of the devices used to measure them and by an analysis of some of the findings that have been reported. One of the tests used to measure field-independence is the Rod and Frame Test (RFT). The subject is seated in a dark room. He faces an illuminated frame and a rod. His task is to adjust the rod to a true vertical position while the frame is tilted, starting from a condition in which both frame and rod are tilted. In another test, the Body Adjustment Test (BAT), the subject is seated in a tilted chair in a room which is also tilted. His task is to adjust his chair to a true vertical position. The Room Adjustment Test (RAT) is like the BAT, but this time the subject must adjust the room to a true upright position. These tests require elaborate apparatus. Consequently, Witkin and his colleagues developed a simpler testing procedure, in which the subject is simply required to find a figure that is encompassed by a larger and more complex figure, that is to say, a figure that is embedded within another figure (EFT). In a series of studies it was found that RAT did not correlate very well with the other three tests, whereas these other three tests had moderate to substantial intercorrelations. Therefore, in developing a "perceptual index" which measured the relative degree of field dependence, the RAT was excluded.

Witkin has shown [41], as have others, that perceptual style as measured by his index is related to the nature of early life-experiences. It has been shown that perceptual style is clearly

Witkin's Rod-and-Frame Test. David Linton

related to sexual roles [42]. Field-dependent subjects have less well differentiated concepts about themselves and their bodies. They tend to be more suggestible. They tend to use more primitive or immature defense mechanisms, like denial and repression.

The perceptual index is also similar to Thurstone's "flexibility of closure" [43] and to other related perceptual measures. The types of personal adaptation made by people with the characteristics of the field-dependent subject are different from those made by people who are not field-dependent; and they seem to be characterized by what is commonly regarded as less mature social behavior.

RESPONSE STYLES   There is a general tendency for people to agree with statements or to accept situations which are vague or indefinite [44]. However, people do differ in this tendency to agree, and studies provided by clinical evaluation or treatment as well as experimental studies seem to confirm the conclusion that those who have this tendency to a high degree are more suggestible, are more field-dependent, and, when psychopathological, tend toward hysterical patterns of personality adaptation (see Chapter 6). Recent studies have shown that, while these characteristics may be present, the agreers have personalities that are more complex than these generalizations would suggest. They seem to be anxious to "please" and hence "agree" but at the same time are "internally" in conflict with this need and see themselves as stubborn, willful, hostile, and competitive [45]. Thus a clinical study by Couch and Keniston revealed that agreers were internally hostile, felt a lack of ego-control, and were otherwise in conflict [46], although to the outside observer they seemed co-operative, respectful, and submissive.

In recent years a great deal of research has been devoted to response styles that have to do with cognitive controls. It would take us too far afield to review these studies in detail, but it may suffice to indicate that most workers conceive of these response styles in terms of the newer *ego psychology* stemming from psychoanalytic theory. In ego psychology, response styles in thinking, remembering, and perceiving are seen as developing out of a relatively conflict-free area of development. These cognitive controls are conceived of as regulatory mechanisms and have been related to general mechanisms of adaptation and adjustment. For example, one principle of cognitive control involves the variable known as *leveling and sharpening*. As the term suggests, this has to do with the degree of differentiation the subject makes in studies involving memory traces. Holzman and Gardner found [47] that subjects who were high in leveling tended to be high in the mechanism of repression. Gardner made a factorial analysis of six measures of cognitive control, using both male and female subjects [11]. This study and related experimental findings suggest that cognitive style may be of very great importance in relation to both methods of coping with problems (see Chapter 4) and defense mechanisms. That response styles, in general, and cognitive controls, in particular, may be linked with cultural practices is indicated by the finding that males differ significantly from females in these patterns of behavior and that cultural differences have been found to correlate with such styles.

SOCIAL DESIRABILITY   One of the problems that has confounded a great deal of personality research utilizing paper-and-pencil tests of personality (see Chapter 8) is the tendency for the subject to respond in such a manner as to appear "socially desirable" [48]. Most subjects tend to answer items so that their responses agree with what social consensus would indicate is a *desirable* response. Much of the recent work in this area was influenced by the reported findings of Edwards, who developed a Social Desirability Scale [49]. As we noted earlier, subjects tend to agree with items when their content is vague. They also tend to agree when the content indicates a socially desirable quality or an absence of obvious pathology, although the latter is not always the case, for some subjects try to "paint themselves" as "sicker" than they really are [50]. Psychologists must be concerned with social desirability, since it might contaminate the validity of personality tests. Messick found that when he analyzed Edwards' Personal Preference Scale, a large portion of the variance in test scores could be accounted for in terms of a tendency to respond in the stereotype of the "achievement-oriented middle class" [51]. The fact is that the tendency to appear "socially desirable" may itself be significantly related to personality makeup; and rather than attempt to get rid of it in personality tests, psychologists are now trying to utilize and control it in such measurements.

The Self as a Personality Attribute

One of the perennial questions asked by philosophers is "Who am I?" All of us have asked ourselves this question many times; and sometimes we feel that we really know who we are, but at other times we may be confused about ourselves. When we think that we know ourselves best, we are sometimes shocked to discover that others don't agree with our self-perceptions. And, sometimes, we learn suddenly that there is something about ourselves that we had never thought was "there," as when we find ourselves giving in to a fit of anger, or when we begin to cry or feel depressed and had no inkling that we were going to feel that way. In psychotherapy, too, the patient frequently finds that there are aspects and levels of the self that he was unaware of or had distorted in some way.

THE SELF: MEANING AND DEVELOPMENT   In psychology the study of the self-concept has received considerable emphasis, particularly in recent years, but no conceptual definition of the "self" has been universally accepted. Carl Rogers, who has been studying the development of the self-concept for many years, utilizing the data derived from counseling people by means of the *client-centered approach* (see Chapter 7), offers the following definition: "[It is the] . . . organized, consistent conceptual gestalt composed of perceptions of the characteristics of the 'I' or 'me' and the perceptions of the relations of the 'I' or 'me' to others and to various aspects of life, together with the values attached to these perceptions . . ." [52]. This is an attempt to define the self in terms of the individual's perceptions of himself as well as his perceptions of his interpersonal relationships and his relationships with the world. We notice that it emphasizes two characteristics of the self: the person's awareness of himself as *he* sees himself and *his* awareness of his relationships with people and situations. We may also notice that, although he speaks of *perceptions,* the self is defined as a *conceptual* Gestalt. Since an individual does not have any *concept* of himself in infancy, and since his concept of himself is founded upon *perceptions* of himself, it would be well to trace briefly how this conceptualization develops.

But before we do so, we might note other characteristics of the self-concept which have been proposed. The self may be defined not only in terms of the person's self-awareness and his awareness of interpersonal events, but it may also encompass other aspects or dimensions. Some writers speak of the *core* of the self as distinguished from the *phenomenological* aspects of the self. In such analyses, the emphasis is upon *different levels* of the self-concept. Individuals differ in how readily, if at all, they can become aware of deeper (or more unconscious) levels of the self. Other writers emphasize the self as *an agent* and prefer to define the self in terms of the social roles that the person employs. Thus, Snygg and Combs believe that the self-concept consists of those ". . . parts of the phenomenal field which the individual has differentiated as definite and fairly stable characteristics of himself" [53]. Still another position with respect to the self-concept has to do with the emphasis placed upon *bodily feelings*. To such people an important characteristic of the self is that which is projected onto one's feelings about one's body, i.e., whether one sees oneself as good-looking, strong, healthy, virile, and so on. And another dimension of the self-concept embraces the dual perceptions of the self as it *actually is* and the self as one *would like it to be*. Symonds speaks of these dimensions as "the self as conceived" and "the self to be realized" [54]. Miller refers to the *actual self* and the *potential self* [55]. Sometimes workers in this field also utilize the dimension of the *ideal self,* to represent the conception that the person reports or feels he would like to be. As we shall see, research on the self often makes use of discrepancies between two or more of these three aspects of the self.

Now we can turn our attention to the development of the self. Before we can have any perception concerning ourselves, we must be able to distinguish ourselves from others. In other words, we must be able to distinguish the "me" from the "not-me." Perceptions of this kind first develop during infancy in an amorphous way as the baby begins to become aware of sensations in his body, but they become somewhat more focused, especially in the second year of life, when the child is able to distinguish the external source of pleasurable or painful stimulation, i.e., when he is able to perceive that "someone out there" who is "not me" is doing something which causes him to experience pleasure or pain. The original locus of the self is thus usually conceived of as somewhere in the body, since this is the referent the child must use in becoming perceptually aware of the internal and the external sources of stimulation as well as the experiences of pain and pleasure [56]. The baby is also able to begin to perceive that, while he is the source of some actions, others are the sources of other actions. We traced in Chapter 3 the conceptions advanced by Erikson to account for the development of a basic attitudinal orientation toward the world. Part of this orientation involves the beginning perceptions of the self as something one can rely upon—as a "feeling" that one can, in favorable circumstances, rely upon oneself with some degree of confidence. Many of these early perceptions are referred to the body, and so it is believed that bodily feelings become the "core" of the early self-percepts. As bodily controls become more efficient, the child learns to master his physical world, and these successful actions mark an extension of the boundaries of the self. Likewise, as the child learns to "deal actively with" the significant people in his life, his sense of self develops, is extended, and becomes more important as a factor guiding his interpersonal behavior.

It is doubtful that these early perceptions of the self are at all well integrated. Rather, the child seems to have many, and sometimes contradictory, perceptions of himself. Only in time are these differing perceptions integrated into self-concepts. The child, even the adult, may have a number of nuclei of self-concepts, so that he senses himself as adept in social situations but feels inadequate in other situations in which he must deal with an authority figure; he feels at ease with men but feels uncomfortable with women; he feels superior in physical activities but feels inferior in intellectual pursuits; and so on. A moment's introspection will reveal that, in most cases, we have self-concepts about ourselves that differ with respect to situation and with respect to time.

We should emphasize that many of our self-perceptions represent distortions of the "objective reality." This is probably true not only because of the vagaries of the self-concept, in general, but because unconscious factors modify the accuracy of our self-perceptions. The way we "feel" about our stature or our physical appearance, for example, colors the perceptions we have about these aspects of our bodies. We may see ourselves as "plain" or even as "ugly," not necessarily because of the realities of our appearance but because of our need to avoid feeling beautiful or handsome—in other words, as a defense against conflicts of which we are only dimly aware or are entirely unaware. Cultural attitudes may markedly reinforce such distortions or even induce them, but unconscious factors are likely to play a more significant role. A brief excerpt from a case study may help to illustrate the role of the unconscious factors in producing such distortions in the self-perception.

An adolescent girl was seen in clinical consultation by one of the writers because she was quite depressed, anxious, and unable to concentrate in her schoolwork. She believed that she was quite ugly and that boys were not interested in her as a consequence, and she attributed her emotional difficulties to these factors. Her self-perceptions as "ugly" rested, she thought, on the presence of a mole on one of her cheeks. As a matter of fact, she had been trying, without success, to induce her family doctor to remove the mole surgically. As seen by both her peers and elders, she was a quite beautiful girl, and, if anything, the small mole enhanced her beauty and gave her face even greater charm. On

605

the basis of clinical study, it soon became apparent that she had severe conflicts over her sexual impulses and had considerable guilt. Actually, it was her sexual wishes and fantasies which were "ugly." Her self-perception as "ugly" gave her a pretext for believing that boys could not be attracted to her and thus enabled her to rationalize her own fear of social contact with them.

The development of language also plays an important part in the development of the self-concept. The child begins to refer to himself as "me," not only when his development is sufficiently sophisticated to enable him to distinguish the "not-me" from the "me," but when his language concepts are extensive enough to designate others by their appropriate pronoun designations (such as "he," "them," and the like) (see [57]). Language symbols form the basis of many kinds of primary conceptualizations about the self, such as being "happy," feeling "sad," and, much later, being "assertive" or being "compliant." Discrete views of the self are conceived in terms of language and are facilitated by them.

A continuing feature of the development of the self-concept is the ability to conceive of oneself as having continuity over time. We, as adults, may take for granted this feeling of continuity in our self-concept and usually have no difficulty in recognizing that we are the same person we were some years ago, despite differences due to developmental factors and learning experiences. Under severe emotional stress, we sometimes may doubt this continuity. Persons suffering from memory loss, as in amnesia (see Chapter 6), temporarily lose this capacity for continuity in the self-concept and feel and act as if they are different persons. There are other types of psychological and organic disturbance which may produce a disruption in the sense of one's self-continuity. The perception of continuity in time of the self-concept is indicative of an extension of the *self-boundaries* and indicates that one has formed some stable components in the self-concept that are not disrupted by changing circumstances or are only transiently disrupted by changes in mood or by illness. The person who is "me" has developed a stable identity.

MEASUREMENT OF THE SELF-CONCEPT   Perhaps one of the simplest ways to measure perceptions or conceptions of the self is by means of *self-ratings*. The subject is given a questionnaire in which he is asked to rate himself on various aspects of the self. In this respect the method is similar to many types of personality questionnaires (see Chapter 8). The self-rating questionnaire may consist of a single dimension of the self-concept, with many examples of behavior on which the subject is asked to rate himself, or it may consist of a number of subscales, so that different aspects of the self may be assessed. Studies have shown that there is a relationship between scores on such self-ratings and adequacy of adjustment. In many cases investigators have obtained *discrepancy scores* by having the subject rate not only himself but also his ideal self or the characteristics of some other well-defined group. Again, it has been demonstrated that, in general, larger discrepancies are associated with greater degrees of maladjustment. In studies of the effects of psychotherapy, it has been found that as individuals improve in their adjustment their self-ratings improve [58], their perceptions of others become more favorable [59], and their discrepancy scores become smaller [60]. In fact, Rogers, who has done and stimulated so much research in this area, believes that changes in the direction of a more favorable self-concept produce changes in adjustive behavior [52].

However, there are difficulties in the use of self-ratings. In the first place, some individuals may tend to distort their self-ratings in order to present a more favorable picture of themselves to themselves and to others. We commented previously on the influence of response set and social desirability as factors influencing such ratings. Some kinds of people are particularly likely to present a false picture of themselve [61]. In the second place, the results on self-ratings depend significantly upon the "situational climate" in which they are obtained and may change as a result of concurrent events in the life of the subject [62]. And, finally, large discrepancies between self-ratings and ratings of "others" do not necessarily reflect poor adjustment. For example, Havener and Izard found that some psychotics showed no greater discrepancy scores than normals [63]. They believed that the reason for this was that these psychotics were less accepting of others than were normals, and thus the relative discrepancy scores for the two groups were about comparable.

A refinement of the self-rating techniques involves the method known as the *Q-sort* [64]. In this procedure the subject is given a series of statements on which he is asked to evaluate himself, but, instead of being asked simply to state that a given statement is true or false (or assign it a simple scale value), he is asked to distribute the statements in several piles. (He is usually given each statement on a separate slip of paper or a card.) Thus, he may be asked to distribute the statements so that pile A, which applies to statements which characterize him *least,* contains only 2 statements, pile B, which applies to statements which characterize him slightly better, contains 5 statements, and so on through piles D and E, each of which contains 18 statements, up to pile H, which applies to statements which characterize him *most* and contains 2 statements. He is forced to distribute his statements according to a normal probability distribution, and each statement can then be given a score depending upon the pile in which it was placed. This technique has certain statistical advantages over the usual self-rating questionnaire, but from the viewpoint of validity it has some of the same problems that all self-ratings have.

By contrast with these two methods, there are approaches which attempt to secure more innerdetermined measures of the self-concept, that is, to utilize methods in which the individual's own frame of reference is explored. For example, George Kelly has developed a Repertory Test, in which the subject is asked to select the names of people he knows or has known who "suggest to you some people you know" who fit each of twenty-four "roles" printed on 24 cards [65]. Thus, card 1 is "A teacher you liked," card 2 is "A teacher you disliked," card 5 is "Your mother," card 12 is "A neighbor with whom you get along well," and card 16 is "A boy you did not like when you were in high school." No name may be listed more than once. The subject is then presented with the cards, three at a time (in various combinations) and is asked to tell in what important way two of them are alike but are different from the third. In this way the nature of the personal constructs, in terms of the characteristics the subject sees as relevant, are determined. Kelly suggests other procedures for eliciting additional analysis of the role constructs that are *significant for the individual subject.* This approach is essentially clinical in its orientation, though the test may be administered in group as well as individual form. Other approaches utilizing a clinical approach make use of projective tests, detailed interviews, and recordings of observed behavior. Clinical approaches have the advantage of defining the self from the inside view of the person as he experiences himself, consciously or unconsciously, but they may have the disadvantage, common to many clinical approaches, that the results are difficult to handle statistically.

SOME ADDITIONAL RESEARCH FINDINGS ON THE SELF As we stated, there has been considerable research on the self in recent years. Some of the findings are of particular interest to us. We noted, in a previous section, some of the aspects or dimensions of the self that various writers have distinguished. Most of these conceptions were founded upon empirical findings from clinical or research studies. Recent attempts to factor-analyze the dimensions of the self have, in general, supported these conceptions. An extension of the meaning of the self-concept, as it operates at the adult level, was provided by a factor analysis done by Smith, who found five clusters in the self-concept: body image, self-esteem, anxiety-tension, independence, and estrangement [66].

The relationship between the concepts of ego and self have also been explored. We will recall that the ego consists of that aspect of the personality which mediates internal drives and relates them to the external world. The newer ego psychology has postulated a sphere of conflict-free operations of the ego based, in part, on genetic and constitutional factors that develop as autonomous functions. Schactel has presented evidence to indicate that there are no conflict-free domains of the ego but that, instead, all behavior is influenced by conflict and that, as the ego learns to master conflict, feelings about the self are enhanced [67].

There is considerable evidence that there is a relationship between mood and changes in the self-concept, as shown in a study by Wessman, Ricks, and Tyl [68]. Moreover, the self-concept has been shown to improve in benevolent or favorable environments [58], whereas it tends to deteriorate in unfavorable environments [69]. During adolescence, the individual is typically subjected to considerable biological and psychological stress. Those individuals who already have positive self-concepts manifest more stability during this adjustmental phase than those with poorer self-concepts [70]. It has also been learned that persons who show greater consistency in their self-concepts over time are much more likely to be well adjusted than those who are inconsistent in this respect [60]. Corroborating research in this respect demonstrates that children who are more anxious tend to have poorer self-concepts than children who are less anxious [71]. Finally, it is interesting to note not only that cultural factors significantly influence the formation of the self-concept, as in the study by Bieri and Lobeck [72] which indicates that Jews perceive themselves as critical and skeptical whereas Catholics see themselves as conforming and acquiescent, but that those who see themselves as more in control of their own fate tend to influence the culture in which they live more than those who see themselves as externally controlled. Thus, a study by Gore and Rotter [73] indicated that Negroes who feel less controlled by external factors are more inclined toward social action than other Negroes.

Present Status of Organizational Theories

No one theory of the structure of the personality is universally acceptable to psychologists. All theories are seen as only approximations to a conceptualization that is adequate for either understanding or predicting significant aspects of behavior. Some theories seem particularly useful in dealing with pathological behavior, whereas others appear to be more useful in dealing with normals. The interaction of the developments in clinical and experimental research are having a catalytic effect in improving our understanding of the nature of man and the nature of his personality structure.

References

1. Freud, S. *Interpretation of Dreams*. In *The Standard Edition of the Complete Psychological Works of Sigmund Freud* (trans. and ed. by J. Strachey). London: Hogarth, 1953. (First German ed., 1900.)
2. Freud, S. *An Outline of Psychoanalysis*. New York: Norton, 1949. (First German ed., 1940).
3. Freud, S. Instincts and Their Vicissitudes. In *Collected Papers,* Vol. IV (trans. and ed. by J. Riviere, A. Strachey, & J. Strachey). London: Hogarth, 1925. (First German ed., 1915.)
4. Hartmann, H., Kris, E., & Lowenstein, R. M. Comments on the formation of psychic structure. In R. S. Eissler, A. Freud, H. Hartmann, & M. Kris (Eds.), *The Psychoanalytic Study of the Child,* Vol. II. New York: International Universities Press, 1946.

5. Stotsky, B. A., & Weinberg, H. The prediction of the psychiatric patient's work adjustment. *J. counsel. Psychol.,* 1956, **3,** 3–7.
6. Singer, J. L., Wilensky, H., & McCraven, V. G. Delaying capacity, fantasy and planning capacity, ability: A factorial study of some basic ego functions. *J. consult. Psychol.,* 1956, **20,** 375–383.
7. Freud, S. *Analysis, Terminable and Interminable.* In *Collected Papers,* Vol. V (trans. and ed. by J. Riviere, A. Strachey, & J. Strachey). London: Hogarth, 1950. (First German ed., 1937.)
8. Hartmann, H. *Ego Psychology and the Problem of Adaptation.* New York: International Universities Press, 1958.
9. Erikson, E. H. The problem of ego identity. *J. Amer. Psychoanal. Assoc.,* 1956, **4,** 58–121.
10. Klein, G. S. The personal world through perception. In R. R. Blake & G. V. Ramsey (Eds.), *Perception: An Approach to Personality.* New York: Ronald, 1951.
11. Gardner, R. W., et al. Cognitive control. In *Psychol. Issues,* **1,** No. 4. New York: International Universities Press, 1959.
12. Piaget, J. *The Language and Thought of the Child.* (2nd ed.) London: Routledge, 1932.
13. Murray, H. A., et al. *Explorations in Personality.* New York: Oxford, 1938.
14. Sears, R. R. Survey of objective studies of psychoanalytic concepts. *Soc. Sci. Res. Council Bull.,* 1953, No. 51.
15. Nothman, F. H. The influence of response conditions on recognition thresholds for tabu words. *J. abnorm. soc. Psychol.,* 1962, **65,** 154–161.
16. Blum, G. S. *A Model of the Mind.* New York: Wiley, 1961.
17. Eysenck, H. J. *The Scientific Study of Personality.* New York: Macmillan, 1952.
18. Allport, G. W., & Odbert, H. S. Trait-names: A psychological study. *Psychol. Monogr.,* 1936, **47,** No. 211.
19. Cronbach, L. J. *Essentials of Psychological Testing.* (2nd ed.) New York: Harper & Row, 1960.
20. Guilford, J. P. *Personality.* New York: McGraw-Hill, 1959.
21. Cattell, R. B. The principal replicated factors discovered in objective personality tests. *J. abnorm. soc. Psychol.,* 1955, **50,** 219–314.
22. Hoskins, R. G. *Endocrinology: The Glands and Their Functions.* New York: Norton, 1941.
23. Kretchmer, E. *Physique and Character.* New York: Harcourt, Brace & World, 1925. (Trans. from orig. ed. of 1921.)
24. Sheldon, W. H. (with the collaboration of S. S. Stevens). *The Varieties of Temperament: A Psychology of Constitutional Differences.* New York: Harper & Row, 1942.
25. Sheldon, W. H. (with the collaboration of C. W. Dupertuis

& E. McDermott). *Atlas of Men: A Guide for Somatotyping the Adult Male at All Ages.* New York: Harper & Row, 1954.

26. Smith, H. C. Psychometric checks on hypotheses derived from Sheldon's work on physique and temperament. *J. Pers.,* 1949, **17,** 310–320.

27. Thurstone, L. L. Factor analysis and body types. *Psychometrika,* 1946, **11,** 15–21.

28. Newman, R. W. Age changes in body build. *Amer. J. phys. Anthrop.,* 1952, **10,** 75–90.

29. Jung, C. G. *The Integration of the Personality.* New York: Holt, Rinehart and Winston, 1939.

30. Eysenck, S. B. G., & Eysenck, H. J. On the dual nature of extraversion. *Brit. J. soc. clin. Psychol.,* 1963, **2,** 46–55.

31. Guilford, J. P. *An Inventory of Factors STDCR.* Beverly Hills, Calif.: Sheridan Supply Co., 1940.

32. Eysenck, H. J. Reminiscence, drive, and personality—revision and extension of a theory. *Brit. J. soc. clin. Psychol.,* 1962, **1,** 127–140.

33. Lewin, K. *A Dynamic Theory of Personality.* New York: McGraw-Hill, 1935.

34. Wright, H. F. The influence of barriers upon strength of motivation. *Contr. psychol. Theor.,* 1937, **1,** No. 3.

35. Zeigarnik, B. Über das Behalten von erledigten und unerledigten Handlungen. *Psychol. Forsch.,* 1927, **9,** 1–85.

36. Ovsiankina, M. Die Wiederaufnahme unter brochener Handlungen. *Psychol. Forsch.,* 1928, **11,** 302–379.

37. Lewin, K., Lippitt, R., & White, R. K. Patterns of aggressive behavior in experimentally created social climates. *J. soc. Psychol.,* 1939, **10,** 271–299.

38. Cartwright, D., & Zander, A. *Group Dynamics: Research and Theory.* New York: Harper & Row, 1953.

39. Witkin, H. A., Dyk, R. B., Faterson, H. F., Goodenough, D. R., & Karp, S. A. *Psychological Differentiation.* New York: Wiley, 1962.

40. Witkin, H. A., Karp, S. A., & Goodenough, D. R. Dependence in alcoholics. *Quart. J. Stud. Alc.,* 1959, **20,** 493–504.

41. Witkin, H. A. The perception of the upright. *Sci. American,* 1959, **200,** 50–56.

42. Bieri, J., Bradburn, W. M., & Galinsky, M. D. Sex differences in perceptual behavior. *J. Pers.,* 1958, **26,** 1–12.

43. Thurstone, L. I. *A Factorial Study of Perception.* Chicago: Univ. Chicago Press, 1944.

44. Messick, S., & Jackson, D. N. The measurement of authoritarian attitudes. *Educ. psychol. Measmt.,* 1958, **18,** 241–253.

45. Asch, M. J. Negative response bias and personality adjustment. *J. counsel. Psychol.,* 1958, **5,** 206–210.

46. Couch, A., & Keniston, K. Yeasayers and naysayers:

Agreeing response set as a personality variable. *J. abnorm. soc. Psychol.,* 1960, **60,** 151–174.

47. Holzman, P. S., & Gardner, R. W. Leveling and repression. *J. abnorm. soc. Psychol.,* 1959, **59,** 151–155.
48. Hanley, C. Responses to the wording of personality test items. *J. consult. Psychol.,* 1959, **23,** 261–265.
49. Edwards, A. L. *The Social Desirability Variable in Personality Assessment.* New York: Holt, Rinehart and Winston, 1959.
50. Messick, S. Dimensions of social desirability. *J. consult. Psychol.,* 1960, **24,** 279–287.
51. Messick, S. Personality structure. *Annu. Rev. Psychol.,* 1961, **12,** 93–128.
52. Rogers, C. R. A theory of therapy, personality, and interpersonal relationships, as developed in the client-centered framework. In S. Koch (Ed.), *Psychology: A Study of a Science,* Vol. III. New York: McGraw-Hill, 1959.
53. Snygg, D., & Combs, A. W. *Individual Behavior.* New York: Harper & Row, 1948.
54. Symonds, P. M. *The Ego and the Self.* New York: Appleton-Century-Crofts, 1951.
55. Miller, D. R. The study of social relationships: Situation, identity, and social interaction. In S. Koch (Ed.), *Psychology: A Study of Science,* Vol. V. New York: McGraw-Hill, 1963.
56. Schilder, P. *The Image and Appearance of the Human Body.* (Psyche Monogr., No. 6.) London: Routledge, 1935.
57. Fisher, M. S. *Language Patterns of Preschool Children.* New York: Teachers College, 1934.
58. Cartwright, R. D. The effects of psychotherapy on self-consistency. *J. consult. Psychol.,* 1961, **25,** 376–382.
59. Suinn, R. M. The relationship between self-acceptance and acceptance of others: A learning theory analysis. *J. abnorm. soc. Psychol.,* 1961, **63,** 37–42.
60. Block, J. Some differences between the concepts of social desirability and adjustment. *J. consult. Psychol.,* 1962, **26,** 527–530.
61. Spiegel, L. A. The self, the sense of self, and perception. In R. S. Eissler, A. Freud, H. Hartmann, & M. Kris (Eds.), *Psychoanalytic Study of the Child,* Vol. XIV. New York: International Universities Press, 1959.
62. Veldman, D. J., & Worchel, P. Defensiveness and self-acceptance in the management of hostility. *J. abnorm. soc. Psychol.,* 1961, **63,** 319–325.
63. Havener, P. H., & Izard, C. E. Unrealistic self-enhancement in paranoid schizophrenics. *J. consult. Psychol.,* 1962, **26,** 65–68.
64. Stephenson, W. *The Study of Behavior: Q-technique and Its Methodology.* Chicago: Univ. Chicago Press, 1953.

613

65. Kelly, G. A. *The Psychology of Personal Constructs,* Vol. I: *A Theory of Personality.* New York: Norton, 1955.
66. Smith, P. A. A factor analytic study of the self-concept. *J. consult. Psychol.,* 1960, **24,** 191.
67. Schactel, E. G. *Metamorphosis.* New York: Basic Books, 1959.
68. Wessman, E. A., Ricks, D. F., & Tyl, M. M. Characteristics and concomitants of mood fluctuations in college women. *J. abnorm. soc. Psychol.,* 1960, **60,** 117–126.
69. Edgerton, S. G. From mortification to aggrandizement: Changing self-concepts in the careers of the mentally retarded. *Psychiatry,* 1962, **25,** 263–272.
70. Engel, M. The stability of the self-concept in adolescence. *J. abnorm. soc. Psychol.,* 1959, **58,** 211–215.
71. Horowitz, F. D. The relationship of anxiety, self-concept, and sociometric status among fourth, fifth, and sixth grade children. *J. abnorm. soc. Psychol.,* 1962, **65,** 212–214.
72. Bieri, J., & Lobeck, R. Self-concept differences in relation to identification, religion, and social class. *J. abnorm. soc. Psychol.,* 1961, **62,** 94–98.
73. Gore, P. M., & Rotter, J. B. A personality correlate of social action. *J. Pers.,* 1963, **31,** 58–64.

SIX MALADJUSTMENT: THE DISORGANIZATION OF PERSONALITY

We have previously considered some aspects of personality development, functioning, and organization. Our study of personality would be incomplete if we did not also discuss how the functioning of the personality becomes disorganized and how, under certain circumstances, this dysfunctioning may be mended. We shall devote the present chapter to the former problem, and the next chapter to the latter.

Disorganization in functioning of the personality, in moderate or in severe degree, is quite common. It has been estimated, for example, that more than one-half of all hospital beds in this

Rational protest or personality disorganization?

Scheier from Monkmeyer

country are occupied by patients who are suffering from some form of psychopathology [1]. Moreover, there is a large proportion of the general population that has some disruptive emotional disturbance that does not require hospitalization. It is not in jest that this has been called "The Age of Anxiety."

The great magnitude of the problem of personality disorganization constitutes an important reason for learning about it. However, there are other reasons for undertaking its study.

Knowledge of maldevelopment of personality function tells us something about the nature of normal function. When we attempt to repair an automobile engine that has broken down, we can learn a great deal about what makes such an engine work properly and, perhaps, how to build a better engine or one that will break down less often. Moreover, the study of the malfunction of an engine—or an organism—gives us a better understanding of its parts. We shall learn, for example, that the defense mechanisms and aberrations shown by persons with severe personality disturbance are also present in normal persons; the differences between the abnormal and the normal may be differences in frequency of occurrence or in patterning of the various defense mechanisms. In any case, we are better able to understand defense mechanisms in the normal person after we have studied them in the abnormal. Then, again, knowledge of the relative contribution of genetic, biochemical, and learning factors in the development of severe mental disorders contributes to a better understanding of these factors in the less severely disordered and in the normal.

This chapter will first consider the frequency of occurrence of the major forms of personality disorder. Then we shall discuss the most severe forms of disorder as well as the less severe forms. Finally, we shall evaluate the nature of normal personality functioning.

Prevalence of Personality Disturbance

It is very difficult to assess the number or percentage of people with personality disturbances. First, there is the problem of defining such conditions. Next, there is the problem of measuring such conditions reliably. And then there is the extremely difficult problem of obtaining representative samples from the total population. As we shall see, definition and classification of personality disorders still leave much to be desired. Methods of evaluation have improved considerably during the past few decades, but the validity of even the improved modern methods is far from perfect. Further, present solutions to the sampling problem involve a number of important assumptions, since it has not been possible to subject a truly representative sample to adequate evaluation procedures. Estimates are therefore based on hospital admissions, referral to mental health agencies, and the like. Reasons for referral to psychiatric clinics vary with social conditions (for example, during unemployment or periods of economic depression, frequency of referral tends to go up), with the community (for example, referral to clinics and admissions to hospitals are relatively greater in urban than in rural communities), and with community attitudes (for example, communities vary greatly in attitudes toward mental health problems and in availability of clinical facilities).

The most accurate data on this problem come from statistics on admissions to hospitals. Prior to 1947 such data were collated by the Bureau of the Census, but since then they have been gathered by the National Institute of Mental Health. Most states, of course, make available detailed analyses of their hospital populations, but methods of codifying such information vary considerably among the several states. In general, the data on admissions to mental hospitals for very serious mental disorders show a steady and rapid increase [2]. Between 1922, when such data became available for the entire country, and 1950, there was an increase of 48 percent, or from a rate of 68.2 per 100,000 of the population to 100.6. Yet we cannot conclude from these data alone that there has been a comparable rate of increase in the incidence of severe mental disorder in the general population. Rates of admission to mental hospitals depend on many variables, such as number of beds available, criteria for admission, the attitudes of the mental health professions, and the attitudes of society in general.

A study of the comparative data on admissions to hospitals in the various states is extremely interesting. These data show that such rates vary considerably, the northeastern states having rates that are well above the average and the southern states having rates that are well below the average. In fact, New York admits about three times as many patients to mental hospitals as does New Mexico or Mississippi. We do not know, however, that these rates reflect a real difference in incidence of mental illness, since the states are not at all comparable in the kinds of variables we noted above.

A more accurate assessment of the nature of this problem can be gleaned from data obtained within one state. Malzberg, who has devoted intensive and continuing attention to the problem of mental health statistics, has made an analysis of such data for the state of New York [3]. He has shown that for the period between 1920 and 1950 (controlling for both sex and age of patients who were admitted) there was an increase of *first admissions*[1] of 37 percent. He interprets his data as supporting the conclusion that ". . . there has been a corre-

---

[1] "First admissions" refers to patients who are hospitalized for the first time in their lives.

sponding increase in the incidence of mental disease" in the population at large. We may dispute this conclusion on the grounds that rates of admissions are influenced not alone by incidence of illness but also by attitudes of society toward placement of people in mental hospitals, by availability of mental hospital facilities, and the like.

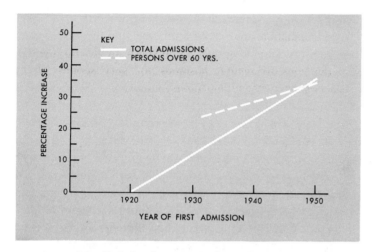

FIGURE 6.1 *Relative increase in first admissions for psychiatric disturbances in New York State. Based on findings in B. Malzberg. Important statistical data about mental illness. In S. Arieti (Ed.),* American Handbook of Psychiatry, *Vol. 1. New York: Basic Books, 1959.*

Several other findings from Malzberg's study are interesting. He shows that about 30 percent of all first admissions in New York are for the psychosis known as dementia praecox (or schizophrenia). This is by far the greatest single group. It is also noted that there has been a significant increase in admission of the aged; from 1930 to 1950, for example, the percentage of first admissions for persons over 60 years of age increased from about 23 percent to about 35 percent. See Figure 6.1 for a comparison of total first admissions with first admissions for persons over sixty years of age. There are important ethnic differences, as well. Negroes had about twice as many admissions as whites, but their admissions resulted from the conditions of *general paresis* (due to syphilitic infection) and *alcoholic psychosis*—conditions that are clearly related to social and economic factors. Jews, who had about average admission rates compared with the admission rates of the general population, had the lowest rate for alcoholic psychosis (close to zero), while the Irish had the highest rate for alcoholic psychosis and the lowest rate for general paresis. The conclusion that seems strongly supportable on the basis of this and related evidence is that the frequency and type of psychosis, at least for some forms of psychosis, is markedly influenced by social-environmental conditions, such as training in social controls, morality, and other social patterns of living.

It is also interesting to note that, contrary to popular conception, rates of discharge from mental hospitals are relatively high, more than 40 percent of all such patients being discharged within a five-year period and most of these within the first year. If one also considers that many patients come from the lowest socioeconomic groups and cannot be discharged because they have no family that can support or guide them after discharge, the outlook (or prognosis) is by no means as discouraging as many people apparently believe it to be.

How about noninstitutionalized persons with some form of personality disturbance? Again, accurate figures are difficult to obtain. According to one estimate, in absolute numbers, some ten millions of persons suffer from the milder forms of personality difficulties, such as *psychoneurosis* and *character disorder* [4]. Rennie made a survey in New York and concluded that about 30 percent of the population had some disturbing personality problems [5]. In what is probably the most thorough and comprehensive research to date, Dorothea Leighton and her colleagues made a ten-year study of an entire county (Stirling) and developed careful sampling and evaluative procedures as part of their research [6]. Table 6.1 presents the major findings on the prevalence of personality disturbance. The numbers in the table are based on representative samples of the area under study. It will be noted that from 11 to 17 percent are rated as "probably well" and from 25 to 43 percent are rated as "doubtful" in mental health, or better. These percentages are far lower than the usual estimates of good mental health in the general population. Excluding the most severe cases of psychiatric disorder, and including only Type II and Type III categories, where maximum information is available, it appears that 74 percent of the population shows at least minor forms of psychiatric disturbance. The percentage for only Type III cases is not much out of line with (although somewhat higher than) the results indicated in previous intensive studies of this kind.

TABLE 6.1. RATINGS OF NEED FOR PSYCHIATRIC ATTENTION

Typology of Need		Percentage Based on Maximum Information Available	Percentage Based on Medium Information Available
Type I:	Most abnormal	1%	3%
Type II:	Significant impairment	38%	17%
Type III:	Probable psychiatric disorder	36%	37%
Type IV:	Doubtful	14%	26%
Type V:	Probably well	11%	17%
Total number of respondents		140	1,010

SOURCE: D. C. Leighton *et al., The Character of Danger: Psychiatric Symptoms in Selected Communities,* New York: Basic Books, 1963, p. 142.

Our sampling of the findings on prevalence of mental disturbances has clearly revealed the very great magnitude of the problem. Such findings have given great impetus to the study of preventive psychiatry as well as to the search for improved methods of treatment. It is certain that the problems of mental health are everyone's concern, since they touch almost all families, and that knowledge of the nature of these problems will assist in their solutions. Efforts are needed to attack these problems at many levels and in diverse ways.

The Major Psychoses

In attempting to convey a vivid idea of the nature of a particular form of *psychosis* (or insanity, as it is sometimes popularly called), Jung wrote in 1903, "Let the dreamer walk about and act as though he were awake and we have at once the clinical picture of dementia praecox" [7]. Dementia praecox is one form of psychosis and is commonly called schizophrenia today. The individual with this condition often acts as though he were in a dream state, and his speech and thinking processes seem similar in many respects to that of the dreamer. The lay person often expresses the same idea when he says, after observing a psychotic person, "He has lost touch with reality," or "He just doesn't seem to be all there." Such characterizations are not necessarily true of all persons with schizophrenia or of all persons with any of the other forms of psychosis. In some psychoses there is little or no loss of reality awareness.

What, then, is a psychosis? Experts in the mental health field have not been able to agree on a definition that accounts for all psychotic conditions or that invariably permits differentiation of such conditions from psychoneurotic or normal behavior. From the clinical viewpoint, a psychosis may be thought of as a gross disturbance in behavior in which any or all of the following major classes of severe disturbance are present:

1. disorganization of the thinking processes
2. inappropriateness in the nature of, or extreme intensity of, emotional reactions, especially of general mood
3. severe distortion in the perception of self or environment
4. loss of control over impulses
5. disharmony between emotion and thought (e.g., the person tells of a tragic event in his life yet appears unconcerned or even happy)

The question which arises is whether such disturbances in psychosis are different in degree or in quality from conditions in nonpsychotic states. No universally accepted answer to this question is available, since each alternative (degree or quality) is acceptable to significant numbers of workers in the mental health field [8]. It is also worth noting that, although a psychosis may be more disabling than a psychoneurosis, this is not invariably the case.

Nevertheless, we may think of psychoses as involving a more profound alteration of the personality than is the case in other conditions because there is a pervasive disruption of the personality even though the individual may still be able to maintain himself in society. The disruption represents a failure in *integrative adaptation* of the organism to internal conditions, or external conditions, or both. Thus, there may be a profound disturbance in perception (as in *hallucinations,* when the person experiences the presence of some external stimulation which is, in fact, not present), or in thinking (as in *delusions,* when the person has some belief that is not supported by available and quite apparent evidence), or in *interpersonal relations* (as in autism, when the person withdraws interest from the world and

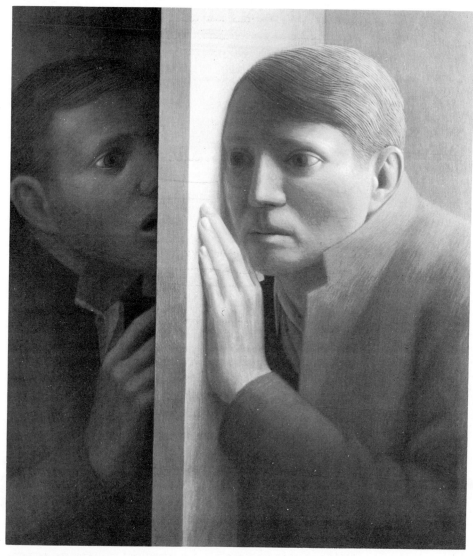

'Voice' Painting by George Tooker. Private Collection.
Courtesy Durlacher Brothers, New York

tends to live within himself). There may also be profound
alterations in the biochemical functioning so that food is re-
fused, the output of urine is doubled, or liver function is
severely disturbed [1]. At the psychological level, Hutt has
suggested that psychosis involves a *fragmentation of the ego,*
that is, that the many functions subsumed under the concept of
ego do not work together smoothly and that some functions are
markedly exaggerated whereas others are markedly inhibited [1].

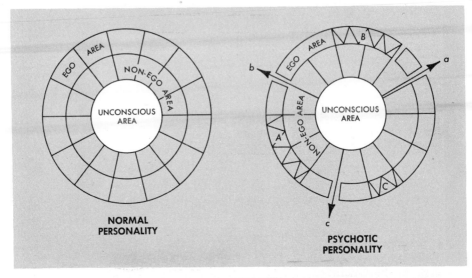

NORMAL
PERSONALITY

PSYCHOTIC
PERSONALITY

FIGURE 6.2   *Schematic representation of the organization of the personality in normal and psychotic conditions. In the normal condition, on the left, the personality is well differentiated; there are many large subdivisions of the ego, and there is good articulation (communication among several areas). In the psychotic condition, at the right, there is less total ego area; some areas of the ego are poorly developed (represented by the cross hatching at A, B, and C). There are "breaks" in the ego (at a, b, and c) so that impulses can "break through" without intervention of ego functions, and there is less well developed articulation among the several areas of the personality.*

Figure 6.2 illustrates, schematically, normal and psychotic ego characteristics.

CLASSIFICATION OF THE PSYCHOSES   The categorization of the functional psychoses which is most widely used in this country is that proposed by the American Psychiatric Association in 1952 [8]. In this classification, functional psychoses are seen as involving "personality disintegration for time, place, and/or person." There are four main subgroups of functional psychoses: *involutional psychotic reactions* (mainly depression occurring during the involutional period of life, providing no previous psychotic reactions have occurred); *affective reactions* (manic-depressive reactions and psychotic depressive reactions); *schizophrenic reactions* (including eight major subdivisions, which we shall discuss presently); and *paranoid reactions* (involving delusional behavior). As will be noted, this scheme of classification is based on reaction patterns, i.e., behavioral manifestations. It is not based on presumptive underlying dynamics, although the classification is the result of long years of clinical study of psychotic patients by many psychiatrists.

There are many problems in such a diagnostic categorization. There is the question of the essential unity of each major subcategory. Clinical evidence has shown, for instance, that many patients who are at first classifiable as belonging to the affective-reaction group later are classifiable as belonging to the schizophrenic-reaction group [9]. There is also the problem of whether these subgroups adequately cover the entire range of functional psychotic reactions.

Eysenck, who has studied personality structure for many years, utilizing factor analysis as his major research tool, has come to the conclusion that two dimensions are necessary to account for the entire range of behavioral adjustments from normal to abnormal [10]. His evidence is interpreted by him to indicate that there is a general psychoticism factor which can be differentiated from the neurotic factor, and that these two factors serve adequately to account for his data. His data show that those tests which discriminate between normals and psychotics do not discrimate between these two groups and neurotics. Some critics have severely criticized Eysenck for both his methodology and his interpretations, but he has continued to maintain his position [11].

In the very recent past, attempts have been made in this country to assimilate and explore anew factor-analytic studies of psychotic reactions. Lorr and his colleagues have conducted a series of studies in their attempt to explore the psychotic phenomenon [12]. Utilizing Guttman's concept of a circular law of behavior [13] for explaining parsimoniously the structure of interpersonal behavior, they have proposed ten syndromes (or clusters of behavior symptoms) to account for all of the rated behavior of the patients in their studies. They employed a 75-item rating scale (The Inpatient Multidimensional Psychiatric Scale) which was applied by expert interviewers to 566 patients in 44 hospitals. It is still too early to say how well this ten-syndrome analysis will stand up under the scrutiny of developmental studies, follow-up studies, and further experimental evaluation.

For the present, we shall continue to follow the clinical

classification proposed by the American Psychiatric Association, recognizing full well that a better scheme may become available in the future.

There are many clinical types of psychoses, and it is not our purpose to treat each of these exhaustively in this volume. Instead we shall concentrate our attention on *schizophrenia,* the most common form of psychosis, and then by way of contrast discuss the *manic-depressive* form. Both of these are classified as *functional psychoses,* by which it is meant that the condition is predominantly attributable to emotional maladaptation, although organic factors may be involved, and that it constitutes a disturbance in the functional aspects of behavior. Another general category of psychoses is called *organic.* These psychoses are severely disturbed forms of behavior in which the condition is primarily attributable to some organic factor. Included in this category are *alcoholic psychoses* (due to the effects on the biochemistry of the body of excessive and prolonged use of alcohol), *senile psychoses* (due to certain effects of the aging process on the central nervous system), *paresis* (due to a neurosyphilitic condition), and *toxic psychoses* (due to the effects of toxic agents). Of course, every functional psychosis involves disturbance in the functions or even the structure of some organ or organs, and every organic psychosis involves disturbance in some function or functions. Nevertheless, the distinction is made to indicate the probable primacy of either the organic or functional factor in the causation (etiology) of the psychosis or to indicate which factor represents the more significant disturbance in an organ or in some functional aspects of behavior.

THE SCHIZOPHRENIAS Schizophrenia takes many forms. As we shall see, there is some doubt that all forms represent the same "disease." Hence, we title this section "The Schizophrenias" to acknowledge the indeterminacy of this question.

Schizophrenia is not only the most prevalent psychosis in our society but is also the psychosis which has been most exhaustively studied—by both clinical and experimental research methods. Yet opinions of experts in the mental health field are sharply divided about its causes. Despite their inconclusiveness, the intensive analyses which have been made of the findings on causation shed considerable light on the phenomenon of "mental illness" and, therefore, of mental health. Similarly, the well-documented studies of the clinical manifestations of the schizophrenias cast the mechanisms of many other abnormal and normal conditions into sharper relief. These are some of the reasons for devoting considerable attention to this topic.

Types of schizophrenia   The classification of types of schizophrenia which is still officially recognized by the American Psychiatric Association is essentially that proposed by Kraepelin some fifty years ago. Basing his analysis upon clinical observations, Kraepelin suggested four main types of schizophrenia: simple, catatonic, hebephrenic, and paranoid [14]. The official classification in this country consists of these four types plus four others which can be regarded as pigeonholes for cases with mixed symptoms or with conditions that vary over time and which therefore do not constitute new categories but are simply categories of convenience for the practitioner.[2] However, even within the four classical categories, patients differ with respect to such factors as severity of the reaction, age of onset of the reaction, and progress of the illness. In other words, not all paranoid schizophrenics are alike with respect to how much they have regressed, or when their illness became manifest, or the likelihood of their recovery or nonrecovery.

THE SIMPLE TYPE.   In simple schizophrenia the individual slowly loses interest in the world around him and becomes increasingly incapable of living up to his former promise. Because of the slow *onset* of this illness, it is termed *insidious*. Moreover, there usually are no dramatic symptoms like delusions or hallucinations. Instead, there is a gradual loss of initiative, there is an increasing inability to work, and there is an increasing poverty of thought. Emotional reactions become increasingly more shallow (*flattened*) and resemble those of a young child in their immaturity. Especially important is the gradual loss of capacity for abstract thinking, so that there may appear to be a condition of mental retardation rather than psychosis.

The simple type of schizophrenia is not really simple at all. This designation indicates that there is no bizzarre behavior. The complex process of regression which underlies the reaction may not halt until the individual reaches a very low level of adaptation and may result in total social ineffectiveness. Many simple schizophrenics spend their adult lifetime in a psychiatric

[2] These are: chronic undifferentiated, acute undifferentiated, residual, and schizo-affective types.

hospital; others become beachcombers, prostitutes, or derelicts. Fortunately, although therapeutic efforts are difficult, modern methods of treatment can do much to arrest the development of this condition or to produce considerable recovery. In this connection, it is important to note that, the earlier the condition is detected and diagnosed and the earlier treatment is provided, the greater are the chances for recovery or at least improvement.

THE CATATONIC TYPE. In sharp contrast to the simple type, the catatonic reaction appears quite suddenly. The reaction usually begins with a period of great agitation and marked excitement which appear to be unrelated to external events in the patient's life. The agitation seems to have no purpose. Following this period, the patient may become increasingly inactive and more stuporous. In both phases the behavior appears bizarre and irrational. In both, the psychomotor sphere of activity is primarily involved. The term "psychomotor" rather than "motor" is employed because the willful or volitional aspects of behavior are disturbed even though the overt manifestation is a great increase or decrease in motor activity. The patient is in extreme conflict and withdraws into preoccupation with his conflicting impulses. Thus, he may be unresponsive to external stimulation (even though subsequently he can tell you the exact nature of this stimulation).

The following excerpt from clinical notes made concerning a catatonic patient may help to concretize this kind of behavior:

Harry, aged 32 years, was brought into the examining room by an attendant. He was literally led into the office since the attendant had to pull him by the arm. He stood where he had been left until the examiner motioned him to a chair and gently helped him into it. Then he sat staring off into space. The focus of the interview was to learn something of his current work interests so that he might be motivated for some appropriate occupational therapy in the hospital. He made no response to questions except to repeat a few of them mechanically. However, he would startle violently whenever there was some noise in the hall outside of the room. At the same time his face remained mask-like in appearance. After some 20 minutes spent fruitlessly in attempting to engage him in some discussion of his interests, during which he became increasingly rigid and motionless in postural adjustment, the interview was ended, and with some prodding he was finally able to be helped out of the room.

Three days later, another interview was attempted. This time he seemed more animated and engaged in a little spontaneous conversation. His muscular rigidity was far less pronounced than during the previous visit. When asked about his vocational interests, he began to respond with the query, "Didn't you ask me about that the last time?" He was asked to tell what he remembered of his last visit and he was remarkably clear about most of the questions he had been asked.

The two phases of catatonia do *not* occur inevitably. Some patients reveal only catatonic stupor. In this condition, they may be extremely negativistic. They may refuse to move or to eat, and they may show extreme insensitivity to painful stimulation. They may withhold their urine or feces. They may stare at a spot on the floor for long periods of time. They may refuse to speak. If they are placed in an awkward position, they may retain this position for hours. Conversely, in catatonic excitement, all motor activities are speeded up. There may be incessant activity. There may be sudden and apparently inexplicable periods of violent destructiveness.

In either phase of catatonia, there usually are both hallucinations and delusions, although the presence of these phenomena may not be overtly noticeable because of the patient's inability to communicate until the stupor or excitement abates. To the catatonic patient, all of his apparently purposeless activity or inactivity has meaning in terms of his inner conflicts. During periods of remission (abatement) of symptoms, he may be able to communicate this meaning.

Catatonic reactions can involve some or all of the above characteristics and phases. In some cases catatonia is a prelude to another type of schizophrenia. In others there may be a sudden recovery with no subsequent relapse. Treatment of catatonic reactions by modern methods, such as electric shock therapy, or drug therapy, especially if accompanied or followed by psychotherapy, often proves very helpful. (See Chapter 7.)

THE HEBEPHRENIC TYPE. The onset of hebephrenic reactions may be slow and insidious, like the simple type, or, as is more common, it may develop quite rapidly, more like the catatonic type. In either case, there is almost always a long history of prior silly or inappropriate behavior, so that the hebephrenic seemed "odd" earlier in life. In general, the behavior of hebephrenics exaggerates that of a young adolescent who is acting queer or silly. More specifically, the course of this illness shows the following characteristics: increasing degrees of inappropriateness of behavior; discrepancies between mood and thought content; manneristic speech and behavior; increasing preoccupation with inner life; hallucinatory behavior and numerous delusions (especially of grandeur); bizarre hypochondriacal ideas (such as a feeling that his brain has shifted to another part of his body); and, above all, very severe desocialization and deterioration of personality. These may be so extreme that the patient is rendered incoherent and has to be taken care of.

Hebephrenia is clearly recognizable to the layman as an abnormality because of its bizarre characteristics. In the early stages it is difficult to distinguish this condition from other types of schizophrenia. In the past such patients were usually seen in psychiatric hospitals in their severely regressed and deteriorated states, living at or near a vegetative or mere existence level. Today many cases of hebephrenia are helped long before this state of regression has been reached. Moreover, increasing numbers of them recover significantly with effective and intense treatment.

THE PARANOID TYPE. This type usually develops later in life than the other types (most commonly in the age range of 30–50 years), and is characterized by the prominence of delusions that characteristically involve anger and suspiciousness. The overt development of these phenomena is preceded by a long history of emotional instability involving suspiciousness of others as well as sadistic and deprecatory attitudes. Gradually, delusional thinking becomes more prominent and is defended with more and more rationalization. Hallucinations are also prominent in the clinical picture. The mechanism of projection (described in Chapter 4) is quite apparent in these individuals. Despite the delusional and hallucinatory behavior of paranoids, they usually do not regress rapidly; many remain at the same level of psychotic involvement for some period of time. Others may recover spontaneously or with therapeutic help. Those who do not recover within the first two years of their acute illness or who do not receive therapeutic help relatively early usually become somewhat more regressed in time. However, most paranoids maintain relatively good contact with reality, except in the areas of their delusions, and are able to channel their energies into useful and productive work. Some paranoids who feel very persecuted and who have a high tension level act unpredictably and are physically aggressive and even homicidal. Unlike hebephrenics, emotional mood is usually closely congruent with ideational content. A central conflict in many cases of paranoid schizophrenia, although quite clearly not in all of them, involves homosexual impulses. According to Freud, the persecutory attitudes of such male paranoids follow the formula:

1. "I love men."
2. This impulse is unacceptable, is "reversed," and is then experienced as, "I hate men."
3. This feeling is then "projected" and therefore is experienced as, "Men hate me."

We noted that the course of individuals with paranoid schizophrenia is highly variable. When the illness progresses, it can assume some of the characteristics of catatonia or hebephrenia or both.

Psychodynamics of schizophrenia reactions Now let us summarize some of the mechanisms employed by schizophrenics and analyze the nature of the conflicts and stresses which they suffer. In doing so, we shall emphasize the differences in intensity and in patterns from less severe forms of mental illness. The similarities will also be noted.

One of the most important processes in schizophrenia is that of regression. We shall discuss later whether this is largely or entirely due to psychological conflict or whether it is significantly influenced by genetic and biochemical factors. In any case, severe regression, as exemplified in hebephrenia, represents a marked failure in adaptive capacities (or in adaptive functions of the ego) and is accompanied by behavior which is similar to that found in the preoccupation of young children with autoerotic fantasies and loss of impulse control. Schizophrenia has been viewed as a process of progressive maladaptation, and it has been suggested that severe anxiety and conflict (which trigger off the regression) cause inadequate neural discharge and poor integration in behavioral responses [15]. In this respect the severe regression we see in many cases of schizophrenia is not essentially different from the moderate or temporary regression encountered in normals and neurotics under conditions of stress.

Not all workers are willing to accept the thesis that regression in the psychotic differs only in degree from the normal to the psychotic population. As we noted previously, Eysenck believes that the hypothesis of one dimension or type of regression is untenable [16]. His data, based on a battery of tests, showed that he could discriminate normals from psychotics but "on the whole" could not discriminate normals from neurotics. Hence he concludes that two separate personality variables are necessary to explain the findings. However, even if we assume that his techniques of factor analysis are valid and that there is a qualitative difference in personality dimensions between psychotics, on the one hand, and normals and neurotics, on the other, it is still possible to conceive that psychotics suffer damage to the ego at an earlier age and consequently manifest a greater degree of regression. Therefore, this regression would be both *quantitatively* and *qualitatively* different. An analogy may be made with the process of reducing the temperature of water, in which differences in degree of the temperature do not produce qualitative change until the temperature gets below the freezing point, when ice is formed.

Closely related to the problem of regression is that of *fixation*. The schizophrenic seems to be fixated behaviorally at an earlier period in his psychodynamic development. During regression, patterns of behavior may be reinstated that are similar to those that were fixated previously. Fixation is not an all-or-none process. Each of us is fixated to some degree in terms of earlier periods of development. Some of these fixations are mild and others are more severe. The schizophrenic, however, has deeper and varied patterns of fixation. Therefore, his behavior tends to fluctuate widely during periods of stress, sometimes exhibiting regression very markedly and other times only slightly. This variability in regression, and in its severity, makes it more difficult for the schizophrenic to test reality accurately. In severe regression he tends to be oblivious of external stress, although he retains awareness of inner impulses and fantasies. In periods of moderate regression he may be much more aware of external reality. The normal individual who regresses slightly during stress may have perceptions that are influenced by needs, too, but he can more easily check them against reality and so obtain more nearly valid perceptual experience. It is the severity of, and variability in, fixation which makes it more difficult for the schizophrenic to test reality. In turn, this facilitates even more regression and less capacity to cope with reality.

Another characteristic observed in the clinical descriptions of the schizophrenic is the *failure of repression*. The patient becomes aware of feelings, impulses, and thoughts and has to express them, often in ways which seem incomprehensible to the normal person. However, we may remember from our discussion in Chapter 4 that repression sometimes fails in both normals and neurotics. Examples of this, we may recall, are slips of the tongue (in which we say something we did not intend to say and are unaware of the "slip") and "normal" hallucinatory experiences (such as those that occur under conditions of sensory deprivation). The young child frequently has hallucinatory experiences, yet this behavior is not regarded as psychotic [17]. The schizophrenic, in contrast, reveals a massive or severe failure of repression. Hence, unconscious material floods his consciousness and further beclouds the accuracy of the perceptions of his environment. This delusional or hallucinatory behavior may be conceived of as attempts to reconstruct a seemingly reality-oriented world, although we who observe this behavior view it as pathological. In these forms of behavior the person tries to project his internal wishes upon the external world (a person or an object) and thereby gain some degree of control over his impulses while satisfying his internal needs.

Other defense mechanisms which are characteristically part of the pattern of schizophrenic behavior are *denial, projection,* and *introjection.* Once again, we must note that normals and neurotics also employ these mechanisms, but in the case of schizophrenics they are predominant in the defensive hierarchy. Not only are they the *preferred mechanisms*—for schizophrenics employ, at times, all of the other defense mechanisms—but denial, projection, and introjection are more fully developed, perhaps as the result of frequent reinforcement. These mechanisms offer some defense against conflict and anxiety, mainly in avoiding the conflict situation. However, they offer little opportunity for reality-testing. Hence, their continual use facilitates regression and produces a vicious spiral of increasing avoidance, more intense conflict, and then more complete avoidance of reality.

Another interesting aspect of schizophrenic behavior, and perhaps one of central importance, is the disturbance in thinking. Although the thought processes of persons with other forms of psychosis may seem strange because they are "frenzied" or show indications of "wandering," they seem understandable to some degree. But the schizophrenic's thinking is often expressed in a weird garble of incoherent phrases and strange words (*neologisms*). For example, one patient, when asked how he

633

happened to be in a psychiatric hospital, replied, "Well, it seems strangulous. But usurpations by others require radio contacts. Our enemies are in there, and they comply but they never feign. Only when it's dark and cold, one must face them." Perhaps the reader may catch a glimpse of the paranoid process in which vague enemies, radio waves, feelings of aloneness, and feelings of impotence are suggested.

The thinking of schizophrenics has been studied intensively. In the early stages of schizophrenia, thinking is likely to be *stereotyped* (use of the same idea or the same phrase over and over again) and *scattered* (sequences of thought are unrelated or illogical). Later it becomes *less abstract* and *more concrete* (that is, concrete things are substituted for abstractions or generalizations). Goldstein has called attention to the *loss of the abstract attitude* and the substitution of a concrete attitude (or the inability to conceptualize) [18]. Arieti believes, however, that the schizophrenic not only withdraws and regresses from abstract to concrete thinking but actively transforms the abstract into the concrete [19]. This change in thinking pattern is not easily reversible, even under drugs, as Senf has shown [20]. When patients were intravenously administered sodium amytal, a drug which induces a "twilight sleep," they improved in responsiveness but did not improve in the precision of their thinking.

Schizophrenic thinking is marked by its infantile character. It employs the types of logic and symbols that are characteristic of the most primitive minds. It no longer follows Aristotelian logic, which is indicative of secondary processes in personality development, but rather shows characteristics of earlier forms of logic; i.e., "paleologic." Von Domarus compares these forms of logic as follows: "Whereas the normal person accepts identity only upon the basis of identical subjects, the paleologician accepts identity based upon identical predicates" [21]. Paleologic would reach the following conclusion based on the following premises:

1. Horses have legs.
2. Dr. Smith has legs.
3. Dr. Smith, therefore, is a horse.

Not only is the logic of the schizophrenic primitive; it is also governed to a great extent by "primary process," that is, it is based on internal needs and does not obey consistent, logical principles.

Arieti believes that schizophrenic thought may be characterized, in general, as showing *teleological regression* [19]. Such thinking is regressive but is purposeful (i.e., is directed toward specific goals). It serves to avoid severe anxiety by the substitution of fantasy for a reality that the patient finds too difficult to cope with. If we examine the schizophrenic's thoughts with this principle in mind, we can sometimes discover the wishes he is trying to avoid.

It is clear that, although schizophrenic thought is disorganized, the intellectual level of the schizophrenic is not necessarily permanently impaired [22]. Only some aspects of the thinking process are severely disturbed. Schizophrenics have difficulty in attending to current tasks, adopting flexible approaches to problems, and persisting in task-completion. Hence they may score lower than might be expected on intelligence tests. However, the quality of schizophrenic thought is different from that of normals. Schilder suggested, some time ago, "The characteristic content of the unfinished thoughts of the schizophrenic is the characteristic for the thought processes of primitives" [23]. In this respect, this psychotic group is quite different from both normals and neurotics, but, as we have indicated, it is not so different from the thinking of very young normal children.

Problems concerning theories of psychosis   Various theoretical explanations have been proposed concerning the causes of schizophrenia, and we shall attempt to summarize them briefly. But before doing this, it might be well to discuss some of the general problems concerning the study of causes which apply to all forms of mental illness or maladjustment. These difficulties are dramatically illustrated in the study of schizophrenia.

We should note, first, that we are dealing with *end products* when we study the clinical forms of schizophrenia. These psychiatric conditions, like most forms of maladjustment, whether severe or mild, are diagnosed and classified on the basis of a *clinical syndrome* (group of symptoms). It is well known, however, that the same symptom may have different causes as well as different meanings in the case of different individuals. The same point is applicable to syndromes [24]. As an illustration, we may note that aggression is manifested differently in different social classes [25] and that aggressive behavior has different significance for different individuals. Hence, when we group people together in a nosological category (like schizophrenia), or even when we group them by subtypes of symptoms, we may be including the end results of many kinds of *processes*. The conditions leading to the several members of each type or subtype may, in fact, be quite different.

It has also been repeatedly established that the outcomes of schizophrenic reactions are markedly different depending upon the nature of the onset of the illness [26]. When the illness develops suddenly (acute condition), the *prognosis* (or outlook) is much more favorable than when it is slow and insidious (chronic condition). Similarly, when the onset is accompanied by intense anxiety (evidence of conflict with which the patient is struggling), the outcome is likely to be more favorable than when this is not the case. Certain questions immediately come to mind. Are these conditions similar with respect to symptoms but different with respect to development and other behavioral outcomes? And if they are, to what extent is the process underlying the disease influenced, for better or worse, by external social or emotional conditions (or other conditions)?

The striking difference in prognosis of different schizophrenics has fostered the development of an over-all categorization of schizophrenics into two major classes: *reactive and process* [27]. The former, with acute onset, have a favorable prognosis; the latter, with slow onset, have a relatively unfavorable prognosis. But how are we to explain the factors that contribute to reactive and to process types of phenomena? Is a "process schizophrenic" merely an individual with more pathology than a "reactive schizophrenic"? Is the reactive type capable of withstanding stresses better than the process type because of compensating factors in his constitution? And if we assume that the reactive type is produced as a reaction to the relatively sudden exposure to anxiety, and not primarily as a result of endogenous factors, why do schizophrenics with lesser amounts of anxiety have such a poor prognosis?

Still another general issue which must concern us is the question of the relative homogeneity or heterogeneity of the different forms of schizophrenia. Many catatonics later develop paranoid and hebephrenic symptoms, or combinations of these symptoms. Others do not. What distinguishes these two types of catatonics? Are we dealing with one or several nosological categories? Are these differences in the course of the catatonic reaction to be explained on the basis of differences in original constitution, differences in the developmental histories, or interactions of these two classes of events? As we shall see in the next section, no single answer is at present universally acceptable. The more we learn about this condition (or these conditions), the more we appreciate the complexity of all mental health phenomena.

Theories of the etiology of schizophrenia   Theories of the etiology of schizophrenia range through the whole continuum from those proposing exclusive genetic determination, at one extreme, to the completely psychodynamic determination, at the other extreme. Each theory attempts to explain the whole range of schizophrenic phenomena, usually making the implicit assumption that what is involved is a single disease or pathological entity. We have suggested that there is serious difficulty with the assumption of a unitary condition. Slater, who has made extensive studies of data from identical and fraternal schizophrenics, analyzed findings supplied by Kallmann [28], one of the foremost proponents of the unitary position, and found that the clinical subtypes of this illness were genetically heterogeneous [29]. Another line of evidence, which considers the age at onset of the schizophrenic reaction, casts doubt on the unitary position. If the condition were unitary, and if hereditary factors were responsible, there should be a high degree of correlation for the age at onset of monozygotic twins and increasingly lower degrees of correlation, respectively, for dizygotic twins and siblings. The evidence on this problem clearly does not support this position [30]. Slater found, in fact, that the correlation for age at onset for monozygotic twins was .54, whereas it was .74 for dizygotic twins. For concordant siblings the correlation was .50. Clearly, such findings, if replicated, must cast doubt on any monogenetic hypothesis.

One could argue, of course, that (1) schizophrenia is genetically determined but the specific forms of expression are not (the latter being influenced by nongenetic factors, such as the nature of stresses) and (2) schizophrenia is not genetically determined, but some predisposition to it is genetically determined. These and other arguments may now be examined as we discuss the various theories.

MONOGENETIC THEORIES. Theories which support this position argue that schizophrenia is a specific, inherited disease and that persons who inherit certain genetic factors will almost

637

inevitably develop the complete clinical manifestations. The general position taken by such theorists is that schizophrenia is attributable to a single recessive Mendelian type of gene. Little or no significance is given to environmental stress as contributing to the illness.

The work most frequently cited in support of this position is that of Kallmann, who in the research already described, as well as in later research based on 953 twins from psychiatric hospitals in New York [31], showed that the incidence of the schizophrenic reaction increased sharply when rates of congruence (that is, agreement among pairs) were considered for pairs of half-siblings, siblings, fraternal twins, and identical twins. The rates rose from 7.0 percent in the first group to 85.8 percent in the last group. Other researchers employing this approach have not been able to achieve results as spectacular as Kallmann, but their findings have been in the same direction. The argument proposed by these workers is that the greater the similarity in heredity, the closer the congruence rate for the incidence of schizophrenia when one member of the pair has schizophrenia.

Many workers have challenged the conclusion of such studies, some arguing that only a predisposition to the illness is suggested by the data, while others indicate that even this possibility is not clearly proved. Koller has reanalyzed Kallmann's data and has shown that they do not support his own hypothesis, even if they are taken at face value [32]. His argument is that if single recessivity is the hereditary basis of schizophrenia, the incidence for siblings should be higher than for the children of schizophrenics, but Kallman's data show the opposite results. Pastore has argued that various methodological errors of a serious nature were made in Kallmann's studies which vitiate his conclusions [33]. The difference in congruence rates for siblings and identical twins can be explained, say many workers, on the grounds that twins have much more similar familial and environmental experiences than siblings, even though all come from the same family. This argument, it must be admitted, does not necessarily account for the difference between identical and nonidentical twins, since both types of twins live in similar familial conditions yet show such a wide divergence in rates (85.8 percent as compared with 14.7 percent). However, nonidentical twins may be of different sexes, may be treated quite dissimilarly by home and community, and may be biologically and genetically quite different. Which of these factors contributes to the illness, and to what degree, is undetermined. Moreover, some investigators, using sampling techniques different from Kallmann's (by sampling community rather than hospital subjects, for example), obtain results in opposition to his. For example, Essen-Möller, in an analysis of results with monozygotic twins only, found that the psychiatric conditions and personalities in *every pair of twins* were divergent and not congruent [34]. In fact, the psychiatric outcomes were divergent for every pair of twins.

An adequate test of the monogenetic hypothesis would require, among other things, that monozygotic twins from schizophrenic parents be separated from each other in *early infancy* and that the separate members of each pair be placed in widely differing types of home conditions (as, for example, in homes with very healthy and stable adults as compared with homes containing schizophrenic adults). Studies of this kind have not been attempted on an experimental basis, for obvious reasons, and have occurred very infrequently on a natural basis. It is noteworthy, however, that this kind of twin-study, investigating hereditary-environmental influences on intellectual development, has tended to indicate greater effect of environmental factors than was anticipated on genetic grounds [35].

PREDISPOSITION THEORIES. In this category may be grouped the diverse theories which propose that what is inherited is either a specific predisposition toward schizophrenia which, when complemented by stressful conditions of living, especially in early life, or when not compensated for by other, more healthful constitutional or environmental conditions, leads to the development of the illness—or to a more general predisposition toward the development of psychopathology.

Meehl presents the most forceful case for this type of position [36]. He postulates a "neural integrative defect" (defined as "an aberration in some parameter of single cell function") as a necessary precondition for the development of schizophrenia. He calls people with this defect *schizotaxics* and states:

All schizotaxics become, *on all actually existing social learning regimes,* schizotypic in personality organization; but most remain compensated. A minority . . . are . . . potentiated into clinical schizophrenia. . . . The schizotype is a person who, having been schizotaxic, because of certain social experiences (and therefore because of learning) exhibits four core behavior traits: cognitive slippage; anhedonia; ambivalence; and inter-personal aversiveness.

"Remaining compensated" means that such individuals have sufficient defenses to avoid becoming actual schizophrenics.

Meehl believes that the four behavior traits are *inevitably* learned under present conditions of life because of the schizo-taxic predisposition and whether schizophrenia develops in a schizotaxic individual depends upon the effects of modifying genes and environmental conditions.

Meehl recognizes certain difficulties with his theory. He indicates, for example, that the genetic basis for the four core traits may be questioned on the basis of recent experimental and psychotherapeutic experiences which indicate that a wide variety of individuals (schizophrenic as well as nonschizophrenic) may either develop the traits or markedly modify them. But there are other questions which pose serious difficulties for this type of theory. If there is a specific predisposition (which schizotaxia implies), how is one to account for sex differences in the incidence of schizophrenia? How is one to account for *marked differences* in the incidence of schizophrenia in differing cultures [37]? Are only the four core traits, singly or in combination, the essence of schizophrenia? And, if so, how is one to account for differences in the incidence of schizophrenia among people who seem to have one of these types of traits (like introversion) [38]? And, is schizophrenia really a unitary disease, as Meehl implies?

SOMATIC HYPOTHESES. Many types of somatic hypotheses have been offered to account for schizophrenia. We can refer to only some of these by way of illustration. Sheldon and his co-workers have suggested that body type (that of the asthenic or ectomorphic) is significantly associated with the incidence of schizophrenia [39]. (See Chapter 5.) This hypothesis has not been confirmed. Moreover, individuals with nonectomorphic personality attributes frequently become schizophrenics.

Biochemical and neuropathological differences have been postulated as the basis for the schizophrenic reaction [40, 41]. A wide variety of suspected factors has been suggested, but none of these has yet been shown to be specific for schizo-phrenia. Similar biochemical phenomena may also be found among nonschizophrenics [42]. Moreover, the conditions may not be necessarily attributable to schizophrenia per se but to its *consequences,* which influence ways of living and therefore body chemistry. Some workers believe that schizophrenia is primarily a metabolic disorder, due to the formation of "taraxein" [43]. This, in turn, is symptomatic of a defect in the oxidizing enzyme system. However, these studies are criticized on the grounds of inadequate methodological controls, and their findings await further confirmation. We must always ask: Is the changed biochemical functioning or neural structure the cause or the result of the psychopathology?

PSYCHOGENIC THEORIES. These theories suggest that some forms of schizophrenia, at least, are attributable to profound disturbances in the functioning of the ego. Such disturbances may result from various types of constitutional inadequacies or from entirely psychological factors. Jung was the first to propose that severe emotional difficulties might produce toxins which damage the brain [44]. Freud believed that due to severe fixations early in life the individual loses the capacity for coping with reality and withdraws libidinal energy from the world. He may never mature beyond the early schizophrenic, narcissistic stage, or he may regress to the early stages of ego development when under stress later in life [45].

Research has amply documented the proposition that pathological family relationships, and, particularly, severe pathology in the mother (who is most important in the young infant's life), characterize the developmental history of many schizophrenics [46]. The significant finding is that the lack of communication between mother and child, due to the highly inconsistent relationship between mother and child, produces in the child either (*a*) severe overt anxiety, which prevents adequate coping with these conditions, or (*b*) extreme withdrawal (autism), often with little overt evidence of anxiety [47]. At least some forms of schizophrenia are seen as an extreme withdrawal from the world. Other forms are seen as regression under external stress, due to the prior fixations, which did not previously precipitate the illness. Still others are viewed as almost heroic attempts by the individual to maintain some form of personality integrity and self-esteem under internal and external stresses during critical periods in the person's life [48]. Such individuals manage to maintain a precarious but "brittle" integration in personality.

Recent psychogenic theorists have attempted to describe psychoanalytic or other psychogenic theories of schizophrenia in terms of specific operations or procedures. Cameron has proposed a "social disorganization theory" in which failure in communication and withdrawal into a pseudocommunity results from social-learning conditions that are definable and objectively measurable [49]. Mednick proposes that intense anxiety, which spreads and generalizes, produces reinforcement of idiosyncratic responses. These in turn lead to psychotic personality organization and development [50]. These idiosyncratic responses are not extinguished because of some genetic factor or because of an "impossible" external situation. This theory would not account for some forms of schizophrenic development in which high anxiety levels do not seem to be present, but it does allow for both genetic and social-learning conditions to interact in the development of schizophrenia.

PRESENT STATUS OF THEORIES. Obviously, the last word has not been written about schizophrenia. We cannot be certain whether we are dealing with a unitary phenomenon or with many different but related phenomena. We are not even certain that all schizophrenic reactions are truly psychotic; certainly some transient "schizophrenic" reactions may not be. It may be that genetic factors contribute in some way toward a disposition for schizophreniform behavior, but it is questionable whether such a disposition is a necessary precondition for the illness. It is questionable whether, if a predisposition is necessary, it leads to general psychopathological and disorganized personality development or to schizophrenia specifically. Social-learning conditions and various types of anxiety reactions have been shown to play a prominent role in many cases of schizophrenia, but the extent of their significance is still open to question.

Psychogenic theories give comfort to psychotherapists, who hope to assist patients by psychotherapeutic means. Somatic theories give comfort to those who hope to find biochemical antidotes for this condition. Increased knowledge will assist both groups of scientists in preventive and treatment programs, but, above all, it will help us to understand more about human behavior, normal as well as abnormal. We need to learn much more about continuities and discontinuities across the whole spectrum of behavior reactions and the mediating mechanisms that are involved in the process of "being human."

THE MANIC-DEPRESSIVE PSYCHOSES This psychosis is characterized by periods of great excitement, increased motor activity, and an elation of mood—or by periods of melancholia, decreased motor activity, and a poverty of thought—or by both conditions, alternately. In contrast to the schizophrenias, there may be little loss of contact with reality. Also in contrast, social and psychological factors apparently have a greater role in precipitating the illness. Moreover, while there is severe regression in this form of psychosis, fragmentation of the ego is *not* a prominent part of the clinical picture, and deterioration into infantile types of behavior is rarely present.

We shall consider briefly the clinical forms of this illness, then consider the underlying psychodynamics, and finally evaluate the etiological factors that are held to be responsible. The classification of mania and depression as circular and opposing phases of a single process was not accepted until 1899 when Kraepelin proposed this method of analysis [51]. Today, however, there is some doubt concerning the unitary nature of this illness.

Depression　The major characteristics of "psychotic depression" are (1) a more or less severe depression of mood; (2) disturbances in the thinking processes, manifested mainly in a slowing-down of such processes; (3) a preoccupation with morbid ideas; and (4) psychomotor retardation, in which all motor movements are slow, e.g., the behavior shows lethargy or stupor. Other indications are slower speech and slower perceptual reactions. Great effort may be needed to accomplish even the most simple, routine task. Along with these primary symptoms there may be, especially in cases of severe depression, marked decrease in physiological functions. Appetite is decreased, sleep is difficult, and there may be a marked loss of weight. In the most severe cases, a state of stupor is reached, patients become mute, and almost all forms of responsiveness are severely restricted. Suicide may be attempted and, noteworthy in this respect, it may be tried just when it appears that the patient is beginning to make a recovery.

In this illness delusions and hallucinations are rare. Rather, the individual complains that he cannot think and that he feels guilty and worthless. When delusions do occur, they often are related to the individual's mood and are self-accusatory or take the form of excessive concern over disease and death.

The depressed patient either consciously seeks support or behaves in such a way as to require an almost inexhaustible amount of help. Nevertheless, except in the most severe cases, the patient is in touch with reality and does not show the

643

disorganized type of thinking so characteristic of schizophrenics.

Mania In many respects, mania is the polar opposite of depression. Its major characteristics are (1) a more or less marked elevation of mood, (2) a disturbance in thinking processes, with an increased pace of ideation, flights of ideas, and an incessant need to talk, and (3) a psychomotor acceleration. There may be physiological symptoms, including loss of appetite, sleeping difficulties, and loss of weight.

Frequently mania is preceded by depression, although the opposite may also occur. It has been suggested that the mania is a defense against feelings of guilt and worthlessness. The manic patient shows a great increase in *apparent* self-esteem. He thinks quickly, brags quite a bit, is boisterous, and is quite socially intrusive in other ways. If he does develop delusions, they are likely to be delusions of grandeur—great abilities, prowess, or wealth. To the average person, such behavior appears to represent only an extreme boastfulness. He may enjoy the unusual "story-telling" capacities of the patient, with his verbal facility. Despite the increased ideational or associational capacity of such patients, their thoughts are shallow or impoverished.

Mixed reactions Some patients not only exhibit successive periods of depression and mania but show periods of *agitated depression, manic stupor,* and other varied combinations of the types of symptoms we have already described. Moreover, although from 30 to 40 percent of individuals who have an attack of either mania or depression never have a recurrence [52], others may have a number of attacks. These may become progressively worse. Still others may develop schizophrenic reactions. Figure 6.3 illustrates some of the types of reactions which occur.

Psychodynamic considerations Many cases of manic-depressive psychosis recover completely after a single attack; only a few deteriorate. When recovery is not spontaneous or when psychotherapy is ineffective, recent advances in treatment have enabled mental health workers to produce rapid and effective recovery by means of electroshock therapy or the use of antidepressant or tranquilizing drugs. (See Chapter 7 for a discussion of these and related methods.) In fact, one of the major distinguishing features of this psychosis from schizophrenia is the much more favorable prognosis.

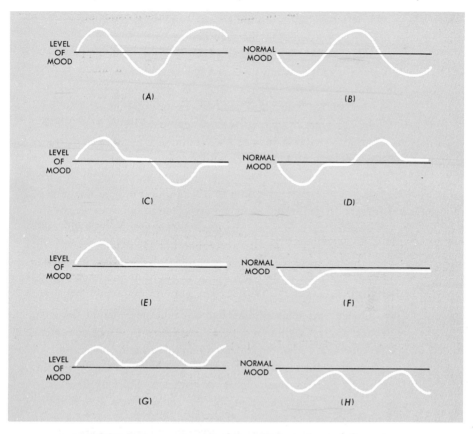

FIGURE 6.3 *Patterns of manic-depressive, manic, and depressive reactions.* (A): *manic-depressive reaction, beginning with mania;* (B): *manic-depressive reaction, beginning with depression;* (C) *and* (D): *manic-depressive reactions with normal interludes;* (E) *and* (F): *single attacks of mania and depression, respectively;* (G) *and* (H): *recurrent attacks of mania and depression, respectively.*

The first systematic attempt to explain the dynamics of depression was offered by one of Freud's disciples, Karl Abraham, who believed that depression was not unlike normal mourning, except that in the latter case one mourned a lost person and, after a period of time, the grief abated [53]. In depression, one feels guilty and really mourns the "lost person" that had been assimilated (incorporated) in one's own personality. Abraham believed that such phenomena in depression presupposed previous fixation at the oral, and to some extent at the anal-sadistic, level.

The modern dynamic conception of psychotic depression is

not very different from the above. Arieti suggests that there is a basic inconsistency in the way depressed patients were treated in infancy [54]. The infant was first "accepted" by the mother—a person with a strong superego who devotes herself *dutifully* to ministering to the infant's needs. In turn, the infant accepted this dependent, succored position. He introjected, at the same time, this moralistic personality characteristic of the mother. During the second year of his life, there is a drastic change in the mother's attitude. Now she makes considerable demands upon her child, even though ministering to his needs to some extent. In turn, the child has to learn to meet the expectations of others—to learn an early sense of duty and responsibility. Nevertheless, he resents the new demands, often showing attacks of rebellion and defiance. At the same time, he is still dependent upon his mother, and simultaneously she is unconsciously resented. Moreover, she makes him feel guilty if he "doesn't behave."

Unlike the schizophrenic, who could never learn what to expect from a highly inconsistent mother with whom communication was very limited, the depressive first learns one pattern of interaction, then is suddenly required to adapt to a new pattern. Despite his fixations, he is nevertheless able to develop a reasonably good ego and, at the same time, a very strict superego.

Depressions are precipitated in later life by an actual or threatened loss of "supplies" (sources of succor). This can be a person or an object that has great significance for the individual. If the patient suffers a sudden loss in self-esteem, he mourns as if he had lost something from within himself. He directs his feelings of hostility toward himself and simultaneously feels guilty. In psychoanalytic terms, there is regression to the oral stage, a renewed demand for "supplies," and a conflict between ego and superego. In this struggle, the superego dominates and the ego is subordinated.

Manic reactions are frequently interpreted as defenses against depression. There is an apparent increase in self-esteem as the individual attempts to fight off the depression. Freud suggested that there is a fusion of ego and superego functions in which, in contrast to depression, the ego is freed to permit drive expression, and id impulses break through [55]. The condition is similar to sleep, when superego controls are relaxed and id material appears in dreams.

Etiology of manic-depressive psychosis   One of the interesting findings about this condition is that its incidence varies greatly in different cultures. According to Eaton and Weil, for example, the predominant psychosis among the Hutterites is manic-depressive psychosis [37]. This sect constitutes a closely knit society which emphasizes moral values, the cohesiveness of the group, and the need for developing "inner-directedness." Externally directed aggression is not tolerated; strict conscience and excessive guilt are reinforced. Other studies show that cultures in which there is a relatively high incidence of this psychosis differ in many of the respects we have discussed above in terms of psychodynamic development [56]. Increases in the incidence of manic-depressive psychosis seem related to socioeconomic factors [57], so that there is a disproportionately higher incidence of this condition than of other psychotic conditions during times of economic depression. Such findings suggest, at least, that this psychosis is precipitated by social-psychological factors or that such factors are related to predispositions for this type of maladjustment.

On the other hand, there are numerous proponents of the genetic viewpoint with respect to the etiology of this psychosis. Studies of families of such people reveal that manic-depressive conditions tend to "run in families" [58]. Some investigators believe that there is evidence of an inherited predisposition [59, 61]; others point out that the data do not support the laws of Mendelian inheritance [58]. Still others believe in the theory of multiple etiologies, some attacks being due to exogenous factors, some to endogenous factors, and still others to combinations of these factors. The evidence for genetic factors is far less convincing than in the case of schizophrenia, but still some kind of biological dysfunction may play an important role in some types of manic-depressive conditions [60].

The Psychoneuroses

A consideration of the many kinds of psychoneuroses will point up the fact that, while biochemical factors may be of some significance in these conditions, the basic contributing factor is psychological conflict. Neurotic conditions vary greatly in severity. Some may present only minor problems in adjustment, while others are utterly intolerable and produce an inability to function effectively in life. The great majority of psychoneurotics are not hospitalized. A few are hospitalized because their doctors wish to make a more exhaustive search for possible underlying physiological factors.

We shall consider, first, the general nature of psychoneuroses, examine some specific examples, and then compare the psychoneuroses with the psychoses.

THE NATURE OF PSYCHONEUROTIC REACTIONS Psychoneuroses take many forms, which differ markedly in their outward manifestations yet have certain features in common. At the base of all such reactions is a continuing high anxiety level resulting from unresolved conflicts. In the case of *anxiety neurotics,* the anxiety is so intense it is almost palpable. These people complain that their condition is insufferable, and they have many physiological disturbances, including such symptoms as depression, headache, feelings of fatigue, tenseness of the body muscles, and difficulty in sleeping (often accompanied by frightful nightmares). In other cases the overt anxiety appears to be mild or is absent. For example, in the so-called *character disorders* or in the "*psychopathic*" *states,* there seems to be a distortion of the ways in which impulses are handled, but there are few, if any, complaints of anxiety. The observer may be unaware that any anxiety is present. These individuals complain that society is intolerant of their needs and not that they are suffering because of internal problems. However, as we shall see, these disturbances in behavior may also result from intolerable anxiety conditions, but the neurosis shields the individual from experiencing the anxiety. In other words, the anxiety has been transformed into aberrant forms of behavior. It is still there, however, as may be confirmed in psychotherapy, when the aberrant ways of behaving (and the defenses) are modified, and the individual begins to experience anxiety directly. In such cases we may think of the anxiety as being latent (see Chapter 4). There are also some types of psychoneuroses in which anxiety is *displaced* into physiological functions or physical organs or takes *symbolic* forms. This occurs in *conversion hysteria;* for example, the individual develops a functional paralysis of the hand although there is no neurological basis for it.

Thus we may say that anxiety, in some form, is at the base of all psychoneurotic conditions. We may also say that the anxiety results from a neurotic conflict. We have previously discussed the nature of conflict, noting that when conflicts are unresolved, and have unconscious components, the individual learns to defend himself against the anxiety by means of inappropriate and stereotyped behavior. But why is the neurotic unable to resolve his conflict? Why does anxiety become so intense that it cannot be dealt with by ordinary means? The answer lies in the fact that neurotic conflicts develop out of situations in which the individual is unable to cope successfully with the external threat that is present. Typically, these situations originate in childhood when the individual's security system is threatened. This may occur when loss of support by the parents (separation anxiety) or fear of severe punishment because of forbidden impulses (castration anxiety) threatens the individual. Then, what was originally an external threat becomes an *internalized threat*. The individual is now afraid of his own impulses since their expression is opposed by his own prohibitions (superego) or by the still all-powerful parents, whose love and support may be lost. The possible range of suitable alternative behaviors becomes limited, stereotyped, and defensive. In turn, such behavior limits further appropriate learning, and the anxiety tends to increase. It may be channeled into symptomatic behavior. This is the nuclear core of the neurosis.

Freud suggested that in neurosis the conflict is between id impulses and superego forces [62]. The ego is the battleground of the conflict, but the ego is not fragmented or destroyed. At the same time, neurosis prevents full participation of all the segments of the personality. The ego is limited in the possible range of its activities because the security of the individual is threatened by his unacceptable drives.

Hutt and Gibby have suggested six criteria of a psychoneurosis [1]. These are:

1. An inadequate resolution of basic and conflicting drives . . . leads to a dammed-up state which is manifested either as anxiety or as some persistent tension condition.
2. There is an eruption of symptoms on a functional basis.
3. Certain persistent and inappropriate defenses are used to permit partial discharge of impulses.
4. There is reduced effectiveness and impairment of some functions.
5. There is a high degree of irrational repetitiveness in the pattern of behavior, even when it is clearly inappropriate to the situation.

6. The neurotic lacks insight into the true causes of his conflict. Hence he often "displaces," "rationalizes," or "reaction forms."

It is possible to classify the psychoneurotic reactions into three main categories on the basis of the nature of the "ego boundary" of the condition. (See Figure 6.4.) By "ego boundary"

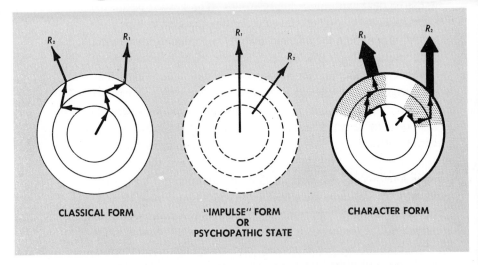

CLASSICAL FORM   "IMPULSE" FORM
                              OR
                      PSYCHOPATHIC STATE   CHARACTER FORM

FIGURE 6.4   *Three categories of psychoneuroses.*

is meant the nature of the system of internal controls through which the expression of impulses is permitted or inhibited. The sensed feelings of such controls enable a person to distinguish between internal needs and external demands—hence, a "boundary." In the "classical forms" of the neuroses, such as anxiety neurosis and conversion hysteria, anxiety is displaced into certain symptoms, but the ego permits the expression of many impulses, at least indirectly. The person experiences some degree of conflict. The ego boundary is well defined in such conditions.

A second category of neurotic conditions includes the "impulse neuroses" and the "psychopathic states"—as in cases of pyromania (fire-setting) and some kinds of sexually deviant behavior (such as nymphomania). In such conditions, the impulse is *acted out*. It is not inhibited or integrated into appropriate patterns of behavior by ego mechanisms. In these cases, impulses are not "experienced" or sensed by the person, anxiety is not experienced, and there usually is no real sense of conflict. Nevertheless, the ego is still reasonably intact. The person is aware of reality and of the nature of his behavior.

The third general form of neurosis is that of the "character disorders." In these instances there is an "armoring of the ego"— a phrase coined by Reich [63]. The patient may seem to be composed and effective, yet he feels somehow troubled. He does not experience internal conflict but is aware that something is wrong. His behavior is overly rigid; he has developed certain excessive character traits, of which he is not fully cognizant. Sometimes such people are constantly aggressive but don't "know" it. Usually, they are not capable of spontaneous feeling. They tend to act as wholes and are not especially sensitive to the impact of external conditions. The "character armor" makes them impervious to many events of everyday life. They are, therefore, characterized as "ego syntonic," i.e., they do not experience much anxiety. Although ego functions are distorted, as in the other forms of neurosis, they are essentially intact.

SOME EXAMPLES OF NEUROTIC PATTERNS We shall discuss a few neurotic patterns in order to provide some "feel" for the phenomena and to illustrate certain mechanisms and symptoms.

Hysteria This neurosis deserves primary attention because it has been studied exhaustively and because it illustrates so vividly some of the mechanisms underlying the symptom-formation of all the neuroses. One of the writers had occasion to treat the hysteric discussed below.

When the patient was first seen, his most distressing symptom was an inability to use his right hand in any form of writing, although there was little disability in the use of this hand in other functions. This symptom distressed him particularly because he was unable to sign checks and other documents. Both of these difficulties embarrassed him since he was often called upon to sign his name in public as part of his usual business activities. Neurological examination was essentially negative, and all other medical conditions were essentially normal.

This 38-year-old married man was a model husband and had been a highly effective executive in business. He was a man of high moral standards, devoted to his wife and family, and had had no prior obvious neurotic symptoms.

In the course of his psychotherapy, it became clear that the symptom had first occurred some 17 months earlier, when he was on a business trip and had occasion to sign a hotel register. Even this memory had been forgotten. What was even more surprising, he had forgotten all the details of that situation—the particular hotel, the nature of the situation at the time, and the events immediately preceding and following the outbreak of the symptom. In other words, his repression had been very effective in blotting out the circumstances of the *precipitating situation*. Still later in psychotherapy he was able to reconstruct the development of his symptoms. At first he had felt only a little numbness in his hand, with slight attendant difficulty in writing on some occasions. Later he became unable to sign hotel registers and experienced considerable anxiety about this. Still later he became unable to sign checks, but his anxiety was no longer as intense as it had been. In fact, although he was embarrassed by his disability, he was rather bland in discussing it.

The major aspects of the underlying psychodynamics, as they were gradually reconstructed, were that he had, for some time, had vague fantasies about having an affair with an unmarried woman who reminded him of his mother, but he fought against such wishes. Later, at the hotel where his symptom first developed, he was intensely driven to have an affair with another woman. This woman also seemed to him to resemble his mother. Thoughts about his sudden inability to sign the hotel register preoccupied him, however, and excluded his thoughts about having an affair.

He had been an only child and was emotionally tied to his mother. She had apparently had an unconsciously "seductive" relationship with her son but had brought him up under conditions of very strict morality. His mother had died about a year before he began to have thoughts about an extramarital affair.

In summary, he had experienced an intense oedipal complex involving his mother and had subsequently repressed his sexual strivings, first toward his mother and later toward other women. (He was usually impotent with his wife.) After his mother's death, there was a breakthrough of forbidden sexual impulses. The conflict was "resolved" by the "conversion reaction" of paralysis of his right hand, which symbolically expressed a prohibition of his sexual wishes. His symptom offered him some relief from his conflicts and brought him the concern of others for his welfare.

This brief case summary contains all of the usual elements found in hysteria. There is fixation at the oedipal level of development, with failure to attain adult genital functions. There is a massive repression of the oedipal "material." Subsequently, when triggered off by some traumatic event, there is a release of impulse and of defensive behaviors accompanied by the formation of the hysterical symptom. When treated successfully by psychotherapy (to which this condition lends itself fairly readily), the oedipal complex is resolved and symptom formation is no longer necessary. This case also clearly portrays the *secondary gain* which the illness provides. The neurosis requires that others treat or help the individual who has become "disabled," while the conflict is unconsciously avoided. The *displacement* of the conflict to a *symbolic manifestation* is also demonstrated.

We stated, above, that hysteria has been more exhaustively studied than any other psychoneurosis. It was known during the age of Pericles, and the term used by the Greeks to describe it, "hysteria," literally means a "wandering of the womb." Thus, hysteria was thought to be a sexual disturbance. Much later, with the development of the biological sciences in the nineteenth century, it was thought to represent some disease of the brain [64]. However, the work of Charcot, and particularly of Janet, in the latter part of that century, who utilized hypnosis to study hysteria, offered evidence that the condition was primarily psychogenic in origin. The use of hypnosis and the re-experiencing of the conflict situation or the use of suggestion could produce alleviation or removal of the symptoms. It remained for Freud and Breuer to propose a theoretical explanation of this condition [65]. Freud showed how psychoanalysis, through the uncovering of emotionally charged memories which had been repressed, could bring about a cure.

In recent years some additional elaborations of the theory of this phenomenon have been developed. For example, Fairbairn states that an outstanding feature of hysteria is "the substitution of a bodily state for a personal problem" [66]. The effect of environmental conditions has been studied. It has been noted that the "classical" forms of hysteria have decreased in some sections of the world, presumably due to changed cultural conditions, and especially the greater tolerance for sexuality and its public discussion [67].

Since the symptoms of hysteria may take many forms, it might be worth considering the possibility that some of the reported decrease in the incidence of "classical hysteria" is more apparent than real. Current forms of the illness may be less obvious than previous ones. With increased sophistication, people may not as easily be capable of expressing their conflicts through gross and obvious symptoms. The major forms of the illness involve physical symptoms (sensory, visceral, or motor disturbances which can take on symbolic meanings) and psychological symptoms (such as amnesia, or loss of memory, hallucinations, somnabulistic behavior, or sleepwalking).

We shall not discuss some of the other types of "classical" psychoneuroses, such as anxiety reactions, phobias, obsessive-

The Timid Soul. Cartoon by H. T. Webster,
courtesy Mrs. H. T. Webster

compulsive reactions, and hypochondriasis (neurotic complaints about the state of one's health). While these differ in some important respects from hysteria, they are essentially similar to it. (Other "classical" neuroses differ especially with respect to the severity of the regression, the amount of overt anxiety, and the types of defense mechanisms employed.) Instead, we shall discuss character disorders and the psychopathic states. These are ego disturbances different from hysteria.

Character disorders Such conditions are often the most difficult of the psychoneuroses for the student to understand.

There are no bizarre or striking symptoms, and frequently the character neurotic is able to function with a reasonable degree of effectiveness. Such individuals manifest, instead, a gross exaggeration of some trait, or group of traits, employed in almost all situations. One example is that of Casper Milquetoast, that is, a person with greatly exaggerated tendencies to be passive and submissive. Another example is that of the "bull in the china shop." Both types are fair approximations of character disorders. They are like caricatures of normal people in whom a particular characterological tendency predominates. Horney has given us some incisive analyses of such people and the traits they are likely to display in contemporary settings [68].

The following is an example of a character disorder. A man, about 42 years of age, was successful in his business ventures. However, he complained that his office help, and often his business associates, took advantage of him. He saw them as demanding, unco-operative, and often aggressive. He seemed to have great difficulty in obtaining their co-operation in business operations. It soon became apparent, in therapy, that he had a great deal of hostility of which he was unaware. He expressed this hostility in many *characterological* ways. He was overly assertive in most of his behavior, slammed doors, sat down and got up with excessive vigor, and demanded things rather than asked for them. At first he seemed to be unable to comprehend that these were hostile ways of behaving. Only after the therapist had gathered sufficient evidence of this kind of behavior, and only after the relationship in therapy had been firmly established, did the therapist call these and other examples to the patient's attention. Later he showed considerable anxiety when doing these things. Finally he realized how much counteraggression he engendered in others by his own style of behavior. After much "working-through" of the sources of the conflict causing the hostility (see Chapter 7), he began to find ways of responding that evoked co-operation instead of counteraggression from others.

How are we to understand this type of individual? In this case we can see that aggression is an overdetermined or exaggerated trait. It is expressed quite rigidly, without appropriate regard for the circumstances in which the individual finds himself. Psychoanalytic theory postulates that chronic character defects result from massive fixation at a particular developmental (libidinal) level. In our case, the facts that support this view are that this individual was raised by a highly moral, punitive, and compulsive mother. As a child, during the anal phase of his development, very strict and excessive measures were employed in his "toilet training." As a result of these and other circumstances at the time, he was fixated at the anal stage of development. He developed to an excess those "modes of anality" which included stubbornness, rigidity in behavior, "demandingness," and other aggressive characteristics. Moreover, these traits became *ego syntonic,* i.e., they operated without any significant degree of awareness and without internal conflict over their manifestation. And, finally, the expression of this behavior was not accompanied by anxiety, although there was anxiety over their indirect effect. There was considerable anxiety later, in therapy, when the patient attempted to change them.

Freud believed that characterological traits were largely the result of libidinal fixations, although he allowed room in his theory for other factors [69]. Neurotic character formation was different from normal character development only in the degree of rigidity with which some character traits were employed. In character neurosis, as in all neuroses, there was basic conflict between ego and superego forces, but the excessive development of particular traits was seen as a defense against anxiety, so that other symptoms were no longer needed.

Abraham [70], and later Reich [71], studied character neurosis more penetratingly and offered additional dynamic explanations as well as new nosological groupings of various character types. In more recent years, Horney emphasized cultural factors in the development of character problems and grouped character tendencies into three main categories: *aggression* (moving against people), *detachment* (moving away from people), and *compliance* (moving toward people) [68]. These are regarded as normal traits when they are present and are used appropriately and flexibly. In character neurotics, however, a single one of these characteristics dominates the individual's behavior and is employed as a defense against highly reinforced impulses.

Others have suggested modifications of this grouping. Riesman, using a social-psychological approach, speaks of inner-directed people, outer-directed people, and tradition-directed people [72]. Fromm, a psychiatrist who followed Sullivan's theoretical orientation, suggests five character groupings: marketing, productive, hoarding, receptive, and exploitative [73]. The emphasis on social-cultural factors is clearly apparent.

Psychoanalysts prefer a grouping which is closely linked to the theory of libido and which is in accord with the nature of traits presumed to be linked to fixations. Thus we find: the *oral*

Protest: involvement and detachment. Wide World

character (one with fixation during this period of development and showing an excess of narcissism); the *anal* character (with fixation at this level, with compulsive and sadistic traits); the *genital* character (with fixation at this level, accompanied by hysterical traits).

Whatever the cultural influences, character disorders may be thought of as neuroses in which the exaggeration of some characterological trend is fixated. Through repression, in an attempt to ward off excessive anxiety, the individual develops pathological ways of behaving. Instead of developing acute symptoms, he overdevelops certain characterological trends. This occurs through identification with the person (and his personal and culturally reinforced characteristics) who poses the threat. Other defenses, such as reaction formation, isolation of affect, and undoing are employed to ward off the anxiety, and the person learns to employ his overlearned traits rigidly and inappropriately. He may, however, use them to advantage some of the time.

Psychopathic states   One of the most intriguing, and at the same time most baffling, conditions is that of the psychopathic states. When a man with good intelligence, full awareness of moral issues, and with an apparently fine background engages in some outlandish criminal behavior, we may look for the explanation in terms of some psychotic or psychoneurotic condition. Yet, if he has no delusions, is in good contact with reality, is fully aware of his conduct, and has no manifest anxiety or other neurotic symptoms, we may feel at a loss to explain his behavior. And, so may he! Experts may agree that he does not fit the psychotic or neurotic criteria, yet they may be unable to agree on the nature of his problem. This is precisely the dilemma that *psychopaths* present.

The term psychopath is not as widely accepted by mental health workers today as it was some two decades ago. It fell into disrepute because it had become a catchall category for a wide variety of vague, ill-understood, and undiagnosable conditions. But it has its champions [74], and if employed with care has certain advantages, as we shall see shortly. As used here, it refers to disturbed behavior which has certain outstanding characteristics:

1. The person acts upon an unknown (to him) impulse, despite the fact that he is fully aware that his act is immoral, antisocial, or inappropriate. Often he feels that he can't prevent himself from engaging in the act.
2. The person acts in callous disregard of the needs of others but is fully aware that he may be hurting others very badly.
3. His antisocial behavior is characterized by irresponsibility.
4. The person is incapable of prolonged and deep interpersonal relationships, although he may be able to maintain such relationships for short periods of time.

5. He does not appear to be able to profit from his experience; that is, although he "knows" what is right, he fails to behave morally, except when it is convenient for him.
6. He expresses no anxiety or conflict about his behavior.

These criteria suggest that we are describing an individual with a psychoneurotic disorder whose major characteristic is impairment of *impulse control*. Some workers in the mental health field prefer the terms "impulse neurosis" and "character neurosis" [75] to "psychopathic states." At any rate, like the character disorder we have discussed in the previous section, there is a defect in the ego, but in this case there is no "armoring" of the ego. Instead, the ego is *excessively permeable*—impulses get through without being experienced by the ego. Hence, unlike other types of neurosis, there is no internal conflict. There *seem to be* no antagonistic sets of impulses from ego and superego. Psychopathic states appear to be more like neuroses than psychoses, in that the individual is disturbed but is not irrational. They do not present the severe regression or fragmentation of ego that is shown in psychoses.

In the official classification proposed by the American Psychiatric Association, the grouping for psychopathic states has been replaced by the category Personality Disorder [8]. This is a very broad grouping of many diverse disturbances, including unstable personality, sexual deviates, alcoholic addiction, speech disturbances, and somnambulism. The person with the condition we have described above as psychopathic would fall within this general category and would be placed within the subgroup designated as "Sociopathic personality disturbance, Antisocial reaction." Thus, this condition is seen as highlighted by antisocial behavior which is *socially unhealthy*. We are treating the condition as one of the subcategories of neuroses, instead, because it more nearly fits the criteria of neurosis than any other category.

Many kinds of behavior can be called psychopathic. Often types of homicide and some types of sexual deviation may also be included. In short, any problem in impulse control that meets the tests we have suggested might be included. In the title of his interesting account of the treatment of such an individual, Linder appropriately called it "Rebel Without a Cause" [76].

And what of the etiology of such conditions? Genetic, psychogenic, and cultural explanations have been offered. The argument for hereditary factors has been documented by New-kirk [77], but most workers in the field are reluctant to accept this kind of explanation for most psychopathic states. In many cases, evidence has been adduced which purportedly shows the great importance of either (*a*) severe trauma in very early childhood or (*b*) early "spoiling" (overprotection) by parents. In others, sociocultural facts have been highlighted [78]. It is possible that, in different cases, different factors are responsible. In other words, since we are dealing with a complex pattern of symptoms, the same general type of behavior might conceivably represent quite different developmental conditions.

Psychopaths are notoriously difficult to treat successfully by the usual psychotherapeutic methods. They sometimes appear to improve in the course of psychotherapy but subsequently regress without apparent reason. However, some patients have been treated successfully and have maintained their improved status for indefinite periods. Treatment is perhaps most success-ful when it is given early (in childhood or adolescence) and when it involves both intensive individual psychotherapy plus group or environmental therapy (see Chapter 7). Fascinating accounts of such programs are contained in books by the Mc-Cords [79] and by Redl and Wineman [80].

The Integrated Personality

Now that we have examined some illustrations of psychoses and neuroses, have considered the dynamic features which charac-terize them, and have discussed etiological factors, we are in a good position to evaluate the nature of "normal behavior." As might be guessed, it is easier to give examples of and criteria for psychopathology than to define normality.

We should begin by emphasizing that normal behavior is not synonymous with conventional or socially accepted behavior. There is a difference between a "rebel without a cause" and a "rebel with a cause." The mature and creative adult seeks to better his own life and the lives of those around him. He is constantly exploring the reasons for the status quo and seeks to improve upon it. Sometimes, in expressing his creativity and individuality, he may run afoul of the conventions. He may be scorned or even reviled, and he will certainly often be misunderstood, yet he may be far healthier than those around him. In short, unique or nonconventional behavior is not necessarily pathological. It may even be healthy.

It is for such reasons that the term *adjustment* has fallen into disrepute. To many psychologists, the term implies acceptance of the social norms as the major criterion of mental health. In this sense, adjustment might mean the subordination of one's own needs in order to conform. Depending upon circumstances, conformity may or may not be appropriate. Of course, if we are to have any kind of reasonable social order, there must be some degree of subordination of self to society's needs. The real question is how to achieve an effective social order without sacrificing man's quest for growth and individuality. Philosophers, politicians, and social scientists have been struggling with this problem for ages. It attains very high priority today when the mass media of communication and the rise of technocracy and automation operate to deny man's individuality and to deny him opportunity for adequate self-expression and self-fulfillment.

We shall use the terms "normal mental health" and "good adjustment" to imply a positive concept which encompasses the most complete possibilities for self-actualization and creative growth. And by contrast with the known conditions of mental illness or psychopathology, we shall try to understand the nature of good mental health. We prefer a definition of the mature person as one who has an *integrated personality,* that is, one who has the capacities for integrating his many inner functions with reality and is able to actualize his potentialities.

Perhaps we shall have to accept the premise that there is no single set of criteria of good mental health. We may wish to agree with Hartmann, a psychoanalyst, who says that "the theoretical standards of health are usually *too narrow* [italics ours] insofar as they underestimate the great diversity of types which in practice pass as health . . ." [81]. Or we might conclude that people can be mentally healthy in some respects but unhealthy in others—that the ideal of complete mental health is only an ideal, and that the degree of mental health is only relative.

TRANSIENT MALADJUSTMENT We have seen that the mere presence of certain symptoms does not necessarily imply that the person is suffering from some form of psychopathology. The

Conformity. Both photos, Wide World

mere absence of symptoms is, similarly, not a sufficient condition to characterize good mental health. Symptoms may occur in a healthy organism as the result of continued stress, and, when the stress is removed, the individual may be free of symptoms again. Even the healthiest organism reacts to the invasion of physical or psychological stress by some *temporary regression* and dysfunction.

Children go through various stages of temporary dysfunction during normal development. During such periods they may be attempting new roles for themselves, as when they leave the stage of infantile dependence and begin to assume some degree of volitional independence [82]. Such periods are normal during the oedipal phase of development, during the early stages of adolescence, and during the later stages of aging. These are ubiquitous phenomena which characterize most, if not all, cultures and peoples.

Hutt and Gibby [1] have labeled such temporary developmental dysfunctions *transient adaptive problems*. They delineate six major types of such temporary maladaptations: (1) those associated with growth; (2) those associated with unevenness in development; (3) those associated with physical illness or disease; (4) those associated with environmental stress; (5) those associated with cultural practice or conflict; and (6) those associated with exceptional capacities.

Temporary dysfunction may be produced by means of biochemical manipulations or by means of temporary, although extreme, stress. Biochemical stress may be induced experimentally by the administration of lysergic acid diethylamide (LSD). In normal persons the drug-induced effect is similar in many respects to the acute symptoms of schizophrenia. They experience severe disturbances in thinking, perception, and feeling. People show wide variations in some specific aspects of the reaction, presumably due to the previous state of the person's defense patterns. Some develop delusional thinking, some lose their sense of self-identity, and some experience peculiar feelings of "depersonalization" (a loss in self-identity). Anxiety seems to be increased markedly in most cases. After a few hours the drug-induced "regression" disappears and normal functions return. One hypothesis to explain these effects is that stimulation of the adrenal glands by drugs increases the activity of the adrenal-pituitary system. In turn, this might render the adrenal cortex resistant to normal activity for a period of time. Other mechanisms which produce these effects have been suggested. A study by Rinkel and co-workers describes these phenomena [83].

Studies such as these suggest that in schizophrenics the pituitary-adrenal system may be defective. Since similar effects can be produced without specific chemical stimulation in normal individuals, such as in cases of severe situational stress, in war conditions [84], or in sensory-deprivation experiments [85], we may conclude that the arousal of severe anxiety is a central and significant factor. Such results are compatible with the psychogenic theories relating anxiety to the development of schizophrenia, but they do not rule out the significance of constitutional factors in other cases.

An analysis of all types of transient maladaptive behavior suggests that psychogenic factors are responsible for the onset of acute symptomatology in many types of neuroses and psychoses. When such stresses are persistent, due to external circumstances, or when they occur at *critical periods,* their effects may tend to be irreversible. Even structural, bodily changes may occur which make reversal of the regressive trend difficult. A person's resistance to prolonged effects of such conditions depends upon his previously learned defense patterns as well as upon his immediate vulnerability to such conditions.

Such considerations suggest that normality may, in fact, be a matter of the degree of internal integration of the personality functions which prevents further disorganization, even though temporarily acute dysfunction may occur under severe stress. They do not, however, eliminate the possible contribution of such other factors as constitutional predispositions, which may be significant in some cases.

NORMAL MENTAL HEALTH   As we have seen, conceptions of good mental health can vary widely. At this stage of our knowledge, Smith's suggestion that empirical research is needed to determine more precisely what combinations of factors are optimal under given conditions is highly pertinent [86]. Rejecting the view that all possible factors predisposing toward good mental health should necessarily be maximized in everyone, he believes that some of these factors can vary inversely under certain conditions. In other words, various combinations of factors might be most beneficial under differing circumstances. He assumes an underlying unitary function, so that excessive development of one set of "healthful" factors may actually impede over-all optimal mental health development, since less energy is available for developing other functions. Hence, the *pattern* of development that is optimal needs to be evaluated, rather than maximum development of each possible factor. This view does not rule out the possibility that certain factors may be more basic than others.

We shall have to be content, for the moment, with a consideration of some of the important criteria of good mental health. Nevertheless, we have seen the critical importance of the concepts of integration and disintegration. Whatever weight we may finally assign to the factors discussed below, the healthy personality must have an integration in its over-all functioning so that it does not become persistently fragmented under internal or external stress. Now, let us examine six proposed criteria of mental health.

Deep emotional cathexis The threat of rejection, as we have learned, is crucial in creating damaging conditions which may lead to psychopathology. Man needs to know that he is loved, and is capable of loving, not only as an antidote to threats of rejection and feelings of aloneness, but as a condition for satisfying what is perhaps the essence of "the human condition." The infant is narcissistic in orientation and in behavior and is utterly dependent upon others for existence and for gratification of his psychological needs. The mature adult has internalized the love of others. He has learned to love both himself and others. He has learned to feel that the needs of others are as important as his own. And in the process, he has developed a stable and secure self-image. Even when he still suffers because of the loss of a loved one (i.e., as in depression or mourning), he "recovers" because of this stability in his self-identity.

Fromm defines mature love as follows [87]: "Love is union with somebody, or something, outside oneself, under the condition of retaining the separateness and integrity of one's own self." Freud conceived of genital maturity in much the same way and saw the successive stages in the individual's capacity to relate as primary for optimal psychological development. In the developmental struggle to attain this goal, the individual learns to master anxiety, to cope with reality, and to express himself in a harmonious interplay of emotions, perceptions, and cognition.

Deep emotional cathexis, involving attachment of libido to other persons or objects, requires the investment of oneself in

665

Love has many forms.

another person on a reciprocal basis. It is not the same thing as the capacity for "joining" groups, which may often be used as a defense against feelings of aloneness and rejection. Nor does it simply involve the "role-playing" of liking someone (we have seen how the psychopath "role-plays" liking someone but does not love him). It does not permit unrealistic suspiciousness and anxiety (as in the cases of schizophrenia and hysteria, respectively) to inhibit effective relations with others.

Certain cultures place a pre-eminence upon self-reliance [89]. Self-reliance can easily be carried to excess, however. It can result in becoming insulated from others. More than this, when carried to excess, it can prevent the true development of autonomy. It may produce rigid adherence to outworn beliefs or practices. True autonomy requires realistic self-regard and appropriate acceptance of responsibility, while, at the same time, it requires capacity for sensitivity to the needs, suggestions, and admonitions of others. The autonomous person reflects a balance of passivity and assertiveness. He is inner-directed, but he is responsive.

Autonomy, viewed in this manner, may be a by-product of the capacity for deep emotional cathexis. In turn, it leads to other primary traits, such as we have discussed in Chapter 5.

Capacity for spontaneity Closely related to the above qualities is the capacity for spontaneity. As Maslow has shown, when people are able to relate to others and are also capable of autonomy, they are capable of spontaneous and creative behavior [89]. Spontaneity, as here conceived, is synonymous with the capacity for flexible and appropriate adaptation to changing circumstances. It requires adequate self-discipline, sufficient emotional security, and flexibility of response (rather than impulsiveness).

We have seen that the essence of the neurotic reaction is that of irrational repetition. In turn, this rigidity in behavior results from excessive anxiety. In the spontaneous individual, the security system is such that either he does not develop excessive anxiety, or he is able to discharge it effectively.

Capacity for tolerating anxiety There is probably an optimal level of anxiety for each individual at his particular stage of development that maximizes his growth and performance. We have seen how important anxiety is in adjustment and development. The healthy adult can be conceived as having either (*a*) a high tolerance for anxiety or (*b*) a low level of inappropriate anxiety—or both.

The individual who was overprotected in early life may, if conditions remain favorable, be able to avoid excessive anxiety reactions. But he may not learn to deal effectively with anxiety. Hence, when he meets external stress or severe internal conflict, he has no readily available techniques for dealing with the sudden emergence of severe anxiety reactions.

On the other hand, the individual who has learned to cope with anxiety reactions under secure emotional conditions is more able to tolerate sudden stresses and conflicts. He is more able to cope with the problems which confront him. Furthermore, he is able to perceive reality more accurately, avoid problems which he is unable to cope with, and find effective ways of meeting his needs without endangering the integrity of his personality.

Capacity for self-insight Little children can usually tell us what "troubles them inside"; many adults have great difficulty in doing so. We have seen how the individual with a character neurosis has difficulty in perceiving that many of his problems "stem from within." Most neurotics have difficulty in determining precisely what it is within themselves that bothers them, although they may be fully aware that they are internally troubled and even that their symptoms are the result of psychological conflict. Some psychotics, on the other hand, seem to have an excessive awareness of "unconscious material." But in none of the phenomena of psychopathology is there an adequate capacity for self-insight. Conflicts either have to be repressed, or, if this fails, the impulses have to be acted out directly or symbolically.

The healthy, integrated adult, on the other hand, is capable of looking *within* as well as *without* with little defensiveness. Usually he is aware of his feelings and is aware of the causes of his behavior. He is also realistically aware of his shortcomings and is able to recognize that, sometimes, something bothers him of which he is unaware. But he does not project the cause of his discomfort upon others. It is this quality of self-awareness, perhaps more than any other, which makes the healthy adult seem rational.

Capacity for empathy with others The ability to know how others feel may not seem very important to the sophisticated intellectual or to the egocentric individual. Yet without this capacity, he is deprived of a considerable body of knowledge—knowledge of others in the human race. This capacity for identifying emotionally with others probably stems from secure emotional relationships in infancy and early childhood. Identification with an emotionally warm and responsive person enables one to learn how to empathize with others.

Effective social adaptation requires that we realistically perceive how others about us feel. Otherwise we, too, may become a "bull in a china shop." Capacity for empathy may also reinforce one's own security, since it provides opportunity not only for realistic perceptions of others but appropriate adaptation to them. As a result, the probability of positive feedback to, and obtaining accurate information about, oneself is heightened.

Capacity for self-actualization   The concept of self-actualization is as old as philosophy itself, perhaps older. It refers to the capacity of the organism to grow, to develop, and to function more efficiently. In modern conceptions of mental health, the concept is differentiated into two motivational components [90]. One component has to do with *deficiency motivation*, i.e., motivation to assure security, belongingness, and self-esteem. These stem from deficits in an individual's interaction with others. Such forces tend to prevent the development of psychopathology in all people. They assist in the therapeutic process of reintegration of the personality when it has become disorganized. The other component involves *growth motivation*, not based on prior deficits. This component leads to self-actualization to the highest degree of which the individual is capable. It is reflected by an ever increasing self-effectiveness rather than by resignation to apathy. Perhaps an even more important aspect of the growth motives is that they are experienced as pleasurable and nonthreatening.

Probably, growth motivation is closely related to the development of conscience and ego-ideal, since it has to do with the development and maintenance of distant goals. The mentally healthy person strives to achieve higher accomplishments, but not because of a neurotic anxiety to be accepted and not out of feelings of desperation and inadequacy. Rather, he experiences positive satisfaction in the growth process itself. Such a person can be said to be more motivated by an intrinsic orientation than by external, extrinsic demands. At an optimal level, development of the capacity for self-actualization produces an individual with very high, sometimes even lofty ideals, and this is a characteristic of our best leaders in all walks of life.   *669*

References

1. Hutt, M. L., & Gibby, R. G. *Patterns of Abnormal Behavior,* Englewood Cliffs, N.J.: Allyn and Bacon, 1957.
2. United States Department of Health, Education, and Welfare. *Patients in Mental Institutions, 1950, 1951.* Washington, D.C.: National Institutes of Mental Health, 1954.
3. Malzberg, B. Important statistical data about mental illness. In S. Arieti (Ed.), *American Handbook of Psychiatry,* Vol. I. New York: Basic Books, 1959.
4. Coleman, J. C. *Abnormal Psychology and Modern Life.* Chicago: Scott, Foresman, 1950.
5. Rennie, T. A. C. Studies in urban mental health. Paper delivered at Amer. Psychiat. Assoc., May, 1955.
6. Leighton, D. C., *et al. The Character of Danger: Psychiatric Symptoms in Selected Communities,* Vol. III. New York: Basic Books, 1963.
7. Jung, C. G. *The Psychology of Dementia Praecox.* (Nerv. & Ment. Dis. Monogr., No. 3.) New York: Nervous & Mental Disease Publishing Co., 1936.
8. American Psychiatric Association. *Diagnostic and Statistical Manual, Mental Disorders.* Washington, D.C.: Author, 1952.
9. Hoch, P., & Rachlin, H. L. An evaluation of manic-depressive psychosis in the light of follow-up studies. *Amer. J. Psychiat.,* 1941, **97,** 831–843.
10. Eysenck, H. J. *The Structure of Human Personality.* London: Methuen, 1953.
11. Eysenck, H. J. Psychoticism or ten psychotic syndromes? *J. consult. Psychol.,* 1963, **27,** 179–180.
12. Lorr, M., Klett, C. J., & McNair, D. M. *Syndromes of Psychosis.* New York: Pergamon Press, 1963.
13. Guttman, L. A new approach to factor analysis: The radex. In P. F. Lazarsfeld (Ed.), *Mathematical Thinking in the Social Sciences.* New York: Free Press, 1954.
14. Kraepelin, E. *Dementia Praecox and Paraphrenia.* (Trans. from 8th German ed.) Edinburgh: Livingston, 1925.
15. Jenkins, R. L. Suturing the schizophrenic split. *Arch. Neurol. Psychiat.,* 1955, **73,** 110–117.
16. Eysenck, H. J. *The Scientific Study of Personality.* London: Routledge, 1952.
17. Weiner, M. F. Hallucinations in children. *Arch. gen. Psychiat.,* 1961, **5,** 544–553.
18. Goldstein, K. Methodological approach to the study of schizophrenic thought disorders. In J. S. Kasanin (Ed.), *Language and Thought in Schizophrenia.* Berkeley: Univ. California Press, 1944.

19. Arieti, S. Schizophrenia: The manifest symptomatology, the psychodynamic and formal mechanisms. In S. Arieti (Ed.), *American Handbook of Psychiatry*, Vol. I. New York: Basic Books, 1959.
20. Senf, R., Huston, P. E., & Cohen, B. D. Thinking deficit in schizophrenia and changes with amytol. *J. abnorm. soc. Psychol.*, 1955, **50**, 383–387.
21. Von Domarus, E. The specific laws of logic in schizophrenia. In J. S. Kasanin (Ed.), *Language and Thought in Schizophrenia*. Berkeley: Univ. California Press, 1944.
22. Kendig, I., & Richmond, W. *Psychological Studies on Dementia Praecox*. Ann Arbor: Edwards Bros., 1940.
23. Schilder, P. *Mind, Perception and Thought*. New York: Columbia Univ. Press, 1942.
24. Hutt, M. L., & Briskin, G. J. *The Hutt Adaptation of the Bender-Gestalt Test*. New York: Grune & Stratton, 1960.
25. Miller, D. R., & Swanson, G. E., et al. *Inner Conflict and Defense*. New York: Holt, Rinehart and Winston, 1958.
26. Zubin, J. S., et al. A biometric approach to prognosis in schizophrenia. In P. H. Hoch & J. S. Zubin (Eds.), *Comparative Epidemiology of the Mental Disorders*. New York: Grune & Stratton, 1961.
27. Garmezy, N., Clarke, A. R., & Stockner, C. Child-rearing attitudes of mothers and fathers as reported by schizophrenic and normal patients. *J. abnorm. soc. Psychol.*, 1961, **63**, 176–182.
28. Kallmann, F. J. The genetic theory of schizophrenia: An analysis of 691 schizophrenic twin index families. *Amer. J. Psychiat.*, 1946, **103**, 309–322.
29. Slater, E. Genetical causes of schizophrenic symptoms. *Mschr. psychiat. Neurol.*, 1947, **113**, 50–58.
30. Slater, E. *Psychotic and Neurotic Illnesses in Twins*. London: H. M. Stationery Office, 1953.
31. Kallmann, F. J. The genetics of schizophrenia: An analysis of 1232 twin index families. In Congrès International de Psychiatrie. VI. *Psychiatrie sociale*. Paris: Hermann & Cie, 1937.
32. Koller, S. Quoted in M. Roth, Interaction of genetic and environmental factors in causation of schizophrenia. In D. Richter (Ed.), *Schizophrenia: Somatic Aspects*. New York: Macmillan, 1957.
33. Pastore, N. Genetics of schizophrenia. *Psychol. Bull.*, 1949, **46**, 285–302.
34. Essen-Möller, E. *Psychiatrische Untersuchungen an einer Serie von Zwillingen*. Copenhagen: E. Munksgaard, 1941.
35. McHunt, J. V. *Intelligence and Experience*. New York: Macmillan, 1961.
36. Meehl, P. E. Schizotaxia, schizotypy, schizophrenia. *Amer. Psychologist*, 1962, **17**, 827–838.
37. Eaton, J. W., & Weil, R. J. *Culture and Mental Disorders*. New York: Free Press, 1955.

38. Michael, C. M., Morris, D. P., & Soroker, E. Follow-up studies of shy, withdrawn children, II. Relative incidence of schizophrenia. *Amer. J. Orthopsychiat.*, 1957, **27**, 331–337.
39. Sheldon, W. H. (with the collaboration of S. S. Stevens). *The Varieties of Temperament: A Psychology of Constitutional Differences.* New York: Harper & Row, 1942.
40. Bellak, L., & Wilson, E. On the etiology of dementia praecox. *J. nerv. & ment. Dis.*, 1947, **105**, 1 ff.
41. Wolf, A., & Cowen, D. Histopathology of schizophrenia and other psychoses of unknown origin. In *The Biology of Mental Health and Disease.* New York: Hoeber-Harper, 1952.
42. Hoskins, R. G. *The Biology of Schizophrenia.* New York: Norton, 1946.
43. Heath, R. G., *et al. Studies in Mind-Brain Relationships: Behavioral Changes with Administration of Taraxein, a Substance Extracted from Schizophrenic Serum.* New York: Grune & Stratton, 1960.
44. Jung, C. G. *The Psychology of Dementia Praecox.* New York: Nervous and Mental Disease Publishing Co., 1936.
45. Freud, S. *Collected Papers,* 5 vols. New York: Basic Books, 1959.
46. Lidz, T., Cornelison, A. R., Fleck, S., & Terry, D. The intrafamilial environment of schizophrenic patients, II. Marital schism and mental skew. *Amer. J. Psychiat.*, 1957, **114**, 241.
47. Lidz, R. W., & Lidz, T. The family environment of schizophrenic patients. *Amer. J. Psychiat.*, 1949, **106**, 332.
48. Arieti, S. *Interpretation of Schizophrenia.* New York: Robert Bruner, 1955.
49. Cameron, N. The paranoid pseudocommunity. *Amer. J. Sociol.*, 1943, **49**, 32–38.
50. Mednick, S. A. A learning theory approach to research in schizophrenia. *Psychol. Bull.*, 1958, **55**, 315–327.
51. Kraepelin, E. *Manic-Depressive Insanity and Paranoia.* Edinburgh: Livingston, 1921.
52. Rennie, T. A. C. Prognosis in manic-depressive psychosis. *Amer. J. Psychiat.*, 1942, **98**, 801.
53. Abraham, K. Notes on the psycho-analytical investigation and treatment of manic-depressive insanity and allied conditions. In H. C. Abraham (Ed.), *Selected Papers on Psychoanalysis.* New York: Basic Books, 1955.
54. Arieti, S. Manic-depressive psychosis. In S. Arieti (Ed.), *American Handbook of Psychiatry.* New York: Basic Books, 1959.
55. Freud, S. Mourning and melancholia. In *Collected Papers,* Vol. IV. New York: Basic Books, 1959.
56. Becker, J., Parker, J. B., & Spielberger, C. D. A note on the relationship between manic-depressive psychosis and inner-directed personality. *J. nerv. & ment. Dis.*, 1963, **137** (2), 162–172.

57. Faris, R. E. L., & Dunham, H. W. *Mental Disorders in Urban Areas.* Chicago: Univ. Chicago Press, 1939.
58. Pollock, H. M., Malzberg, B., & Fuller, R. G. *Hereditary and Environmental Factors in the Causation of Manic-Depressive Psychosis and Dementia Praecox.* Utica, N.Y.: State Hospital Press, 1939.
59. Slater, E. T. O. Genetics in psychiatry. *J. ment. Science,* 1944, **90,** 17.
60. Kraines, S. H. *Mental Depressions and Their Treatment.* New York: Macmillan, 1957.
61. Matz, P. B., & Willhite, O. C. A study of manic-depressive psychosis among ex-service men. In *Manic-Depressive Psychosis,* Vol. XI. Baltimore: Williams & Wilkins, 1931.
62. Freud, S. *Introductory Lectures to Psychoanalysis.* New York: Boni & Liveright, 1920.
63. Reich, W. *Character Analysis.* (3rd ed.) New York: Orgone Press, 1949.
64. Briquet, P. *Traité de l'hysterie.* Paris: Baillière, 1859.
65. Breuer, J., and Freud, S. *Studies in Hysteria.* New York: Nervous and Mental Disease Publishing Co., 1950.
66. Fairbairn, W. R. D. Observations on the nature of hysterical states. *Brit. J. med. Psychol.,* 1954, **27,** 105–125.
67. Chodoff, P. A re-examination of some aspects of conversion hysteria. *Psychiatry,* 1954, **17,** 75–81.
68. Horney, K. *The Neurotic Personality of Our Time.* New York: Norton, 1937.
69. Freud, S. Three essays on the theory of sexuality. In *The Standard Edition of the Complete Psychological Works of Sigmund Freud,* Vol. VII (trans. and ed. by J. Strachey). London: Hogarth, 1953.
70. Abraham, K. The influence of oral eroticism on character formation. In H. C. Abraham (Ed.), *Selected Papers on Psychoanalysis.* New York: Basic Books, 1955.
71. Reich, W. *Character Analysis.* (2nd ed.) New York: Orgone Press, 1945.
72. Riesman, D. *The Lonely Crowd.* New Haven: Yale, 1950.
73. Fromm, E. *Man for Himself.* New York: Holt, Rinehart and Winston, 1947.
74. Cleckley, H. *The Mask of Sanity.* (2nd ed.) St. Louis: Mosby, 1950.
75. Alexander, F. The neurotic character. *Int. J. Psychoanal.,* 1930, **11,** 292–311.
76. Linder, R. *Rebel Without a Cause.* New York: Grune & Stratton, 1948.
77. Newkirk, P. R. Psychopathic traits are inheritable. *Dis. nerv. System,* 1957, **18,** 52–54.
78. Aichorn, A. *Wayward Youth.* New York: Viking, 1935.
79. McCord, W., & McCord, J. *Psychopathy and Delinquency.* New York: Grune & Stratton, 1956.

80. Redl, F., & Wineman, D. *Controls from Within.* New York: Free Press, 1954.
81. Hartmann, H. Ego psychology and the problem of adaptation. In D. Rapaport (Ed.), *Organization and Pathology of Thought.* New York: Columbia Univ. Press, 1951.
82. Ausubel, D. P. *Ego Development and the Personality Disorders.* New York: Grune & Stratton, 1952.
83. Rinkel, M., Hyde, R. W., Solomon, H. C., & Hoagland, H. Experimental psychiatry. II, Clinical and Physio-chemical observations in experimental psychosis. *Amer. J. Psychiat.,* 1955, **111,** 881–895.
84. Grinker, R. R., & Spiegel, J. P. *Men under Stress.* Philadelphia: Blakiston, 1945.
85. Kubzansky, P. E. The effects of reduced environmental stimulation on human behavior: A review. In A. D. Biderman & H. Zimmer (Eds.), *The Manipulation of Human Behavior.* New York: Wiley, 1961.
86. Smith, M. B. Optima of mental health. *Psychiatry,* 1950, **13,** 503.
87. Fromm, E. *The Art of Loving.* New York: Harper & Row, 1956.
88. Riesman, D., Glazier, N., & Denney, R. *The Lonely Crowd.* New Haven: Yale, 1950.
89. Maslow, A. H. Personality problems and personality growth. In C. Moustakas (Ed.), *The Self.* Harper & Row, 1956.
90. Maslow, A. H. Deficiency motivation and growth motivation. In M. R. Jones (Ed.), *Nebraska Symposium on Motivation.* Lincoln, Neb.: Univ. Nebraska Press, 1955.

SEVEN   REORGANIZATION OF THE PERSONALITY

We have referred at several points in the previous chapters to various methods of treatment used to provide some relief from excessive anxiety, behavioral difficulties, and symptoms. Now we shall discuss some of the salient features of various approaches to treatment and evaluate the present status of such methods.

Treatment methods may be classified in terms of the *therapeutic mode,* such as *somatic* or *psychological,* or they may be classified in terms of the *basic unit* for therapeutic intervention, such as *individual* or *group.* They may be subdivided further in terms of the kind of psychological treatment that is provided. We shall begin our discussion by considering some illustrations of psychotherapy for individuals. Then we shall proceed to psychotherapy applied to groups of people. Finally we shall consider some aspects of somatic treatment.

Commonalities in Diverse Forms of Psychotherapy

All forms of individual psychotherapy have in common the aim of assisting the individual to lead a more effective life and to reduce the ravages or impairment caused by the psychopathology. Although they may differ considerably in some respects, they attempt to help the person function at a higher level of efficiency or with less discomfort. Sometimes the aim is not only to assist the individual but to protect society from the real or imagined dangers which the individual's behavior presents. This point should be emphasized because society's needs, as distinguished from the individual's, cause difficulties for the therapist —sometimes in quite subtle ways.

As we have seen in preceding chapters, society is not always willing to tolerate individualistic expression of a person's behavior, even though it is clearly not pathological. Society tries to protect its own security by requiring compliance with its conventions, mores, and laws. Although most people are able to accept this requirement, it often interferes with those who are "unconventional," "individualistic," or "radical." Many of these people are not psychologically disturbed, but their behavior threatens society. Of course it is also true that many persons rebel against society because of neurotic problems. In other words, not all unconventional and individualistic persons are "sick," but some are.

This complicated issue is directly relevant to the first commonality in all forms of psychotherapy. The primary obligation of the therapist—as distinguished from the policeman, the teacher, the parent, or the minister—is not to protect society but to assist the individual to maximize his potentialities, which are impaired by his mental malfunctioning. Thus, the therapist has a *unique role* in his therapeutic orientation. He must maintain an *amoral* (not immoral) attitude toward his patient's behavior. He must observe the behavior of the patient closely and understand it objectively. At the same time, he must assist the individual in resolving his conflicts and achieving greater personal and social effectiveness. He cannot *judge* or seek to

Normal roles can be shifted in extraordinary situations.

control. He cannot confuse his own role with the differing roles of the custodians of society's security. Yet, the therapist is a member of society himself and to some extent has interiorized its values. He is therefore likely to try to impose society's attitudes on the patient, even if unwittingly. Thus, each psychotherapist needs special training (some say he needs personal therapy or psychoanalysis) to sensitize himself to, and to deal effectively with, the patient's conflicts without imposing upon him the very moral directives that may have contributed to the patient's problems. Another way of stating this position is to indicate that the therapist must be trained to maintain his *integrity as a therapist,* in terms of the specific role he plays for his patient.

This position is not shared by all therapists. Some view the central problem in psychogenic illness as an insufficient development of conscience, and not as a conflict between superego and id. Such therapists view their function as one which requires the teaching or reinforcement of the major cultural values. Mowrer, for one, takes this position in conformity with his own views on personality development [1]. We shall have more to say about this viewpoint later in this chapter.

A second commonality in most forms of psychotherapy is the characteristic *relationship* which develops between patient and therapist. The psychotherapist seeks to establish a trusting, warm, and reciprocal relationship with his patient. Both enter the therapeutic situation with the common purpose of helping the patient to achieve more effective functioning. The patient expects that he can rely upon the therapist's skills, his understanding, and his support to assist him in gaining this objective. The therapist expects that the patient is motivated to achieve some behavioral changes and is willing to make some sacrifices to achieve this. Under favorable circumstances, these conditions prevail at the beginning of therapy. Even then, however, there are some negative aspects to the relationship. Although the patient is consciously motivated to change, he is also resistant to modifying his defenses and major adaptive techniques, since these have had a certain value for him. His disturbed behavior may have brought him certain secondary gains. Moreover, his preformed attitudes toward people are carried into the therapeutic relationship. He may have difficulty trusting people, or he may trust them naïvely. He may expect to become entirely dependent upon the therapist, or he may be unduly fearful of any close relationship. He may even expect the therapist to perform some miracle or expect to be changed without having to experience any anxiety or discomfort.

As therapy progresses, the nature of the relationship often becomes much more complex. More and more of the patient's unconscious (or unknown) needs are projected on the therapist as the patient begins to feel more free in expressing them. He may expect the therapist to represent some unconscious ideal and feel disappointed when he learns that he is not perfect. He may demand more and more of the therapist's sympathy and tolerance. In psychoanalytic terms, this highly complex situation is termed *transference,* i.e., the patient transfers to the therapist all of his unconscious and unresolved needs and, to some degree, relives his old conflict within the therapeutic relationship—and, as in real life, consciously expects to be disappointed, rejected, humiliated, or otherwise frustrated.

Most therapists expect that, in the beginning, the emotional relationship will be an essentially positive one, so that there may be a good basis for initiating therapy. They also expect that the relationship will become more complex. Often the patient will become very hostile, demanding, and provocative. We shall have more to say about this phase of the relationship in subsequent discussion of psychoanalysis. Finally, in successful therapy, the complex, ambivalent relationship is resolved as it is worked through, and the patient learns to respond more objectively in terms of realities. Figure 7.1 shows the nature of the changing patient–therapist relationships during the course of psychotherapy.

A third commonality in almost all forms of psychotherapy involves the *emotional climate* of the therapeutic sessions. This commonality follows closely from the previous two points. The attempt is made to provide a *supportive, understanding,* and an accepting climate. This should help the patient to express his feelings and thoughts more freely, since these are received not only without moral judgement but also without rejecting the patient for having such characteristics. In turn, this usually helps to reduce the patient's anxiety and enables him to perceive more clearly both the nature of his inner conflicts as well as alternative ways of behaving. In other words, it is believed that this kind of climate helps to reduce anxiety and provide for the possible extinction of neurotic methods of responding.

A number of research studies have shown that this last factor

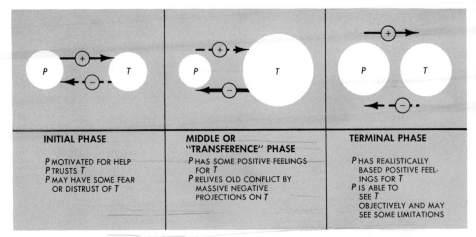

INITIAL PHASE	MIDDLE OR "TRANSFERENCE" PHASE	TERMINAL PHASE
P MOTIVATED FOR HELP	P HAS SOME POSITIVE FEELINGS FOR T	P HAS REALISTICALLY BASED POSITIVE FEELINGS FOR T
P TRUSTS T	P RELIVES OLD CONFLICT BY MASSIVE NEGATIVE PROJECTIONS ON T	P IS ABLE TO SEE T OBJECTIVELY AND MAY SEE SOME LIMITATIONS
P MAY HAVE SOME FEAR OR DISTRUST OF T		

FIGURE 7.1 *The three typical phases during psychotherapy, with their varying patient-therapist relationships.*

has significance in reducing neurotic or other emotional conflicts and the concomitant symptomatic ways of responding. For example, in a study by Rioch and her colleagues, eight untrained married women were trained for a two-year period to provide, among other things, just such a climate for psychiatric patients. In characterizing their therapeutic technique, Rioch states, ". . . they pleasantly reassure, protect, and sympathize . . ." [2].

Although they did more than this, of course, these eight lay-therapists were trained to be sensitive to and accepting of their patients' verbalizations. Above all else, they were supportive. As judged by means of a series of criteria, they were able to provide as much therapeutic help as would have been expected from experienced, professional therapists. Rioch states, ". . . as therapists they have all performed some useful service to patients during this past year, and none of them has done anyone any harm."

Closely related to the above commonality in therapies is a fourth attribute of psychotherapy. Therapy provides an opportunity for *catharsis* and for *ventilation* (*or expression*) *of feelings*. Catharsis is the broader of the two terms. It refers to the emotional reliving of conflict-laden experience. Ventilation, on the other hand, refers to the opportunity for discharge of pent-up emotions, although there may be no actual "reliving" of the conflict. When such behaviors are permitted or encouraged in an emotionally accepting and supportive relationship, conflicts tend to be reduced, if not resolved, and neurotic patterns tend to become alleviated. Levy has shown that when conflicts are of recent origin, children can be greatly aided simply by encouraging them to re-experience the conflict in a *play situation* [3]. The technique involves providing suitable play and creative art materials by means of which the conflict situation

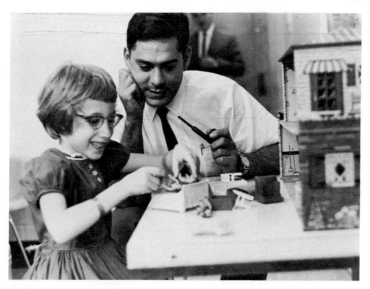

Play therapy. Irwin Cohen from Jewish Board of Guardians, New York

can be re-enacted and re-experienced under supportive, therapeutic conditions. Interpretation *need not* be offered in such circumstances. Many therapists believe that, for adults, the verbal expression of feelings, the discharge of the concomitant affect, and the response by the therapist which provides support and understanding (some call it empathic understanding) encourage therapeutic change and growth. Thus, Carl Rogers, who is the founder of the so-called "client-centered" school of therapy [4], Franz Alexander, who was a leader of the neo-Freudian school of psychoanalysis [5], and Wolpe, who is a leader in a form of behavior therapy which utilizes the learning principles involved in reciprocal inhibition[1] [6], accept this viewpoint and offer supporting evidence for it. (Of course, these therapists differ considerably in how they view the nature of the whole therapeutic process, as we shall see later.)

[1] See page 698 for a discussion of this term.

Two other characteristics of therapy which are not universal, but are nevertheless widespread, are *interpretation* and *insight*. The former term refers to the attempts made by the therapist to provide some degree of understanding of the nature of the patient's conflicts. Often some explanation of the causative factors in the development of these conflicts is also provided. "Insight" refers to increased awareness by the patient of the nature of his behavior and the underlying conflicts which generate it. Some therapists believe that insight, to be effective, must be not merely *intellectual* but *emotional,* i.e., accompanied by emotional reliving of some aspect of the conflict. Other therapists, like Rogers, decry the use of interpretive statements by the therapist, believing they only tend to impede the process of therapeutic change. However, Rogers, who favors simply reflecting the feeling being expressed by the patient, has been challenged by some who believe that any reflection of feeling involves at least some degree of interpretation. The therapist must interpret the communication by the patient, and he must attend to and select certain aspects of the communication. Moreover, the *way* in which he responds, whether by gesture and postural adjustments during the interview or by verbal communication, may implicitly suggest his own interpretations of what he has observed. Most therapists would agree that, in the complex interactions of therapy, the therapist is bound to provide some interpretative frame of reference and that, as a result, the patient gains some degree of insight into his problems.

"Uncovering" Psychotherapies

One broad classification of types of psychotherapy is that which is centrally characterized by its goal of "uncovering" the sources of conflict. Presumably this orientation is based on the assumption that "uncovering" is a necessary precursor to resolving conflicts. As we have implied in previous discussion, not all psychotherapies are equally directed to this goal. The aim may be more limited, such as eliminating objectionable symptoms or increasing the tolerance for frustration. In some forms of psychopathology, or at some points in the therapy of some patients, "uncovering" may be regarded as unwise or even dangerous. For example, when a patient is precariously holding on to reality, as in incipient psychosis, the anxiety produced by further exposing the patient to painful conflicts may cause him to become dramatically worse.

Psychoanalysis may be regarded as a method of treatment which attempts to produce a profound reintegration of the personality as it eliminates the underlying psychopathology, and it is the classical model of "uncovering" psychotherapy. As a matter of fact, psychoanalysts of the Freudian persuasion often argue that their treatment is not psychotherapy at all. Psychoanalysis differs from other forms of treatment in that it attempts to uncover more deeply repressed material and emphasizes the analysis of the transference between the analyst and the patient. Of course, it follows the Feudian theory of personality development and psychopathology. We prefer to use the term psychotherapy for all forms of treatment, as does Kubie [7]. The aim of psychotherapy is improvement in the emotional adjustment of the individual by some form of specific psychological intervention.

Some of the other schools of psychotherapy which are based on differing theories of psychopathology and personality development (see Chapter 5), such as the Jungian, Rankian, Sullivanian, and Adlerian, also aim at uncovering unresolved conflicts and resolving them. In some cases, an even deeper type of uncovering may be attempted, as in Jungian analysis, which includes efforts to analyze the "collective unconscious" as well as the individual unconscious (see Chapter 5). In other schools of psychotherapy a more circumscribed type of analysis may be provided. Many of these focus the therapeutic analysis on current central conflict areas, that is, on the present difficulties of the patients. Thus far we have been referring to the schools of therapy which have diverged from classical psychoanalysis, i.e., to the neopsychoanalytic schools. Certain nonpsychoanalytic forms of psychotherapy also attempt to uncover internal conflicts, although their therapeutic approaches may rely upon quite different techniques. For example, client-centered psychotherapy, as developed by Carl Rogers [8], and Gestalt psychotherapy [9] are approaches based upon different theories. We shall examine some of these approaches in terms of therapeutic *technique* and therapeutic *process*.

FREUDIAN PSYCHOANALYSIS In the ideal case, when a full analysis is considered feasible, this form of psychoanalysis

683

attempts a highly ambitious goal: the uncovering of all major areas of repression and the reconstruction of the personality so that it can function with minimal use of defenses. Such an analysis typically requires more than two years of therapeutic work, more frequently three to five years. Sessions are held at least three times per week; more commonly there are five to six sessions per week. It can easily be seen that not all patients are sufficiently motivated or have adequate finances to engage in such an effort. A thorough Feudian psychoanalysis requires that the patient be motivated to engage in prolonged therapeutic work designed to do much more than merely make him more comfortable by eliminating some symptoms or learning to tolerate stress more easily.

After a relatively short "trial period," during which the patient and psychoanalyst evaluate the nature of the psychopathology and test the patient's suitability for analytic work, the formal analysis begins.[2] The patient is instructed to "tell everything that comes to mind" without censoring any thoughts or feelings, no matter how objectionable or embarrassing they may be. This is the Freudian principle of *free association*. When the patient attempts to follow this rule, he finds that this is an extraordinarily difficult task. He may be unable "to let go" of control of his thoughts, he finds it difficult to verbalize marginal thoughts and feelings, he may have to recount in obsessive manner all events occurring between sessions, and he may digress whenever he feels intense emotions beginning to develop.

In these and many other ways the patient manifests *resistance* to the uncovering process. Resistance is understood as evidence of the struggle of the patient in exposing to conscious awareness those painfully associated experiences which have been repressed. The main job of the analyst during this period is to help the patient learn to "free-associate" and to overcome his resistance. There are many techniques involved in this process, but essentially they involve the analyst's focusing on the evidence of the patient's resistance. In this process the analyst tries to help the patient become less "guarded" and less defensive. He assumes that the patient's motivation to be "cured," the nonthreatening climate of the therapeutic session, and sup-

---

[2] Many modern psychoanalysts initiate psychoanalysis directly after the initial consultation(s) with the patient, without the formality of a "trial period."

port by the analyst during the process of uncovering will help the patient to become gradually more aware of his conflicting impulses and his "painful" repressions.

During this initial phase of the analysis, the patient learns that it is fully acceptable to express any feeling, no matter how abhorrent it may seem to be. He also learns that the analyst will *not* give advice or suggest better modes of behavior. Although the climate of the sessions is accepting and supportive, the analyst is essentially *passive* except when it is necessary for him to work through the patient's resistances. The patient often feels anxious: he does not know "where he is going"; he gets no active assistance in solving his dilemma; he finds the analyst is more or less like a *blank screen,* and this can be highly frustrating.

Quite often the patient becomes worse during this period. Not only does his anxiety increase, but he also *regresses* as more and more material from his childhood experiences is uncovered. Sometimes he "acts out" his impulses, that is, he engages in some forms of behavior toward his analyst or others before he has fully understood or integrated his conflicting impulses. In time, a *transference neurosis* develops. This is a situation in which the patient projects his unconscious fantasies upon the relatively "neutral" analyst. He may like his analyst, but he also experiences certain frustrating moments, as well. This means that the analyst is experienced as behaving like other important and frustrating people in his own life, typically his parents and other significant individuals. In this highly charged and ambivalent situation, the patient is able to experience vividly the repressed and conflictful material which his neurosis enabled him to ward off. At the same time, his current feelings, which actually are re-enactments of older experiences, provide basic material for the analyst and the patient to work on.

The next phase of the analysis then begins. The analyst now becomes much more active, offering interpretations when needed, to help focus and define ever more clearly and completely the areas of unconscious conflict. In this interpretative process, the analyst attempts to "peel off" the defensive layers, starting with those conflicts which are closest to awareness and then offering insights into more deeply repressed conflicts. In the course of this work, the Freudian analyst makes use of many kinds of evidence of the patient's "unconscious" conflicts, e.g., dreams, slips of the tongue, "acting-out" behavior, and even postural and other physical behavior adjustments.

In the course of this interpretation, the "transference" is gradually worked through and the patient no longer has the need to project unresolved conflicts. Behavior is no longer dominated by irrational, unconscious needs. In short, psychoanalysis ends when "Where id was, ego now is," to slightly paraphrase one of Freud's dicta.

In addition to "resolving the transference," many, if not most, contemporary psychoanalysts deal extensively with the patient's ego problems [10]. In this process, problems of everyday functioning are analyzed in terms of the patient's patterns of defenses. Behavior is evaluated to determine the relative degree of independence which the patient has developed. Many other modifications in the terminal phases of psychoanalysis have been introduced in recent years [11].

Thus far we have presented the classical picture of psychoanalysis as it is applied in cases of psychoneuroses. There are many variations from this general strategy when other kinds of psychopathology are encountered. In cases of borderline psychosis and in fully developed psychotic conditions, some analysts attempt first to build up the strength of the patient's ego and his capacity for reality-testing [12]. Others, believing that there are deficiencies of a grave nature in superego functions of psychotics, may attempt to act as an alternative or supplementary superego [13]. But in all Freudian psychoanalytic work, the Freudian theory of personality development and of psychoanalysis is applied. To emphasize a few of the basic correlates, this involves: interpreting behavioral manifestations of the unconscious, using free association and related techniques to elicit and uncover repressed material, analysis of the transference situation, and, finally, assisting in development of healthy ego functions, especially in the latter stages of analysis.

Psychoanalysts claim their greatest therapeutic success for cases of hysteria, anxiety neurosis, and obsessive-compulsive neurosis [14]. As judged by their own criteria, they usually claim complete recovery, or substantial improvement, in about 60 percent of such cases. When slighter degrees of recovery are considered, the percentage of success is even higher. The relative success of this method of psychotherapy will be considered more fully in the section entitled "A Comparison of Various Forms of Psychotherapy."

OTHER ANALYTIC TYPES OF PSYCHOTHERAPY By way of illustration, we shall review briefly a few of the many variants of classical Freudian psychoanalysis and some aspects of neo-psychoanalytic therapy. Our aim is not to provide a comprehensive summary of each of these approaches but rather to document some principles and processes, as found in other therapies, which may differ from Freudian psychoanalysis.

Rankian psychotherapy Otto Rank was a member of Freud's closest coterie for a number of years. He broke with the Freudian group because of differences in regard to both personality theory and therapeutic strategy. In 1924, with the publication of his book *The Trauma of Birth* [15], he began to propose some basic differences from Freud's views. Chief among them at this time was his emphasis upon the importance of *separation anxiety,* which was exemplified by the birth process and the child's struggle to exist outside the mother's womb. Later, in his other writings, he indicated that the appropriate differentiation of the self from others, as a unique and secure individual, was the essence of the healthy personality. This enabled the person to function in a spontaneous and even creative manner. Central in this development was the early emergence of the infant's *will,* as it sought to express itself. The emergence of the will gradually enabled the self to become more fully differentiated as a separate structure. However, the expression of the child's will was frustrated by the physical and psychological realities (especially as represented by the mother), thus fostering the emergence of the *counter will.* When the expression of counter will is too harshly dealt with and is associated with guilt reactions, neurotic development is likely to result and the child learns to fear the loss of love excessively [16].

For these reasons, psychotherapy is seen as a clash of wills or a duel between patient and therapist. But the therapist, unlike the (neurotic) parent (or other important authority figures in the patient's life), *accepts* the expression of the patient's counter will as a positive force. The therapist does not deal with resistances by attempting to counter them or subdue the patient. Rather, resistance is seen as an attempt by the patient to express his individuality more fully. This leads to another shift in emphasis during the course of therapy. The therapist focuses on the *current interpersonal situation* as the most relevant datum for therapy. Historical uncovering is not only insignificant but is likely to lead to avoidance of the present emotional

687

relationship. What matters is how background experiences are dealt with here and now. The insight concerning past development is not the central task.

The therapist's *active task* is to be constantly alert to the current implications of the patient's emotional behavior. He seeks to accept the patient while at the same time helping him to become deeply aware of the meaning of his behavior. The therapist makes no effort, however, to change the patient; this would only encourage the reinforcement of counter will tendencies, and excessive counter will leads to neurotic difficulties. Although active interpretation is maintained throughout therapy, the patient is left free to do what he wishes about his behavior.

Two other points need emphasis in this short account of Rank's approach. One is that the *implicit meaning* of the patient's emotional reactions must be dealt with, and not merely the content of his communication. The other is that *separation anxiety* is considered the central theme from the initiation of therapy until its conclusion. In thus focusing on current feelings and the separation problem, Rankians believe that it is often possible to reduce the length of therapy to far less than the extended analysis found necessary by Freudians.

Vivid accounts of the nature of Rankian transactions may be found in two books. One, by Allen, describes in detail the therapeutic management of emotionally disturbed children [17]. Another, by Taft, discusses the application of Rankian principles to casework as it is carried out by psychiatric social workers [18]. Rank's formulations have had a profound impact upon therapists of many persuasions and have led to many therapeutic and social-psychological research studies.

Sullivanian psychotherapy   Another great figure in the psychotherapeutic world, regarded by some as second only to Freud, was Harry Stack Sullivan, a clinical psychiatrist. His theoretical formulations opened the door, even wider than did those of Rank, to clinical study and research concerning the specific influences of cultural factors on personality development and psychopathology and to the complex nature of interpersonal relations [19].

Sullivan divided the various human drives into two main groups: (1) the pursuit of *satisfactions* (the biological needs of man for survival) and (2) the pursuit of *security* (the psychological needs of belonging, acceptance, and feelings of well-being). Frustration in the pursuit of security, caused by social conditions and by other persons who, because of their own emotional disturbances, are determiners of such conditions, is seen as the main determinant of psychopathology. In infancy, anxiety is experienced empathically and contagiously through contact with an overly anxious mother. Subsequently this anxiety may be reinforced by other types of frustrating social conditions. The development of excessive anxiety severely restricts the maturation of the *self-system* (i.e., the integrated patterns of coping with reality) as a secure and happy one. In order to maintain some degree of security, the individual develops pathological *self-dynamisms* (i.e., the "relatively enduring systems of energy transformations" by means of which the individual restricts the input of anxiety-laden information). But, in the process, he develops what Sullivan terms *parataxic reaction patterns*. These are patterns of perception in which the individual reacts to others not in terms of the reality of the others' behavior but rather in terms of *fantastic personifications* of others (these are similar to but broader than transference reactions). Psychopathology is thought to be, in the main, the result of excessive development of unrealistic perception, which, in turn, tends to preclude adequate reality-testing and self-correction of behavior.

Threats to the security system originating out of faulty interpersonal experiences result in two other types of pathological behavior reactions. The first of these is the self-dynamism of *selective inattention*. By this means the individual restricts awareness of anxiety-laden stimuli. Perception is focused on what is not painful, and that which is painful is denied awareness. In acute anxiety this dynamism is assisted by the process of *dissociation*, which is roughly equivalent to repression, thus causing gross distortion in one's awareness of the current reality.

Sullivan worked extensively with schizophrenics, although he was also greatly interested in obsessional cases. Thus, his clinical experience was in marked contrast with both Freud's and Rank's, who dealt extensively with psychoneurotics. Parenthetically, it may be noted that his work with hospitalized psychotics (rather than with nonhospitalized psychoneurotics) may have been partly responsible for the difference in his theoretical orientation from Freud's. Like Rank, he believed that the therapist had to be intensely active. But Sullivan also believed that the therapist was more than an active and merely objective observer. He also was a *participating observer*. Not only was the patient's behavior to be analyzed during therapy, but the personality reactions of the therapist were grist for the same mill. The *interpersonal relations* between patient and therapist were the objects of scrutiny, and the reciprocal nature of these interactions was stressed. This meant that the therapist had responsibility in communicating relevant aspects of his own ideas and feelings to the patient.

Like Freud, Sullivan believed it was necessary for the therapist to be fully informed about the patient's previous psychological history. The therapist must be in a position to understand the origins of the patient's dissociations and selective inattention. However, therapy proceeded primarily on the basis of testing and correcting these maldeveloped dynamisms through the process of *consensual validation*. This meant that direct interpretations of examples of the patient's dissociations had to be offered and evaluated, thus leading to the relinquishment of pathologic security operations. Extensive use was made of the patient's *marginal thoughts* (passing and peripheral thoughts) during the interview sessions. The patient was encouraged to try to capture thoughts and feelings which were not directly in focus and to discuss dreams as means of demonstrating the nature of his distortions and helping to correct them. However, free association was not encouraged, since it was felt that much more decisive and direct data could be obtained by skillful use of the current interpersonal situation and directed questioning. Fromm-Reichmann, in her book on the application of these principles to what she terms intensive therapy, illustrates how this is done in a flexible manner consistent with the basic premises. [20].

This approach is reputed to be relatively successful for the types of patients Sullivan worked with. It has led to intensive research on the nature of interpersonal behavior [21] and to operational definition of many of the variables involved in such behavior. The use of consensual-validation methods in reducing anxiety has become an active area for current research efforts.

Adler's psychotherapy Alfred Adler, one of the early disciples of Freud and the first to break with him openly, presents a sharp contrast to the "schools" of psychoanalysis discussed thus far. By contrast with Freud, his theory of personality development seems naïvely simple. Giving little or no emphasis to biological and hereditary factors, it places the major emphasis on the individual's *sense of inferiority* and on the healthy or neurotic ways in which the individual learns to deal with this problem. Yet, at the same time, Adler presents a paradox, for he was the first analyst to emphasize the *individual life-style*. This was conceived as the central problem for therapeutic analysis and as such laid the groundwork for *character analysis*. *Character analysis* involves examination of the patient's general modes of adaptation in contrast with *symptom analysis,* which focuses on specific behavioral disturbances. Adler's grasp of the concept of the *life-style,* as we shall see, was indeed profound and constituted the basis for a radically different type of therapeutic strategy. Fortunately, there is a penetrating restatement of Adler's theoretical premises and therapeutic approach in the book by the Ansbachers [22].

Adler believed that the struggle against feelings of inferiority was the keystone to the understanding of neurotic behavior, and not frustrations of the sexual drives. The human infant is, in fact, helpless for a long period of time and perceives himself as helpless and dependent. These feelings of helplessness may be reinforced by some actual physical inferiorities (diseases or defects) and by the environment, which may frustrate the individual. In dealing with these real and perceived inferiorities, the individual develops his own, unique style of life. Neurosis consists of substituting *fictitious goals* (i.e., unrealistic goals) and an abnormal style of behavior for a realistic set of goals and a healthy style. The central task of psychotherapy is not that of resolving specific conflicts but rather that of uncovering the neurotic life-style with its fictitious goals and teaching the patient to substitute another, more suitable set of goals. The patient is assisted in modifying his life-style. In this process, the patient must learn to have more *courage* in facing his reality problems and to develop more *common sense* in dealing with them. (Adler uses the two italicized words unabashedly.)

It should be emphasized that for Adlerians there is a *functional unity* of the whole individual. By means of careful diagnostic procedures (which Adler specified), and by means of such techniques as directly confronting the patient with specific evidence of his neurotic style and its inappropriate goals, the therapist attempts to re-educate the patient and encourage him in attempts at new modes of behavior. Social interest and participation are similarly encouraged. Analysis of the transference reactions of the patient to the therapist is not regarded as significant. The therapist uses his knowledge of the patient's neurotic style, and its causes, to teach him new ways of living and of coping with his real problems. In this whole program, uncovering of patterns of behavior is attempted, but specific attention is not directed to resolving repressions or to analyzing specific unconscious conflicts.

Although there are a considerable number of practicing therapists of Adlerian persuasion, relatively little research effort has been made to test their hypotheses. A shift in this direction may be detectable in recent years, however. One example of an Adlerian hypothesis which emphasizes the possibility of rapid diagnosis and rapid therapeutic change is that *consciously selected early memories* which the patient is asked to provide depict his current life-style and make possible predictions about his present behavior. This was tested by Berman, who was able to find evidence which confirmed it [23].

Nonanalytic and Behavioral Therapies

Let us now examine two examples of therapy which adopt a differing perspective of the nature of personality development and the strategy of treatment. The examples we shall discuss have little in common with each other except that, in both, little or no emphasis is given to unconscious factors in behavior. They have been greatly influenced by the orientation of experimental psychology and attempt to base their formulations on generally accepted principles of learning theory.

CLIENT-CENTERED THERAPY (ROGERS) Carl Rogers is a psychologist who was trained in educational psychology and in clinical counseling. Out of his clinical work, as well as his philosophical orientation toward life (he received training in liberal theology at the Union Theological Seminary), he approached psychotherapy (he first preferred the term "counseling") as a task to be shared by co-equals, the counselor and the "client" (as Rogers first called him). This approach emphasized *permissiveness* and *nondirectiveness* in the client-counselor relationship and was influenced by the Rankian conceptions of psychotherapy. It was also influenced by many other therapeutic theorists (notably Sullivan) and philosophers (notably John

Dewey). In the beginning, Rogers believed that no specific personality theory was responsible for his orientation, preferring to wait upon research data before offering his own theory [24]. Eleven years later, in 1951, he offered his first systematic attempt at such a formulation. It was based on a number of research studies dealing with different aspects of the client-centered approach [25]. In the early stages of his work, Rogers specified some necessary attributes of those clients whom his approach to therapy might benefit. It was assumed that not all clients were capable of profiting from this experience. The criteria used for selecting appropriate clients included: an adequate level of intelligence, freedom from family control, and absence of very severe emotional problems. As time passed and experience with the method and its research findings became available, Rogers chose to discount the significance of these or any other kinds of restrictive criteria. For the past several years he and his co-workers have worked intensively with schizophrenics, for example. However, it is still probably true that most Rogerian counselors treat college students in counseling bureaus and primarily attract moderately disturbed individuals whose emotional problems are centered in adjusting to academic work and the college situation.

Although the nature of client-centered therapy has changed over the past 25 years or so, in essence it has preserved certain characteristics. The client is aware of the need for change in his behavior because of a discrepancy between his self-concept and his perceived experience. The counselor provides an opportunity, in a permissive and shared relationship, for the client to express his feelings. The main therapeutic task is for the therapist to empathize as fully as possible with the client and to reflect or communicate this understanding to the client in an accepting manner. The therapist takes *no responsibility* for directing the client's feelings, perceptions, or other aspects of behavior. All of these are left up to the client. The client initiates therapy, continues it at his own pace, and terminates it when he feels ready to do so. The therapist does not attempt to diagnose, evaluate, or offer authoritative suggestions. Basically, he only reflects the feelings expressed by the client. He makes no conscious effort to interpret.

This apparently simple formula for therapeutic change does appear to work for some people [26]. It represents an extension to the therapeutic field of the general approach advocated by theorists who maintain a phenomenological point of view [27]. In this view the individual's behavior is thought to be entirely determined by his own perceptions of his experiences, and it is therefore not necessary to understand any unconscious forces that are presumed to underlie behavior. What matters, exclusively, is how the person *experiences and perceives his world.*

Rogers holds that when the client-centered viewpoint is maintained, the individual's self-actualizing tendencies (his growth tendencies), which have been blocked or distorted, are released, and, consequently, change will occur. The change produces a closer fit between the person's view of himself and his perceptions of the environment. The faulty self-perception is corrected, and a harmonious and more integrated self-concept, consistent with one's experience, results. Then there is less discomfort and less need for defensive behavior. Figure 7.2 depicts the kind of change which is expected following successful client-centered therapy.

One of the most important contributions by Rogers and his followers was the initiation of their own extensive research program and the stimulation of research in the whole field of therapy. This group formulated relatively precise hypotheses about the nature of therapeutic changes that were expected and proceeded to test them. They made tape recordings of therapeutic sessions and thus were able to examine minutely many aspects of therapeutic interchanges and of changes reported by the client in self-percept. They were able to study the behavior of the therapist as well as that of the client. They analyzed many aspects of outcomes of the therapeutic process.

As illustrative of their research on therapy, a few examples may suffice. It has been possible to show that, when therapy was successful, as judged by objective criteria, there was change in the self-concept in the direction of greater congruence, as postulated [28]. Rogers and Dymond, in their volume summarizing both theory and research [26], were able to define certain necessary conditions for change and the sequential order in which these changes occurred. In a recent study on 28 cases seen in a college counseling center at Chicago, therapeutic change was found to be a function of the therapist's empathy for the patient, the patient's motivation to change, and the interaction of these variables [29]. Some aspects of these findings have been confirmed in research with schizophrenics [30], in which it was found that such patients, when treated by

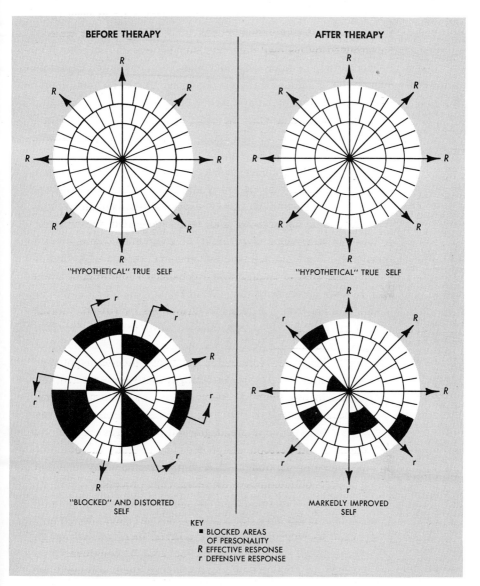

BEFORE THERAPY

AFTER THERAPY

"HYPOTHETICAL" TRUE SELF

"HYPOTHETICAL" TRUE SELF

"BLOCKED" AND DISTORTED
SELF

MARKEDLY IMPROVED
SELF

KEY
■ BLOCKED AREAS
    OF PERSONALITY
R EFFECTIVE RESPONSE
r DEFENSIVE RESPONSE

FIGURE 7.2   *Changes in the self following successful client-centered therapy compared with the true self.*

therapists who are skilled in empathy, tend to improve, but, when treated by therapists who are not so skilled, tend to get worse.

We shall not attempt, at this point, to evaluate either the effectiveness of this therapeutic approach or the adequacy of the research. This is a highly complex problem and would require intensive study of the data and the theory. Some important questions that need to be considered may be raised, however. Most of the work done by Rogerians has been with nonhospitalized, self-referred, and moderately "disturbed" young adults (although by no means all of it). To what extent would this approach be useful to other kinds of patients? Is this approach more effective than other approaches either in terms of basic personality change or in duration of results? Rogers himself has recently noted that therapists disagreed very markedly on what the most important aspects of the patient-therapist interaction were and even on what the goals of therapy were. He was shocked by this, stating, "It meant that our differences ran far deeper than I had presumed" [34]. And what of the criteria of therapeutic change? This has been a perennial problem for all the therapeutic approaches and is still largely unresolved. Should we estimate degree of improvement in terms of objective personality measures, or by other means? Are the conditions described by Rogers the minimal characteristics of all effective therapy? Are they necessary as well as sufficient in some or in all cases? No one has the answer to these and other questions, although if one reads the therapeutic literature one can find innumerable examples of therapists who write as if the answers were known. The research by Rogers and his colleagues has posed these questions for all therapeutic schools— and posed them with dramatic forthrightness.

BEHAVIORAL THERAPIES In recent years psychologists and others interested in behavioral change have sought to translate learning-theory concepts into procedures which might be useful in therapy; many take their cues from laboratory work with animals. Most such people have been dissatisfied with traditional therapeutic concepts and techniques, labeling them "mystical," "obscure," and "unscientific." They have attempted, instead, to utilize concepts and methods which were capable of more precise definition and more adequate experimental manipulation. We shall discuss these approaches under the general heading "behavioral therapy," since they all involve relatively specific analysis of the components of the neurotic behavior and try to modify this behavior through application of learning principles. However, not all therapists whom we subsume under the caption "behavioral therapist" operate in this manner. Some utilize psychoanalytic concepts, some apply social-learning theories, and some apply methods which can best be described as "educational."

In 1950 Dollard and Miller [31] and Mowrer [32] published books in which they tried to apply learning principles to the process of therapy. In the case of Dollard and Miller, relatively traditional psychoanalytic concepts were *translated* into operational learning-theory terms. For example, the Freudian concept of the *pleasure principle* was translated into the concept of *positive reinforcement,* and the concept of *transference* was considered *stimulus generalization.* In the first of these translations the pleasure principle, which Freudians regard as an innate tendency of the organism to respond in terms of maximizing immediate pleasure, is conceived of as the learning of avoidant responses to reduce momentary anxiety. This reinforces the neurotic response, which temporarily offers less pain (anxiety) and more "pleasure." The second translation involves stimulus generalization from one stimulus to another which previously did not evoke the response. For instance, attributes of important persons in the patient's previous experience generalize to the therapist, who may have some, but not all, of these attributes. On the other hand, Mowrer presented alternative analytic formulations for the traditional psychoanalytic ones. He provided a modified set of concepts of the learning process to account for the paradox of neurotic behavior. (See the present authors' *Psychology: The Science of Behavior* for a description of Mowrer's current learning theory.) Attempts along these lines have continued. For example, in 1953 Dollard, Auld, and White illustrated the application of learning principles to therapy by offering a detailed analysis of the complex process of psychotherapy with actual case material [33]. And in 1963 Alexander, one of the founders of the Chicago psychoanalytic school, offered his version of the application of learning theory to psychoanalytically oriented psychotherapy [34].

On the other hand, some psychologists have abandoned psychoanalytic concepts entirely, preferring to conceptualize all of the therapeutic interactions in learning-theory terms. They have discarded, as misleading, concepts of the unconscious, the ego, and transference. Among these people, Wolpe was the first to offer both an explanation of the origin of neurotic behavior and the modification of this behavior entirely in terms of simple

697

learning principles [6]. Wolpe believes that most, if not all, neurotic behavior can be eliminated by means of the principle of *reciprocal inhibition*—which we shall examine in a moment. The extent of his disagreement with psychoanalysis can be gauged from his statement: "The truth is that after 60 years of expanding influence, psychoanalytic theory still, in almost every particular, consists of nothing more than speculation; none of its major propositions has passed any [empirical] tests" [35]. This disregards, it seems to us, the experimental confirmation of at least some of the psychoanalytic hypotheses.

Let us examine Wolpe's position in some detail. Wolpe, a psychiatrist, had observed that the neurotic behavior of animals was reduced or eliminated when they had pleasurable feeding experiences in the presence of anxiety-producing stimuli. From this he reasoned that, in the human, a response that was evoked by an anxiety-conditioned stimulus might be eliminated if the human were induced to respond simultaneously in some manner that was antagonistic to the anxiety response. Thus, he believed that the bond between the anxiety-evoking stimulus and its response could be weakened if the person were required to respond, in this situation, with an alternate and more pleasurable kind of behavior. The first step in the therapeutic program was to obtain a list of stimuli ranked in terms of severity of inappropriate anxiety produced by them. The list was unique for each patient, of course. Then the patient would be induced to respond to the lowest-ranked, least noxious of these stimuli with an antagonistic response. For example, the patient would be placed in a hypnotic trance, or taught to relax deeply, and told to imagine the low-anxiety stimulus (or stimulus situation). If the patient succeeded in maintaining the state of relaxation, that is, if he did not respond with anxiety, he would then be asked to respond to the next, more anxious, stimulus in another relaxation session. In this manner the dosage of the anxiety-associated stimuli would be increased until the patient was able to tolerate all anxiety-inducing stimuli in that category. He called this therapeutic task the "unmaking of functional neurotic connections" by the process of reciprocal inhibition.

Wolpe used a variety of methods for reducing the "connection" between stimuli and their anxiety responses. He employed "assertive responses," "sexual responses," "respiratory responses," and "motoric responses" as antagonists to the anxiety response. In the beginning he concentrated his work on phobias.

Later he used this approach for many other kinds of neurotic behaviors. He states that his results have been highly successful, claiming as high as 91 percent success in phobic cases, with an average of 10 sessions needed to obtain "success" [36]. He has invited research verification of the effectiveness of his methods, and a new journal is currently reporting studies of this kind (*Behavior Research and Therapy*).

However, the usefulness of Wolpe's approach remains open to clinical and empirical verification. This method may have some utility with respect to "biotropic" conditions, i.e., conditions involving the autonomic nervous system in which the goal of therapy is the removal of symptoms [37]. There is a question as to the applicability of this method to "sociotropic" conditions, i.e., those which involve complex social-cultural problems. Eysenck, a British psychologist who has also been experimenting with conditioning methods, raises other issues [38]. He believes that methods of "classical extinction" of responses, like Wolpe's reciprocal inhibition, may be effective for conditions such as phobias. However, he believes that other methods are necessary for conditions which are not essentially autonomic nervous system responses. Conditions like homosexuality, perversions, and alcoholic addictions, he thinks, can be treated by shaping new response patterns in the problem situation by *partial reinforcement*. Competing, antagonistic responses would be induced in the presence of appropriate stimuli and reinforced, or rewarded, on an intermittent basis; i.e., the responses would sometimes be rewarded and would sometimes not be rewarded. It has also been argued, by dynamically oriented psychologists, that symptom removal without resolution of the underlying conflicts produces, at best, a displacement of the symptom. Therefore, anxiety is only temporarily reduced. It may even make the person's total behavior more maladaptive in time. For these and related questions, we need careful research evidence.

A Comparison of Various Forms of Psychotherapy

If the student has become somewhat bewildered by the profusion of claims and counterclaims made by the various proponents of differing schools of psychotherapy, this is entirely understandable. It is clear that the experts do not agree on the goals of therapy. Nor do they agree on the essential ingredients of the therapeutic process, although, as we have seen, there is some consensus on some of them. The past few decades have been marked by a proliferation of research studies, some of them trivial, some of them irrelevant, but quite a few of real significance. To date, research has been most profitably applied to relatively simple aspects of the total therapeutic program, such as measuring some types of change (as in studies of self-perception), measuring patient and therapist interactions (as in studies of degree of empathy), and measuring specific attributes of the patient and of the therapist.

Our discussion of the nature of psychopathology in Chapter 6 revealed the enormous complexity of these phenomena and the difficulties in diagnostic assessment of such conditions. From this perspective we can see that it is quite possible that markedly differing therapeutic aproaches are needed for different types of cases. For example, it is quite difficult to see how Rogerian therapy could be applied effectively if the patient is unmotivated for therapeutic change (as in psychopathic states or in catatonic withdrawal). Psychoanalysis has been shown to be ineffective for most types of schizophrenia, and psychoanalysts working with such patients, as at the Menninger Foundation, have had to modify this approach considerably to achieve some degree of success [39]. Adlerian therapy seems to be effective for certain kinds of cases and is thought to be relatively more effective than other approaches when problems of the patient's "life-style" are involved. As we have noted, behavior therapy has claimed remarkable effectiveness with certain kinds of phobic patients. All therapeutic approaches seem to have some degree of success in reducing anxiety, but reduction of anxiety, while perhaps basic, does not by itself guarantee effective therapeutic change.

Where does this leave us at present? Obviously, we are not in a position to answer this question. Certain considerations seem important to emphasize, and some provocative speculation may be profitable at this point. In order to address ourselves to this task, let us first consider an actual case of an individual as he presents himself for psychotherapy.

This young man of 24 years, a graduate student, complains that he has begun to find that he is ineffective in his studies. Try as he will, he finds it difficult to complete term papers, and he has a gnawing sense of his own incompetence. He claims that even when he was more successful in his studies, during undergraduate days, he still felt himself to be inadequate, although he "knew" he had very superior intelligence. In the early, exploratory sessions of therapy, some new complaints begin to emerge. The most striking of these is his feeling that he is "about ready to fall apart," i.e., to lose self-control and possibly become psychotic. Now he admits to periods of severe depression, starting at or shortly after the beginning of puberty. He also speaks of shyness with girls and tendencies to withdraw into his own world of private fantasy. Reluctantly he admits to severe and terrifying nightmares which he has been unwilling to discuss heretofore because their content involves homosexual orgies, and such thoughts are morally reprehensible to him.

As this man proceeds with uncovering therapy, many underlying layers of conflict emerge. With great affection he recalls his highly competent mother, who managed his life with skill and success, always guiding him to what she considered the "right" decisions or the "right" behavior. He recalls how he despised his father, who assumed a passive role in the home and seemed totally ineffective in relation to his mother. Still later, this man's hatred for his mother is dramatically expressed, and his concealed fear of offending her becomes apparent. Subsequently, he remembers some experience with his father, when they had outings alone, but he also remembers returning home and being afraid to tell his mother how much he had enjoyed his father's companionship. In working through these ambivalent feelings toward both parents, he becomes aware of feelings of panic concerning his conscious homosexual urges and, simultaneously, begins to express great anger toward the therapist. This helps him to keep the therapist at a distance. His thinking now assumes paranoid coloring, but his contact with reality is maintained. Despite, or possibly because of, these strong affects, he finds that he can now apply himself easily to his schoolwork. After a considerable additional period of therapy, he is finally able to achieve comfortable intra- and interpersonal effectiveness.

Although we have only begun to sketch some of the major aspects of this man's communications in therapy, we can already see how complex are the determinants of his behavior. However, rather than attempt to evaluate the precise nature of the psychopathology, let us consider some of the therapeutic tasks which his case presents.

Cases of this kind seem to present some obvious and important differences from other cases, such as those involving relatively restricted phobias, simple hypertension, or gastrointestinal complaints. The former involve the "total personality" with more diffuse psychological, motor, and cognitive phenomena.

701

The latter, typically, involve more circumscribed, more local-ized, and perhaps relatively focused autonomic disturbances. It is also well known, to anyone who has had extensive psycho-therapeutic experience with diverse types of clinical problems, that some cases present, at first, what seem to be restricted disturbances (as in cases of apparently simple obsessive-com-pulsive phenomena) but turn out to be cases involving complex and severe ego fragmentation (when it is discovered that the obsessive behavior "conceals" a profound schizophrenic reac-tion pattern).

Thus, when attempting to compare the effectiveness of differ-ing approaches to psychotherapy, it is very important to equate for comparability of psychopathology. In a number of attempts to compare the relative effectiveness of different forms of therapy (see, for example [40]) this primary requirement of adequate research design has not been met. These considerations lead to the following summary comments.

1. Comparison of the relative effectiveness of different thera-peutic approaches must control carefully for comparability of psychopathology.

2. Closely related to this first point is a second general consideration: The relative effectiveness of therapies must be evaluated in terms of the types and degrees of improvement. The case described above did have counseling during his under-graduate days. He did learn to feel a little better about himself. But the improvement did not last. Nor were any of the "deeper" problems dealt with in this earlier counseling.

3. A third point concerns the focus of the therapeutic inter-action. In listening to, and trying to understand a patient, what aspects of personality functioning (overt versus covert, rational versus irrational, concrete versus symbolic, etc.) are attended to by the therapist? It seems clear that different schools of therapy *select* aspects of the communication between patient and thera-pist in different ways. Both their explicit and implicit philos-ophy and psychological orientation train them to respond to different kinds of behavior. Studies of the Sullivanian type of therapy have shown that this bias of the therapist influences the type of interaction. Even in standardized testing situations, communication can be greatly influenced by both the explicit and implicit stimulus values of the psychologist [41]. Not only does the therapeutic orientation of the therapist produce such effect, but so does the nature of the therapist's personality [42].

4. Therapeutic approaches differ in terms of the degree of responsibility and/or authority which the therapist assumes. In the case illustration we have given, a number of issues along this line become evident. What responsibility should or must the therapist assume for a person with depressive trends or with a person who seems to be on the edge of a psychotic breakdown? Does he need to evaluate the probability of some dangerous homicidal or suicidal acting-out or of severe disorganization of the personality? And should he take any steps to counteract such trends? Such problems present moral and strategic issues on which the different schools of therapy diverge widely.

5. In the course of therapy, progress may be markedly influenced by the therapeutic strategy. Some patients leave therapy because they need, or feel they need, some direction by the therapist and do not obtain it. Are such patients necessarily bad therapeutic risks, or is the therapeutic approach at fault? Can we assume that providing a warm, accepting, and empathic understanding will necessarily produce exposure of significant unconscious material? Is it necessary for the therapist to help actively in working through the patient's resistances and to prevent him from avoiding or distorting reality so that anxiety does not become intolerable? Rankians and Rogerians seem to differ markedly from Freudians and Adlerians on this issue. Will some patients leave therapy with false feelings of comfort, not because they have resolved their underlying problems, but with relief because they did not have to face them? In our case illustration, would the several layers of the problem have been exposed, exposed more slowly or more rapidly, or exposed more deeply, if permissive or behavioral therapy had been tried? These are questions that need empirical study.

6. How much awareness need the therapist have concerning his own "blind spots"? Some schools of psychotherapy require that the therapist himself be analyzed and have intense personal supervision so that he can resolve his own conflicts or at least become sensitive to his own defenses. Other schools minimize or neglect this aspect of training. How important is it? How does it affect therapeutic change? We have some evidence which indicates that this factor is quite important [43]. Involved in this issue is the more basic philosophical problem of the approach to scientific study of the personality; i.e., should we consider persons as "objects" with their own immutable characteristics, or should we view persons as adaptive organisms whose be-

havior can only be understood in terms of interacting fields of forces of the person and those with whom he is interacting?

(7.) Another general issue which has received very little attention in empirical studies, although there is ample clinical commentary about it, concerns the significance of the *setting* in which therapy takes place. Psychoanalysts speak of the pre-transference effects of the status of the psychoanalyst or of the institute in which he functions. Psychologists have studied some of the effects of the "setting" upon behavioral performance [44]. There are many possible factors in the therapeutic setting: the reputation of the therapist(s); the reputation of the clinic, hospital, or center; the physical characteristics of the therapy room; the frequency and distribution of therapy sessions; the anticipated duration of therapy. Such factors may affect the patient's expectations, and, in turn, the patient's expectations may affect his selection of the therapist and the setting in which he functions. Patients frequently comment that they wish to retain some degree of privacy and therefore decide to seek therapy outside a clinic or hospital. Others prefer to be treated by a doctor of medicine or by a male therapist. Still others wish to have careful diagnostic assessment before they commence therapy. These examples are indicative of the probable influence of the "setting" in relation to patients' expectancies.

Let us turn now to another orientation in comparing the various approaches to psychotherapy. Increasingly, therapists of many persuasions are seeking to codify the nature of their therapeutic operations and to define them more explicitly and precisely. Increasingly, attempts are being made to understand the nature of therapeutic change in terms of learning principles. Since the human organism inherits only general behavior tendencies, the precise nature of his performance must depend significantly upon the interrelationship between the individual and the environment to which he is exposed. At the least, what is known about learning principles can assist in maximizing the relearning situation that constitutes therapy. At the most, all of therapy can be understood in terms of such principles. However, we must recognize that therapy is, in fact, a highly complex learning task. We do not yet have the knowledge which enables us to predict the learning principles that would be appropriate for specific individuals at different stages in their therapeutic progress. One great danger of the advocacy of the learning-theory approach to therapy is that the need to "opera-tionalize" may cause oversimplification of the therapeutic prob-lem. In the process, scientific progress may be retarded rather than accelerated. It is even appropriate to ask whether learning theory can ever be expected to account for all therapeutic change. As we know, most learning theorists use the simplest kinds of experimental situations in order to understand these before applying learning principles to more complex situations. The caution of such theorists can serve as a warning to those who would recklessly extrapolate their results to psychotherapy.

Most, but not all, therapeutic schools recognize the great importance of reducing excessive anxiety in order to assist the individual. It seems to us that, for many clinical conditions, maintenance of anxiety, at tolerable limits for the patient, enables him to develop more accurate perception of the nature of his conflicts and to attempt new methods of dealing with them. This control of the intensity of the anxiety may be dealt with explicitly by the therapist, as Wolpe does, or it may be handled through the utilization of a permissive and accepting therapeutic atmosphere, as Rogerians and many others do. It may be necessary, in some pathological conditions, and at some stages of therapy, for others to attempt to *increase* the anxiety reaction in order to stimulate some favorable changes. For instance, when the patient attempts to avoid awareness of conflicts (as in some psychopathic states) or when his symp-toms offer temporary neurotic satisfactions (as in cases of hysteria), such a strategy may be indicated.

But, there is a fundamental question as to whether anxiety manipulation, in any fashion, is a *sufficient condition* for thera-peutic change. Can we assume that all individuals are capable of improving their functioning, once neurotic patterns have been established, if only anxiety is lessened? Is not some kind of directed learning necessary, at least in some cases? This appears to be necessary in psychosis, in character disorder, and in psychopathic states or severe problems of impulse control. And if some form of directed learning is necessary, how is it to be provided? The followers of Adler provide suggestions for the re-education of the patient. The Freudians call attention to the patient's resistance, and especially to the transference relation-ship, as well as provide suggestions for ego re-education. The behavioral therapists use some form of explicit conditioning.

705

There are other forms of therapy than individual psycho-therapy, and it is to some of these that we now turn our attention.

Group and Environmental Therapy

Treatment of individuals in groups had its beginnings in about 1905. At first this method had as its major aim the building of morale through identification with the leader of the group and with the other members. Pratt, who fostered this approach with individuals suffering from pulmonary tuberculosis, thought of it as *repressive-inspirational* therapy [45], because it attempted to change behavior by example and illustration without uncovering unconscious conflicts. A few years later, Marsh, who was a minister at the time, utilized this approach with psychoneu-rotics. He subsequently received training as a psychiatrist and applied this kind of group therapy to psychotics, calling it the "psychological equivalent of the revival" [46]. In 1911, Moreno developed a method which he called psychodrama [47]. In this approach a number of patients were asked to "role-play" certain kinds of conflict situations. The patients and staff members acted these conflicts out in a dramatic setting on a stage, with other patients present. The chief aims of this method were to develop spontaneity in expressing feeling and to become more fully aware of conflictful material that had been warded off from awareness. In the 1930's, Wender [48] and Schilder [49] applied psychoanalytic principles to group therapy. In World War II, great impetus was given to group therapy, chiefly because of the need to treat large numbers of patients eco-nomically. Since then, group methods have proliferated, and considerable research attention has been given to group proc-esses and to outcomes of group therapy. Social psychologists contributed significant increments to our psychological knowl-edge of the nature of group structure and group interactions. Cartwright and Zander summarize the theories and research up to 1953 [50]. A more recent and quite general summary of socially oriented efforts at inducing psychological change is provided by Lippitt, Watson, and Westley [51].

There are a number of quite different orientations toward the functions of a group for purposes of therapy. For some, like

Moreno's psychodrama. Moreno Academy, Beacon, New York

Wender, "The premise of group psychotherapy is that the human individual is a 'group animal,' seeking a satisfying niche in his social setting" [48]. For them, the group provides for special kinds of interactions among members—not available in individual therapy—which can be focused on by both patients and therapist. For others, the group as such is not studied, but the individual experiences of each member of the group are dealt with [52]. Still others utilize the group for inspirational purposes or as an educational experience in which didactic instruction in mental health problems is given [53].

In the past decade or so, theoretical and research attention has been given to the therapeutic effects of the nature of the "hospital environment" as it influences patients' behavior [54]. It has been shown that the kind of relationships existing among hospital personnel, and between them and patients, as well as the kinds of authority and communication channels that exist, can influence the rate of recovery. The characteristics of the community and relationships with psychopathology have also

707

been studied by sociologists, psychiatrists, and psychologists [55, 56, and 57].

Group therapy seems to have certain kinds of advantages which may complement or even supplement individual therapy. In the first place, it provides for *economy,* since more patients can be seen by fewer therapists. In the second place, it can provide the *emotional support of the group* for members who are fearful of exposing themselves in individual therapy. Of course, there are some patients who are unduly threatened by exposure in a group; but others derive support from a group in which similar problems are being experienced and similar feelings are expressed. Perhaps more important than either of these advantages is that the group provides opportunity for each individual to relate to and interact with a number of different people. Thus, the *complexity of his reactions* can be observed at first hand as the patient reacts differentially to different people, as he responds to criticism or support, as he feels competitiveness or co-operation, and so on. In individual therapy, the patient can only talk about these varying behavioral reactions. They cannot be observed directly, and neither patient nor therapist can experience them directly. Finally, *group process,* involving the overt and implicit interactions within the group (such as the formation of cliques, the taking-over of leadership, and so on), can be experienced and dealt with, whereas only two-person communication is possible in individual therapy.

It may be helpful to conceptualize group therapy in terms of the nature of the interrelationships among patients and therapist. Figure 7.3 illustrates three kinds of group patterns In *A,*

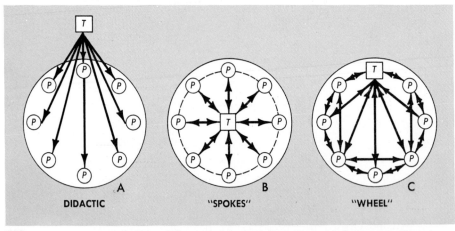

DIDACTIC   "SPOKES"   "WHEEL"

FIGURE 7.3   *Schematic plans of three types of therapy groups.*

the therapist is outside and "above" the group. The lines of communication go, almost exclusively, from him to the patients. There is little interaction among the patients. This is the model of group therapy which has been called repressive-inspirational. The therapist is either a "teacher" and presents "information" which may be useful for the patients, or the therapist is a "leader" and exhorts, inspires, motivates, and the like.

In *B,* the therapist is also a central figure, but now he is within the group, and the lines of communication go directly from him to each patient. They also go directly from each patient to him, as well as from each patient to every other patient. This is the model of psychoanalytic and other types of group therapy in which the reactions of the group, the interactions of patients and therapists, and the interactions of patients among themselves are foci of the therapeutic work. The group is now being utilized as a source of information as well as a means of therapeutic change. Sometimes patients help one another more than the therapist can help them. Sometimes the therapist can make use of reactions of the group to a particular patient. In these and other ways the domain of data available to both patient and therapist can be greatly extended over that which is available in individual therapy.

In *C,* the therapist is essentially another member of the group. Within the group, communication is readily available to all members. The therapist is a member of the group and adds his resources (training and personality) to it, but he does not dominate it or lead it. This is the model of client-centered or permissive therapies applied to groups. The group works on its own problems, making whatever use it wishes of all of the members of the group.

From inspection of these three types of group organizations, it can be seen that different uses tend to be made of the group and of members of the group. In type *B*, called the "Spokes" type, since the organization resembles a wheel with radial spokes, it would be expected that strong transference reactions between patients and therapist would be maximized because of the focus of the group on the therapist. The group is also likely to become a vehicle for transferences among members of the group. The type *C* group, called the "Wheel" type, would not be likely to generate so much patient-therapist or even patient-patient transference since the therapist is not a central figure and patient-patient interactions are not necessarily maximized.

However, it might generate more "group feeling," more group cohesiveness, and more permissive expression of feeling than type *B,* because "group" reactions are maximized. The type *A* group would be used, mainly, for didactic teaching purposes and would enable the inspirational or exhortatory therapist to maximize his effects. Psychoanalysts tend to use type *B* groups, while Rogerians tend to use type *C.*

It has been learned from experience that groups of types *B* and *C* should usually have from six to eight members. The criteria for selection and composition of the group have also received some research study. These findings suggest that some kind of balance in the personality of the members must be achieved if the group is not to disintegrate. For example, the group should not be overbalanced with either verbally aggressive or very shy individuals. In the former case, there would be a likelihood of disruption of the group, due to excessive competitive behavior. In the latter case, the shy members, unless there were at least two, would tend to withdraw within or from the group or participate to a minimal degree. There is less agreement on such variables as sex, educational level, socioeconomic status, and type of psychopathology. Some have found that heterogeneity is not undesirable, while others tend to disagree [58, 59]. Groups of psychotic hospitalized patients have been found to benefit from all three types of group-therapy programs. Fox has come to the conclusion, contrary to a previously held belief, that criminal offenders can be helped by group therapy and that such therapy is more effective than individual therapy because it provides more opportunity for learning appropriate social roles [60]. It has been found that even imprisoned sexual psychopaths, a group that is notoriously difficult to treat, were able to improve sufficiently to be returned from prison to society by means of group therapy. About 66 percent of a group of 120 such cases showed this amount of improvement [61].

All therapeutic viewpoints are represented in programs of group therapy [62]. Furthermore, many have been combined. For example, Gestalt and psychoanalytic positions were combined by Bach, who has provided us with an excellent rationale for his methods and with criteria for the selection of suitable patients for such work [58]. Others have used Sullivanian concepts in their approach. Coffey [63], in studying the process of group behavior, following this orientation, has distinguished

710

sequential phases in group therapy: (1) an early period of defensiveness; (2) a later stage of "confiding," in which fantasies and unconscious roles are communicated and tested out; and (3) a final integrative-prospective period, in which conflicts are resolved and new self-concepts emerge. These phases characterize the group's process and not necessarily each member of the group.

Variants of the group-therapy program have also been developed. Slavson, a leader in such modifications, describes what he calls "activity group therapy," originally used with children manifesting deviant patterns of social behavior [64]. In an arts-and-craft type of setting, children were encouraged to join the "club" and engage in projects of their own choosing. They tended to express their feelings freely and even enjoyably and, as a result, were helped in understanding their internal conflicts and in integrating new roles for themselves. Extensive work with delinquent and aggressive children has been done by Redl, who is psychoanalytically oriented. He has directed considerable research toward unearthing the types of specific therapeutic techniques that are most helpful. He has also elaborated the mechanisms of group behavior that facilitate constructive behavioral change as well as those that are destructive [65]. In recent years, family therapy (or *conjoint therapy,* as it is called), with several members of the family, has been successfully applied.

The field of group therapy is an active one. Most of the concepts employed still lean heavily upon those that have been carried over from individual therapy. Current research programs are beginning to develop new concepts and idiosyncratic techniques and are testing them out in a great variety of group settings.

Somatic Methods of Treatment

The recent developments in the medical and health sciences have furnished us with a variety of chemical methods of treatment. We have reached the age of "wonder drugs," in which extraordinary changes in behavior can be induced through the use of medication. Although the use of such physical methods and drugs is restricted to licensed physicians, research teams composed of psychiatrists, physiologists, chemists, and psychologists are engaged in trying to evaluate the effectiveness of such methods of treatment.

Exorbitant claims have universally been made for almost all chemical methods of treatment when first introduced. Such claims were followed, after extensive research with the method, by sobering re-evaluations. The findings to date may be summarized as follows:

1. Chemical methods of treatment are most effective with cases of recent origin.
2. With cases of long-term or chronic psychopathology, chemical methods of treatment are most effective in reducing agitation and excessive states of excitement, thus making such cases more "manageable."
3. Chemical methods of treatment are most effective in reducing the severity of symptoms but are not likely to have great effect upon the basic problems or in producing significant improvement in ego functions.
4. Such methods have relatively little effect in changing disorders of thinking, although they may reduce hallucinations or delusions. They appear to have little value in the psychoneuroses, except in helping to reduce anxiety. Even here, chronic anxiety states are not relieved.
5. They are sometimes useful in helping to make patients accessible for psychotherapy. Some patients, like those who are severely depressed or agitated, who would otherwise not be able to respond to such treatment, can be sufficiently helped to make other psychotherapeutic methods available.
6. In general, the most lasting and significant effects have been produced in cases of uncomplicated depression.
7. There is a danger of unfavorable side effects, sometimes only temporarily disabling, but occasionally fatal.
8. There are highly significant differences in the ways patients, even in the same pathological category, respond to such methods. The criteria for the selection of a drug for a particular patient are therefore quite difficult to apply.
9. In most instances, combined chemical and psychotherapeutic treatment is the best procedure.

We shall do no more than highlight some of the specific somatic methods of treatment, referring to specialized summaries or other types of references whenever possible. Our aim, here, is merely to introduce the student to this technical field and provide some "feel" for its methods.

SHOCK THERAPIES   The shock therapies were in prominent use for a while until more effective and less drastic methods, especially the various drug therapies, became available in recent years. These methods have in common the feature that the patient is induced to go into "shock," in which, usually following a period of unconsciousness, there are convulsions and spasms, followed by regression in behavior to more infantile modes of responding, such as infantile speech and thumb-sucking, and after which, especially with the repeated application of shock treatment, there are changes in the emotional tone and the symptomatic forms of behavior.

Shock can be induced chemically or electrically. Chemically induced shock was introduced by the Viennese psychiatrist, Sakel, who employed the hormone *insulin* [66]. In insulin shock there is a temporarily reduced blood-sugar level. Complicated changes in physiological reactions follow, including abnormal neural activity and motor seizures. The metabolism of the brain, especially of the higher centers such as the cortex, is profoundly altered. After a series of such treatments there may be improvement in the patient's condition. Insulin treatment was used most extensively with schizophrenics, although it has also been employed with neurotic cases showing intense anxiety. Many studies of the effectiveness of insulin shock have been made, but the results are not universally accepted because of problems with research design. In one typical study, in which careful control was employed for a treated and an untreated group, Bond and Rivers found that with insulin-shock treatment 54 percent of hospitalized patients made a "social recovery" (i.e., were able to make some social adjustments), whereas without insulin-shock treatment only 20 percent made such a recovery [67]. Moreover, in a follow-up study made five years later, a significantly higher proportion of the treated than the untreated cases maintained their improvement. These favorable outcomes have not been reported by other workers, however.

Electroshock treatment can be given either at convulsive or subconvulsive levels. An electrical current is applied to the head through two electrodes. The amount of applied voltage and the duration of application determine whether or not a convulsion will be produced. As with insulin shock, a number of treatments are given, depending upon the patient's response to the procedure. The greatest improvement tends to occur in disturbed, emotional, psychotic states, especially in psychotic depression, but electroconvulsive therapy has been used for many other conditions. There has been considerable discussion of possible organic brain damage caused by electroshock therapy, but most studies have failed to reveal anything other than transient constriction of blood cells without damage to nerve cells. However, memory changes do occur, and there are indications of organic damage when electroencephalographic studies of the brain are made. A very thorough summary of clinical and research findings with electroshock therapy has been supplied by Kalinowsky [68].

DRUG THERAPIES An exceedingly great variety of drugs has been employed in the treatment of all types of psychopathologies. Of these the most widely known, and apparently the most useful, have been the tranquilizing drugs. For example, chlorpromazine, one of the phenothiazine compounds and commonly known as a tranquilizer, has been extensively employed in the treatment of schizophrenia and depression. However, it is no longer used alone in cases of depression because such individuals tend to become much more severely depressed and to stay that way. In such cases, electroshock therapy and a tranquilizer are combined. In evaluating the effectiveness of chlorpromazine with schizophrenics, Hoch states, "In our experience, 10 to 15 per cent of schizophrenic patients improve to such a degree that they can go back to the community and function adequately" [69]. The use of this drug is attended by possible complications, among which the development of jaundice and a drop in the white blood count are the most serious.

Various drugs have been used successfully in the treatment of depression. Recently a highly effective drug, *imipramine hydrochloride* (Tofranil), has been reported. This drug is reputed to be most effective in cases with endogenous (or essential) depression, and very few side effects have been reported thus far. Moreover, there have been a number of research studies which confirm this drug's usefulness [70, 71].

PSYCHOSURGERY This euphonious-sounding term for drastic surgical procedures was coined to indicate that the purpose of the surgery was to produce psychological consequences. Various types of brain surgery have been used, the most common ones involving the frontal lobes of the brain. In *prefrontal lobotomy* fibers connecting prefrontal areas with certain sub-cortical limbic-system areas are severed. In *prefrontal lobectomy* the prefrontal neocortical regions are actually removed. The intent is to change the emotional reactions of the patient by this disruption of nerve connections. Such measures are employed only when there are highly persistent and intense emotional tensions which are disabling or dangerous for the patient. Even then they are used only after other methods have proved to be ineffectual. Klebanoff and his colleagues report, after careful review of the research literature, that, although results vary with both the type of surgery and the condition of the patient, reduced capacity for abstract thinking results, together with significant loss in memory and capacity for sustained attention. Personality changes are particularly likely to be profound, with the development of apathy and depression quite common [72]. Freeman, one of the world's leading authorities on psychosurgery, states, ". . . psychosurgery reduces creativity, sometimes to the vanishing point" [73]. Clearly, psychosurgery is a drastic measure, at best, and its possible use needs extended and very careful evaluation in any given instance.

Varieties of Mental Health Personnel

Some degree of understanding of the nature of the therapeutic process may be gained from an examination of the varieties of personnel involved in such programs. Such people are usually classified into professional and subprofessional categories. The presumption, of course, is that the major therapeutic contributions are made by professionally trained personnel, but, painful as it may be to some, this is not necessarily always the case. Clifford Beers, the founder of the National Mental Hygiene Movement in this country and himself a former psychiatric patient who spent considerable time in psychiatric hospitals, attributed his recovery largely to the acceptance and support he gained from an attendant in one of these hospitals. We should at least note that during a considerable portion of their time in mental hospitals, patients are in the company of, and are under the supervision and even guidance of ward attendants, volunteer workers (usually, interested adults in the community), and other nonprofessional personnel. There are also semiprofessional personnel, usually with carefully specified training at the college level, such as occupational therapists and physical therapists.

MEDICALLY TRAINED PERSONNEL Time was when the only professionally trained personnel who treated people with psychopathology were psychiatrists. Until recently, most laymen still thought of the psychiatrist when a psychotherapist was needed. Although the picture has changed, psychiatrists are numerically the largest single group of psychotherapists.

A psychiatrist is a member of the medical profession whose specialty is the diagnosis and treatment of people suffering from psychopathology. Following his internship as a doctor of medicine, he follows a psychiatric residency program, usually for three years. This training is offered in selected teaching hospitals and clinics, where he obtains diagnostic and therapeutic experience under careful supervision. After a period of suitable experience, and after passing rigid oral and written examinations under the auspices of the American Board of Neurology and Psychiatry, he is known as a diplomate in psychiatry.

The psychiatrist is the only mental health worker (except for medical psychoanalysts) who is trained, and legally qualified, to administer drugs and use other forms of somatic therapy, such as electroshock treatment. In cases of severe psychopathology which require careful medical supervision and somatic treatment, at least as part of the total treatment program, he is the one who has the legal responsibility for the patient.

Considerable controversy has arisen concerning the appropriateness of the training of psychiatrists, mainly on two counts. One is that he spends many years in training as a physician and comparatively little time in the study of psychopathology, developmental psychology, personality therapy, personality diagnosis, psychotherapeutic theory, and kindred subjects. The argument is that much of the medical training is unrelated to the practice of psychiatry, that medical training may actually reduce an individual's effectiveness in the practice of psychotherapy, and that too little training is offered in many areas of personality, psychopathology, and psychotherapy [74]. In terms of actual practice, these areas pre-empt most of the psychiatrist's time. Some psychiatrists have proposed a new program of training, involving more psychology and less medicine, which would lead to a degree of doctor of clinical psychology. This would be a combined medical and psychological program. Up to the present time this proposal has not gained wide acceptance or support. It has also been argued that psychiatrists should receive training in research methodology—an area that is now almost completely neglected in their training—because of the great need to evaluate psychotherapeutic methods and to discover new or better methods of treatment.

THE PSYCHOANALYST   The term psychoanalyst was originally applied only to persons who successfully completed training under the auspices of a Freudian psychoanalytic institute. Today many schools of psychoanalysis exist, such as the Jungian, Adlerian, and Sullivanian. Their trainees also use the appellation of psychoanalyst.

Some psychoanalytical institutes admit nonmedical personnel for training, but in the United States the American Psychoanalytical Association limits its training to doctors of medicine. This is not the case in some European countries. In this country, the psychiatrist (or other medically trained person) who wishes to become a Freudian psychoanalyst is admitted to training after evaluation of his suitability, and he then undergoes a personal psychoanalysis. In the later stages of his training, he undertakes psychoanalytic treatment of patients under conditions of very close supervision. He also attends seminars and case discussions in which he receives further indoctrination and theoretical training in this specialty. Of all professional workers in the mental health field, the psychoanalyst (Freudian) receives the longest and most intensive training in treatment methods. He also is trained extensively, through his own psychoanalysis, to be highly sensitive to his own conflicts and to expressions of conflict in others.

Other schools of psychoanalysis follow relatively similar plans of training, but some admit nonmedical personnel (chiefly psychologists and psychiatric social workers) as well as physicians, and their training programs in some cases may be less intensive.

Many psychoanalysts do not utilize somatic treatment with their patients, referring such cases to physicians or psychiatrists when such treatment is indicated. Most believe that the psychoanalyst's and the physician's roles should be carefully differentiated. For the patient, the two offer highly different kinds of

717

treatment programs. The patient expects the physician *to do something to him,* whereas in psychoanalysis the patient *must learn to do most of the work himself,* since the psychoanalyst is relatively passive and inactive.

THE CLINICAL PSYCHOLOGIST   This is the youngest of the professions involved in the psychotherapy of emotionally disturbed individuals. Although there were some clinical psychologists in this country prior to World War II, these individuals were, for the most part, psychodiagnosticians, that is, they administered and interpreted psychological tests. If they engaged in psychotherapy, they usually did so under direct supervision by a psychiatrist. Some practiced independently after they had obtained training in psychotherapy on some individual basis or through some informal type of apprenticeship.

As a result of the great need for psychotherapists which became evident during World War II, universities began to offer programs leading to the doctoral degree in clinical psychology (Ph.D). Today, there are many universities offering such programs. These programs are constantly undergoing revision as a result of discussion based on experience and research findings, but in the main the Ph.D. program involves approximately four to five years of graduate training, including personality and behavior theory, research, and clinical experience.

All psychologists, including the clinician, are expected to be psychologists first. This means that they must receive training in the major areas of psychology: statistical methods, research methods, learning theory, motivational theory, sensory and perceptual theory, and the physiological background of behavior. They are expected to acquire substantial knowledge in these areas as well as understanding of the theoretical issues. They receive training in the specialized domain of clinical psychology. This includes courses and seminars in diagnostic methods, psychotherapeutic theory and practice, developmental psychology, personality theory, and psychopathology. In addition to field practice given in conjunction with their courses, they are required to complete a year's internship with diagnostic and therapeutic experience under carefully supervised conditions. And finally, they must complete a dissertation based on research to demonstrate competency in this area. Following the completion of the degree, and with the acquisition of further suitable clinical experience, they may apply for examination for diplomate status to the American Board of Examiners in Professional Psychology and take the oral and written tests required for this kind of certification. They may also apply for certification or licensing in their own state (twenty-five states now have legal provisions of this kind).

Clinical psychologists may practice independently, do either diagnostic or therapeutic work or both, and engage in research. Their basic training differs from all other professional workers in the mental health field in several important respects, among which training in research procedures, personality theory, general psychological theory, and psychological methods of assessment are particularly relevant. Unlike psychiatrists and most psychoanalysts, they do not have any specific medical training and are unable to prescribe drugs or offer somatic treatment. They more frequently work with relatively less disturbed people (especially in school systems and in community clinics with adults), but they also work with patients who are severely psychoneurotic or even psychotic.

As might be expected on the basis of their training, clinical psychologists tend to be much more diverse in their approach than most workers in the mental health field. Some emphasize learning theory in their therapeutic approach, others may follow psychoanalytic approaches, and still others follow approaches based on perceptual theories. They vary widely in their utilization of psychological tests [75]. Increasingly, many attend post-doctoral institutes of different kinds to improve their clinical skills and keep abreast of new findings.

THE PSYCHIATRIC SOCIAL WORKER Growing out of the wide scope of social-work activities, there developed the specialization known as psychiatric social work. Such workers have been employed in a wide variety of social agencies but most commonly have functioned in mental hygiene or psychiatric clinics, departments of psychiatry in hospitals, and in family service agencies.

Their professional training, leading to a Master's degree in social work with a subspecialty in psychiatric social work, is typically a two-year program beyond the bachelor's degree. This training includes course work in such subjects as casework process, personality development, and psychopathology. They are required to have a year's field work in an appropriate psychiatric agency as part of their training. This training is noteworthy for the close liaison between the school of social work and the agencies providing the field-work experience. The supervised casework experience is of high quality, and there is close supervision of the trainees. In recent years some schools have offered additional graduate training, often in conjunction with departments of psychology and psychiatry, leading to a Ph.D. degree in social work. This program places emphasis upon research in psychiatric social-work problems.

The psychiatric social worker, in the past, was usually a member of the psychiatric team, usually with a psychiatrist and a clinical psychologist. In such roles they have worked with the senior psychotherapist, taking on responsibility for one member of the family while the senior psychotherapist assumed a therapeutic role with another—usually the more critically disturbed member. Sometimes, especially in child guidance or mental health clinics, they have assumed the entire therapeutic task. Frequently they limit their role to assisting patients to deal with environmental problems more effectively or to reduce the severity of their conflicts through emotional support and acceptance, catharsis, and a minimal amount of interpretative work. By virtue of their relatively limited training and responsibility, they have been keenly aware of their own limitations in uncovering deeply repressed material and have referred patients needing more intensive therapy to more qualified therapists. In more recent years the scope of their therapeutic work has increased. Some psychiatric social workers have established themselves in independent practice, most frequently in group practice. In some social agencies the major role assigned to such workers, however, has been in providing service for the intake of patients and in preparing a psychiatric social-work history to assist the therapist.

THE PSYCHIATRIC NURSE   The field of psychiatric nursing is changing rapidly, so that statements made about it today will probably be inaccurate within a few years. At the present time, training programs in nursing vary markedly from one state to another. There are two basic paths to accreditation as a nurse. One involves a three-year program in an accredited training institution in which practical training as a nurse, plus course work, leads to a diploma in nursing. Attendance in college is not required. Registration as a nurse is dependent upon passing an examination given by the state nursing board. The other involves a college program of four or five years in a nursing school and leads to a degree in general nursing.

Psychiatric nursing is learned in an apprenticeship setting, usually in a psychiatric hospital. Sometimes there is also a formal program involving courses and seminars which offer training in interview methods, adjustment, and psychopathology. The basic principles of individual and group psychotherapy are also taught.

The psychiatric nurse is expected to minister to the patient's physical needs but to be aware, at the same time, of the implications of the patient's behavior from a therapeutic viewpoint. She must be able to communicate effectively with the patient, offer emotional support when needed, report to the physician or psychiatrist evidence of significant behavior, and carry out the regime of psychiatric nursing care on the ward that is prescribed for the patient's benefit. Quite often she is the first person to become aware of important changes in the patient's behavior. These might, in some instances, lead to attempts at suicide or to violent "acting-out" of conflicts. She might have to take emergency steps in such situations and then report the behavior to the physician in charge.

The nursing profession is constantly evaluating its training program and attempting to make it more effective.

COMMENTS ABOUT MENTAL HEALTH PERSONNEL   It should be obvious that all types of mental health workers share some common attributes. For example, they all have to learn the significance of various types of disturbed personality reactions, they all must learn to listen attentively and supportively, they must know when to encourage or to limit the expression of emotional material, and they all have to be able to respond in terms of the patient's therapeutic needs. The lines of demarcation between the skills employed by the several disciplines are, in many instances, quite hazy. The lines of responsibility may more often be fixed by tradition and awareness of status than by skill or competence. Although there are some obvious and apparently important differences in skill, training, and length of instruction, it becomes an empirical question to determine how significant these differences—and others—are in relation to therapeutic effectiveness. We are a long way from knowing the answers to this question, and one of the factors that tends to impede accumulation of research evidence along such lines is, quite frankly, that of "vested interests." Although we believe that differences in training and careful methods of certification and licensing are very important, we don't know if this is the complete solution to the problem.

Aside from differences in training, there are also apparently important differences among the professions in selection of candidates. Some professions require college graduation or even postcollege education before specialized training is offered. Completion of such training is probably significantly correlated with level of intelligence, with habits of disciplined study, motivation for success and status, and with other personality variables. The mental health field must be as candid about such matters as it asks patients to be in their psychotherapeutic sessions. It should examine itself critically and be willing to assess the importance of current standards and practices by adequate research methods. Fortunately there are many signs that significant portions of the membership of all the mental health professions are alert to such issues and are seeking to initiate programs for such evaluations.

References

1. Mowrer, O. H. Biological vs. moral "frustration" in the causation of personality disturbance. Chapter 20 in O. H. Mowrer, *Learning Theory and Personality Dynamics.* New York: Ronald, 1950.
2. Rioch, M. J., *et al.* National Institute of Mental Health pilot study in training mental health counselors *Amer. J. Orthopsychiat.,* 1963, **33,** 678–689.
3. Levy, D. M. Release therapy. *Amer. J. Orthopsychiat.,* 1939, **96,** 713–736.
4. Rogers, C. R. Psychotherapy today or where do we go from here? *Amer. J. Psychother.,* 1963, **17,** 5–16.
5. Alexander, F. The dynamics of psychotherapy in the light of learning theory. *Amer. J. Psychiat.,* 1963, **120,** 440–448.
6. Wolpe, J. *Psychotherapy by Reciprocal Inhibition.* Stanford, Calif.: Stanford Univ. Press, 1958.
7. Kubie, L. S. Medical responsibility for training in clinical psychology. *J. clin. Psychol.,* 1949, **5,** 94–100.
8. Rogers, C. R. *Client-Centered Therapy.* Boston: Houghton Mifflin, 1951.
9. Perls, F., Hefferline, R. F., & Goodman, P. *Gestalt Therapy.* New York: Julian Press, 1951.
10. Menninger, K. *Theory of Psychoanalytic Technique.* (Men-

ninger Clin. Monogr. Series, No. 12.) New York: Basic Books, 1958.

11. Alexander, F. *Fundamentals of Psychoanalysis.* New York: Norton, 1948.
12. Bychowski, G. *Psychotherapy of Psychosis.* New York: Grune & Stratton, 1952.
13. Wexler, M. The structural problem in schizophrenia: The role of the internal object. In E. B. Brody & F. C. Redlich (Eds.) *Psychotherapy with Schizophrenics.* New York: International Universities Press, 1952.
14. Fenichel, O. *Problems of Psychoanalytic Technique.* Albany: Psychoanalytic Quarterly, 1941.
15. Rank, O. *The Trauma of Birth.* New York: Robert Bruner, 1952.
16. Rank, O. *Will Therapy and Truth and Reality.* New York: Knopf, 1947.
17. Allen, F. H. *Psychotherapy with Children.* New York: Norton, 1942.
18. Taft, J. *The Dynamics of Therapy.* New York: Macmillan, 1933.
19. Sullivan, H. S. *The Interpersonal Theory of Psychiatry.* New York: Norton, 1953.
20. Fromm-Reichmann, F. *Principles of Intensive Psychotherapy.* Chicago: Univ. Chicago Press, 1950.
21. Heider, F. *The Psychology of Interpersonal Behavior.* New York: Wiley, 1958.
22. Ansbacher, H. L., & Ansbacher, R. R. (Eds.). *Superiority and Social Interest: A Collection of Later Writings of Alfred Adler.* Evanston, Ill.: Northwestern Univ. Press, 1964.
23. Berman, L. A. The projective interpretation of early recollections. Unpublished doctoral dissertation, University of Michigan, 1957.
24. Rogers, C. R. *Counseling and Psychotherapy.* Boston: Houghton Mifflin, 1942.
25. Rogers, C. R. *Client-Centered Therapy.* Boston: Houghton Mifflin, 1951.
26. Rogers, C. R., & Dymond, R. F. (Eds.). *Psychotherapy and Personality Change.* Chicago: Univ. Chicago Press, 1954.
27. Snygg, D., & Combs, A. W. *Individual Behavior: A New Frame of Reference for Psychology.* New York: Harper & Row, 1949.
28. Raimy, V. C. Self-reference in counseling interviews. *J. consult. Psychol.,* 1948, **12,** 153–163.
29. Cartwright, R. D., & Lerner, B. Empathy, need to change, and improvement with psychotherapy. *J. consult. Psychol.,* 1963, **27,** 138–144.
30. Truax, C. B. Effective ingredients in psychotherapy: An approach to unraveling the patient-therapist interaction. *J. counsel. Psychol.,* 1963, **10,** 256–163.

31. Dollard, J., & Miller, N. E. *Personality and Psychotherapy.* New York: McGraw-Hill, 1950.
32. Mowrer, O. H. *Learning Theory and Personality Dynamics.* New York: Ronald, 1950.
33. Dollard, J., Audl, F., & White, A. M. *Steps in Psychotherapy: Study of a Case of Sex-Fear Conflict.* New York: Macmillan, 1953.
34. Alexander, F. The dynamics of psychotherapy in the light of learning theory. *Amer. J. Psychother.,* 1963, **120,** 440–448.
35. Wolpe, J. Psychotherapy: The non-scientific heritage and the new science. *Behav. res. Ther.,* 1963, **1,** 23–28.
36. Wolpe, J. Quantitative relationships in the systematic desensitization of phobias. *Amer. J. Psychiat.,* 1963, **119,** 1062–1068.
37. Murray, E. J. Learning theory and psychotherapy: Biotropic versus sociotropic approaches. *J. counsel. Psychol.,* 1953, **10,** 250–255.
38. Eysenck, H. J. (Ed.). *Experiments in Behavior Therapy.* New York: Macmillan, 1964.
39. Wexler, M. The structural problem in schizophrenia: The role of the internal object. In E. B. Brody & F. C. Redlich (Eds.), *Psychotherapy with Schizophrenics.* New York: International Universities Press, 1952.
40. Eysenck, H. J. The effects of psychotherapy: An evaluation. *J. consult. Psychol.,* 1952, **16,** 319–324.
41. Gibby, R. G., Miller, D. R., & Walker, E. L. Examiner variance in the Rorschach protocols of neuropsychiatric patients. *Amer. Psychologist,* 1952, **7,** 337–338.
42. Holt, R. R., & Luborsky, L. *Personality Patterns of Psychiatrists.* New York: Basic Books, 1958.
43. Eckstein, R., & Wallerstin, R. S. *The Teachings and Learning of Psychotherapy.* New York: Basic Books, 1958.
44. Hutt, M. L. The effect of varied experimental "sets" upon Rorschach performance. *J. proj. Tech.,* 1950, **14,** 181–187.
45. Pratt, J. H. The principles of class treatment and their application to various chronic diseases. *Hosp. Soc. Service,* 1922, **6,** 401 ff.
46. Marsh, L. C. Group treatment of the psychoses by the psychological equivalent of revival. *Ment. Hyg., N. Y.,* 1931, **15,** 328–349.
47. Moreno, J. C. *Who Shall Survive?* New York: Nervous and Mental Disease Publishing Co., 1934.
48. Wender, L. Dynamics of group therapy. *J. nerv. & ment. Dis.,* 1936, **84,** 54–60.
49. Schilder, P. Results and problems of group therapy in severe neuroses. *Ment. Hyg., N.Y.,* 1939, **23,** 87–98.
50. Cartwright, D., & Zander, A. *Group Dynamics: Research and Theory.* New York: Harper & Row, 1953.

51. Lippitt, R., Watson, J., & Westley, B. *The Dynamics of Planned Change.* New York: Harcourt, Brace & World, 1958.
52. Slavson, S. R. *An Introduction to Group Therapy.* New York: Commonwealth Fund, 1943.
53. Klapman, J. W. *Group Therapy: Theory and Practice.* New York: Grune & Stratton, 1946.
54. Vitale, J. H. Mental hospital therapy: A review and integration. In J. H. Masserman (Ed.), *Current Psychiatric Therapies,* Vol. II. New York: Grune & Stratton, 1962.
55. Stanton, A. H., & Schwartz, M. S. *The Mental Hospital.* New York: Basic Books, 1954.
56. Jones, M. *The Therapeutic Community: A New Treatment Method in Psychiatry.* New York: Basic Books, 1953.
57. Caplan, G. (Ed.). *Prevention of Mental Disorders in Children: Initial Explorations.* New York: Basic Books, 1961.
58. Bach, G. R. *Intensive Group Psychotherapy.* New York: Ronald, 1954.
59. Corsini, R. J. *Methods of Group Psychotherapy.* Chicago: William James Press, 1964.
60. Fox, V. Group methods in criminology. *Group Psychother.,* 1962, **15,** 40–55.
61. Cabeen, C. W. & Coleman, J. C. Group therapy with sexual offenders: Description and evaluation of group therapy program in an institutionalized setting. *J. clin. Psychol.,* 1961, **17,** 122–129.
62. Frank, J. D., & Powdermaker, F. B. Group psychotherapy. In S. Arieti (Ed.), *American Handbook of Psychiatry,* Vol. II. New York: Basic Books, 1959.
63. Coffey, H. S. Group psychotherapy. In L. A. Pennington & I. A. Berg (Eds.), *An Introduction to Clinical Psychology.* (2nd ed.) New York: Ronald, 1954.
64. Slavson, S. R. (Ed.). *The Fields of Group Psychotherapy.* New York: International Universities Press, 1956.
65. Redl, F., & Wineman, D. *Controls from Within.* New York: Free Press, 1952.
66. Sakel, M. Insulintherapy and shock therapies. *Congr. int. Psychiat.,* 1950, **4,** 163 ff.
67. Bond, E. D., & Rivers, T. D. Insulin shock therapy after seven years. *Amer. J. Psychiat.,* 1944, **101,** 62.
68. Kalinowsky, L. B. Convulsive shock treatment. In S. Arieti (Ed.). *American Handbook of Psychiatry,* Vol. II. New York: Basic Books, 1959.
69. Hoch, P. Drug therapy. In S. Arieti (Ed.), *American Handbook of Psychiatry,* Vol. II. New York: Basic Books, 1959.
70. Kuhn, R. The treatment of depressive states with G 22355 (imipramine hydrochloride). *Amer. J. Psychiat.,* 1958, **115,** 459–464.
71. Lehmann, N. E., Cahn, C. H., & Verteull, R. L. The treat-

ment of depressive conditions with imipramine (G 22355). *Canad. psychiat. Assoc.,* 1958, **3,** 155–164.

72. Klebanoff, G. S., Singer, J. L., & Wilensky, H. Psychological consequences of brain lesions and ablations. *Psychol. Bull.,* 1954, **51,** 1.

73. Freeman, W. Psychosurgery. In S. Arieti (Ed.), *American Handbook of Psychiatry,* Vol. II. New York: Basic Books, 1959.

74. Kubie, L. J. Elements in the medical curriculum which are essential in the training for psychotherapy. In L. J. Kubie (Chairman) *Training in Clinical Psychology.* New York: Josiah Macy, Jr. Foundation, 1947.

75. Rubinstein, E. A., & Lorr, M. (Eds.). *Survey of Clinical Practice in Psychology.* New York: International Universities Press, 1954.

EIGHT ASSESSMENT: INTRA- AND INTERPERSONAL BEHAVIOR

General Problems

Throughout this book we were constantly confronted with two basic methodological problems: (1) How can we construct adequate definitions of behavioral variables? (2) Assuming adequate definitions of variables, how can we assess them with reliability and validity? In this chapter we shall examine these questions in details. We shall consider both individual and group variables. We shall concentrate on definitions and assessment problems for the "individual variable" of intelligence, such personality variables as "dependence," and "ego strength," and the "interpersonal variable" of "attitudes."

We have indicated at numerous points throughout this book that a behavioral variable is really nothing more than hypothesis about behavior. Such variables can be conceptualized in terms of measurable overt behavior, or in terms of covert factors which are *inferred* from directly observed behavior. In either case, we first need to define clearly the behavior to be observed. Having done so, we make the assumption that the observations or measurements tell us something about the variable presumably being studied.

If we wish to measure an individual's intelligence, we must have at least a working definition of this variable. As will be noted later, this is not a simple matter. However, we should mention that the type of definition used determines the method or methods used for assessment. One might think of intelligence as a single attribute of the individual which can predict behavior in certain types of situations. Samples of behavior are obtained, each of which is thought to be an indicator of "intelligence." The more samples of intelligent behavior the individual manifests, the more likely is the person to possess a high level of intelligence. Holding such a view, a test for intelligence could be merely a collection of tasks, such as solutions to problems or answers to questions. The tasks would be chosen so that their solution required "intelligence," and one might simply add up the number of tasks correctly solved.

On the other hand, intelligence can be viewed as a quality of mental functioning. That is, one could hold that the more intelligent person approaches problems differently than the less intelligent person. Therefore, assessment of intelligence requires making judgments as to the quality of mental processes within the individual. Such judgments require the obtaining of behavioral samples, but they are used as a basis for inference about more complex mental phenomena rather than as samples of intelligence in themselves.

If the above analysis seems complicated, we should be aware that the problem is actually even more complicated. Another knotty issue relates to the question of whether behavioral variables *exist within the individual* or are the result of *an interaction of factors in the individual and his environment.*

This issue can be seen more readily in relation to personality variables such as "dependence," although it is also relevant in relation to presumably intrapersonal variables such as "intelligence." We know that "dependent behavior" is determined by the person and the total situation. In other words, this variable, and many other personality variables, can be conceived of as determined by the interaction of an individual with his environment rather than as simply an individual characteristic [1, 2].

Still another general consideration should be noted. The measurement of any behavior variable is significantly affected by the observer (or examiner) making the assessment. This problem is really directly related to the more general problem of the interaction of the individual with his environment, but it deserves special attention. We must take into account the possible influence of the observer who is measuring the behavior under observation. In other words, measurement of behavioral phenomena cannot be conceived of as a mechanical procedure in which the obtained results are independent of the observer. Rather, the observer, no matter how hard he may try to be an inconspicuous or insignificant part of the environment, is a *participating observer* and is influencing the phenomenon being assessed.

A few examples of the influence of the participating observer may make this point more meaningful. In the case of both "objective" and "projective" tests of personality (see pp. 765–777) the results may be significantly influenced by the personality of the examiner [3, 4], even though the administration of the test is "standardized." When intelligence tests are administered, the motivation of the examinees, and hence the test results, are influenced by the kind of examiner administering the test [5]. When standard interviewing procedures are used, the obtained results, and therefore the inferences made about the interviewees, vary as a function of the color of the interviewer's skin, his economic status (as inferred from the interviewer's appearance), and other personal attributes [6, 7]. Thus, results of assessment are influenced, sometimes very little, sometimes greatly, by the appearance and behavior of the examiner.

We should stress, once more, that the assessment of any personality characteristic is closely related to theories about the characteristic itself. Behavior should not be observed without certain formal or implicit theoretical assumptions. Adequate evaluations of data about assessment cannot be made without consideration of the underlying theoretical models upon which the procedures are predicated. These models must involve both theories about the variable and theories of its assessment.

Now, perhaps, the reasons for sampling the three types of attributes will be more meaningful. We shall consider "intelligence" first, as an example of an intra-individual attribute. Then we shall discuss the measurement of social-personality attributes. Finally, we shall discuss group and social-behavior phenomena, such as political behavior, as examples of interpersonal attributes. In each case, we shall try to make explicit certain assumptions about the definition and measurement of the variable so that the phenomena in question may themselves be more fully comprehended.

The Assessment of Intelligence: Background

The approach to the problem of assessing "general intelligence" illustrates some of the issues we have been discussing. Although the nature of intelligence has been long and exhaustively studied, there is still no universal agreement as to whether it is best conceptualized as a single attribute of the person or as a cluster of several independent attributes. As we shall see, the specific methods which have been utilized to assess intelligence were influenced by assumptions held by those devising the instruments. Tests that have been developed to measure this phenomenon reflect these differing assumptions and theories.

We shall also note how prevailing cultural attitudes significantly influence developments in theory and methods. More specifically, the needs of a society affect the approach which the scientist uses in attacking a problem. In the case of intelligence tests, Alfred Binet developed his test of intelligence because society required some method for selecting "slow learners," who could then be offered different kinds of educational treatment.

BINET'S CONTRIBUTIONS   In 1905 Binet and Simon published a Metrical Scale of Intelligence, which is usually thought to represent the turning point in the development of measures of intellectual capacities. For Binet this contribution was actually but one more paper on the general problem of evaluating intelligence of children. He had been working on this assessment problem for many years. His 1905 contribution reflects an interesting convergence of work in assessment which was influenced by diverse contemporary social factors.

Before Binet's work a number of approaches to the nature and assessment of intelligence had been investigated. These included the measurement of reaction time and many other kinds of rudimentary indices of physiological reactivity. These simple quasiphysiological indicators were thought to be measures of some quality of efficiency of the entire nervous system and therefore to represent an index of the efficiency of mental activity. They reflected the prevailing spirit of the psychological laboratories in Germany. These laboratories were dedicated to a physiological orientation in studying psychological phenomena. It was believed that investigation of the most uncomplicated behavioral phenomena was the most promising approach to the scientific study of human behavior. It is doubtless true that much of present-day psychology was strongly influenced by this German tradition. However, this dedication to investigation of the simplest aspects of behavior limited the types of tests used to evaluate mental efficiency. Unfortunately, these simple measures of physiological responsiveness failed to correlate with generally accepted criteria of intellectual ability, i.e., intelligence as rated on the basis of accomplishment and on the basis of the age of the person tested (it is assumed that older children have more intellectual ability than younger ones).

Binet's approach to the problem of finding a method to determine intelligence was not strongly influenced by the prevalent Germanic traditions in experimental psychology since his training had been clinical rather than academic. His early professional experiences were obtained in working with patients in a neurological clinic. His professional traditions were French rather than German, and, as luck would have it, he did not read a word of German. Consequently, most of the German psychological and philosophical literature was not readily available to him.

On the other hand, because of his fluent English, Binet was able to read the contributions of the school of philosophers known as the British Associationists. These men also furnished the roots of the modern theories of learning. In any case, in Alfred Binet we find a merger of many sources—influences from French medicine, influences from the British philosophers, and, perhaps surprisingly, influences from the field of law. Binet had received formal training in law and received a degree in this subject. His interest in medicine stemmed from a long family tradition. He had become interested in the work in hypnotism being done by Charcot and had worked in Charcot's laboratory doing research in abnormal psychology. Coincidentally, as we noted in a previous chapter, this same laboratory had an early and profound effect upon the theoretical formulations of Sigmund Freud.

Binet gradually became interested in studying the differences in degrees of brightness of children. He had embarked on a research program to measure intellectual activity in children ten years before he published the Metrical Scale of Intelligence. Unhampered by the restrictive views of the "tidy science" of the German laboratories, and relying upon his own clinical experience and intuition, he started programs aimed at evaluating not only memory but the vividness of memory, the span and nature of attention, and the ways in which people use images, among other things. His assessment techniques were aimed at finding indices of underlying characteristics believed to exist in everyone. Since he knew that many kinds of mental activity occurred, why not measure them and find which ones were related to intellectual capacity? This is just what he set out to do.

Due to his many contributions in child psychology, Binet was chosen to be on a commission established by the Minister of Public Instruction of France to consider the problem of selecting children for special training who had less than average intelligence. The actual report of the commission was vague, and this probably acted as a spur to Binet, who devoted the remainder of his life to developing tests which would be effective predictors of learning in school. As his work progressed through countless hours of examining and interviewing children, many items were added and then eliminated from the formal test developed by Binet and Simon. Theoretical considerations were minimal, and the ever-present criterion of usefulness became paramount. Items were selected for inclusion if they helped to discriminate the bright from the dull children or if they differentiated older ones from younger ones. Thus there was almost no attempt to preselect specific types of items on some general theoretical basis. Items were included which tapped all kinds of mental characteristics. The Binet test was essentially designed for the specific educational purpose of selecting mentally retarded school children.

MENTAL AGE   One of Binet's contributions was the development of the concept of mental age. His rationale for the concept of mental age was approximately the following. Given a pool, or collection, of items of varying difficulty, it is found that older children will answer more of them correctly than younger children. This allows the items to be ordered by categories of increasing difficulty. Items which all of the tested children can answer correctly would represent the easiest end of the scale. Items which none of them could answer would represent the most difficult. Furthermore, the items can be examined to determine which can be answered by children of a given age (assuming all are in the same academic grade). With this information it is then possible to evaluate the mental ability of an individual child on the basis of the items which he can answer correctly. To do this, the entire test is given to a child. Then one determines which items are failed and which are passed, and an "age level" is then established for the child.

For example, let us assume that we have given the test to a seven-year-old child and have found that he can answer all of the questions that are usually passed by seven-year-old children. We might also find that he could pass all of the questions usually answered by eight-year-old children and some of the questions answered by nine-year-old children. Therefore, his mental abilities would be slightly better than that of the average eight-year-old child. Binet suggested that this evaluation could be called "mental age." Arbitrarily, a child's mental age would be determined by the highest level of questions he could pass that were typically passed by children of a specific chronological age. Furthermore, as a more precise criterion, he specified that a child would be assigned a mental age which corresponded to that age category in which he could pass at least 50 percent of the questions. If the boy in our example could pass half of the nine-year-old questions, his mental age would be estimated as nine years. If he could pass less than half of these items but half or more of the eight-year-old items, he would be assigned a mental age of eight years. Therefore, the use of mental tests such as that developed by Binet results in a mental-age score which is used as an indicator of the child's mental accomplishment. Table 8.1 illustrates the calculation of the mental age for three individuals.

It should be noted that mental age is a measure of actual intellectual attainment. It tells what level of functioning on

TABLE 8.1. THREE EXAMPLES OF BINET'S METHOD OF OBTAINING THE MENTAL AGE

Test Items Arranged in Order of Ascending Difficulty	Year Level of Items	Passes and Failures by Item		
		Child A (7 yrs.)	Child B (7 yrs.)	Child C (11 yrs.)
1		+	+	+
2		+	+	+
3	7	+	+	+
4		+	+	+
5		+	+	+
6		+	+	+
7		+	+	+
8	8	+	+	+
9		+	+	+
10		+	+	+
11		+	+	+
12		−	+	+
13	9	−	+	+
14		−	+	−
15		−	−	−
16		−	−	−
17		−	−	−
18	10	−	−	−
19		−	−	−
20		−	−	−

+ = Item Passed
− = Item Failed

Child A obtains a mental age of slightly more than 8 years (Bright)
Child B obtains a mental age of about 9 years (Bright)
Child C obtains a mental age of about 9 years (Dull)

mental tasks the individual is able to reach. By using the chronological age of the examined individual as a point of reference, we can get an idea of his relative superiority or inferiority. Returning to our example, if a child of seven years reaches the nine-year level on a mental test, we consider him to be "bright." If a nine-year-old has a mental age of nine, we consider him "average." If an eleven-year-old attains a mental age of nine, we consider him "dull."

INTELLIGENCE QUOTIENT Since mental age is a measure of level of accomplishment, it must be considered in relation to chronological age to obtain a measure of relative accomplishment or "degree of brightness." This was what we did, of course, in the preceding paragraph in a crude way. Another way of doing the same thing and of obtaining a quantitative measure of degree of brightness is to obtain the ratio of the mental age to the chronological age. This would give a measure of a person's relative intellectual accomplishment for his age and would give us a numerical value. For example, if a boy of seven years had a mental age of nine, this ratio would be $9/7$ and would represent the numerical value of 1.29. We can remove the decimal point in this ratio by multiplying it by 100. We would then have what is conventionally called an intelligence quotient. This quotient would be 129. Similarly, for a boy with a mental age of nine and a chronological age of twelve, the intelligence quotient would be $9/12 \times 100$, or 75. The intellectual quotient, or I.Q., score can be represented in symbolic terms as follows:

$$\frac{\text{M.A.}}{\text{C.A.}} \times 100 = \text{I.Q.}$$

where M.A. stands for mental age and C.A. stands for chronological age.

Several things should be noted about such scores. First, they are measures of intellectual brightness, inasmuch as they represent accomplishment relative to age. Second, since the level of mental accomplishment is always divided by the factor of chronological age, the obtained quotient *could* be relatively constant over time, providing relative mental accomplishment remained constant over time. Whether it is or is not a matter for empirical research will be discussed. Third, the score is dependent upon some measure of mental age. Therefore, the method used to assess mental age is of vital importance. There are many kinds of tests which provide estimates of mental age, and different tests might provide different measures of mental age. One should always include the name or type of test that was utilized in the statement of the obtained I.Q. score.

The computation of an I.Q. score is usually done quite differently today from the earlier procedure, which used the original I.Q. formula noted above—to which there are several objections. In the first place, the I.Q. score was used to predict an individual's mental age at later stages in his development. This procedure made the assumption that rate of mental development is contant—an assumption that has been shown to be unwarranted. Moreover, the ratio assumes a number of characteristics in the two factors in the ratio; chief among these is the assumption that the units of mental age are equivalent for the entire range of mental development. This assumption has been shown to be untenable. And, finally, the formula is inapplicable at the upper age levels when, because of the shape of the mental-growth curve, mental-age units no longer increase proportionately with chronological age. For these and other reasons, the individual's intelligence test score is nowadays referred to a specially developed table (for each intelligence test) that permits comparison of his score with a distribution of scores on the test made by other individuals of his own age. The I.Q. score is then derived from the table. This type of procedure tends to avoid some of the problems involved in the old method.

MENTAL TESTS IN AMERICA   The approach to assessing intelligence by Binet and Simon was further developed in the United States by Terman at Stanford University. In 1916 he published the first version of what is now a most well-known *individual intelligence test,* called the Stanford-Binet Intelligence Scale. This test was revised in 1937 and again in 1960. This was necessary to improve the predictive capacities of the instrument and to revise some of the tests items because of social and cultural changes occurring in these intervals. It has been learned that responses to "intelligence test items" are influenced by such factors. Consequently, they must be selected so as to be applicable to specific social-cultural conditions.

There is little doubt that the United States is the most "test-conscious" country in the world today. The popularity of mental tests in this country increased sharply during the period of World War I, largely in response to the needs of the military forces to select and train soldiers for jobs in the military services. It was during this war that the first *group intelligence scale,* the Army Alpha, was developed. A similar impetus to the development came from the educators who were instrumental in fostering the development of a group intelligence test for children, the National Intelligence Test, following the war. Moreover, this development was probably based, in turn, on the attitudes which prevailed in the United States. Testing for ability seemed congruent with the belief that efficiency and hardheaded practicality are essential in life and especially in business. To many, therefore, psychological evaluation represented a method of extending practicality into the management of human affairs. Today, people are evaluated by many kinds of tests for many types of traits and characteristics. They have become the indispensable tool for an assessment-oriented culture.

The most widely assessed psychological characteristic is intelligence. We shall, therefore, discuss some of the critical issues concerning the concept of intelligence and its measurement.

Intelligence: General Considerations

DEFINITIONS McNemar has suggested, with tongue in cheek, that no definition of intelligence is really necessary, since everyone knows it is "the thing the other guy lacks." [8]. This attitude concerning the nature of intelligence is not new. Many years ago another psychologist put it this way: "Intelligence is what intelligence tests test." In short, psychologists have not been able to agree on a definition of the term "intelligence." This may seem surprising, since there has been more work done with psychological tests purporting to measure intelligence than in any other area of behavioral research. On the other hand, the obvious lack of agreement in defining intelligence may obscure a fairly basic agreement regarding the nature of the concept. This is probably the case, since there are certain things that we expect people of superior intelligence to do better, or more frequently, than less intelligent ones. Current intelligence tests are correlated with and predict, with fair accuracy, the rate of academic progress, the level of general scholastic ability, and even many aspects of vocational and professional success. In other words, intelligence tests tend to do those things which we expect them to do if they were measuring something called intelligence. Such facts support the view that, despite the difficulty in providing a universally acceptable and scientifically precise definition, most of us tend to "understand" the term reasonably well. There is still the question whether what we think intelligence tests test is the "real" phenomenon of intelligence.

The lack of formal agreement on the word intelligence stems in part from the fact that different psychologists tend to hold quite different views about its theoretical properties. One major group of psychologists believes that it represents a general trait of mental ability. Another group holds that intelligence is not one kind of general intellectual ability but is, in fact, only a catchall phrase that represents, poorly at best, a collection of highly specific psychological abilities. This latter group argues (1) that the term intelligence should be abandoned, since it only leads to the misconception that there is some general trait (intelligence), and (2) that the predictive usefulness of a total score, like the I.Q., is less powerful or useful than predictions made from each of the specific mental qualities that go into the total score. This argument is often called the "one versus the many." The controversy has a long history and is still very active. Later in the chapter, when discussing modern developments in research in assessment techniques, we shall return to this issue (pp. 743–746). For the present, however, we should note that this type of controversy has made it difficult to establish a general definition of intelligence.

THE CONSTANCY OF INTELLIGENCE   Since the I.Q. score is a ratio of ability to age, it is possible that this measure might remain constant over a number of years. This would indicate, presumably, that a person's intellectual brightness is also fairly constant. In general there are two ways in which such a constancy could be exhibited. In the first, a group of people could be evaluated on tests yielding an I.Q. score; this group could then be retested over the course of years to determine whether the I.Q. score of these people remained constant. In the second, instead of measuring the same group repeatedly, it might be possible to compare *equivalent* groups of people at different times; the major problem in using this method would be to obtain equivalent groups.

Generally speaking, the correlation in obtained I.Q. for the same group of subjects retested over a period of time reveals a fairly high degree of relationship. There is less constancy in I.Q. for groups of brighter people than for the duller ones [9]. The degree of correlation also depends upon several other factors, such as the time interval between tests and the age of the subjects when first tested. Scores on intelligence tests given during infancy or early childhood are notoriously poor predictors of later intelligence level.

From the data available it appears that various patterns of change in intelligence test scores are found in individuals retested many times in long-term studies [10]. Some individuals show gradual improvement over the years. Others show gradual decline over similar periods. Still others show irregular patterns. Some individuals, of course, show relatively constant scores.

The basic question is, What factor or factors contribute to the relative constancy or variability in I.Q. over a span of years? It would be a happy event if changes in measured intelligence could be associated with significant changes in the environment of the persons being measured. Considerable evidence has been accumulated purporting to demonstrate the influence of favorable social-psychological environments in improving the rate of intellectual development and of unfavorable factors in depressing this rate. Although this evidence is highly important, some investigators have not found such corresponding alterations [11]. The issue is by no means a closed matter. Many psychologists believe that as we obtain more knowledge of the relationship between personality functions and measured intelligence we will better be able to isolate the important environmental correlates of changes in brightness.

The problem of determining the constancy of I.Q. scores is significant for two reasons. First of all, if the results of intelligence-testing are to be utilized in educational planning and counseling, there must be a firm basis for the assumption that a current measure of intelligence has predictive validity for the future. In the second place, if I.Q. scores remain constant over the years despite variability in environmental conditions, this finding would lend support to the position that intelligence is a genetically determined, unitary trait. It is to the second point that we shall now turn our attention.

GENETIC INFLUENCES Men have long been interested in the extent to which their intellectual capacities are determined by genetic factors and the extent to which they are determined by environmental factors. As we have indicated, the issue has not been resolved. The argument continues, and protagonists for each side are able to cite empirical evidence to support their positions. One of the reasons the debate has continued without resolution is the difficulty of obtaining well-controlled observations of subjects of known genetic backgrounds tested at the same time and at the same ages who have lived under well-defined environmental conditions. Thus, research study has been piled upon research study, but they differ significantly in population and controls. The studies that provide evidence for the greater influences of heredity are found to have certain "fatal flaws" when examined by proponents of the environmentalist camp, and vice versa.

The history of research on the inheritance of mental ability can be traced back for centuries. One of the more interesting studies was that made by Francis Galton in the nineteenth century. Galton was a grandson of Erasmus Darwin and the cousin of Charles Darwin (an interesting example of three famous men in the same family occurring in three generations). He became interested in the observation that genius seemed to run in families. In his own highly creative work Galton developed a program to identify men who could be called "eminent." After establishing his criterion of eminence, he calculated the frequency of occurrence in the population at large. Using this figure as a baseline, he then looked for the frequency of occurrence in families in which one member had been identified as eminent. He found that the rate of achievement of eminence in such families was much higher than in the population at large. He also found that, the closer the family relation to the eminent man, the greater was the likelihood of becoming eminent. Galton recognized that this kind of study, by itself, was inconclusive, since those who were closest in relationship to the eminent man were most often the closest to him in a physical sense and thus might share in whatever effects a beneficial environment might provide. Thus, there would be a confounding of genetic and environmental factors.

One of the indications of the genius of Galton was his ability to find ways to test his hypothesis that genetic factors were important for attaining eminence. He accumulated evidence to show that the rate of attainment of eminence was no higher in America than in England, despite the higher educational levels in the United States. In a more unusual analysis he found that the adopted "children of the Pope," who were given every kind of educational and social advantage in the schools of the Vatican, achieved positions of eminence less frequently than did the relatives of eminent men. Another innovation of Galton's was his use of the study of twins. He recognized the difference between similar and dissimilar twins, although he did not have enough information to know that there were in fact two kinds of twins—identical and fraternal.

STUDIES OF FAMILIES The evaluation of genetic influences upon intelligence has usually taken advantage of the fact that identical twins have the same genetic material and that fraternal twins have more dissimilar genetic determinants than identical twins but are more alike than pairs of brothers or sisters. It was believed that comparison of the similarities of identical twins and of fraternal twins would demonstrate possible differences in genetic backgrounds. It should be noted that this argument assumes the presence of essentially similar environments, both in the uterus before birth and in the external world after birth, for both kinds of twins.

It would appear that both heredity and environment play important roles in determining the measured intelligence of an individual. Research findings indicate that the differences in measures of intelligence are greater for fraternal than for identical twins and that certain types of performances required on intelligence tests are more greatly influenced by heredity than other types of performance [12]. Another finding is that the correlation between the intelligence scores of adopted children and the scores of their "true" parents is greater than the correlation between their scores and those of their adoptive parents [13]. The correlation of an adopted child's intelligence test score and his true mother's intelligence level remains relatively constant despite the fact that the absolute intelligence scores of the children exceed the absolute scores of their mothers [14]. The fact that the children's scores are higher may reflect the effect of a more favorable environment for the development of the child's intellectual capacities.

The size of the obtained correlation depends upon the relative similarities in environmental experiences to which children are subjected. For example, it has been shown that when *unrelated children* are adopted into the same home, their intelligence test scores correlate about .65 [15]. This degree of correlation is comparable to that of siblings reared together [16]. It is also close to the size of correlation usually reported for fraternal twins [16]. It should also be noted that, in the study cited above [14], it was found that when foster children were adopted into homes that were superior in socioeconomic status to that of their true parents, the correlation in intelligence test scores between these children and those of their true parents was .00. When siblings are reared apart, their intelligence test scores are much lower than when they are reared together [15]. Finally, it should be noted that a favorable environment is reflected in the gradual increase in measured intel-

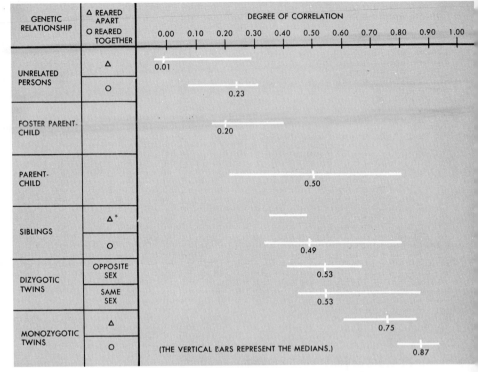

FIGURE 8.1 *Medians and ranges in correlation coefficients for "intelligence" test scores from 52 studies. Asterisk indicates insufficient studies to obtain a median. Adapted from L. Erlenmeyer-Kimling & L. F. Jarvik. Genetics and intelligence: a review. Science, 1963, 142, no. 3595, p. 1478. Copyright 1963 by the American Association for the Advancement of Science.*

ligence; this has been found in Negro children who moved to the North from relatively poor environmental experiences in the South [17].

Such findings leave no doubt that environment plays an important role in the manifestations of intelligence as measured by our current tests. They suggest, too, that the effectiveness with which an individual functions is significantly influenced by the experiences to which he is subjected—especially experiences during the formative periods of his life.

Another important question is whether or not there are genetically established differences between Negroes and whites. This issue has not been completely settled. There are reports which show consistent, although minor, differences among the racial groups [e.g., 18, 19]. Some psychologists believe that these small differences may represent genetic differences in psychological functions. The majority of psychologists believe, however, that these differences reflect the superior educational and family backgrounds of the white subjects tested. In any case, measured differences among racial groups produce such small differences in measured scores that they are insignificant when compared with the much larger variability within any racial or ethnic group.

Considering the problems inherent in establishing equivalent groups in terms of genetic makeup as well as in terms of favorable educational and emotional environments, it would seem that any attempt to establish the relative contributions of the genetic or environmental contributions to intelligence would be futile. Perhaps the best way in which to view the problem would be to say that nature, in terms of the hereditary material, sets an upper limit of intellectual capacities which can be approximated more or less closely by more or less favorable environmental circumstances.

Figure 8.1 summarizes the findings of fifty-two studies in which correlation coefficients in intelligence were obtained for different types of genetic relationships.

The Dimensions of Intelligence

One question that has been a source of controversy among psychologists for many years, in fact since the pioneering work of Binet, is whether or not intelligence should be viewed as a "single dimension" of "behavioral effectiveness" or whether it should be viewed as a collection of many highly specific characteristics. As will be noted below, in our discussion of the tests commonly used to measure intelligence, most instruments have various subtests whose scores are "summed" to determine an overall index of intelligence. The mere existence of the subtests, which usually are made up of apparently similar tasks, reflects the view that there are separate kinds of abilities, each contributing in its own fashion to intelligent patterns of behavior.

Historically, Binet believed that intelligence was a very complex, multifactored ability and designed a test which had items of all kinds and varieties of tasks in the hope that, by using a large number of such items, the likelihood of sampling the appropriate dimensions of personality would be high. On the

743

other hand, Galton believed that intelligence was a unitary characteristic of the individual.

In England the psychologist Spearman argued for the concept of a general intelligence variable at the turn of the century. He called this global factor "g," although he did not maintain that this was the sum total of all intellectual abilities. This theory of a general intellectual ability was also dominant in American psychology until about 1938, at which time Thurstone attacked the concept of "g" by presenting evidence that no such global factor existed when the responses of individuals to a battery of tests were analyzed by a statistical method called "factor analysis" [20].

FACTOR ANALYSIS: THE METHOD   Factor analysis is a statistical procedure which can be used to obtain a description of sets of dimensions or factors which describe a given set of data in new ways (see pp. 573–578). Often these factors are thought to represent fundamental or basic dimensions on which people, or tasks, exist and which can only be observed by the use of special techniques. However, this is not warranted, and the results of factor analysis only produce a set of hypothetical factors derived mathematically from the data used in the analysis. Since they are derived by known mathematical procedures and their application is compatible with mathematical rules and assumptions, there is an appealing logical basis for the use of factor analysis. Nevertheless, there are many kinds of assumptions one can make about the mathematical models involved, and these assumptions make vast differences in the outcome of the analysis. Thus, there are many kinds of factor analyses, and on a logical basis there is little reason to prefer one over another. The important criterion of the factor-analytic method is its usefulness to us as students of behavior.

Despite the difficulties inherent in factor analyses, some psychologists believe that the factors produced by a given method represent psychological realities. The factors have been thought of as "entities"—primary, fundamental attributes of behavior. Other psychologists tend to think of factors only as more or less useful descriptive devices for understanding and cataloguing behavior. This latter, more conservative viewpoint seems to be more in keeping with the difficulties inherent in the final resolution and interpretation of the results obtained from the method.

All of the foregoing has had as its purpose the establishment of sufficient background to discuss a much debated issue about intelligence: Should intelligence be viewed as a single attribute of the person, or should it be viewed as a collection of independent attributes, each of which is significantly related to performance?

INTELLIGENCE: HOW MANY FACTORS?   The differences which exist among individuals in the expression of intelligent behavior have always been recognized. The question is, "How should these differences be expressed?" When factor analysis was developed, it was hoped that this method could be used to describe more perfectly the number and nature of dimensions on which intelligence is exhibited.

One of the earliest of the leaders in the mental test movement, Spearman, postulated a two-component theory of intelligence [21]. He believed that every person has a number of highly specific abilities but that there is a positive correlation among the specific abilities. This correlation among specific attributes was thought of as the second component, a general factor of mental ability which he labeled "g." Actually, there can be no doubt that each of us has developed highly specific techniques for dealing with our environments. These represent the highly specific characteristics described by Spearman. However, Spearman noted that there were families of abilities, usually clusters of similar specific abilities, which represented something more than the idiosyncratic sets of specific characteristics and something less than the "g" factor.

As noted above, it was in 1938 that an attack was seriously made upon Spearman's "g." In this year Thurstone presented data from factor analyses of intelligence tests which seemed to prove that a general factor, operating among specific factors, did not exist [20]. Thurstone found a set of factors which were like families of specific abilities. He called these factors the Primary Mental Abilities. Some of these factors were:

V = verbal comprehension
W = word fluency
N = numerical ability (speed and accuracy in simple arithmetic
    operations)
S = spatial relations
M = associative memory
P = perceptual speed
I = inductive reasoning

These factors have been found in many subsequent factor analyses and can be thought of as common dimensions among mental test results. However, Thurstone's factors were found to be correlated with each other [22], and of course it was just this sort of correlation among abilities which had been the basis of Spearman's "g." Furthermore, many other studies produced data from which it became apparent that some general correlation is usually found among the responses of subjects to batteries of intelligence test items. Thus, it is perhaps best to conclude that intelligent behavior can be thought of as existing at three levels:

1. Highly specific individual patterns of responses to specific situations.
2. Families, or groups, of specialized responses, as represented in Thurstone's Primary Mental Abilities.
3. A general factor representing the correlation among the more specific characteristics of levels 1 and 2.

Given these three levels of intelligence, one can then ask, "To what extent are measures at each of three levels useful in predicting behavior?" After examining the nature of samples of subjects used by different investigators, Hunt concluded that while the most specific factors (level 1) are seldom likely to be of use in predicting behavior, the group factors (level 2) tend to be more useful in older children and adults, whereas the general-ability factor (level 3) is more useful in young children [23]. Furthermore, it appears that we should not look upon the level 2 factors as indicative of any necessary, absolute, and unalterable dimensions of behavior. Rather, they would appear to be only more or less useful descriptive categories which may be modified over time through experience or training.

Some Widely Used Tests of General Mental Ability

A great many tests of intelligence have been developed since Binet's early instrument, and volumes would be needed to describe and evaluate them all. There are many technical factors that the psychologist considers in selecting a test, or a battery of tests, when evaluating an individual or a group. Careful evaluation of intelligence requires more than the proper administration of a "standard" test. The test must be suitable for the individual in terms of his social and cultural background, in terms of his age and intelligence level, and in terms of his general physical, sensory, and linguistic development. For example, the Stanford-Binet Scale would not be suitable for the intelligence evaluation of a foreign-born adult recently arrived in the United States because his linguistic and social experiences would be quite different from those upon whom this test was standardized. As another illustration, this test would not be suitable for a deaf or a blind individual, since it assumes normal sensory capacities and experiences.

Our purpose in this section will be to introduce the student to some widely used tests of mental ability and then to discuss some problems in their administration and interpretation.

CLASSIFICATION OF INTELLIGENCE TESTS   As we have already learned, tests may be designed for administration to individuals or to groups. Some tests can be used either way. Hence our first major categorization of such tests is: *individual vs. group*. The next general category involves the content of the tests. Some tests involve the use of language. They require comprehension of oral or written directions and the capacity to make oral or written responses. Other tests do not use verbal content. The subject responds to items which require perceptual discriminations, manipulation of objects and materials, and other nonverbal responses. Test instructions can be given in pantomime, although a limited use of oral explanation, of a very simple kind, may also be employed. Thus our second category of tests, based on content, is: *verbal vs. nonverbal* (or performance).

The third category of tests is based on the age and intelligence level of the subjects. Some tests are useful with people over a restricted range of age, while other tests attempt to measure individuals of widely varying ages. However, when a test is restricted to a specific range of ages (and hence to a restricted range in mental maturation), it may be classified on this basis. There are *infant tests, tests for children,* and *tests for adults.* Some tests, like the Stanford-Binet Scale, include materials suitable for a wide range of ages. Such tests may be called *wide-range* tests.

There are other categories of tests which are occasionally used. For example, since some tests emphasize speed of response while others emphasize power (level of attainment), tests may be categorized as *speed tests* or *power tests*. In   **747** general, the classification of a test tells us something about the population for which it is designed and something about its content or nature.

THE STANFORD-BINET INTELLIGENCE SCALE; L-M FORM   This is an *individual* intelligence test, essentially *verbal* in content, and applicable through the *age range* from two years, six months to eighteen years [24]. It is called the L-M form because it represents a combination of most of the better items from the 1937 edition of this scale, which contained two forms, L and M. It had been found that, with the passing of time, some of the items from the older scales were inappropriate because of changes in cultural conditions which were important for answering the questions correctly. Other items omitted were either too easy or too difficult. The 1960 edition was made up of the most discriminating and relevant items from the earlier scale. In standardizing the new form (testing the items for validity and age placement), 4,498 subjects were examined. Two criteria of objective validity were used: (1) an increase in the percentage of subjects passing the item with increasing age of the subjects; (2) high correlations of the separate items with the total test score.

The items of this scale are placed at "age levels," i.e., each item is placed at a year level for which it is appropriate in terms of difficulty. In the standardized administration of the test, the examiner begins his test with that age level at which he believes the subject can pass all of the items. He then continues his testing at higher age levels until he reaches that level at which the subject fails all of the items. The assumption is made that the subject would have passed all items from levels below the one at which he passed all items (the *basal age*) and would have failed all items above the level at which, in fact, he failed all items (sometimes called the *maximal age*). Thus the assumption that items are well ordered on the basis of mental age required to pass the items is an important one. If the examiner has reason to suspect that the assumption is not valid, he may test below the basal age or above the maximal age.

After the administration of the test has been completed, the examiner calculates the subject's I.Q. score. In the older editions of this test, the subject's mental age was first obtained by use of the following steps. Starting with the basal age, additions were calculated in terms of proportion of tests passed at higher age levels. Then, the usual formula for I.Q. (M.A./C.A. × 100) was applied. In the 1960 edition, however, conversion tables are provided for obtaining I.Q. scores from the raw score based on the number of items passed at different levels.

The content of the test varies at the different age levels. In part, this is inevitable with a scale that extends over a wide chronological age range and tests abilities from the lowest levels of brightness (*mental retardation*) to the highest levels of brightness (*very superior* or *genius*). In infancy, some mental functions have not emerged or are so primitive that they cannot be tested very effectively. According to Terman, at the upper age levels, intelligence is chiefly manifested in the ability to perform conceptual thinking. He therefore believed that language, which is "the shorthand of the higher thought processes," is "one of the most important determinants of the levels of the processes themselves" [9]. Therefore, at lower levels of chronological age, this important dimension of intelligence can only be inadequately tested.

Test content has been classified in many ways. A useful classification of test content was tentatively proposed by Porteus [25]. He grouped the items on the basis of the kinds of mental functions they seemed to measure. These are:

1. *Memory* (ability to repeat a series of digits, ability to repeat sentences of varying lengths, ability to reproduce visual designs, etc.)
2. *School attainments* (items involving arithmetic ability and reading)
3. *Verbal ability* (vocabulary, verbal reasoning, verbal comprehension, etc.)
4. *Common knowledge* (problems of fact; interpretation of pictures, ability to evaluate similarities among different concepts, detection of absurdities in pictures)
5. *Practical judgment and abilities* (tests of manipulative skill, ability on form boards, ability to draw, etc.)

The Stanford-Binet Scale is both verbal and nonverbal, although the relative contribution of each of these aspects varies at the different chronological age levels. McNemar, in attempting to construct a nonverbal test using the items from this scale, found that there were no truly nonverbal items, or almost none, at age levels VII, XI, and XIV, and that the test was essentially verbal [26]. As might be expected, the validity of the test, as judged in terms of specific predictive criteria, varies at the different age levels.

The primary purpose of this test, like the original test by Binet and Simon, was to predict progress in schoolwork. Extended research over the years has demonstrated that the test

FIGURE 8.2 *Administration of bead-chain test from the Stanford-Binet. The examiner first makes up a chain in a particular pattern using wooden beads of different shapes. He removes it from sight, and then asks the subject to reproduce the pattern from memory.*

does this very well. However, many psychologists have objected to the test as a measure of "general intelligence" precisely because it is essentially a scholastic-aptitude test; that is, it both samples and predicts scholastic ability [23]. In any case, its predictive validity for school accomplishment is limited at the lower age levels, and it has limitations with individuals who are not similar in cultural and educational background experience to the standardization group.

THE WECHSLER INTELLIGENCE SCALES These scales are among the most widely used individual intelligence tests in this country. They are based on different assumptions about the nature of intelligence and on different methods of test construction than the Stanford-Binet. Moreover, they came into being because of different needs. Whereas Terman was interested in predicting school performance, Wechsler was more interested in the usefulness of his test as a clinical instrument.

At present there are two Wechsler scales: the Wechsler Adult Intelligence Scale (commonly designated the WAIS) and the Wechsler Intelligence Scale for Children (commonly designated the WISC). These tests are outgrowths from and revisions of the original Wechsler-Bellevue Scale (1939) and the modified Wechsler-Bellevue Scale (1949). These earlier scales were intended primarily for adults, since it was felt that the Stanford-Binet was of limited usefulness in the adult range. More important, Wechsler wanted to develop a test that would be more useful in clinical practice. In such work it was often necessary to evaluate the level of intelligence of patients with quite diverse social-educational backgrounds, with limited use of the English language, and with various psychiatric and physical handicaps. One of the methods used to evaluate the test, both during its construction and, later, in research on its validity, was to compare the measure of intelligence which it yielded with the judgment of the psychiatrist and the clinical staff (a method referred to as "concurrent validity").

Wechsler's clinical work at the Bellevue Hospital in New York City often was concerned with the evaluation of illiterate people, social misfits, psychiatric cases, and patients who were suspected of having seriously impaired mental functions. This orientation undoubtedly motivated him to construct a test that would (1) contain ample nonverbal content and (2) have samples of sufficiently different mental functions so as to permit better clinical evaluation based on variability among the functions. Later we shall have more to say about each of these functions of the test. At this point it is sufficient to emphasize Wechsler's orientation for the test so as to understand something of the basis of its difference from the Stanford-Binet.

Our discussion will be limited to the WAIS, but the theory of test construction and the test's content and applicability are quite similar to the WISC. The WAIS was published in 1955. It consists of two sections, a Verbal Scale and a Performance Scale. Each of these two scales consists of several subtests. The WAIS is not an age scale, like the Stanford-Binet; the items of the test are not grouped by chronological age. Instead, it is a *point scale,* and the items are grouped in terms of similar content into a number of subtests, arranged in each subtest from easiest to most difficult. Subjects are usually given *all of the subtests,* and *all of the items within each subtest,* until items are reached which are so difficult that none are passed. A score on

751

the test consists of the number of points a subject has earned on each subtest. These subtest scores are converted into *standard scores* for each subtest (so that the scores from all subtests are comparable).

The *Verbal Scale* consists of six subtests: Information, Similarities, Comprehension, Digit Span, Arithmetic, and Vocabulary. The Information subtest contains items the adult is presumed to have learned about in the course of everyday experience, for example, who is President of the United States and what is the population of the United States. The underlying theory is that the ability to learn and remember such information is correlated with intelligence. The Similarities subtest requires the analysis of similarities between words. For example, the subject is required to tell how air and water are alike. The Comprehension subtest involves "common-sense judgments." The Digit Span subtest contains a series of digits. The subject is asked to repeat them from memory after they have been spoken by the examiner. This subtest also contains another series of digits which subjects are asked to reproduce in reverse order. The Arithmetic subtest has items requiring arithmetical reasoning which the subject solves without the use of pencil and paper. The Vocabulary subtest is just that—the subject must explain the meaning of words. Wechsler recommends that the Vocabulary subtest be considered an alternate when one of the other subtests is not applicable, and that each subject, therefore, be given only five of the six subtests from the Verbal Scale.

The *Performance Scale* consists of five subtests. There is a Block Design subtest in which subjects are asked to make designs with colored blocks which resemble those shown on test cards. A Picture Arrangement subtest requires subjects to arrange cartoon-like pictures printed on cards so that they tell a story in pantomime. There is a Picture Completion subtest in which subjects are asked to tell what part is missing from each of a set of pictures. An Object Assembly subtest requires subjects to put together pieces of wood to form a profile of a face, or a hand, or other figures. There is a Digit Symbol subtest in which subjects are asked to follow a code and fill in symbols for a large number of digits as rapidly as possible, using a code system given at the top of the page.

Subjects earn a point score on each subtest. These are then converted into standard scores. The five scores for the Verbal

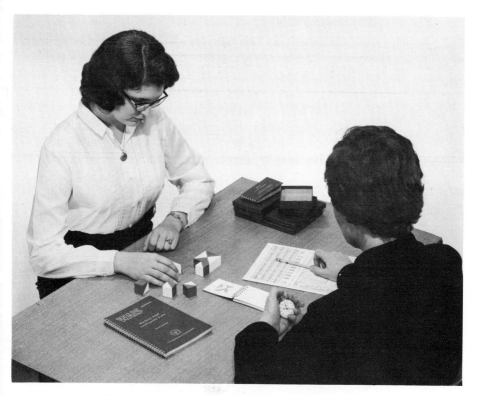

FIGURE 8.3 *Administration of the Block Design Test from the* WAIS. *Courtesy of The Psychological Corporation.*

Scale are then summed, and by means of a conversion table provided for the age group of the subject a Verbal I.Q. score is obtained. A Performance I.Q. score is similarly calculated. Finally, the total score, based on all of the subtests, is converted into a Full Scale I.Q. score.

Now let us examine some of the distinguishing features of this test. In the first place, we note that it places equal emphasis upon verbal and nonverbal content, unlike the Stanford-Binet, which heavily emphasizes verbal content. An approximate I.Q. score can therefore be obtained even when the subject is unable to respond in English. Perhaps more important is the assumption that equal weight should be given to verbal and nonverbal aspects of mental ability (i.e., in the Full Scale I.Q. score). This raises the question as to the degree of relationship between the two major components of the scale. This relationship between verbal and nonverbal components varies slightly in different age groups. In general, verbal and nonverbal I.Q., as measured by the test, correlate about .80 [27]. This would indicate that these scales have much in common. However, the Verbal I.Q. correlates with the Stanford-Binet about .75, while the Performance I.Q. correlates with Stanford-Binet only about .65. Since reliability for each of these measures is very high, it appears that the Verbal I.Q. score is more closely related to the Stanford-Binet I.Q. score than is Performance I.Q. score. Typical findings also indicate that the Full Scale I.Q. score correlates about .80 to .85 with the Stanford-Binet. In general, therefore, it appears that WAIS and Stanford-Binet are closely related. However, two important differences emerge when results are more closely inspected. The first is that the correlations reported above are not found when groups of adults who are exceptional in background educational or cultural experience are compared. The second is that when I.Q. scores obtained by these tests on the same subjects are compared, the Stanford-Binet yields higher I.Q. scores for superior subjects and the WAIS yields higher I.Q. scores for inferior subjects. Considering all of these findings, it appears that the two tests do not entirely measure the same phenomena and that the Performance Scale of the WAIS measures different aspects of the intellectual processes than does the Stanford-Binet.

The latter conclusion is reinforced by factor-analytic studies of responses to the WAIS. For instance, in one study ten factors were isolated which corresponded roughly to the ten subtests [28]. Another study showed that, with increasing age of subjects, fewer factors could be isolated, but, even at ages above 55 years, at least three factors were necessary to account for the data. These factors were labeled verbal-abstract, concrete-performance (i.e., motor and nonverbal), and immediate memory. [29]. Since a number of different factors were obtained, Wechsler did accomplish one of his original purposes: to provide a richer and different sampling of mental functions than the Stanford-Binet.

Another important difference of the WAIS from the Stanford-Binet lies in the fact that the same items of the scale are given to subjects of every age. This allows for more effective comparison of subjects at different age levels. And still another difference between the tests is that ten different subtest scores, directly related to one another, are available. Only one score is available for the Stanford-Binet. This last point requires some amplification.

From a clinical viewpoint, the availability of ten subscores on the WAIS, if these are relatively independent, leads to certain important possibilities. For example, if personality disturbances differentially affect different subtest scores, there is the possibility that uneven patterns of scores on the subtests may be diagnostically useful in detecting such personality problems. As one example of such phenomena, it has been shown that high anxiety levels influence the subtest results differentially. Hence, the test can be used in evaluating the presence of intense anxiety that may not be overtly or clinically observable. It has also been shown that wide differences in I.Q. scores obtained from the Verbal and Performance scales are indicative of other kinds of personality disorders, depending upon which score is higher. For example, such results may involve mental deterioration due to disease, atypical background experiences, or severe inhibition of interpersonal relations. The careful clinician must be very cautious, however, in drawing conclusions from the pattern of subtest scores alone, especially if the pattern is not highly irregular. Rather, he will consider his formulations as working hypotheses to be checked carefully against other clinical and life-history data.

OTHER TESTS OF INTELLIGENCE The Stanford-Binet and Wechsler tests are examples, not only of very widely used intelligence tests, but of very carefully standardized tests. Great care was used in selecting items for these tests, in obtaining representative samples for trying out the items, in item placement, and in developing suitable norms or scoring systems. Detailed manuals of instructions for administering, scoring, and interpreting the results have been prepared. There are a number of other well-developed individual and group intelligence tests which differ in some important respects from these two. The research psychologist and the clinician give much thought to the problem of selecting the type of test most suitable for the population to be tested and most appropriate in terms of the uses to which the test results will be put. We shall now examine very briefly a few other tests in order to provide some appreciation of the variety available.

Tests for infants A number of standardized tests of "mental development" are available for infants. It is possible to obtain measurements of rate of development as early as 18 days of age. However, such tests are not likely to measure the same

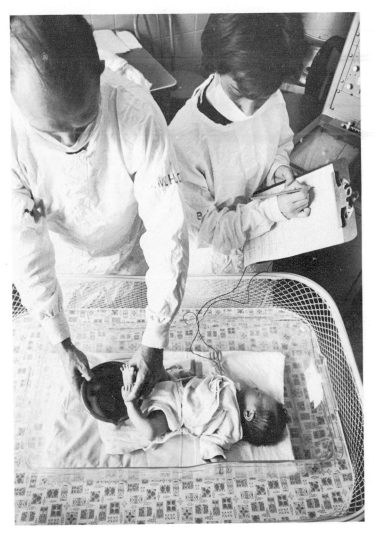

Measuring an infant's response. Guy Gillette

kinds of functions measured by intelligence tests designed for use with older children and adults. This is due to the fact that until certain mental processes have developed to the point at which they are measurable, no amount of ingenuity on the part of the tester can assess them. Tests involving reasoning are not applicable until this ability has matured and until the subject is able to give sustained attention to the task of problem-solving, can comprehend complex directions, and, for many tasks, can employ verbal concepts with some degree of facility. Of course, it is possible that certain infantile behaviors could be good

756

predictors of the operation of these immature abilities. For example, age of crawling could be correlated with mental reasoning as tested in later childhood. The failure to obtain high correlations between infant scores and test scores of intelligence in later years makes this a remote possibility. Another factor which makes prediction of later mental development from tests administered during infancy difficult is that the reliability of the measures is relatively low. In turn, this is due both to the variability in development of mental abilities during infancy and to the obvious difficulties in obtaining co-operation from the very young subjects during testing.

One of the most widely used developmental schedules for infants and young children is that developed by Gesell and his co-workers at Yale University. (At present there is a separate unit called the Gesell Institute of Child Development.) There are four basic schedules, with an age range from four weeks

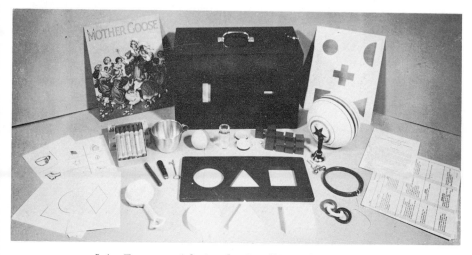

FIGURE 8.4 *Test materials for the Gesell Developmental Schedule. Courtesy of The Psychological Corporation.*

through six years, which are based on longitudinal studies of the same children. The schedule of *motor* development includes the behaviors of creeping, walking, and other more mature forms of motor behavior. The schedule of *adaptive behavior* includes items involving visual and other sensory stimuli and requires the infant to make some adaptive response to them, such as responding to a dangling object. The *language schedule* includes items of communication and comprehension as well as the child's total response to such situations. The *personal-social* schedule includes response to social situations, including feeding, playing, and toilet habits. The responses in each area of development are evaluated on the basis of norms for age groups and are interpreted in terms of the relative degree of acceleration or retardation in each area. In effect, these schedules, based on the concept of construct validity, are a refined method of observation of commonly used items of behavior. No single, over-all measure of developmental rate is furnished.

In contrast to the Gesell Developmental Schedules is the *Cattell Infant Intelligence Scale,* which is a formal intelligence test for ages two to thirty months. It consists of some items from form L of the older Stanford-Binet, some items from the Gesell Schedules, and some original items developed by Cattell. At the lowest levels the test depends essentially upon sensory-motor tasks, but at the upper levels more complex mental phenomena are evaluated. The test yields an I.Q. score. Both the author and other researchers have found the test to have very little predictive value when given to children below one year of age [30]. After the first year the test shows a low correlation with the Stanford-Binet, but it is very limited in predicting later I.Q. scores on intelligence tests within the school age range [31].

In general, it has been found that infant tests of intelligence are most useful for research purposes and for clinical evaluation of abnormal development and adjustment. They have very limited predictive validity for mental ability in adulthood. They are most effectively used by experienced observers and clinicians, who evaluate the responses to test items, together with other information, to make important *qualitative* judgments of the infant's behavior in arriving at a better understanding of his current adjustment and development.

Intelligence tests for special purposes A number of tests have been developed to serve purposes other than the prediction of scholastic success. We shall discuss two of these "intelligence tests." The quotation marks are used because there are many who would disagree that some of these tests measure intelligence as the term generally is understood.

Porteus published his test, the *Porteus Maze Test,* in 1915 and reviewed most of the research done with the test since that time in his book published more than forty years later [32]. As the name implies, this test consists of a series of mazes of increasing difficulty. The mazes are printed on paper, one to a page, and the subject is required to trace a path with a pencil from a starting point to the exit from the maze. The age range of the test is from the three-year-level to the adult level, although Porteus and other workers agree that the test does not discriminate different degrees of intelligence at the adult level.

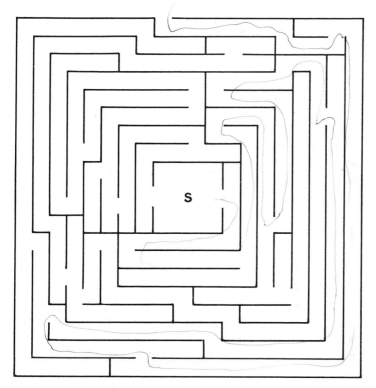

FIGURE 8.5 *A maze from the adult level of the Porteus Maze Test. Courtesy of Dr. S. D. Porteus and The Psychological Corporation.*

Porteus developed this test, in part, because he was dissatisfied with what he thought was an overemphasis in other intelligence tests on verbal ability and scholastic achievement. He wished to have a test that would emphasize "common sense," instead. He believed that good performance on the mazes involves "prudence" and "foresight," or planning ability. His clinical experience involved the evaluation and guidance of mental defectives, and he believed that their progress could be predicted more accurately on the basis of a test which measured the "social sufficiency" of his subjects rather than on the basis

759

of one that relied exclusively upon verbal reasoning. Over the years it has been learned that verbal tests of intelligence, like the Stanford-Binet, predict educational progress better, while the Porteus predicts social and "practical" adjustment better [33]. Some workers regard the test as a measure of social maturity. It is most widely used in the assessment of retarded individuals and delinquents.

Two scores are available. One is a mental age based on the age level of the most difficult mazes which the subject can complete successfully. The other is a Q score. This is based on qualitative aspects of the subject's performance: evidence of slovenliness and impulsivity, evidence of disregard of instructions, and evidence of careless habits of work. The Q score may be of value in predicting effectiveness in some real-life situations, such as the ability to work at a job efficiently [32, 33]. Thus, Porteus was able to demonstrate that his test bore out a judgment made by Thorndike, another famous educational psychologist, that a test of mental functions that was less verbal than the widely used verbal intelligence tests would be a better predictor of "practical adjustment" [34].

Another type of special-purpose "intelligence test" is the *Peabody Picture Vocabulary Test.* It consists of a series of pictures. The subject is asked to indicate which of four pictures, in each instance, represents the best response to a stimulus word (vocabulary). It takes only about fifteen minutes to administer and does not require verbal responses by the subject. It was designed to test the intelligence of individuals who were physically or verbally handicapped, and it has been used most extensively with institutionalized children, particularly mentally retarded individuals.

This test has a fairly good correlation with the Stanford-Binet (correlations of about .70 are usually reported). It does predict scholastic performance of mental retardates with some degree of success [35], and, although it has limited reliability in the higher ranges of mental retardation, it has been found to be a useful test in cases in which other tests are not applicable.

PROBLEMS OF ADMINISTRATION AND INTERPRETATION   It is not difficult to see that the proper administration and interpretation of intelligence tests are complicated problems requiring a great deal of technical competence and special training. We shall highlight a few of these problems in order to introduce the

MERRILL PALMER SCHOOL

AIGNER FROM MONKMEYER

Testing.

MERRIM FROM MONKMEYER

BAHNSEN FROM MONKMEYER

student to some interesting complexities of this area. No matter how valid a test may be for some specified purposes, it is only through the appropriate selection of a test (or tests), its competent administration and scoring, and, above all, through expert interpretation of the results in the light of the individual's particular situation that meaningful results may be expected.

We have already indicated that the test must be selected so that it is suitable in terms of similarity in background between the standardization population and the subject. In addition, the test must have demonstrated validity for the criterion to be predicted.

The administration of a test poses other problems. Aside from familiarity with the specific instructions for administering a particular test, the examiner must be alert to a number of other factors. One of these is the *motivation of the subject.* Infants are naturally unco-operative and easily distracted. Psychopaths frequently resist taking any tests. Many people are unduly afraid of taking intelligence tests because they do not wish to expose suspected deficiencies or limitations. The examiner must take the motivational condition of the subject into careful consideration and either provide suitable conditions to motivate him effectively or, failing this, make appropriate allowance for the unsatisfactory condition. In some instances it may be impossible to obtain meaningful results, and no evaluation can be made. In any case, the results of the test are always influenced, sometimes more and sometimes less, by the nature and intensity of motivation of the subject. This must always be considered in interpreting results. As Mandler and Sarason have indicated, people with high anxiety drives are not likely to obtain intelligence test scores that are truly commensurate with their abilities [36].

Another factor concerns the physical condition of the subject. Sensory deficiencies may interfere with performance on some tests. Fatigue may be another debilitating factor. Physical illness may reduce either rate or accuracy of performance. Again, as with motivation, the examiner must make allowance for such conditions and qualify his evaluations accordingly. In doing this he may make use of research findings with the test given under varying conditions, and he may use his own research or clinical experience with the test.

A special problem concerns the possible influence of type or degree of psychopathology upon intelligence test performance.

Obviously, psychiatric patients who are highly distraught or who are psychologically inaccessible present very special problems in assessment. But even the usual test directions may have differential effects upon subjects who are only moderately disturbed. For example, Hutt compared the intelligence test results obtained with the Stanford-Binet Scale given, under two conditions of administration, to children who differed only moderately in adjustment [37]. All children were given the specific items of the scale under precise conditions of the test administration by expert examiners, but the experimental group was given the total test by what was called the "adaptive method," while the control group was given the test under standard conditions, or, as it is called, the "consecutive method." The essential difference between these two methods is that, in the former, the *order of the items* of the test is so administered that failure and success experiences on the test are alternated, whereas, in the latter, the order of the items is such that there is a progression from easiest to most difficult items. Hence, in consecutive testing, the child is faced with a constantly increasing, and therefore frustrating, series of test experiences. When the results of the two types of testing sequences were compared, it was found that there was no significant difference in average I.Q. scores under the two conditions. However, when the total of 640 cases was subdivided into extreme groups of well-adjusted and poorly adjusted children—equated, on other bases, in intelligence levels—it was found that a group of poorly adjusted children, when tested consecutively, obtained I.Q. scores that were 18 points lower than a group of poorly adjusted children who were tested adaptively. This and other related findings indicate that the usual test administration unfavorably and significantly depresses the I.Q. when subjects have a relatively poor adjustment.

Still another general factor involved in test administration concerns the characteristics of the examiner: sex, skin color, appearance, personality attributes, and the like. There is little doubt that these characteristics may influence the obtained I.Q. score and must therefore be taken into consideration in evaluating the meaning of the results of the testing.

When we turn to interpreting test results, we encounter many problems that are too technical to discuss effectively in an introductory text. We can note, however, that far more than an evaluation of the numerical scores is involved. The qualitative aspects of performance need to be fully considered in order to arrive at a proper appreciation of what the scores represent. For instance, two subjects may both fail an item such as, "Why should you avoid going around with bad company?" But one subject may say, "I don't see any reason why you shouldn't go with bad company," while another may respond, "Because they are all older than you." Answers such as these may give the examiner insight into the nature of the person's mental processes as well as provide information about his values and attitudes.

Interpretation really implies that there has been a careful review of the test findings, both quantitative and qualitative, considered in the light of the conditions under which the test was given, and evaluated in terms of the subject's own personal history. Moreover, it may be necessary to consider the findings from a particular test, or test battery, in relation to other measures of intellectual functioning and effectiveness. Finally, this total evaluation must be summarized in terms of various possibilities and contingencies under which the predictions are likely to be true or false. In short, the judgment of the examiner plays an important role in interpreting the results of even the best-constructed tests for a particular individual who is being assessed.

The Measurement of Personality

Considerable research effort and ingenuity have gone into the development of methods of measuring personality reactions. These methods range all the way from *objective tests,* which attempt to devise questions which can be scored entirely objectively, through *standardized interviews,* the response to which can be coded for relatively objective scoring or which can be evaluated clinically or subjectively. In between there are *projective tests, observational procedures,* and *role-playing procedures* —each of which provides data about the behavior of people. These methods vary on the dimension of objectivity of the analysis. They also vary in other ways: type of data elicited, degree of reliance upon normative information, and types of evaluations that may be made. All measurement techniques have in common the aim of providing more precise and more valid measures of well-defined aspects of personality reactions.

The one-way screen: an observational procedure.
Merrill Palmer School

We shall discuss some examples of objective and projective methods of assessing personality. Our aim will be to provide some insight into the kind of theoretical and methodological issues which are involved as well as some knowledge of the kinds of evaluations which are possible.

OBJECTIVE TESTS OF PERSONALITY   Objective tests of personality attempt to eliminate the need for subjective evaluations made by the examiner. They also attempt to minimize the effect of the examiner upon the responses which are obtained from the examinee, which, as we shall see later, may be considerable in some kinds of assessment. Often this is done by giving the subject a paper-and-pencil examination, using a standard form with carefully prescribed instructions in a neutral setting. Evaluation of personality characteristics is accomplished by counting the responses to certain sets of questions in much the same way that intelligence test scores are determined. In theory, many dimensions of personality can be evaluated by the same questionnaire, although how many useful dimensions can be abstracted from any single test is a matter for empirical research.

The aim of developing objective tests for personality assessment is to eliminate or reduce the presumed error of human judgment of the examiner. Advocates of the objective instruments might argue that, through the use of objective scales, items which serve a useful role will be determined through correlations with empirical criteria. Predictions from the tests can be unequivocally tested. Furthermore, the test is entirely public and communicable, characteristics which are desirable for any "science of behavior."

With an enthusiasm based in part on the considerations just mentioned and in part upon the general movement of Behaviorism, which minimized the importance of subjective phenomena generally, many tests of personality were developed in the 1930's and 1940's. Like the tests of intelligence, many were developed to assist the military services select individuals during periods of wartime crisis. For example, one of the first scales was that developed by Woodworth during World War I [38]. Psychiatric descriptions of traits found in neurotic or psychotic patients were made into a questionnaire of 116 items. Subjects were asked to rate each item as it applied to themselves.

Most objective personality scales are self-report in nature; that is, subjects indicate which of the items apply to themselves or how frequently they "have" a characteristic described in an item. In short, they provide self-descriptions in an objective way by indicating applicable attributes.

A moment's reflection will make it obvious that the number and types of questions which could be given to subjects are almost beyond calculation. The types that are used, therefore, are chosen with certain specific goals in mind. Most often these goals are easily related to the purpose of the test, as in the case of Woodworth's early questionnaire, which was designed to weed out potential neurotics and psychotics from military service. Other goals for which tests have been constructed are to discriminate and provide diagnosis for those with mental disorders, to describe personality structure and mechanisms for more effective counseling and guidance, and to find better ways to describe personality. In this last case, the persons developing the test are primarily interested in using the test for theory-development and basic research.

Since the mental-testing movement has been very active in America for more than forty years, a large number of objective personality tests have been developed, and a wealth of research centered about each has been done. To begin a superficial review of each would be beyond the scope of this book. We shall therefore discuss only a few of the more prominent tests of current and historical interest for illustrative purposes.

THE MINNESOTA MULTIPHASIC PERSONALITY INVENTORY (MMPI) This test was designed to be of assistance in the diagnosis of mental dysfunction by reflecting the type of disorder and the intensity of the problem [39]. The method of test construction was to obtain subjects who reflected the abnormalities to be investigated. These subjects were chosen on the basis of consensus among clinical workers. Each case was carefully chosen to be representative of a specific type or intensity of disorder. Then 550 test items were given to this group and to a control group of normal subjects.

The 550 test items were divided into 26 groups or subsets of items. The items asked the subjects to tell about their general health, neurologic symptoms, motor movements and co-ordination, habits, family and marital relationships, as well as various psychological characteristics. From these items, scales were obtained by ascertaining which ones discriminated subjects with specific types of psychological disturbances from those with other psychopathologies and from normal subjects.

On the basis of weights assigned to test items, various scales of personality characteristics have been developed. Nine of these scales have been used very widely. These scales are defined as follows:

1. *Hypochondriasis* (Hs)   Subject reports being worried about bodily functions. Often associated with past history of exaggerated physical complaints.
2. *Hysteria* (Hy)   Subject reports being worried about paralyses, gastric or intestinal complaints, attacks of weakness, fainting, or even epileptic attacks.
3. *Depression* (D)   Subject reports being in depths of depression, discouraged, and without self-confidence.
4. *Hypomania* (Ma)   The subject reports he is overproductive in both thought and action. Often this may go along with trouble resulting from attempting too much and from a disregard of social conventions.

767

5. *Psychopathic deviate* (Pd)　The subject's responses reflect an absence of deep emotionality. Nothing seems to matter. He may be intelligent but likely to lie, to cheat, or to be addicted to drugs. Crimes may be undertaken without interest in personal gain.

6. *Paranoia* (Pa)　Subject is suspicious, oversensitive, and has delusions of persecution.

7. *Psychasthenia* (Pt)　These responses are typical of those with phobic or compulsive behaviors. Subject may have queer thoughts or ideas from which he cannot escape.

8. *Schizophrenia* (Sc)　Subjects who give responses scored as unusual and bizarre are high on this scale. Generally, these responses reflect a dissociation of the subjective life of the individual from reality.

9. *Masculinity–femininity* (Mf)　This scale tends to differentiate masculine–feminine psychological characteristics between men and women in the normal group of subjects.

A number of other scales have been developed and found useful in clinical practice. Three of these are especially important in the routine analysis of this test's results. One is the Question Score (?). Since subjects are asked to respond to each item of the test in terms of "Yes," "No," and "Cannot say," it is possible to summate the number of ? scores of "Cannot say" scores. Tests with abnormally high ? scores are considered invalid since they cannot properly be compared with the standardization group. Another score is the Lie Score (L), which indicates the number of improbable answers given by the subject. These are answers which indicate denial of symptoms or behaviors that are so ubiquitous that denial is indicative of evasion. And finally, there is a False Score (F), which indicates that the subject gave far more than the usual number of extremely rare responses and thus was careless, or was trying to fake his answers, or was otherwise responding invalidly.

The MMPI is the most frequently used objective personality test in current clinical practice. It has also been used widely in research, and special scales, such as those purporting to measure "social desirability," "anxiety," and the like, have been devised from responses to the items for such purposes. Nevertheless, the validity of the test has been questioned sharply. For one thing, there are a number of studies which indicate that the test fails to correlate as well with psychiatric judgment as is claimed [40, 41]. For another, the test scores do not give much information about the nature of the personality problems or their psychodynamics, beyond a label of type or types of psychopathology.

The authors of the scale are well aware of its limitations and have made various efforts to provide more meaningful and more detailed types of analyses. In their *Atlas*[1] they provide many methods for analyzing this test in terms of profiles or patterns on the various subscales and in terms of clinical examples of sophisticated analyses using the test results as a basis [42]. Some research studies have shown the values of some of its original or derived scales in predicting significant behavioral correlates. As we noted in Chapter 3, Taylor developed an anxiety scale from responses to this test and was able to use it in predicting differential learning among anxious and nonanxious subjects [43]. Schubert, basing predictions concerning the oral fixations among college smokers on Freudian theory, found that smokers scored higher on the manic and psychopathic-deviate scales [44].

Objective tests of personality, like the MMPI, have an important place in clinical work, but thus far they have not been able to replace the use of projective tests, which we shall discuss next, or other clinical procedures. They have greater use in mass programs of testing and in experimental work.

PROJECTIVE TECHNIQUES   Another type of assessment device, first introduced and used extensively by clinical psychologists and later studied and utilized in experimental studies of personality, is the *projective test*. As the name suggests, projective tests attempt to maximize the extent to which subjects attribute internal needs to the test stimuli to which they are responding. Subjects are presented with more or less ambiguous stimuli, and it is then assumed that responses are largely determined by internal needs. An excellent illustration of projection in response to an ambiguous stimulus may be obtained if the student simply asks people to look at a drifting, hazy, and fleecy cloud and to tell what it looks like. It will be noted that people vary quite widely in *what* they see, *how* they see it, and *where* in the clouds they see what they are reporting. It will be noted that

[1] The *Atlas* is a handbook for the clinical interpretation of this test's results.

such factors as the mood, recent experience, and basic personality characteristics will influence responses.

Of course, almost any test may be used projectively in the sense that qualitative aspects of the response may be examined. We gave an illustration of the "projective use" of varying responses to a formal intelligence test item in a previous section of this chapter. When a subject responds to the question, "Why should you avoid going around with bad company?" the response may simply be scored in terms of its correctness or incorrectness or the response may be evaluated qualitatively in terms of what it reveals about the subject's personality. However, projective tests are so constructed that the subject is compelled to respond to the test in ways which give indices of feelings, needs, and values, whether he is aware of them or not. Some years ago Hutt proposed that projective tests might be classified on the degree to which the stimulus material was *structured,* i.e., on its relative degree of ambiguity [45]. On this basis tests could be classified as *highly structured* (in which the stimulus had a clear and common meaning to most subjects); *partially structured* (with moderately ambiguous stimuli); and *unstructured* (with very ambiguous stimuli).

Projective tests are presumed to be most advantageous in revealing unconscious information about the subject and his inner dynamics. How well they do this is a matter for empirical research. At the present time such tests are in very wide use, especially by clinical psychologists. There is considerable evidence that experience and extensive research are leading to improved projective tests, with more efficient methods of administration and assessment.

We shall discuss briefly three of the most widely used projective tests of personality.

THE RORSCHACH PSYCHODIAGNOSTIC TEST   This test, popularly referred to as the Ink-Blot Test, was developed by a Swiss psychiatrist, Hermann Rorschach. He was interested in the experimental study of perception as it was related to various forms of psychopathology. Inkblots had been used in psychological studies before this time, but the main focus of the earlier research had been on the nature of the associations evoked by these stimuli. Rorschach was interested, instead, in the nature of the perceptual responses—in other words, in how responses were determined rather than in the content of the responses.

FIGURE 8.6   *A Rorschach-like inkblot.*

The test, as now used, consists of ten inkblots selected on the basis of extensive preliminary testing with more than 400 subjects, both normal and abnormal. (See Figure 8.6.) Half of the blots are made with various colors. Some of the colors are very vivid. The others are achromatic. The test is usually administered individually. The subject is shown each card in turn and is asked to tell what he sees in the inkblot. This is called the Free Association phase of the procedure. After all ten cards have been administered, the examiner presents each card once again, this time seeking to ascertain how much of the blot was used for each response, what aspects of the stimulus were used in making the response, and the precise nature of the content of the response. This is called the Inquiry phase.

In scoring the test, the examiner evaluates each response in terms of *location* (whether all or part of the inkblot was used), *determinants* (whether form qualities, color qualities, shading effects, and background were used and in what combination), and *content* (the category of the response itself in terms of concepts used). A great many variants of scoring, both quantitative and qualitative, have been developed and explored.

The analysis of the test yields many types of evaluations: level and functioning of intelligence; type of psychopathology; typical traits and defenses; areas of unconscious conflict; characteristics of ego functioning; and the like. Both the test variables and the predictions made from them, separately and in combination, have been studied in all kinds of institutional, school, and cultural settings. More than 2,000 publications dealing with the inkblot test have been published.   *771*

Today, more than forty years after the introduction of the test, opinion on its validity is still divided. The evidence seems to indicate that judgments based on this test concerning an individual's psychopathology can be made with reasonable success by experienced clinicians. The accuracy of predictions concerning specific traits and defenses seems far less certain. It has also been difficult to assess the extent to which evaluations are ordinarily influenced by the examiner's observations of the subject during testing. The administration of the test and the behavior of the subject during testing yield rich data along these lines. Analyses of "blind" evaluations, i.e., those made on the basis of test responses alone, indicate that such evaluations are usually less effective than those based on both observational and test data. There is serious question about some of the specific variables for which the test can be scored, and many improvements on the original test variables have been proposed. Some of these are very promising. For example, test scores related to intensity of hostile impulses and indices of anxiety have shown excellent promise. And experimental studies of the test have brought a rich harvest of important information about the nature of the perceptual processes and have led to verification of some fundamental qualities attributed to the test.

As illustrative of some recent research efforts, we may note that the test was able to predict tolerance of severe stress. Subjects were exposed to eight hours of total isolation [46]. There was a significant correlation between scores on the Rorschach test which measure the control of primary processes (see Chapter 4) and tolerance of perceptual isolation. The test differentiated between those individuals who were able to maintain secondary effective goal-oriented process thinking despite the stress and those who could not do so because they were too dependent on support from reality. As another example of the value of the test, it was demonstrated that, as hypothesized, the individual's responsiveness to emotional stimuli becomes significantly restricted during old age, and this produces increasing poverty in mental associations; further, new modes of defensiveness are created [47].

One of the special problems in the use of this test is that examiners tend to find relatively more evidence of psychopathology than is actually present and less evidence of healthy or effective functioning.

A recent development in inkblot techniques designed to avoid some of the pitfalls of the Rorschach test, and which introduces more objective and extensive scoring of variables, is the Holtz- man Inkblot Technique [48, 49]. This test consists of two parallel forms of 45 inkblots each. The subject makes only one response per card. The range of the test is from the preschool level to the superior adult level. Twenty-two variables have been developed and have high internal consistency. Factor analysis of response reveals six factors that appear in most samples of individuals who have been tested. The test seems to offer excellent promise for evaluation of important aspects of the personality, but additional corroboratory research is still needed.

THE THEMATIC APPERCEPTION TEST (TAT)   This is an example of tests that have "partially structured" stimulus materials. It was developed originally as a device to measure fantasies [50]. The patterns of the responses were carefully analyzed by Murray, about three years later, on the basis of his own theory of personality, and were then offered as a means of assessing needs and personality traits [51]. Since that time (1938), many methods of evaluating responses to the TAT have been de- veloped, and investigators have claimed that the test yields measures of impulse control, severity of conflict, and ego strength, as well as general personality traits and needs.

The test consists of 29 cards, each having a printed picture, and 1 blank card. Figure 8.6 illustrates the type of test materials which are utilized. The examiner selects 19 pictures and 1 blank card in presenting the test to a particular individual. The selection of particular cards is based on the appropriateness of the cards for either male or female subjects and for either children or adults. The subject is asked to tell a story about each card, indicating what is happening, how the people in the picture are feeling and thinking, what happened before, and how the story will end. He is asked to do the same thing with the blank card.

An example of the content and possible interpretation of the response to one card (the boy and violin) is the following (the subject was a fourteen-year-old male delinquent):

Somebody wants to make that boy learn to play the violin, but he ain't gonna do it. That's a sissy thing, anyway. His "old lady" is making him do it. So he's sitting there, figuring out how he's gonna get out. (Q: What happens?) They get into an awful fight

FIGURE 8.7 *A test card from the Thematic Apperception Test. From H. A. Murray.* Thematic Apperception Test. *Cambridge, Mass.: Harvard Univer. Press. Copyright 1943 by the President and Fellows of Harvard College.*

and his "old lady" beats him up, but he doesn't do it anyway. Later he gets himself a drum.

In one method of analysis, the *"hero"* can be identified as the subject himself. He is seen as an oppositional and rebellious individual. The *theme* of the story concerns the conflict between mother and son and suggests the son's view that the mother is excessively demanding and intolerant. The *outcome* of the conflict is that the son finally triumphs and has his own way. This kind of analysis, relating to the *theme* and *conflict,* helps the clinician to diagnose areas of conflict and methods of dealing with them.

Test content may be analyzed in many different ways, some qualitative and others quantitative. Scores representing dependency needs, aggressive needs, and the like may be obtained [52]. Many attempts to validate the measures of specific traits and defenses have been made [53]. On the whole, these measures seem to offer considerable research promise and have been found useful in clinical work. The problems of validation are similar to those encountered with the Rorschach test. One special problem is that the content of fantasy material is relatively unstable, since it is significantly influenced by recent events in the individual's life. This makes the problem of prediction especially difficult.

Various revisions of the TAT have been developed. One of these, a revision developed exclusively for use with children, is the Michigan Picture Test. In this test, scores are based, not on content, but on formal aspects of the performance, such as: the relative frequency of past-, present-, and future-tense verbs; action by the central figure that is predominantly centripetal (forces acting upon him) or centrifugal (his active encounter with external forces); and the relative use of personal and impersonal pronouns. These scores are related to dependency, withdrawal, self-assertion, emotional maturity, and level of internal tension. A general tension index score, indicative of the degree of maladjustment, may be obtained [54].

THE HUTT ADAPTATION OF THE BENDER GESTALT TEST A different approach to the projective measurement of intellectual and personality factors is found in this test. The test stimuli are derived from figures published by Wertheimer in 1933. Wertheimer was a Gestalt psychologist, interested in the phenomena of perception. There are nine simple line drawings, each on a separate card. (See Figure 8.8.) The subject is shown each card in turn and is requested to make a freehand drawing of it. After completing this phase of the testing, he is shown the cards again. This second time he is asked to modify the figures, as much or as little as he wishes, so as to make them more pleasing to him. In the third phase of the test, he is asked to give his associations to the original and modified figures.

This visual-motor test was first employed by Bender to investigate the kinds of abnormalities of perception and motor performance displayed by patients with various physical and psychological disorders. Hutt later developed various methods

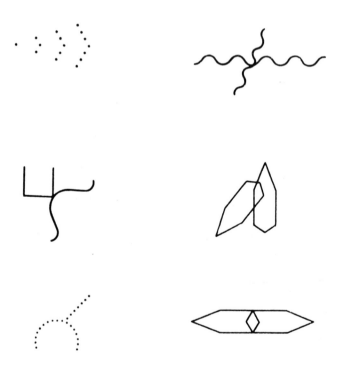

FIGURE 8.8   *Test figures for the Hutt adaptation of the Bender Gestalt Test. Courtesy of Grune & Stratton, Inc., N.Y.*

for utilizing the test projectively on the assumption that the underlying personality organization would influence the kinds of distortions made in the drawings [55]. Such factors as amount of increase or decrease in the size of the figures (related to approach versus withdrawal tendencies), degree of change in orientation of the figure or rotation (related to depressive and euphoric mood swings), and difficulty with closure of the figures (related to capacity for relating to people) were investigated clinically and experimentally. The data from the association phase of the test were used to explore areas of conflict and defense.

The test was utilized extensively during World War II, especially in the study of brain damage, severe reaction to stress, differentiation of neurotic from psychotic conditions, and similar problems. It has been used extensively ever since [56]. Methods for estimating intellectual level (for children and retarded adults) have been developed. Although some aspects of the qualitative analysis and some quantitative scores have been reasonably well validated, other problems of validation are far from settled and will require considerable research study. However, the test has been very useful as a source of rich hypotheses about psychopathology in patients.

Attitudes: Their Nature and Meaning

A third type of variable presenting special problems of assessment and definition is that of attitude. Useful concepts about the nature of attitudes enable us to describe changes in attitude and suggest ways in which they can be changed.

First, we must agree on what attitudes are. By attitudes we mean the beliefs, feelings, and action tendencies of an individual or group of individuals toward objects, ideas, and people. An action tendency refers to a disposition to respond in a certain way toward an object or person. Generally speaking, we will tend to approach and interact with objects toward which we hold favorable attitudes and to shun or avoid objects toward which we have unfavorable attitudes. It should be noted that a person's verbal report of his attitudes may not always correspond to his actual responses toward the object. A person could report that he does not believe in the principles or actions of the Ku Klux Klan and yet might support them financially or assist them in other ways. Therefore, any definition of attitude must take into consideration other things than a person's verbal responses.

While most attitudes are complex, they often can be described as favorable or unfavorable toward the object of the attitude. It should be remembered that the components of an attitude contributing to this favorable or unfavorable reaction are seldom as logical to the observer as they are to the holder of the attitude. In other words, it is often possible to point to inconsistencies in the beliefs, feelings, and action tendencies of others, whereas the components of our own attitudes seldom seem inconsistent but, rather, support the "obvious" logic of our positions.

Changes in attitude, and the degree or direction of change, demand techniques capable of establishing reliable and valid measures. Accordingly, psychologists and other social scientists devote much time and attention to sampling techniques and instruments designed to measure attitudes.

Two major types of attitude-measuring instruments have been devised, namely, scales and questionnaires. The former tend to be more frequently used in studies of social issues, the latter in application of research to social phenomena. Prior to a discussion of scales and questionnaires, a brief comment about sampling is necessary.

THE SAMPLE The results of any attitude-measurement technique upon a sample of subjects will be generalized to, or compared with, a larger population, since, almost always, it is impossible to examine every individual in a population under study. Therefore, some subgroup of the larger population is selected for testing. It is hoped that the sample will faithfully represent, and be "typical" of, the larger population. In a national election the population with which we are most concerned is the total number of persons who actually vote. For a new product, the population of potential users is most important. Various techniques have been developed to draw a sample that will adequately represent the larger population.

Kish [57] has described methods called simple random sampling, probability sampling, area sampling, stratified sampling, and cluster sampling, among others. As is almost obvious, the selection and size of the sample are partly a matter of practical affairs: budget and time. But some systematic method of selecting the sample from the universe of the population is essential if the results are to have reliability and validity.

In drawing a simple random sample, the size of the population—such as the number of voters in the country—is known. A number can be assigned to each one. Those to be interviewed will be determined on a chance basis, as if numbers were drawn by chance. Those whose numbers are drawn will be included in the sample. In the probability sample, selection of respondents is based on a knowledge of the groups of people comprising the population. Estimates might be made of the number of people in different religious faiths in the general population. Then samples might be drawn from each religious group at random, with the stipulation that the number selected from each religious group be in proportion to the total number of such individuals in the population. It is, in other words, a statistical refinement of the random sample technique. Area sampling selects its respondents from geographical boundaries that are defined and identifiable; most often the individuals selected in area sampling are identified by dwelling units within the area. (See Table 8.2.)

TABLE 8.2. TYPES OF SAMPLING AND SELECTION PROCEDURES

Sample	Chance Selection
Random	From total population
Probability	From subgroups of population
Area	By geography
Stratified	From strata with specific characteristics
Cluster	From concentration within segments

Stratified sampling divides the population into subpopulations called strata. From each stratum a sample is selected. For example, subsamples might consist of product-users versus non-users of a product, or teen-age males and teen-age females, or almost any variable in the characteristics of a population about which one hopes to obtain data leading to a solution of the problem investigated. Cluster sampling requires the selection of respondents from defined groups or areas. Selecting a sample from five cities, eight blocks, three classes of general-psychology students, or, for that matter, any other selected and defined segment of a population is the essence of cluster sampling.

Regardless of the method of sampling and the statistical refinements introduced to reduce sampling errors, the ultimate

779

value of the sample obtained depends upon the methods used to determine attitudes. When using interviews, one cannot hope to obtain adequate information without paying great attention to the briefing, supervising, and auditing of field interviews. Unfortunately, this fact is too often overlooked. Many methods have been devised for conducting "standard interviews" and for controlling for the many kinds of extraneous variables which can enter into an interview. As might be anticipated, however, the problems become much greater when interviews are conducted by large numbers of interviewers.

SCALE MEASUREMENT Different scaling methods exist, and four methods used in attitude measurement will be briefly described, namely: the Thurstone, Likert, Guttman, and Osgood methods. When using the Thurstone method, subjects are presented with a number of statements reflecting various degrees of favorableness toward a topic such as birth control, communism, religion, etc. Each statement is assigned a mathematical value, say from one to eleven, on the basis of judges' ratings of the statement. The subject's attitude is measured by adding together the score of the statements chosen. The numerical weight assigned to each statement is the average weight of a group of judges. In the following sample, the second statement has a weight of 5.5. This means it was probably placed in the categories 5 or 6 by most judges. The third statement with a weight of 10.6 is a strongly negative statement and was placed at the end of the scale.

An example of such statements to measure attitude toward the church is [58]:

(.5) I feel the church is the greatest agency for the uplift of the world.
(5.5) Sometimes I feel the church is worth while and sometimes I doubt it.
(10.6) I regard the church as a parasite on society.

As can be seen, the lower the numerical value of the statement, the more favorable is the statement about "the church." A subject's responses on other statements about "the church" or religion can be summed to find the degree of favorableness indicated by the responses.

The Likert scale has the subject assign one of the following responses to statements: (5) strongly approve, (4) approve, (3) neutral, (2) disapprove, and (1) strongly disapprove. The attitude measurement is then a sum of the values assigned to the statements. An example of this type of procedure would be:

In the interest of permanent peace, we should be willing to arbitrate absolutely all differences with other nations which we cannot settle by diplomacy.

Strongly Approve	Approve	Undecided	Disapprove	Strongly Disapprove
(5)	(4)	(3)	(2)	(1)

Guttman [59] has proposed a method in which the scale has a special cumulative property. For example, a subject who responds positively to the eighth item of a ten-point scale ranging from favorable to unfavorable will have responded positively to all other seven items. The subject who responds to the fourth item will have responded positively to only the first, second, and third preceding items. In practice, the construction of a scale which justifies this assumption of cumulative endorsement has many difficulties because there are many dimensions of attitudes. However, the scale does present an interesting methodological departure from the Thurstone and Likert methods.

A fourth method of attitude measurement has been proposed by Osgood, Suci, and Tannenbaum. It is known as the Semantic Differential [60]. (See Table 8.3.) The method requires the

TABLE 8.3. ILLUSTRATION OF A SEMANTIC DIFFERENTIAL FORM

angular	. . . .	rounded
weak	. . . .	strong
rough	. . . .	smooth
active	. . . .	passive
small	. . . .	large
cold	. . . .	hot
good	. . . .	bad
tense	. . . .	relaxed
wet	. . . .	dry
fresh	. . . .	stale

SOURCE: C. E. Osgood. The nature and measurement of meaning. *Psychol Bull.*, 1952, **49**, 229.

respondent to rate the associative meaning of a word or statement. A series of descriptive polar terms is presented below the "to-be-rated" item. Subjects indicate by a mark, on a line connecting the polar descriptions, the degree to which the item is like one or the other of the polar descriptors. The polar terms are made up of many pairs of words. Words often used are good-bad, rough-smooth, weak-strong, small-large, tense-relaxed, wet-dry, fresh-stale, cold-hot, fair-unfair, etc.

This method is especially valuable in determining the degree to which different groups of subjects tend to agree on the meaning of words or statements. The pattern of responses on the polar descriptors reflects the associations of the subjects to each item tested. It is interesting to note that about one-half of the variance of ratings of different words is contributed by the evaluative dimension with "good" and "bad" as the polar extremes.

THE QUESTIONNAIRE The questionnaire is probably the most widely used instrument to measure attitudes. A questionnaire can be either structured or unstructured.

The structured questionnaire asks a question and provides several possible answers. The person being interviewed is encouraged to select the most appropriate answer from among those provided. The unstructured questionnaire primarily asks questions, but no suggested answers are offered. The latter technique provides more freedom to the interviewees but is more difficult to analyze when large groups of subjects are used. The interviewer is provided with the questionnaire and contacts the people selected to be in the sample. Interviews are usually conducted on a face-to-face basis but can be done via the telephone or by mail. The decision as to which type of interview to use is based on the problems being studied and other practical factors.

Sometimes interviewees are asked to rate responses on a numerical or verbal scale so that the intensity with which the attitude is held may be indicated.

ATTITUDE FORMATION Which of the different methods is used on any occasion depends in part upon the views held by the investigator about the formation of attitudes and the ways in which they can be changed.

A large part of our social lives is dominated by attitudes. These are sometimes predictable from the relationships we have had with others, particularly members of our families, our friends, our teachers, our neighbors, and our religious advisers. Of course the family contributes to the formation of our attitudes. Attitudes toward the opposite sex, toward religion, toward education, toward occupations, toward political parties, and so forth may be the result of our accepting or rejecting the attitudes held by members of our family.

Our neighborhoods have certain structures in terms of housing, cultural facilities, religious groupings, and possibly ethnic customs. Further, there are neighbors. The neighbors as adults or children tolerate, reinforce, or punish certain attitudes and behavior. As a result, we are New Yorkers, Midwesterners, Southerners, etc. Depending upon personality and environmental factors, we may accept or deny environmental influences. Conformity or rebellion may arise as the result of our adjustment to environmental pressures.

Our present economic and occupational position and aspirations for the future also contribute to our attitudes. In part they may influence our attitudes toward unions, management, and our beliefs about certain proposed legislation. Our entire socioeconomic background influences our present and future attitudes. When we believe that certain objects or actions may act to lower our economic status, our attitudes toward them may become less favorable. When other objects or actions seem likely to improve our economic status, they often seem more favorable to us. While attitudes do not respond in perfect relationship to economic considerations, some attitudes are bound to our views of the relationship between the attitude's object and probable economic changes. Attitudes toward some objects can be changed by changing this relationship.

Attitudes are influenced by information we receive from various sources. When this information is congruent with our predispositions and previous judgments, we often develop a more favorable or positive attitude toward the new object, idea, person, or group. However, when the information, no matter how received, is incongruent with our predispositions, the source may be judged as unreliable and have little effect upon our attitudes. Actually, present attitude structures are quite resistant to change by additional information. Apparently it is easy to question the credibility of information which goes against former attitudes or to forget or distort the information.

All forms of mass communication—television, radio, newspapers, and magazines—"feed" their audiences large quantities of "information." In part, the presentation of news or information is constructed so as to cater to the attitudes of their audiences. In turn, the audience selects the specific form of mass communication that best reflects its attitudes on various subjects. Items of interest range from sex and the teen-agers, crime, divorce, politics, religion, dope addiction, and civil rights to pornographic literature. The material we select helps us to either substantiate our opinions or establish new ones.

The impact of information upon attitudes depends upon the subject's impressions of the source and the manner in which the information is presented. Kelman and Eagly [61] report the results of two experiments. In the first, three communications to a group of Negro college students were the same. However, one-third of the students heard the tape-recorded communication from a communicator represented as pompous, paternalistic, and authoritarian. The second had a communicator represented as a modest, humble, and objective scholar (a college professor). The third group heard from a person represented as a Negro minister who spoke as a member of the Negro community. The "negative" speaker was consistently judged lower in trustworthiness, expertness, general attractiveness, and representativeness than the other two speakers.

In the second experiment, high-school students heard taped messages emphasizing the juvenile delinquency problem. A "negative communicator" projected the image of an ignorant enemy, while the "positive communicator" projected the image of one who would be personally attractive to a teen-age group. The main conclusion drawn is that "the tendency to perceive communication content in line with one's attitude toward the communicator is most likely to come into play when the communicator arouses strong feelings." Kelman and Eagly hypothesize that "misconception is a function of the degree to which the incongruous situation raises questions of *self-definition* in the subject."

The mass-communication media are effective though non-scientific in changing attitudes. They represent particular points of view about foreign countries, the United Nations, color television, the President, taxes, federal aid to education, dieting, smoking, fashion, and art. They act to form attitudes or change existing ones.

ATTITUDE CHANGE Changes in attitudes can be classified as changes of direction or changes in intensity. The change most readily obtained is a change in intensity of a pre-established attitude. When a person is for (or against) an object, idea, or person, it is rather easy to change the intensity of the attitude as long as it remains in the same direction.

Achieving a change in direction of attitude, that is, from favorable to unfavorable or vice versa, is usually more difficult to achieve, although it is possible.

As recently summarized by Krech, Crutchfield, and Ballachey [62], attitude modifiability is a function of seven characteristics of attitudes, namely: (1) extremeness, (2) multiplexity, (3) consistency, (4) interconnectedness, (5) consonance, (6) strength and number of motives served by the attitude, and (7) the importance of the values to which the attitude is related.

The more extreme the attitude, the less likely it is to be changed. The more complex the attitude, the less likely it is that a change in direction of attitude will occur, but the more likely it is that a change of intensity in present direction can be made to occur. Attitudes with consistency among their various components tend to be more stable than attitudes with inconsistent components. The more an attitude is interconnected with others, the less likely is change to occur. For example, if one is a conservative in many walks of life, then changing conservatism in any one area will not be readily accomplished. When an attitude exists in a consonant relationship with other attitudes, attitude change is not likely to occur. Since attitudes can serve many motives and needs of an individual, the possibility of change will depend upon the number and strength of the motives served. And last, the closer the attitude is to the basic values held by an individual, the less likely is change to occur.

Changes in attitudes may occur when there is an imbalance or disequilibrium among various belief systems. This disequilibrium initiates change, and change operates to restore equilibrium. Generally speaking, models of attitude change can be based on theories of equilibrium restoration known as dissonance models [63], balance models [64], or congruity models [60]. In many respects the models have a great deal in common.

The essence of these theories is that incongruity, dissonance, and imbalance among attitudes are conditions of disequilibrium, and under such conditions attitude changes occur in the direction of reducing these states.

ATTITUDES IN BUSINESS Probably those with the greatest interest in measuring attitudes which reflect public opinion are companies engaged in marketing products for the consumer. This field is known as "market research" or "consumer psychology." It represents a link between business and the public. Information about the attitudes of purchasers is of interest to manufacturers, retailers, advertising agencies, and the mass-communication media who sell advertising time or space.

Bogart [65] lists the types of research performed in this field as follows:

(1) To determine the position of competitive brands in the market, both in terms of actual unit or dollar sales and in terms of consumer awareness and acceptance; (2) to study the prevailing consumption patterns of different segments of the population in relation to particular products and brands; (3) to understand the tastes and motivations that underlie opinion and behavior in the marketplace; (4) to evaluate the influences on consumer action and attitudes, including the opinions and activities of the retailer and the effects of display, promotion, and advertising; (5) to determine how successfully various techniques of persuasion and communication appeal to popular tastes and thereby influence the purchase of goods and services; (6) to compare the opportunities that various media provide for communication with different segments of the public.

This is an area of applied research which is preoccupied with the practical nature of the problem rather than its theoretical implications; it is thus likely to be more descriptive than analytic.

What are the issues involved when a company attempts to measure consumer reactions toward its own and its competitors' products? Immediately we are in the realm of attitude measurement. There are those who legitimately engage in the business of measuring attitudes of consumers. They may work either on the staffs of large corporations or as consultants to them. These people provide information which will allow more effective marketing of products and services by their clients.

Today there is a lot of talk about the "images" of corporations. These are merely the total of the various attitudes held by people toward these companies. Advertising attempts to build or change these images. Market research tends to find both the favorable and unfavorable attitudes toward these companies and to suggest ways in which favorable attitudes can be enhanced and unfavorable attitudes can be reduced.

Those engaged in this business do not try to mislead consumers, for the very sound business reason that they "cannot get away with it." The few companies who try to misrepresent their products sooner or later suffer from the backlash of consumer reaction. It is true, however, that some advantages are taken by exaggerating certain claims or by presenting claims in ambiguous fashion. Such instances should not be included in the ethics of the more reputable business organizations and should never be tolerated by the professional social scientist working in this area.

The successful experiences that a consumer has with a brand will probably lead to another purchase. If unsuccessful, the consumer will be likely to switch brands. The essence of consumer research is simply to measure the variety of attitudes and experiences that consumers have. With the knowledge then available, business policies and practices can more or less objectively conform to the reality of the situation.

Another area of great concern relates to the unfulfilled needs of the consumer. At one point in time, only a few years ago, frozen foods were unknown. A controversial question is whether frozen foods sold well because of certain unfulfilled needs or desires on the part of the consumer or whether someone with a bright idea created the need or desire for them. It is often presumed that consumer needs, real or imagined, result from "deficits" in life. These deficits may not be of vital concern but represent a product or service for which people will pay. Should beer be marketed in bottles or in cans? If in cans, how should they be opened for most appeal?

The discovery of a latent or unfulfilled need in the consumer population is obviously more economical and profitable than it is to cajole a consumer into using a product or a service which he does not need. The introduction of men's toiletries, especially the cologne type of after-shave lotion, is another illustration. Do manufacturers and advertisers create a need for this product, or has it existed among consumers as a desire to be complimented for their odors by women? Color television is another example. It has been around for a number of years, and there is no doubt but that it will someday replace black-and-white television. There has not been an overwhelming demand for it in its early stages. As the popularity of color television increases, we might ask whether color television was foisted on the consumer, and a need for it created, or whether there was a pre-existing need which was fulfilled.

PUBLIC-OPINION AND POLITICAL POLLING One of the great American games is to predict election results. Surveys are conducted and appear in newspapers and magazines. Readers regard such publications as news, and since most people are interested in predictions and make many of their own, the interest in the results of such surveys seems high. Naturally, the winner of the poll reacts favorably to them, while the loser disregards or disclaims them.

A more serious aspect of political polls is the confidential poll sponsored by a political organization. A candidate has a need for advance knowledge, on the basis of which he and his advisers may plan tactics and strategy and may often decide which stand on which campaign issues shall be emphasized, minimized, or even avoided. Such polls and their results are rarely, if ever, revealed to the public. They are used by the political candidates and their parties to determine, as well in advance as is possible, the attitudes of the public on the various issues. Such polls also are used in measuring the "image" of the candidate. The action based on this image leads to attempts on the part of speech-writers and publicists either to improve or change the image of the candidate.

There are those who favor political polling because they say that it allows the candidate to be more effective and to more accurately estimate the temper of the public. There are others who believe that this is unfair and who argue that polls influence elections by their very publication.

Another subject of investigations into political behavior is the characteristics of those who vote. Among the variables related to frequent voting in elections are high income, high education, being a male, and being an older resident in the community. Variables related to infrequent turnout at the polls are low income, low education, being a woman, being young (under 35), and normal political situations. Religious affiliations are important. More Jews vote in most elections than do Catholics. The explanatory factors for rates of voting turnout are, (1) factors affecting the relevance of government policies to the individual, (2) factors affecting access to information, (3) factors relating to group pressure to vote, (4) factors relating to pressure not to vote [66].

Another problem to be studied is whether the voter will change his attitude during the course of a campaign. Conducting surveys at several points during a campaign, and analyzing voter approval or disapproval of campaign issues, allows trends to be spotted. For example, racial inequities are important issues to Negroes. One paradox in the relationship between race and political affiliation is that most Negroes have voted Democratic since the New Deal era of the 1930s while many Southern Democrats have taken an anti-Negro position over the same period. A major swing to Republicans or a closer identification with Democrats on the part of Negro voters would surely have an effect on the future of American politics.

PREJUDICE   Prejudices are attitudes. Half-humorously, prejudices are other people's attitudes that we don't share. The prejudices of others are, therefore, often called "wrong" or "bad" [67]. Prejudices have an important impact on all of us and on our interpersonal relations. Almost everyone is in favor of reducing prejudice, but not everyone is willing to admit that his attitudes are prejudices. Someone who is anti-Negro, or anti-Semitic, or anti-anything can present "facts" to prove that he is not prejudiced. This reflects an almost universally unfavorable attitude toward "prejudices" in our society.

Intelligence does not insulate us from basing our behavior on factors other than rational analysis and decision. In other words, people with varying degrees of intelligence often share the same attitudes and hold them with similar intensities. Justifications of attitudes are often a function of the rationalizations used to justify the attitudes held for other reasons.

For any person, attitudes are related to motives, values, personality, and emotions. The individual has internal needs and reacts to external social pressures. In coping with the environment, internal needs are manifested through wants, aspirations, and expectancies. To other people a person expresses and defends his attitudes. When attitudes are weak, he may not even choose to defend them; but when his attitudes about an idea, object, person, or group are intense, he will often use many kinds of defense mechanisms to appear logical, lofty, and righteous.

Racists hold intense attitudes. Often they are rabid reformers and claim to be "idealists." Others do not agree with their ideals and insist that they have no ideals at all.

One's attitudes or prejudices are related to the groups with which one identifies. People at all ages belong to many groups, of a formal or informal variety. This is reflected in clubs (good?) and gangs (bad?). We have "good colleges" and "poor colleges." Which are which depends in part on *who* and *what* you believe. Think of the large number of organized groups: Republicans, Democrats, P.T.A., fraternities, Daughters of the American Revolution, CORE, KKK, Black Muslims, Anti-Defamation League, anti-vivisectionists, etc. Such organizations tend to have some rabid and inspired members, and for each there are antagonistic nonmembers who would not join for any reason. On the other hand, most organizations have many passive members who belong but do not participate in group roles.

We may ask, How does it happen that groups can have staunch supporters, passive onlookers, and rabid attackers? Only part of the answer comes from social approval or immediate gratifications. The other part of the answer must stem from the attitudes held prior to joining the group. Individuals expect the group to help them achieve certain goals, or they find support for their attitudes from the similar attitudes of others. The satisfaction in finding a number of people with similar attitude structures should not be underestimated as a motivating factor.

Summary Statement

In this chapter we have seen how psychologists have attempted to conceptualize such behavior variables as intelligence, personality, and attitude. The theories which underlie the measurement of such variables influence, sometimes to an extraordinary degree, the methods used in their assessment. Sometimes the methods of assessment prejudice the kinds of results which are achieved. It may seem, therefore, that we are constantly caught within the web of our own creation. To a certain extent this is undoubtedly true. Nevertheless, the more precise we can be about both our theories and our methods of evaluating them—in other words, the more explicitly we understand fully the nature of our investigations into behavioral phenomena—the more likely we are to be critically aware of the limitations of our knowledge, on the one hand, and of needed new directions for our explorations.

In science, theory and prediction go hand in hand. We may choose to conceptualize our understanding of man in terms of forces within him or in terms of interactions between man and his environment. In either case we are not able to ascertain the "whole truth." In each case different kinds of measurements or evaluations and predictions emerge. Measurement, if valid, enables us to assess phenomena more adequately. But in the end, it is the man who uses the measuring devices who must decide what he wishes to learn about man and in what direction he wishes him to travel.

References

1. Hutt, M. L., Gibby, R., Milton, E. O., & Pottharst, K. The effect of varied experimental "sets" upon Rorschach test performance. *J. proj. Tech.,* 1950, **14,** 85–103.
2. Eron, L. D. A normative study of the Thematic Apperception Test. *Psychol Monogr.,* 1950, **64,** No. 9.
3. Postman, L., Bronson, W. C., & Gropper, G. L. Is there a mechanism of perceptual defense? *J. abnorm. soc. Psychol.,* 1953, **48,** 215–224.
4. Baughman, E. E. Rorschach scores as a function of examiner differences. *J. proj. Tech.,* 1951, **15,** 243–249.
5. Windle, C. Psychological tests in psychopathological prognosis. *Psychol. Bull.,* 1952, **49,** 451–482.
6. Cantril, H. *Gauging Public Opinion.* Princeton, N. J.: Princeton Univ. Press, 1944.
7. Whittaker, E. M., Gilchrist, J. C., & Fischer, J. W. Perceptual defense or response suppression? *J. abnorm. soc. Psychol.,* 1952, **47,** 732–733.
8. McNemar, Q. Lost: Our intelligence? Why? *Amer. Psychologist,* 1964, **19,** 871–882.
9. Terman, L. M. & Merrill, M. A. *Measuring Intelligence.* Boston: Houghton Mifflin, 1937.
10. Jones, H. E. The environment and mental development. In L. Carmichael (Ed.), *Handbook of Child Psychology.* New York: Wiley, 1954.
11. Goodenough, F. L., & Maurer, K. M. *The Mental Growth of Children from Two to Fourteen Years; A Study of the Predictive Value of the Minnesota Preschool Scales.* Minneapolis: Univ. Minnesota Press, 1952.
12. Vandenberg, S. G. The heredity abilities study: Hereditary components in a psychological test battery. *Amer. J. hum. Genet.,* 1962, **14,** 220–237.
13. Burks, B. S. The relative influence of nature and nurture upon mental development: A comparative study of foster parent–foster child resemblance and true parent–true child

resemblance. *Yearb. Natl. Soc. Stud. Educ.,* 1928, **27** (Part I), 219–316.

14. Skodak, M., & Skeels, H. M. A final follow-up study of one hundred adopted children. *J. genet. Psychol.,* 1949, **75,** 85–125.
15. Skeels, H. M. Mental growth of adopted children in the same family. *J. genet. Psychol.,* 1950, **77,** 3–9.
16. Freeman, F. N., Holzinger, K. J., & Mitchell, B. C. The influence of environment on the intelligence, school achievement, and conduct of foster children. *Yearb. Natl. Soc. Stud. Educ.,* 1928, **27** (Part I), 103–217.
17. Lee, E. S. Negro intelligence and selective migration: A Philadelphia test of the Klineberg hypothesis. *Amer. sociol. Rev.,* 1951, **16,** 227–233.
18. Shuey, A. M. *The Testing of Negro Intelligence.* Lynchburg, Va.: J. P. Bell, 1958.
19. Dreger, R. M., & Miller, K. S. Comparative psychological studies of Negroes and whites in the United States. *Psychol. Bull.,* 1960, **57,** 361–402.
20. Thurstone, L. L. *Primary Mental Abilities.* Chicago: Univ. Chicago Press, 1938.
21. Spearman, C. "General intelligence" objectively determined and measured. *Amer. J. Psychol.,* 1904, **15,** 210–293.
22. Thurstone, L. L., & Thurstone, T. G. *Factorial Studies of Intelligence.* Chicago: Univ. Chicago Press, 1941.
23. Hunt, J. McV. *Intelligence and Experience.* New York: Ronald, 1961.
24. Terman, L. M., & Merrill, M. A. *Stanford-Binet Intelligence Scale.* Boston: Houghton Mifflin, 1960.
25. Porteus, S. D. *The Practice of Clinical Psychology.* New York: American Book, 1941.
26. McNemar, Q. *The Revision of the Stanford-Binet Scale: An Analysis of the Standardization Data.* Boston: Houghton Mifflin, 1942.
27. Guertin, W. H., Rabin, A. I., Frank, C. H., & Ladd, C. F. Research with the Wechsler intelligence scale for adults. *Psychol. Bull.,* 1960, **59,** 1–26.
28. Saunders, D. R. On the dimensionality of the WAIS battery for two groups of normal males. *Psychol. Repts.,* 1959, **5,** 529–554.
29. Green, R. F., & Berkowitz, B. Changes in intellect with age. II, Factorial analysis of Wechsler-Bellevue scores. *J. genet. Psychol.* 1964, **104,** 3–17.
30. Cattell, P. *The Measurement of Intelligence of Infants and Young Children.* New York: Psychological Corp., 1947.
31. Cavanaugh, M. C., *et al.* Predictions from the Cattell Infant Intelligence Scale. *J. consult. Psychol.,* 1957, **21,** 33–37.
32. Porteus, S. D. *The Maze Test and Clinical Psychology.* Palo Alto: Pacific Books, 1959.

33. Dentler, R., & Mackler, B. The Porteus Maze Test as a prediction of the functioning abilities of retarded children. *J. consult. Psychol.,* 1962, **26,** 50–55.
34. Thorndike, E. L. Intelligence and its measurement: A symposium. *J. educ. Psychol.,* 1921, **12,** 124–127.
35. Wolfensberger, W. The correlations between Peabody Picture Vocabulary Test and achievement among retardates. *Amer. J. ment. Def.,* 1962, **67,** 450–451.
36. Mandler, G., & Sarason, S. B. A study of anxiety and learning. *J. abnorm. soc. Psychol.,* 1952, **47,** 166–173.
37. Hutt, M. L. A clinical study of "consecutive" and "adaptive" testing with the Revised Stanford-Binet. *J. consult. Psychol.,* 1947, **11,** 93–103.
38. Woodworth, R. S. *Personal Data Sheet.* Chicago: C. H. Stoelting Co., 1917.
39. Hathaway, S. R., & McKinley, J. C. *The Minnesota Multiphasic Personality Inventory.* New York: Psychological Corp., 1942, 1947, 1951.
40. Benton, A. L. The MMPI in clinical practice. *J. nerv. & ment. Dis.,* 1945, **102,** 416–420.
41. Modlin, H. C. A study of the Minnesota Multiphasic Personality Test in clinical practice. *Amer. J. Psychiat.,* 1947, **103,** 578–769.
42. Hathaway, S. R., & Meehl, P. E. *An Atlas for the Clinical Use of the Minnesota Multiphasic Personality Inventory.* Minneapolis: Univ. Minnesota Press, 1951.
43. Taylor, J. A. A personality scale of manifest anxiety. *J. abnorm. soc. Psychol.,* 1953, **48,** 285–290.
44. Schubert, D. S. P. Personality implications of cigarette smoking among college students. *J. consult. Psychol.,* 1959, **23,** 376.
45. Hutt, M. L. The use of projective methods of personality measurement in Army medical installations. *J. clin. Psychol.,* 1945, **1,** 123–140.
46. Goldberger, L. Reactions to perceptual isolation and Rorschach manifestations of the primary process. *J. proj. Tech.,* 1961, **25,** 287–302.
47. Ames, L. B. Age changes in the Rorschach responses of a group of elderly individuals. *J. genet. Psychol.,* 1960, **97,** 257–185.
48. Holtzman, W. H., Thorpe, J. S., Swartz, J. D., & Herron, E. W. *Inkblot Perception and Personality.* Austin, Tex.: Univ. Texas Press, 1961.
49. Holtzman, W. H. Inkblot perception and personality: The meaning of inkblot variables. *Bull. Menninger Clin.,* 1963, **27,** 84–95.
50. Morgan, C. D., & Murray, H. A. A method for investigating fantasies: The Thematic Apperception Test. *Arch. neurol. Psychiat.,* 1935, **34,** 189–306.

51. Murray, H. A., *et al. Explorations in Personality.* New York: Oxford, 1938.
52. Mussen, P. H., & Naylor, H. K. The relation between overt and fantasy aggression. *J. abnorm. soc. Psychol.,* 1954, **49,** 410–412.
53. Henry, W. E. *The Analysis of Fantasy.* New York: Wiley, 1956.
54. Manual. *Michigan Picture Test.* Chicago: Science Research Associates, 1953.
55. Hutt, M. L., & Briskin, G. J. *The Hutt Adaptation of the Bender Gestalt Test.* New York: Grune & Stratton, 1965.
56. Tolor, A., & Schulberg, H. C. *An Evaluation of the Bender Gestalt Test.* Springfield, Ill.: Charles C Thomas, 1962.
57. Kish, L. *Selection of the Sample in Research Methods in the Behavioral Sciences.* (Ed. by L. Festinger and D. Katz.) New York: Holt, Rinehart and Winston, 1953.
58. Sargent, S. S., & Williamson, R. C. *Social Psychology.* New York: Ronald, 1958.
59. Guttman, L. The basis for scalogram analysis. In T. Stouffer *et al.* (Eds.), *Measurement and Prediction.* Princeton: Princeton Univ. Press, 1950.
60. Osgood, C. E., Suci, J., & Tannenbaum, P. H. *The Measurement of Meaning.* Urbana: Univ. Illinois Press, 1957.
61. Kelman, H. C., & Eagly, A. H. Attitude toward the communicator, perception of communication content and attitude change. *J. pers. & soc. Psychol.,* 1965, **1,** 63–78.
62. Krech, D., Crutchfield, R. S., & Ballachey, E. Z. *Individual in Society.* New York: McGraw-Hill, 1962.
63. Festinger, L. *A Theory of Cognitive Dissonance.* New York: Harper & Row, 1957.
64. Abelson, R. P., & Rosenberg, M. J. Symbolic psychologic: A model of attitudinal cognition. *Behav. Sci.,* 1958, **3,** 1–13.
65. Bogart, L. Inside marketing research. *Pub. Opin. Quart.* 1963, **4,** 562–577.
66. Lipset, S. M., Lazarsfeld, P. F., Barton, A. H., & Linz, J. The psychology of voting: An analysis of political behavior. In *Handbook of Social Psychology.* Cambridge, Mass.: Addison-Wesley, 1954.
67. Stein, D. D., Hardyck, J. A., & Smith, M. B. Race and belief: An open and shut case. *J. Pers. & soc. Psychol.,* 1965, **1,** 281–289.

INDEX